Giants

of Enterprise

**SEVEN BUSINESS INNOVATORS
AND THE EMPIRES THEY BUILT**

RICHARD S. TEDLOW

HarperBusiness
An Imprint of HarperCollins*Publishers*

Portions of the chapters on George Eastman and Charles Revson appeared in somewhat different form in respectively: "The Beginning of Mass Marketing in America: George Eastman and Photography as a Case Study," *Journal of Macromarketing,* vol. 17, no. 2 (fall 1997); and "Intellect on Television: The Quiz Show Scandals of the 1950s," *American Quarterly,* vol. 28, no. 4 (fall 1976).

Grateful acknowledgment is made to the following organizations for the photographs that appear in this book: portrait of Henry Ford, © CORBIS; portrait of Sam Walton, courtesy of Archive Photos; portrait of George Eastman, © Bettmann/CORBIS; portrait of Andrew Carnegie, courtesy of Archive Photos; portrait of Robert Noyce, courtesy of AP/Worldwide Photos; portrait of Thomas J. Watson, © Bettmann/CORBIS; portrait of Charles Revson, courtesy of Archive Photos.

HarperCollins books may be purchased for educational, business, or sales promotional use. For information please write: Special Markets Department, HarperCollins Publishers, Inc., 10 East 53rd Street, New York, NY 10022.

FIRST EDITION

Designed by Nancy Singer Olaguera

Library of Congress Cataloging-in-Publication Data
Tedlow, Richard S.
   Giants of enterprise : seven business innovators and the empires they built / Richard S. Tedlow.—1st ed.
      p. cm.
   Includes bibliographical references and index.
   ISBN 0-06-662035-X (hc)
      1. Businessmen—United States—Biography. 2. Executives—United States—Biography. 3. Capitalists and financiers—United States—Biography. 4. Entrepreneurship—United States—Case studies. 5. Big business—United States—Case studies.

HC102.5.A2T43 2001
338'.04'092273—dc21
[B]   2001024462

02 03 04 05 RRD/❖ 10 9 8 7 6 5 4

This book is dedicated to my
beloved and loving wife

Joyce R. Tedlow, M.D.

Wir sind durch Not und Freude
*gegangen Hand in Hand . . .**

* Through sorrow and joy
   we have walked hand in hand . . .
   —Joseph Karl Benedikt Freiherr von Eichendorff (1788–1857)
      "Im Abendrot" ("At Sunset")

CONTENTS

ACKNOWLEDGMENTS

In compiling a list of people who helped me in the course of writing this book, I am quite struck by how many to whom I owe gratitude. It has been my great good fortune to have as friends and colleagues so many who supported this project.

Helen Rees, my agent, first showed confidence in this book, and her advice from start to finish has been indispensable. She put me in touch with Adrian Zackheim, senior vice president and associate publisher at HarperBusiness, and we struck a deal with Helen's assistance over the phone in a matter of about a minute. Adrian and his team, including Joe Veltre, have had a deep understanding of what I have tried to do with *Giants of Enterprise*.

I had been thinking about this book for many years, but the actual writing began about the time that Kim B. Clark became dean of the Harvard Business School in 1995. Much of the collegiality from which I benefited was the result of his goals and aspirations for the school. *Giants* was funded by the Division of Research, where Ken Froot, year after year, was unfailingly generous. Each chapter of this book has been presented at a seminar at the school, and many improvements have resulted. I received advice and ideas from many members of the faculty. These include Carliss Baldwin, Adam Brandenburger, Al Chandler, John Deighton, Bob Dolan, Susan Fournier, Linda Hill, Geoff Jones, Bob Kennedy, Rakesh Khurana, Nancy Koehn, Anita McGahan, Huw Pill, Forest Reinhardt, Mike Roberts, Dick Rosenbloom, Julio Rotemberg, Bill Sahlman, Walt Salmon, Debora Spar, Don Sull, Dick Vietor, Jonathan West, David Yoffie, and Abe Zaleznik. A special note of thanks is due to Tom McCraw, the leader of the business history enterprise at the Harvard Business School.

On the school's staff, I would like to express my gratitude to Chris Albanese, Chris Allen, Kim Bettcher, Jeff Cronin, Chris Darwall, Sarah Eriksen, Walter Friedman, Courtney Purrington, Kathleen Ryan, and Margaret Willard.

Many scholars, businesspeople, and personal friends lent a welcome helping hand. These include Jim Amoss, Ann Bowers, Kathy Connor, Lillian Cravotta-Crouch, Bob Cuff, Bill Donaldson, Lynn

Groff, Andy Grove, Reed Hundt, Richard John, Analisa Lattes, Erik Lund, Sandy Lynch, Darlene Mann, Susan McCraw, Gordon Moore, Pendred Noyce, M.D., Rowena Olegario, Cliff Reid, Martin Revson, Barbara Rifkind, Arthur Rock, Linda Smith, Charles Spencer, Irwin Tomash, and Les Vadasz.

My greatest debt of gratitude is owed to my wife, Joyce. A psychiatrist, Joyce supplied intellectual insight concerning the subjects of this book and a great deal of emotional support to its author. She did this in the midst of a challenging situation with regard to her health. She never lost faith.

Man's character is his fate.

—Heraclitus, as quoted in Charles H. Kahn, *The Art and Thought of Heraclitus: An Edition of the Fragments with Translation and Commentary*

At last I had authority to give directions over the whole scene. I felt as if I were walking with destiny, and that all of my past life had been but a preparation for this hour and for this trial.

—Winston Churchill, after being appointed prime minister of Great Britain, June 10, 1940, quoted in Martin Gilbert, *Churchill, A Life*

INTRODUCTION THE BIG PICTURE

This is a book about what Americans do best—founding and building new businesses. It is about men who broke old rules and made new ones, who built new worlds, who were determined to govern and not to be governed,[1] who exploited tools and techniques of which their contemporaries were only vaguely aware to serve markets which in some instances they had to create. The seven men portrayed in these pages were individuals of extraordinary inner drive and competitiveness living in a country and culture which encouraged those traits and channeled them into business enterprise. Each in his own way was an outstanding person, living in a nation which allowed him to give full vent to his talent. These men in this country were as free as anyone can be in this world.

Had these seven men been Italians, perhaps they would have become composers; and the world would have seen a second Verdi rather than mass-marketed photography. "He wept for us; he loved for us," was D'Annunzio's farewell to Verdi in his memorial.[2] Had they been Russians, perhaps they would have been novelists. On September 27, 1867, when he was in the midst of the "Great Labor" which became *War and Peace,* Tolstoy wrote his wife: "God grant me health and peace and quiet, and I shall describe the battle of Borodino as it has never been described before."[3] Had they been Portuguese, perhaps they would have been navigators; Germans, soldiers; Japanese, servants of the state; Romanians, gymnasts. And so forth.

America has produced people able to do all these things (just as these nations have all produced businesspeople); but, speaking generally, America as a nation and a culture has not distinguished itself as the best in any of them. Isolated instances of excellence spring up in a variety of endeavors all over the world, sometimes in pretty unexpected places. When one takes the long view, however—say, 250 years—it is fair to assert that America has been the best in starting and nurturing companies. This, therefore, is a book about the best of the best.

Why these seven? The most important reason is that their lives and careers span a lengthy period of time. Andrew Carnegie was born in 1835. He became a force in the business world in the 1860s. The last two biographies are of Sam Walton and Robert Noyce, both of whom died in the 1990s. So their careers provide the opportunity to see how founding and building companies in the United States changed over time.

The seven biographical essays in this book are divided into three sets. The first set—Carnegie, Eastman, and Ford—illustrates the transition from the United States as a developing country to world leadership. The second—Watson and Revson—illustrates leadership in an industrial marketer (IBM) and a consumer marketer (Revlon) during the middle decades of the twentieth century. The third—Walton and Noyce—provides the same contrast between a consumer business (Wal-Mart) and an industrial business (Intel) toward the end of the century. They also show different leadership styles in the oldest of industries (retailing) and the newest (semiconductor electronics). These seven portraits will enable us to explore in the concluding chapter the fundamental changes in the demands on business leaders from the Civil War to 1990.

Another selection criterion was regional. Business leaders act differently in different parts of the United States. Andrew Carnegie was born near Edinburgh, Scotland, and made his fortune in Pittsburgh. George Eastman was born in upper New York State and established Kodak's headquarters in Rochester. Ford was born and spent his working life in the Detroit suburb of Dearborn. Watson, like Eastman, was born in upper New York State and spent his working life in New York City. Revson was born in Boston and, like Watson, established his firm's headquarters in New York City. Walton was born in Kingfisher, Oklahoma. Wal-Mart's headquarters in Bentonville, Arkansas, gives us a glimpse of business south of the Mason-Dixon line. Noyce was born in Denmark, Iowa, and established Intel in Santa Clara, California, in the heart of Silicon Valley.

Some, not all, of these business leaders were profoundly influenced by their sense of place. It is as difficult to imagine Bob Noyce in Bentonville as it is Sam Walton in Silicon Valley. The same could be said about putting Charles Revson in Dearborn and Ford in New York. Though traveling widely from an early age, Eastman was a son of Rochester, to which he was devoted. To this day, Kodak is headquartered in Rochester; and the company's current critics wonder whether there is too much of Rochester in Kodak and whether the company might have to move to save itself.

There was nothing inevitable about the careers of any of the seven men in this book. If Andrew Carnegie had never left the Pittsburgh cotton mill where he got his first job, no one would be asking: Why was there no Carnegie in American history? Carnegie, indeed, is among the unlikeliest characters in the nation's past. For eight decades, historians have been puzzling over him. In the 1940s and 1950s, a widely used American history textbook described him as the "most typical figure of the industrial age."[4] Three decades later, received wisdom from the history profession was that Carnegie was "in every way exceptional."[5] Carnegie died in 1919, so this change in opinion was not the result of anything he did.

There was nothing inevitable about Carnegie Steel, about the camera, about nail polish, or about the integrated circuit. No theory of institutions which does not take account of the talent, genius, idiosyncrasy, and, at times, idiocy of the individual leader can explain how America came to do best what it does best. By the same token, it is no accident that the individuals whose careers are described and analyzed in this book flourished in the United States. It was this society which both provided the encouragement for them and refused to erect the barriers which might have prevented them from fulfilling their destiny. This book is thus the story of individuals and institutions. But the individuals take center stage, while the institutions, both public and private, provide the background.

The institutions of the United States from the Civil War to the present have provided a great deal of latitude to the entrepreneur. The result has been a society in which the goal seems to be to give everyone an equal chance to become unequal.

The freedom to engage in entrepreneurial activity has been broad, but it has not been limitless. Antitrust is one example. The Sherman Act, which made it a federal crime to enter into a "conspiracy in restraint of trade," became law in 1890. Andrew Carnegie simply ignored it in the 1890s. Quizzed about it by a congressional committee, he said: "Do you really expect men engaged in the active struggle to make a living at manufacturing to be posted about laws and their decisions, and what is applied here, there, and everywhere? . . . Nobody ever mentioned the Sherman Act to me, that I remember."[6] Carnegie paid no price for this insouciance. He boasted of it. A century later, Bill Gates took precisely the same attitude, and it cost his company's shareholders over a quarter of a trillion dollars. Times change. Rules change, too.

None of the seven protagonists can be called "typical." There is no typical American business executive; and if one should be found, his very typicality would make him even more atypical. When one studies CEOs of American businesses in large numbers,[7] what is most impressive is their variety within certain limits which I will describe momentarily. They have been born and raised in all parts of a nation the size of a continent. Some have been born and raised abroad. They have adhered to a variety of religions and denominations. Their career paths have been markedly different, as have their educational backgrounds.

These observations are true for executives during the past century and a half with some important caveats. The first is race. The history of African American business enterprise in the United States is a fascinating subject. With some rare, recent exceptions, however, black men and women have not been given the opportunity to lead a large American corporation. The same is true of women. A study of the CEOs of the two hundred most important American industrials in 1917 reveals not one African American or woman.[8] Even today it is rare to find a member of one of these two groups (which, obviously, overlap—i.e., there are black women) leading a large American firm. In the year 2000, only three CEOs in *Fortune* magazine's list of the five hundred largest American firms were women.

In 1932, Frank W. Taussig, a senior economist at Harvard, published along with a colleague, coauthor Carl S. Joslyn, the results of an extensive investigation of the social origins of America's business leaders. The study concluded by declaring that "every lad with energy, ambition, and intelligence, no matter how meager might be his educational equipment, found it possible to gain a foothold in the business world and to work his way up to a higher position."[9] It is noteworthy that two scholars would, after conducting such a meticulous and expensive study, come to this conclusion because it was inaccurate at the time and in fact has never been true.

Indeed, the Taussig and Joslyn conclusion is self-refuting. The phrase "every lad" leaves out the female half of the American population. There is no mention of African Americans in their book, but there can be no question that from the end of slavery in 1865 to the present blacks have been sharply underrepresented among America's corporate elite. The fact that Taussig and Joslyn could have made this assertion about "every lad" illustrates that women and blacks, over half the population, did not count. Both groups were involved in business as employees and as owners. But as top executives of major corporations, they have historically made up a very small percentage.

Taussig, Joslyn, and many others who have marveled at the openness and fluidity of the American economy were not unintelligent. They, like everyone else, were merely products of their times. They did not see the exclusion of well over half the American population from the American business elite as evidence of what it was: exclusivity. They took for granted that some groups were simply "beyond the melting pot."[10] This was axiomatic.

What struck them and has impressed many other observers was not who was "out" but who was "in." You could run one of America's great corporations if you were, for example, a self-educated Russian Jew. This was true in an overwhelmingly Christian nation in which the national language was English and the legal traditions which governed economic enterprise relied heavily on English foundations. The Russian Jew in question was David Sarnoff, creator and for many years the virtual dictator of RCA, the Radio Corporation of America.[11]

Now merely a brand name and not a terribly important one, RCA was among the nation's key companies from the 1920s through the 1980s. It stood athwart the communications industry, which was highly visible because of the entertainment it provided (RCA owned NBC at a time when there were only three networks) and which was also vital for national defense. Communications technology could enable ships at sea to keep in touch and transform an army from a mob into a coordinated fighting unit. It is inconceivable that Sarnoff could have risen to a position of such pivotal importance had he remained in Russia or had he emigrated to, say, Japan.

Thus when we speak of the freedom of access to American corporate power, we must be clear that such access was extraordinarily liberal for those who were within "acceptable" boundaries and closed tight against those who were outside them. Caucasian men were in—even if they were Jews like Charles Revson, even if they were impoverished immigrants without much formal education like Andrew Carnegie, even if they were born and raised far from the centers of national corporate power and capital like Sam Walton. Blacks and women were out.

The selection of the seven people discussed in this book was guided by this irreconcilable, brute fact. The white men portrayed are very different people. But gender and skin color they do have in common. There is plenty of room for books about the history of leading figures among women and blacks in American business. There are a wealth of untold stories that deserve an audience. People wanting to learn those stories will, however, have to read a different book from this one.[12]

Another factor governing the selection of men to portray is that they no longer be living. This decision is quite important and deserves some explanation. History is a democratic discipline. Any literate person can write it. You don't need technical training. You don't need mathematical notation. All you need is judgment, the willingness to work, and some help from friends.

It is no wonder that historians are not terribly good at predicting the future. No mathematical model will be presented in the pages that follow to help you figure out who will be the business titans of 2010. You will find no magic formula for decoding where the markets will be down the road.

Some businesspeople may find this a bit frustrating. Capitalists, it has been said, "are people who make bets on the future. The essence of capitalism is a psychological orientation toward the pursuit of future wealth and prosperity."[13] This, then, is a history of people who, as Robert Noyce put it, exerted every effort not to be encumbered by history so they could go out and do something wonderful.

History does, however, make one contribution to the effort to learn about business that is quite valuable. Historians have the advantage of perspective and context. We know what happened. We know what the answer turned out to be.

Contrast that to the situation in which other students of business find themselves. In early October of 1929, world-famous Yale economist Irving Fisher said that "stock prices have reached what looks like a permanently high plateau."[14] They hadn't. In 1970, *Sales Management* magazine declared that the five large domestic tire manufacturers had a "virtually unthreatened hold on U.S. tire sales." By 1988, four of the five had been forced out of the industry.[15] In October of 1986, *Fortune* magazine featured Ken Olsen in an article saying that a few entrepreneurs, like "Wal-Mart founder Sam Walton, have done better for their shareholders or made themselves richer than Olsen. But none has created as mighty or important an industrial enterprise as DEC. And on that basis, *Fortune* considers him the greatest success." This quotation can be found in a biography of Olsen entitled *The Ultimate Entrepreneur*.[16] When *Fortune* published that encomium, DEC was the largest employer in the Commonwealth of Massachusetts. In 1992, however, Olsen was forced out of the company he had founded.[17] In 1998, what was left of DEC was sold.[18] Today, DEC no longer exists. Ken Olsen is now viewed as one of the biggest failures in business, the computer executive who could not imagine why anyone would need a computer on his desk. He turned out to be the "ultimate" entrepreneur indeed, but in an ironic rather than a literal sense. Certainly no one today would compare him favorably with Sam Walton.

At this writing, GE's Jack Welch would be judged by many commentators to be the nation's greatest businessman. Some would call him the greatest businessman of the twentieth century. But if General Electric proves incapable of digesting the many acquisitions it has made, people will change their minds. Shortly before the end of his tenure as GE's CEO, Welch made a very large purchase, acquiring Honeywell in the year 2000 for over $30 billion. If that acquisition fails to generate the hoped-for economies, market power, and profit, the legacy of Jack Welch will be a good deal less impressive than his reputation is today. And the truth is that the Honeywell deal is so big that no one knows whether it will work.[19]

To the charge that historians know what they know only because hindsight is twenty-twenty, I cheerfully plead guilty. The wisdom derived from hindsight is precisely what the study of history brings to business. There is no other field of human activity—including entertainment, sports, high fashion, or politics—which is so riddled by fads as business. Every day there is a newspaper headline, every week there is a magazine story, and perhaps with the Internet we will soon be saying every hour there is yet another "guru" that touts a new hero of business or a new method of solving problems which date back not merely ten years but far longer. At the least, the study of business history can prompt an executive to ask of each new "solution" to problems that can never be solved but only managed: How really lasting is this approach, this idea, this company?

Historians are no better than anyone else at assessing the present. They are failures at divining the future. But they simply can't be beat when it comes to predicting the past. Coca-Cola shouldn't have changed its formula in 1985. See? Right again. Thus it is not by accident that the executives selected for this book are no longer living.

Various questions are discussed in each of the biographical studies in this book. The different answers the executives arrived at not only shed light on their particular individual makeup but also show how the demands to be met in order to do great things in the business world changed over time.

One such question has already been discussed. That is antitrust. Andrew Carnegie could ignore it. Thomas J. Watson Sr. (the man who made IBM great) could not. Neither could Bill Gates. The issue of antitrust is only the most obvious manifestation of business-government relations. All seven of these entrepreneurs had to learn to manage the government at the same time that the government in the form of a regulatory agency, a congressional committee, or criminal or civil litigation was seeking to manage them. These relations could become extraordinarily complex and contradictory. To select just one example, Watson stood virtually at the gates of the penitentiary in 1914 for criminal antitrust violations. By the 1930s, in sharp contrast, the federal government, through social security and other programs which demanded the accumulation and analysis of large volumes of data, became a key consumer of IBM's goods and services; and Watson, in a Republican business world, became an ardent supporter of Franklin D. Roosevelt. By the mid-1950s, antitrust troubles loomed yet again. The government, it appeared, giveth with one hand and taketh with two.

Other issues also recur. These include the process of growing a business from a start-up to a large, bureaucratic firm, the recruitment and training of a cadre of managers, the management of labor relations, and the different points of view from which the entrepreneur sees the world as he ages and new challenges arise.

Another important theme linking the seven chapters is vision. These are seven stories about men who saw things others did not and made the most of their insight. They used tools that were available to others as well, but used them with greater skill.

For what purpose? To win. To own. To control. To create. This is the story of seven capitalists seizing opportunities in spite of what others saw as constraints.[20]

These seven were all risk takers, innovators, experimenters. They were all more hungry for success than they were afraid of failure. They all had the courage to change not only when things were going badly but, and this is much more difficult, when things were going well.

They were all men of extraordinary self-confidence, deriving either from an innate sense of security (Noyce and Walton) or from distrust of the judgment of others (Revson). Whatever the reason, they believed in themselves. Experience proved this belief justified. They came to feel there were no limits to their talent, a belief that sometimes caused them to run amok in later life (Ford).

All that said, when we change our angle of vision from the role these men played in business and in the world at large to who they were as individual human beings, we discover remarkable variety. These were very different people, with different backgrounds and different strengths and weaknesses. It is difficult to imagine a dinner with all seven of them present.

They had at least two things in common. They were business titans in their time. And they were American. Why choose these seven upon whom to focus to learn more about American business leadership and how it changed over time? Some reasons have already been advanced. More will become apparent as you read on. But I would suggest that a better question than Why these seven? is: Why not these seven? To that question, the only answer is: No reason in the world. These seven men have a lot to teach us about business, organization, the struggle for individual autonomy, and the ability to spot a new technology and run with it.

In August of 1866, a *New York Times* correspondent reported from Nebraska that the building of the transcontinental railroad was an expression of "genuine American genius."[21] The following chapters narrate examples of "genuine American genius" as well. In their industries, these were the men who assaulted the new frontiers.

In Britain, men and women of great achievement are honored by titles sprung from the nation's medieval past. Artists, scholars, soldiers are knighted or ennobled. When the English political philosopher John Locke was asked to draw up governing documents for the American colonies, he suggested that a complicated and well-ordered, titled, aristocratic hierarchy, in part hereditary, would be just the thing. There were to be "signories," "baronies of the nobility," "landgraves," and "caziques."[22] But the United States, which institutionalized so much of its British heritage (including many of Locke's ideas), turned its back on titles. The U.S. Constitution explicitly prohibits granting them.[23] The duchess of Kent awards trophies at Wimbledon. No queen of Queens plays that role at the U.S. Open in Flushing Meadow.

In Italy in 1901, thousands of people lined the streets to witness the late Giuseppe Verdi being carried to his final resting place. The royal family was there, as were leading politicians, dignitaries, and ordinary citizens. Great Italian opera composers including Mascagni, Leoncavallo, and Puccini were there. Arturo Toscanini led the orchestra and chorus of La Scala, one of the world's premier opera houses, in a famous Verdi chorus, *Va, pensiero*. Spontaneously, the crowd joined in, and the beautiful melody of the chorus rose to Heaven that day.

Such a scene is inconceivable in the United States. Thousands of citizens lining the streets and spontaneously singing a chorus of a great American composer of serious music? I don't think so. The people who matter here, who really matter, the true aristocrats, the people who people in the know want to know, are the people in this book. They were made possible by American culture and institutions. At the same time, they were so important that they shaped that culture and those institutions.

Would America mark the passing of a great composer? Try to name a great American composer of concert-hall music. It isn't easy. But at Henry Ford's funeral in 1947, the governor of Michigan ordered flags on state buildings lowered to half-mast. The state legislature halted business "in commemoration of the passing of a great man."[24] Thousands showed up for Ford's funeral, not for some composer's. The founders and builders of giant enterprises are as special here as the creators of great opera are in Italy.

The lives of these seven men serve as a lens through which we will see the history of American business unfold.

PART ONE

The Rise to Global Economic Power

ANDREW CARNEGIE

GEORGE EASTMAN

HENRY FORD

INTRODUCTION

The three executives profiled in this section take us from a time in which the United States was an economic power distinctly of the second rank to an era when we were the dominant force in the world in terms of output, income per capita, and technological progress. The first business leader we discuss, Andrew Carnegie, was born in Scotland in 1835 and emigrated with his family thirteen years later. With this simple observation, we encounter a phenomenon of fundamental importance. From Carnegie's time down to the present day, the United States has benefited enormously from what has been the greatest voluntary mass movement of human beings in the history of the world.

Of course, the great irony of America during Carnegie's early years here was that not all the immigration from which we benefited was voluntary. A mere forty-five miles south of Pittsburgh, where Carnegie settled, was Virginia, a slave state. Cheek by jowl with the hotbed of entrepreneurial activity which was Pittsburgh in the late 1840s was a society where some men, to paraphrase Abraham Lincoln's immortal second inaugural address, wrung their bread from the sweat of other men's faces. Carnegie was acutely aware of this fundamental contradiction in the American polity, and from the beginning he was an ardent advocate of the abolition of slavery.

Once Carnegie got to the United States, there was less standing in his way than there would have been in other countries. And Carnegie knew it. As he grew older, he embraced the United States and American ways with all the fervor of the convert. He enjoyed teasing, touting, and sometimes taunting his European friends with the superiority of his adopted land. He began a book in 1886 with what was to become a famous line: "The old nations of the world creep on at a snail's pace; the republic thunders past with the rush of the express."[1]

When Carnegie began his rise to fortune in 1848, Great Britain had the world's leading economy. As late as 1870, Britain produced more steel than the rest of the world combined. Carnegie made steel his own industry, and he thundered past his native land with the rush of an express. In 1900, the year before Carnegie's retirement, the United States produced twice as much steel as Britain,[2] and a lot of that steel was from Carnegie's own mills. It was the highest-quality, lowest-priced steel available anywhere.

As a man, Carnegie presents many issues which we will encounter repeatedly. How he dealt with these issues—including how he treated those who helped him early in life, how he treated his partners, how he treated his labor force—defined who he was. So also did his passionate desire to hold on to the past (he bought a huge estate with a castle in Scotland) and to "thunder" into the future. Each of the people portrayed in this book had to come to terms with their own wealth. Each became far richer than they had any right to expect when they were young. Carnegie had his own unique response to this situation.

Carnegie was part of a set of business titans born in the 1830s who later became known, fairly or not, by the unlovely label of "robber barons." J. P. Morgan, for example, was born two years after Carnegie. John D. Rockefeller was born in 1839, two years after Morgan. Our next chapter deals with a man nineteen years Carnegie's junior, George Eastman.

Eastman is never referred to as a "robber baron," and the differences between Carnegie and him are striking. Carnegie was an extraordinarily voluble man, writing articles and books that had a wide circulation. He had a zest for life; he was greedy for it and could not get enough of it. Pittsburgh was not big enough to hold him; he divided the two decades of his retirement between his magnificent Scottish estate, where he entertained the world's notables, and his sumptuous house in Manhattan. Carnegie would have made the Faustian bargain to live life again.

Eastman, by contrast, was remote. This man who made his fortune commercializing photography was hidden. He wrote innumerable letters but few if any articles and no books. His most intimate business associate was a man named Henry Alvah Strong, who could appreciate him but never (as Strong himself acknowledged) understand him. His closest bond was with his mother; but his affection for her was not, as far as one can judge such things on the basis of limited information, fully and satisfactorily reciprocated. Eastman is the only business leader in this book, and one of a mere handful of chief executive officers of major corporations in American business history, who never married. Despite being much celebrated not only in his hometown of Rochester but around the world as well (his Kodak camera was marketed everywhere) George Eastman was a lonely man in later life. In old age, having outlived his friends and in failing health, he was not thinking about a Faustian bargain. He committed suicide.

Extraordinarily generous with his great wealth, Eastman directed his often-anonymous philanthropy toward health care, education, and culture. He had a highly developed aesthetic sense. He did more than compete in the photographic industry; he transformed it. He put a camera, the Kodak Brownie, into the hands of everyone who had $1.00 in disposable income and an interest in taking pictures.

Eastman Kodak was founded in 1880, and George Eastman was in the vanguard of businessmen who marketed consumer products (as opposed to selling to other businesses) which were, and this is very important, branded.

The 1880s was the decade that saw an explosion of branded consumer goods introduced to the mass market. Procter & Gamble had been around since 1837, but Ivory Soap floated in 1879. American Tobacco was founded in 1882. Coca-Cola and Johnson & Johnson were both founded in 1886. Heinz and Campbell Soup were also founded in the 1880s. In one product category after another, nationally branded, packaged products became dominant. In cameras, it was Kodak.

This move to brands was unprecedented. Very few brands marketed prior to 1880 survived for long. There are some exceptions, like Wedgwood, but not many. However, if we look at the above list of branded products created in the 1880s, they are all still with us. Why? What happened?

The 1860s was the decade of Civil War and political collapse. During the 1870s, the United States was struck by a devastating depression. By the 1880s, the union of the states was secure and the depression over. Just as important, the telegraph and railroad networks had reached a stage of maturity which permitted access to a national market.

Anything which collapses barriers of time and space opens up vast new opportunities for entrepreneurs with insight and the daring to act. Eastman had both. Eastman Kodak would have been impossible without the railroad and the telegraph, the two technological marvels of the age. Some believe the Internet will play a similar role in the twenty-first century, and for the same reason. It permits the movement of data with unprecedented speed and economy.

In the 1880s, Eastman had the wind at his back. But so did everyone else. What made him (and a few select others) stand out was that he knew how to sail. The 1880s were the real beginning of the American cornucopia, of an economy that produced a great deal of what people wanted, things like inexpensive cameras, as opposed solely to the food, clothing, and shelter that they needed to survive.

The third entrepreneur in this section, Henry Ford, became as famous as anyone ever born in America. When he and his company were at their high tide, in the early 1920s, the place of the United States in the world had changed completely. When Andrew Carnegie reached our shores, the United States had a classic colonial-type economy, exporting agricultural products and importing manufactured goods, trying to protect itself with tariffs, and running the constant risk of losing the gold in the treasury because of chronic balance of payments deficits in a world of fixed exchange rates.

By the early 1920s, the United States was the world leader in what were then the industries of the future, especially automobiles and electricity. Henry Ford not only dominated the automobile industry from 1908 until the mid-1920s, his methods of production became the marvel of business. He became more than a man; he became a movement. Fordism is a word translated into many languages, and many people who spoke these languages made the pilgrimage to his gigantic industrial complex on the River Rouge in the Detroit suburb of Dearborn.

During the mid-1920s, no one in the United States was worried about the nation's status in the global financial system. The United States emerged from World War I as a creditor nation for the first time in its history. We became an export engine and also built production facilities overseas. Ford had a factory in England as early as 1911.

Henry Ford, more than any other individual, put America on wheels. He liberated a rural nation from place. He put a car within the reach of the masses. Motorized transportation changed America's cities as well. In 1900, 2.5 million tons of horse manure and sixty thousand gallons of urine were deposited on the streets of New York City every day.[3] Think about it.

The problem with Ford was that he believed his own press

notices. Perhaps more than any other figure in America's business past, he suffered from the madness of great men. His dismal life story following 1927 is an eloquent testimony to the wisdom of the fear of the founding fathers of unchecked power.

The careers of these three men—Carnegie, Eastman, and Ford—take us from America as a backwater to America at a peak in its history. Their careers posed problems to each which in some ways were similar. But they came up with very different solutions.

1 ANDREW CARNEGIE

From Rags to Richest

*You seem to be in prosperity. Could you lend an admirer a dollar &
a half to buy a hymn book with? God will bless you. I feel it. I
know it. . . . P.S. Don't send the hymn-book, send the money. I
want to make the selection myself.*[1]

MONEY

Sometime between 1886 and the turn of the century, Andrew
Carnegie was visiting his widowed sister-in-law Lucy at the estate
his late brother had bought in Dungeness, Florida, just off the coast
of the border between Florida and Georgia. Andrew and Lucy got
along well. He had named his first blast furnace for the production
of pig iron after her (it was the custom in the iron trade to name fur-
naces after women); and she had named one of her sons (she and
Tom were the parents of nine children) Andrew.

During this visit, Lucy was complaining to her bemused brother-
in-law that her son Andrew neglected to write her from the college
which he was attending. Without missing a beat, Carnegie told her
that he could induce a response from the young collegian by return
mail. He was sure enough that he bet her $10, a wager to which she
immediately agreed.

So Andrew drafted what has been described as a "nice, newsy"
letter to his nephew and namesake. He added a postscript that he
was enclosing a check for $10 as a gift. He then deliberately left the
check out of the envelope.

In no time, young Andrew Carnegie wrote back to his uncle,
gratified by the gift but distressed that it had not been enclosed.
Carnegie triumphantly presented the letter to Lucy; she paid him the
$10 she had lost on the bet, and Carnegie sent that $10 off to his
nephew.[2]

Andrew Carnegie and John D. Rockefeller were the two greatest

American businessmen produced during the nineteenth century. They were the two richest and the two most powerful. As individuals, however, it would be hard to imagine two people less like one another. Carnegie was ebullient; until the very end of his life he was incurably optimistic; he was by turns genuinely sincere and hypocritical, intensely realistic and grandiose. Slightly manic, he was a man of enthusiasms which could be painlessly transformed into wholly different enthusiasms. He was capable of physical exertion, but he was also a physical coward. He was loyal; he was fickle. He could love. He could betray.

There was an unbridgeable gulf between the man he wanted to be and the man the business world rewarded him for being. This is a critical attribute of Carnegie's career, and one which he shares with many another businessperson. There can be no better illustration than what Joseph Frazier Wall called "the most traumatic and highly publicized episode in his business career,"[3] the bloody lockout of labor at the Homestead plant in 1892.

Carnegie had an insatiable thirst for public approbation, a need which comported ill with his insatiable thirst for money and power. He wrote incessantly, and what he wrote was as liberal and fair-minded as the image he wanted to have of himself. In April of 1886, he wrote in *Forum* magazine that "my experience has been that trades-unions, upon the whole, are beneficial both to labor and to capital."[4]

Not many employers were publishing words like that in 1886. The month after the April article, the Haymarket "riot" occurred, placing labor and radicalism in the same boat to much of middle-class America. Nothing daunted, Carnegie rushed back into print. In his "Results of the Labor Struggle" in August of 1886, he wrote: "To expect that one dependent upon his daily wage for the necessities of life will stand by peaceably and see a new man employed in his stead, is to expect much. There is an unwritten law among the best workmen: 'Thou shalt not take thy neighbor's job.' "[5]

These sentiments struck a profoundly responsive chord among workingmen, and Carnegie was lionized for them by unions. The Brotherhood of Locomotive Engineers named a division after him and conferred upon him an honorary membership, which Carnegie happily accepted:

As you know, I am a strong believer in the advantages of Trade Unions, and organizations of work men generally, believing that they are the best educative instruments within reach. . . . I feel honored by your adopting my name. It is another strong bond, keeping me to performance of the duties of life worthily, so that I may never do anything of which your Society may be ashamed.[6]

The reaction of Pittsburgh's business community, dominated as it was by Carnegie's principal partner, Henry Clay Frick, and Frick's banker, Judge Thomas Mellon, can be imagined. Unions were anathema to these men and to the old-time ironmasters at the center of Pittsburgh's business economy.

Labor violence was endemic in Pittsburgh. There was a lockout in the city's iron mills in 1874–1875. This was followed by the "Great Labor Uprising" of July 1877. During the course of the riots at the time, twenty or more Pittsburghers were killed by National Guardsmen. Paul Krause, the leading historian of labor in Pittsburgh during this era, has written that the 1877 riot was to employers "a palpable reminder that the Paris commune might yet come to the United States."[7]

The Pittsburgh Bessemer Steel Company was formed in October 1879 by some of the most successful industrialists in Pittsburgh. The company's goal was to put up a state-of-the-art steel mill to compete with the "ET," as Carnegie's Edgar Thomson mill came to be called. The site they chose for the mill was Homestead, close to the ET.

From the first, Homestead experienced labor troubles, or from labor's point of view what would be better labeled "owner troubles." Unlike the ET, Homestead was unionized from the start. The Amalgamated Association of Iron and Steel Workers (AAISW) was engaged in a combination of a strike and lockout during the first quarter of 1882. Conflict flared up periodically thereafter, and by the following year the owners were ready to sell to Carnegie.

Carnegie was ready to buy. The Homestead mill was the most modern in the country; and Carnegie, always looking to the future, was not unaware that Homestead could produce structural steel, in addition to rails. He bought the mill at cost, offering to pay the investors in cash or stock. Only one investor took stock. The amount was $50,000. In a decade and a half, that $50,000 in stock was worth $8 million.[8]

The sources do not tell us the number of people to whom Carnegie made the proposition to purchase Homestead. According to Wall, "representatives of five manufacturing companies" had been involved in creating the Pittsburgh Bessemer Steel Company in 1879.[9] It is remarkable that despite the record he had already achieved by 1883, only one person wanted to become Carnegie's partner. Carnegie once said that "I am sure that any competent judge would be surprised how little I ever risked. . . ."[10] As with so many of Carnegie's pronouncements about his own career, this was quite untrue, however. Many of the people who declined to become his partner believed in 1883 that Bessemer steel manufacturing was a very risky business indeed. They took the money and ran.

All but one of the former owners of the Homestead mill were out of the picture by the end of 1883, but labor strife was very much still in the picture. For all his fine words about unions, Carnegie did not want organized labor at any plant of his. His effort to break the AAISW resulted in the Homestead lockout of 1889. The union prevailed.[11] The story was to be quite different three years later when the contract came up for renewal.

When Carnegie came face-to-face with the implications of his fine words about unions, he walked away from them. Six years after his articles were published in *Forum,* labor unrest once again came to Homestead. Carnegie decamped to a remote retreat in Scotland, leaving Henry Clay Frick in charge of his properties. Frick and Carnegie both knew that to accumulate the money and power they lusted after, they had to keep production costs and prices lower than any of their competitors. The AAISW stood athwart that strategy. As one Carnegie partner put it, "The Amalgamated placed a tax on improvements, therefore the Amalgamated had to go."[12]

Frick was unsentimental. He had no compunction in using every tactic which Carnegie's magazine articles had condemned to break the strike and destroy the union. Here was precisely that conflict, between the man Carnegie wanted to see himself as and the man that business reality demanded he be, that was an ongoing theme in his life. More than once, his actions contradicted his words. With Walt Whitman, he could have said:

Do I contradict myself?
Very well, then, I contradict myself;
(I am large—I contain multitudes.)[13]

There was an antic quality to Carnegie that was lacking in his contemporary, Rockefeller. Unlike Carnegie, Rockefeller contained within him no need to please. Nor was there any need to boast. Carnegie kept a file labeled "Gratitude and Sweet Words." It is hard to imagine such a file in Rockefeller's office. Carnegie yearned for intellectual respectability. Rockefeller, who personally founded two universities (Rockefeller University and the University of Chicago) and one college (Spelman College), and who gave a fortune to other institutions of higher education, could not have cared less.

Alice Roosevelt Longworth, Theodore Roosevelt's oldest child, said of her father that he had to be the "bride at every wedding, the corpse at every funeral."[14] One could conceive of a remark like that about Carnegie. After he retired from active business, he received an award called the "Freedom of the City" from some fifty-seven British cities. The previous record had been held by William E. Gladstone, a man who had served as the nation's prime minister on four separate occasions. Not even Winston Churchill, whom mature historical judgment has rightly denominated the "saviour of his country,"[15] accumulated as many Freedoms as did Andrew Carnegie.[16]

The power which resided in the persons of Rockefeller and Carnegie came from opposite traits. It is easier to be at home with Carnegie. We have met people like him. His goals, his needs, his pleasures are like ours, except increased by the scale on which his wealth allowed him to live. His fortune turned him into a magnified man.

Rockefeller was magnified by his wealth as well. So completely, however, was he self-contained that the menace he posed to an adversary was never defined. It was left to the adversary's imagination. And Rockefeller knew how to stimulate that imagination. He was the master of the "look of stone." You could become petrified in his presence. Or you could simply seem to disappear, so little did he need you around. The result was that when you negotiated with Rockefeller or when you tried to trap him on the witness stand, you invariably became your own worst enemy.

If you walked into a meeting room at which Rockefeller were present, you probably would not guess that he was the boss. He made it a practice not to sit at the head of the conference table. If there were a couch in the room, he might recline on it. He might seem almost to doze off. Almost. If he heard a number he did not like, a raised eyebrow might result.

Carnegie commanded the limelight. Rockefeller preferred operating from the shadows. Rockefeller once said: "I never had a craving for tobacco, or tea and coffee. I never had a craving for anything."[17] How different from Carnegie. One can scarcely imagine him making such a pronouncement. It would probably be easier to list the things Carnegie did not crave than those he did.

Rockefeller's statement was not quite correct. He did have at least one craving—one that he shared in full measure with Andrew Carnegie. These two men had one very important thing in common.

Rockefeller and Carnegie craved money. They craved the power it brought them, even in little things. (Remember how Carnegie managed to get his nephew to send him a letter.) They craved the luxury. The freedom. The self-esteem. The vindication. These two men craved money; and more than anyone else in nineteenth-century America, they knew how to get it.

ANDREW CARNEGIE
New Frontiers

On November 25, 1835, in the Scottish village of Dunfermline, about fifteen miles across the River Forth from Edinburgh, Margaret Morrison Carnegie gave birth to her first child, a son the parents named Andrew. The birthplace was a small cottage that served as both home and workplace for Andrew's father, William, and his mother, Margaret. Both parents came from politically radical families; but Will, unlike Margaret, was shy by nature.[18]

Shy or not, Will Carnegie, as a weaver of damask linen, was among the aristocrats of labor. His work was a true craft which demanded the dexterity and flexibility of an organist and the aesthetic sensibility of an individual of genuine artistic discernment. To be a truly talented handloom weaver of damask designs, as Will

Carnegie was, meant not only "minding" one's own loom and over-seeing first one, then two, then three others with all the attendant clatter and racket and the interpersonal problems that are natural to life in a small business, but also producing a superior product by "making a reality of the beauty he felt within himself." For that to happen, the beauty had to be there in the first place, and in Will Carnegie's case it apparently was. His work fascinated his son, who fully expected to follow in his father's footsteps.[19] This was a future that was not to be.

Will Carnegie comes down to us through the years as a kind and decent man. A sweet man. A man who, though shy, could assert himself to protect his family in the face of sufficient provocation.[20]

Sadly, tragically, Will was without those qualities which were vital in facing the evolving world of the nineteenth century. These were qualities which his wife did possess and which his eldest son learned from her and to which he made many additions himself.

Will Carnegie was a textbook example of what not to do in the face of radical change. He was also a man about whom no one today would have any recollection were it not for the achievements of his son. Will, his family, and his in-laws, the Morrisons, were passionate advocates of the "Charter," a political manifesto the purpose of which was to democratize the United Kingdom. This passion for political freedom Andrew Carnegie never abandoned. During the Spanish-American War of 1898, he was horrified at the imperial designs of the McKinley administration on the Philippines. When he learned of the plan to pay Spain $20 million for the islands after they had been conquered, he offered to buy them from the president and set them free. He meant this offer to be taken seriously.[21]

Carnegie could afford such gestures by 1898. But the Philippines had as little to do with the fate of Carnegie Steel as the Charter did with the fate of Will Carnegie and his fellow handloom weavers. Their problem was not the monarchy, nor the House of Lords, nor rotten boroughs. It was new technology, specifically, steam. It was steam-powered weaving mills, which could not be voted away or wished away, that destroyed Will Carnegie's world, making him and his friends technologically obsolete.

After Andrew was born, Will's business was brisk briefly; but the inexorable and foreseeable results of steam power soon made themselves felt throughout the world of handloom weavers. Will Carnegie began a dreadful economic descent. It lasted for more than a decade in Scotland and then continued in the United States. He cleaved to the old ways. He felt trapped, losing a world he loved in which the combination of beauty, skill, and the rhythm of his hand-operated wooden machinery provided comfort to a gentle man who found sustenance in routine. In place of this world he was losing, he faced the unknown. Finally, reality became undeniable. "Andra," he told his son in the winter of 1847–1848, "I can get nae mair work."[22] From that moment, the power in the family shifted from father to mother and never shifted back.

With tears and borrowed money, Will, Margaret, Andrew, and Tom Carnegie became four of the 188,233 Britons to emigrate to the United States in 1848. Tom, born in 1843, was a gentle young boy. (Separating Andrew and Tom was the birth of Ann in 1840. She died the following year.) Glasgow's port was depressing, the day of departure was depressing, the ship was depressing. Will Carnegie was already "a tired and defeated man."[23]

Margaret Carnegie, to the contrary, was, one senses, in a controlled rage. Life had dealt her a heavy blow. She would get back her own and more than her own. With the odds against her, she never gave up. As for her oldest son, he was smart, shrewd, charming, self-confident. He fit into the brave new world hand in glove.

"Slabtown." The name says it all. That is where the Carnegie family ended up in the late summer of 1848. They were not alone. Margaret had relatives in Allegheny, Pennsylvania (the location of Slabtown), and Scottish immigrants who preceded them lent a helping hand. The Carnegies were poor—very poor—but not quite destitute. Their home was a hovel, but not quite a hellhole. Allegheny, Pittsburgh, and the environs were ugly and just plain awful. But there were worse places in the world then, and there are now.[24]

Over against this bleakness was an upside. Margaret had an iron will. Andrew had limitless energy and ambition. There was room in the United States for a young fellow like that in 1848.

Margaret and Andrew knew how to work. Margaret betook herself to a shoemaker and fellow resident of Slabtown named Henry Phipps and asked for homework, which he gave her. Andrew went to work soon thereafter as a bobbin boy in a cotton textile mill owned by a Scotsman. Pay: $1.20 a week. In 1901, he was worth

$300 million. Poor, benighted Will Carnegie went into the mill, too. He could not stand the place, but it was his assignment to keep an eye on his young son. Soon, another job presented itself. A family friend who manufactured bobbins offered Andrew a job firing the boiler of the steam engine. The steam engine, frightful though it was, Andrew could deal with, even though it meant long hours alone in the cellar of a cacophonous factory for this most gregarious of youths. Soon thereafter, the bobbin manufacturer found he needed some help in the office; and Andrew became a clerk. To see to it that he was earning the $2.00 a week he was paid, the manufacturer assigned Andrew the additional task of dousing bobbins with a protective coat of oil. This he could scarcely bear. In his autobiography, which he wrote at the end of his life and was published posthumously, he still recalled vividly how the smell of oil nauseated him. "But if I had to lose breakfast, or dinner, I had all the better appetite for supper, and the allotted work was done."[25]

Next to Carnegie, Norman Vincent Peale was a clinically depressed pessimist. The cellar of a factory in Pittsburgh, Pennsylvania, at the dawn of the Industrial Age was arguably not a good place to be. To flee factory production in Scotland, travel thirty-five hundred miles, and wind up in another factory does not seem like progress. To have lived in a country just long enough to learn to love it dearly and then to find oneself a foreigner with almost no formal education in a raw new land with no heritage, no rules, no place to fit in, and in a city so uninterested in itself that you could not find a park near where you lived—these are not circumstances that would fill most hearts with joy. To have a father so defeated that he returned to the only occupation which brought him solace, handloom weaving, even though there was no market for his cloth, hardly helped matters.

What was a brick wall to Will Carnegie was a triumphal arch to his oldest son. He was a free man in a free land. Nothing could stop him. One new frontier after another—that was America to young Andrew Carnegie.

Andrew, after a twelve-hour day, went to downtown Pittsburgh, where he and some friends persuaded a local accountant to teach them double-entry bookkeeping. Andrew turned out to have an affinity and an affection for mathematics. A chance encounter through his uncle brought the boy to the attention of the O'Reilly

Telegraph Company. The company needed another messenger boy. Andrew radiated talent. He was hired on the spot. Within months of arriving in Slabtown, Andrew had his third job; and this one had potential. Soon Andrew was making $11.25 a month; quickly after that, $13.50. While the other boys did their work competently at best, Andrew was a whirlwind. The result? "Two years after arriving in America," Carnegie biographer Harold C. Livesay observed, "the Carnegie family had rebuilt their fortunes: they enjoyed a total income greater than they had ever known in Scotland; they had repaid the borrowed passage money . . ."; and they owned their own home.[26] "For Andrew," according to Joseph Frazier Wall, "'America was promises,' promises of growth [and] opportunity. . . ." "Everything around us is in motion . . . ," Carnegie wrote to a Scottish relative;[27] and no one was moving more quickly than he.

There were plenty of young telegraph messengers in the United States in 1849, and the attitude of most of them was not surprising. The work seemed inherently dull: coming to an office every morning, cleaning it up, and then running all over town, rain or shine, delivering messages to people more important than you. What job could have a less promising future?

This was another case of brick walls and triumphal arches. Carnegie saw nothing but opportunity in his new job. He got to learn, at no cost, who in Pittsburgh was growing and where the action was. He came to know a great deal about the city's business community in no time at all.

On his own, with no lessons, he learned telegraphy. He mastered it; he was quicker than anyone else. His salary climbed to $25 a month. Soon Pittsburgh newspapers hired him. Andrew Carnegie, in his mid-teens, was becoming the center of information in a booming metropolis where news meant money. The newspapers paid him to keep them up to the minute.

One evening in the spring of 1852, Andrew rushed to the wharf with some dispatches to be sent by riverboat down the Ohio to Wheeling and Cincinnati. There, future met past in an unexpected and startling encounter. Andrew saw his father headed toward Cincinnati to try, and doubtless to fail, to sell a few tablecloths he had woven. Will Carnegie was almost forty-eight years old, and he could not afford a cabin. He was going to spend the night on deck. Andrew bought him passage in a cabin, and the two exchanged kind words.

There cannot have been a better illustration of the triumph and the tragedy of industrialization and immigration. Will Carnegie was a sweet, loving, gentle man, a perfect description of an individual for whom there was no place in the New World. Will Carnegie's life in America was a long, slow decline. He clung to his weaving as the world passed him by. His son was a bold experimenter, a true "go-getter."[28] The New World was made for him, and at the same time he helped to make it.

Will Carnegie—how Dickensian his first name sounds, for it was the lack of the will to adapt which spelled his downfall—kept weaving for three years after the encounter with his son. Then he finally gave up. On October 2, 1855, about a year after he became a naturalized American citizen, he died.

The passage in Carnegie's autobiography which deals with this meeting at the wharf is subject to multiple interpretations. On the face of it, nothing could be more appropriate or touching. This passage is important and worth quoting at length:

> I remember how deeply affected I was on finding that instead of taking a cabin passage, [my father] had resolved not to pay the price, but to go down the river as a deck passenger. I was indignant that one of so fine a nature should be compelled to travel thus. But there was comfort in saying: "Well, father, it will not be long before mother and you shall ride in your carriage."
>
> My father was usually shy, reserved, and keenly sensitive, very saving of praise (a Scotch trait) lest his sons might be too greatly uplifted; but when touched he lost his self-control. He was so upon this occasion, and grasped my hand with a look which I often see and can never forget. He murmured slowly:
>
> "Andra, I am proud of you."
>
> The voice trembled and he seemed ashamed of himself for saying so much. . . . My father was one of the most lovable of men, beloved of his companions, deeply religious, although non-sectarian and non-theological, not much of a man of the world, but a man all over for Heaven. He was kindness itself, although reserved. Alas! he passed away soon after returning from this Western tour just as we were becoming able to give him a life of leisure and comfort.[29]

Harold Livesay, in his brief but engrossing Carnegie biography, asserted that Will Carnegie's "wife and elder son clearly thought him a failure, their love and respect gradually changing to shame and contempt." Livesay referred to the passage just quoted as evidence. "This was faint praise indeed," Livesay wrote, "from one who abandoned religion as a boy, spent his Sundays iceskating, reading, or riding horses, scoffed at the idea of heaven and at those who preached it, embraced the evolutionary dogmas of Herbert Spencer, and boasted of his own achievements as a 'man of the world.'"[30]

Margaret Carnegie, who came from a proud and rebellious family, could hardly have viewed her husband, who was six years her senior, as a success. Their situation had called for adaptation, and he had not adapted. She was working like mad to keep a roof over their heads, while he was pursuing a terminally quixotic path.

Andrew was a ball of fire who seemed not at all to mind being the head of the house. It was he, after all, who was to care for his father, not the other way around. Over half a century after the event, Carnegie remembered his father expressing pride in him and ascribed to his father shame at so doing. One can reread that passage and without too great a leap see Andrew expressing pride in himself and being ashamed of his father.

Will Carnegie was not a fool; and although there is no evidence that his family belittled him for it, his failure in the New World was hardly a state secret. Will was a failure, and he knew it. Andrew, whose long life was (with a few exceptions) one success after another, did not understand failure. It was not in this most self-confident of people to understand it.[31] To be sure, he could understand failure intellectually; and doubtless on that same plane he could sympathize with it. But he could achieve no true understanding of it. Asking him to understand failure would be like asking a color-blind person to see the colors to which he or she was blind.

One expert on power in business who is also a psychoanalyst has described Carnegie as an "Oedipal victor."[32] That is to say, he had seen his father pushed aside by circumstances, had seen him fail, and had taken his place by his mother's side in every way but physically. Andrew Carnegie said in 1897 that his "childhood's desire was to get to be a man and kill a King."[33] On page 10 of an autobiography which is 372 pages long and was completed in 1914,

Carnegie wrote, "As a child I could have slain King, Duke, or Lord, and considered their deaths a service to the state and hence an heroic act."[34]

Such boyhood fantasies are not uncommon. But to see them in some sense acted out in the case of a father who fails when a boy is twelve and dies when he is nineteen is noteworthy. And then to see the son bond so closely to the mother that she advised him in business matters and spent all her time with him is more noteworthy. And then to realize that there was no chance of this man marrying while his mother lived is more noteworthy still.

Andrew Carnegie met the woman who was to be his wife, Louise Whitfield, in 1880. A genuine affection grew up between the two; but the romance was successfully blockaded by Andrew's mother, who could marshal the same single-minded intensity in the service of her goals as could her son. Only the calm and patience of Louise and her instinctive understanding that there would be no wedding while Carnegie's mother lived made the match possible.

The story of the courtship hardly reveals Carnegie as a model of impetuosity.[35] It was not until April 22, 1887, that Carnegie and Louise were wed. Carnegie's mother, the indomitable Margaret Morrison Carnegie, had passed away on November 10, 1886. Carnegie was fifty-one. His bride was thirty. On March 30, 1897, Louise Whitfield Carnegie gave birth to the couple's only child, a daughter. The child's name? One hardly need ask. It was, of course, Margaret. They probably would have named the child Margaret if it had been a boy.

Louise and Andrew loved each other genuinely, and they were both devoted to their daughter. The marriage was a success because Louise understood the role which being the wife of a great man called upon her to play. Her husband knew he had things pretty much his own way, and at those rare instances when she did make a special request he acceded.

Louise Carnegie was a woman of tact, but she also had a long memory. She told Carnegie's earliest major biographer that Andrew's mother was the most disagreeable woman she had ever known.[36]

Carnegie was a many-sided man. He was lavishly talented. But there was one trait which was virtually absent in him, the absence of which was very useful to success in business in the nineteenth century and perhaps today. What did the Oedipus of Sophocles himself do when he discovered he had murdered his father and married his mother? He gouged his eyes out. Why? Because, among other reasons, he was overwhelmed by that which was as much a stranger to Carnegie as was failure. Guilt.

Moment of Truth

Let us remind ourselves of the earlier quotation from Carnegie's autobiography about the fate of his father. Carnegie had seen his father off on a riverboat and had purchased for him a cabin passage. It might as well have been the River Styx. The father was never to return as a force in the son's life.

A new father figure now came upon the scene, and he is described in the very next sentence of Carnegie's autobiography following the encounter at the wharf: "After my return to Pittsburgh it was not long before I made the acquaintance of an extraordinary man, Thomas A. Scott, one to whom the term 'genius' in his department may safely be applied."[37] All his life, he was a hero-worshiper, hardly a stereotypical trait for a "robber baron."[38] In 1904, he established a Hero Fund to honor the "true heroes of civilization," whom he described as "those alone who save or greatly serve" their fellow human beings.[39]

Thomas Alexander Scott, the man Carnegie proclaimed in his autobiography to be a "genius," was the most important individual in Carnegie's business career. Always hungry for knowledge, Carnegie had enjoyed only four or five years of formal education. It was Tom Scott who took a liking to the seventeen-year-old "white-haired Scotch devil," as he affectionately referred to Carnegie. It was Scott who introduced Carnegie to what in the early 1850s was the nation's leading corporation . . . Scott who hoisted Carnegie above the many people who worked for the Pennsylvania to the acquaintanceship and then the early friendship of the coterie of executives who ran the company . . . Scott who taught the poor immigrant how many ways there were to make money . . . Scott—strikingly handsome, impeccably groomed—who modeled for Carnegie how to look and how to act in the world of affairs.

I believe that Andrew Carnegie would have been a success even if Scott had never met him. Obviously we will never know. Carnegie was effectively fatherless at an early age and thus had no one to soften the impact of an overbearing and at times disturbingly selfish mother. He was denied what, as Wall puts it, "should have been part of the normal education of an adolescent boy" with regard to sex.[40] The result was somewhat greater uneasiness concerning sexuality than might have been the case had his biological father been Tom Scott rather than Will Carnegie. Living in a city with the mores of the frontier, Carnegie was, Livesay informs us, "a small boy and a short man (five-feet-three-inches full-grown at a time when the average American male stood five-feet-seven)."[41] What if his grandiose fantasies had gotten out of hand when he was young, rather than when he had already established his fortune? "Carnegie," according to Wall's perspicacious observation, "above all else was a romantic. Like all nineteenth-century romantics, he glorified the improbable event, and he denied the predictable pattern. . . ."[42] This complete surrender of the bureaucratic to the charismatic is not necessarily a recipe for success in business.

We need only look as far as Carnegie's younger brother Tom to see that there was nothing inevitable about success in the new land. Tom, the "beautiful white-haired child with lustrous black eyes, who everywhere attracted attention,"[43] eight years his brother's junior, was the only member of the family who was not struck, because of his youth, by the enormity of becoming a refugee from a beloved homeland in the disastrous year of 1848. It was he, rather than his older brother, whom one would have expected to have an easier adjustment to the United States.

However, Tom Carnegie had more of his father than his mother in him. He became chairman of the Carnegie enterprises, but there was no doubt that the real power resided with his brother. Andrew did not have a formal title in his company, but owned a majority of the stock. Tom Carnegie never met a counterpart to Tom Scott. His mentor was his older brother. Tom was both a competent and likable individual. Andrew trusted him, and depended on him during his long absences from the business for his European travels.

Joseph Frazier Wall, whose *Andrew Carnegie* is and will remain the standard work on its subject for years to come, contains an aside concerning relations within the Carnegie family which is exceptionally difficult to understand. Writing of the late 1860s and 1870s, Wall observed: "With each passing year, Margaret [Carnegie, the boys' mother] became more possessive of her older son [i.e., Andrew] and more demanding of his attention. Tom, *whom Andrew always felt his mother secretly favored*, had successfully broken free of Margaret's domination."[44]

What are we to make of the italicized phrase? Wall provides no reference for it. And without a specific reference, it is difficult to evaluate and, in the end, difficult to accept. The italicized phrase raises two questions: First, did Andrew really feel his mother favored his brother? And second, was his putative perception of this secret favoritism justified?

The answer has to be no to both of these questions. Andrew himself was devoted to Tom after his fashion. He loved him as much as a narcissistic, selfish, and voracious man could love anyone. That is to say, he relied on Tom and used him; but he had no idea how to be a true friend to Tom's inner self. Surrounded by a large family and a lot of friends, Tom Carnegie was a lonely man. He turned to drink for companionship. The bottle was for Tom what the loom was for his father, a retreat from life's harsh realities.

This is how Wall described Margaret Carnegie as a young woman:

> Although she always quietly deferred to her father, a more perceptive observer than William [i.e., her husband] might have sensed the great strength of will and determination that Margaret possessed. Intensely loyal to those whom she loved, and fiercely possessive of all that she could call her own, Margaret could on occasion display a ruthless determination that William would never understand.[45]

If not quite Lady Macbeth, Margaret Morrison Carnegie was no Mary Poppins. There is no clear evidence that she was ever cruel to the weak, but she gravitated to the strong. It was Andrew, therefore, who was the focus of her attention. There is no indication that she had any objection to Tom's getting married. Indeed, the precise date of the wedding is noted neither by Wall nor by any other biographer.[46] Wall does not even note the precise date of Tom's birth or death.[47]

Only Andrew knew how to handle the powerful if sometimes disguised tidal wave of Margaret's affect. It was he and perhaps only he who knew how to please her. The Carnegie family not only had to recoup its fortunes and more, but everybody in Dunfermline had to know it.[48]

Margaret Carnegie lived with Andrew for almost two decades after Tom's marriage—from 1867 to 1886 (when Tom and Margaret died within the space of a month). There is nothing in the extensive record that suggests that Andrew felt competitive with Tom, whom, as we have mentioned, he liked but to whom he condescended, for his mother's affections. One is forced to conclude that Wall, who was right about so many things, was simply wrong about this.

I have explored this issue at some length because it is important in understanding Carnegie's view of himself and therefore his approach to his mentor, Tom Scott, and later to his partners and his employees. The hero-worshiping Carnegie commonly referred to his mother as a "heroine." His descriptions of her were extravagant even by nineteenth-century standards.

In truth, Andrew Carnegie had only one hero and knew only one genius. He encountered that individual each time he looked in a mirror. The place he held in the heart of his "heroine" undoubtedly contributed to his self-regard. In the words of Sigmund Freud, "A man who has been the indisputable favorite of his mother keeps for life the feeling of a conqueror, that confidence of success that often induces real success."[49]

Let us now return to the story of Tom Scott and Andrew Carnegie.

Like Carnegie, Scott was a self-made man. He was born in the hamlet of Loudon in Franklin County in eastern Pennsylvania on December 23, 1823. When he was ten, his father died, leaving behind a widow and eleven children, of whom Scott was the seventh. The Pennsylvania Railroad was founded on April 13, 1846, and in 1850 Scott became the station agent at Duncansville. It was on December 10, 1852, an important date in the history of American business, that the Pennsylvania Railroad reached the city of Pittsburgh. Thomas Alexander Scott became the third assistant superintendent of the Western Division of the Pennsylvania and was based in Pittsburgh. Tom Scott found himself running a major portion of what was to become one of the most profitable businesses in the nineteenth century.[50] "Quick-witted, dapper, handsome, and well-met"[51] though he may have been, Scott had a big job; and he was going to need help. Where would he find it?

A glance at a map will show that by American standards Pennsylvania is not that large a state. Today, it ranks thirty-third out of fifty in area. But to executives in 1852 trying to run a railroad over its mountains and through its valleys on iron (not yet steel) rails, and over its rivers and streams on bridges often made of wood with locomotives and rolling stock which were primitive even by the standards of the next generation, it looked large, indeed. To run such a railroad required up-to-the-second information. That meant the telegraph. The suave Mr. Scott often found himself scurrying over to O'Reilly's telegraph office to see where his trains were, to hear the heart of his railroad beat between Pittsburgh and Altoona, eighty-three miles to the east, and the headquarters of Herman Lombaert, the general superintendent and Scott's boss. The Pennsylvania had only a single track covering that distance; therefore, scheduling was literally vital.

It soon became clear to Scott that he needed a telegraph office of his own. He received permission from Pennsylvania president J. Edgar Thomson to set one up. The choice of office manager was easy. Scott had met Carnegie at O'Reilly's, and it was love at first sight. Carnegie, said to be the third person in the United States to learn to take messages by sound rather than having to transcribe the rolls of dots and dashes which Samuel F. B. Morse had assumed would be necessary,[52] was a quick study. He was also a born problem solver. And Scott was a man with more than his share of problems.

Scott asked one of his assistants about Carnegie's availability, but was told that Carnegie was fully employed at O'Reilly's. Carnegie did not need others to speak for him when his interests were concerned, and it certainly was not his wont to let grass grow under his feet when opportunity knocked. "Not so fast," he said as soon as he heard of the conversation. "He [Scott] can have me. . . . Please go and tell him so."[53]

On February 1, 1853, Andrew Carnegie became an employee of the Pennsylvania Railroad as Mr. Thomas A. Scott's clerk and telegraph manager. His salary was now $35.00 a month, up 40 percent from the $25.00 he was making at O'Reilly's. He was seventeen years old. When he was thirteen, he was making $1.20 a week.

More important than the money was the position. Carnegie stood at the epicenter of transportation and communication for one of the fastest-growing manufacturing districts in the United States.

He had, as if by magic, become the protégé of a man whose origins were almost as humble as his own, and whose rise would be almost as meteoric as his own was to be. On top of all this, he had himself. He was an adolescent of remarkable talent. He was bold in its exploitation. He was charming and ingratiating. In short, he was on his way.

Within a few days Carnegie was becoming known within the top tier at the Pennsylvania. Soon he started meeting the movers and shakers themselves. He was off to Altoona, his first trip of any length since the "flitting" from Scotland, to pick up the monthly payroll. While in Altoona, Carnegie had the opportunity to meet Tom Scott's boss, the aforementioned Herman Lombaert.

Lombaert's reputation was the reverse of Scott's. As would be said today, Lombaert lacked "people skills." "Rather stern and unbending" was how Carnegie characterized his reputation.[54] No wonder Carnegie was shocked when Lombaert invited him to tea with his wife that evening. "I stammered out something of acceptance and awaited the appointed hour with great trepidation." Lombaert introduced him to his wife as "Mr. Scott's 'Andy.'" "I was very proud indeed of being recognized as belonging to Mr. Scott."[55] Andy belonged. He was something of a pet, but he belonged. And all thanks to Mr. Scott. "Mr. Scott was one of the most delightful superiors that anybody could have and I soon became warmly attached to him. He was my great man and all the hero worship that is inherent in youth I showered upon him."[56]

Scott's faith in little Andy was repaid in extraordinary fashion soon after Carnegie's employment. An accident on the Eastern Division resulted in the halting of trains all along the line. Carnegie discovered this immediately as he arrived at work, but "Mr. Scott was not to be found. Finally," as Carnegie recalls in his autobiography, "I could not resist the temptation to plunge in, take the responsibility, give 'train orders' and set matters going. . . . I could set everything in motion." And he did, tapping out order after order and signing them T.A.S. rather than A.C.[57] This was the telegraph, not the telephone; no recipient of an order could know who was really sending it.

A lot was at stake: "I knew it was dismissal, disgrace, perhaps criminal punishment for me if I erred." When Scott, having heard of the accident, hurried into the office, Carnegie laid out the situation for him in every detail—"freights, ballast trains, everything." Scott "looked in my face for a second. I scarcely dared look in his." But soon Carnegie learned from a third party that Scott was bragging about "what that little white-haired Scotch devil of mine did." After that, "it was very seldom that Mr. Scott gave a train order."[58]

Soon thereafter Carnegie was introduced to J. Edgar Thomson, president of the Pennsylvania; and soon after that it became clear that Andrew Carnegie was going to be looking at life from the other side of the wide and deep chasm dividing rich from poor. Following his father's death, Carnegie was approached by Tom Scott with an idea for an investment. There was one small difficulty. Scott needed $500 to make this investment on Carnegie's behalf. Carnegie recalled in his autobiography that "five hundred cents was much nearer my capital. I certainly had not fifty dollars saved for investment, but I was not going to miss the chance of becoming financially connected with my leader and great man. So I said boldly I thought I could manage that sum."[59] Boldness paid off big in the United States.

In his autobiography, Carnegie writes that his next stop was his heroine mother. Somehow, she came up almost immediately with the $500 required. But then, a last-minute hitch—another $100 was to be paid "as a premium." As Carnegie writes, in response to this last-minute call, "Mr. Scott kindly said I could pay that when convenient."[60]

The problem with this remarkable story is that in one essential it is inaccurate. Five hundred dollars was a fortune in 1856. One could not simply go running around town and scare it up. Tom Scott advanced Carnegie the full amount for the purchase of ten shares of Adams Express Company stock. Carnegie's mother had nothing to do with it. The sum was $610.

The investment paid off, but that was hardly the point. The point was that through the investment Carnegie learned that money could make money. "Eureka!" he cried when he received the first dividend check. "Here's the goose that lays the golden eggs." None of his friends "had imagined such an investment possible." In an instant, Carnegie was transformed from employee to capitalist—thanks to Tom Scott.[61]

Carnegie felt the pulse of America. As he repeatedly marveled, everything was on the move. Tom Scott was an important mover, and late in the autumn of 1856 he was promoted to Herman Lombaert's job. He was now the general superintendent of the Pennsylvania Railroad. This meant he had to move to Altoona, and of course Mr. Scott's Andy came along, but at a new salary of $50 a month.

Scott was in motion again in 1859, this time to a vice presidency of the Pennsylvania. When Scott moved up, the issue of what would happen to Mr. Scott's Andy asserted itself: "What was to become of me was a serious question. Would he take me with him or must I remain at Altoona with the new official [i.e., Scott's replacement]? To part with Mr. Scott was hard enough; to serve a new official in his place I did not believe possible. The sun rose and set upon his head as far as I was concerned."[62]

Scott went to Philadelphia to talk things over with the Pennsylvania's president, Thomson. An able, dour, and formidable man, Thomson had met "Mr. Scott's Andy" when he was a young "phenom" in the railroad's Pittsburgh telegraph office. But to promote this twenty-four-year-old to the superintendency of the Western Division of the Pennsylvania Railroad . . . that was quite a leap.

Scott, nevertheless, sold the move to Thomson; and he certainly had no trouble selling the idea to Carnegie. As of December 1, 1859, the deed was done.[63]

Now Carnegie was the line manager of a key component of the transportation infrastructure of the United States. His salary was $1,500 a year. Perhaps the most remarkable thing about this munificent sum was that it really did not matter anymore. Carnegie had learned, thanks to Scott and the Adams Express investment, how easy it was to make money. Indeed, one's money could make money, while one's work brought one "glory."[64]

In 1858 or 1859, under obscure circumstances, Carnegie managed to make an investment in the Woodruff Sleeping Car Company. His one-eighth interest in this company was the true "start of the Carnegie fortune." Wall and Carnegie's first major biographer, Burton J. Hendrick, are in agreement on this point.[65]

Soon after the fall of Fort Sumter in April 1861, the secretary of war asked Tom Scott to leave the Pennsylvania to come to Washington and see to it that the capital's rail connections with the Union were not severed by secessionists in Maryland. Scott needed staff support, and for one last time Mr. Scott's Andy followed the man on whom the sun rose and set. After some harrowing adventures, Scott and Carnegie succeeded in securing the railroads to the capital. Carnegie was involved in transportation and communication support for the First Battle of Bull Run. He suffered sunstroke in July, and received a gash across his face while repairing telegraph wires. In all, he spent May to September of 1861 in Maryland, Washington, D.C., and Virginia. With military reorganization, he was able to return to Pittsburgh and the superintendency of the Western Division of the Pennsylvania.

The Civil War years were good to Carnegie. "Good," indeed, hardly describes them. By the end of 1863, he was a very rich man. He had continued his investing, and his money was making a fortune for him. His total income in 1863 was $42,260.67. His salary from the Pennsylvania that year was $2,400.00. He no longer needed a salary. He no longer needed the Pennsylvania Railroad. He no longer needed Tom Scott. Not quite thirty years of age, he could do quite well on his own in the business world.

Although he no longer needed Scott or Thomson, with whom he also became closely associated, he certainly enjoyed their company as investors. Carnegie invested in railroads, bridge building, a myriad of other enterprises, and a variety of securities from the time he left the Pennsylvania Railroad on March 28, 1865, until he at last determined in 1872 and 1873 that his business future was in steel.

By no means did all those investments have happy outcomes. Tensions did develop at times between Carnegie and his friends. Those years proved, though, if there had ever been any doubt, that Carnegie was an outstanding businessman. He could grasp the essentials and make money for himself and his friends in a variety of industries.

The odds are that Carnegie would have been a great success as a manipulator of money. But at heart, he was a man of the real, rather than the financial, economy. In 1872, he had become convinced that steel would lie at the center of the world of real work. "My preference was always for manufacturing. I wished to make something tangible."[66]

In December of 1868, Carnegie sat himself down and created a personal balance sheet. He was thirty-three years old. It had seemed by that early age that he had already lived a dozen lives. He listed his investments. They came to $400,000. The little acorn planted less than a decade previously with Tom Scott's money and ten shares of Adams Express had grown into a mighty oak. The returns from those investments were a staggering $56,110. Carnegie was one of the richest men in the nation. Carnegie, comments Wall, "had eagerly accepted Scott and Thomson as his mentors, and their values had become his values, their goals his vision of success."[67]

Nevertheless, having achieved the American dream, Carnegie was unsatisfied. "Most of the successful men he had encountered were men with but one ambition—money. . . ." But Carnegie wrote to himself the following: "Man must have an idol—The amassing of wealth is one of the worst species of idolatary [sic]. No idol more debasing than the worship of money. *Whatever I engage in I must push inordinately* therefor should I be careful to choose that life which will be most elevating in its character."

Wall finds this "self-analysis" to be "surely unique in American entrepreneurial history" for its revelatory self-awareness. For Wall, the central challenge of Carnegie's life was not the amassing of wealth, but rather the reconciliation of his radical Scottish heritage with the reality that in the New World all that had seemed so unattainable in the old was granted without even the necessity of a request. The hunt—the hunt for ever more money and power—which motivated so many entrepreneurs generated in Carnegie "moments of ennui and restlessness that few of his associates could understand."[68]

I believe Wall is incorrect in taking Carnegie completely at his word and in his explanations for these "moments of ennui and restlessness." First of all, such feelings were not unique to him. J. P. Morgan described himself in similar terms.[69] Second, it is at least possible that what Carnegie was yearning for was not so much an escape from the idolatry of money (an appreciation of the power of which he kept with him to his last breath) as an escape from loneliness. He had lots of business associates and, of course, his mother. But he had no wife, no children, not even a home. He was living in a hotel in New York City when he took stock of himself.

For whatever reason, Carnegie was experiencing some inner turmoil. Like so many big businessmen, he was at the same time adept at self-deception and deeply insightful. He could not have been more right in divining that he would "push inordinately" anything he did. In order for him to satisfy that need, however, he could not allow himself to pursue half a dozen different business interests, no matter how successful they might be.

No one ever had to tell Andrew Carnegie that it was important to think big. That was in his marrow. But he understood that to think big in the coming era—to be the king of the era of steel—meant marshaling all his resources. Sideshows had to be discontinued. All his intellectual energy, all his financial resources, all his business connections had to be focused on a single goal. However big the steel industry was to be, he would be bigger. This was his route to the fulfillment of his destiny. This is how he would quiet the restlessness within him.

Just as this great effort was getting under way, the banking house of Jay Cooke and Company failed on September 18, 1873, setting off a financial panic of monumental proportions. This soon translated itself into the real economy, causing an untold number of business failures and resulting in what was probably the worst depression in the country to that time. It was at this very moment, just when Carnegie had resolved his midlife crisis and had begun worshiping the idol of steel, that his moment of truth came.

Tom Scott had gotten himself into a dangerously exposed financial position. To make a very long story short, Scott had decided to build a railroad, which was to be called the Texas and Pacific, from the Louisiana-Texas border to the Pacific Ocean. He embarked upon this project without the proper financing in place and against Carnegie's advice. To finance a project of this magnitude on the basis of short-term loans was to Carnegie imprudent in the extreme. Scott had thought he could pull the grand project off. Like so many other nineteenth-century entrepreneurs, Scott could not find the fine line between luck and the iron logic of business success. To him and to others, Carnegie, for example, was basically lucky.

Carnegie was indeed lucky, and he knew it. He never depended on his luck, however. He depended on his unexcelled shrewdness as an analyst of business opportunities, on his salesmanship, and on his ability to manipulate people.

For the Texas and Pacific scheme to succeed, luck was a prerequisite. But when the Panic of 1873 struck, Tom Scott's luck ran out. He found himself deeply in debt, and he needed the endorsement of men of standing on his loans. But Carnegie had already put a quarter of a million dollars into this project, a project in which he had never believed in the first place. This he had done "for fellowship's sake," one might say. How much further was he to go? Was he to sacrifice his own ambitions in steel? What did he owe this man who had lifted him out of obscurity?

This was an extraordinarily complex moment. Or it *should* have been a complex moment. It certainly *would* have been for most people. This is how Carnegie, to whom we can always turn first for part of the truth, describes the situation he faced. Tom Scott "telegraphed me one day in New York to meet him at Philadelphia without fail. I met him there with several other friends. . . . A large loan for [Scott's] Texas Pacific had fallen due in London and its renewal was agreed to by Morgan & Co., provided I would join the other parties to the loan."[70]

The Morgan referred to was Junius S. Morgan, J. P. Morgan's father and, in 1873, the head of the banking house that bore his name. Carnegie's business relations with Morgan had begun in the summer of 1868, when he was a transatlantic bond salesman. Carnegie found selling bonds an easy and pleasant way to pass the time. It was one of the many activities at which he excelled, and he and Morgan made a lot of money together. This "white shoe" house had come to trust the youthful Carnegie.

It is a pity no one at this meeting recorded it in detail. The lack of a record compels us to turn to our imagination. We cannot even be certain who was in attendance. Who were the "several other friends"? Who were "the other parties to the loan"?

From what we can gather, present at the meeting, in addition to Scott and Carnegie, was the Texas and Pacific's chief engineer, the experienced Civil War veteran Grenville M. Dodge.[71] Dodge, who was respected by everyone from Sherman to Grant to Lincoln, had played a key role (perhaps the key role) in constructing the Union Pacific after the Civil War.[72] One historian describes the "hastily called meeting" as an "emotionally charged conclave at which the careers of Thomson, Scott, Thaw, McManus, Baird, Houston, and Carnegie hung in the balance. . . . The arguments lasted all day and most of the night."[73] Most of the people mentioned were probably at the meeting. Thomson, however, probably was not. One imagines Carnegie would have noted him specifically if he had been there.

What we do know is that Scott, the "genius" upon whom the sun "rose and set,"and other investors with whom Carnegie had made money in the past were applying to him for assistance. Scott was as close to a father figure as "his Andy" had ever really known. Indeed, in the business world, the alliance of these two men had, according to Wall, "long been regarded . . . as something as fixed and dependable as that which united the Rothschild family. . . ."[74]

Scott was not only a lifelong friend and business ally of Carnegie, he was also the close friend (as was Carnegie) of the president of the Pennsylvania Railroad, J. Edgar Thomson, who had held that position for two decades, having taken office on February 3, 1852. Thomson and other officers of the Pennsylvania were investors in Scott's Texas and Pacific and had endorsed some of his notes "out of friendship."[75] Scott himself in September 1873 was the senior vice president of the Pennsylvania. As the second in command, he was Thomson's presumptive successor. Thomson was sixty-five years old in September 1873. He was tired and ill.

These facts are noteworthy because the Pennsylvania Railroad was probably the most important business organization in the nation to a man going into the steel business in Pittsburgh in 1872–1873. First of all, it was a consumer of rails. Rails were to be the heart of the steel business for much of the remainder of the nineteenth century. Second, the Pennsylvania was by far the most efficient way to ship freight in and out of Pittsburgh. The city and all who manufactured goods in its environs were dependent upon it. Its rates could make or break a company. In other words, this meeting would have been crucial simply because Scott was a big shot at the Pennsylvania, even if he and Carnegie had never previously met.

Imagine, then, Andrew Carnegie at this meeting in late September of 1873. He is surrounded by the decision makers at a railroad that is critical to him. He is bound to the central character in the drama (i.e., Scott) by the strongest of emotional ties. He is probably the youngest man at this meeting, and he is surrounded by men all of whom were probably taller than he. There was, one imagines, no time for beating around the bush. Doubtless pleasantries were brief, and Scott probably got right to the point with words such as: "Will you join our friends and push this great venture forward?" This is pressure. Real pressure from every quarter.

In his autobiography, Carnegie records his response: "I declined." He continues: "I was then asked if I would bring them all to ruin by refusing to stand by my friends." We can only imagine the tone of voice in which such a question would be asked. No wonder that Carnegie recalled this as "one of the most trying moments of my whole life."

It may have been "trying," but it was not confusing or complex for Carnegie. He had no doubt before, during, or after this meeting about what course of action he would take; and he was not a man who could be either cajoled or browbeaten. He writes: "Yet I was not tempted for a moment to entertain the idea of involving myself."

Why not? Let Carnegie speak for himself: "The question of what was my duty came first and prevented that. All my capital was in manufacturing and every dollar of it was required. I was the capitalist (then a modest one, indeed) of our concern. All depended upon me. My brother with his wife and family, Mr. Phipps and his family, Mr. Kloman and his family, all rose up before me and claimed protection."

Carnegie's reference to "our concern" was to his fledgling iron and steel enterprise. He had entered into partnerships with the above-mentioned people. These partnerships were unincorporated, and liability was unlimited. If Carnegie signed Scott's notes, he asserted, not only would his own house collapse, but so would the houses of people who had trusted his judgment.

His decision would impact not only him, but others. If he went bankrupt, they might, too. The "duty" that "came first" was to his new partners, not to his original mentor.[76]

Next, Carnegie expressed a disdain for Scott's proposition that approaches the aesthetic in nature:

> I told Mr. Scott that I had done my best to prevent him from beginning to construct a great railway before he had secured the necessary capital. I had insisted that thousands of miles of rail lines could not be constructed by means of temporary loans. Besides, I had paid two hundred and fifty thousand dollars cash for an interest in it, which he told me upon my return from Europe he had reserved for me, although I had never approved the scheme. But nothing in the world would ever induce me to be guilty of endorsing the paper of that construction company or of any other concern than our own firm.

Scott's project, in other words, was stupid in the first place. He had been warned of its impracticality. He had allocated a quarter of a million dollars for this adventure to Carnegie, "which he told me upon my return from Europe," even though Carnegie had not approved the plan. Scott had, in other words, taken Carnegie for granted. Of course, he was used to this. When he went to Altoona, he took "his Andy." When the Civil War broke out and Scott went to Washington, he took "his Andy." But now it was 1873. "His Andy" had become an independent capitalist with a transatlantic reputation, and he was using this event to announce to the world that he was going places, but that no one was taking him anywhere. It is noteworthy that once again Carnegie uses the language of morality. In the previous paragraph, he speaks of his "duty." In this passage, he uses the word "guilty," but the guilt is associated not with denying Scott help, but with the possibility of providing it.

Carnegie next asserted that whatever action he took could not have saved the situation. Scott's ship was going to sink. Carnegie positioned his only choice as to board it or to stay on dry land: "I knew that it would be impossible for me to pay the Morgan loan in sixty days, or even to pay my proportion of it. Besides, it was not that loan by itself, but the half-dozen other loans that would be required thereafter that had to be considered."

Scott probably suspected Carnegie's feelings prior to this meeting. Yet it must have come as a shock to have "his Andy" say no to him unequivocally face-to-face. Could he believe what he was hearing? He turned to his own mentor, partner, and boss, J. Edgar Thomson, to try again. Thomson laid it on pretty thick. On October 3, he wrote Carnegie:

> You should tax your friends, if you have not the means your-self, to meet the calls for the Texas concern. . . . The scheme in itself was good enough, but it has been most wofully [sic] mismanaged financially, Scott having acted upon his faith in his guiding star, instead of sound discretion. But Scott should be carried until his return, and you of all others should lend your helping hand when you run no risk—If you cannot go further. P.S. I shall be glad to get out of this Texas matter with a loss of three times your subscription.[77]

We know from Carnegie's autobiography—and Thomson should have known at the time—that from Carnegie's point of view he ran a very considerable risk by endorsing Scott's notes. Nevertheless that phrase—"you of all others should lend your helping hand"—that phrase had power. But no words existed to change the adamantine Carnegie's stand. As far as the other appeals were concerned, Carnegie, as Livesay writes, "would have none of the 'guiding star' foolishness. . . ."[78] Scott had failed to understand what Carnegie always knew so well. Luck was a luxury, not the basis for a business. Luck had to be a "nice to have," not a "need to have."

Let us return to Carnegie's recounting of this momentous meeting. His refusal to back Scott

> marked another step [the two had had some recent sharp disagreements] in the total business separation which had to come between Mr. Scott and myself. It gave me more pain than all the financial trials to which I had been subjected up to that time. It was not long after this meeting that the disaster came and the country was startled by the failure of those whom it had regarded as its strongest men. I fear Mr. Scott's premature death can measurably be attributed to the humiliation which he had to bear. He was a sensitive rather than a proud man, and his seemingly impending failure cut him to the quick.[79]

Wall recounts this episode in detail and with his accustomed sensitivity. He concludes that "the pain" to which Carnegie refers in the previous passage,

> if not a sense of guilt, persisted, and even when Carnegie was an old man, writing his autobiography, he could not ignore this episode as he did the many other unpleasant incidents of the past. He felt compelled to recount the whole story and once again justify his decision. His concluding sentence to the story showed that the pain was still there: "I fear Mr. Scott's premature death can measurably be attributed to the humiliation which he had to bear." This passage is notable for being one of those rare instances in his autobiography in which Carnegie expressed regret for things past.[80]

As usual, Wall's narrative is authoritative and richly documented. Once again, however, I find that his analysis raises questions. The questions center precisely on the issue of Scott's "premature death" and "humiliation."[81]

For starters, how great was Scott's "humiliation"?

On November 5, 1873, a $300,000 note came due which Scott and some of his friends who were parties to it could not pay. This was bankruptcy. According to one account, Scott "brought the major creditors together and persuaded them to allow him to retain control of the concern to see what he could salvage for them. So great was the blow to Scott's reputation that he felt obliged to present his resignation to the Pennsylvania's board three days later."[82]

Clearly, this was not good news. On the other hand, although the Texas and Pacific as well as its construction company were bankrupt, Scott, for reasons which are unclear, apparently was not personally bankrupt. Moreover, the days when people were jailed for debt were long gone by the 1870s in the United States. Hundreds, thousands, of railroads, banks, other businesses, and industrials went through bankruptcy in the nineteenth century, only to rise from the ashes. Even Jay Cooke, whose bankruptcy in 1873 led to the panic and depression of that year, resulting in injury to millions, was discharged from bankruptcy in 1876; and by his death in 1905 he had accumulated another sizable estate.[83]

Thomson blamed Scott not only for his own mismanagement, but for involving the Pennsylvania Railroad in his failed investments. On the other hand, Thomson chaired the board meeting at which Scott's offer to resign was considered; and he advised that the acceptance of this offer was neither "necessary or desirable."[84] It is not unlikely that Scott's resignation and its rejection were merely matters of form.

It should also be noted that the Texas and Pacific did not lose all its value. It played a role in the railroad battles of the Southwest for years. Financier Jay Gould bought Tom Scott's holdings in the railroad in April 1881.[85]

Thus, it is true that Scott had suffered a "humiliation." But it is difficult to conclude from the historical record that this humiliation was devastating or lasting. Texas and Pacific securities surely never lived up to the inflated dreams of their promoters in 1871, but a decade later they were not worthless. As early as October 1875, Scott and one of his partners "were able to advertise their willingness to purchase at par all the notes which bore their joint endorsement."[86]

J. Edgar Thomson died on May 27, 1874. The following week, on June 3 to be precise, Tom Scott was elected president of the Pennsylvania Railroad. The board did not jettison him with the removal of his longtime partner and protector, Thomson, from the scene. He obviously was not a humiliated, wounded, or ineffectual man in the eyes of the board a mere half a year after the Texas and Pacific default. The board had chosen him to head the road through what were going to be the predictably difficult times of a major depression.

The 1870s were years of extraordinary challenges for the Pennsylvania. It was dueling not only with competitors but with big shippers like John D. Rockefeller. It endured a major strike which began in Pittsburgh on July 19, 1877, and was accompanied by riots and the destruction of a great deal of railroad property.[87] Despite all these trials, the Pennsylvania during Scott's tenure in office "was able to earn enough . . . to pay a cash dividend in each year, though they did not come with periodical regularity as they formerly had, and in 1878 were reduced to two per cent."[88]

Scott retired from the Pennsylvania Railroad on June 1, 1880. A history of the Pennsylvania notes, "He was still only 56 years old, but he had been in bad health for at least two years, his ailment probably caused or aggravated by the troubles of 1877."[89] Scott died the following year at the age of fifty-seven.

Where does all this leave Carnegie's recounting of the end of his relationship with Scott? Where does it leave the analysis of Carnegie's views by historians?

Scott clearly suffered a business setback when his Pacific railroad project fell through. Every such defeat is, I suppose, a humiliation to a proud, self-made man who prefers victory to defeat. But in light of Scott's later career, it can definitely be said that he did not suffer a crippling or lasting humiliation.

What are we to make of Carnegie's confession of pain and regret at perhaps having contributed to Scott's premature death? We must dismiss this confession completely. First of all, death at fifty-seven can hardly be called premature in nineteenth-century America. Carnegie's own brother Tom was forty-three at his death in 1886. (And Carnegie had a sister, Ann, who lived for only a year and who is not mentioned at all in his autobiography.) One could make a much better case that Carnegie, with his hectoring criticism and his insistence on "pushing" not only himself but especially those over whom he had power "inordinately," took a terrible toll on his younger brother, whom Carnegie described as "born tired."[90] Not surprisingly, there is no acknowledgment of pain or guilt in this case, where it might have been more than a little appropriate.

Tom Scott lived for almost eight years after the break with Carnegie, from September of 1873 to May 21, 1881. He spent almost all of that time as president of the nation's most important railroad. Those were tough years for him, but they would have been for anyone running that railroad. The Pennsylvania's historians speculate that the great strike of 1877 might have contributed to the loss of his health. They do not mention Carnegie.

To see a man claim to have done good deeds that he did not perform would not surprise the reader of an autobiography. Nor would it surprise us to read of his denial of evil for which he was actually responsible. But in his autobiography, Carnegie expresses remorse for what he treated as tragedy, Scott's humiliation and premature death, despite the fact that he had no connection at all with the latter and rather a convoluted relation to the former. It is rare indeed that one reads an autobiography in which a man takes the blame, however indirectly, for events for which he bore no responsibility.

Why?

At that fateful meeting in September of 1873, Carnegie came of age as a tycoon. Note how he refers in his autobiography to "the total business separation which *had* to come between Mr. Scott and myself."[91] Carnegie knew this had to happen. He believed in his own judgment more than anybody or anything else. He was not going to follow Tom Scott or any group of men. Others would follow him. As Wall says: "The year 1872–1873 marks the great transitional period of Carnegie's life. It was then that he made the decision to concentrate his business interests and specialize in the manufacture of steel. *Old associates had to be cast aside.*"[92]

In psychological terms, Carnegie had killed Scott off as a father figure. He did not need father figures anymore. That meeting was a triumph. Carnegie was proud of it. In later life, Carnegie came to enjoy Wagner's music.[93] Like Siegfried, he had slain a dragon. Like Siegfried, he had confronted his own Wotan and pushed him aside. It is for these reasons, rather than because of any lingering guilt, that he remembered the break the way he did. No other explanation makes his obvious inaccuracies comprehensible. Carnegie was proud, not at all regretful, of his ability to think straight and to be hard when that was what success demanded. His own father never would have passed this test. He would have given way to sentiment. But in this climactic contest between mercy and money, Carnegie chose the latter.

What were the results of Carnegie's "great refusal" to endorse the loans? Soon after returning to New York from Philadelphia, "rumors reached him of the doubts clouding his name in Pittsburgh." The chief doubters were at the Exchange Bank, from which Carnegie was borrowing heavily to put up his first steel mill at Braddock, Pennsylvania, the mill that he was to name Edgar Thomson. The bankers knew that Scott was a plunger; they thought that, as had always been the case in the past, Scott and Carnegie were joined at the hip; and they feared that through Carnegie the virus of insolvency would spread to their bank.

Carnegie hopped on the first train to Pittsburgh. According to biographer Burton J. Hendrick, "The scene that followed in the directors' room partook of that dramatic character which was dear to Carnegie's heart. A slight figure sat firmly in his chair, surrounded by dignified inquisitors who proceeded to apply the screws."[94] As always, however, Carnegie proved quite adept at dealing with the sadism aimed at him. When the directors of the Exchange Bank turned the screws, they did not find Carnegie's thumbs in them.

As Wall put it, "The answers he [Carnegie] gave were not what the bankers expected to hear."[95] They had expected that he had gone along with his old friends. They were prepared to lecture him on the irresponsibility of speculating in securities with other people's money because of the pull of sentiment. Instead, Carnegie delivered that very lecture to them. He was, he could truthfully say, innocent of allowing sentiment to cloud his clear-eyed view of what Hendrick called "fundamental principles." Carnegie "rose from the cross-examination a new man—new, at least in the estimation of his own community. The steel maker whom the bankers had regarded as the weakest and most likely to collapse with hard times suddenly appeared as practically the only one who could successfully ride the storm."[96]

In 1911, an expert on the steel industry evaluating Carnegie's special genius said that an important part of it lay in his realization that "the real time to extend your operations was when nobody else was doing it." That was usually during depressed times when money was tight. And that is why Carnegie made his famous remark seven years after his retirement that "the man who has money during a panic is the wise and valuable citizen."[97] (Even in old age, he maintained his puckish, wise-guy sense of humor.) With his bank credit secured and having demonstrated in the Scott episode what he was willing to do to show that behind the "headstrong exterior there lay a calculating brain,"[98] Carnegie never had trouble securing funds for the rest of his life. He could build when others could not. That meant he could build more inexpensively than they. That meant his costs would always be lower and his profits higher than the competition.

PIONEERING PAYS: WHERE THE MONEY CAME FROM

We are so used to thinking of Andrew Carnegie as a boy wonder, as indeed he was, that it takes us aback to realize that before he became an entrepreneur he was an organization man. As he himself once said, poor people go to work early in life. He was no exception. He was in that Pittsburgh cotton mill when he was thirteen, in 1848.

By early in 1853, however, he was working at the railroad. Not just any railroad, either, but the largest and most important business organization in a basically unorganized, rural nation populated predominantly by small farmers. We have seen how between 1853 and his retirement from the Pennsylvania in 1865, he climbed a clearly delineated ladder of success rung by rung.

Carnegie was doing much else besides advancing at the railroad during these years. He was a fabulously successful investor. One of his most important investments, given his future career, was in the Piper and Schiffler Company, which was organized as a bridge-building concern in February of 1862. Carnegie assured the partners whose names the firm bore that there would be plenty of business for bridge builders, especially builders of railroad bridges, after the Civil War; and he took a fifth interest in the business for $1,250.[99] In retrospect, Carnegie's prediction appears obvious. But life is not lived in retrospect. At any rate, the following year Carnegie's investment returned $7,500. [100]

Bridge building became one door through which Carnegie passed on the way toward his interest in iron. Piper and Schiffler officially became the Keystone Bridge Works on May 1, 1865, shortly after Appomattox and the assassination of President Lincoln. The old world of slavery was gone forever. The new world of industrial capitalism on a national scale beckoned, and Keystone had a continent before it. Keystone specialized in iron bridges. To the prescient, it was clear that iron would replace wood. It was sturdier. It was fireproof. It could be built to last. By the close of the Civil War, business was booming at Keystone.[101]

Carnegie went to Europe for a grand tour after Keystone was reorganized. He returned to Dunfermline, visited other cities in Britain, and saw the sights on the Continent. He attacked the Old World like a one-man invading army, effervescing about what he saw and thoroughly exhausting his companions. Childlike in his unabashed enthusiasms, Carnegie would remain an avid tourist his whole life. For most of his adult life, he took extended vacations and kept track of his business interests through written reports. He was not at all a hardworking man by modern standards.[102]

Carnegie's biography is a history of cutting-edge technology in the nineteenth century. He saw his father's craft displaced by a steam-powered textile mill. He mastered the telegraph soon after its invention. He was in the right place at the right time when the railroad revolution began. Carnegie understood well the needs of railroads. His

> interest in the manufacturing of rails was at this time [i.e., at the time of his 1865 European tour] of minor significance compared with his other business ventures, but he had no difficulty in seeing the potential advantages of holding the American patent rights for any process that would improve . . . cast iron rails. . . . For cast iron, being brittle and inflexible, was severely affected by extremes in temperature, and with the ever-increasing weight demands of American railway traffic, the problem of weak, easily cracked rails was becoming more acute each year. . . . An all-steel rail would, of course, be the answer, but in these pre-Bessemer days such a rail was prohibitively expensive.[103]

What the railroads needed was a strong, durable metal that could be relied upon in any weather. The costs they incurred for laying rails, building bridges, and buying locomotives and rolling stock were immense. The magnitude of the railroad industry by the late nineteenth century was unprecedented in history. The price of any product failure was also unprecedentedly high. What the railroads needed, in other words, was steel.

The properties of steel were hardly news to Americans on the threshold of the railroad boom which greeted the end of the Civil War. Depending on precisely how it was defined, steel could trace its ancestry to well over a millennium prior to the birth of Christ. By 500 B.C., liquid steel was being produced in India. Although steel was in use in Europe in the Middle Ages, it was not until 1740 that Europeans rediscovered the art of producing liquid steel.[104]

Iron, along with cotton textiles and steam, played a key role in the first Industrial Revolution in Britain during the last forty years of the eighteenth century. Steel did not. It was too expensive and difficult to produce. It was appropriate for springs in high-quality timepieces, tools, small parts of machines, or for expensive cutlery[105] but not for production in a volume at a price that a railroad could use.

Between 1850 and 1872, the role of steel changed forever. The single most dramatic moment in this transformation came by accident, and it was reported to the world by Sir Henry Bessemer in August of 1856. He had discovered how to remove impurities in pig iron without heating it between layers of charcoal and without labor-intensive puddling. Instead, steelmakers could force cold air into a converter full of molten pig iron, causing the oxygen in the air to bind with the carbon in the pig iron; the carbon would then remove itself, as it were, automatically. Excess silicon, a substance we will encounter at the conclusion of this book, could be expelled in the same fashion.[106]

The market was there: the railroads. The product was there: steel. What was needed was an economic method for product to meet market. Sir Henry Bessemer's paper "The Manufacture of Iron without Fuel"[107] pointed the way, but there were all kinds of problems that had still to be overcome before large-scale manufacture could be attempted. These problems were both legal and technical. The Bessemer breakthrough was another example of a dictum which would later in the century be so eloquently articulated by

Thomas Edison: a patent is an "invitation to a lawsuit."[108] Among the most important technical problems was the removal of phosphorus from iron ore. In addition to these issues, there was the challenge of acquiring raw materials for steel manufacture in volumes that had previously been unimaginable.

The three most important raw materials were iron ore itself, limestone, and coke. Limestone shortages were not a problem. The midwestern United States was well endowed with iron ore; and even when it was shipped to Pittsburgh from as far away as the upper Great Lakes, its quality rendered the transportation costs economical.

Coke, coal which had been baked to remove sulfur and phosphorus, was another matter. It was heavy and bulky. Shipping it long distances was not an option. Fortunately for Pittsburgh and fortunately for Carnegie, about thirty-five miles south and west of Pittsburgh down the Youghiogheny (pronounced "Yuck-a-gain-ee") River lay the town of Connellsville, Pennsylvania. Connellsville was situated in the midst of a large seam of superb coking coal. The coal was transformed into coke by being baked in dozens of beehive ovens. The dominant figure in coal, coke, and ovens in Connellsville was an empire builder on Carnegie's scale named Henry Clay Frick.[109]

Frick proved a brilliant, brutal, unreconstructed capitalist. His desire to expand his operations and to keep his costs down were equal to Carnegie's. He and Carnegie became partners late in 1881. One important cost that the coke and steel business shared was labor. Both men knew this cost had to be kept low. Both knew how to control it. The difference between the two was that Frick was a man utterly without illusions about what that meant. Carnegie, on the other hand, was quite simply a hypocrite about the workingman. Hypocrisy, it has been said,[110] is the tribute vice pays to virtue. Frick felt no need to pay such a tribute. Carnegie did. It was on the shoals of this difference that one of the most successful of business partnerships eventually ran aground. For the present, however, the point is that once the H. C. Frick Coke Company was connected to the Carnegie Steel interests not through markets but through ownership, the stage was fully set for a spectacular increase in Carnegie output and profit.

This Carnegie complex on the Allegheny and Monongahela Rivers, which meet at Pittsburgh to form the Ohio, did not grow older, it grew better. By the turn of the century it was able to manufacture steel at a price and a quality unmatched by any other organization anywhere.

Some statistics help tell the story. The Edgar Thomson steel mill became operational in 1875. That year, it accounted for 2.25 percent of Bessemer rail production in the United States, which amounted to 259,699 gross tons. The final full year of Carnegie ownership, 1900, Edgar Thomson's share of U.S. output had soared to 26.30 percent. And that share was of a vastly larger market. U.S. output of Bessemer steel rails was 2,383,654 gross tons, an order of magnitude increase representing a compound annual growth rate over the last quarter of the nineteenth century of 9.3 percent.[111]

Carnegie's defining characteristic as a businessperson was his combination of foresight and his acceptance, even his welcoming, of change. It is hard to know the truth about the future of a business and the market it faces. It is equally hard to cast aside old views in the face of that truth and act. Sunk costs are costs a business has incurred which cannot be recovered and which therefore should exert no influence on future decisions. Everyone in business knows that definition. Few have the courage to act on it. Carnegie did. He once told Charles Schwab, one of his protégés, to demolish and replace a brand-new rolling mill when Schwab told him that there was a better design.[112]

For a decade after the completion of the Edgar Thomson works, the market for steel was mostly for rails. Thereafter, the market began to shift toward structures as America's cities grew, a growth made possible by the maturation of the railroad network. In 1888, Bessemer rail production accounted for not quite half of the steel produced in the United States. In 1900, that figure had dropped to under a quarter. This change in end use necessitated changes in production processes from minor alterations in plant layout to major transformations from Bessemer to open-hearth steelmaking. Carnegie welcomed this change in the market because, like the hedgehog in Sir Isaiah Berlin's parable, he knew one big thing.[113]

What "one big thing" did Carnegie know that others did not? Sometime between 1868 and 1872, he came to understand that steel was destined to change the material basis of civilization.[114] The man who could be the low-cost, high-quality supplier of this commodity would be the richest man in the world (so much for losing sleep about idolizing money) and the greatest of businesspeople.

What I want to emphasize is not merely that Carnegie understood this fact. He understood it with an immediacy, an urgency, matched by no one else. He understood that no investment in this industry was too great if it contributed to his dominance of it.

From the start, every sign reinforced his faith. The Edgar Thomson works—masterfully designed by the greatest industrial engineer of the age, Alexander L. Holley, and built during the depression of 1873, thus costing three-fourths what it would have cost if constructed a few years earlier or later[115]—was an immediate success. The first order it received was for two thousand steel rails from the Pennsylvania railroad.[116] The president of the Pennsylvania at this time, let us recall, was Thomas A. Scott. He had lived through Carnegie's "humiliation" of him two years before well enough to forget all about it where business was concerned.

The gigantic mill appears to have been profitable after a mere six months. "Where is there such a business!" was Carnegie's famous exclamation.[117] In the quarter century from the opening of Edgar Thomson to 1900, the Carnegie Companies never had an unprofitable year. In 1875, Carnegie made $18,600; in 1900, $40 million.[118]

How did he do it?

First of all, he was right about steel and right about America. He had an unquenchable faith in the future of both. Here we see Carnegie the hedgehog.

We can call him a visionary, as indeed he was. There are many visionaries in the world, however. The simple sad fact is that asylums are filled with people who have visions. But Carnegie was right. He knew he was right. His knowledge was based both on his vision and on cold, hard facts.

Carnegie was not particularly technologically inclined. As he himself said, he had "no shadow of claim to rank as an inventor, chemist, investigator, or mechanician."[119] But he knew what he did not know and therefore had to buy or hire. He may not have known chemistry; but he knew how to hire a chemist, "a learned German, Dr. Fricke, and great secrets did the doctor open up to us." Mines said to be producing high-quality ironstone actually were turning out an inferior product, and vice versa. "The good was bad and the bad was good, and everything was topsy-turvy." At a key moment in the operation of a blast furnace, too much lime had been used to cleanse iron ore which was unexpectedly pure. The result: The furnace "met with disaster. . . . The very superiority of the materials had involved us in serious losses."[120]

"What fools we had been!" But then, Carnegie reported with undisguised glee, there was this consolation: We were "not as great fools as our competitors. It was years after we had taken chemistry to guide us that [others said] they could not afford to employ a chemist." The truth was "they could not afford to be without one." Never penny-wise and pound-foolish, Carnegie knew that what others thought was extravagant was in fact economical.[121]

What Carnegie had to know personally and what he knew better than anyone else was costs. One could not control a market, although Carnegie was a superb salesman, but one could, one had to, control costs.

Carnegie had not wasted his twelve years working for the Pennsylvania Railroad. "[B]ig trains, loaded full, and run fast."[122] The Pennsylvania was the best-managed company in the country, and one of the keys to its success was control of its costs.

It was the elite railroads like the Pennsylvania that first figured out sophisticated methods of cost accounting. Carnegie took this knowledge to the steel industry. He knew more about the implications of a high-fixed-cost business than any of his competitors. It was really very simple: "Cheapness is in proportion to the scale of production. To make ten tons of steel would cost many times as much as to make one hundred tons. . . . Thus the larger the scale of operation the cheaper the product."[123]

This unbending reality carried with it two implications: control costs and keep the mills running. To use Carnegie's own words: "Cut the prices; scoop the market; run the mills full. . . . Watch the costs and the profits will take care of themselves."[124] Carnegie reiterated his credo at every opportunity. "Run our works full; we *must* run them at any price. . . . Cost if it can be had, but any price for cash or undoubted buyer. Keep this in mind—all other considerations secondary."[125]

Flowing logically from these principles was Carnegie's capital expenditure policy. Specifically: Hire the best engineers to design the plants. Spend what needs to be spent to keep operating costs low. Only the slimmest margins were necessary, and in fact only they were desirable. The lower the margins, the lower the price. The lower the price, the larger the market. The larger the market, the greater the scale economies. The greater the scale economies, the greater the competitive advantage.

Precepts like these are easy to state and simple to understand in hindsight, but only one in a million businesspeople could live by them. Carnegie not only held the right convictions; he had the power and the courage to put them into practice.

The power came from ownership. Until he sold his holdings to J. P. Morgan in 1901, Carnegie's companies (which had a variety of forms and names through the years) were privately held. These companies were governed by an "Iron Clad Agreement" which forced any owner who wanted to monetize his assets to sell his stock to the firm at book value. This was but a tiny fraction of what the stock would have been worth at any time from 1875 to 1901 on an open market. Carnegie always personally owned more than 50 percent of his firm. He could and did force his "partners" to dance to his tune.

One needs not only courage to build during a depression. One needs money. And Carnegie always had plenty because he did not pay dividends, to the consternation of his partners. He had money, and he never had to go on bended knee to Wall Street for it.

In addition to all this, Carnegie was an exceptionally ruthless man. He fired executives with ease and without qualm. "Give him a trial," he once said about a potential hire. "That's all we get ourselves and all we can give to anyone. If he can win the race, he is our race-horse. If not, he goes to the cart."[126] His attitude toward labor, when judged by what he did rather than by what he said, was not distinguishable from that of his peers. Carnegie is such a seductive personality that it is easy to wrap oneself in a gauze of sentimentality when thinking about him. But to do so is to deny reality.

"Pioneering don't pay" is a much-quoted Carnegie saying. Like so much of what he said, this proved a very poor description of what he did. Andrew Carnegie was a pioneer in many ways, and pioneering paid very well indeed for him.[127]

THE DERANGEMENT OF POWER

"Let me tell you about the very rich," Scott Fitzgerald wrote in 1926. "They are different from you and me."[128] Ernest Hemingway responded in a 1938 story, "Yes, they have more money."[129] In this well-known exchange, Fitzgerald was right, and Hemingway was wrong. The rich really are different. Not necessarily better, but different. They are different from other people who work in the corporations that made them rich. They are different from other people in the nation. They are different from who they themselves were before they became rich. The principal reason is that with great wealth comes power.

On April 5, 1887, John Emerich Edward Dalberg-Acton, Lord Acton, wrote a letter to Bishop Mandell Creighton in which he said, "Power tends to corrupt and absolute power corrupts absolutely."[130] These words are so often quoted that their import can prove elusive. Every day, every man or woman with power should ask not "Am I being corrupted by power?" but rather "In what ways am I being corrupted by power?"

What one learns from studying American business tycoons is that Lord Acton's dictum can be modified with benefit. Power does more than corrupt. It does something more subtle and insidious. The word I choose to describe the impact of power is that it "deranges."[131]

Corruption and derangement are not mutually exclusive, but "derangement" brings an added dimension to an understanding of the impact of power. Corrupt people often know they are corrupt. But deranged people are denied that self-knowledge. They do not know the multifarious methods by which the world conspires with their own grandiosity to make them deranged, that is to say, to change the lens through which they apprehend the world around them.

The problem is not merely that powerful people are surrounded by yes-men. Of course they are. Author Mel Gussow wrote a biography of Hollywood mogul Darryl F. Zanuck with the delightful title *Don't Say "Yes" Until I Finish Talking*.[132] Yes-men are so anxious to please that they will agree no matter what the boss says. Thus, there is no need for him or her to finish speaking. Yes-men are easily spotted. Their approval can be discounted; or, if the person of power is sufficiently insecure, he or she can bask in their flattery.

Derangement, however, is not caused by the yes-man type. It is caused by the courtier who is clever or frightened enough not to be detected. These are the people who arrange a world of continual approbation for the person of power. They see to it that he or she never loses time in a traffic jam and never has cream served with coffee if milk is preferred. The courtier makes perfect for the powerful those little things which bedevil normal folk. In the process, they abstract the powerful from the real world with which even the relatively wealthy of the upper middle class must cope.

The room changes, the feeling changes, the geography changes, in the presence of the powerful. Euripides said that "a slave is he who cannot speak his thought."[133] If that is true, bondage flourishes even today in the American corporation, the Thirteenth Amendment to the Constitution[134] to the contrary notwithstanding. Even people who do not want to play courtier censor themselves in the presence of the boss.

Do not think this kind of behavior is restricted to old-time smokestack companies. Not long ago I was at a firm in California where everyone was "empowered." The CEO was running the business not merely to make money, but "to benefit humanity." The people in that firm were walking on eggs because they could not figure out where the CEO was coming from.[135]

The derangement of power is heightened by interactive effects. CEOs spend a lot of time with each other. Bill Gates and Warren Buffett are friends. Do you think that friendship helps either man to a greater understanding of what life is like for people whose net worth is not numbered in eleven figures?

As we know, Andrew Carnegie came to the United States with no money and very little going for him other than his own drive. It was not long, however, before he met, did business with, and became friends with the most important businessmen of his era: Scott, Thomson, George Pullman, Junius Morgan,[136] and others. It was not long before he began making the acquaintance of important political figures and of men of letters. These celebrities were not merely trophies. He enjoyed them. They expressed part of his nature, just as Henry Clay Frick—cold, stoic, ruthless—expressed another part of his nature.[137]

A great strength of Carnegie's from a business if not from a moral point of view was what we might label "strategic amnesia." In the face of disaster (of which, by the way, he experienced precious little in a long life), Carnegie could just forget. The most severe labor strife at any of his properties was the Homestead lockout of 1892. Carnegie talked and published incessantly. He always wanted to present himself to the world and to himself as a liberal-thinking, liberal-minded man capable of fully appreciating reasoned argument, even if it did not conform to his own views. The idea that wealth and power might have to be fought for, that the struggle for them might literally result in physical conflict, was anathema to Carnegie's thinking. He believed in the "survival of the fittest" but not through fisticuffs. Carnegie's convoluted denial of his share of responsibility for Homestead is as artfully self-deceiving as his reinvention of his relationship with Tom Scott.[138]

Carnegie embraced Charles Darwin via his own made-to-order interpretation of Herbert Spencer's version of the master's writings. Biographer Wall writes that Carnegie's discovery of evolution "came as a thrilling revelation."[139] In his autobiography, Carnegie recalls reading Darwin and Spencer with the result that "light came as in a flood and all was clear. . . . 'All is well since all grows better' became my motto, my true source of comfort."[140] As Wall writes, "'All is well, since all grows better' was for [Carnegie] the satisfying distillation of thirty volumes of Spencer's philosophical speculation."[141]

In his classic *The American Political Tradition: And the Men Who Made It,* Richard Hofstadter wrote that he was "here analyzing men of action in their capacity as leaders of popular thought, which is not their most impressive function."[142] If politicians are not "impressive" as "leaders of popular thought," how much truer is that of businesspeople? American business leaders have only rarely been men or women who were thought leaders among the populace, not to mention in academic circles. As Hofstadter said of politicians, it could also be said that businesspeople generally have been oriented toward action rather than contemplation. Businesspeople can often be highly intelligent. More rarely, however, are they intellectuals in the academic sense, nor would intellectualism necessarily assist them on the job.

The distinction Hofstadter draws between intelligence and intellect is arbitrary but useful. Intelligence "is an excellence of mind that is employed within a fairly narrow, immediate, and predictable range; it is a manipulative, adjustive, unfailingly practical quality. . . ." Intellect, by contrast, Hofstadter believes to be "the critical, creative, and contemplative side of mind. . . . Intellect evaluates evaluations." The intellectual not only works with ideas; he or she plays with them. Ideas have an integrity of their own for the intellectual who therefore approaches them not only with "playfulness" but with "piety" as well. The business executive, on the other hand, "lives *off* ideas, not for them. His professional role, his professional skills, do not make him an intellectual. He is a mental worker, a technician."[143]

This is relevant to understanding Carnegie because he yearned almost touchingly to be more than a mere moneymaker. When he toted up his assets at his home in New York City's sumptuous St. Nicholas Hotel late in 1868 and realized just how rich he really was, that discovery seems to have been depressing rather than exhilarating. It had nothing like the impact on him of his discovery of evolution. Carnegie had met only one successful businessman who could quote from memory a line of Shakespeare or Burns. He loved the hunt and he loved the money, but he did not love the men in the hunt for the money. "He could not help comparing these business associates with the heroes of his childhood, Uncle Tom Morrison, Uncle Lauder, and his father, men who would discourse at length upon topics drawn from history, literature, politics."[144]

What Carnegie did not appreciate was that these "heroes of his childhood" were big men in a very little world. "Uncle Tom Morrison, Uncle Lauder, and his father" would never have their views scrutinized before a skeptical public. More important, they were never men of sufficient power to attract close comparison between what they said and what they did. Carnegie's mother was quite happy to forget their hot air (where, after all, had it landed them but in a shack in Slabtown) and enjoy the tangible fruits of her son's success. But Carnegie wanted to be a force in the world not only of steel but also of ideas and of politics. The derangement of his power in the one paved the way for his making a fool of himself in the other.

Carnegie was a great businessman. He had precisely the intelligence Hofstadter described. He understood better than anyone else the opportunity presented by the production economies of and the demand for steel. No wonder he exclaimed: "Where is there such a business!" Nowhere else but in oil, where John D. Rockefeller had established his dominance.

Here, in steel, was the basket into which Carnegie would put all his eggs. It was the basket he would watch intensely. This proved to be the great battle of his life. He knew how to fight and he won. After he retired, Congressman A. O. Stanley remarked to him, "I believe you would have captured the steel trade of the world if you had stayed in business." Carnegie answered, "I am as certain of it as I can be certain of anything."

We do not have to take Carnegie's word for it. Elbert H. Gary, who first competed against Carnegie and then became chief executive officer of United States Steel, which included Carnegie's firm, said, "It is not at all certain that if the management that was in force at the time had continued, the Carnegie Company would not have driven out of business every steel company in the United States."[145]

With the triumph in steel came money in amounts never before seen. When J. P. Morgan bought Carnegie Steel and created United States Steel in 1901, he expressed an interest in meeting Carnegie to shake hands on the biggest business deal ever. He invited Carnegie down to his famous lair at 23 Wall Street. Carnegie responded that it seemed to him to be equally far from 23 Wall Street to 5 West Fifty-first Street (which is where Carnegie lived at the time) as it was in the opposite direction. If Morgan wanted to see him, in other words, he was welcome to make the trip. And Morgan did, in order to announce: "Mr. Carnegie, I want to congratulate you on being the richest man in the world!"[146] Carnegie's ego, never small, seemed to grow larger with each dollar.

Carnegie gave away the great bulk of his fortune, and much of his generosity did and continues to do a lot of good. As a member of a university faculty, I am personally quite pleased that the Teachers Insurance and Annuity Association exists.[147] His philanthropies flattered his vanity, but that does not make them any the less worthwhile. His generosity was genuine and principled. He believed it was a disgrace to die rich.

The quintessential illustration of how power deranged Carnegie lay not in his philanthropies, but rather in the vocation that absorbed so much of his energy for the two decades between his retirement and his death. What vocation could engage a man of his energy and wealth who had already scaled the greatest heights in the most important industry of his age, an industry which had not even existed when he was born? How does one suppose the richest man in the world would spend his time? Andrew Carnegie devoted himself to nothing less than the quest for world peace. In this quest he was as complete a failure as he was a success at making money in the steel industry. He was worse than a failure; he was a fool.

Before we can understand how such a shrewd man could transform himself into a clown, it is worthwhile contemplating how Carnegie lived, what his daily reality was like. Carnegie did not work hard from 1880 onward. He took frequent extended vacations in Europe. True, he kept an eye on the business through reports which were regularly sent to him. He was so knowledgeable that these reports sufficed. He knew what the key indicators for the success of the business were. He knew when he was being overcharged by suppliers or shippers. He knew when competitive threats arose. He knew what deals to make and when to take a pass. And he knew how to harass his junior partners into working like slaves while he enjoyed a special life of his own creation.[148]

Andrew Carnegie was not only a self-made man, he lived in a self-made world. The glitterati of two continents were his grateful guests at his magnificent castle in Scotland, Skibo. The estate was a "fixer-upper," and Carnegie was able to pick it up for a mere £85,000. He was looking for a place that had a view of the sea, a trout stream, and a waterfall. What Skibo did not have, Carnegie could build. There is no evidence that James Hilton was ever a guest, but Wall makes the place sound like Shangri-la:

> It lay in Sutherland County, in the far northeast corner of Scotland on the Firth of Dornoch. Two rivers, the Shinn and the Evelix, lying twenty miles apart, formed the boundaries of this estate. Although Skibo is in the same latitude as Juneau, Alaska, it is protected by the long narrow firth and the surrounding hills of Sutherland from the cruel east winds off the North Sea. The air is soft and mild throughout most of the year, rhododendrons have been known to bloom in January, and, in a country where there is little competition for such honors, Skibo has more hours of sunshine a year than any other part of Scotland.
>
> The ancient castle of Skibo lay in ruins when Carnegie first drove up the long winding road from the little village of Bonar Bridge. There was no waterfall on the estate, but the

sea was there, gleaming silver in the distance, the sun was shining, and the thousands of acres of empty moor were a hazy green with only a slight lavender suggestion of the deep purple heather that would later bloom. Here at last was his Scottish highland home, and Carnegie immediately began making plans for the building of a new baronial castle—and a waterfall.[149]

It was the summer of 1897. Carnegie was sixty-one years of age. On March 30, he had become a father. He had lost none of his youthful vigor. Just as his business interests were approaching their climax, so his domestic life was entering a new phase. It was in this context that the desperate desires of his partners and competitors and the gentle prodding of his wife combined to tip the balance toward the domestic and pave the way for the sale to Morgan.

Running Skibo was an operation of gigantic proportions. One number tells the tale. There was a staff of eighty-five.[150]

In 1902, the Carnegies moved into their new mansion on Fifth Avenue at Ninety-first Street. This, their winter quarters, was a town house, and not on the scale of Skibo. This is not to say it was small. It was four stories high with three basement levels. Plenty of space for guests here, too. There were sixty-four rooms. Wall writes, "The entire house was a marvel of technological planning for that day." For example: "Air was brought in from the outside, filtered, and then heated or cooled to exactly the proper temperature." The fee for the architects was a million and a half dollars.[151]

This, then, was how Carnegie, who in 1891 had published an article entitled "The Advantage of Poverty,"[152] lived. What could be further removed from the darkest and most satanic of mills on the banks of the Allegheny and the Monongahela? When one of Carnegie's many idols, Herbert Spencer, was lured to Pittsburgh, he remarked: "Six months residence here would justify suicide."[153]

Carnegie was a stranger to Pittsburgh during the last two decades of his life. No matter how wild one's fantasies, the world of business does demand at least some discipline. With that gone and his immense wealth to make him a man hard to ignore, Carnegie's shrewdness seemed to wither as his self-deception grew.

There is nothing wrong with supporting world peace. Nor should one need credentials in order to be heard in such a cause. Yet the enormity of the challenge would seem to call for at least a touch of humility. If there were one trait Carnegie's nature and career failed to engender in him, that was it.

His naïveté, his foolishness, is nowhere better illustrated than in his attitude toward Kaiser Wilhelm II of Germany. This is not the place to discourse at length on the kaiser. He is one of those important historical actors about whom there is little disagreement. He was a vainglorious child who built up a huge military establishment that contemporaries as well as historians knew was meant to be used. Wilhelm II was bellicose and stupid, and one would hardly have thought that Carnegie could have seen in him a kindred spirit. But Carnegie never really did see him. All he saw was his dream.

The dream was that at a meeting of the kaiser and Theodore Roosevelt, Carnegie would outline his plan for world peace and the kaiser and president would warmly embrace it. The kaiser, Carnegie felt, was the key man. "Much has been written and said of the Emperor as a menace to the peace of Europe," he told a peace conference in 1907, "but I think unjustly. So far, let me remind you, he has been nearly twenty years on the throne and is guiltless of shedding blood."[154]

Later that year Carnegie reported to the principal of the University of St. Andrews, "I had three interviews with the German Emperor and dined with him twice—a wonderful man, so bright, humorous, and *with a sweet smile*. I think he can be trusted and declares himself for peace."[155] Also in 1907, a busy year for the cause of peace, Carnegie sent the kaiser a copy of "my speech putting the peace of nations on him," accompanied with a two-paragraph cover letter. The first paragraph read: "In my reveries you sometimes appear and enter my brain. I then imagine myself 'The Emperor' and soliloquize as per enclosed."[156]

Where was the man who had so deftly negotiated with Junius and J. P. Morgan, George Pullman, Henry Clay Frick, and John D. Rockefeller? During his career, his astuteness was matched by few. Business was his métier; politics his hobby. If ever a shoemaker should have stuck to his last, it was Carnegie. But money, he had told himself as a young man, was "the worst species of idolatry." If he was compelled to push something inordinately, the accumulation of wealth was insufficiently satisfying. World peace: that was another matter.

The results were reveries about Kaiser Wilhelm II, a man about whom the most forgiving of commentators have had precious little good to say. Historian Gordon A. Craig describes Wilhelm II as "a kind of perennial Potsdam lieutenant, whose love for uniforms was so intense that he is reported to have insisted on wearing full admiral's regalia to performances of *The Flying Dutchman,* who dined to *Ulanenmusik,* and who preferred military companions, military manners, and military advice to any other." Wilhelm's mother correctly felt that he harbored political views that would be calamitous for Germany.[157] An odd repository, indeed—this man—for reveries about peace.

The darker the world scene became, the sunnier everything seemed to Carnegie. He was one of two Americans who presented the kaiser with a memorial expressing "cordial congratulations upon your twenty-five years of peaceful and prosperous reign. . . . We thank your Imperial Majesty as the foremost apostle of peace in our time. . . ." This was in June of 1913. In his autobiography, Carnegie writes:

> As I approached to hand him the casket containing the address, he recognized me and with outstretched arms, exclaimed:
> "Carnegie, twenty-five years of peace and we hope for many more."
> I could not help responding:
> "And in this noblest of all missions you are our chief ally."[158]

Perhaps the presentation took something like this form, but Carnegie is very much in fantasyland as well. The kaiser never did anything "with outstretched arms." His left arm was atrophied at birth.[159]

One could go on with Carnegie's misadventures in the cause of peace. Certainly seeing the phrase "peace in our time" in the memorial to the kaiser brings chilling forebodings of the equally naive Neville Chamberlain returning from his meeting with Hitler in Munich in 1938.

The point I wish to make is simply that Carnegie's quest for peace was not about peace, it was about Carnegie. When World War I broke out, he seemed to take it personally. His "heroes" had failed him. And there was no denying that he was wrong. He could not rewrite history successfully in this instance, as he had so often in his business life. He had to face facts, and this man whose whole life had been sunshine finally had the opportunity firsthand to learn what failure and depression were.

The power that he had wielded since the mid-1860s had so deranged his judgment that he had come to believe that he could solve the problem of human aggression. Who was to contradict him? He had so much money that he could not be ignored. The men of standing who thought him a fool almost always said so behind his back. The men who agreed with him were happy to spend time at Skibo.

CONCLUDING THOUGHTS

For all his foibles, one cannot look back upon the eighty-three years of Andrew Carnegie's life without awe. From rags to richest.[160] If he allowed himself to think that he could make world peace, how much crazier was that than his fantastic ascent after his first transatlantic crossing on the *Wiscasset* in 1848? He was to cross the Atlantic sixty-five more times. Could anyone have guessed that there would be so many such journeys? Or that never again would he travel steerage?

Andrew Carnegie was a great man. He saw new frontiers where others saw nothing at all. His zest for life and his ability to enjoy himself excite respect and envy.

Though a great man, Carnegie was not always a good man. Indeed, one of the intriguing aspects of his life story is the extent to which being great and being good were mutually exclusive. His relationship with Tom Scott raises this conflict, and that is a situation which admits of no simple resolution. How much, when all is said and done, do you really owe your mentor in the world of business? When Scott met Carnegie in 1852, they developed a friendship built on business. When Scott tried to push Carnegie into the Texas and Pacific investment twenty-one years later, he was offering a business relationship built on friendship. The two are quite different. The former permits the exercise of acumen; the latter prohibits it.

In the Homestead situation, Carnegie's actions are less defensible. Here we see a direct clash between Carnegie the good, the friend of the workingman, and Carnegie the great, the owner of low-cost plants which allowed him to become the king of steel. There is nothing inherently good about unions, and most managers prefer doing without them. The problem lies not there, but with the fact that Carnegie fled to an inaccessible Scottish hideaway, leaving a surrogate, Henry Clay Frick, to do the dirty work in breaking the Amalgamated and to take the heat at the risk of his life.

In his moments of truth, Carnegie chose greatness over goodness when the two came into conflict. In business, they come into conflict often.

From the first, when he wanted to be a man and kill a king, Carnegie had a certain grandiosity. Thinking big can result in great achievement. It can also result in delusion. By the last two decades of his life, his fortune so cushioned him from reality that there was no brake on his fantasy world. When he was in business, there were always men willing to publish hurtful truths about him. Some would tell him such truths to his face and go as far as to menace him physically.[161] Even though, with his "strategic amnesia," Carnegie could slough this criticism off, it was still there. It was a fact.

When he departed business, this fact disappeared. Now his reveries were unchecked. So much had already transpired in his life which was improbable; why believe that anything could be denied him?

Carnegie's quest for peace was not really a new chapter in his life. Rather, it was an exaggeration of the derangement which his money and power had been generating since the 1860s. It alerts us to watch for the same syndrome in other great men of business.

We shall find it without having to look too far.

ANDREW CARNEGIE

November 25, 1835	Andrew Carnegie is born in Dunfermline, Scotland.
May 17, 1848	The Carnegie family sails from Scotland.
1848	Andrew Carnegie's first job: a "bobbin boy."
1851	Carnegie has become a telegraph operator.
February 1, 1853	Carnegie joins the Pennsylvania Railroad as Thomas Scott's clerk and telegraph manager.
December 1, 1859	Carnegie becomes superintendent of the Western Division.
February 1862	Piper and Schiffler Company formed for building railroad bridges. Carnegie takes a one-fifth interest. Later reorganized as the Keystone Bridge Company.
March–May 1865	Kloman & Phipps merges with Cyclops to form the Union Iron Mills, which is later reorganized as Carnegie, Kloman & Company, although still known as Union.
March 28, 1865	Carnegie resigns from the Pennsylvania Railroad.
1873	Construction of Carnegie's Edgar Thomson steel mill at Braddock begins.
1881	Carnegie invests in the Frick Coke Company.
October 1883	Carnegie acquires Homestead.
April 22, 1887	Carnegie marries Louise Whitfield.
November 1890	Carnegie acquires the Duquesne Steel Works.
June 29, 1892	Homestead lockout.
July 1, 1892	Reorganization and further consolidation of the Carnegie holdings into the Carnegie Steel Company.
January 1901	Carnegie agrees to sell his holdings to J. P. Morgan for $480 million. Carnegie's personal share is $300 million.
August 11, 1919	Carnegie dies in Lenox, Massachusetts.

2 GEORGE EASTMAN and the Creation of a Mass Market

PROLOGUE

"To my friends My work is done—Why wait?"[1] At ten minutes to one o'clock on the afternoon of Monday, March 14, 1932, just after writing these words in an unsteady hand on a piece of yellow lined paper, George Eastman committed suicide. He was fastidious about it.

He put the cap back on the fountain pen with which he had written the note. He smoked a cigarette and carefully extinguished it. He folded a wet towel over his chest apparently to prevent powder burns. He shot himself in the heart. He knew exactly where to point the Luger automatic because he had asked his personal physician to outline his heart on his chest not long before.[2] The sewing basket of his beloved mother containing two of her gloves was next to the note. Nearby was another Luger, just in case the first one misfired. Oddly enough for such a precise man, the note itself was, in one sense, slightly misleading.

THE EASTMAN FAMILY

George Eastman was seventy-seven years of age when he died. His family history was interwoven with the nation's. The ancestors of his mother, Maria (pronounced "Mah-rye-ah") Kilbourn, disembarked in a Dutch settlement in Connecticut in 1635. Three years later, Roger Eastman emigrated from Wales to what today is Franklin, New Hampshire. Among Roger's descendants were generals in the Revolutionary War (on the American side); Senator Daniel Webster; Francis Amasa Walker (an early president of the Massachusetts Institute of Technology); the Colgate brothers, Sidney and

Arthur, of the packaged goods company by that name; and George Washington Eastman, George Eastman's father.

George Washington Eastman was born on the family homestead in Marshall, near Waterville, in Oneida County, New York, on September 9, 1815. He was the youngest of ten children. Maria Kilbourn, the youngest of seven, was born six years later on a nearby farm. The Eastman and Kilbourn families had already intermarried by the time George and Maria became man and wife on September 25, 1844.

Eastman discovered in himself an "aptitude for penmanship," which he had begun teaching both in schools and as a private tutor early in the 1830s, in addition to working on the family farm. In 1842, he moved to Rochester and advertised himself as a penmanship teacher.[3] During the 1840s, Eastman also began teaching bookkeeping and accounting. With the help of some relatives, he found himself running a business school, Rochester's first "commercial college"; he coauthored some textbooks on the subjects he taught.[4]

Maria was not unhappy in Rochester, but she preferred the countryside; and in 1849 Eastman moved the family to a ten-acre farm between Waterville and Utica, which he purchased for $3,000. He opened a commercial college in Waterville also; and so the early 1850s found him running two schools separated by 120 miles, as well as a farm. Eastman lived in Rochester while his family lived in Waterville for the better part of each year.[5]

In the midst of these entrepreneurial activities, the family was growing. Ellen Maria was born on November 4, 1845. On August 6, 1850, came Emma Kate. Apparently a son died soon after birth in 1852. On July 12, 1854, George Eastman was born.[6]

We have precious little information about life in the Eastman family. Though entrepreneurial, the father seems to have been a bit depressed as well. The long absences from his family may have been dispiriting. It is difficult to believe a more congenial living situation could not have been devised. Life in these early years did not seem to be hard from a financial point of view. Nor was it devoid of the beauty of nature; roses and fruit trees adorned the Waterville farm. But something seems to have been missing.

What comes through the scanty record is joylessness. "I never smiled until I was forty," George Eastman recalled in 1920. Precise as always, he added: "I may have grinned but I never smiled."[7] This observation is worth thinking about. The contrast with Carnegie and Sam Walton and Bob Noyce (whom we will meet later in this book) is stark. The remark is typical of Eastman. He knew he had missed something important in his early life. But he seems clinical rather than bitter in describing it.

Illness, especially infectious and contagious diseases, and early death were common experiences before the era of modern medicine; and the Eastman family suffered its share of both. Not only did one of Maria's children die in infancy; another, Emma Kate, was stricken with infantile paralysis when barely a year old and bore the crippling effects of the disease until her death in 1870.

George Washington Eastman, who, according to his son's biographer Elizabeth Brayer, "seemed to have the American dream at his fingertips,"[8] saw that dream start to slip away in 1857. The reasons are unclear. His health began to deteriorate when he endured an attack of inflammatory rheumatism and was housebound for a time. Eighteen fifty-seven was also the year of a financial panic which led to sharply depressed business conditions in the North.

In 1858, Eastman sold the Waterville business; two years later, after some difficulty, he also sold the Waterville home. The family was back in Rochester to stay. "Then," writes Brayer, "total calamity." Eastman died, reportedly of a "brain disorder," on May 2, 1862.[9]

It is not clear how close to the American dream G. W. Eastman ever really did come. The business he chose held out only limited profit potential, unlike the one his son entered. Even if it had prospered prior to 1857, which one cannot determine, the business and along with it the fortunes of Eastman's family began to deteriorate after that year. Eastman may have dreamed big dreams as a younger man, but he never seemed able to pull everything together. That was true both professionally and personally. If he had a master plan for building his business, it never became known. In his personal life, for most of each year he accepted voluntary exile from the home which should have been the haven for his heart. He could not have been much of a father to his son. When he was not away from the family, he was at home ill. This was at a time when his wife had a child in delicate health to nurture.

When G. W. Eastman died, his son was seven years old. The downward glide in social and economic standing which commenced in 1857 turned into an abrupt tailspin in 1862. Stuck in Rochester, Maria took in boarders to make ends meet. Then she moved to less expensive quarters. Brayer asserts that the "family's condition was more shabbily genteel than grindingly poverty-stricken, even though poverty is the myth helped along by Eastman's own selective memory."[10]

Brayer is an authority on matters such as this, but it is remarkable if she is right and "Eastman's own selective memory" wrong. His father left the family not with assets but with debts, a fact which the son is said to have resented.[11] The taking in of lodgers was indeed common, but it was also commonly a source of friction in the family circle. And the income generated could not have been great. Maria Eastman came from a large extended family; and, although there is no record of it, one wonders if family members lent a helping hand at times of particular distress.

GEORGE EASTMAN AS A YOUNG MAN

George Eastman spent seven years in public school and then quit to go to work as an office boy for an insurance firm at $3 a week. His responsibilities included cleaning out the cuspidors.[12] It was 1868. Eastman had less formal education than his mother, a rarity among American tycoons.

Eastman was physically rather small. Most of his life he was described as shy, but that description seems not quite right. He had no trouble on the job market. He worked hard: sixty hours a week. He enjoyed making money, and he enjoyed spending it on clothes and on travel. He was generous with his family, especially his ill sister; and he financed membership in the Episcopal Church to please his mother. It is worth noting that Eastman did not wait to become rich before becoming generous.[13] He loved reading, traveling, and the outdoors. By 1873, he had visited Chicago, New York, many of the towns in between, and had fished and sailed off the New England coast. We have already seen how, soon after his arrival in the United States, Andrew Carnegie marveled that "everything around us is in motion." Eastman's many travels at an early age exemplify this phenomenon.

In addition to traveling, Eastman also attended lectures, subscribed to such publications as *Harper's,* and—though it seems too portentous to be true—became an avid reader of one "Oliver Optic." Oliver Optic was the pseudonymous author of Horatio

Alger–type books, the theme of which was enthusiasm for travel or science which led to adventure.[14] Indiana Jones is the modern-day equivalent of an Optic hero.

In the workaday world, once again, we see Eastman's supposed shyness brought into question by his actions. He asked for a raise (for some men a paralyzing experience); not receiving it, he decamped to another insurance agency. By 1869, in his fifteenth year, he was making $6.00 a week. He was seen as a "comer" in his new job, and he eventually became a partner in the firm.[15]

After a childhood in which he had sustained more than his share of bad breaks, things had begun to go Eastman's way. A fire engulfed a large part of Chicago in 1871. Some businesses which had been locally insured found their insurers going bankrupt. The lesson: Take out insurance policies in numerous cities. They were not going to burn down all at once.[16] Rochester was apparently a prime choice, and young Eastman soon found himself writing "new policies to the amount of three-quarters of a million or more."[17]

It was in 1871 that Eastman's economic climb began. He was making $41.66 a month from his insurance company and another $8.00 a month as a fireman in his spare time. He held a mortgage that was generating interest and had small investments in real estate.[18] He could care for his mother, the center of his emotional universe; and he had money for other interests as well.

In 1874, one of his mother's boarders told Eastman of a job opening at the Rochester Savings Bank. This was not long after the Panic of 1873 had sent national income plummeting and unemployment rising. Jobs were scarce; job seekers were not. Eight men applied for the bank position of "clerk at a salary of $700." The supposedly shy Eastman apparently had no trouble asserting himself to be the best man for the job. He got it. By January of the following year, he had been promoted to second assistant bookkeeper, and his annual salary had increased to $1,000.[19]

According to a biographer of Benjamin Franklin, "In any age, in any place Franklin would have been great."[20] Could the same be said of George Eastman? Did he have the unique key capable of opening the unique lock on the door of success in the United States of the last quarter of the nineteenth century? Or did he have within his person a set of characteristics that would have enabled him to succeed "in any age, in any place"?

Numbers speak to successful businesspeople. Sometimes, the success of an entrepreneur can be captured by his understanding of one number or of a simple arithmetic relationship. For John D. Rockefeller, the focus of his business was the fact that the larger the refinery he built, the lower his costs became. With a refinery capacity of five hundred barrels a day, unit costs were $0.06 a gallon. At fifteen hundred a day, they were $0.03 a gallon. "This relationship of scale to costs has remained central from that date [i.e., the 1860s] to this."[21] Rockefeller's understanding of this critical dynamic drove his business strategy.

A handful of numbers also formed the core of Andrew Carnegie's mastery of the steel industry. This was how he put it:

> The eighth wonder of the world is this:
>
> two pounds of iron-stone [i.e., iron ore] purchased on
> the shores of Lake Superior and
> transported to Pittsburgh;
>
> two pounds of coal mined in Connellsville
> and manufactured into coke and
> brought to Pittsburgh;
>
> a little manganese ore,
> mined in Virginia and
> brought to Pittsburgh,
>
> And these four and one half pounds of material
> manufactured into one pound of solid steel
> and sold for one cent.
>
> That's all that need be said
> about the steel business.[22]

According to Henry Bessemer, who, as we know, introduced Bessemer steel to the world in 1856, the price of steel prior to the commercialization of his steelmaking process was £50 to £60 a ton or about $240 to $288.[23] At one pound for one cent, steel cost $20 a ton.

Henry Ford was, in David Riesman's shrewd observation, a man "obsessed by time."[24] In Ford's case, the critical measurement was the amount of time required to build a Model T in his great plant at Highland Park. In the autumn of 1913, it took twelve hours and twenty minutes to assemble the chassis. The following spring, it took one hour and thirty-three minutes.[25] If a competitor to Ford was still running at the 1913 rate in 1914 . . . or at half the 1913 rate . . . or at a quarter of the 1913 rate . . . that competitor was face-to-face with bankruptcy.

Before numbers can matter, one has to keep track of them. With care and precision, John D. Rockefeller began keeping his Ledger A in 1855. He was sixteen years old. He had just taken some courses at Folsom's Commercial College in Cleveland (the kind of institution which Eastman's father had wanted to create) and had begun his business life, as did George Eastman, as a bookkeeper.[26]

Eastman began his account book on March 7, 1868. He was thirteen years old. Brayer refers to the "meticulous entries and Spencerian script" in which he "kept careful records of every cent earned and spent."[27] What strikes the modern reader of Eastman's account book is the artistic flourish, especially embodied in the display of the word "Inclusive." Perhaps noting this sort of detail is the kind of overinterpretation which would not be made if Eastman had grown up to be just an average businessperson. But he did not. He grew up to define an industry, and one of the puzzles about him is here. Why George Eastman? Why not someone else?

From his childhood, we can discern traits which would serve an entrepreneur well in late-nineteenth-century America. The first and most important has already been mentioned, a fluency with numbers. One can add to this his energy and intensity. Eastman had considerable powers of concentration. There was a remarkable freedom from worry about him. As a youth, he set out in the world with no connections. He was willing to do what it took to do a job well, even if it meant cleaning cuspidors. He was not hamstrung by pride. Nor was he crippled by fear. If he were paid less than he felt himself to be worth, he walked out and found work elsewhere. We can infer that he did not hold himself in low regard. But he could not have been arrogant either. The bankers who hired him had choices. One doubts they would have selected a braggart.

Then there is his wanderlust. Unlike the majority of Americans at the time of his youth in the 1860s and 1870s, Eastman was, like

Carnegie, a city boy. From the first, however, he wanted to enjoy the country as well as the city. Travel was arduous in the United States at this time: the very word comes from the French *travail*, meaning "toil."[28] But this young fellow covered a lot of ground.

Despite all he saw, Eastman kept returning to Rochester. In the course of his life he traveled the world, but he had his taproots in Rochester. His famous house there is a remarkable statement of place and of home. Perhaps it was the power of his attachment to Rochester which enabled him to travel as far as he did both professionally and geographically. Moreover, through his philanthropies, the beneficiaries of which included the Eastman School of Music and the University of Rochester, he brought the sophistication of the cosmopolitan world to the banks of the Genesee River.

In 1877, Eastman was preparing for yet another trip. This was to Santo Domingo, in the Caribbean. The goal of the trip was not to escape one of Rochester's winters. Rather, Eastman wanted to explore the possibilities of investing in land. An acquaintance at the Rochester Savings Bank suggested that he take a camera along to record what he encountered.[29]

Eastman decided not to make this particular trip.[30] He did, however, purchase photographic equipment. That is how the great journey of his life began.

MAN AND HOUR MEET

The representation of what people see in pictures has been going on for so long that the desire to do it must be innate in the human race. People have drawn pictures since before history began. This activity unites us with one another, and it differentiates us from animals. They don't draw; we do.

It is a profound and awesome experience to see an ancient drawing on the wall of a cave. Some human being stood by that wall and had the urge to reproduce the form of, say, an animal he or she had just seen. Why? Why was not merely seeing the animal satisfying? In what way did the creation of the image of the animal give it meaning to the artist?

People have been trying to capture reality through the creation of images forever. A picture stops time. A self-portrait can give you that power to see yourself as others do. But not really. Time actually continues. And no picture, of oneself or of anyone or anything else, is the same as the reality of that person or thing.

The Belgian surrealist René Magritte once painted a picture of a pipe (the kind one smokes, not the kind one uses for plumbing). Below the pipe, on the canvas, he wrote in a large, flowing script: *"Ceci n'est pas une pipe."* At first this subscript is confusing. Why paint a picture of what is unmistakably a pipe and then write on the canvas that this is not a pipe? The reason is that it is indeed not a pipe. It is a picture of a pipe. The painting is entitled *The Betrayal of Images.*[31]

Many volumes have been written about photography since its invention, and some of the most creative artists in the world have chosen to express themselves through it. A camera is not merely a toy, nor is it only an instrument of magical technology, although it combines both toylike and magical properties. Like other great media of artistic expression, a photograph can touch people of different backgrounds, cultures, and languages.

Thus, a photograph (and the camera and film which make it possible) is not just another product. Writing about Eastman, one historian observed: "The mysterious internal process that drew him [Eastman] at once to become deeply involved with the camera is beyond this historian's probe. It is enough to say that the young bank clerk began to spend increasing amounts of time behind the lens and in the developing room, and to read everything he could lay hands on concerning photographic techniques."[32]

The problem is that this is not quite "enough," because photography is a special kind of business. Eastman was not manufacturing a basic commodity like oil or steel, as did Rockefeller and Carnegie. He was not producing the elemental needs of food, clothing, and shelter. No one "needs" a camera in the same sense that they do these three things. Nor was he making money by manipulating money. These options were open to him, especially the latter, given his decade of experience in insurance and banking.

One of the important questions about Eastman's life and career is: Did he choose to devote himself to photography solely or primarily because it was a business opportunity, or was there something special to him about capturing an image in time on film? We will never know, but my guess is that the latter is closer to the truth than the former. Henry Alvah Strong, Eastman's first backer, is a good example of someone for whom a camera was a profitable toy, nothing more. If all Eastman wanted was, like Strong, to have money, he had already proven that there were other ways than photography for him to make it.

Eastman did not choose this industry because he was an artist. He is hardly mentioned in books about photography as art.[33] He definitely had an aesthetic sense, but it was personal and undisciplined. Nevertheless, it is hard to believe that to Eastman this was just another business.

Perhaps this is the moment for some amateur psychology. George Eastman never knew who he was. A lot of people do not know who they are; but one senses that for Eastman, this lack of self-knowledge gnawed at him, especially in adolescence and early adulthood.

Eastman's childhood was brief. Due to his father's death, he was the man of the house at an early age. He was not quite eight. He could not have gained much self-knowledge at home. His mother seems to have been a rather unhappy woman and something of a cipher. His father was a failure, a state for which Eastman, like Carnegie, had precious little patience. Early pictures of Eastman make him appear like a man experimenting with "possible selves."[34] This man grew up, metaphorically, in a home without mirrors. A picture is a kind of mirror.

In other words, Eastman, in my opinion, did not go into this business just for the money. One is reluctant to make this statement. The list of businesspeople who have claimed not to be money motivated is long, and their claims are unconvincing. Rare indeed is a man like Standard Oil executive Henry Huttleston Rogers, a contemporary of Eastman, who described himself in Who's Who simply as "Capitalist" and who once told a congressional investigating committee, "We are not in business for our health but are out for the dollars."[35]

With Eastman, to the contrary, it actually seems to have been true. He unquestionably enjoyed money; but there were easier ways of making it than by competing with minimal capital and training in a new, uncertain, technology-intensive industry. Looking back on his career from 1930, he said, "All I had in mind was to make enough money so that my mother would never have to work again."[36] There was something about this industry that captured him.

Since ancient times it has been known that some materials faded and some darkened when exposed to light. Not until the early eighteenth century in Europe, however, did experimentation with light-sensitive chemicals, including especially compounds of silver, begin in earnest.

The daguerreotype, developed in France and originally described in print in 1839, was the first product which to a modern eye looks like a legitimate precursor to a photograph. Not surprisingly, interest in the daguerreotype was immediate. Henry Bessemer was then a young man of twenty-six. Later in his life he wrote, "I well remember how the world was startled by the great discovery of Daguerre; how few minds could at the first moment of its announcement, realise the wondrous fact that by the aid of chemistry combined with knowledge, he had seized upon and trapped the fleeting shadow on his silvery plate and held it there immovable forever."[37] Experimentation with improvements on this involved process was vigorous.

By the mid-1850s, the "wet collodion"[38] process was available to photographers for the preparation of photographic negatives.[39] A contemporary article entitled "The Wonders of Photography" described the wet collodion process this way:

> The negative is made on clear, crystal glass, first polished and well cleaned with powdered rotten-stone or alcohol, coated with a creamy mixture of ether, alcohol, gun-cotton, and sundry bromides and iodides, and dipped into a bath of pure water and nitrate of silver, after remaining in which a few moments, the collodion film becomes highly sensitive to the light, being impregnated with the silver solution, which makes it turn black whenever light is permitted to strike it.

The plate was then immediately taken into a darkroom, where a solution was poured over it and the image began to appear as a negative. This was washed and fixed[40] with another solution, and dried and varnished. It then was taken to the printer, where the negative was pressed against a sheet of paper which had been treated with egg white, dried, floated on a silver solution, dried again, and then exposed to fumes from ammonia. The negative and the paper were pressed together in a wooden frame and exposed to bright light. The positive image would then appear on the paper because the areas which were dark in the negative protected the paper's surface from exposure to the light. In order to prevent the entire paper image from turning black, the paper had to be further treated with a solution of hyposulfate of soda and water. After this, it was washed again and toned by being placed in a solution of chloride of gold and other chemicals. It was given a final washing, then dried, trimmed, pasted onto a stiffer card, dried again, pressed, and polished.

I am going into this detail to make a number of points. First, taking a picture in the mid-nineteenth century was not easy. Think of the expertise involved in the process just described. This was an unforgiving proposition. A wrong move during any part of it meant a poor photograph or none at all. One had to take lessons from a master before one could take a picture.

In 1871, an English physician published experiments on a gelatin silver bromide emulsion to substitute for collodion. This invention has been described as "epoch-making," even though its inventor did not understand its implications. Improved by others, "the rapid gelatin dry-plate ushered in the modern era of factory-produced photographic material, freeing the photographer from the necessity of preparing his own plates. . . . [Gelatin dry-plates] could be stored for long periods and made possible truly instantaneous photographs with exposures of a fraction of a second."[41]

By pure chance, Eastman happened to become interested in photography at a technological inflection point in its history. He learned the wet collodion process in the fall and winter of 1877–1878. If he had taken up photography just a year or two later, he never would have acquired this grounding in the history of the craft. Charles Bennett published some of his advances in dry-plate emulsion in March 1878 in the *British Journal of Photography*, to which Eastman had begun subscribing in the previous month.[42]

Why was this sequence of events important? First, it inspired in Eastman's inquisitive, entrepreneurial mind the question of what might be next. If improvements of this magnitude were possible, what opportunities might further open up? Eastman saw firsthand at an early age what a step-function change in technology could mean.

"The English article," Eastman later said, "started me in the right direction." In his spare time (he held a full-time job at the

Rochester Savings Bank), he began working on his own dry-plate emulsion formula. He did not succeed at first; so he tried, tried again. Eventually, he did quite well. His first goal was simply to make it easier for himself to take pictures, "but soon I thought of the possibilities of commercial production."[43] Perhaps we should also note a certain similarity with Carnegie's commitment to the steel industry. In the 1860s, steel was manufactured by the pound. But in the early 1870s, only half a decade before Eastman's interest in photography, the Bessemer process transformed the production and economics of steel. Carnegie, like Eastman, benefited immeasurably by seeing both sides of the inflection point in the industry in which he was to make his fortune.

Second, and this is also through the merest chance, the two masters who taught Eastman the wet collodion process turned out to be important in his business career. One of these was George Monroe, a professional photographer whom Eastman paid $5 for lessons. He would call on Monroe fifteen years later to work for him when an important lieutenant abandoned him in order to start a competing firm.

Eastman's other teacher was one of the only two amateur photographers in all of Rochester. He was a patent attorney named George B. Selden. This is the same George Selden who on November 5, 1895, was granted patent number 549,160 for an "improved road engine" powered by "a liquid hydrocarbon engine of the compression type." This was the most important patent in the history of the automobile industry. If Henry Ford had not fought and broken it,[44] there probably would be no Ford Motor Company today; and the automobile industry would have had a distinctly different history. The point is that George Selden knew about patents. That knowledge proved important. Success in the photography industry without a shrewd patent strategy was not possible.

When George Eastman purchased his camera and the associated equipment on November 13, 1877, it cost him $49.58. When we add the $5.00 he paid for lessons, we see that he spent $54.58 to become a photographer.[45] In 1900, the Eastman Kodak Company brought out the Brownie. It cost $1.00, and you did not need lessons to learn to use it. The film for it cost 15 cents. These are the numbers that mattered most in Eastman's business career: $54.58 and $1.15.

In addition to the price, another big difference between what

Eastman bought to take a picture and the camera he brought to the market at the turn of the century concerned paraphernalia. Here is what was included in Eastman's starting kit in 1877:

> the heavy camera itself, together with a tripod, plus plates, paper, boxes for storing negatives, and a tent that he could set up as a darkroom, [and] also the furnishings of a small chemistry laboratory—nitrate of silver, acetate soda, chlorides of gold, sodium, and iron, collodion, varnish, alcohol, litmus paper, hydrometer, graduate, evaporating dish, funnel, bristle brush, scales and weights, and washing pans.[46]

Compare this to the Brownie of 1900, which was a small, light little box which came equipped with unexposed film.[47]

Given the cost and the complexity, it is not surprising that the number of amateur photographers was small. The most influential market was the professionals. And members of many professions have often proven resistant to change. They had to master the mysteries of all that equipment Eastman bought. Those mysteries constituted a barrier to new competition. Their mastery was the source of their income. Every profession, to paraphrase Bernard Shaw, is a conspiracy against the laity.[48] Photography was no different.

George Eastman did not set out with a clear idea of the direction in which he wanted to move the trade. He was not like a scientist who has as a goal the discovery of a cure for a disease and for whom all the intermediate steps are merely means to the end. Eastman started out working with means. Only step by step did an end clarify itself. Unlike Edison with the lightbulb, Ford with the automobile, or Steve Jobs with the computer, Eastman set out neither to change the world nor to change his industry. He set out because the idea of staying put never seems to have entered his mind.

THE BIRTH OF A BUSINESS

In late 1877 and early 1878, Eastman realized that the dry plate was going to change photography. His goal was to come up with his own dry-plate formula which would outperform the others on the market. By the summer of 1878, he was conducting experiments from the time he left the bank at three in the afternoon until breakfast. He could not have gotten very much sleep.[49] His work habits seem more appropriate to Silicon Valley software engineers than to our stereotype of the slower-paced life of 125 years ago.

Entrepreneurs have been defined as businesspeople who are opportunity driven rather than resource constrained.[50] The opportunity was for a better formula. The resources by which Eastman was constrained included every resource one can imagine: connections, capital, education, equipment, and time. But he did not let the constraints dominate the opportunity.

Eastman was not by nature a pure researcher.[51] He was not interested in chemistry for its own sake. His "method was empirical in the strictest sense: What seemed to work, he kept; what did not, he tossed."[52] In a matter of months, he came up with an emulsion which he believed represented an improvement on anything on the market.

Applying the emulsion to a glass plate for photographic purposes proved to be difficult. Eastman therefore set about to create a machine to coat glass plates with his new emulsion. It seems that he had as much of a knack for mechanical contrivances as for chemistry, and by the summer of 1878 this device was complete.

Eastman traveled to Britain in June of 1878 to apply for patents (apparently) on both the emulsion and the coating apparatus. Britain was the center of the photographic industry at the time, but it is still unclear why it should have been his first stop. Back in the United States, George Selden advised Eastman to patent his inventions here as well. Eastman followed Selden's advice, but eventually Selden's lack of aggressiveness got on his nerves. In 1887, he replaced him, explaining: "We want a *fighter*."[53]

Both these areas, emulsion making and production machinery, were targeted by Eastman as arenas for continuous improvement. New emulsion formulas, new machines, and new patents came quickly from the loft above a music store which Eastman called his factory. All the while that this was going on, Eastman continued his progress at the bank.

By April of 1880, Eastman was using his patented machine to produce dry-plates for photography coated with his patented emulsion at 73 State Street in Rochester's financial district. He "took pride in being handy. He did everything himself, from hiring to firing, from inventing, mixing, and building to selling, bookkeeping, and corresponding."[54] Meanwhile, he was doing well at the bank, earning promotions and raises in salary.

It is an indication of the freedom which characterized the lives of Americans in 1880 that Eastman could create a business without the need to consult lawyers, bankers, and accountants. In 1879 and 1880, he made a total of $4,000 running a company which had no legal existence.

By the end of 1880, Eastman decided to change that. Earlier in the year, he had tried to persuade his former employer at the insurance agency to join him as a partner. His inquiry was politely declined,[55] a very expensive mistake.

Eastman also approached a well-known Rochester businessman named Henry Alvah Strong, and Strong decided to bet on Eastman. The relationship between Strong and Eastman proved to be extraordinarily fruitful. Strong was one of the few individuals who spanned the yawning gulf between Eastman's persona as a professional man of the business world and his inner delicacy. He became the bridge between the public side and the private side of George Eastman.

Eastman's instinct for the development of his company and for the construction of his own career served him extraordinarily well in his early years. The great majority of business start-ups fail, and most of these failures take place soon after firms are founded. Eastman Kodak survived its infancy and childhood, and did so in style. Why?

Entrepreneurs are usually thought of as risk takers. They are said to take big risks for big rewards. In fact, most entrepreneurs embrace the rewards but try to avoid the risks. (Most, not all. Some are thrill seekers and get a kick out of the risk.) The problem with risk is that it is . . . risky. The extent of risk can sometimes be quantified, and the degree of risk associated with different courses of action calculated. But the fact is that when the calculation is completed, there is an irreducible element of luck involved when a risk is taken.

Coming out of the nineteenth century, we encounter some of the nation's most famous entrepreneurs running from risk and embracing certainty as quickly as they could. Marshall Field, for example, founded a great retail dynasty. In discussing his business, he once observed that "there were never any great ventures or risks, nothing exciting whatever." When Field moved his store from Lake Street to State Street in Chicago, he knew his relocation was a sure thing because his friend Potter Palmer was a real estate tycoon who had decided to reconfigure Chicago's entire business district. Field was "in" with the "in crowd." His prior knowledge of the plans of his friend and onetime partner Palmer took the risk out of store site selection for him.[56]

John D. Rockefeller's fortune was based upon capturing scale economies in oil refining and negotiating preferential transportation rates from the railroads. He had a little trouble getting off the ground. He once complained of having "worn out the knees of my pants" in the search for credit.[57] But this phase of his career did not last long. Soon, bankers were chasing him down the street and pleading with him to "use $50,000."[58] Why the change? Because Rockefeller had eliminated much of the risk from his business. His unmatchably low costs had turned Standard Oil into a sure thing. Similar stories could be told of Carnegie in steel and Ford in automobiles. These men placed their firms astride the choke points in their respective industries. They established, through the achievement of low costs, formidable competitive positions. Keep in mind that like all generalizations, this one has exceptions. Robert Noyce, whom we will learn about later in this book, made a point of speaking of the "technologist" (rather than the entrepreneur specifically) as someone who was "comfortable with risk." But Noyce was more of a daredevil than most successful businesspeople.

Thus, the voyage of many a great entrepreneur is, among other things, the voyage away from risk, which can never be completely eliminated from a new venture, and toward certainty. How can we chart George Eastman's voyage?

Eastman hedged his bets from the beginning. He did not throw caution to the winds and abandon his job at the bank the first time he touched a camera. Not until September 5, 1881, four years after he took his first picture, did Eastman feel free to ditch his job at the bank, where he felt he was being treated unfairly.

By 1880, Eastman had worked his way up to the position of first assistant bookkeeper at the Rochester Savings Bank. He was earning $1,400 a year, a substantial amount of money at the time, especially for a twenty-five-year-old man whose first wage had been $3 a week. It was in 1881, however, that one of those defining events, one of those moments of truth, which so many entrepreneurs experience transpired in Eastman's life. His immediate superior left the bank, and Eastman expected to receive the promotion for which he felt himself amply qualified. But he was passed over in favor of a relative of one of the bank's directors. "It wasn't fair," Eastman told the *New York Times* many years later. "It wasn't right; it was against every principle of justice."[59] Eastman had the exquisite pleasure of returning to the bank years later, this time as a trustee.

This was the moment that the rubber band snapped for Eastman. He was a free man. He did not have to put up with what he viewed as unfair and not right. In the America of 1881, there was no place in which either by law or custom Eastman had to stay if he did not want to. He walked out of that bank, just as he had quit the insurance firm in 1874. This time, however, he had what was beginning to look like a promising direction to which to turn: the Eastman Dry Plate Company, in a new location at 101 and 103 State Street in Rochester. Now, after four years of rubbing up against photography and learning about it, had come the moment to, as Andrew Carnegie liked to say, "put all your good eggs in one basket, and then watch that basket."[60] Like Carnegie and Rockefeller, Eastman did not start out in the business, or even in the industry, in which he would make his mark. He got to know the industry while doing something else. That meant long hours holding down two jobs, but it greatly weakened the enemy of so many businesspeople—risk.

EASTMAN AND STRONG

A striking difference between Eastman on the one hand and Ford, Carnegie, Rockefeller, Field, and a host of other entrepreneurs on the other hand is the robustness of Eastman's business relationships once his company was founded. Often, business relationships, especially early ones, crack up. Rockefeller and Clark, Carnegie and Frick, Ford and Malcomson, Field and Leiter—none of these partnerships endured. Why did these and so many others fail to withstand the test of time? Why did Eastman's relationship with Henry Alvah Strong flourish up until Strong's retirement in 1901 and until his death in 1919?

Think of the entrepreneur as we have defined him, reaching out for opportunities and overcoming constraints. Eastman saw an opportunity in photography. The field was moving fast. Experimenters were sharing their innovations with one another, after the fashion of the "home brew" get-togethers in the early days of the personal computer. Photography was interesting, intriguing, and fun. Rarely have such adjectives been applied to bookkeeping. It seems never to have entered Eastman's mind that this was a field he should not enter because of his lack of professional training or social standing. In most other countries, such issues would at least have been considerations. The fluidity and openness of Eastman's surroundings could not be better illustrated by the fact that this particular dog did not bark.

Whatever the opportunity the entrepreneur detects, he is going to need money to exploit it. If he is not independently wealthy, that money, to state the obvious, is going to have to come from some other individual or some institution. It is noteworthy that during the second half of the nineteenth century, capital was often available to projects with potential and with an enthusiastic promoter. To return to an example mentioned previously, Rockefeller needed money at first, but soon thereafter investors were lining up to place their funds with him. And the same is true of Eastman. In his career, he was never capital constrained. Moreover, the source of the capital for these entrepreneurs of the second industrial revolution was rarely the Wall Street or State Street investment machine. It was usually local money at first, supplemented by retained earnings as the enterprise prospered.

The money was available. But the precise terms of the deal by which the entrepreneur gained access to the needed funds were varied. In nine cases out of ten, the source of funds and the entrepreneur had different financial, business, and psychological goals. When these differences became unresolvable, the young enterprise spiraled downward into crisis. A noteworthy feature of Eastman's business was that no crisis along these lines ever occurred. The reason is the relationship between Eastman and Strong. The bond between these two men is difficult to decode.

Strong was an eighth-generation descendant of Elder John Strong, who arrived in Dorchester, Massachusetts, on a ship from England (the *Mary and John*) in 1630. Ancestors and relatives included the patriot Nathan Hale; Caleb Strong, the governor of Massachusetts in the early nineteenth century; and Washington Hunt, the governor of New York from 1850 to 1852. (A distant relative from South Coventry, England, was an ancestor of the late Lady Diana Spencer, formerly the Princess of Wales.)

The Strong family resided in Rochester from the city's beginnings. Hulda Strong was the first schoolteacher in what was then Rochesterville in 1813. Another Strong married the town's first postmaster. Other members of the family were physicians, newspaper editors, businessmen, politicians, and public figures.[61]

Strong was a navy paymaster during the Civil War. On his return to Rochester, he went into his uncle's buggy whip business. He acquired his uncle's ownership interest and formed a partnership with another Rochesterian. By 1880, this firm was said to be the second-largest buggy whip manufacturer in the United States, employing a hundred people to turn out almost a million whips a year and generating excess cash in search of a home.[62]

Strong placed $1,000 with Eastman on December 23, 1880. Strong was to be president of the fledgling Eastman Dry Plate Company, Eastman the treasurer. Strong invested an additional $1,000 in January, and another $1,873 in March. By August of 1881, Strong had invested more than $5,000.[63] Why? What were his goals?

We do not know Strong's financial goals. We know now, of course, that the buggy whip industry was a good one to exit; but that was far from obvious in 1880, when there were a lot of horses in the United States and hay to feed them was among the nation's largest agricultural commodities. The first stirrings of the automobile did not come until the 1890s, and it was only with the introduction of the Model T in 1908 that the demise of the horse and buggy became a certainty.

Strong did not invest out of any interest in photography. He knew less than nothing about the new industry. He did not take a picture until May of 1888.[64] As an individual, Strong seems to have been a blowhard and a bit of a phony. As Brayer puts it, "There was always something faintly bogus about Strong's personality, something about his grandiose verbalizing (not to mention his girth) that had a touch of Falstaff to it."[65]

As a businessman, Strong had his limits, to put it kindly. For some odd reason, he fell in love with Tacoma, Washington. He invested large sums in enterprises there which he was incapable by training or inclination of managing properly. He pledged the one asset of incontestable value, his Eastman stock, to secure some of these investments. In 1894, Strong's Tacoma enterprises collapsed. Eastman stepped in, liquidated what he could, and redeemed the stock. This forms an interesting contrast with Carnegie, who, as we have seen, would not play the financial savior for his mentor Tom Scott.[66] Eventually, Strong's seemingly worthless investments increased in value and began to generate cash for the surprised Eastman. Sometimes good deeds do pay off.

Eastman brought Strong back to Rochester and kept him on as president of what was by then the Eastman Kodak Company. Eastman expressed "great relief" at having Strong back at home.[67] Strong remained as president, with Eastman as treasurer, until Strong voluntarily stepped down to while away the days playing golf with friends such as John D. Rockefeller. He continued as the president of the New York operating company and as vice president and treasurer of the New Jersey corporation for many years thereafter. Strong never really knew much about the business, and these positions seem to have been principally ceremonial. He devoted the last two decades of his life to having fun.[68]

The relationship between Eastman and Strong is important and puzzling. Successful entrepreneurs are often people who leave others behind. Strong and his $5,000 were vitally important to Eastman in 1880 and 1881. In return for his funds, Strong became the president of the company. When the Eastman Dry Plate Company first sold stock to the public in 1884, Strong received 750 shares to Eastman's 650. It appears that the only thing Strong brought to the party was money. By 1894, when Strong was speculating in Tacoma, he was worthless to Eastman's business. Yet Eastman saved him and at no small cost. Why?

Eastman was able to save Strong without ruining himself. Nevertheless, there are a number of similarities with the story of Carnegie and Scott. Strong, like Scott, undertook his new ventures against the advice of his onetime protégé. Eastman, like Carnegie, was in a complicated financial situation when Strong came to grief. Eighteen ninety-four was the trough of a severe depression. Eastman was about to leave for a vacation when word reached him of the idiotic situation into which Strong had sunk. Why not let the old fellow stew in his own juice?

Perhaps there were business reasons for Eastman's solicitude. Strong had mortgaged his Eastman Kodak stock. A large block of stock was, for the first time, in the hands of outsiders. Strong had been the model of a passive owner. He had never interfered. Might new owners be looking for something more in the way of dividends than Strong had asked?

If thoughts like this were on Eastman's mind, there is no evidence of it. Instead, everything points to sentiment. This is not to suggest that Eastman was a nicer person than Carnegie or that he was softer. Eastman was not the self-conscious social Darwinist that Carnegie was, but America never produced a tougher businessman. "Peace," Eastman once wrote, "extends only to private life. . . . In business it is war all the time."[69] He walked his talk. He used industrial espionage when he felt it was called for, and denied competitors access to needed resources and marketing outlets when he could.[70]

Marion Gleason, a pharmacologist at the University of Rochester and the wife of the man Eastman hired as his personal organist, once said to Eastman: "I envy you, your ability to be hard when you need to be." Eastman replied: "Yes, one has to be hard, hard in this world. But never forget, one must always keep one part of one's heart a little soft."[71] Strong benefited from the soft side of Eastman's heart.

Eastman was hard when he felt he had to be and when he felt he was in the right. When he was hard, his hardness seemed divorced from emotion. The deprivation of emotion was part of his hardness. Eastman could be quite clinical. When he discovered, for example, that Henry M. Reichenbach, one of his most important and trusted employees, whom Eastman had plucked out of the University of Rochester and given the opportunity of a lifetime, was planning to betray him by leaving to establish his own firm, Eastman found out and wrote immediately and simply:

> Dear Sir:
> Your services are no longer required by this company.
> Yours truly,
> Geo Eastman[72]

No lecture on ingratitude; no expression of hurt feelings. It was as if Reichenbach had fallen off the edge of the earth.

For Strong, the rules were different. True, as noted, there were business reasons for Eastman to get along with him. At least until

1894, Strong owned more stock than Eastman himself. Together with Strong, Eastman controlled the majority of shares even as his company became more widely held. Eastman Kodak was able to grow into a major industrial corporation with millions of dollars in assets while under the control of a stable partnership that lasted almost four decades.

This stability, when combined with Kodak's virtual monopoly over parts of the industry by the turn of the century, could have led to calcification and stasis. Instead, Kodak was among the most vibrant and progressive of companies during the late nineteenth and early twentieth centuries. One pillar of this stable dynamism was the unshakable alliance of Eastman and Strong.

But the feelings of these men for one another went deeper than commercial relationships. It would be easy to say that Strong was a father figure. This would not be wholly inaccurate, but neither would it be the whole story. Eastman's father was born in 1815. Strong was born in 1838, just sixteen years before Eastman, although the gap in their ages seemed greater. Strong was always trying to introduce Eastman to young women. This was a role a father might play. Eastman never really dated and never married, one of the very few major figures in American business of his time of whom these things could be said.[73]

Beyond this, however, to say that Strong was a father figure obscures more than it reveals. Relations between fathers and sons are almost always complex. When business is added to family, this dyad can become explosive. Love and money often do not mix. The connection between Strong and Eastman seems, rather, to have been one of unalloyed affection. Perhaps in his role as surrogate father Strong never threatened Eastman's relationship with his mother as every biological father, in a sense, does.

Eastman was devoted to his mother. When she died on June 16, 1907, at the age of eighty-five, he said that he "cried all day. I could not have stopped to save my life."[74] She was forty-one when her husband died. By 1880, when her son had a financial competence, she was almost sixty. He became the center of her life and her sole support and caretaker. However, from what one can gather, she seems to have been reserved and withholding in response to her son's generosity and spectacular success. Maria Kilbourn Eastman did not have an easy life for sixty years. In her old age, though, she lived amid surroundings which few people ever enjoy. Instead of celebrating a son who was one of the wealthiest men on earth, she was gnomic. When Eastman said, "We're millionaires now, Mother," she did not trouble to interrupt her knitting, saying only, "That's nice, George," and apparently did not pause to note that Eastman could have said "I" rather than "we." Later she said to her nurse, "George's money came too late for me to enjoy."[75] The lifelong bachelor Eastman adored his mother in an extravagant, Victorian manner. She seems to have been less than fully appreciative of his accomplishments. She was a woman who could not be pleased.

To this bleak picture Strong presents a stark contrast. A hail-fellow and glad-hander, he was generous with his affection. He was different from Eastman in every way. He was outgoing, while Eastman was not; he was a gambler, while Eastman was cautious; he was unguarded, while Eastman was shrewd; he was a big, rambling man physically, while Eastman was slight and younger-looking than his age. Perhaps it was because of these differences, rather than in spite of them, that Eastman was able to enjoy Strong's friendship.

Strong appreciated Eastman. "You are a queer cuss, Geo," he wrote him in 1888, "and I know you never want any sympathy or comfort from your friends . . . but I want you to know that I, for one, appreciate the mountains of care and responsibility that you are constantly called to overcome . . . and if I never express it in words, it may be a source of comfort to you to know that I am always with you heart and hand."[76] Strong's recognition of Eastman's ability to concentrate intensely and to carry the load was not unique. Others began to understand Eastman's talents soon after he got involved in the industry. What is remarkable is that Eastman was able to accept Strong's appreciation of him.

MANUFACTURING AND MARKETING

Eastman's friendship with Strong not only reveals part of the man; it also, as noted, protected the business. The Eastman Dry Plate Company set out to become the best dry photographic plate producer in the country. This meant a commitment to producing the best gelatin-coated glass plates. It also meant the most skillful marketing of the product. Eastman understood more quickly than anyone else in the industry that coordination of production and distribution was going to be essential. He also understood that competitive advantage could be achieved at any point in the "value chain" and that it could just as well be lost at any point.[77]

The transition from the wet collodion to the dry-plate process was a revolution. The essence of the revolution was that dry-plate photographic materials did not have to be prepared and photographs did not have to be developed on-site. The business model demanded by the wet collodion process was decentralized production and development of photographic plates because each photographer had to manage these tasks personally and simultaneously with the taking of the photograph. What could be centralized was the distribution of photographic supplies. Therefore the biggest, most important firms in photography were the marketers of photographic equipment from stores and "depots."

With dry-plate photography, plates could be stored both before and after exposure. This meant that the plates could be centrally manufactured and scale economies could be captured. In the dry era, therefore, the manufacturer became the "channel commander" of the industry, the key player in the value chain, replacing the distributor in that role. This is as important as any change that can take place in an industry. It would be as if some technological change in the automobile industry made it more important what dealer you purchased your car from than who manufactured the car you bought.

Moreover, once dry-plate photography became a reality, experimenters quickly began looking for a carrier base other than glass. What these experimenters discovered was that celluloid, a type of nitrocellulose usually thought of as the first plastic, could be produced as film which could replace the glass plate. Film could be delivered in a roll. Roll holders thus of a sudden became important in the industry.

In the early years of the Eastman Dry Plate Company, Eastman and William H. Walker, a difficult individual who was granted an ownership interest in the company and a seat on the board, concentrated on developing and patenting what they viewed as the three basic elements of photography: the film, the process of filmmaking, and the roll holder. They succeeded, and the company did very well from the start.[78] Eastman's competitive methods and his basic business philosophy were, in the early 1880s, rather traditional. He did his best to patent everything he could and went to great lengths to buy the patents of others. He entered into pools to control price and output. He began buying other companies, sixteen of them at least, to control competition.

Both the chemistry of Eastman's emulsions and mechanics of his roll holders were patented. Of the two fields, chemical and mechanical, the former proved the more delicate and the more valuable. During the course of the 1880s, emulsion formulas quickly came to be seen as a key element of success in the industry. They therefore became the most closely guarded secrets. The sharing, amateur, home brew phase of the photography industry was over for good.

Patents are as old as law, and pools restricting price and output are as old as business. Pools have been illegal in the United States since the passage of the Sherman Act in 1890. Eastman Kodak lost at least one major antitrust suit. An exasperated Eastman once said that he did not understand the antitrust laws and did not know anyone who did.

The thrust of the Sherman Act was to prevent price fixing and monopoly. It was among the factors driving Kodak and other firms such as Du Pont away from agreements with direct competitors and toward vertical integration.[79] Independent of the Sherman Act's influence, Eastman had begun to realize during the late 1880s and the early 1890s that pools and patents had limits as devices through which to organize an industry. The problem with pools, and even with purchasing competitors, was that there was nothing to stop some other firm from entering the market for the specific purpose of being bought out. This pattern had already established itself in the railroad industry, and by late in the nineteenth century it was spreading to industrials.

Patents are still important in the photography industry, but they have plenty of defects to accompany their virtues. First, they generate lawsuits. Second, a patent is a public document, tipping off the rest of the industry to a company's direction. If a patent can be "invented around," the information it transmits may cost the company dearly. If the traditional methods of competition were coming under question, what new way could be found to create and sustain industry leadership?

By the mid-1880s, Eastman had clearly given birth to a business. He was an intensely hard worker, extraordinarily knowledgeable, and tenacious. He was attracting some first-class talent to work with him. He was off and running. But where was he running to?

George Eastman wrote thousands of letters during the course of his long life. Through conversations with friends which have been preserved in memoirs and in numerous, lengthy court proceedings, we have, when added to all these letters and Elizabeth Brayer's comprehensive biography, evidence of Eastman's thinking year by year. Until 1887 or 1888, Eastman and his employees were working so intensely, especially on the delicate problems involved in the preparation of emulsions for coating plates or film, that there seems to have been limited time devoted to the big picture, so to speak. Eastman pushed his colleagues with such forcefulness that a rather large number of them collapsed under the strain. Chemistry . . . roll holders . . . patents . . . lawsuits . . . trade secrets . . . spies . . . suppliers . . . distributors . . . employees . . . competitors . . . foreign rights . . . domestic statutes—this list of words dominated Eastman's waking moments. On any given day, their relative importance might change; but Eastman was always putting out fires in one place or another. Sometimes these fires were not merely metaphoric. Photographic chemicals were inflammable and explosive. Eastman's State Street plant was engulfed by fire in 1888 and closed for two months.[80] One reason that has been suggested for the nervous problems of Eastman's colleagues is the neurological effects of the fumes from emulsion making. He and his company were running very hard to stay in place. What was missing from Eastman's company was a galvanizing idea—what has come to be known today by the rather infelicitous phrase "Big Hairy Audacious Goal," or "BHAG."[81]

As the 1880s began, the market for photographic equipment consisted of two segments: the professional portrait photographer and what was known as the serious amateur. Given how difficult photography was, any amateur had to be serious. Whether undertaken for profit or for enjoyment, photography demanded patience, knowledge, and work.

Step by step and not in accord with any master plan, changes were taking place in the various elements of the industry that would make it easier to take a picture. In 1878, taking a picture required money and care. A decade later, your film could be made for you and developed for you. The camera itself had so shrunk in size during the 1880s that it was no larger than a briefcase. In 1883, the "Detective Camera," so named because it was sufficiently unobtrusive that it could supposedly be used in undercover police work, was patented.

The industry in general and Eastman specifically were building a better mousetrap, but the world was not beating a path to their doors. In the words of the leading historian of the industry, Reese V. Jenkins, the great majority of Americans in the early 1880s "never entertained the thought of taking a photograph, let alone pursuing the complicated operations of developing and printing that were required following exposure."[82] But what would happen if the average person could take a picture without all those "complicated operations"? No one knew. In fact, no one even knew that this was a question worth asking.

We must pause and emphasize this moment because it has been repeated many times in different industries from 1880 to the present day. How can one know whether a technologically new and formerly unimagined product will appeal to a mass market? How do you know anyone would want a refrigerator? An air conditioner? A radio? Air travel? A personal computer? What will these products or services do for the mass buying public? How can they be distributed? How advertised? How sold? How priced? The business history of the twentieth century in the United States was the history of the introduction of new products. These questions had to be answered for such products to capture a mass market. Before they could be answered, they had to be asked. And before they could be asked, someone had to start thinking in a way different from his peers, orthogonally to the way in which production and marketing issues had been conceptualized in the past.

The term "paradigm shift" is used rather offhandedly today. The man who gave the word "paradigm" its current meaning is the late historian of science Thomas S. Kuhn. Here is what he meant:

> Consider . . . the men who called Copernicus mad because he proclaimed that the earth moved. They were not either just wrong or quite wrong. Part of what they meant by "earth" was fixed position. Their earth, at least, could not be moved. Correspondingly, Copernicus' innovation was not simply to move the earth. Rather, it was a whole new way of regarding the problems of physics and astronomy, one that changed the meaning of both "earth" and "motion."[83]

Prior to the 1880s, part of what people meant by the word "photography" was an elaborate chemistry set and all those "complicated operations" Jenkins wrote about. But what would photography be if you could have the picture without the expertise?

What Eastman discovered was that nothing happened. As he put it: "When we started out with our scheme of film photography, we expected that everybody that used glass plates would take up film, but we found that the number that did this was relatively small and that in order to make a large business we would have to reach the general public and create a new class of patrons."[84]

Eastman would have to "create," to use his word, a mass market. He had been rejected by the professionals and the serious amateurs. But how big was the potential market beyond them? No one knew. Eastman himself well understood that no one needed a camera or a picture for physical survival. Photography was a luxury. Could it be democratized? Eastman thought so. He began working on a simple camera which targeted a mass market in the summer of 1887. By December, his "little roll holder breast camera" was ready for a name. He called it Kodak. He had always liked the letter "K," which was the first letter of his mother's maiden name. He wanted a brand-new, unique word in order to meet the trademark requirements in England; and he also wanted a word easy to pronounce. Including the case in which it was sold, the new Kodak was 6½ inches by 3¼ inches by 3¾ inches. Price: $25.

But Eastman was selling more than a camera, he was selling a service as well. The $25 Kodak came already loaded with a roll of one hundred frames of unexposed film. All the photographer had to do was turn the key to get to the next frame, pull a cord to cock the shutter, and push a button to take the picture. When all one hundred frames had been exposed, the photographer sent the camera back to Rochester, where the Eastman Kodak Company unloaded it, developed the pictures, reloaded the camera, and sent the pictures and the camera back to the customer. Price for this service: $10.[85]

This was the turning point in the history of photography.

The fire at the plant halted production in the late winter of 1888. Nevertheless, by the end of June the new Kodak was being shipped from Rochester. Eastman had not merely managed his company to this point. He had been actively and aggressively involved in every aspect of the Kodak: from conception through production to marketing, down to the point of naming the product and composing (or at least selecting) the slogan which, in one brief sentence, communicated to the customer a great deal of information about this breakthrough: "You press the button and we do the rest." The name of the product and its slogan, both created without market research, quickly became world famous. The brand name still is. The slogan has been recognized as among the greatest ever.

More important than any of this, it was Eastman's wholehearted embrace of the Kodak concept which made it possible. At last, the Eastman Kodak Company was no longer just doing business from one day to the next, putting out fires. Now it was guided—inflamed—by the power of an idea whose time had come.[86] An experience like this does not take place often in a major company.

Eastman quickly began to realize that he had in his grip something fantastic. He gave one of the first Kodaks to Henry Strong, who was off to enjoy himself on the banks of Puget Sound. Remarked Eastman: "It was the first time he [Strong] had ever carried a camera, and he was tickled with it as a boy over a new top. I never saw anybody so pleased over a lot of pictures before. He apparently had never realized that it was a possible thing to take pictures himself."[87]

Eastman went to Minneapolis in July for the annual photographers' convention. He had the pleasure of seeing the Kodak awarded the medal as the invention of the year. Later that month, he said that the Kodak seemed likely to become "the most popular thing of the kind ever introduced."[88] Dealers were stocking out all over the country.

For a decade Eastman had been panning for gold. He had steadily moved upstream and found ever larger nuggets. In 1888, he struck the mother lode. He staked his claim (patenting everything in sight) and invested every penny to make this strike pay off. It is during this period—the introduction of the Kodak camera in 1888 and of a new, improved celluloid film—that Eastman began to speak in grand but not unrealistic terms about the opportunity before him. "Success," he said, "means millions."[89] Referring to the new celluloid film slated for the market in 1889, he said that if he could control it through patents "I would not trade it for the telephone."[90] In an often quoted remark, Eastman said in 1894 that "the manifest destiny of the Eastman Kodak Company is to be the largest manufacturer of photographic materials in the world or else go to pot." The company had its Big Hairy Audacious Goal.

Each of these declarations may have been grand, but they were not grandiose. Success did mean millions, many millions. Kodak sales rose from an estimated $510,000 in 1889 to just under $900,000 in 1895, with profits that year of $185,000 and dividends of over $40,000. (This was in the middle of a depression.) Sales reached $9.7 million in 1909, a year in which Kodak accounted for almost 43 percent of all U.S. photographic sales.[91]

It was during the 1890s that Eastman began to think about new ways to compete. We have already discussed the problems with pools and patents. No one was more aware of these than Eastman, who knew as much about his business as any executive ever has. What he gradually began to realize was that the central problem with pools and patents was the static conception of the firm upon which they were based. Pools, with some very rare exceptions, will not work in the long term. Market conditions change too much; and, as noted, any pooling agreement is a standing invitation for a new firm to enter the industry. Patents cannot last too long either, because they have a statutory expiration date. And they serve as an advertisement for the most sensitive and confidential views of a company's leadership.

This is not to say that patents all of a sudden became unimportant. One is reminded that when Mark Twain's Hank Morgan got hit on the head with a crowbar and woke up as the Connecticut Yankee in King Arthur's court, "the very first thing I did, in my administration [as "The Boss"]—and it was on the very first day of it, too—was to start a patent office; for I knew that a country without a patent office and good patent laws was just a crab, and couldn't travel any way but sideways or backwards."[92] For obvious reasons, patents were and remain of vital importance. However, although Twain might have been right in asserting that without a patent system a country was a mere "crab" that could only move "sideways" and "backwards," it was not necessarily true that with a patent system a country would move forward.

Eastman came to understand that the best way to maintain leadership was to turn his company into a moving target. He wanted to build a business capable of creating "a rapid succession of changes and improvements. . . . If we can get out improved goods every year nobody will be able to follow us and compete with us. The only way to compete with us will be to get out original goods the same as we do."[93] Eastman wanted Eastman Kodak to become what in current parlance would be called a "learning organization" characterized by "continuous improvement." This goal could be achieved with the help of patents, but not with patents alone. Pools, under this new concept of the corporation, became not only unnecessary, they were a hindrance.

How does a company turn itself into a "learning organization"? One way is to involve itself through hiring and philanthropy with institutions of higher education. Eastman hired Henry M. Reichenbach in August of 1886, before he finished his undergraduate training at the University of Rochester. For over five years, Reichenbach proved one of the key people in conquering technical hurdles and driving Eastman's company forward. Reichenbach betrayed his benefactor in 1891 and paid the price, industry obscurity. But this turn of fortune did not sour Eastman on the University of Rochester, whose leading benefactor he became, or on universities in general.

With the introduction of the Kodak, production facilities had to be rapidly expanded. On October 1, 1890, ground was broken for Kodak Park, three miles north of the center of Rochester. This industrial park grew with the needs of the company. To a remarkable degree, the fate of Rochester for the next century would be interwoven with Eastman Kodak.

To replace Reichenbach as plant manager, in the process assuming the far larger responsibilities associated with the burgeoning Kodak Park, Eastman appointed twenty-one-year-old Darragh de Lancey directly out of MIT. De Lancey worked like a fiend until his nervous breakdown in 1898. He himself hired three other MIT graduates to help with the exuberant but exhausting work. Eastman was so impressed with what he saw that he wrote an MIT chemistry professor, "I have a great deal of confidence in the material you turn out at your institution."[94] This was the beginning of a relationship which would prove invaluable both to Eastman Kodak and to MIT, to which George Eastman became one of the most generous donors.

A second way to create a learning organization is to go into the learning business. Eastman Kodak had long had facilities for testing its products. In 1912, goaded, some believe, by a remark by Carl

Duisberg, the head of the German chemical giant Bayer, Eastman decided to invest in basic research at Kodak Park. He told the man he chose to head this new effort, the Englishman Charles Edward Kenneth Mees, that "your job is the future of photography."[95] Eastman had said this many years before to Reichenbach. It was true in the late 1880s but truer in 1912. The Brownie, selling for $1.00, with a roll of film for an additional $0.15, had been introduced in 1900. Eastman Kodak was to sell millions of them.

As noted earlier, the 1880s were the years that perspicacious businessmen seized upon the value of a brand. Not only Kodak but a host of other branded products introduced into the market during that decade are still dominant at this writing. The name "Coca-Cola" is among the most valuable properties in the business world.

From the beginning, although there was nothing in his background to suggest this kind of insight, Eastman appreciated the importance of a brand. The name Kodak, the advertising and merchandising behind it, and the continuous improvement of the product itself were in the 1880s vital components in brand building.

Equally important was the understanding that there was a mass market for photography whether the mass market understood it or not. Instinctively, Eastman knew that he could "create a new class of patrons," and that once he did, they would be his for life. Every businessperson's dream, brand loyalty, would have been achieved.

The greatest single stroke in this campaign came in 1900 with the introduction of the Kodak Brownie. Like the Model T Ford or the six-and-a-half ounce, hobble-skirted bottle of Coca-Cola, the Brownie defined a whole product category. It only cost $1.00. Think of it. On November 13, 1877, George Eastman purchased a camera at a cost of $49.58. It was so difficult to use that he had to pay $5.00 for lessons. But in 1900 you could do the exact same thing that Eastman had done twenty-three years earlier, now for a mere $1.00. And this was in a far wealthier and more populous nation. As for lessons: "You push the button and we do the rest."

Suddenly, the whole country went through the transformation that Henry Strong experienced back in 1888: "He was tickled with it as a boy over a new top. He apparently never realized that it was a possible thing to take pictures himself."[96] Invented as a child's plaything, a new top, it captured the imagination of millions.

Aggressively marketed through public relations as well as advertising, it became an icon, a part of people's lives. Years after they bought or were given their first one, they treasured fond memories of the pleasure it provided them.[97] Not until instant photography a half century later did it find a rival. This was real brand power and true American marketing. What had been a preserve of the few had, in less than a quarter of a century, become easily available to the masses. It took the masses a few years to realize they wanted to take advantage of this easy availability. But once they did, that special magic transpired which happens for one brand in a million. Americans made the Kodak Brownie their own.

In 1985, the late Roberto Goizueta, who had a fabulously successful career as CEO of Coca-Cola, committed one of the biggest business blunders in recent memory. He changed the Coca-Cola formula. Public outrage was so great that, despite all the money, prestige, and ego that had been invested in the formula change, there was no option but to reintroduce the original formula. What was the lesson of this famous incident? Goizueta said that he learned that Coca-Cola did not own its brand. The consumer did.

It is useful to modify this analysis slightly. The truly great power brands are owned neither solely by the company nor by the customer. They are "co-created"—both the company and the customer interact to create some amalgam that no single individual thought up.[98] There is no better advertising than word of mouth; and when the customers assume some share of ownership, the brand benefits greatly from what they say to one another.

This is the core dynamic of mass marketing, which American firms stumbled upon by accident. Brand marketers can spend millions shouting about their product and its benefits. This shouting, if there is enough money and cleverness behind it, will have considerable reach. A minute on the Super Bowl will be seen by a lot of people (especially in the first quarter of the game).

What those advertising dollars will not generate is richness of customer interaction. That Super Bowl minute lasts only sixty seconds. A lot of viewers will not pay much attention to it. But once the co-creation process begins, consumers do take a sense of ownership, and at no cost to the company.[99]

An example of richness, which the Kodak Brownie still enjoys, are the pages on the Internet devoted to it which ask you, among other things, to "share your stories." One page is entitled "The Brownie Camera @ 100: A Celebration."[100] Few brands last ten years, much less a hundred, and fewer still of the thousands introduced are celebrated in such a fashion.

"The Brownie Camera Page" is managed not by Kodak but by an aficionado: "A public service page and labor of love maintained by Chuck Baker. This page is dedicated to Brownie photographers everywhere: past, present, and future."[101] This page contains a large amount of information about the product, including when each new model was introduced, what kind of film it used, and so on. You can learn, for example, that the "Brownie Pliant Six-20 was a folding rollfilm camera that was believed to have been sold only briefly in 1939." Chuck Baker offers "A special thanks to Damien Liew of Australia for this information!"

Who is Damien Liew? Someone to whom the Kodak Brownie meant enough that he must have compiled an awful lot of information about it. And finally the devotion paid off. He is on computer screens all over the world. You can't have mass production and mass marketing without mass consumption. And "mass consumption" is an artificial construct. The "mass" is a host of individuals, millions and millions of Chuck Bakers and Damien Liews. It was George Eastman who set this process in motion. But it has been people like them who kept the ball rolling.

The low price of the Brownie when it was introduced in 1900 demanded economies in every part of the business, for profit was to be made on volume, not on paper-thin margins. To compete, you had to be able to meet Kodak's price, an impossible task for a start-up firm. Kodak had been working its way to this cost position for two decades, using retained earnings. To meet its business model, you would have had to borrow a lot of money from J. P. Morgan. And even if you did, how could you create the organizational capabilities Kodak had built up over the years? Where would you find another George Eastman?

All this, then, is a portrait of the new competition of the twentieth century. Low margins, low prices, high volume, scale economies, continuous improvement, the learning organization. A far cry from the pools of the olden days.

By 1912, the company was the most important firm in photography, far ahead of whatever was in second place. Theory suggests that monopolists limit output, keep prices high, and stifle innovation. In practice, however, people matter. George Eastman became more curious, not less, as his industry grew. Color film . . . motion pictures . . . the future seemed without limit. It was that limitless future for which he was going to compete by making investments with unpredictable outcomes. He and Charles Mees agreed that no commercial property should be expected from the new research laboratory for ten years.[102]

SUCCESS

In the three decades from 1880 to 1912, the career of George Eastman was remarkable. He began in photography while still a bookkeeper at a bank. He was making $1,400 a year. Was that a lot of money? Horatio Alger's *Fame and Fortune* concludes with the hero earning that salary (plus the income from $2,000 in savings).[103] Eastman bought himself a camera because someone suggested that it would be worthwhile for him to record in pictures a trip he was going to take. To this, as to so many other suggestions, he responded, "Why not?"

Eastman quickly moved on from curious individual to serious amateur. Remember that in the late 1870s an amateur had to be serious. At this juncture, two important events did not take place. First, Eastman did not decide to become a professional photographer. He could have. He had the skill and the interest. But if he had become a professional photographer, chances are he would have viewed the industry from the inside to such an extent that he would never have driven the changes for which he was eventually responsible.

The second event which did not take place was that he did not decide to remain an amateur photographer and a professional banker. This, too, could have easily happened. A man could live very well on what Eastman was making at Rochester Savings in 1881. Even though he did not receive the promotion he felt was due him that year, he probably would have received one soon thereafter. And even if he had not, there were other banks. The Rochester Savings Bank was his third employer. He could have gone on to a fourth.

My guess is that he would have been a success either as a professional photographer or as a professional banker/amateur photographer. In the second role, especially, one can envision Eastman achieving a considerable measure of wealth. There is always room in business for people who know how to make money from money.

Why bring these counterfactual propositions up? Because both of them are more likely career paths than the one Eastman chose. There was nothing inevitable about his electing the road less traveled. As the British historian Frederick W. Maitland has cautioned, in an observation which is deceptively simple: "It is very hard to remember that events now long in the past were once in the future."[104] An informed observer in 1880 would have been more likely to predict one of the two careers just mentioned than the career Eastman ultimately pursued.

There are no statistics for new business formation in 1880 which compare the United States to other nations. It is a fair guess, however, that there was more such activity in the United States than in Britain, Japan, or anyplace in between. The incentives were there. The models were there. The irrational belief (given the number of failures) was there. And the penalties for failure were not as great as they were elsewhere.

All that having been said, it is still the rare individual who would have given up that sure thing at the bank to start a new company in a new industry. Although the penalties for bankruptcy may not have been as great as they were in other nations, failure, as we saw in the case of Tom Scott, was no fun.

A lot of famous American entrepreneurs have had firsthand experience with failure. Just five years before Eastman founded his Dry Plate Company in Rochester, Henry John Heinz filed for bankruptcy in Pittsburgh. What was it like for Heinz in 1875 to watch the dream of a company of his own dissolve into a nightmare? As 1875 drew to a close, creditors accused Heinz of fraud and twice had him arrested. One entry in Heinz's diary in November read: "I have two thousand dollars to meet tomorrow, and not a penny to meet it with." He broke out in boils.

On December 17, 1875, Heinz declared bankruptcy. Soon thereafter he wrote in his diary: "No Christmas gifts to exchange. Sallie [his wife] seemed grieved, and cried, yet said it was not about our troubles; only she did not feel well. It is grief. I wish no one such trials. I have no Christmas gifts to make. . . . I feel as though people are all pushing us down because we are bankrupt. Such is the world."[105]

True, you were not thrown in jail for bankruptcy. Nor were you denied the chance to try to found a business again. (Heinz did, and things worked out better the second time.) Nor did you lose the right to vote. Because these things did not happen, more people did take a chance as entrepreneurs here than in other countries. A culture, with institutional support, of founding new businesses is a distinctive trait of the American business world. Nevertheless, judging from Heinz's experience, unless you enjoy boils, failure was not much fun.

The truly remarkable aspect of Eastman's early career is that he seems never even to have worried about failure, despite seeing examples of it all about him and despite the decline of his own father. It would be interesting to know more about domestic relations in the Eastman household from 1857, when George Washington Eastman was felled by inflammatory rheumatism, to 1862, when he died. During those years, while Eastman was progressing through childhood, he saw the man of the house decline from breadwinner to bread eater. He was transformed from the family's solution to the family's problem. Maria seems to have had a stoic disposition, but it is hard to believe she did not have ways of making known her displeasure with the turn her life was taking. Given Eastman's feelings about his mother, the fear of her displeasure may have loomed at least as large as the social disapprobation or legal entanglements that failure would have meant. But he moved ahead, seemingly without fear.

Thus, from curious individual turned serious amateur and experimenter, Eastman quickly moved on to entrepreneur. He established the Eastman Dry Plate Company; and though not the sole proprietor or even the president, he was the moving spirit and the indispensable man.

Eastman entered this industry with a serious deficiency. He had no formal training in chemistry. But he did not let this stop him. Eastman was interested in opportunities, not constraints. What he did not know, he learned. He devoured technical journals. This is difficult. Try it. But it was necessary. To supplement what he could teach himself, he hired college-trained chemists. He had no prejudice against formal learning, although such prejudice was commonplace among businesspeople in his era and is not unknown today. More impressive, he had sufficient self-regard such that he was not threatened by the strengths of others. Dislike for formal training is often little more than envy or thinly veiled feelings of inferiority. So he hired Henry Reichenbach.

When Reichenbach left him, taking trade secrets in the process, Eastman could easily have tarred all college-trained individuals with the same brush. One can easily imagine him thinking: "They never had to fight to bring a business into being. They have had easy lives. They don't know the meaning of loyalty."

There is no trace of such sentiments from Eastman. Instead, he went back to college, this time to MIT. In a time when "no Irish need apply" was common policy, Eastman hired a man named Darragh de Lancey. As rare as a firm which welcomed people of Irish descent to high positions was one which welcomed women. Eastman hired Harriet Gallup out of MIT in 1894. The early history of Eastman's companies is a remarkable testament to the value of being a genuine equal opportunity employer. He was going after people who could get the job done. That was the criterion for employment.[106]

If Eastman did not smile until he was forty, the first time he smiled was sometime on or after July 12, 1894. That was an eventful and worrisome year. The failing Strong had to be rescued from his misadventures on the West Coast. Eastman Kodak's own numbers were not what one might have wished. The company was suffering along with the country through the great depression of the 1890s.

Nevertheless, there was reason to smile. The company had a vision and the resources to make that vision a reality. It was a global force, establishing plants overseas. It was the principal factor in transforming the United States from an importer and a follower in the photographic industry to an exporter and a leader.

By 1894, Kodak Park had been established. It continued to grow as Eastman invested in the future. Rochester emerged as the photography capital of the world. In the late 1890s, Eastman proved himself master of yet another key element of modern business. Not only could he manufacture, he could market. He placed advertisements in the general circulation press for a new, low-priced product aimed at a mass public. The magnitude of this strategic change deserves emphasis. Even today, with all the tools of marketing science at their command, it is one of their most difficult tasks for businesspeople to predict what advertising will be successful; and it is remarkably complicated to figure out the effect that advertisements exert. Furthermore, associated as it was with bogus patent medicines and "cancer cures" which were often merely alcoholic beverages, the reputation of advertising as a trade in the late nineteenth century was abysmal.

Nevertheless, Eastman embraced it. He showed a genius for copywriting, editing, and media selection which nothing in his background suggested he possessed. His advertising was brilliant in a way that only a simple slogan can be. "You press the button . . ." is remembered even today. It communicated a message. It was pithy to the point of being poetic.

From curious individual, to experimenter, to entrepreneur, to manufacturer, to marketer—but Eastman's odyssey as an executive was not yet complete. In the first decade of the twentieth century, Eastman began the process of gradually shifting managerial responsibilities to others. The first general manager of Eastman Kodak other than Eastman was Frank William Lovejoy. Another MIT-trained chemist, Lovejoy was hired by de Lancey to work at Kodak Park in 1894, the same year Harriet Gallup signed on.[107] In the early 1900s, Lovejoy moved from his technical headquarters at Kodak Park to Kodak's administrative offices to act as Eastman's general assistant.

As the day-to-day complexities of running a global enterprise multiplied, Eastman decided that professional help was needed in management, just as it had been in manufacturing and in marketing. In 1914, he traveled to Boston to meet with the dean of the Harvard Business School (which had been founded six years previously). He told the dean he wanted to hire a quality student. Apparently, Eastman only had to interview one, Marion B. Folsom. He offered Folsom a job at $100 a month. After some hesitation, Folsom accepted and spent the rest of his career at Eastman Kodak.

As Eastman slowly withdrew from active involvement, he was always on the lookout for sharp people, especially young people, who would come to the company and meet tomorrow's challenges. By 1919, he was hiring consulting firms to help assure him that the management of Eastman Kodak was as effective as its marketing and manufacturing. This was the three-pronged investment—in manufacturing, marketing, and management—which historian

Alfred D. Chandler Jr. has described as essential to the building of a large enterprise capable of sustaining itself.[108]

Before departing our discussion of Eastman as a businessman, a word must be said about his labor policies. In 1898, the company, awash in profits, turned its attention to the workforce. A reorganization had just netted Eastman personally almost a million dollars. From this amount, he set aside over $175,000 for distribution to the company's almost three thousand employees. This gesture was accompanied by the following note: "This is a personal matter with Mr. Eastman and he requests that you will not consider it as a gift but as extra pay for good work."[109] Eastman did this during an era in which one of Andrew Carnegie's ironmasters said: "I have always had one rule. When a workman sticks up his head, hit it."[110] To say that this example of what came to be known as "welfare capitalism" was remarkable in its time is an understatement. Eastman took this money out of his own pocket. Neither he nor his firm were under duress. There was no quid pro quo.

As he eased himself toward passing the torch to the people he had trained, Eastman accomplished the succession with a seamless flow. Here again we have the story of a whole host of problems which did not take place. As outsiders looking at Eastman's retirement and the transit of power to a new generation, it is easy to assume that because no problems were evident in the process, the process is problem-free by nature. It can be hard to grasp how something works until it breaks. The reader of these words takes the functioning of his or her eyes for granted. One does not give one's sight a thought. However, if one's vision suddenly blurred, one would find oneself learning a lot about the workings of the eye and the nature of sight.

History helps us understand some of the recurring problems with executive succession. People feel guilty. No matter what their public statements, many ambitious executives in a company the size of Kodak at its reorganization in 1919 must have felt that it was time for the "old man" to step aside. When he does, the connection between one's inner thoughts and objective reality can be disquieting. People feel insecure. The man whom for years they had looked to for answers will no longer be around. People often idealize their leaders. They endow them with qualities of wisdom and compassion which they may or may not possess because of the need for security, the need to believe that life makes sense.

These urges to have the leader go and to have him stay, contradictory though they are, can exist simultaneously. This makes the period of actual departure—which, especially after a lengthy tenure in office, people know has to happen, but also do not believe ever really will—a time of potential emotional confusion.

There is also the issue of rivalry. Different factions will often form within a company, each backing different leaders. When one is chosen, others are left out. If the contestants are of approximately the same age, that means the loser in all likelihood will never rise to the top spot. The risk of defections from the company, either forced by the triumphant winner or voluntary by the disappointed losers, is high at this moment. A company encounters the danger of a hemorrhage of its finest talent.

None of the challenges just enumerated above are merely imagined. All have taken place. The potential for difficulty is heightened when the departing leader is the founder of the company, the leading citizen of the city in which the executives live, and, to use a trite phrase which in this instance is accurate, a legend in his own time. Founders of companies are famous, notorious, for not knowing when to leave, for looking over the shoulders of their successors, and even, if their ownership position permits, for returning to power well after their abilities have ebbed. Henry Ford did all these things. Eastman avoided them all.

In 1919, when Eastman Kodak was formally reorganized along functional lines with a management team of nine reporting to Eastman, he was sixty-five years old. His mother had been dead for twelve years. Henry Strong, Eastman's best friend, died that year. Eastman was close to some of his relatives. He had a wide circle of friends and numberless acquaintances. Through his philanthropies he had made himself one of the nation's most important people in the worlds of medicine and of music.

But Eastman had no wife. No children. The "supreme happiness of life," Victor Hugo wrote, "is the conviction that we are loved. . . ."[111] That true communion for which there is no substitute, Eastman, for all his wealth, did not have—and by 1919 it was clear that he never would have. The temptation for this man to mistake the company that bore his name for his family might have been dangerous. He did not fall prey to it. Once again, the story of Eastman's success is the story of failure which was avoided.

In 1923, Eastman wrote to a director of the Eastman Kodak Company in Britain:

> We are getting old and have got to pass over the divide before many years. I am sixty-nine but do not as yet feel my age and am still going strong. When I go I hope I shall have things in shape so they will go on just the same. What I would like to do is just fade out of the picture and not go out with a bang. There is a lot of young blood in the Company and I am trying to organize it so people will say after I am gone that the old man was not the whole thing after all.[112]

Eastman began taking longer vacations. His absences from the office also increased. Recalled the head of the Development Laboratory who had an office next to Eastman's in the Kodak Office Tower: "Then there came the time when he [Eastman] was in his office less and less frequently. It came to be news when he was there. The word would go round—Mr. Eastman is in today. Somehow or other, that made it a better day for all of us. Finally he came no more."[113]

LIFE AFTER KODAK

In 1925, his final year of active engagement on a regular basis in his business, Eastman told a group of employees: "What we do in our working hours determines what we have in the world. What we do in our play hours determines what we are."[114]

Eastman was able to leave the company in such a positive fashion because he was not only retiring *from* something. He was also retiring *to* a host of interests which he had been cultivating for years. As he grew older, wealthier, and more widely known, Eastman could travel in style and meet anyone who interested him. Twice, in 1925 and in 1927, he went on a safari in Africa. On the second trip, at the age of seventy-three, he shot an elephant and a white rhinoceros.

No matter how many miles he traveled, he always came home to Rochester. There he built an exceptionally appealing house. This house, which is today open to the public, is located at 900 East Avenue, not far from the business district, the University of

Rochester, and Kodak Park. The Eastman house was (and is) real, authentic, and richly textured to reflect who Eastman was and what he found beautiful. Unlike the gigantic architectural piles which oppress Newport, Rhode Island, this house, with its beauties and unique touches, was (and remains) a distinct statement of Eastman the man, rather than merely a showcase of what he possessed. Despite its use for many formal events, Eastman's house was actually a home. He made it what he wanted it to be, personally and precisely attending to renovations and additions over the years.

The house was equipped with all the modern amenities: electric lighting, phonographs, and motion picture projectors, as well as a 1903 Otis elevator. Although he was willing to spend any amount on his home, Eastman bought few antiques for it. He was perfectly happy with copies of objets d'art. His indifference toward the quality of the furnishings for the house reflects an attitude similar to that he held toward music. His organist's comment that Eastman "made no pretense to know anything *about* music . . . he knew exactly what he liked and did *not* like"[115] could just as easily apply to his perspective on art and antiques.

Eastman was a lover of organ music and hired Harold Gleason as his personal musician to play for him every morning at breakfast, as well as at frequent luncheons and evening recitals. Although his guests often disapproved of his taste in music (he was known for his love of Wagner and his dislike of Bach), he nonetheless insisted on choosing the musical programs himself, though he pretended to no expertise on the subject.

The conservatory is exquisitely decorated with fine antiques, which seem to have been chosen simply because Eastman liked them and not to fit any decorative scheme. Indeed, the room is rendered almost comical by the enormous elephant head mounted above the windows, which look out onto the garden. This head is a trophy from his 1927 African safari. The entire house is filled with such trophies of his hunting expeditions, though none approaches the scale of the elephant head. In nearly every room there is an ashtray made of the hoof of some large animal, and skins are draped over some pieces of furniture.

Eastman's art collection, like so many elements of his home, reflected his personal taste, not those of esteemed critics. The paintings are primarily portraits, representing a variety of styles and periods. One of the grandest of these is a portrait of his mother, which is hung above the fireplace in the spacious, airy living room. Eastman decorated his house for himself and filled it with objects, plants, and colors which he himself enjoyed, irrespective of whether they would appeal to the many guests he entertained there. His home was his expression of himself, designed for him and by him.

THE SUICIDE REVISITED

This chapter began with Eastman's suicide note and with the assertion that it was not quite accurate. Wherein lies the inaccuracy?

Eastman committed suicide as a deliberate, premeditated act because of a sense of depression that he saw no reason to believe could be ameliorated. He was in failing health. He was afflicted with a progressive deterioration of the lower spine which had already led to urinary incontinence, a condition he found deeply distressing. Eastman was seventy-seven when he shot himself. Anyone who lived to that age during those years lived to see most close companions die. New friends, true friends, were hard to make for a man growing more physically frail and socially self-conscious.

Here we can locate the real cause of his suicide. It was not that his work was over. That really had been finished for at least seven years. Had he wanted to do so, Eastman could have retired after World War I. Kodak was on very firm footing. His investment in it would only grow in value.

Eastman loved Eastman Kodak, but I am not willing to say that he loved business per se. Business was war. Business was hard-hearted. Business was the dark side of Eastman's Manichaean life.

It took Eastman a long time to learn about play, but once he did he discovered how much fun life could really be. His creativity was expressed through his house; his adventurous side, by his travels; and his desire to leave the world a better place than he found it, by his munificence. It was at leisure that Eastman, as he himself said, expressed who he was. This was the bright side of his life. What his work determined was what he would have.

I believe Eastman committed suicide not because his work was over, but because his age and his physical condition meant that his play was over. His suicide was a rational act.

In our discussion of Carnegie, we talked of the entrepreneur discovering new frontiers, encountering moments of truth, and being subject to the derangement of power. Eastman clearly saw new frontiers in the industry which he dominated. What others could not imagine, he transformed into reality: a camera for everybody. He also had his share of moments of truth. Walking away from his job at the Rochester Savings Bank was one. Realizing that he had to create demand through active marketing even though he had a product so good that it seemed people should have flocked to it automatically was another.

But of that most unattractive of traits, the derangement of power, Eastman showed very little evidence. He never seemed to lose his grip on reality despite his enthusiasm for his business, an enthusiasm without which there would have been no business. Unlike Carnegie or Ford or Watson or Revson, Eastman showed no trace of cruelty despite his wealth and power. He seems never to have made a fool of himself. This stands in stark contrast to our first visionary, Carnegie, and to our next one, Ford.

Theodore Roosevelt once said, "How very fortunate we have all been. . . . We have encountered troubles and at times disaster and we can not expect to escape a certain grayness in the afternoon of life—for it is not often that life ends in the splendor of a golden sunset."[116]

George Eastman was a man who did so much that was right in his life. His actions were so consistently appropriate to his age and stage. One cannot help thinking how much better and more deserved it would have been had his heart simply stopped beating and fate had allowed him a peaceful, natural death.

GEORGE EASTMAN

July 12, 1854	George Eastman is born.
March 8, 1868	Eastman goes to work at a Rochester insurance firm.
April 1874	Eastman leaves to work for the Rochester Savings Bank as a junior bookkeeper.
November 1877	Eastman takes his first photograph.
January 1, 1881	Eastman Dry Plate Company is officially founded as an ongoing enterprise.
September 5, 1881	Eastman quits his job at the Rochester Savings Bank.
Early fall 1884	William Hall Walker and Eastman apply for patents on the three basic elements of the roll film system.
October 1884	Eastman Dry Plate and Film Company incorporated.
June 1888	Eastman places the first Kodak camera on the market. The camera is advertised with the slogan "You press the button and we do the rest."
August 27, 1889	The first roll of nitrocellulose film goes on sale.
October 1, 1890	Construction of the Kodak Park factory in Rochester begins.
May 1892	Eastman Kodak Company formed.
1900	Eastman introduces the Brownie camera.
1925	Eastman resigns as president of Eastman Kodak Company.
March 14, 1932	Eastman commits suicide.

3 HENRY FORD
The Profits and the Price of Primitivism

HENRY FORD AS A WORLD-HISTORICAL FIGURE

"I will build a car for the great multitude," Henry Ford said early in his career, "constructed of the best materials by the best men to be hired after the simplest designs that modern engineering can devise . . . so low in price that no man making a good salary will be unable to own one—and enjoy with his family the blessing of hours of pleasure in God's great open spaces."[1] This elegant, eloquent passage ranks among the finest statements of corporate purpose in American business history.

We have here a distinctively American declaration. In European countries in the 1890s and early 1900s, the automobile was primarily viewed as a product for the rich.[2] Henry Ford wanted to give it to the "great multitude." What is more, he did not set out to give the multitude a flimsy imitation of the real thing. The people were going to get the best. And the best was not going to cost them an arm and a leg. They were going to get the best for less.

At his funeral, one of Ford's eulogists compared him to Abraham Lincoln: "Abraham Lincoln and Ford mean America throughout the world—log cabin to White House—machine shop to industrial empire."[3] The similarity this eulogist suggests dealt with social and economic mobility, but the comparison of Ford to Lincoln extends further than that attribute alone.

After Lincoln's assassination, Ralph Waldo Emerson said that in Lincoln the middle-class nation had found its middle-class president at last. In a sense, Henry Ford, like Lincoln, was a dedicated servant of the middle class. His goal as a businessman was to make their lives better by providing inexpensive, quality transportation. If he did that, many other problems would take care of themselves. Ford succeeded in his goal. However, it was not only what he did, but also how he did it, that contributes to his Lincolnesque quality.

In the autumn of 1916, John and Horace Dodge, minority

shareholders, brought suit against Henry Ford to compel him to distribute more of the Ford Motor Company's profits as dividends. What follows is an excerpt from Ford's testimony on the witness stand. He was being questioned at this point by the lawyer for the plaintiffs:

Q. You say you do not think it is right to make so much profits? What is this business being continued for, and why is it being enlarged?
A. To do as much [good] as possible for everybody concerned.
Q. What do you mean by "doing as much good as possible"?
A. To make money and use it, give employment, and send out the car where the people can use it.
Q. Is that all? Haven't you said that you had money enough yourself, and you were going to run the Ford Motor Company thereafter to employ just as many people as you could to give them the benefits of the high wages that you paid, and to give the public the benefit of a low-priced car?
A. I suppose I have, and incidentally make money.
Q. Incidentally make money?
A. Yes sir.
Q. But your controlling feature, so far as your policy, since you have got all the money you want, is to employ a great army of men at high wages, to reduce the selling price of your car, so that a lot of people can buy it at a cheap price, and give everybody a car that wants one.
A. If you give all that, the money will fall into your hands; you can't get out of it.[4]

As we saw in Andrew Carnegie's career, the demands of business can divide a man between what he has to do to be a success and the way he wants to present himself to the public. In the exchange just quoted, one can imagine Ford getting a kick out of playing the rube, the hick just off the farm. He was no grasping robber baron. He seems more than happy to have this city slicker lawyer[5] "accuse" him of making cars available to everybody, paying his employees well, and just having money fall into his lap as a result.

From the point of view of image, Ford's performance could not be beat. This was no Henry Clay Frick (who was still alive and a member of the board of United States Steel when Ford testified) sneaking Pinkertons into a factory in the dead of night to force good, "horny fisted sons of toil" from their jobs. This was pure American Gothic—the businessman as benefactor of humankind.

One can imagine this scene in a Frank Capra movie or in a tale by Joel Chandler Harris. But as actual history, there is a fantastic element to it. Of all the businessmen in American history, only Henry Ford can be imagined saying such things on the witness stand. He embodied a shrewd simplicity, a mother wit that was rooted in the earth of America and could not be taught (but could be untaught) to a smart-aleck graduate of a sophisticated, highfalutin university.

From a business point of view, however, Ford paid a price for this posturing.[6] Capitalism has rules, and in his munificence he was violating them because some of the money with which he was being generous belonged to other people. The attorney questioning Ford could not have cared less about public relations. Although Ford's words might look just charming to the press and the public, the plaintiff's lawyer was playing only to an audience of judges. The very words just quoted helped cost Ford the case. In the opinion of the Supreme Court of the State of Michigan:

> There should be no confusion (of which there is evidence) of the duties which Mr. Ford conceives that he and the stockholders owe to the general public and the duties which in law he and his co-directors owe to protesting, minority stockholders. *A business cooperation is organized and carried on primarily for the profit of the stockholders.* The powers of the directors are to be employed for that end. *The discretion of directors is to be exercised in the choice of means to attain that end and does not extend to a change in the end itself,* to the reduction of profits or to the nondistribution of profits among stockholders in order to devote them to other purposes.[7]

As a result of the loss of this suit, a loss caused at least in part by Ford's posturing, Ford was forced to declare larger dividends than he wished. (Much of these dividends went into his own pocket, as the largest shareholder.) It was this decision which prompted Ford to buy out all the minority shareholders and gain complete control of the company.[8] Ford's buy-out has had ramifications down to the present day. The Ford Motor Company was not taken public until January of 1956. At this writing, just over 40 percent of the voting stock is still controlled by the Ford family.[9]

Americans liked the Model T Ford. "Like" is not a strong enough word. They loved it.[10] Many millions of them also loved the man who made it. He seemed to be one of them. As historian Thomas K. McCraw has written, people seemed "to imagine that they knew him [Ford] personally, and to trust him not only as a representative of the common man, but as himself the common man."[11]

This was the same face that Lincoln showed to the public. "I happen, temporarily, to occupy this White House," he said in a talk to the 166th Ohio Regiment. "I am a living witness that any one of your children may look to come here as my father's child has."[12] This is as much a comment about identity as it is about mobility. Lincoln was not only saying that he held (temporarily) the nation's highest office and that the children of his listeners had an equal chance to do so as well. He was also saying that no matter how far he had traveled, part of him had never left home.

Something like this characterized the relationship between Henry Ford and his public. By the early 1920s, when to be a millionaire was to be wealthy beyond imagination, Henry Ford was a billionaire. Only John D. Rockefeller and Andrew Carnegie among Americans had amassed fortunes on his scale. He was probably one of the dozen richest people in the world.

Yet Ford never made Americans feel inferior to him in ways that Americans have feared inferiority. He did not want servants in his home. As he explained, "I still like boiled potatoes with the skins on, and I do not want a man standing back of my chair at table laughing up his sleeve at me while I am taking the potatoes' jackets off."[13]

Ford plainly and proudly positioned himself as the champion of the farmer. "The Model T, more than any other, was the farmer's car."[14] He also wanted to be thought of as the champion of Main Street and hard work against Wall Street and capital. "Did you ever see dishonest calluses on a man's hands?" he once asked. "Hardly. When a man's hands are callused and women's hands are worn, you may be sure honesty is there. That's more than you can say about many soft white hands."[15] It was those "soft white hands" that grasped not hammers or hoes, but stocks and bonds. They were the hands of capital. They were the hands not of people who created value, but of people who relaxed and enjoyed life while their money made money.

Ford was not viewed by the American people as a rich man. Yet he was at least as rich as Rockefeller, who was excoriated for amassing his wealth. Ford was richer by many times than the soft, white-handed J. P. Morgan. Yet when he visited Morgan's house, he said, apparently without a trace of irony, "It is very interesting to see how the rich live."[16] One gathers that Ford, who exhibited false consciousness in so many ways, did not view himself as rich. Think of Abraham Lincoln and then think of a businessman. Henry Ford is the only one who could be comfortably seen in the same sentence. (The one other possibility is Thomas A. Edison, but he will always be remembered more as an inventor than as a businessman.)

One does not want to push a comparison between Abraham Lincoln and Henry Ford too far. Perhaps the relationship between the two was best expressed by, of all people, Gerald Ford. A longtime member of the House of Representatives from the congressional district centering on Grand Rapids, Michigan, and no relation to Henry Ford's family, Gerald Ford played a unique role in American history. On December 6, 1973, he was confirmed as vice president of the United States, to succeed the discredited Spiro T. Agnew, who had been taking bribes. Ford assumed office in the shadow of the Watergate scandals, as a result of which Richard M. Nixon was forced from the presidency in 1974.

Gerald Ford took the oath of office as vice president in the chamber of the House of Representatives in the Capitol. He said, in the only memorable line he ever spoke: "I am a Ford, not a Lincoln."[17] What Gerald Ford was saying (in this complicated pun designed to manage expectations) was that he was "basic transportation," and not the class of the field. This was true of both Gerald Ford and Henry Ford. They were unable to transcend themselves. Lincoln was able to and did so. In any case, we want to be careful about pushing this analogy too far. Abraham Lincoln is, it need hardly be said, without compare among Americans. Henry Ford, in the end, was a disappointment as a human being.

Nevertheless, in the great years of the Model T, thinking of Ford and Lincoln in the same sentence is not risible. Both were figures of world-historical importance. Both were, in their own fields, "Great

Emancipators." The late Jonathan R. T. Hughes, an economic historian who was quite hardheaded in his view of Henry Ford, conceded: "Ford liberated the common man on a greater scale than any hero in history. Ford said that of Edison. But it applied to Ford himself."[18]

Unfortunately, this was not the whole story, as Hughes well knew. Ford's biography, he wrote, illustrated "how the possession of great wealth in the hands of a barely literate bigot could do untold harm."[19] In few other people do the arguments for and against capitalism illustrate themselves so starkly. Henry Ford's story is the story of the profits and the price of primitivism.

There has been more written about Henry Ford than about any other American businessperson. There are numerous reasons for this attention. One is that the product his business manufactured occupies a unique place in our lives. The automobile is the most expensive branded product most people ever buy. Indeed, it can be considered the most expensive consumer good most people buy. Their homes cost more; but home buyers usually view that purchase as an investment which, if properly maintained, will appreciate in value.

In addition to its core function of transportation, which did indeed emancipate the populace, the automobile has taken on the added dimension of making a statement about its owner. "Much of modern property," as historian Donald F. Davis has noted, "is inconspicuous and therefore of little value in defining . . . status. . . . The automobile, by contrast, is exceptionally visible and mobile. . . ."[20] "Automobiles evoke passion," Davis declared; and this visibility is one of the many reasons why.[21]

The second reason so much has been written about Ford is that he encouraged interest in himself. Yet another putatively shy business magnate, Ford wrote (or had written for him) as many as six books and also owned a magazine.[22] Ford was a publicity hound on other fronts as well.

Lastly, Ford lived a very long life. He was born on July 30, 1863, in the month of the battles of Gettysburg and Vicksburg in the middle of the Civil War. He died on April 7, 1947, in the Atomic Age. During the bulk of the first four decades of this century, he was the absolute master of an enormously valuable corporation which had an immediate impact on the lives of hundreds of thousands of workers, suppliers, and distributors, and of millions of consumers of this "passionate" product.

If there is a single theme that pervades the ocean of words that have been written about Henry Ford, it is puzzlement. As one historian has observed, Ford's "personality . . . continues to elude us: was he a simple man erroneously assumed to be complex, or an enormously complex individual with a misleading aura of simplicity?"[23] Another historian entitled a chapter about him "Genius Ignoramus."[24]

According to the standard work on Ford and his company by Allan Nevins, Frank Ernest Hill, and their team,[25] Henry Ford was a man "of vision and of visions."[26] In their choice of words, they may have been more right than they knew. Anne Jardim, author of a Ford biography from a psychoanalytic standpoint, observed that his "choices of action bore a *visionary* stamp which testified more to *a burning need to do what he had to do* than to any rational appraisal of the opportunities that lay open to him."[27] It is this element of compulsion in his makeup which seems the most striking aspect of Ford's character. Beset by his compulsion, Ford was free of self-questioning.

In the chapter on George Eastman, I asked whether it could be said of him what was said of Benjamin Franklin: that in any age in any place he would have been great.[28] This was certainly true of Franklin and may well have been true of Eastman. It is doubtful, however, that Henry Ford's mixture of personal traits would ever have served him as well as they did in Detroit, Michigan, in the United States of America from 1899 to 1914. Genius is an overused word, and it is hard to say whether Ford possessed it. But he certainly was remarkably talented as a mechanic. He was a highly competent individual who lived a self-respecting middle-class life from birth into his early forties. There is no reason to believe that the last half of his life would not have been a lot like the first half had it not been for the birth of the automobile industry and the contrast between his view of the business and that of his competitors.

Call it stubbornness or obsession. At the birth of the automobile industry, Henry Ford understood two things. The first was that the United States needed an inexpensive car. The second was that anyone who wanted to build such a car would have to fight like hell to do so. He would have to fight his financial backers, who would constantly push him toward building heavier, more expensive models. He would have to fight his competitors, who had arrayed themselves under license of the Selden[29] Patent in the Association of

Licensed Automobile Manufacturers, and who demanded that everyone in the industry play by the "gentlemanly" rules they made. He would have to fight engineering barriers which stood in the way of manufacturing enough inexpensive yet rugged and dependable vehicles to make an acceptable profit while keeping the retail price low. In fact, he would have to fight everything and everybody with one exception. The exception was the consumer.

Evidence of consumer demand for a low-priced, self-propelled road vehicle was plentiful. The best example is the early career of Ransom E. Olds. Born in Geneva, Ohio, in 1864, Olds was living in Lansing, Michigan, when he bought an interest in his father's machine shop. Olds's early experiments with horseless carriages used steam power; but in 1896, the same year that Henry Ford completed his quadricycle, Olds built his first vehicle powered by a gasoline engine[30]

With the backing of Samuel L. Smith, Olds incorporated the Olds Motor Works on May 8, 1899.[31] There was no clear idea of what the product would be, but the allure of the high-priced market was evident in company deliberations. "In 1899 and 1900, Olds and his staff came up with about eleven different automobile models, ranging in price from $1,200 for a two-passenger trap [a trap is a body style] on up to $2,750 for a four-passenger brougham [a brougham is a closed four-wheel carriage with an open driver's seat in front]."[32] These were high prices. In June of 1899, by contrast, the steam-powered Locomobile was advertised for $600.[33]

In 1901, Olds decided to concentrate his efforts on the inexpensive runabout.[34] This became the "merry Oldsmobile," famed in song[35] and story. Known as the "curved-dash Oldsmobile" because the floor curved upward in front of the vehicle to form the dashboard,[36] the car proved remarkably popular.

Reliable sales figures are hard to come by. According to Donald F. Davis, 400 Oldsmobiles were sold in 1901 and then 2,500, 4,000, 5,500, and 6,500 in 1902 through 1905, respectively.[37] Davis states that "between 1899 and 1903 Olds paid cash dividends of 105 percent *and* raised its capital (through reinvested profits) from $350,000 to $2,000,000."[38]

Judging from these sales figures, it must have looked as if Oldsmobile, which was the oldest surviving American automobile nameplate until General Motors announced its discontinuance in

2000,[39] was destined to emerge as the giant firm of the industry. Even if the unit sales were only half the estimates just reported, they were high indeed considering that there were only about 4,200 automobiles sold in the entire country in 1900; and Oldsmobile's sales trend certainly was in the right direction. Oldsmobile's "market mastery of the lower price-class did not go uncontested, but most of its competitors did not have its financial resources and manufacturing experience."[40]

As so often happened, however, the vision of the bonanza awaiting the low-priced car dissolved like a mirage for Oldsmobile. Olds himself was forced out of the company early in 1904 by a wealthy backer who wanted to produce higher-priced vehicles. Olds reentered the industry by founding Reo, but this firm never competed in the low-priced field.

Olds understood one of the two things which Ford understood. There was a market in the United States for low-priced cars. Others saw this as well. Seeing it took shrewdness, perhaps, but not genius. What Ford had which others did not was an understanding that he would have to fight a host of foes to serve that low-priced market.

Henry Ford's personal peculiarities, or, depending upon the view one adopts, his personality disorder, served him perfectly at this critical juncture in the history of the industry. He became utterly inflexible in his quest for the car for the "great multitude." Inflexible though he was in his goal, that is how flexible he was in the means by which he sought it. He went through two companies and eight models before he had the Ford Motor Company producing the Model T. Once the Model T was commercialized in 1908, demand exceeded all but the wildest dreams. From this circumstance flowed consequences which have shaped the modern world: the Highland Park plant, the moving assembly line, interchangeable parts, and the $5 day, to name just a few.

HENRY FORD AND THE PROBLEM OF PERSONALITY IN HISTORY

If the Highland Park plant was as important as just suggested, and if Henry Ford was the owner of the company that owned the plant, the question of who he was presents itself to us for our consideration. If the industry drove the modern world, if the Ford Motor Company drove the industry in these crucial early years, and if Henry Ford dictated the policy of the company, then surely the author owes the reader an explanation of who Ford was and why he did what he did.

Reasonable though this requirement may be, it is not possible to satisfy it fully. "Wonders are many on earth," Sophocles wrote, "and the greatest of these / Is man."[41] Each individual is a congeries of contradictions, complexities, and (sometimes) complexes. When a man rises to the eminence of Henry Ford, he has the opportunity to act out his impulses without the civilizing imperatives of getting along with other people. Within his kingdom, Henry Ford could make the rules, and no one could say him nay. With this kind of freedom, or license, his personal strengths and weaknesses could express themselves without limit.

For the historian, the problem of his or her profession is difficult in proportion to the degree of generality with which a subject is being discussed. Take, as an example, the Civil War in the United States. The historian can say with geometric certainty that the war began in 1861 and ended in 1865 and that the Union won. These are facts, and anyone who denies them is simply wrong.

When we get down to the level of individual battles, things become a bit more complicated. Take the following hypothetical. Let us say that we are narrating the sequence of events on a battlefield. Let us say that an officer's memoirs inform us that at a certain time the enemy launched an attack at a certain place. Probably our first effort would be to seek corroboration for this memoir. If we found another officer in a position to view the scene writing a similar story in his memoirs, we would feel more comfortable in recording as truth the launching of the attack at the place and time described.

If the second officer's memoirs differed in material respects from the original account, we would have cause for concern. If the second officer agreed, we would feel more confident. The more closely he agreed, the better we would feel. Unless, that is, the agreement between these two officers were *too* close. If they used the same words, we would assume that one copied from the other or that they both copied from a third source. Thus, it would appear that there is a similarity which vindicates and a similarity which discredits. But how similar is too similar?[42]

When we get down to the level of the individual human being, historians find themselves in ever-deepening waters. Let us return from the Civil War battlefield to the world of Henry Ford. We know a lot of facts about his life. We know when he was born and when he died, how he acquired control over the Ford Motor Company, and how skilled a mechanic he was.

But this is hardly satisfying. Henry Ford changed the world. There were "at least 57 plants engaged in making motor cars" in the United States in 1900.[43] No one knew whether gasoline, steam, or electricity would emerge as the dominant source of power. In addition to those who owned plants or, more accurately, sheds for automobile production, there were thousands of other Americans dreaming big dreams about this industry at this time. Almost all of them failed. Ford succeeded. Why? Who was Henry Ford?

This is not an idle question. The chief executive officer of an automobile company in 1905 was not the faceless bureaucrat of half a century later. "Early auto manufacturers often attached their own personal prestige to this product in order to distinguish it from hundreds of competing cars. . . ."[44]

Reputation can be manipulated, but, sooner or later, reality must be faced. In reality, Ford said many things and took many actions which were inconsistent, self-defeating, and bad for business. It would not be difficult to assemble a set of quotations which would make him seem simply like an idiot. Here, for example, is an explanation Ford is said to have given to reporters of his belief in reincarnation: "When the automobile was new and one of them came down the road, a chicken would run straight for home—and usually be killed. But today, when a car comes along, a chicken will run for the nearest side of the road. That chicken has been hit in the ass in a previous life."[45]

Perhaps the historian need not worry about such a statement. It is doubtful that it affected the sale of even one car, although it is indicative of rather odd thought processes.

Other statements Ford made and other aspects of how he conducted himself were not only revealing of the man but had a definite impact on the business. That impact was not always negative. Ford's identification with the working person, his permanent estrangement from Detroit's upper crust (symbolized by his decision to live not near them, but instead more than a dozen miles away in a "gloomy mansion in Dearborn"),[46] his devotion to what was hard, real, and tangible—all these traits helped him to be the only automobile pioneer to keep focused on the great mass market.

There was, however, another side to this man: combative, vindictive, and mean-spirited. Nowhere was this more clearly illustrated than by his virulent anti-Semitism, an attitude which needlessly injured the company, not to mention the Jews who were its target for years, and which we will discuss presently. With this, as with so many other of Ford's beliefs, the historian's standard narrative tools do not serve to explain very much.

A good example of the problem Ford's personality poses is his pacifism. This is a belief that he trumpeted with increasing bombast as World War I dragged into 1915. When he was told of the torpedoing of the *Lusitania* in May of that year, he observed: "Well, they were fools to go on that boat, because they were warned." Canadian-born James Couzens, a man unafraid of Ford and whose organizational skills were vital to the company, had Allied sympathies and may have wanted the company to supply the Allies. Ford himself publicly stated he would burn his factory to the ground rather than supply war materiel.[47]

Ford kept up a steady stream of pacifist pronouncements throughout the summer and fall of 1915. "I hate war, because war is murder, desolation, and destruction," he announced.[48] Each such declaration angered the indispensable Couzens further. Finally, in October, Couzens quit. He left the industry altogether and entered politics, eventually becoming a senator from Michigan.

Ford later explained that it was time for Couzens to leave. His mind, Ford alleged, was not on his work. He had political ambitions that "didn't mix with holding a job in the Ford Motor Company." When they had their final argument about publishing Ford's pacifist views, Ford said to himself, "Fine. That's a dandy way to get out of it."[49]

Did Ford really hold pacifist views? Or was he parading them merely as a way to force out a rival for the leadership of the firm, a man whose personal power Ford may have found menacing?

Getting rid of Couzens cannot be all there was to it, because once Couzens quit, Ford's pacifist adventure continued unabated. In late November, Ford chartered his famous "Peace Ship," the *Oscar II,* to sail to Europe to bring peace to the warring nations. On

November 22, Ford visited the White House, where he found President Wilson cordial but noncommittal. Shortly before setting sail, Ford announced that the soldiers in the trenches should call a general strike.[50]

The *Oscar II* departed from Hoboken, New Jersey, on December 5, 1915—a fool's errand if ever there was one. When Ford arrived in Oslo on December 18, he said nothing for five days. He then called a press conference to explain that his new tractor was unpatented and that armaments makers could realize greater profits on tractors than on the instruments of war. Ford betrayed not the slightest inkling of the causes or potential consequences of the greatest armed conflict in history. Observed one attendee at the press conference, "He must be a very great man who permits himself to utter such foolishness."[51] The similarity to Carnegie is striking.

Was Henry Ford—this man who told the world that war is nothing but murder, who said he would burn his factory (at the time among the world's largest) to the ground before he would accept war-related business, who (without relation to company politics, Couzens having already left) risked and reaped the opprobrium of the world for spending half a million dollars to charter an ocean liner with a vague notion that somehow peace would result—a genuine pacifist? In the Nevins and Hill study, chapter 2 of the volume on this period is entitled "Peace Crusade." The reader turns the page to see chapter 3, which is entitled "Production for War." "The transformation of Henry Ford from peace angel to Vulcan took less than a week," they explain. Louis P. Lochner, a doctrinaire pacifist who spoke with Ford on January 30, 1917, learned that Ford had not closed the door on efforts for peace. On February 3, Lochner said that Ford "laughed at the idea of any danger of war," although he also said he would support any decision the president made. On February 5, two days after President Wilson broke diplomatic relations with Germany, Ford said, "I cannot believe that war will come"; but if it did he promised to "place our factory at the disposal of the United States government and will operate without one cent of profit."[52]

This statement was half true, the half about producing war materiel for the government. The Ford Motor Company became a major defense contractor in 1917 and 1918. The half that was not quite true was the part about "one cent of profit." The company made $8,151,119.31 before taxes from war contracts. As principal stockholder, Henry Ford's own personal after-tax income from the war was $926,780.46.[53] Not "one cent of profit" was ever repatriated to the federal treasury.

If one is to stick with historical narrative, one finds a man who, for an extended period of time, was a belligerent pacifist—if that is not an oxymoron—willing to see his factory burned down rather than accept an order for a bullet. Then, suddenly, having virulently opposed a reasonable plan for preparedness which had been backed by the nation's chief executive, Ford changed his mind completely and for no apparent reason. "I am a pacifist first but perhaps militarism can be crushed only with militarism. In that case, I am in on it to the finish."[54]

Why the change? Historian David Hackett Fischer has warned historians against asking "why" questions: "A 'why' question tends to become a metaphysical question. It is also an imprecise question, for the adverb 'why' is slippery and difficult to define. Sometimes it seeks a cause, sometimes a motive, sometimes a reason, sometimes a description, sometimes a process, sometimes a purpose, sometimes a justification." Fischer prefers historians to stick to the empirically resolvable questions of who, where, when, what, and how.[55] Fischer's observation is well taken, but it is also limiting, sometimes excessively so. The problem with it can be seen in the present instance—the question of Ford and pacifism.

It seems to me inescapable to ask: Why did Ford change his views from pacifist to pro-war? Why did he promise to take "not one cent of profit" from war contracts and then make and keep over $8 million for his company and almost $1 million personally? What, moreover, happened to his pacifism during World War II, when his firm built a gigantic bomber plant from scratch?

Fischer is right that we can never know the answers to these questions empirically. There is no "answer" to the puzzles of Henry Ford's personality. We can, however, offer informed speculation and invite our reader to make his or her best guess.

The Nevins and Hill chapters dealing with the Peace Crusade and its abandonment for war manufacture, while complete to the point of exhaustion, leave the reader hungry for a little more explanation and a little less detail.[56] The most obvious question is: Was Ford really a pacifist or was his pacifism a means to some other end? The Nevins and Hill answer is that Ford was a sincere pacifist and that his views on the subject were quite in tune with the spirit of the age. Ford, we are informed, "grew up in an era marked by an increasing devotion to peace." Leading American statesmen had been crusading for peace for more than a decade prior to World War I. "Pacifism in the United States . . . was thus not only respectable but little short of triumphant." Ford had not embarked upon a "wild, perverse crusade." To the contrary, "millions in spirit marched with him."[57]

True, Nevins and Hill provide us with some alternative possibilities. Ford may have wanted to rid himself of Couzens, and the provocation of his public pacifism may have been a convenient pretext. But Couzens resigned on October 12, 1915,[58] and Ford remained a very noisy pacifist until February of 1917.

Later, when discussing the Peace Ship misadventure, Ford said that he "got a million dollars worth of advertising out of it" and that he had found new markets for his tractor.[59] These objectives could have been achieved without the farce of the Peace Ship, and certainly cannot account for the months of Ford's pacifism preceding it.

Indeed, Ford's public posturing between 1915 and 1918 makes little sense. He complained that Couzens had been absent a great deal from the plant prior to his resignation. "If a man has a job with us," Ford said, "he must stick to it. . . ."[60] He claimed that Couzens had been there only 184 days the previous year—"I have," he said, "had a check kept on him."[61] I do not know how many days Ford spent in the plant, but his complaining about attendance to the business and his own sailing off to Europe are hardly consistent.

Prior to the voyage, Ford arranged to see Woodrow Wilson. Ford found Wilson a "small man" when he declined to give the Peace Ship a more hearty endorsement.[62] The following year, however, when Wilson specifically requested it, Ford ran for the U.S. Senate from Michigan. Previously a nominal Republican, although he may never even have bothered to vote,[63] Ford ran as a Democrat. It was Wilson's desperate hope that the Senate would have a Democratic majority.

Ford did not campaign, spent almost nothing, and did not seem to care about the outcome. Throughout, he "remained inert."[64] In the event, this political naïf, making no speeches and spending no money, running with the backing of an unpopular president in a Republican state which had not elected a Democrat to the Senate since before the Civil War, won 48 percent of the 440,000 votes cast.

After this remarkable performance, Ford took it upon himself to destroy the man who defeated him. Spending far more time, energy, and money on this effort than he did on the Senate race itself, Ford subjected his opponent, Truman Newberry, to an attack so merciless and so effective that Newberry, having, in his words, "suffered the tortures of hell," resigned his Senate seat in 1922.[65]

If the flamboyantly erratic behavior just described were limited to a particular arena (say, politics) or to a particular period of time (say, 1915 to 1922), it could perhaps be dismissed as a strange misadventure in the long life of a successful man. On the contrary, however, this kind of mania is more typical than exceptional.

With regard to labor unions, Ford, thought of in his early years as the greatest friend of the working person among industrialists, had by the 1930s infiltrated his factories with spies with underworld backgrounds to monitor his workforce. He was one of the most ardent antiunion employers in the United States in the late 1930s. He had organizers beaten up, and it is the merest luck that there were no killings at the River Rouge. He threatened, once again, to close the whole company rather than allow labor to organize his factories. Only the pleading of his family is said to have prevented this.

Then, suddenly, after foolishly fighting the unions and the government for years, Ford gave in. And when he did, he granted the United Automobile Workers the most generous contract in the industry. The about-face forced Nevins and Hill to ask a "why" question: "Why had Henry Ford thus suddenly reversed his whole past policy?" Their attempt to answer this perplexing question is not convincing to me. One wonders whether they themselves found it so.[66]

From the the second decade of the twentieth century until his death in 1947, Henry Ford behaved irrationally with regard to a variety of matters, some directly related to the business, some far removed. These episodes or areas of irrationality widened and increased in frequency as he aged. That he was already subject to such bouts in the years 1910–1919 is nowhere clearer than in the story of his pacifism.

Any attempt to discuss Ford's pacifism as if Ford were thinking straight is doomed to failure. The narrator will wind up with an inconsistent story if forced to summarize Ford's own inconsistencies. The historian must bring something more to the discussion than questions of "who, where, what, when, and how." He or she must ask: Why did Ford act as he did?

Psychiatry and its allied disciplines cannot supply a satisfying answer. First, we are lacking in the intimate detail of the life of even as well-known a man as Henry Ford to develop a coherent clinical picture. Even if we had access to all the information we might want, psychiatry is far from an exact science. Provided with the same clinical data, different psychiatrists and the different schools of psychiatry will deliver different diagnoses and prescriptions.[67] Though psychiatry may not be able to supply us with answers, it can do the next best thing. It can supply us with questions to help us uncover what is going on when a powerful man acts in ways that are clearly not rational.

Was Ford really a pacifist? When he said he was, did he mean it? Did he, to borrow a chapter title from Erik H. Erikson's study of Martin Luther, understand the meaning of "meaning it"?[68] The answer is no. As Anne Jardim has pointed out, "for all his protestations, Ford was not a pacifist in any real sense: his were not the beliefs of a Quaker." She explains what role his supposed belief played: "*Pacifism for him was a means of expressing emotion unencumbered by conviction. . . .* The belligerence, earlier turned against war and the makers of war, was now expressed in waging it."[69]

This seems to me, if not the "answer" to the Henry Ford conundrum, a key point to grasp in thinking about why he acted the way he did. Ford was without introspection. He was not psychologically minded. For reasons which we will never know fully, he was in the grip of impulses which were at times wonderfully creative but which were often, especially as he grew older, aggressive and destructive. Unaware as he was of his own inner makeup, he careened from one "conviction" to another, blithely innocent of the contradictions thus displayed to the world or of the confusion such behavior caused to those close to him.

Jardim's key observation—Ford's "emotion unencumbered by conviction"—ruled the life of this man. He stands as the perfect example of someone who never understood the meaning of "meaning it."

When he expressed pacific beliefs, he did not mean them. What he needed was an outlet for his aggression. When it became more convenient to supply the military, he undertook that task with the same aggressive attitude. What mattered was to find a cause to express his emotion, not the cause itself. It is comical that such a man spoke so much and wrote (or had written for him) so many books and articles. He could have random "beliefs," but never a coherent system of beliefs. Seen in this light, his endless inconsistencies had a consistency about them. He was not insincere on purpose. He was, rather, a collection of shifting emotions he did not understand.

No discussion of the peculiarity of Ford's enthusiasms or of the intensity of his free-floating anger would be complete without attention to his anti-Semitism, which was mixed up in some indecipherable way with his pacifism. Ford hated Jews with the same inconsistency that he approached other matters. In this case, however, the impact of his passionate confusion was greater and more long lasting; his advocacy uglier.

Late in 1918, Ford purchased a little publication called the *Dearborn Independent*. On May 22, 1920, for no particular reason that anyone has been able to figure out, the magazine embarked on a campaign of anti-Semitism which has been described as "the first systematic anti-Jewish agitation in the United States."[70] David L. Lewis describes how Ford used the pages of his magazine to assert his opinions :

> "[I]nternational Jewish banking power" had started the war [i.e., World War I—blaming Jews for the war is an indication of the association in Ford's addled brain between his pacifism and anti-Semitism] and kept it going . . . Jews were plotting "to destroy Christian civilization," and . . . most Jews were "mere hucksters, traders who don't want to produce, but to make something out of what somebody else produces." While protesting that most Jews were not producers, the auto king employed thousands of Jews in his plants; "we see that they work, too," he told a reporter, "and that they don't get into the office." . . .
>
> The *Independent* . . . revived that hoary forgery, *The Protocols of the Wise Men of Zion*, which contended that Jews everywhere were conspiring to attain world domination. . . .

Jewish interests were held responsible for a decline in public and private morals, for intemperance, for high rents, short skirts, rolled stockings, cheap movies, vulgar Broadway shows, gambling, jazz, scarlet fiction, flashy jewelry, [and] night clubs. . . . [C]harges were leveled against many prominent Jews. Bernard M. Baruch, for example, was proclaimed the "pro-consul of Judah in America," a "Jew of Super-Power," the head of a dictatorial conspiracy.[71]

When Henry Ford spoke, people listened. Reporters duly scurried to Baruch to get his response to these charges. Baruch, who had a sense of humor, said that he could hardly be expected to deny them.[72] He could imagine worse accusations than being possessed of "Super-Power."

But the truth is there was nothing funny about Ford's campaign. In the early 1920s, he compiled articles from the *Dearborn Independent* and had them published in a volume entitled *The International Jew*. This collection was widely distributed not only in America but also in Europe, where it was translated into many languages and "eagerly seized upon" by bigots from France to Russia.[73] But the greatest impact of this repulsive little volume was in Germany. Baldur von Schirach, who became the "Youth Leader for the Nazi Party" in 1931 and, after Hitler came to power, the "Leader of Youth in the German Reich," read *The International Jew* when he was seventeen. At his trial in Nuremberg in 1945, he said, "You have no idea what a great influence this book had on the thinking of German youth. . . . The younger generation looked with envy to the symbols of success and prosperity like Henry Ford, and if he said that Jews were to blame, why naturally we believed him."[74]

Von Schirach is not the kind of man one takes at his word, and citing Ford at his war crimes trial served to indict the United States to some degree for Nazi anti-Semitism.[75] There can be no doubt, however, that Ford was useful to the Nazis in the 1930s, before World War II and the Holocaust. He was the only American favorably mentioned in the American edition of Hitler's *Mein Kampf*.

Hitler wrote that "one great man, Ford, to their exasperation [i.e., to the "exasperation" of American Jews] still holds out against them."[76] Hitler would have been an anti-Semite without Ford, but the truth is we will never know how much damage Ford did. He was among the world's most famous people, and he was prominently associated with the "average man" at the "grass roots" of society. Hitler's ability to cite such a prominent figure as having views similar to his could only have helped him.

Yet, suddenly, Ford reversed his public stance and apologized. The apology was unconvincing and probably caused by business considerations. It is true, however, that Ford seemed to treat some individual Jews well; and he was puzzled when Jews broke off friendships with him because of what he was saying about them. According to one authority, Ford was an anti-Semite to the end. That may be true, but it is unclear if he really understood what anti-Semitism was. His own conduct in this regard often showed confusion and inconsistency.[77] At one point, he offered to help resettle European Jewish refugees, a humanitarian project in which the U.S. government was notoriously uninterested.

Ford's anti-Semitism was well known in the United States among the general public and much resented by some Jews into the 1960s. Few people today know of it. Nevertheless, the impact of Ford's attitude toward Jews is very much alive if you know where to look. No need to go to a library. *The International Jew* is on the Web. You can read *The International Jew, The World's Foremost Problem* "Abridged from the original as published by the world renowned industrial leader, HENRY FORD, SR:" at http://flinet.com/~politics/antisemi/internatjew.html (the address at this writing). It remains as repulsive as the day it was published.

Anti-Semitism was hardly new to Western civilization when Henry Ford began advocating it. It had been endemic for centuries. In the twentieth century, however, anti-Semitism became a defining and defiling passion. The Holocaust that it made possible will live forever as a stark illustration of how thin the veneer of decency is in the human race. The Holocaust would have occurred without Henry Ford, but he contributed more to the insanity that led to it than any other American businessperson. His actions illustrate the cost of the severance of power from responsibility.

Henry Ford possessed the obstinacy of the confused man. When he seized on an idea, he could pursue it with a single-minded tenacity and faith in himself which did seem to be able to move mountains. It was Ford who succeeded in the low-priced market while all others failed, and it was Ford who created Highland Park. He was a mechanic's mechanic, as astute with inanimate objects as he was obtuse with human beings.

If Henry Ford had died in February of 1914, after the announcement of the $5 day, he would be remembered almost without qualification as a man of true greatness. His flaws were noticeable in his first half century of life, but they would have been forgotten. Instead, Ford lived on to 1947, surrounded as he grew older by a corps of yes-men outdoing themselves in telling him what he wanted to hear rather than what he needed to understand. As his wealth grew and his fame engulfed the whole world, he lost all perspective. No life better exemplifies the derangement of power. Anyone who attempted to tell him the truth risked dismissal.[79] He cheated on his beloved wife.[80] He drove his only son to an early grave.[81]

As early as 1923, Samuel S. Marquis, the dean of Detroit's largest Episcopal Church and, for a time, the manager of Ford's Sociological Department (or what today would be called personnel or human resources) wrote of Ford that "in his presence no one is ever entirely at his ease. . . ."[82] In part, this was simply because he was the boss. But it was also because people never knew how he really felt or what he would do. Ford himself did not know either.

Honoré de Balzac once wrote, "Behind every great fortune there is a great crime." Peter Collier and David Horowitz, two journalists who have written a splendid book on the Ford family, observed: "Old Henry, perverse as always, reversed things: the fortune came first and then the crimes."[83] Therein lies the puzzle and the tragedy of Henry Ford.

CHILDHOOD, BOYHOOD, YOUTH

Henry Ford was born on July 30, 1863, nine years after George Eastman. His father's father, John Ford, had emigrated from Ireland in 1847. His eldest son, William, born in 1826, was Henry Ford's father. Ford's family was Protestant and traced its origins to England, perhaps to Somerset and Devon. Two of John Ford's brothers had arrived in Dearborn, Michigan, in 1832; and that is where John took his large family.

Henry Ford's mother, Mary Litogot, was the foster daughter of Patrick O'Hern, a prosperous Dearborn farmer who had emigrated from County Cork around 1830. Mary's biological father, whose background was Dutch or Flemish, died in an accident in the 1840s, and the childless O'Herns gladly took in the young Mary (she had been born in 1839). "They gave her the warmest love and devotion and she returned them a full and happy affection."[84]

On April 25, 1861, William Ford, by this time a farmer of some standing in Dearborn, took Mary Litogot, thirteen years his junior, to be his wedded wife. The marriage seemed to be a happy one from the outset, as were the relations with the extended family, especially the O'Herns. The Fords and O'Herns owned a lot of land in Dearborn and its environs, and they were prosperous.

The couple's first child was born in 1861 and died in infancy the following year. The second child, Henry, was born in 1863. After Henry came four more sons and two daughters. The last son died almost immediately, and his mother followed him to the grave twelve days later. Prior to this catastrophe, for his first thirteen years, Henry Ford's childhood seems idyllic.

When the first Fords reached Dearborn in 1832, it was wilderness. When Alexis de Tocqueville began his epic sojourn in the New World in 1831, he wanted to see the frontier, and he found it in Detroit, which was as much a French city as an American one. Dearborn, on Detroit's southwest border, was forest. Michigan was not admitted to the Union as a state until 1837.

This new land—"gigantic, savage, yet aglow with promise"[85]— grew at a staggering pace. In 1830, the population of Detroit was 2,222, of Michigan, 31,639. In 1860, the respective populations were 45,619 and 749,113.[86] European settlers cut down the trees, built railroads, and violated the virgin land with the plow. Farms were inexpensive to purchase and clear. As transportation improved, Michigan prospered. America, the whole Western world, was renewing itself there.[87]

In addition to farming, William Ford worked on the Michigan Central Railroad. He was not solely a manual laborer; he was also a skilled carpenter. It was hundreds—thousands—of William Fords who built Michigan into an economic power and one of the bulwarks of the Union in 1861. Tocqueville's recollections of Michigan are of a hard land settled by rough-hewn people. By the time of Henry Ford's birth, the demands of the environment were still manifest. Nevertheless, an element of the "garden" had replaced the wild Michigan being settled:

The child Henry Ford toddled about on the Dearborn farm amid pleasant surroundings. The land, though a stiff clay and somewhat hard to work, was fertile. Beyond the yard with its pump, beyond the evergreen shrubs and the orchard, well-cultivated fields were broken by patches of timber. Wild flowers bloomed in the fence corners and on the margins of the woods; butterflies rose from moist patches of the earth, and dragonflies circled marshy pools; on spring mornings the meadowlarks, song sparrows, brown thrushes, catbirds, bobolinks and bluejays raised a merry din. Gazing out over the April fields with . . . his father, the boy at times heard the lusty drummings of the partridge, or saw the bird as it whirred into sudden flight. He became familiar with the small wild animals of the region: rabbits, skunks, raccoons, foxes, minks, and muskrats.[88]

In later life, Ford, thinking of these days, jotted down his first memory. It was of "my father taking my brother and myself to see a bird's nest under a big oak twenty rods east of our home and my birthplace." Ford believed this little excursion took place in June 1866. His father carried his year-old brother, John; but Henry, almost three, was just old enough to be able to "run along with them." Ford could remember "the nest with four eggs and also the bird and hearing it sing."[89]

Ford transformed this bucolic little world into a center of industry to rival, if not surpass, the Ruhr. By the 1920s, his two-thousand-acre industrial complex, located at the mouth of the River Rouge, a few miles from the old homestead, employed a hundred thousand people. Ford owned it all personally, no stockholders and no partners. Of course, Ford changed more than Dearborn, Detroit, and Michigan. More than any other individual, it was he who put America on wheels. By making it possible for so many people in the world to move, he moved the world. He was the Copernicus of cars.

Ford's early years were full of exploration and discovery and wonderment. William and Mary Ford's marriage seems to have been a genuine love match. Mary ruled the roost in a manner that was lovingly serious or seriously loving, depending upon how one looks at it. "Fun we had and plenty of it," recalled Ford of his youth; but his mother "was forever reminding us that life cannot be all fun.

'You must earn the right to play,' she used to say to me. . . . 'The best fun follows a duty done.'"[90] Mary Ford taught her son how to read. Both she and William recognized a precocity with regard to things mechanical in the boy. Mary's influence on Henry was profound and enduring. "I have tried to live my life as my mother would have wished," he said in 1923.

A full decade after Mark Twain's beloved daughter Suzy died suddenly and unexpectedly of meningitis in 1895, Twain remarked: "It is one of the mysteries of our nature that a man, all unprepared, can receive a thunder-stroke like that and live."[91] No one in the Ford family had mastered the language as Twain had, but their feelings must have been much like his in March of 1876. Mary was expecting her eighth child. She had never had trouble in childbirth before. At thirty-seven, she was not young, but she was not old.

The child, a son, was lost at birth on March 17. A doctor was called in. No one knew what was wrong. Nothing could be done. Henry Ford's mother died on March 29, 1876. Her epitaph read:

> Dearest Thou has left us. It is thy loss we deeply mourn. But it is God that hath berieved [sic] us. He can all our sorrows heal again. In Heaven we hope to greet thee, where no farewell tears are shed.[92]

Years later, Ford said the house became like a watch without a mainspring,[93] a touching expression of grief even if slightly jarring in its use of a mechanical, inanimate simile. He remained on the farm at Dearborn until 1879, but his years of innocence were at an end. He had discovered how hard life could be.

Ford was thus not quite thirteen when his mother died. Puberty is a time both of burgeoning sexuality and the beginnings of the desire to be treated as an adult in an adult world. His mother's eighth pregnancy was a vivid statement of his parent's ongoing physical intimacy. As a thirteen-year-old, he might well have had complex feelings about his father's sexual freedom with his mother. This freedom and her death could have been associated in his mind, at least in his unconscious thoughts.

Admittedly, this is speculation. But we do need some way to explain Ford's misrepresentation of his father's later assistance to him. We also need some help in understanding why Ford harbored within him such anger, anger which found full vent, to the detriment of everyone, including himself, in his later life.

Four months after his mother died, Henry was in Detroit with his father. He saw a vehicle powered by a steam engine making its way along the road. It was a magic moment, "a sight almost as astounding to the boy as if Elijah's chariot of fire had suddenly appeared."[94] He remembered that sight for the rest of his life. He had found something new to love soon after his mother's death. And, unlike a person, a machine could not die and abandon a loved one.

Ford spent a couple of more years on the farm and attending school. But he grew to dislike farm life, with its repetitive drudgery and boredom, especially with the "mainspring" gone. "I never had any particular love for the farm," he said in something of an understatement. "It was the mother on the farm I loved."[95]

Ford left home in 1879 to seek his fortune in Detroit. This also marked the end of his formal schooling. Jonathan Hughes exaggerated in calling Ford barely literate. He could read and write, and his love letters to his bride to be, Clara Jane Bryant, are real and touching. Ford was, however, quite "unschooled." From the moment he received his first watch as a gift, he felt he had no further need for books. "Machines are to a mechanic what books are to a writer," he later said.[96]

Ford was fascinated by watches. He could take them apart and put them together with ease. He was enchanted by other machines as well, such as the steam road engine. He was born to be a mechanic. He was patient, systematic, and careful with machines, to which description must be added that he possessed true talent in this realm.

Neither Eastman nor Ford had much formal schooling. Eastman, however, became a knowledgeable and even wise man in his later years. What he did not learn formally, he made up for on his own. Few observations are more indicative of Eastman's discernment than his assessment of Henry Ford late in 1916. Ford, he wrote in a personal letter concerning the Peace Ship, "makes me both sick and tired."[97]

Eastman and Ford both idealized their mothers, and both had problems with their fathers. Eastman's father died when he was a mere child. His feckless business career left the family not with assets but with debts. There is no record of Eastman looking back on his father's life longingly or lovingly.

Ford's relationship with his father is difficult to decode because Ford himself was so confused about it. When not corroborated, Ford's own recollections of his father are unreliable. Ford wanted the world to believe that his father opposed his leaving the farm and opposed his interest in automobiles. There is an element of truth in this assessment. But there is also convincing evidence that William Ford was not nearly as oppositional as his son would have had everyone believe. Ford's memory of his youth from the vantage point of his later years appears to be laced with inaccuracies.

There is evidence that William Ford wanted his eldest son to take up farming in Dearborn. There is also evidence that the father was unimpressed at best by his son's early attempts to build an automobile. Nevertheless, the most striking aspect of the relations between father and son is the son's consistent misrepresentation of his father's attitude and actions toward him.

How do we know this? Our best witness is Margaret Ford Ruddiman, a sister of Henry's. Born in 1867, Mrs. Ruddiman was interviewed extensively in the early 1950s for the corporate archives which the Ford Motor Company founded in Dearborn in February 1951.[98] Her "Reminiscences," collected after Henry's death, have the ring of truth.[99] They are measured and precise. Moreover, they are, in those instances where it is possible, corroborated by third parties. Her observations deserve to be quoted at some length: "For many years, I have been very concerned about the stories indicating a lack of understanding between Henry and Father. Henry and I discussed this many times, but he put off doing anything about correcting the stories. . . ."

Mrs. Ruddiman is stating the case quite mildly. Ford was the principal exponent of the stories. "There were family discussions," she recalled, "and differences of opinion as there are in all normal families, and no doubt there were many times when Father questioned the wisdom of Henry's decision but at no time were there any serious quarrels. . . ."[100]

Time and again, Ford spoke about having to fight his way to mechanical brilliance, to sneak away from home to Detroit, and to set himself up in the automobile business. In fact, his father obtained a position for Henry at the Flower Brothers Machine Shop in Detroit, his father put him in touch with wealthy Detroiters who invested in his first automobile company, and his father offered to invest his own money in the venture, an offer the son refused.[101]

One does not have to accept the whole of Jardim's interpretation of Henry Ford's personality to be impressed with the acuity with which she has analyzed the discrepancies between Ford's recollections of his early life and what that early life was in actuality. Although his father did have disagreements with Henry, Mrs. Ruddiman was right. These conflicts were not beyond the realm of the normal. On balance, William Ford was supportive, even though his son's desires ran contrary to his own.

It is precisely here that the problem resided. It was not that the father thwarted the son. It was that he supported him. By supporting him, by offering to invest in a business that would take Ford away from the farm, the father sent a message that he was willing to do without the son, that he was willing to, in a sense, abandon the son. In the innumerable reversals in his memories of his youth, Ford painted a picture of himself abandoning his father by turning to mechanical pursuits and decamping from the farm to Detroit. He thus erased a narcissistic injury and transformed it into a courageous declaration of independence through which he invented not only a car but himself. And he did this by himself, without the help of a deceased mother or an oppositional father. The psychic injury done to Ford by his father's "abandonment" of him, expressed, for example, in his father's willingness to support financially his automobile company, was conveniently reversed. It was the son—in Henry Ford's fantasy re-creation of his childhood, boyhood, and youth—who abandoned the father.

Why does any of this matter? First of all, the historian shares the impulse of Mrs. Ruddiman to set the record straight. Second, one is forced to ask how wrong Ford's pronouncements might be on other matters if they were this wrong on his upbringing.

More important, Henry Ford was a man who, especially as he aged, experienced a great deal of trouble getting along with other men. At first this tendency evidenced itself in a penchant for practical jokes and in a mean streak. By the late 1910s, Ford found it difficult to deal with men who did not kowtow to him. Couzens had to go. The rambunctious Dodge brothers had to go. Many members of the team that enabled the Ford Motor Company to function in an organized way and to expand globally were expelled between 1919 and 1921. These included the head of advertising, the assistant secretary and general attorney, the treasurer, the auditor, and the head of personnel. Also included were Norval Hawkins, the man who built the sales system and dealer network, and William S. Knudsen, from manufacturing.[102] Hawkins and Knudsen were quickly hired by General Motors, of which Knudsen eventually became president.

During the 1920s, it became steadily more difficult for a man to work for Ford, especially if that work entailed personal contact, and maintain his self-respect.[103] Jardim said that Ford's "attitude to the men around him at times bordered on the sadistic. . . ."[104] In this, she understated the case. Ford moved well across that border. In later life, he was a sadist pure and simple.

The one man whom Ford would not fire and who was incapable of leaving him was his son, Edsel. Edsel paid the price. "Mr. Ford," recalled an executive, "was unmerciful in embarrassing Edsel." Once, at a meeting with four or five executives about a technical matter, Edsel began to explain to his father what was in the works. Hardly had be begun to speak when his father got out of his chair, said, "Edsel, you shut up!" and left.[105] There is no record of Ford's own father ever humiliating him in such a way. Henry Ford II (the grandson of Henry Ford I and the son of Edsel Ford) blamed his grandfather and his grandfather's cronies, including a Gothic surrogate son named Harry Bennett, for his father's death.[106]

The lives of average men are filled with people to whom they have to answer. Average people must keep their darker impulses in check to be effective in the world. For Ford, with his limitless wealth, the lack of an internal control mechanism met no external control. He was free, but for him that meant freedom to regress.

But we anticipate our story. As Collier and Horowitz put it, Ford's fortune came before his crimes. And the story of his early success in the automobile industry is as inspiring as the story of his later failures as a human being is depressing.

HENRY FORD THE YOUNG ADULT

Henry Ford divided his time between Detroit businesses and the Dearborn farm during the 1880s. Ford did not dive right into the automobile industry. In the 1880s there was no automobile industry into which to dive. The sound of machine shops suffused Detroit, and Ford found work in a number of them. At night, he worked on watches.

In Detroit's machine shops, Ford got to know engines. Only a few years after George Eastman began devouring the *British Journal of Photography,* Ford was scrutinizing "in the English and American magazines which we got in the shop the development of the engine and most particularly the hints of the possible replacement of the illuminating gas fuel by a gas formed by the vaporizing of gasoline." In fact, Ford, like others, was probably more interested in steam than gasoline as fuel. Steam transformed the world in the nineteenth century.[107] Ford worked, read, listened, bided his time.

The most important event in Ford's life in the 1880s took place early in 1885. He was at a party in Greenfield, near Dearborn, when he met Clara Jane Bryant. The oldest of ten children, Clara, eighteen years of age, was brought up on a local farm. A courtship ensued. Clara and Henry were married at St. James Episcopal Church in Detroit on April 11, 1888. It was her twenty-first birthday. The marriage lasted until Henry's death a year short of six decades later. Clara always had faith in Henry, and she was able to satisfy his "hunger for understanding and affection."[108]

There is some controversy about the extent of Ford's experimentation relating to a "horseless carriage" while he and Clara lived in the comfortable "square house" on the Dearborn farm. It is clear that he maintained an interest in engines and in road vehicles. It was in order to pursue this interest that he decided to leave the farm once and for all. Although the conservative Clara was unhappy, she was so supportive that she never mentioned her qualms. William Ford was unhappy as well, but he accepted the situation. In September 1891, Henry and Clara moved off the farm, this time for good. Henry got a job with Detroit's Edison Illuminating Company, where he rapidly rose to chief engineer, making $100 a month.

The Fords were prosperous enough to move from the rooms they first occupied to a two-family home just walking distance from Edison Electric. At the back of the lot was a shed, which Ford, whose interest in motor vehicles was turning into an obsession, transformed into his personal workshop. He worked long hours at Edison Electric. He then came home to his wife, to his son, and, most importantly, to his shed. He worked into the night, but it was a pleasure. "I cannot say it was hard work. No work with interest is ever hard."[109] By 1893, Detroit was pulsing with interest in machinery. The self-propelled road vehicle was proving a lightning rod for

Ford and for other mechanics. It would take a decade, a very eventful decade of invention, before the Ford Motor Company was finally established.

Meanwhile, Ford's family seemed a happy one. His only child, Edsel, was born on November 6, 1893. The distinctive name the Fords chose for their child deserves a comment. The son was named after a school friend of Henry's, Edsel Ruddiman. Ruddiman was a more apt pupil than Henry. By the time of Edsel Ford's birth, Dr. Ruddiman was an established chemist-pharmacist, having proceeded with his higher education long after Henry dropped out of school. He was bright and a good deal more successful than the "rather shiftless farmboy-turned-mechanic who, at the age of thirty, was spending most of his nights tinkering in a back room or laughing and joking with boys."[110] Ford admired Ruddiman. He would soon become a member of Ford's extended family when his brother, James, married Ford's sister Margaret (who was four years Ford's junior). The name "Edsel" itself has roots in Old English. Its original meaning was "from the rich man's house."[111] This is certainly not why the Fords chose the name.

The reason for this digression is that in September of 1957, the Ford Motor Company brought out a new automobile called the Edsel. Although the name was not remarkable in the nineteenth century, by the 1950s it had become not quite quaint, neither antique, but rather odd. Its attachment to one of the great new-product flops in the twentieth century will not do much to revive it.[112] Outside of the Ford family, in which Edsel Ford named his first son Henry Ford II, Henry Ford II named his only son Edsel Ford II, and Edsel Ford II named his first son Henry Ford III (born 1980), one doubts that Edsel will be a commonly used name in the future.

At any rate, during the 1890s, Ford, like Eastman early in his career, held down two jobs: salaried master mechanic by day and freelance experimenter and inventor by night. By 1896, the work was overpowering in its grip. Ford felt that he was on to something new, different, and better than others who were experimenting with the horseless carriage.

By May of 1896, his friends "often wondered when Henry Ford slept." Clara feared he would have a nervous breakdown, but characteristically kept her fears to herself. The result of all this was the emergence, between two and four o'clock on the morning of June 4, of the quadricycle.[113] Henry Ford had done what not one top automobile executive in the world could do today. He had built a complete car with his bare hands.[114]

Ford drove his quadricycle out to his father's Dearborn farm. Charles B. King, an industry pioneer who had been working with Ford, took the trip with him. His father was not merely unimpressed; he felt, according to one account, embarrassed. Recalled King, "I could see that old Mr. Ford was ashamed of a grown-up man like Henry fussing over a little thing like a quadricycle." Henry, said King, was "heartbroken."[115]

A half century later, Ford's sister Margaret Ruddiman remembered that Sunday sojourn in Dearborn. Her father, "a conservative farmer of those times," did indeed decline to take a ride. Nevertheless, she maintained, William Ford "was very proud of Henry's achievement. He talked about it to us at home and he told his neighbors about it . . . [and] on later trips of Henry's to the farm, Father rode in the car."[116]

Whether or not Ford was heartbroken on that Sunday in June more than a century ago, he emerged from the day undaunted. Although there was a lot of skepticism both in Detroit and around the country about self-propelled motor vehicles in general and about gasoline-fueled engines specifically, there was also growing interest. In the Northeast and in the Great Lakes states, entrepreneurs were looking for backers to help them finance the production of carriages which did not need horses to move.

Ford continued his two jobs: at the Edison Illuminating Company, where he was making $1,900 a year, and in his shed. In August he attended a convention of Edison companies in New York. There he met his idol, Thomas Alva Edison himself. He had the chance, which he seized with alacrity, of explaining his ideas to Edison. Edison, the great man of electricity, was enthusiastic about Ford's ideas, even though they had at their center not electricity but gasoline.[117]

Ford, inspired, returned to Detroit. Things began to happen fast. He sold his quadricycle for $200 and used the proceeds to begin work on his next car. The clear goal, however, was not "one-off" vehicles for local businessmen. Ford knew that he wanted to go into volume production. While he was redoubling his automotive efforts, he was also becoming a more important resource at the Edison Illuminating Company, which was expanding.

On August 5, 1899, the Detroit Automobile Company was incorporated. The first automobile firm in the city, it had more than a dozen investors, including, with the help of the intercession of Ford's father, the mayor. The investors composed an "elite group."[118] Ford was the superintendent, and he was granted a small amount of stock although he paid in no capital.

"Once to every man and nation / Comes a moment to decide . . . ," says the hymn. In Henry Ford's life, that moment came in August of 1899. Not even he could continue to hold down two ever-more-demanding jobs. Here is how he put it: "The Edison Company offered me the general superintendency of the company but only on condition that I would give up my gas engine and devote myself to something really useful. I had to choose between my job and my automobile. I chose the automobile, or rather I gave up the job—there was really nothing in the way of a choice." There was no real choice in Ford's view, "For already I knew the car was bound to be a success."[119]

How certain was it that Detroit's first venture into an industry just about to be born would succeed? Ford had a friend at Edison Illuminating named David M. Bell who had worked on Ford's two cars. Ford thought highly enough of Bell to try to take him along in the new venture.

"Dave," Ford said, "you'll grow with the business."

"What business?" replied Bell, who elected the security of a regular paycheck with an established firm.[120] Some people have the stomach for entrepreneurship; others do not. The difference could not be better illustrated than by this little incident.

Ford's assertion to the contrary notwithstanding, nothing was more uncertain than the success of his new car. Indeed, there does not seem to have been a clear definition of what would have constituted success. At the minimum, it had to mean the survival of the Detroit Automobile Company as an ongoing enterprise.

By that rather low standard, the Detroit Automobile Company failed. Ford himself became frustrated with the quality of its vehicles, and in January of 1901 the company suspended operations. A total of $86,000 had been spent, and precious little product had been sold. A number of Ford's investors were, however, sufficiently impressed with him to continue backing him. He was beginning to make a name for himself.[121]

Ford tried again. Racing lent luster to his name. On October 10, 1901, he beat the then famous Alexander Winton in an exciting two-man confrontation in Detroit. "That race has advertised him far and wide," Clara wrote her brother. Investors were attracted to a man and machine who did what Ford and his car did that October 10. Some of the same men who had financed the Detroit Automobile Company rallied around Ford again. This time, the enterprise was called the Henry Ford Company. Ford served as the engineer and was given a $10,000 interest in the firm, which was incorporated on November 30, 1901. The Henry Ford Company, however, fared no better than the Detroit Automobile Company. Ford left it on March 10, 1902, at which time it ceased to use his name.[122]

In August the Henry Ford Company became the Cadillac Automobile Company, as Ford's former backers now put their money on Henry M. Leland. After its share of ups and downs, Cadillac was purchased by the newly formed General Motors on August 20, 1909, for $4.75 million, almost all in cash. The Lelands, father and son, ran Cadillac within General Motors until 1917. They were forced out; and in January of 1920, they founded the Lincoln Motor Company. In 1922, Ford bought Lincoln. They took over from Ford in 1902; he from them two decades later. The worm had turned.

Henry Ford thus failed twice as a businessman before his eventual success. The brief histories of the Detroit Automobile Company and the Henry Ford Company highlight some of the problems of entrepreneurship from the investor's point of view. What industry are you going to invest in? At the turn of the century there was a lot of interest in automobiles. However, the majority of Americans believed an automobile would never be more than an expensive plaything for the rich.[123] Moreover, the wagon business was prospering in the late 1890s. Between 1894 and 1899, according to the president of the Carriage Builders Association, 350,000 carriages had been sold in New York City, compared with 125 cars. The idea that the car would someday replace the horse was "a fallacy too absurd to be mentioned by intelligent men."[124]

Even if, in the face of the conventional wisdom, an investor was foolhardy enough to put his money into an automobile company, which one did he choose? Between 1890 and 1930, hundreds of companies entered the industry.[125] At this writing, there are three domestic manufacturers left. Three, that is, if one includes Chrysler, which, after the Daimler merger, should be considered more a German than an American company.

One of these three is the Ford Motor Company, but Ford's rocky start highlights another problem for the entrepreneurial financier. Ford made no money for his investors in his first two companies and cost some of them quite a lot. The fate of the investors in his third company was quite different.

Consider, for example, the happy story of James Couzens's sister. When the Ford Motor Company was being organized, Couzens was desperately in search of cash to fund his own investment; and his sister, Rosetta, was kind enough to lend him $100 of the $300 she had saved from her income as a public-school teacher in Chatham, Ontario. Rosetta Couzens was not "in" with any elite group of investors, nor did she know anything about automobiles. When Henry Ford bought out his minority stockholders in 1919 and 1920, Mrs. Rosetta Couzens Hauss received $262,036.67 for that $100, a powerful argument for being your brother's keeper.[126]

The entrepreneurial financier must worry about what industry to invest in, what company to invest in, and when to invest. These three critical decisions must be made without the kind of detailed information an investor would normally want. To answer any of these three questions incorrectly is to spell failure. That is why so many people are conservative investors. There are risks in that course as well, however. What would have happened to your money if, in 1899, you had put it into a wagon manufacturer?

THE MODEL T FORD AND THE BIRTH OF THE AUTO-INDUSTRIAL AGE

Henry Ford was undiscouraged by the fate of the Detroit Automobile Company and the Henry Ford Company. The modern Ford Motor Company was incorporated on June 16, 1903, a month and a half prior to Henry Ford's fortieth birthday. A decade later, he was the undisputed leader of the industry, possessor of a fortune beyond calculation, and well on his way to world fame.

In 1903, the Ford Motor Company began manufacture on Mack Avenue in Detroit in rented shops, which appear in photographs to resemble small shacks. The handful of company employees could be easily captured in a photograph and counted. From these cramped quarters, the company quickly moved on to Piquette

Avenue,[127] and from there to the gigantic complex at Highland Park. Highland Park opened at the beginning of 1910 on a sixty-acre tract of land in a township just north of Detroit. The complex was completed six years later when its sixty acres could hold no more buildings.[128] By that time, more than 30,000 people worked there, as compared with 125 at Mack Avenue in 1903.[129]

The English language fails to supply the superlatives contemporaries groped for to express their impressions of Highland Park. And Highland Park was small compared to the huge industrial establishment that Ford built on a two-thousand-acre site on the River Rouge, south of Detroit. In 1929, there was an average hourly workforce of 98,337 at the Rouge.[130] The machine produced first at Highland Park and then at the Rouge, the Model T Ford, became the most famous automobile in the history of the industry.

Prior to Ford, the automobile had been predominantly a high-priced luxury item assembled in small numbers by skilled craftsmen. But Henry Ford developed a vision of what the car should be. That vision is expressed in the first paragraph of this chapter. These sentiments remained familiar into the mid-1990s because the Ford Motor Company continued to use Ford's words in its television advertising.[131]

The Ford Motor Company manufactured eight different models of cars between 1903 and 1908: the Models A, B, C, F, K, N, R, and S. At times, the company manufactured multiple models simultaneously. For example, the Model C Runabout listed for $800, the Model F Touring Car for $1,000 ("with physician's closed coupe" for $1,250), and the Model B for $2,000 during 1904–1905.[132]

During these early years a sharp disagreement developed within the fledgling firm about which market it should serve. The financier behind the Ford Motor Company was Alexander Y. Malcomson, a coal dealer who owned 255 shares (the same number as Henry Ford). Malcomson's friends and relatives also invested.[133] As did so many other capital providers in the early years of the industry, Malcomson favored targeting the upscale market. He "had fallen in love with the design of the [costly] six-cylinder Model K. . . ." There was some evidence that the market for automobiles lay in the high-priced range.[134] Malcomson was a willful man. He was not cut out to play Henry Alvah Strong to Henry Ford's George Eastman.

Ford, on the other hand, held fast to his dream of "a car for the common man." And "dream" is precisely what it was, because it was very difficult to see at the time how Ford's vision could be turned into a profitable business reality.[135] As Charles E. Sorensen, who became Ford's production chief, later recalled, "Ford merely had the idea; he had no picture in his mind as to what the car would be like, or look like."[136] Ford fought for his inexpensive car, and "directors' meetings grew stormy. Much pounding of the table took place, and the little group . . . sometimes broke up angrily."[137] Ford proved to be an extraordinarily effective infighter. He put himself in a position to buy Malcomson's 255 shares, which he did in 1906. By the fall of 1907, he owned a majority of the shares. The company was already setting sales records with the Model N. The next great step was to concentrate, climactically, on the Model T.[138]

The Model T was the automobile that put America on wheels. When it was finally discontinued after almost twenty years in 1927, 15,458,781 had been produced.[139] The Model T made Henry Ford a billionaire. And Henry Ford made the Model T. Of course, he did not do it alone. He did it with the help of hundreds of suppliers, thousands of dealers, and tens of thousands of factory workers. He did it with the help of a collection of exceptionally talented engineers. As one historian has remarked, "Henry Ford possessed an uncommon gift—or was unusually lucky—in attracting to his company well-educated mechanics who believed that 'work was play.'"[140] As "Cast Iron Charlie" Sorensen put it, if work had not been play for these men, "it would have killed them. They were as men possessed. They often forgot to eat."[141]

We would deprive ourselves of the lessons Henry Ford's life has to teach if we allowed his later failings to obscure his vision and his talent. The myriad interpersonal problems only moved to center stage later in his life. In the years of the Model N and in the early years of the Model T and Highland Park, the Ford Motor Company must have been one of the most exciting places to work in the history of industry. If Henry Ford's career had concluded with this era, he would hold a place in the American pantheon beside the greatest figures in nation's past.

Evaluating Ford during these years, Nevins and Hill have written:

> [Ford] evolved from his intuitive processes of thought certain large conceptions which, more than anything else,

account for his spectacular early success. One, of course, was his idea of a car for the masses, built in quantity, and sold at ever-lower prices as consumption grew. Another was his determination to expand his plant, his production, and his sales at a steady pace, in defiance of those who wished to call a halt. He meant to make as many cars as possible at the lowest prices. . . .[142]

Not every student of Ford views him as imposingly as he is being presented here. John Kenneth Galbraith, for example, believes that Ford has been overrated. It was James Couzens, in Galbraith's view, who made the Ford Motor Company the success that it was in the early years; and after Couzens left in 1915, the "company was never so successful again."[143]

Couzens was indeed a remarkable individual who rose from a modest family background to become a millionaire and a U.S. senator from Michigan. According to Nevins: "From childhood Couzens had shown . . . a precise and almost furious industry, a hot temper, and a determination to succeed. As a youth he reproached his mother for letting him be born in Canada. 'I can never become King of England,' he said sharply and quite seriously, 'but if I had been born in the United States, I could be President.'"[144]

Couzens was the business brains of the organization and deserves his full measure of credit for its success. But while there were many James Couzenses, there was only one Henry Ford.[145] An appreciation of this fact is vital because Ford's vision of what an automobile should be and what an automobile company should do has suffused the Ford Motor Company from his day to our own.

Ford's vision found a reflection in Robert S. McNamara's career at the company. The Falcon, which premiered in 1960, was McNamara's car. A journalist has described the Falcon as "a completely utilitarian vehicle . . . no-frills economy transportation . . . [available] only in solid colors, not any of those ghastly two- or three-tone jobs."[146] (This, of course, recalls Henry Ford's famous declaration that "any customer can have a car painted any color he wants so long as it is black.")[147] "He [McNamara] wears granny glasses and puts out a granny car," wrote one automobile reporter. Perhaps that was true. But the Ford Motor Company produced more than 435,000 units[148] of this "modern version of the Tin Lizzie"[149] during its first year on the market; and on June 3, 1960, McNamara, the man with the "granny" glasses, became the president of the Ford Motor Company at the age of 44.[150]

The product policy of the Ford Motor Company in its early years was the manufacturing and marketing of a single automobile, the Model T. From first to last, the market for the Model T was comprised of customers needing "basic transportation."[151] "It takes you there and brings you back" was the popular slogan which Henry Ford liked so much about the car.[152] In 1908, when the touring car debuted at $850, an advertisement boasted accurately: "No car under $2,000 offers more, and no car over $2,000 offers more except trimmings."[153] During World War I, in which it did yeoman service, the Model T earned for itself an encomium to the cadence of "Gunga Din":

> Yes, Tin, Tin, Tin
> You exasperating puzzle Hunka Tin,
> I've abused you and I've flayed you
> But, by Henry Ford who made you
> You are better than a Packard, Hunka Tin.[154]

In Henry Ford's view, the Model T was the automobile the public *should* want; and it was the embodiment of what an automobile *should* be. An automobile was an appliance that took the owner from place to place. It was not a style item, and it had no fashion content. In order to produce his simple car for transportation for the masses, Ford led his colleagues in the transformation of automobile manufacturing from craft production to mass production. The hallmarks of the latter included interchangeable parts, the moving assembly line, the standardization of work assignments, and a highly systematized approach to manufacture.[155]

"The way to make automobiles," Ford told one of his partners in 1903, "is to make them all alike, to make them come from the factory just alike—just like one pin is like another pin when it comes from a pin factory, or one match is like another match when it comes from a match factory."[156] This statement is misleading. First, not all Model Ts came from the factory just alike. Second, the Model T did change over time, especially in the 1920s.

In order fully to understand the Model T, we must first gain an understanding of what a "model" was from 1908 through 1927. Not every Model T was precisely the same in every respect. The Model T was not as standardized as a pin or a match.

Up until about 1930, "model" referred to a chassis, engine-suspension, power-train combination. The "body" of a model was an independently specified item.[157] From October 1, 1912, to August 1, 1913, for example, a consumer could purchase a Runabout (which had seating capacity for a driver and for a passenger), a Touring Car (which had seats for two in front and two to three in back), a Town Car (which featured a compartment at the rear of the car, thus separating the passengers from the driver), and a Delivery Wagon. The prices for these vehicles varied considerably. The Runabout listed for $525, the Touring Car for $600 (almost 15 percent higher), the Town Car for $800 (over 50 percent more than the Runabout), and the Delivery Wagon for $625.[158] By 1915, one could buy a chassis, apparently without any body at all, for $360.[159] In fact, the Model T attracted a good deal of publicity for its off-the-road uses. "News stories frequently told of a stationary Model T providing power for motors which did everything from running newspaper presses and telephone exchanges to pumping water and exterminating gophers."[160]

The Ford Motor Company made a great deal of money selling parts for the servicing of the ever-growing number of Model Ts on the road. Much of the service provided on the Model T was self-service. "If the Model T engine stumbled, [owners] simply looked for the cause in the question-and-answer booklet the company provided and fixed the problem. For example, they might drain the gas tank and pour the fuel back through a chamois to strain any water out. The bottom line: If a part didn't fit properly or was installed slightly out of tolerance, the owner was expected to fix it."[161]

The irony here is that while turning the workers who produced its automobiles into something akin to de-skilled machine tenders, the Ford Motor Company expected its customers to have considerable craft knowledge. Henry Ford himself had an "artisan mentality."[162] In 1910, the year the Highland Park plant opened, only 46 percent of the population of the United States lived in cities of twenty-five hundred or more.[163] Farmers and the residents of small farm communities had a basic familiarity with mechanical machinery because harvesters, mowers, reapers, twine binders, and other mechanical implements had been part of their lives through much of the nineteenth century. Such people were far more adept at dealing even with the complicated parts of their automobiles than most modern drivers are when the "check engine" light flashes on their dashboards.[164]

Not only could the Model T's early owners manage their cars; they also learned how to customize them. Some five thousand accessories were available to Model T owners during the years of its production. Canvas or leather radiator covers, a variety of interior heating devices, shock absorbers, clamp-on bumper bars, electric side lamps, exhaust deflectors, coil and distributor ignition systems, "non-fouling" spark plugs, a variety of carburetors, and crown wheel and pinion sets were just some of the devices available to the enterprising Model T owner. Prior to Ford's adoption of the electric self-starter, a mechanical apparatus was sold which enabled the driver to start the engine while seated behind the wheel. If an owner was willing to crank-start the car but wanted the task made easier, he or she could purchase a "non-kick" device. This item was sold by the Non-Kick Device Company of Kansas City. Advertisements explained: "Better than insurance because it prevents sprained wrists, broken arms with their pain and suffering, inconvenience and doctor bills." All this for a mere $2.50.[165] And finally, the matter of paint. Not everyone wanted their Model T in black. Therefore, an aftermarket grew up for paint shops. When all of this is considered, one realizes the variety that existed in this vehicle.

The Model T changed over time. The Model T has been described as "fundamentally unchanged" from 1909 (there had been some alterations from the introductory version of the previous year) to the discontinuance in 1927.[166] The accuracy of this statement depends upon the definition of "fundamentally." Historian David A. Hounshell lists a set of changes which deal both with the styling of the automobile and with the substance of the engine itself.[167] Despite these advances, there is a consensus among historians and executives that the Model T was outmoded by the mid-1920s. In Hounshell's words: "The ignition, carburetor, transmission, brake and suspension systems, as well as the styling and appointments, made the T appear antique. Genuine engineering improvements . . . had been made by other manufacturers. . . ."[168]

According to the man who built General Motors, Alfred P. Sloan Jr.: "There is a legend cultivated by sentimentalists that Mr.

Ford left behind [in the Model T] a great car expressive of the pure concept of cheap, basic transportation. The fact is that he left behind a car that no longer offered the best buy, even as raw, basic transportation."[169]

The points to be emphasized here are that although there were a number of different Model T body types with significantly different prices, I have not found any indication that the Ford Motor Company aimed at pricing one kind of Model T very low to facilitate the purchase of an entry-level product and then growing the consumer to a more expensive type. No one, in other words, was planning to price the Runabout low in the hope that someday the consumer would trade it in for a Touring Car.

By the same token, no one at Ford changed the Model T during its years on the market in the hope of making obsolete the automobiles already owned by the driving public. Change was never a selling point for the Model T. To the contrary, when Ford changed the Model T, the company sought to hide those changes behind weasel words. That is because the Model T, as Hounshell has pointed out, "was as much an *idea* as it was an automobile."[170] Every product begins as a concept.[171] In this case the concept—the "idea"—"was an unchanging car for the masses."[172] The Model T was conceived of as the answer to the sensible citizen's need for basic transportation. The company therefore feared publicity for the changes that it did make and introduced them in a "hush-hush atmosphere."[173]

THE PLANT AT HIGHLAND PARK

When the Model T was introduced on October 1, 1908, it was state of the art. A dozen men were responsible for its design, and the guiding force was Henry Ford. The Model T and the plant that produced it were his monuments. One could exhaust the English language of its adjectives without capturing their impact. The original price of the Model T was $825 for the Runabout and an additional $25 for the Touring Car. Even at this price, which was higher than Ford's goal and higher than the prices of other cars had sold for previously, the automobile represented real value for the dollar.[174]

In the early years of the industry, model runs in the hundreds were very long. A model which sold a thousand units was a smashing success. The 1908 Model T sold 5,986 units. Eight short years later, when Ford had pushed the price of the touring car down to $360, the Model T sold over 575,000 units.[175] The industry had changed forever. What came to be known as "Fordism" made it possible for the automobile industry to become the most important industry in the twentieth century.

By 1917, Ford had sold 1.5 million Model Ts. Demand had exploded as prices dropped. Increased demand had been met not with price increases, but with increased output and price cuts. The virtuous circle of modern capitalism was being established. As prices dropped, demand increased. As demand increased, output increased. As output increased, costs dropped due to scale economies, the learning curve, and purchasing economies. As costs dropped, prices could be cut again. Meanwhile, profit was soaring because what was lost on margin was made up a thousandfold on volume. Without knowing it, Ford was applying to his business the principles which Carnegie had applied to his.

The plant at Highland Park opened on January 1, 1910. Some of what comprised this plant was not new. Moving lines of work in process had existed elsewhere. So had special-purpose machinery which turned out interchangeable parts. So had scheduling designed to keep everything flowing smoothly. Never, however, had all these things been put together on such a gigantic scale to manufacture a machine as complicated as the Model T Ford. Individual musicians had played partitas on clavichords. Highland Park was the *Symphony of a Thousand*.

To switch from a comparison to Gustav Mahler, the composer of the *Symphony of a Thousand*, to a Wagnerian metaphor, Highland Park was the *Gesamtkunstwerk*, the total artwork, of the automobile industry. In Wagner, every aspect of an opera (or "music drama," as he called his later work) was designed to assist every other aspect—the singing, the acting, the chorus, the movement on stage, the sets, the stage design, and the 107-piece orchestra. When Wagner could not find an instrument that produced the sound he wanted, he designed it himself and had it built for him. All this effort was aimed at telling a story which would not be another standard-issue "lover betrayed/revenge exacted" melodrama, but which would move the audience to new heights of aesthetic sensibility and which would touch them in new ways. A great deal of what Wagner did had been done before. No composer, however, had done it all the way he had. None had aimed for so lofty a goal. None had been so unwilling to settle for less than the best. None had put everything together to create a total artwork.

That is the story of Highland Park. The decision to concentrate on a single model enabled Ford designers to install special-purpose machine tools. In the words of David A. Hounshell, from whose authoritative account much of this treatment is summarized: "[T]he machine tool industry was capable—perhaps for the first time—of manufacturing machines that could turn out large amounts of consistently accurate work. . . . [Ford] did not compromise on this issue. . . . [T]his accuracy provided the rock upon which mass production of the Model T was based."[176] A contemporary expert remarked that "the Ford machinery was the best in the world, everybody knew it." Competitors observed that Ford could purchase specially designed machines and tools without regard to cost because of volume.[177]

Precision, interchangeable, special-purpose parts were a hallmark of Highland Park. Mass production of the Model T without them would have been impossible. So, by the way, would have been servicing after the sale. The Model T was built in one place, but it was sold and driven all across a 3-million-square-mile nation. By 1916, Ford had about eighty-five hundred dealers; and those dealers had to be able to replace worn parts. Without perfect interchangeability, mass marketing would not have been possible.[178]

One study insists that the "key" to mass production was this interchangeability of parts and the ease with which these parts could be attached to one another. The Model T was "designed for manufacture," in modern terms.[179] Perhaps the moving assembly line has been overemphasized because that was what was most obvious to an observer at Highland Park. If that is true, there is no need now to underemphasize it. The moving assembly line was as much the "key" to mass production as interchangeable parts manufactured by specially designed machines. They were both essential.

Ideas about moving the work to the man rather than the man to the work had made their way to the Ford Motor Company as early as 1907.[180] No one, however, had the big picture in mind. Here is how Charles Sorensen, who was among the pioneers and who worked for Ford for four decades, recalled the events from the vantage point of 1954: "Henry Ford had no ideas on mass production.

He wanted to build a lot of autos. He was determined but, like everyone else at that time, he didn't know how. . . . [H]e just grew into it, like the rest of us. The essential tools and the final assembly line with its many integrated feeders resulted from an organization which was continually experimenting and improvising to get better production."[181] This passage explains a great deal. Ford did not know the means. No one did. But he sure knew the end: "He wanted to build a lot of autos." Ford and his colleagues "just grew into it." They embraced experimentation and continuous improvement. They were flexible, open to new ideas, and by 1913 moving very fast.

Sorensen said Ford could not explain what had taken place until 1922. The moving assembly line—or, more accurately, lines, because there were many of them—was the product of pure induction. "The achievement came first," said Sorensen. "Then came logical expression of its principles and philosophy."[182] Hounshell has written that "the development of the assembly line at Ford was so swift and powerful that it defied accurate, unambiguous, timely documentation. . . . Within a year of the first line, virtually every assembly operation at Ford had been put on a moving line basis; and those early ones had been radically revised."[183]

The first moving line may have been for flywheel magneto assembly on April 1, 1913. As Hounshell put it, the installation and operation of this line

> somehow seemed another step in the years of development at Ford yet [also] somehow [seemed to have] suddenly dropped out of the sky. . . . Even before the end of that day, some of the engineers sensed that they had made a fundamental breakthrough. . . . Twenty-nine workers who had each assembled 35 or 40 magnetos per day at the benches (or about one every twenty minutes) put together 1,188 of them on the line (or roughly one every thirteen minutes and ten seconds per person).[184]

This was just the beginning. The magic months were in the fall of 1913 and the winter and spring of 1914. Engines, axles, and even the chassis were all put on moving assembly lines. Productivity increased at rates which staggered the imagination. Prior to the installation of a moving assembly line for the chassis in October of 1913, assembly took twelve hours and twenty-eight minutes. In the spring of 1914, the same task could be accomplished in one hour and thirty-three minutes.[185]

A business journalist who visited Highland Park in 1913 asked his readers to imagine what an output of 200,000 automobiles in one year meant: 800,000 wheels and as many tires; 400,000 cowhides; 2 million square feet of glass; 90,000 tons of steel; 6 million pounds of hair for seats. It meant one Model T, with its five thousand different parts, emerging from the factory every forty seconds of every working day. It meant five trains forty cars long leaving the factory loaded with Model Ts every day.[186] If this were possible, what more might be possible? A great deal. The article citing these statistics was written *before* the chassis was put on a moving assembly line. Just one decade before this article was written, the Ford Motor Company had been founded in a collection of small shacks with a handful of employees. Nevins and Hill called mass production at Highland Park "a new world force . . . destined to affect all economic and social life."[187] They were correct.

If the Highland Park story ended here, it would be revolutionary enough. We have not yet, however, even mentioned what made this plant and its owner world famous. On January 5, 1914, Ford stood by a window at an office in the plant as Couzens read a news release to reporters from three Detroit newspapers:

> The Ford Motor Co., the greatest and most successful automobile manufacturing company in the world, will, on Jan. 12, inaugurate the greatest revolution in the matter of rewards for its workers ever known to the industrial world.
>
> At one stroke it will reduce the hours of labor from nine to eight, and add to every man's pay a share of the profits of the house. The smallest amount to be received by a man 22 years old and upwards will be $5 per day. . . .

The language of the press release was flowery, but deservedly so. There had just been a wage boost to $2.34 a day on October 1, 1913, which represented a 13 percent increase over previous rates. Now, without violence, without pressure from a union, and without coercion from anyone, the Ford Motor Company was more than doubling what was already a competitive wage.[188] A mere twenty-two years prior to this announcement, the Homestead lockout had taken place.

Ford and Couzens knew this announcement would make for good publicity, as their phraseology suggests. But they had no idea of the impact it would have. They thought of it essentially as a local story, which is why they gave releases only to the local press.[189] In fact, it was the biggest news story to originate in Detroit up to that time, and it made Henry Ford's name recognized around the world.

There were operational, business reasons for the $5 day. Working at Highland Park was no picnic, and the more mechanized the plant became, the less control a laborer had over his or her life from one minute to the next. As a result, turnover at the company was a staggering 370 percent in 1913. Ford had to hire 50,448 people to maintain an average labor force of 13,623.[190] A more stable and better compensated labor force could and apparently did result in production efficiencies.[191] But these were not the only reasons for the pay hike. Somehow, Ford and Couzens simply felt it was the thing to do. One newspaper described Ford as someone "who has declined to forget that the distance between overalls and broadcloth is very short."[192] There may be some truth here.

Unlike so many modern executives, Ford actually understood personally how to produce what his company sold. So there was a certain kinship with overalls. Probably more important, there was a definite rejection of broadcloth. He made a point of turning his back on Detroit's social and business elite. Indeed, his munificent wage did not make their lives any easier, as their own employees considered what they were being paid.

The $5 day was the culminating gesture in Henry Ford's turning the world upside down. As demand increased, prices dropped even though supply could not keep up. That is not supposed to happen; but we have seen it before, both with Carnegie and Eastman. Monopolists are not supposed to innovate. But Highland Park was the most innovative plant in the world at a time in which Henry Ford owned the market in which he competed. In the face of a docile, unorganized, and unskilled workforce, Ford more than doubled wages.

Considered together, plunging product prices and rising wages painted a picture of a society unknown to economic theory. If the promise which seemed to be revealing itself on the Ford Motor Company's horizon proved reachable, the human race would be headed neither for a Hobbesian war of each against all nor a Marxist war of one class against another. Rather, there might be no classes at all if the working class made enough money to consume the products it manufactured. Turning workers into consumers. That was the promise of Highland Park on January 5, 1914.

If there was a turning point in Henry Ford's life in the realm of interpersonal relations, it may have been on the occasion of the announcement of the $5 day. Prior to 1914, Ford had his foibles; but they seem larger than life now only because he himself grew to mythic proportions. In context, up until 1914, Ford was an approachable man who, mean streak notwithstanding, was a hard-working hail-fellow-well-met.

The "ocean of publicity" on which Ford set sail and the thousands of letters he received released something inside him which would have been better kept under lock and key. According to David L. Lewis, an insightful historian of Ford's image, the $5 day "was instrumental in changing the manufacturer's image of himself. Ford's modesty became a thing of the past." Whereas he had once declined to comment on matters concerning which he knew nothing, he soon began to believe that his was a wisdom which surpassed understanding. Disquisitions on matters as far removed from auto manufacturing as the gold standard or the theory of evolution became commonplace. "As Ford almost indiscernibly began to shed his modesty, he developed an insatiable appetite for headlines. No other Ford executive was allowed to share them."[193]

It is hard to imagine the Henry Ford of 1903 or of 1913 chartering a Peace Ship; but in 1915 it happened. A crusade against Jews was inconceivable in 1910, but Ford launched one in 1920. The Henry Ford of 1903 and 1913 could work with the most assertive personalities in the industry. He had enough self-confidence that he could not only tolerate their weaknesses; he could exploit their strengths in order to achieve his goals.

By 1921, he had chased them all away. All but Edsel, who could not stand up to him. If he had been as flexible and open when the Model T was coming to the end of its life as he had been when his company gave birth to it, there is every reason to believe that the Ford Motor Company would have remained the towering giant of the industry. But he was not.

THE LONG, SLOW DEFLATION

The situation of the Model T in, say, 1923 bears some similarities to that of Coca-Cola in 1985, the year of the famous formula change. In both cases, the brand had succeeded so well that its managers feared that consumer confusion would result if a change were made in the product. Coca-Cola told the public when it tried to change its formula that "the best has become even better," an assertion which proved unconvincing, to put it mildly.[194] Thus, during the 1920s, when General Motors was exploiting to the hilt the idea of change in the automobile (a lot of which was in fact cosmetic), the Ford Motor Company was concealing the changes in the Model T (some of which were substantive).

The Ford Motor Company did make a noteworthy change in its product line in 1922 when it purchased the bankrupt Lincoln Motor Company. The Lincoln was an expensive car, with one model selling for as much as $6,000 in 1921, when the Model T was listing for about one-twentieth of that price. The founder of Lincoln, Henry M. Leland, had in 1904 become the chief executive of the newly formed Cadillac Company, the successor of the Henry Ford Company, which, it will be recalled, Ford himself departed in 1902.[195] Leland was apparently a true craftsman, much admired for his exacting standards. "He was a fine, creative, intelligent person," Alfred Sloan later said of him. "Quality was his god."[196] Leland was not, however, a successful business executive, which is why he had to sell to Ford. The acquisition was hailed as the marriage of "the manufacturer in quantity production" and "the master of fine things mechanical."[197]

The marriage was short-lived. By June of 1922 the Leland family was out. The Lincoln Motor Company was not operated as a separate division. It was absorbed completely into Ford. Lincoln production remained under ten thousand units annually throughout the 1920s.[198] At no time was it suggested that the Ford and the Lincoln could become a team, with the young owner of the former eventually growing into the older and wealthier owner of the latter.

Down until the discontinuance of the Model T, the best evidence suggests that the Ford Motor Company's product policy amounted to three principles. The first was to sell a car that worked—to customers who knew how to work it. The second was to change the car, but not quickly enough to maintain technological parity with the competition and to resist as far as possible concessions to such frivolities as were involved in style and fashion. The third was price.

Of the four basic elements of the marketing mix—product policy, pricing, marketing communications, and distribution—the Ford Motor Company focused exclusively on two, the product and the price. As the product was stealthily improved, the price was steadily cut. On October 1, 1911, the Model T Runabout listed for $590 and the Touring Car for $690. On December 2, 1924, by which time a total of slightly under 11 million Model Ts had been sold, the Runabout listed for $260 and the Touring Car for $290, representing declines in price of more than one-half compared to when these vehicles had been introduced.[199] (For purposes of context and comparison, a good household refrigerator cost $450 in 1924.)[200] As far as marketing communications were concerned, Ford relied primarily on the plentiful free publicity that the Model T generated. From 1917 to 1923, the company spent no funds on advertising.[201] With regard to distribution, the company pursued a consistent policy of increasing distribution outlets, thus increasing price competition among its distributors and enraging them.[202] Ford's own contempt for retailers, including automobile dealers, was boundless.[203]

As the 1920s progressed, however, price cutting proved less effective in increasing Model T sales. While Ford struggled to maintain volume, Chevrolet sales were skyrocketing. In just one year, from 1925 to 1926, Chevrolet sales increased from 470,000 to 730,000; and this despite a price increase from $510 to $525.[204]

Even Henry Ford had to bow to the inevitable. There is a memorable photograph of his son, Edsel, driving the 15 millionth Model T off the assembly line, with Ford as the passenger. The look on his face, his slouching posture, and his body language in general say it all. The Model T, born when Ford was in the prime of his life (at age forty-five), was dying as he was approaching old age (at sixty-four).

The Model T was a very tough act to follow. "Sixty-four today and the biggest job of my life ahead" is what Henry Ford said on July 30, 1927.[205] During the two-decade Model T era, the Ford

Motor Company had pursued a strategy of cost minimization with a single-mindedness which foreclosed other options. The company had ignored the vital necessity of "balancing the hoped-for advantages from . . . cost reduction against a consequent loss in flexibility and ability to innovate."[206]

Thus, when competitive pressures and market demand made innovation imperative, the costs in terms of dollars, disruption to the organization, and competitive position were staggering. Almost all of the 5,580 parts of the Model A of 1927 "were entirely new." Therefore, "the mechanism of all Ford plants had to be rebuilt from the ground up. Factory layouts were changed; new construction work to fit these alterations was hurried forward; fresh power arrangements, with countless new electrical connections, were made; better conveyors were installed; machine tools of radical new design were made or ordered in thousands."[207]

It was the biggest transformation of a manufacturing facility in the history of American industry. In order to effectuate it, Henry Ford, the man "obsessed by time,"[208] who all his life loved to tinker with watches and who made his fortune by reducing the time it took to assemble an automobile by orders of magnitude, had to shut down the factories at the River Rouge for six months in 1927.[209] In business terms this was a disaster. Estimates of the cost of the shutdown range from $200 million to $250 million.[210] It has been suggested that the whole economy slowed as potential car buyers waited to see Ford's new Model A before deciding on their next purchase.[211]

The Model A won acclaim at its introduction late in 1927, and it is still admired. It represented a giant step forward from the Model T. The Model A brought Ford technological parity with both General Motors and Chrysler, as well as parity in terms of unit sales, which had collapsed in 1927 with the plant shutdown and model changeover.[212]

However, the process of change at Ford in the late 1920s was dreadfully wasteful. The reasons were numerous. There was little if any coordination between people who today would be called design engineers and production engineers. Such coordination was crucial because of the history of the Model T. Not only the tools and the machines in the River Rouge, but the configuration of equipment and people had all been specifically designed with the Model T in mind. The River Rouge was a gigantic Rubik's Cube which had been solved for the Model T. The needs of the Model A meant a rearrangement of all the colors. Extensive advance planning to solve the great riddles thus created was vital, but there was none.

In addition to this, political issues within the firm destroyed goodwill and creativity. Henry Ford had lost touch with reality to too great an extent to find the easiest methods to solve difficult problems. Edsel Ford had good sense and goodwill, but not the power which his title (he was president of the company) implied. Charles Sorensen seized the transformation from T to A as an opportunity to expel rivals from the firm. The process was characterized by politics, ill will, and smashed careers. Work may have been play in the company's early years, but there was nothing playful about this model change. Given all this, it is more than a little remarkable that the Model A achieved the success that it did.[213]

Apparently, the Model A was supposed "to be marketed as a recast and updated Model T."[214] By the late 1920s, however, the Model T was finished both as a product and as an "idea." General Motors was demonstrating that it could mass-produce a changing product rather than a static one. By so doing, it shifted the basis of competitive advantage in the U.S. automobile industry.

Henry Ford predicted 10 million Model A's would be produced. Edsel Ford predicted 20 million. Charles Sorensen guessed 50 million.[215] But on December 7, 1931, Henry Ford announced the introduction of the new Ford V-8. The V-8 first appeared in showrooms on March 31, 1932.[216] The Model A sold 4,320,446 units.[217] This would be an outstanding performance in comparison with anything except its predecessor.

The Ford V-8, according to Sorensen, a man in a position to know, was Henry Ford's "last mechanical triumph." According to Nevins and Hill: "Neither Ford nor many of his contemporaries were aware of any diminution in his powers, but the truth was that he was now [i.e., by about 1934] living in a world that had absorbed all the improvements his own generation had made, and in an industry led by younger men of greater vigor than his."[218]

The halo of Henry Ford's greatness still stood atop the company. But people do not purchase cars for that reason alone. Nor do the most talented people choose a firm at which to make their careers for such a reason. The capacity for introducing new products at the Ford Motor Company had fallen behind the times.

To be sure, Ford sold many motor vehicles during the Great Depression. From 1932 (the year of the introduction of the V-8) through 1941 (the last full year of production prior to conversion for the war), the Ford Motor Company produced worldwide almost 10 million vehicles. However, in the domestic market, Ford's share was consistently below (often way below) General Motors's and some years below Chrysler's. In unit share in 1937, for example, Ford accounted for 21.37 percent, Chrysler for 25.44 percent, and General Motors for 41.79 percent.[219] Ford was the most vertically integrated firm in the industry with the attendant high fixed costs, and it could not absorb sharp gyrations in output without dire financial consequences. In 1929, when the company sold 1.4 million passenger cars, it made $90 million. Two years later, when it sold half a million cars, it lost almost $50 million. From 1927 to 1937 inclusive, the Ford Motor Company lost almost $95 million, while General Motors was making $1.9 billion.[220] The company was slowly and unknowingly drifting into insolvency.

The depression was not without further changes in established products and the introduction of new product lines. The Lincoln was available in twenty-one body types in 1934.[221] The following year, the Lincoln Zephyr was introduced. Described by a sales executive as "a sensational, completely new motor car," the Lincoln Zephyr had a smaller engine and chassis than the standard Lincoln and listed at $1,275, twice the price of a Ford V-8 and no small sum in the mid-1930s. In the view of Nevins and Hill, despite the gap between the V-8 and the Zephyr, the latter "invaded the medium-priced field, essentially giving the Ford dealers a third car."[222] Sales of the Zephyr exceeded twenty-five thousand in 1937, which, quoting Nevins and Hill, was "an excellent showing for a medium-priced car, which promised well for the future."[223]

The Zephyr failed to live up to expectations. Instead of generating plus business for the company, it cannibalized sales of the fully loaded Lincoln. The Zephyr's rising price (the least expensive model on the market listed for $1,360 during the 1939 model year) could not have helped. "By tacit consent the Zephyr did not survive the war period. . . ."[224]

The only lasting addition to the Ford Motor Company's product line during the depression was the Mercury. Announced on October 6, 1938, the Mercury had been specifically positioned "to *expand,* not to divide, the business which belongs to Ford and Lincoln Zephyr." A clear effort was thus being made to copy the product policy of General Motors and Chrysler. The price of the Ford V-8 for the 1939 model year ranged from $540 to $920, of the Mercury from $920 to $1,180, and of the Lincoln Zephyr (as noted) from $1,360.[225]

The Mercury started slowly, but 1938 was a very bad year for the industry in general. Passenger car sales collapsed during the "Roosevelt Recession" from 3.9 million in 1937 to 2.0 million in 1938. Sales increased to 2.9 million in 1939 and 3.7 million in 1940; and as they did, Mercury captured a reasonable share. Mercury sold over 65,000 units in 1939, over 80,000 in 1940, and almost 82,000 in 1941. With U.S. automobile sales that year at about 3.8 million, Mercury's 2.2 percent share was considered a "respectable accomplishment."[226] Oddly enough, there is little evidence that the Mercury was organized as a full-fledged division. And at the time of the Mercury introduction, the Ford Motor Company was competing against one of the most efficiently run divisionalized firms in the world, General Motors.

The divisionalization of General Motors was an organizational innovation of exceptional value. It allowed the company to capture a customer for the whole course of his or her car-buying life. Divisions permitted the company to market cars "for every purse and purpose"—a product line caricatured by *Fortune* as "Chevrolet for the hoi polloi . . . , Pontiac . . . for the poor but proud, Oldsmobile for the comfortable but discreet, Buick for the striving, Cadillac for the rich."[227] This array gave General Motors flexibility in the face of macroeconomic conditions over which it could exercise little control. When times were good, as in the late 1920s or the post–World War II era, General Motors could rake in big profits with its high-margin "mid-priced" trio of Pontiac, Oldsmobile, and Buick. The Detroit dictum of "big cars, big profits; small cars, small profits" was borne out by these road cruisers. At the pinnacle of the line was the Cadillac, a high-priced car aimed at a market wealthy enough to be relatively immune from economic cycles. Even this, explained Alfred P. Sloan Jr., would be a "quantity-production car." General Motors "would not get into the fancy-price field with low production." The company did not intend to compete with European specialists. At the low end was the workhorse of the team, the Chevrolet.

Priced close to or just above the Ford, the Chevrolet was positioned as a first purchase for those entering the automobile market. In depression years, the corporation could count on the "Chevy" to pick up the slack left by those who in better times might have purchased a mid-priced car, but for whom bad times meant that money had to be saved where it could.[228]

A key element of General Motors's product policy was that each entry be differentiated both from the competition through superior features and from other corporation entries through pricing. Sloan understood that prior to his becoming CEO, GM's product line had been marked by its "irrationality." The company had been competing against itself. Sloan's idea was to rationalize its array of products so that the company would compete against its competitors.[229] Division managers would still compete against one another. However, the metric for this competition would be how well each division did against the other automobiles in its price class, not how many units it could steal from other GM divisions. This goal has not always been realized either at GM or at other divisionalized firms.

Whatever its inherent flaws, General Motors's organization was far superior to Ford's. The Ford Motor Company seemed merely to hope that a division would act the way a GM division acted without the planning, the effort, and the history that GM enjoyed. When the Mercury was created, new Ford Motor Company sales chief John R. ("Jack") Davis announced that a new corps of salespeople should be hired to devote "their entire efforts to this field" and that the car should be supported by its own service organization. Nevertheless, some dealers thought of the Mercury as "an overgrown Ford."[230] They probably felt that Mercury sales would be generated at the expense of Ford's rather than Pontiac's, Oldsmobile's, or Dodge's. As with the Lincoln Zephyr, merely saying a new car occupied a distinct class of vehicle did not make it so in the customer's mind.

In their overview of the company on the eve of World War II, Nevins and Hill observed that "the Ford organization in 1940 was still dynamic. It must not be confused with that of 1945."[231] Yet the chapter in which these sentences appear is entitled "A Company in the Doldrums."[232] The chapter title is more accurate than the sentences within it. Henry Ford's treatment of his son, Edsel, steadily degenerated as the 1930s drew toward their close. The sway of Harry Bennett, an evil man with no place in a legitimate business enterprise, was on the increase. Bennett joined the Ford Motor Company after leaving the navy in 1918. By the 1930s, he had worked his way thoroughly into Henry Ford's good graces and exercised remarkable power over personnel decisions in the company.[233] Henry Ford suffered a mild stroke in 1938, at the age of seventy-five;[234] and even though its effects seem to have been minimal, Ford's condition could not have helped a firm so completely under his personal control.

However deep in the doldrums the Ford Motor Company may or may not have been at the outset of America's entry into World War II, there can be no question that it was poised on the precipice at war's end. Henry Ford suffered a second, more severe stroke in 1941. According to Sorensen, he had obsessions which crossed the line into hallucinations. Wrote Nevins and Hill, "The years of the Mad Hatter were beginning; anything could happen."[235]

Ford created an unnecessary and destructive conflict between his son Edsel and Harry Bennett, who became, for lack of a better term, an "anti-son." Edsel, locked into a lifelong pattern of trying to please a man who had become impossible to please, died on May 26, 1943, aged forty-nine. The cause of death, in the words of Nevins and Hill, was "a complication of ailments: stomach cancer, undulant fever, and a broken heart."[236] To the shock of almost everyone, eighty-year-old Henry Ford decided to assume the presidency of the company himself. His ideas for the future were not encouraging. "We've got to go back to Model T days," he told a longtime associate. "We've got to build only one car. There won't be any Mercury, no Lincoln. No other car."[237]

Henry Ford II, Edsel's oldest son, was released from the navy to return to Dearborn in the summer of 1943. From that time, when he was not quite twenty-six years old,[238] until September 21, 1945, when he became president and CEO, the Ford Motor Company went through the dark night of the soul. Some of the company's most able, loyal, and experienced executives left, either because they were fired or because they quit. "Few happenings in plant affairs were now strictly rational."[239]

The tasks facing the young and inexperienced Henry Ford II were daunting. First, he had to push his grandfather aside, and Henry Ford I was not a man to let go easily. A firm shove was required from his wife, Clara, and from Edsel's widow, Eleanor.

When his grandfather finally called for him, Henry Ford II had both the courage and the wit to dictate terms. "I told him I'd take it only if I had a completely free hand to make any changes I wanted to make," he later recalled. "We argued about that—but he didn't withdraw his offer."[240]

In the process of ridding the company of its founder, Henry Ford II also had to expel the man who had wheedled his way into his grandfather's confidence and who posed the threat of taking over the company, Harry Bennett. Bennett, a pugilist with well-known connections to Detroit's underworld, had bested all previous adversaries. This battle, at last, he lost. Henry Ford II showed no little courage in achieving this goal. By the time of reconversion to civilian production, therefore, the young Ford had already undergone a baptism by fire. But his most difficult task lay ahead. He had to get the company back into condition to compete. Its great rival, General Motors, was the nation's largest industrial. It had performed outstandingly as a war contractor. It was well positioned for peace, while the Ford Motor Company was poor in product, processes, and people.

There had been rumors of problems at Ford; but when young Henry and the executives he hired began to examine the company with care, they discovered that the rumors understated reality. The stories are legion. When asked for statistical projections, a bookkeeper innocently replied, "What would you like them to be?"[241] "Can you believe it?" Henry Ford II later exclaimed. "In one department they figured their costs by *weighing* the pile of invoices on a scale."[242] The price for nonmanagement in the mid-twentieth century was not trivial. The company was hit with a $50 million tax surcharge for excess profits because no one had filed forms necessary for war contractors.[243] The most tangible no-confidence vote was cast by the employees, "who, sensing the end, were carrying off tools, parts and anything else they could lay their hands on—a problem symbolized by the crane that had to be rented to retrieve a piece of equipment one . . . executive had stolen and then reassembled piece by piece in his basement."[244] Quite literally, the company was coming apart.

For anyone inclined to believe that great men strive to destroy what they have built before they die, there is plenty of evidence in the career and life of Henry Ford.

THE FINAL ACT

Ford had been in both physical and mental decline for years prior to Edsel's death in 1943; but his son's passing devastated him, his wife, and his daughter-in-law.[245] Ford became fixated on the death. It haunted him. He could not get it out of his mind. At times, he could not believe it had actually happened.

Edsel's widow and even Clara Ford herself held him partially responsible. Clara, for a time, froze Henry out of her life. This woman, who had known of her husband's infidelity and who had borne it with remarkable aplomb,[246] could not bear this. "The old couple, after fifty-five years of marriage, scarcely spoke to one another; they could not discuss Edsel at all."[247] Perhaps the most surprising thing was that in a rare instance of insight into the impact he had on others, Ford himself seemed to grasp that he bore some of the responsibility for his son's death. Eventually, Clara allowed her husband back into her life. One morning, late in June 1943, she said: "Henry, the peonies are in bloom. We need a big jar of them for the front hall. Let's go and see what we can find." They did not speak much that morning, but they were reconciled.[248]

It took two more years for Ford finally to leave his company. In the time that remained to him between the accession of Henry II in 1945 and his own death in 1947, his deterioration continued. He sometimes sank into a confused and agitated state, but was then able to pull himself together.

The day of Ford's death as well as the day of his funeral had their share of ironies. Henry and Clara had recently returned from their mansion in Georgia. Ford seemed invigorated to be back in Dearborn. His mansion there, Fair Lane, was on the banks of the River Rouge, not far from the place of his birth or from his gigantic plant. Alone among the great men of the automobile industry, Ford always remained deeply rooted in Detroit. The same is true of his family to this day.[249]

The Rouge was flooded on April 7; and although Fair Lane, thirty feet above it, was quite safe, the generating plant that provided the house with electric power was flooded. That evening, Clara read to Henry by candlelight.[250] The man who had done as much as anyone to define the twentieth century died in surroundings reminiscent of earlier, simpler times.[251]

Ford began to feel physically uncomfortable at around 11:15. The maid, Rosa Buhler, describes the scene: "When I came into the bedroom I saw that Mr. Ford was dying. We propped him up and he put his head on Mrs. Ford's shoulder just like a tired child. He tried to fold his hands, as if in prayer. She kept saying, 'Henry, please speak to me.' I said to her, 'I think Mr. Ford is leaving us.' She seemed paralyzed. I felt his pulse and listened to his heart. I told Mrs. Ford, 'I think he has passed away.'"[252]

Henry Ford died of a brain hemorrhage at 11:40 on the evening of April 7, 1947. The funeral was three days later, and it was virtually a state occasion. Michigan's legislature interrupted its business "in commemoration of the passing of a great man." The governor ordered flags on state buildings lowered to half staff. In Detroit, the "common council directed that a large portrait of Ford, draped in mourning colors, be displayed on the front of the city hall for thirty days, and that mourning posters be displayed on buses. All motorists in Detroit were requested by the council to come to a complete halt as Ford's body was lowered into the grave."[253]

The display was altogether appropriate. The earth trembles when a great man is laid to rest, and if any place owed Henry Ford a debt of gratitude it was surely Detroit. A number of American cities experienced a boomtown stage in their early years. But because of the automobile industry Detroit grew by a factor of six when it was already a big city. Its population was 305,000 in 1900 and 1,837,000 in 1930. Only Chicago and Los Angeles among American cities experienced similar growth during this period. The reason in Detroit's case is simple: Henry Ford.[254]

Thousands of people crowded around St. Paul's Episcopal Cathedral on the morning of the funeral, April 10. Ford's earthly remains were transported from there to the unpretentious Ford Cemetery at 15801 Joy Road in Detroit. Ford's casket was not placed in a Model T, which would have been a fine gesture, or even in a Lincoln. Rather, he was carried to his final resting place in a 1942 Packard, nestled amidst the Lincoln limousines.[255]

Packard! The automobile that represented everything in the industry (and in local Detroit society) which Henry Ford had stood against and triumphed over. The "Ask the Man Who Owns One," snotty, twelve-cylinder automobile for "the royals and the rich" Packard.[256] The car that Czar Nicholas II, the queen of Spain, the emperor of Japan, and the Aga Khan all owned at one time or another. King Alexander of Yugoslavia had owned forty-eight of them.[257] What a travesty for Henry Ford to have gone to his grave in a Packard.

The day that Packard took Henry Ford to the cemetery, all the automobile assembly lines in the United States stopped for one minute. It has been estimated that 7 million workers paused on that day.[258] Nothing like this had ever accompanied the death of an American businessman in the past. Nothing ever will again. An appropriate gesture for the Copernicus of cars.

John Kenneth Galbraith has written that Henry Ford was not a businessman: "On this the evidence is decisive, and if there is any uncertainty as to what a businessman is, he is assuredly the things Ford was not."[259] There is some truth here. Ford certainly was a man who gave up "taking care of business" long before he relinquished power. In this, it should be said, Ford was not unique. To say that Ford was not a businessman is, however, not quite right.

It is undeniable that Ford was recognized by hundreds of millions of people around the world as a businessman and as a distinctly American specimen of the genre.[260] Ford was a fantastic exaggeration of the best and the worst in business. As Galbraith also wrote: "That Ford was a tenacious man, none can doubt. [In his early years, that tenacity] did him great service. Later, it did him equal disservice." Moreover—and in this also Ford was far from unique as a businessman—"success had made him immune to counsel and advice; for too long he had seen eccentricity and even mere foolishness pictured as genius and had believed it."[261] Ford provides as stark an illustration of the derangement of power as one is likely to find. How many men would be able to withstand the world's flattering their vanity for four decades?

Henry Ford was an extremist. When he was good, he was great; when he was bad, he was dreadful. He seemed, especially in his later years, to bounce back and forth rather than to mature as his power and position increased. He "outgrew the usefulness of his personality."[262]

Henry Ford was an oversteered car.

HENRY FORD

July 30, 1863	Henry Ford is born in Wayne County, Michigan.
1879	Ford quits school and leaves home to find work in Detroit.
1882	Ford returns to the family farm in Dearborn, Michigan.
April 11, 1888	Ford marries Clara Jane Bryant.
1891	Ford begins working for the Detroit Edison Illuminating Company.
June 4, 1896	Ford completes and test-drives his first automobile, the quadricycle.
August 5, 1899	The Detroit Automobile Company is incorporated. Ford serves as its superintendent.
January 1, 1901	The Detroit Automobile Company suspends operations.
November 30, 1901	The Henry Ford Company is incorporated, with Henry Ford serving as the engineer.
March 10, 1902	Ford leaves the Henry Ford Company, the name of which is changed.
June 16, 1903	The modern Ford Motor Company is founded in Detroit.
October 1, 1908	Ford introduces the first Model T.
January 1, 1910	The Highland Park Ford plant opens on a sixty-acre property north of Detroit.
1913	The Ford Motor Company introduces moving assembly-line production.
1919	Edsel Ford becomes president of the Ford Motor Company, although his father still wields the real power.
Late 1927	Ford introduces the Model A.
April 7, 1947	Henry Ford dies of a brain hemorrhage in Dearborn, Michigan.

PART TWO

The Heart
of the
American
Century

THOMAS J. WATSON SR.

CHARLES REVSON

INTRODUCTION

On February 17, 1941, Henry R. Luce, the entrepreneur who founded *Time* magazine and a host of other publications, including *Life* and *Fortune,* declared to the world in an editorial that if Americans were to be true to their heritage and destiny, the twentieth century would be the "American Century."[1] The United States had it all—a highly intelligent and motivated citizenry, the world's leading economy, military might, a stable and just political system, and (in Luce's view) commitment to a moral course of action in its internal affairs and its foreign policy. The time had come for the nation to grasp the reins of leadership which others had let slip from their hands. Luce was proclaiming that Andrew Carnegie's dream had come true. "Democracy" had indeed become "triumphant," thundering past the creeping snails of the Old World with the rush of an express.

When Luce wrote his American Century editorial, the United States was on the cusp of economic achievements at which its history had hinted but which were awesome nevertheless. The nation had languished in wretchedness during the Great Depression in the 1930s. Franklin D. Roosevelt was describing a prostrate state when he said the only thing we have to fear is fear itself. The unemployed worker stalked the land. The greatest problem posed by the depression was unemployment. It was a problem that burned itself into the national memory and made the 1930s the darkest decade of the twentieth century for business. If there has been a consensus in American politics, it is that such a downward crash in the business cycle can never be permitted again.

If Luce had written his American Century manifesto just three years earlier, in the midst of the "Roosevelt Recession" of 1938, he would have been laughed at, if not ignored. In 1941, however, things were looking rather different. The turnaround in American economic performance in just a few short years was simply astonishing. A quarter of the workforce was unemployed in 1933. As late as 1938, about 19 percent of the workforce was still on the job market. In 1944, the unemployment rate was 1.2 percent.

In terms of output as well, the 1930s to the 1940s saw a transformation from chump to champion. From 1929 to 1932, real gross national product declined by almost 30 percent. World War II brought a complete rebound from this trough. The reasons were technological, organizational, and a demand—war—which simply had to be satisfied. The magnitude of the achievement is vividly illustrated by the story of aircraft. In the two decades prior to 1939, 13,500 military planes had been manufactured in the United States. In May of 1940, President Roosevelt called for the production of 50,000 aircraft per year, without, it should be said, having the slightest idea how this feat could be accomplished. He would leave such details to others. Informed observers called Roosevelt's goal impossible of achievement. Yet this nation produced 48,000 aircraft in 1942, and twice that many in 1944.[2]

During World War II, the formerly inconceivable came to seem commonplace. American hegemony in a world wracked by wartime devastation only increased. In 1950, seventeen out of every twenty automobiles produced in the world came from the United States. Almost 40 percent of global economic activity that year was accounted for by America. In one industry after another following World War II, American firms rose to global dominance. As late as 1960, over seven-tenths of the sales of the world's two hundred largest corporations accrued to American firms. More than 60 percent of those two hundred firms had their headquarters in the United States. So what would have sounded ridiculous in 1935 sounded plausible in 1941 and 1942 and seemed proven by 1960.[3] The American Century, indeed.

In this section of the book we encounter one industrial marketer and one consumer marketer who played their parts in turning Americans into a "people of plenty."[4] Thomas J. Watson Sr. was not the founder of IBM, but he was its organizer and the man who made it a great company. It was Watson who put the company on the road to leadership in information processing. Charles Revson founded Revlon, in its time the most dynamic force in the cosmetics industry.

Why these two companies in these two industries? Why these two men? We have encountered this question before, and a reasonable response remains: Why not?

This is a book about empire builders, about "imperial selves" in the land of equality. It is not about those who go with the flow of history but those who swim upstream. It is about individuals who came from nowhere to achieve wealth and power through businesses that reflected who and what they were. It is about how they made their money, what they did with it, and what it did to them. It is also about people whose careers and behavior reveal distinctive characteristics of the system of doing business in America. It is about men who were outliers, typical in no sense.

Could others have been chosen, other magnified men who, because of their success in business, were much envied but not well understood? Yes. Robert Wood Johnson of Johnson & Johnson, who admired Revson's advertisements, would be one.[5] Henry J. Kaiser, who was probably one of IBM's customers, would be another.[6]

There are others. But not *many* others. Watson and Revson stand out. It is through this distinctiveness that we can learn a lot about those few executives who bestrode the business world like colossi.

Like so many tycoons, Watson was born in upper New York State. His roots were firmly in the nineteenth century; and his mentor, the charismatic—if slightly "touched"—John H. Patterson, seemed far more like the robber barons of old than the gray flannel executives of the mid–twentieth century. In Watson's career, we can see the transition from the executive as "mad genius," which Patterson personified, to the programmed executive corps of the most programmed of companies.

We also see with Watson the development of a science of selling. Engineers had worked on railroads and in factories in the nineteenth century and on "engines" before that. But the thought that an engineering approach could be brought to selling was new in the twentieth century. In the vanguard was Watson, who was as convinced that there was "one best way" to sell as Henry Ford was that there was "one best way" to manufacture. IBM achieved industry leadership at least as much because of its army of blue-suited, white-shirted salesmen as it did because of its technology.

Under Watson's leadership, IBM became a global force in the business world. He was as attached to his company as any executive ever has been. His identification with it and commitment to it were complete. He devoted himself to work until he was eighty-two years old in 1956. Six weeks after he turned the reins over to his eldest son, he died.

With Charles Revson, we encounter our first executive who was completely a product of the twentieth century. Born in Boston in 1906 of Russian Jewish immigrant parents, Revson, like all the executives who precede him in this book, never had a college education. Like the others, however, he donated a good deal of his vast wealth to institutions of higher education.

The early years of Revson's life were very hard. His family was not a happy one. Money was scarce. His own personal life was, it must be said, sordid. But he was a business talent of the first magnitude.

The Revlon Nail Enamel Company was founded on March 1, 1932, in the teeth of the Great Depression, which we have just discussed. Revson had some help from relatives, but if ever a company were a one-man story in its early years, this was it. Somehow, against all odds, with the great hopes of the "New Era" of the 1920s dashed and the country in a virtual state of mourning over its economic plight, Revson took a product which had formerly not been used by reputable women, nail polish, and made of it the basis for his own company's greatness.

Revson not only had to battle first a failed economy (in the 1930s) and then a world war (one would hardly assume that nail polish or other cosmetics would qualify as national necessities), he also had to battle himself. Crude and sometimes cruel, he was possessed of almost none of the abilities and characteristics which one learns in modern business schools are essential for success. No formal technical knowledge. No people skills. No formal analytic acumen. (Revson is alone among the seven executives in this book in not being noted for his enjoyment of working and playing with numbers.) Thus there is a great deal that this rather melancholy man did not bring to the party.

What he did have, however, he had in such abundance that it overwhelmed his shortcomings and made success possible. First, he was passionate about the product. Although innocent of the formal study of chemistry, he was an avid experimenter, recalling in his way an earlier day of American inventiveness.[7] Second, he had a vivid understanding of the difference between what his company manufactured and what benefit the customer purchased. In the factory, according to a well-known saying often attributed to him, we experiment with chemicals. In the beauty parlor, we sell hope.

Third, Revson was able to change with the times. He built his business through the early years on the basis of color advertisements in magazines. The advent of television changed the nature of competition in the industry.

As we have already noted in discussing the railroads and telegraph, anything that collapses space and time in the movement of people, products, or information changes how business is done. In its own sphere, television was as dramatic a business breakthrough as anything that had preceded it. Television brought your product directly into your customer's living room with an intimacy and, at first, a credibility matched by nothing else.

We could study the impact of television by focusing on the builders of the three original networks: David Sarnoff at NBC, William Paley at CBS, or Leonard Goldenson at ABC. Instead, we will take the rather less orthodox approach of showing what television meant to a whole class of products: consumer packaged goods. Individually, these products were economically unimportant compared to the other industries whose stories we are telling. Collectively, however, they represent a great deal of business activity. Moreover, all these products which fulfilled "wants" more than "needs" meant a lot not only to Americans, but to hundreds of millions of people abroad who, like us, wanted to be "people of plenty" and partake in the American cornucopia.

Revson and Revlon leave us with many questions about morality in business. The company's use of television brings these issues into focus. The most famous program it sponsored was the fixed quiz show *The $64,000 Question*.

In addition to providing portraits of two giants of enterprise at mid-century, these two chapters show the most advanced methods of the era for interpersonal selling (IBM) and mass marketing (Revlon).

4 THOMAS J. WATSON SR. and American Salesmanship

MAN AND MONUMENT

"Thomas J. Watson Sr. Is Dead; IBM Board Chairman was 82" was one of the headlines in the *New York Times* on June 20, 1956. The subheading read: "'World's Greatest Salesman' Built [$]629 Million Company—'THINK' Slogan." This two-column article appeared on the front page, quite a rarity for the obituary of a businessman.[1] The funeral took place on June 21, and it was crowded. "Watson Funeral Attended by 1,200," reported the *New York Times*. "Overflow Crowd at Brick Church Hears Tribute to IBM Industrialist."[2] Watson had been an elder of the Brick Presbyterian Church for sixteen years. One of the three other life elders was John Foster Dulles, secretary of state of the United States. Dag Hammarskjöld, secretary general of the United Nations, was in attendance. So were David Rockefeller, grandson of John D. Rockefeller; Grayson Kirk, president of Columbia University, on whose board of trustees Watson had served for almost a quarter of a century; Democratic Party stalwart and Franklin D. Roosevelt's postmaster general in the 1930s, James A. Farley; Bernard Gimbel, president of Gimbels; Philip D. Reed, chairman of the board of General Electric; Charles F. Kettering, one of the greatest inventors in American history and largest individual holder of General Motors stock (at the time the bluest of blue chips); General Lucius D. Clay, commander in chief of U.S. Forces in Europe and military governor of the U.S. zone in Germany from 1947 to 1949, the years of the Berlin Airlift; Arthur Hayes Sulzberger, president and publisher of the *New York Times*. . . . In a word, there were a lot of important people present.

Not all of the forty-two honorary pallbearers were able to attend, but their names adorned accounts of the funeral, and they also were people who mattered: Bernard Baruch, financier and adviser to presidents; Sherman M. Fairchild, CEO of Fairchild Camera and Instrument and the largest individual IBM stockholder;[3] Admiral Richard E. Byrd, naval aviator, explorer of the North and South Poles, best-selling author; corporate executives; university presidents; and others. President Dwight D. Eisenhower had already issued a statement lauding Watson, "this truly fine American." "I have lost a good friend, whose counsel was always marked by a deep-seated concern for people." The First Lady wrote a separate, unpublished letter to Mrs. Watson on behalf of herself and the president.[4]

New York is a big city, and it did not grind to a halt on the day of the funeral. On the other hand, twelve hundred people at the corner of Park Avenue and Ninety-first Street must have caused something of a stir. Doubtless, cars were parked for many blocks, including two blocks to the west, at Ninety-first Street and Fifth Avenue, the block occupied by the home Andrew Carnegie purchased soon after his retirement, where his widow lived until her death, a decade before Watson's.[5] One wonders whether cars were parked north of Ninety-sixth Street on Park Avenue. Ninety-sixth and Park is no ordinary intersection in New York City. Ninety-sixth Street is a great gulf, created because the plantings in the median strip on Park Avenue disappear, giving way to the railroad tracks that emerge from the tunnel to Grand Central Station, fifty blocks to the south. When you crossed Ninety-sixth Street in the 1950s, you walked from one of the world's most prestigious and expensive neighborhoods into Harlem.

Part of the Watson story is as simple as walking from the north side of Ninety-sixth Street and Park Avenue to the south, from poverty to wealth, from being a cog in the system to being at the center of it. Watson met many challenges to cross that street. But there was one challenge he did not have to meet. Racism. Watson was a Caucasian Protestant of northern European origin. Most Harlemites are not.

Watson was buried in the Sleepy Hollow Cemetery near Tarrytown, New York, about thirty miles north of New York City, which is also Andrew Carnegie's last resting place. For Watson, the choice of the cemetery was perfect. He was born in upper New York State. His company had extensive facilities up and down the Hudson River valley. Towns such us Poughkeepsie greatly benefited as IBM's growth exploded during the final years of Watson's life and in the three decades following his death.[6] The same was true on the New York side of the border with Pennsylvania. IBM had a very large facility in, for example, the town of Endicott. It is not surprising that Charles F. Johnson, president of Endicott-Johnson, had traveled to the city for the funeral.

At the funeral service, the minister described Watson as "peculiarly loyal to his past. He never separated himself from it or from the small upstate town where he was brought up."[7] Yes and no. Each of the seven men portrayed in this book had complicated relations with his past. Watson had his company invest heavily in what during his lifetime was the nation's largest state. But he was, if anything, more "peculiarly loyal" to the future. For a business to prosper, Watson insisted, it had to "look into the future and study the demands of the future." To achieve this objective, in 1929 he established the Future Demands Department, the purpose of which was to lead the way toward "the creation and development of new products to cover new fields."[8] Watson always insisted from the very beginning that IBM would have a global reach and that it would be immortal.

"This business of ours has a future," Watson told the "100% Club" (composed of the top salesmen from the previous year). "It has a past of which we are all proud, but it has a future that will extend beyond your lifetime and mine. This business has a future for your sons and your grandsons and your great-grandsons, because it is going on forever. Nothing in the world will ever stop it. *The IBM is not merely an organization of men; it is an institution that will go on forever.*"[9]

Watson gave the speech from which this excerpt is taken in January 1926, four decades before his death. At the time, IBM was a tiny speck on America's corporate landscape. Until two years previously it had been known as Computing-Tabulating-Recording. International Business Machines was a far grander name, matching Watson's great expectations.

There are as many ways to lead as there are leaders. A speech like the one quoted above, and Watson gave thousands of them over the course of his career, would be inconceivable from Carnegie, Eastman, or Ford. Of the seven executives in this book, only Sam Walton can be imagined thinking and communicating as Watson did on that winter's day in 1926.

If the eulogist at Watson's funeral was not quite accurate in emphasizing his respect for the past over his belief in the future, the headline writer for the *Times* could not have been more right. " 'World's Greatest Salesman' " is what the headline read. The phrase is in quotations, indicating that it is a claim and a belief rather than a proven fact. Such a description can never be a proven fact, but there can be no question that Watson would be on any short list of the greatest salesmen ever.

Watson's powers of persuasion were awesome. Not only could he persuade customers to buy his products; he could persuade his employees that they were capable of exceeding their own expectations. He could persuade men of great wealth and power to do things they did not want to do.

Here is one example. On February 9, 1931, George Eastman was the guest of honor at a banquet at the Hotel Commodore in New York City. The event was the annual celebration of the Society of the Genesee, an organization of leading figures from the Genesee River valley region of upstate New York. (The Genesee River runs through Rochester.) Over a thousand admirers attended.

Eastman's loathing for this kind of event was without bounds. By the time this one took place, he was in ill health and depressed. There is nothing one can think of about a trip to New York City in the depths of winter during the Great Depression which would be designed to cheer him up. For a decade, the Society of the Genesee had been asking Eastman to be its guest of honor, and Eastman had been turning the invitation down. "After a decade of saying, No, No, No, he capitulated to . . ." To whom? To Thomas J. Watson. Like so many other great executives of the turn of the century, Eastman had been influenced by Watson's mentor, John Henry Patterson. Patterson had created a program for employees to suggest improvements in his company, National Cash Register, and Eastman imported the practice to Eastman Kodak in 1898. Watson met Eastman sometime between 1899 and 1903, and he earned Eastman's admiration. When Watson asked, and kept asking, Eastman at last "capitulated."[10] Watson was the toastmaster, and his speech was graceful and gracious. He praised Eastman's ability and his philanthropy and described him accurately as having "a devotion to sound business principles seldom met with in the maelstrom of industrial life. . . ."[11]

Let's revisit the *Times* headline. It was selling, not technology, that made the papers. This is ironic because IBM was, for many years, at the center of the most technology-intensive of industries. But it is also accurate. Selling and marketing were the heart of IBM's competitive advantage as the industry grew.

LEARNING ABOUT BUSINESS

The most influential man in the life of Thomas J. Watson Sr. was John Henry Patterson, the founder of the National Cash Register Company. Watson was twenty-one years old and unemployed when he hired on as a salesman for NCR's Buffalo office. His first two weeks were unproductive. As a result, his boss, NCR's agent in Buffalo, John Range, berated him with such vituperation, such abandon unmitigated by even a drop of the milk of human kindness, that Watson later said he was waiting for Range to calm down so that he could resign.[12] But Watson did not resign.

After humiliating him, Range's demeanor changed completely. "As easily as Range had turned on his rage, he turned it off and warmly, without apology, comforted Watson."[13] Range offered to take Watson out on the road and teach him how to sell. Watson, shrewd and astute, learned quickly. He soon was a fixture in that world-unto-itself of traveling salesmen. This squad of gypsies had as their only real home the products they carted through city streets and around the countryside to sell.

In a year Watson was one of NCR's top salesmen in the East. By 1899, at the age of twenty-five, he was outselling Range himself; and Patterson selected him for the position of agent in NCR's Rochester branch office.[14] This was one year before George Eastman—located, as we know, in the same city—introduced the Kodak Brownie.

NCR had about 160 branch offices in 1899, and Rochester was among the poorest performers. One of the problems was competition. Rochester was one of those places where NCR did not exercise a monopoly.

Watson's competitive methods were crude but effective. Once he heard a salesman for the Hallwood Company, the principal adversary, mention that the following day he planned to call on a prospect twenty miles away. Why this remark was made we do not know. What we do know is the price of being unguarded in the vicinity of Thomas J. Watson Sr. The next day, Watson encountered this salesman on the road to see the prospect's business. Watson and the salesman were traveling in opposite directions. Watson was on his way back to town, having already made the sale. Watson said he had considered this salesman a friend. But nothing stood between Tom Watson and business.

Watson spied on the competition, posting "spotters" near their offices. He taught the people with whom he worked how to sabotage competitive products so they would malfunction. He intimidated prospective customers of the competition by threats of pending lawsuits for patent infringement. His success at using such tactics—most of which are illegal today, many of which were illegal at the time, and some of which could aspire to no ethical standard higher than the law of the jungle—constitutes an eloquent refutation of the notion that ethics pays.[15] Ethics may well pay, but Watson's early career showed that unethical behavior could have its rewards as well. His success in Rochester brought him once again to the attention of John Henry Patterson. Patterson summoned Watson to NCR headquarters in Dayton in October 1903.

Patterson believed with an evangelical fervor impossible to convey through the medium of the mere written word that every cash register sold in the world should be manufactured by his company. Moreover, every sale should be of a new NCR machine. Thus, he viewed the development of a market for used cash registers as the devil's own work. He decided to muster an army of God to stamp this market out. Standing at Armageddon and leading the battle for the Lord was none other than young Watson.

The plan Watson implemented was simplicity itself. He started in New York City, where he became friendly with one Fred Brainin. Brainin operated a secondhand cash register store at 124 East Fourteenth Street in Manhattan. Soon, a new store opened on Fourteenth Street. This one was called Watson's Cash Register and Second Hand Exchange.[16]

Brainin had only one problem which Watson did not have. But it was a big problem. Brainin was in business to make money. His goal was profit. Watson did not have that objective. He was in business to put Brainin out of business. His pricing policy was to sell for less than Brainin. When it became obvious to Brainin that he could not stay in business against such an aggressive competitor, Watson offered to buy him out on the condition that he agree not to reenter the business. Brainin agreed. All the money Watson needed was laundered from Dayton through Rochester. In city after city, Watson put one secondhand dealer after another out of business in the same way.

Watson's activities were but a part of Patterson's grand plan to monopolize the market. The second was the wholesale use of patent litigation. For Patterson, it really was not whether you won or lost but how you played the game when it came to lawsuits. As he put it:

> If a patent is granted to the Lamson Company [a competitor], we will bring suit. If we lose, we will take it to the Court of Appeals. It will take five or six years of litigation and probably cost Lamson $100,000 before they would have a legal right to use their special key arrester and key coupler, and we would still have the right to go on using the key arrester and key coupler.[17]

The "competition department," at first known as the "opposition department,"[18] at NCR undertook every imaginable means of unfair competition, in all probability including physically assaulting competitors' employees. (Evidence concerning physical violence was ruled irrelevant in court proceedings.)[19] "Knockout" salesmen fanned out across the country selling machines that were copies of competitors' machines, but did not work. These men would discourage purchasers of competing machines from paying for them and offer to defray legal expenses if they were sued. They were instructed on how to sabotage competing machines which had already been purchased.[20] And spies were placed everywhere. Many a competitor found his employees being paid by NCR. The company boasted of this kind of activity, publishing a "Knocker Catalogue."[21] As Patterson himself said, "We do not buy out. We knock over!"[22]

Everyone knew this was illegal; and in 1911 and 1912, the federal government got around to doing something about it. On February 22, 1912, John H. Patterson, Thomas J. Watson, John J. Range, and more than two dozen other top executives of the National Cash Register Company were indicted for violating the Sherman Antitrust Act.[23] The defendants were all found guilty. On February 13, 1913, they were sentenced to a year in jail, the maximum under the law. All were fined $5,000 except Patterson, whose fine was twice that amount.[24]

In a just world, the guilty parties would have served these sentences and paid the fines. Both were well deserved. But we do not live in a just world. All appealed, and all escaped punishment for no good reason.[25]

The chief executive officer, one is tempted to say the ringleader, of the National Cash Register Company now deserves some additional attention. John Henry Patterson has often been called the "father of modern salesmanship."[26] That may not be a scientifically accurate title, but there is no question that Patterson was a high-impact individual in the American business world.

Patterson served in the Civil War and graduated from Dartmouth in 1867, but it is difficult to imagine him as a student or a soldier. Both roles demand at least a degree of disciplined respect for the views and instruction of others. He displayed no hint of such an attitude during the second half of his life. He left no reminiscence of the army. Of college, he said: "What I learned mostly was what not to do. They gave me Greek and Latin and higher mathematics and Edwards on the Will—all useless."[27]

What Patterson wanted was "small words and big ideas."[28] Thus began a lifelong distrust of college men, who wanted, Patterson felt, fat pay and fast promotions they did not deserve. According to Stanley C. Allyn, who spent half a century with NCR, becoming chairman of the board in 1957, the only exception to the prejudice was the University of Wisconsin, fortunately for Allyn his alma mater.[29]

In 1868, Patterson got himself a job as a toll collector on a canal near Dayton. The job was not trouble-free. Canal boat captains made a practice of lying about the tolls they had and had not already paid. And Patterson had no way to protect himself against being suspected of shortchanging his employer. "John Patterson did not take honesty for granted. He took nothing for granted."[30] He devised a system of receipts to mitigate these problems.

The next step was to go into the business of supplying coal to Daytonites. Like so many other entrepreneurs, Patterson held two jobs simultaneously: founding this business while still taking tolls. In partnership with his brother, he managed to differentiate his company from the competition. He had an aversion to bookkeeping, but he possessed a remarkable knack for solving business problems through the creative use of information. He obtained the highest-quality coal available, devised a system to ensure that customers received what they ordered, and also developed receipts which guaranteed that he was paid for what he delivered.[31]

In his coal business, Patterson quickly began to show that flair which set him apart when he went into the manufacture of cash registers. He wanted to endow even as naturally dirty a business as coal delivery with a certain panache:

> When he began to make money, [Patterson] bought the best horses he could find . . . [and] fitted them out with gold- and silver-trimmed harnesses. He had the carts painted brown and put "Patterson & Co." in big gold letters on their side. . . . [He] had already sensed the importance of an air of prosperity; one of his maxims was that before a man could be prosperous he had to look prosperous.[32]

It was not only important to be industrious, it was important to *seem* that way. Appearance, in a nation with no titled aristocracy, no formally inherited status, was vital to success. It was the concentration on the power of appearance to influence not only others but also one's true inner self that Patterson had in common with Benjamin Franklin and that Thomas J. Watson Sr. shared with both. This is a recurring theme among great American salespeople. The idea that "what seems to be" can be transformed into "what is" was a core belief of Mary Kay Ash, founder of Mary Kay Cosmetics, as we shall see later in this book.

After various arguments and unpleasantries, Patterson sold his interest in the coal business in 1884. He had transformed an investment of $40,000 and a lot of hard work into a mere $16,000. He was not penniless; but he had no prospects, no direction. He was forty years old.[33] Patterson was in Colorado Springs with his brother looking to invest in land when he was visited by an epiphanic moment. The clouds parted and there, in heaven, was the cash register.

The immediate occasion was an encounter with an eastern merchant on a long vacation. Patterson asked how the merchant could leave his business for a lengthy period. The answer was that he owned cash registers which produced punched paper from which a statement of his business could be generated.[34] He had the information he needed without the necessity of being on-site. Where, inquired Patterson, were these marvelous machines manufactured? Eleven hundred five miles back east in a city called Dayton, Ohio.

Patterson was not unfamiliar with cash registers. He had begun using them in his coal business in 1882.[35] He purchased twenty-five shares at $50 per share out of a total of three hundred shares available at the time of the National Manufacturing Company, which produced cash registers, in 1883.[36] Patterson was impressed with the utility of cash registers, but he apparently did not recognize in them the business bonanza that he felt he saw in 1884. With his brother, Frank, in tow, Patterson hustled back over those 1,105 miles and bought the cash register company from its owner, George Phillips, for $6,500. The transaction took place in a New York minute.

That same day, Patterson was laughed at for making what was supposedly the worst purchase imaginable. The company, his acquaintances told him, was a shambles. So disheartened was he that he returned to the seller, George Phillips, the following day and tried to get out of the deal. He offered Phillips $100 to cancel the contract. Phillips was not interested. How about $500? Still not interested. Then Patterson offered him $2,000, almost a third of the purchase price. Phillips's reply could not have been very encouraging. "He said to me," Patterson later recalled, "'You have bought this stock. If you had paid for it and I had turned it over to you, then if you were to hand it back to me and say, "George, I will make you a present of this stock," I would not take it.'"[37]

This exchange must have been markedly different from the conversation that Phillips and Patterson had the previous day on this very subject when Phillips sold him the company. The man who became the teacher of some of the greatest salespeople in American business history had just proven that he could be quite a sucker for somebody else's sales pitch. If Phillips's words hurt, Patterson did not show it. He said he would prove Phillips wrong. On November 22, 1884, Patterson took over the National Manufacturing Company, which he quickly renamed the National Cash Register Company.[38]

The factory Patterson had purchased was not much more than a large room, forty feet by eighty feet. There were thirteen employees. But the whole business was in such disarray that it was difficult to say what was in the poorest shape. Patterson decided that sales were the key to everything. As Richard H. Grant, one of Patterson's many alumni who went on to successful careers elsewhere, put it: "Remember, good salesmanship is what makes the smoke come out of the chimneys."[39]

So Patterson set about to discover the secrets of selling. Claims of originality have been made on behalf of others for most of what is described below. The truth is that someone somewhere adopted each of the procedures that Patterson instituted at the National Cash Register Company during his four decades at its helm. But no other company integrated all of them. And no other company had as strong a linchpin as Patterson—shrewd, astute, charismatic, mercurial, and very, very odd.

Before describing Patterson's sales system, it is necessary to provide some context both about the salesmen with whom he would work and the product they would be called upon to sell. The National Cash Register Company did not employ its own field sales force. It could not afford to do so. Rather, Patterson sold through selling agents, independent businessmen who sold other merchandise as well. (When he bought NCR, Patterson had a grand total of one full-time agent.)[40] The agency arrangement was common at the time, and it is not uncommon today. The agency system was not completely replaced at NCR by company-owned branch offices until World War II.[41]

Working through agents had some advantages. First among these was financial. The sales offices and associated overhead were paid for by others. Those others were already located in the geographic areas in which they sold, so it was not unreasonable to expect them to know the territory. An Alabamian would probably know more about prospective purchasers in Montgomery than would someone dispatched from Dayton or transferred from Seattle.

The agency system had, however, the defects of its virtues. With lack of ownership came lack of control, which is, in fact, why the system was changed in the 1940s.[42] Patterson quickly developed specific views about how to sell, how a salesman should present himself, and how an agency should be managed. He did not, however, have the power to order agents with whom he had contractual relations, rather than whom he employed directly, to run their businesses precisely in accord with his program.

This was a source of endless frustration and aggravation because soon after he got into this business, Patterson became convinced that he had discovered the best way to sell. Indeed, he felt he knew the only way to sell. Any deviation would result in a decline in productivity. Patterson was the marketing analogy to Frederick W. Taylor, the engineer whose "Principles of Scientific Management" were soon to be presented to the world as the solution to the problem of production.[43] All Patterson had at his disposal to convince his agents of the efficacy of his methods was persuasion, not hierarchical command. Fortunately for him, Patterson's powers of persuasion were considerable.

The product these agents sold was fairly new in 1884. Some businessmen, such as the eastern merchant Patterson had met in Colorado Springs and Patterson himself in 1882, had used cash registers; but they were new to most people. Two experts in the early development of the cash register have rightly commented on the difficulty of determining "who was the first at anything."[44] A company was founded as early as 1859 to make an "alarm cash till."[45] It was not until the late 1870s, however, that inventors began experimenting with a device similar to the cash register which NCR would make famous. The Ritty brothers, John and James, patented their "Incorruptible Cashier" in 1879, and this is thought to be "the real beginning of the cash-register business."[46]

Selling the cash register presented numerous challenges. Store owners needed it, but they did not know that they did. There were probably a considerable number of stores, especially in rural areas, in which cash itself was rarely used. Shopkeepers knew their customers, and transactions were recorded in credit books with settlements being made only occasionally.[47] For stores that were accustomed to cash, it was not immediately obvious why a register was superior to a drawer, perhaps secured by a lock.

The cash register salesman was saying to his customer that savings would result in the future from real money that the shop owner had to spend in the here and now. Thus, although the cash register was palpable enough, the salesman was selling an abstraction: future savings. For the shop owner, that promise was speculative; but the price for the register was real and immediate.

The biggest problem in making the sale was the person who operated the cash register itself. Clerks hated cash registers. Their purchase was considered an aspersion on the honesty of all who worked in the store. People felt righteously indignant. The cash register could upset the social equilibrium of the establishment that installed it. Its purchase

was often the signal for a walkout. [A cash register sales-
man] was apt to be thrown out of the place. If he did get to
the proprietor and sold him a machine, then the clerks tried
to double-cross the register in every possible fashion so as to
get it taken out. In a number of localities, clerks and bartenders formed organizations to prevent the sale and use of
cash registers and passed around information as to what to
do to make the machines appear inaccurate.[48]

Clerks watched for envelopes that bore "National Cash Register" on the return address and disposed of them before the proprietor saw them, making direct mail advertising tough. Discovering
this, Patterson removed his company's name from the envelopes,
only to discover that mail postmarked "Dayton" was being
destroyed. He had to have his mail shipped to agents in other cities
and posted from them.[49]

Nobody needed a cash register. They cost money, but the long-
term savings could not be guaranteed. The clerks who used them
hated them. Here were some real selling hurdles.

HOW TO SELL

It was against this sea of troubles that Patterson took up the arms of
his method of salesmanship. The most important components of the
Patterson approach to selling were guaranteed sales territories for
the independent agents and precisely quantified sales quotas, which
had to be met every year.

Like many other elements of Patterson's program, guaranteed
sales territories were not a new idea. But it is doubtful that prior to
Patterson, anyone had been so evangelical about it. The goal was
for the salesman to achieve complete penetration of his territory.
One tough sale in an assigned territory was more valuable, in Patterson's view, than two easier sales in someone else's territory. So
much did Patterson believe this that he established an institutional
disincentive to poaching on someone else's market. Any sale made
in a particular agent's territory was credited to that agent whether
or not he actually made it.[50]

The reason for this policy was that agents would be willing to
share their knowledge with one another if they knew that by coop-

erating they would be helping themselves make the whole of NCR greater than the sum of its parts. If, on the other hand, they thought they would be divulging trade secrets which would be used against them in their own territories, they would obviously be inclined to keep their own counsel. "Business," Patterson declared, "is founded on confidence; success on cooperation."[51]

This is logical enough and probably what Patterson did tell himself. But soon after he got into this business, Patterson came to believe that he had all the answers about selling. Since he knew everything, it was up to him to teach everybody. What was there for one agent to learn from another?

Guaranteed territories served other needs, rational and emotional. Strict quotas and the concomitant determination of a salesman's commission would be hard to manage if everyone were selling everywhere. Patterson may have been even more concerned that the challenge posed by new territory would distract the salesman's attention from his real purpose. He once said that "if you allow a man to run into open territory he would rather spend a week getting one order than to get an order in his own territory in three days."[52] Patterson never explained why he felt a salesman might act in this irrational fashion. Perhaps his view was that a salesman was by nature a territorial imperialist, and that impulse had to be contained.

Moreover, Patterson was what in the parlance of the 1960s would be called a "control freak." His desire to "program" the lives of others followed a pattern which was predictable to his contemporaries. He dealt with people in three stages. First, he shattered their spirit and obliterated their previous identity and self-conception. Then he re-formed them, built them up, buttressed their self-esteem, and paid them lavishly. Then he fired them.

Patterson's obsession with control did not exclude his attitude toward himself. "He who overcomes others is strong," he said, "but he who overcomes himself is mightier."[53] Not surprisingly, Patterson was a food faddist, a health nut, and an exercise fanatic. He once fasted for thirty-seven days (or so it is said); he experimented with vegetarianism; he was a guest at the famous sanatorium of Dr. John Kellogg in Battle Creek, Michigan; and so on. Patterson was as concerned with his skin and musculature as with his digestive system. He bathed five times a day. Following his thirty-seven-day fast, he went in search of a physical trainer to restore his health and found in London (probably around 1906) a cockney gymnast and rub-down specialist named Charles Palmer. To the alarm of everyone, Patterson brought Palmer back to Dayton.

When he was forty-four in 1888, Patterson married Katherine Dudley Beck. Little is known of their brief relationship. Mrs. Patterson died of typhoid fever in June 1894, leaving her young son and infant daughter not only motherless but virtually orphaned.[54] Patterson was "helpless" in the face of his offspring. "He knew nothing whatsoever about children," and so they were brought up by relatives.[55]

Patterson's family was "the Cash" (as NCR was often called) and also, for a time, the menacing Mr. Palmer. Palmer, according to author William Rodgers, "claimed to have occult powers, with a special capacity for detecting the true character of people by studying their physiognomy." Patterson made Palmer a member of the NCR board. Palmer's physiognomic determinations came to have a say in personnel decisions. To object to his harsh health routine was to invite dismissal, as Hugh Chalmers discovered. The Dayton press raised "pointed questions" about the relationship of Palmer and Patterson.[56] Strict rules combined with the random violation of them is a method to exercise control through fear. That was Patterson's regime within NCR. That was what he tried to export to his salesmen as much as his lack of ownership of the agencies would permit.

Patterson's second selling principle was the establishment of strict sales quotas which had to be met every year. If a salesman made the grade, he was inducted into the Hundred Point Club, with the attendant ego and economic satisfaction. Samuel Crowther, Patterson's biographer, described this "Club" as the most famous of his innovations.[57] Members were celebrated, and no expense was spared at the annual conventions of these star performers.[58]

Like exclusive territories, commission selling was not new. Once again, however, Patterson pushed the approach to its limit and introduced a new twist. Patterson wanted cash register salesmen compensated on a commission basis solely, with no base salary. In the 1880s, according to Crowther, straight commission selling was fit only for "canvassers" and "life-insurance agents" and was not considered "respectable."[59]

Patterson's attitude was strictly "pay for performance." Salesmen got paid when they sold, not when they failed to sell. The interesting twist mentioned above was that Patterson genuinely wanted his salesmen to succeed. He wanted them to be rich and to look and act that way, and he wanted their wives to enjoy the pleasures of money. Patterson knew he could control men who wanted money if he made it possible for them to earn it. Once again, he was ahead of his time. Today, this is called "golden handcuffs."

At first, NCR agents had trouble comprehending Patterson's attitude. Other employers were none too happy with it either. Agents assumed that the Cash, like so many other businesses, was more interested in keeping expenses down than in getting sales up. They figured that if they made too much money because they sold too many cash registers, the company would cut their commissions.

Patterson never would have entertained such a retrograde notion. It was among his cardinal principles that everyone associated with him should make money through him so that he could control them. When a New York salesman let up because he thought he had earned all NCR would pay him, the New York agent, who had gotten the picture, told him: "You're a fool. If you can sell a million dollars in a week, we'll hire a brass band to take your commission to you. We can't make any money unless you do."[60]

A cash register is a durable good; and it is sold not like a camera, to the general public, but rather to other businesses. Patterson was an industrial marketer, but he had the soul of a mass marketer. He wanted to create new consumers for his product, just as Eastman and Ford did. Constantly raising the quota hurdle produced this effect. The quota was also vital because Patterson had to invest in fixed special-purpose assets in order to manufacture the machine he sold. If he could not predict sales, which the quota facilitated, he ran the risk of either investing too much or too little in his factory and of being caught with excess inventory or stocking out.

Historian Alfred D. Chandler Jr. has argued that the defining characteristic of the modern corporation has been the coordination of mass production with volume distribution.[61] Here is what this problem looked like to Patterson in 1888. The previous year, he said,

it was thought that orders for registers would increase to thirty daily. So confident were all the representatives of accomplishing this result that the factory, *at large expense,* was prepared to meet such a demand.

A large amount of new machinery . . . was bought . . . and new men trained. . . .

Instead of thirty orders daily we are receiving on an average about seventeen orders daily. We turned off part of our force and still have accumulated over three hundred registers. What shall we do? Stop the factory?[62]

Just like Andrew Carnegie, Patterson understood that he had to keep the plant running full and steady.

The salesman was expected to meet his NCR quota every year. Patterson's rejection of the idea of market saturation was complete. If the sales potential of a territory with a population of two hundred thousand was five hundred machines, a salesman who could sell fifty machines one year should be able to do at least as well the next. By the time everyone who ought to have bought had done so, the time would have come for a new and improved register.[63]

This business philosophy had at least two important implications. First, it was necessary for NCR to create and produce new and improved models. This the company strove to do. When Patterson bought NCR in 1884, it sold "exactly two types of register." Sixty years later, NCR marketed machines in more than six hundred styles and sizes,[64] a perfect example of the product proliferation which was a hallmark of marketing during the twentieth century.

The second implication was that used cash registers were a major threat to sales growth through the quota system. Let us return to the estimate that every territory with a population of two hundred thousand should account for sales of five hundred machines, and that a salesman in such a territory should be able to sell fifty a year. One cannot conclude that NCR could wait ten years to bring out a new model. That conclusion assumes that no other company was selling cash registers and that every customer needed a more sophisticated register than he already owned.

If there was a demand for cash registers, and the Cash was doing everything conceivable to develop the market, other companies would build machines and try to reap where NCR had sown. There were reportedly 5,400 cash registers in operation in 1887. By 1890, that number had leaped to 16,395.[65] A market growing at a compound annual rate of 45 percent in units is going to invite competition. There were no patents or proprietary processes to keep competitors out; and barriers to entry in terms of capital requirements, although not negligible, were not high enough to protect high profits for long.

The second assumption, that all customers will need the new and improved version, has to be wrong. The stores in any territory were highly varied. A less expensive secondhand machine would appeal to a large segment of almost any geographic market. That is why competition had to be stamped out and the secondhand business eliminated by fair means or foul. And that is how we have met Thomas J. Watson Sr. at the outset of his career at the Cash, busy at work eliminating secondhand competition.

The Cash meant far more to Watson, however, than training in state-of-the-art unfair competition. He also learned about selling, sales training, inspiration and motivation, and business leadership. When I joined the faculty of the Harvard Business School in 1979, I was told that IBM had the greatest sales force in the world. You can draw a straight line from IBM's sales force that year to the sales force Patterson developed at the Cash ninety years earlier. Watson civilized Patterson's methods and made them more appropriate for the twentieth century. But he always acknowledged Patterson as the master. It was selling, even more than technology, that made IBM great in its glory years. It was selling that Watson learned from Patterson, which is why we are paying so much attention to his activities at the Cash.

Patterson migrated quickly from an admitted novice at selling to the man with all the answers. His most important teacher was his brother-in-law Joseph H. Crane, who was known as Ohio's best wallpaper salesman. Crane told Patterson in 1885 or 1886, at a time when one could still speak to Patterson this way, that "you have a good product, but you don't know how to sell it."[66] Patterson hired Crane, and Crane wrote "How I Sell National Cash Registers." This booklet, known as the "Primer," became the bible of selling at the Cash. Everyone was expected to know it and to abide by it. Anyone who deviated from it could expect to be cross-examined on his reasons by Patterson.

The Primer is a classic of managerial advice. It is intensely practical. The reader is told what to do and why, as well as what to avoid. For example: "When you go to a town, stop at the best hotel and get the best room you can [to demonstrate the cash register to prospective purchasers]." Commenting on his own advice, Crane observed: "You are representing a first-class concern—do it from the shine on your shoes to the room you occupy. Look it. Have the virtue, but assume the virtue if you have it not."[67] This passage captures the flavor of all the advice which NCR gave its salesmen through the Primer, newsletters, and conventions. Be first class. Even if you are not by nature, act that way. Avoid false economies.

The Primer told the agent how to approach the prospect, how to set the scene for the sale, and how to close the sale. (As NCR executive Richard Grant put it, "Quote the price without a quiver.")[68] It also prepared him for sales resistance and told him how to counter it. "Forget yourself," warned the Primer. "You must interest the prospect in the register and what it will do for him, or he will not buy it."[69]

In 1887, Patterson began circulating *The NCR,* a house publication in which he exhorted his salesmen to ever greater accomplishments and expanded upon the principles in the Primer. Here is a list of what not to do which Patterson prepared:

Don't advertise the Register as a thief catcher.

Don't try to make out all clerks are stealing.

Don't do all the talking.

Don't answer a question except with the truth.

Don't wait for a man to come to your office to buy.

Don't stop calling on a man if he says he doesn't need one when you know he does.

Don't think people in your territory are harder to sell than anywhere else. We know by experience they are not.

Don't try to sell a systematizer without a system.

Don't imagine we make any more money than any [other] retailer when they sell the same amount. Our expenses are terrible in comparison.

Don't think you can handle a territory of 1,000,000 inhabitants. It has been proven to us that a small territory is more profitable than a large one.

Don't think a firm is doing too much business to use our registers. There are but few exceptions where they cannot be sold.

Don't fail to write us when any points come up that you are not familiar with.

Don't remain idle.

Don't read these once, but twice. We want you to make money and don't want you to fail.

Don't forget while trying to sell a storekeeper to call attention to our credit books for registering credit sales.[70]

The two italicized points in this text deserve emphasis because they are so integral a part of enterprise in the late nineteenth and early twentieth centuries. First, tell the truth, only and always. Patterson, Crane, and the others wanted their salesmen to be honest. They believed it bolstered their self-respect and that it was good for business.

While thus exhorting the troops, the top officers in this company violated the antitrust laws blithely, without a second thought. Theirs were not merely technical violations. What Patterson, Watson, and their team did was not just illegal, it was unethical. Thus we see one of the many paradoxes of American enterprise. Rocksolid honesty and base corruption marched forward hand in hand.

The second point—we want you to succeed and we want to help you do it—showed the collaborative aspect of business enterprise. Alfred P. Sloan Jr. once said that he was never "interested in business relationships that are not of benefit to all concerned."[71] This was true for Patterson as well and applied within the corporation as well as in relations with customers. Another paradox: To compete successfully, cooperation was vital. That was an additional reason Patterson did not want salesmen poaching on one another's territories.

Not only were "do's" and "don't's" continually circulated through the system; so also were the endless objections to purchases from prospective customers. Among the more widely told tales was of the old grocer in Kentucky who would have nothing in his store not mentioned in the Bible. One salesman recited the Lord's Prayer to this merchant. When he reached "Lead us not into temptation," he paused to say that a Higher Power had brought him to this moment. The great virtue of the cash register was that unlike an open cash drawer, it recorded transactions publicly so that all, the proprietor and the customer as well as the salesclerk, could see. Moreover, that punched tape kept track of every sale. What better way to lead a potentially wayward youth—and what young person in this world of sinners was not at least potentially wayward—away from temptation than to install what might be thought of as an anti-temptation machine? The sale was made.[72]

One of Joseph Crane's cardinal rules was never to hesitate. But even the greatest salesman was bound to encounter questions for which he was unprepared. What then? Crane himself responded in such situations with: "Why, that's just the very reason you should have one."[73]

No wonder Crane was such a great salesman. This response was brilliant. It was always at the ready, thus satisfying the rule never to hesitate. Furthermore, it was quite confusing. A prospect has just advanced a reason why he should not buy a register. He encounters not hesitation, not argument, not refutation. Rather, he is told that his reason not to buy is actually the reverse of what he thought it was. Instead of fighting with a customer, a fight which could never be won, Crane put the customer in the position of fighting with himself while agreeing with the salesman.

Sales training at the Cash extended beyond the tips just enumerated. The company established its first formal training school ten years after Patterson bought it. The first campus was on Patterson's farm, in a cottage under an elm tree. There were thirty-seven students. The faculty was Joseph H. Crane.[74] Patterson had his own theory of education. His two principles were "to teach through the eye" and to "contrast the right with the wrong way."[75] He believed in simplicity and concreteness.

Patterson was a showman as well as someone who liked to see little shows acted out. He was demonstrative to the point of being histrionic. Once, he took a sledgehammer and demolished a malfunctioning cash register. He was known to remove people's desks from their offices and set them afire. It is said that no reading of Patterson's speeches could convey the impact of his message.

> Standing before an easel, red chalk in hand, [Patterson] would be making some sales point when, crushing the chalk in his hands, he would rub it vigorously over his face and

hair and throwing his arms up, looking like a tousled but well tailored Comanche, shout at the top of his lungs:

"Dramatize, verbalize!"

An executive reported that Patterson would shout, "Kill them . . . crush them!" when talking about the competition. "I have seen him knock a table down and smash it, tear off his collar, take a pitcher of water and smash it against the floor."[76]

A key to the Patterson theory of education was role-playing. He himself would play the prospect when a salesman made his pitch. The salesman should have been thoroughly trained to educate the customer in why the product would be good for him. His training should have included watching playlets of selling situations staged with actors. Drugstores, grocery stores, and other retail outlets were built at NCR in Dayton, and skits in these replicas were designed to illustrate how to sell. These playlets, according to one admittedly rather fawning account, "compared favorably with a full-fledged play." In one photograph, there was a cast of three actors and nine actresses in an apparel store.[77]

The focus was always on concreteness and detail. Thus, the salesman was expected to have precisely $7.16 with him in real cash. This was the amount needed to make the change for each demonstration. The company provided a purse to carry this amount in proper denominations.[78] Everything that Patterson learned at college he simply stood on its head in his own system. Patterson's methods exacted a price. Seasoned salesmen often felt humiliated and left the company. Truly talented people, not only Richard Grant and Thomas Watson but, by some estimates, dozens of others, were fired or walked out.

Patterson himself was as full of contradictions as only a blindly self-confident man could be. He insisted that salesmen were made, not born, but he also believed that whoever made them had to have material to work with. He envisioned himself as more than a businessman. He was a monument to the city of Dayton (which did erect a monument to him). He extended himself and the company to the great benefit of the city when the Miami River overflowed its banks, causing the Great Flood of 1913. But he had no compunction in shutting down NCR's factory as part of an infantile dispute with local newspapers, thus throwing two thousand innocent workers out on the street.[79] This Patterson did despite trumpeting his concern for the workingman and supplying clean water, toilet facilities, and a well-lighted plant for their work. When Stanley Allyn, the aforementioned future CEO of the Cash, first walked into the company's main hall in Dayton in 1913, a huge poster arrested his attention. Its title was *Eighty-two Reasons Why National Cash Register Is a Good Place to Work*. Reason Number Five deeply impressed him: "No relatives employed in the business." It would have been better had he been impressed by one of the other eighty-one. Patterson's successor as CEO of the Cash was none other than his son Frederick.

No more dramatic illustration of Patterson's fickle nature exists than his relationship to Watson. Watson well knew Patterson's creed that any man the Cash needed too much should be fired. Watson's life for more than a decade with NCR was dodging bullets, trying to become more important without becoming unemployed.

Watson's first real trouble came in 1907 or 1908. It was the height of Patterson's war on Dayton, and of the accusations of the Dayton newspapers that Patterson and his henchman Charles Palmer were ruining the company and the city with it. Hugh Chalmers, who could be described as the Cash's chief operating officer, had become increasingly disgusted with Palmer's humiliating dictates. When he rebelled, Patterson immediately fired him, igniting a lifelong mutual hatred. Watson was closely associated with Chalmers; and like Chalmers's other friends, his neck seemed to be on the chopping block.

One day, Watson came to work to find his office occupied by another executive and his staff nowhere to be seen. Watson kept coming to work on succeeding days to find the same situation. He made no objection, not even a comment. He visited branch offices. When he bumped into Patterson in Dayton, the two were cool but civil. Watson was shrewd enough never to ask why he had been publicly and deliberately slapped in the face by losing his office. This was real humiliation, but Watson took it without a peep of protest.

In 1908, Patterson departed with Palmer for a two-year sojourn in Europe. For no apparent reason, he promoted Watson to sales manager. For two years, Watson had the NCR sales team to himself. Sales doubled. When Patterson returned in 1910, he was well pleased with Watson. He gave him an expensive motor car (a Pierce-

Arrow) and a house. He took him around the country to visit NCR agencies.[80]

In 1912, the NCR executive corps was indicted en masse. The departed Chalmers took sweet revenge as the principal witness for the prosecution. Thirty-seven years old, indicted and awaiting prosecution, Watson met Jeannette Kittredge, who was to become his wife. Miss Kittredge was nine years Watson's junior, and a member of a socially prominent and prosperous Dayton family. Patterson and her father were friends. They lived near one another and belonged to the same country club. She was ready to get married when she and Watson began dating. Watson, nearing forty and encouraged by his mother back in his hometown of Painted Post, New York, was about ready also. There was one problem, however. Watson and his colleagues were found guilty on February 13, 1913, and he was looking down the double barrel not merely of a hefty fine but of a year in jail.

Miss Kittredge understood the situation, but she was a determined woman. She was almost 30 years old. It was time to get married—indictment, conviction, or acquittal notwithstanding. When Watson told Patterson that he had become engaged, Patterson, according to author William Rodgers, "was genuinely delighted" and said he had been hoping for the match.[81]

On Tuesday, March 25, 1913, Dayton was clobbered by the Great Flood. Patterson had predicted this catastrophe many years previous to it. That is why he built NCR's facilities on high ground, and they were spared the ravages to which so many structures in that city of 130,000 were subjected. Patterson's prediction of the flood was not strictly long range. It rained hard all day Monday and all Monday night. On Tuesday at 6:30 in the morning he went to the roof of the NCR office building and did not like what he saw. Then he drove to the riverbanks. On his return, he predicted a flood that day and said that the company must prepare itself to care for displaced persons.[82]

The flood came, the company was prepared, and numerous Daytonites benefited. Praise showered down on Patterson and his company after the rains stopped and the floodwaters finally receded. Even his former journalistic adversaries lauded him. The lockout a number of years earlier and the escapades associated with Palmer were forgiven and forgotten. A cry rose up from the stricken city that its leading citizen should also be forgiven any antitrust pec-cadilloes he may have been involved with. The two most important factors in saving Patterson from the antitrust penalties he had incurred were his activities during the flood and the change in the administration in Washington from William Howard Taft to Woodrow Wilson.

For Watson, the flood marked the end of his career at NCR. He, too, had labored mightily on behalf of Dayton during the disaster. He married Jeannette Kittredge on April 17, 1913, in her family's home, which two weeks earlier had been partially flooded.[83] The newlyweds went on a honeymoon, and on their return moved into a summerhouse which Patterson gave them near his own home.

As so often happened with Patterson, the closer you got to him, the more danger you courted. It fell to Watson to make preparations for the mammoth Hundred Point Club Convention in July of 1913. An indication of the difficulties involved is that Watson's assistant, who was originally assigned this task, had a nervous breakdown. At the great event, Watson spoke; "and, stammering a bit, but project-ing sincerity and an affinity for the problems of a salesman, he evoked applause."

So far, so good. But hardly had he finished speaking when Pat-terson strode upon the podium for a few unscheduled remarks. He was lavish in his praise of Richard Grant (who had spoken before Watson). The language he used and his mode of presentation made clear that it was time for Grant's day in the sun and that Watson was finished. The internal exile that followed must have been hell. But Watson had survived an episode like this once before, and he was not one to give in easily. This time, however, things were differ-ent: "After being systematically humiliated, after enduring it for many months, after having done so wonderfully well all that he was directed to do and having been convicted as a criminal for doing it, Thomas Watson was fired."[84]

When contemplating John Henry Patterson, the most lasting impression is not his sales methods, not his efforts to improve work-ing conditions in his factory, not his version of welfare capitalism. Neither is it his peculiarities (to put it kindly), the compulsion to fire those who got close to him professionally or personally, the imposi-tion of the charlatan Palmer on hardworking people trying to make a living, the bizarre superstitions such as the belief in the special significance of the number "five."[85] Not even the easy embrace of illegal business practices is what is uppermost in one's view. Rather, the most lasting impression is the extraordinary personal impact of the man. For all his strangeness, Patterson built a great company from nothing against extraordinary odds.

The July 6, 1921, issue of *The NCR* published a banner headline: "96,756 Points in June." Patterson is pictured with his arms spread before a huge board (perhaps fifteen feet by ten feet) filled with cards from the 266 agents and salesmen who reached or exceeded 125 percent of their quota. Everything on the cover is ordered and symmetrical, including Patterson himself, with his large, perfectly trimmed mustache. What is not in keeping with the symmetry of the printwork and photograph is the message in the caption. In large flowing script, as if it were written on one of Patterson's easel demonstrations, appears:

> I am proud of you—
>
> John H. Patterson[86]

The effect is, even at this far remove, very powerful. Patterson is not smiling. I have seen no picture of him smiling, nor have I seen a picture of any NCR function at which anyone was smiling. Business was business. Patterson's self-presentation in this picture was severe but satisfied—for now. If this is how he looked when he was satisfied, what was he like when he was unhappy? One would not want to find out. Patterson was a year short of his own death when this picture was taken. He was seventy-six. But he looked ageless. He appeared utterly certain of himself.

It is a testimony to the magnetism of this grizzled old Civil War veteran that Watson eagerly subordinated himself to him. That is the last such relationship Watson would have for the rest of his life. Being fired by Patterson was a personal cataclysm for Watson. Almost forty years of age, he was not a young man. He had just gotten married; and on January 14, 1914, Jeannette gave birth to Thomas J. Watson Jr.

The child would not be brought up in the home Patterson had given his father. The family had to move out of it. Money was not a problem, at least not an immediate problem. Patterson, always free with a dollar, had given Watson a $50,000 cash severance, a munificent figure.[87] Nor did job offers seem to be a worry. Being fired from NCR was so common that it carried little stigma, and Watson seems to have risen high enough to have made an impression on the business world independent of the company. Some of the nation's leading firms were interested in him. The problem was that he was not interested in the jobs they were offering him. These "were salaried jobs and Watson was a commission man. He wanted his income equated to individual accomplishment."[88] He had felt this way since his youth back in Painted Post.[89]

The worst part of this episode was neither fear for the current situation nor a lack of opportunity for the future. It was the shock of being severed from the man who was never in doubt. Watson had spent a career at NCR watching fine men fired for no particular reason, "yet he could not seem to relate [that] knowledge to his own fate."[90] That very separation probably made it possible for Watson to remain at NCR as long as he did.

Why suffer such shock at something so predictable? Perhaps it is the human condition. Here is a passage from Tolstoy's masterpiece *The Death of Ivan Ilyich*:

> In addition to the speculations aroused in each man's mind about the transfers and likely job changes this death might occasion, the very fact of a death of a close acquaintance evoked in them all the usual feeling that it was someone else, not they, who had died.
>
> "Well, isn't that something—he's dead, but I'm not," was what each of them thought or felt.[91]

Maybe that is what Watson felt (rather than thought—one doubts this sort of thing rose to the conscious level with him). "He's fired, but I'm not." Now, however, it was Watson's turn.

Despite the pain of all this, Watson possessed the remarkable graciousness to write a letter of warm encouragement and support to his successor as sales manager, Richard Grant. He told Grant it was "a source of great satisfaction for me to leave knowing that you are to take up my work here. . . ." It was, he wrote, "my earnest desire to see you make a better record as sales manager than I made."[92]

Watson's son wrote: "Oddly, Dad never complained of this treatment and revered Mr. Patterson until the day he died."[93] This was quite unlike Hugh Chalmers, who, as we have noted, shared a mutual hatred with Patterson after Patterson betrayed him. Instead of anger at Patterson, Watson, according to his son, always blamed another executive at NCR, Edward Deeds, for "whispering" to Patterson just before the 1913 convention that Watson was becoming exceptionally popular in the company. Their paths crossed several times in later life, but Watson never spoke to Deeds again.[94]

We will never know whether Deeds acted as Watson suspected; but even if he did, it hardly makes sense to blame him for Patterson's actions. Watson "revered" this man for whom he almost went to jail, so he exported the responsibility for the most hurtful of Patterson's acts to someone else. "Nearly everything I know about building a business," Watson told his son on more than one occasion, "comes from Mr. Patterson."[95] That is true.

It was from Patterson that Watson learned to put selling in the driver's seat of the corporation. Like Patterson, Watson emphasized sales training. Patterson had his Hundred Point Club for salesmen who met quota. For Watson, it was the 100% Club. The similarities could be pushed further. When the Watsons moved from their Manhattan apartment after the birth of their second child, Jane, they moved to the wealthy New Jersey suburb of Short Hills. Patterson's home in Dayton was named Far Hills. When Watson bought a thousand acres thirty miles away from Short Hills, he called the estate Hills and Dales. Back in Dayton, the NCR country club was called Hills and Dales.[96]

Watson's copyings from the Cash were everywhere to be seen, both in operations and in the more cosmetic aspects of business. Most important was that, purposefully or not, Watson the individual bore the same relation to the International Business Machines Company that Patterson did to the Cash. Both men dominated their organizations. Both were big spenders on themselves and on others. Both were born monopolists and were hounded by antitrust problems. Both demanded, explicitly or implicitly, so complete an allegiance to their own intensely personal views of how business should be done and how life should be lived that working for either made an employee subject to an imperialism of the soul that is unappealing to someone brought up in a free country.

Both were publicity hounds. Both had grandiose views about the impact they could have not only on their industries but on society. Both demanded and attracted sycophants. William Rodgers marveled that Watson required "but seemed often not to hear praise few men would tolerate."[97] This is less surprising when one realizes that the same could have been said of Patterson. Both had no compunction about striding to a podium unscheduled to upstage whoever was speaking. Watson, in other words, regularly did to others what Patterson did to him at the disastrous NCR sales convention of 1913. Neither had a sense of humor. Neither had a sense of irony. Both were paternalistic. Both were extraordinarily successful. Both men were, in a sense, totalitarians.

Watson was not the lunatic Patterson was. He was not as bedeviled by superstitions about magic numbers or diet as was Patterson. He had a successful, if often tempestuous, family life and did not need to rely on a supporting crutch such as Charles Palmer (or, in Henry Ford's case, Harry Bennett) for companionship.

Nor was Watson's policy toward executives as unerringly destructive of his company's future as was Patterson's. Like Henry Ford, Patterson fired his best people. What might have happened had he not done so? In May 1914, after less than half a year of unemployment, Watson became the chief executive officer of Computing-Tabulating-Recording. He renamed the company International Business Machines in 1924. Under his leadership, IBM turned in a spectacular record.

Patterson had always justified his firing of top performers with the excuse that no business institution should be overly reliant on a single individual. But the worst violator of his principle was he himself. He was the great motive force at the Cash; and when he died, that force left as well.

Patterson had always prided himself on being able to predict economic depressions and overcome them with increased selling effort. By luck, his superstitions proved accurate in 1893, and the Cash survived that dismal decade in style. Patterson died on May 7, 1922; and there would never again be a CEO at NCR capable of accurately guessing business cycles. In 1930, the first full year of the Great Depression, NCR profits were cut in half. Profits at IBM increased 10 percent and exceeded the performance of NCR for the first time, $7.4 million to $3.6 million. The profit comparison during the depression decade is striking. From 1930 through 1940 inclusive, IBM made a total of $83.5 million. NCR made $16.1 million. The returns on sales were even more dramatically lopsided. IBM's sales did not exceed NCR's until 1940 ($46.3 million versus $39.9 million). Just as John Patterson had set out to prove George Phillips wrong for underestimating the cash register business back in 1884, so Watson in 1914 "had vowed to build a larger and more successful company than Patterson."[98] He succeeded.

Watson was the man Patterson could not afford to fire.

ON HIS OWN

In a way, Tom Watson had been on his own since early in his life. His family emigrated from Scotland to Ireland to New York State, where he was born on February 17, 1874. One biographer has noted that Watson's family was always on the move,[99] and that was true in many ways. Part of his extended family settled in Brooklyn and converted to Catholicism, causing a schism with Watson's Scots-Irish Presbyterian father. A name change resulted—Watson was actually born Thomas J. Wasson—but the name was changed back soon after his birth.

Watson was born on a farm near East Campbell, New York. Where is that? Five miles from Painted Post, the town Watson thought of as home. In other words, it was in the middle of nowhere, nineteen miles from Elmira and not far from the Pennsylvania border. He was the fifth of five children and the only son of Thomas and Jane Fulton Watson.

Watson's relationship with his father has been described as "not always . . . easy. The senior Watson was stern and domineering, and both were fiery, quick-tempered men, strong in their opinions, and proud."[100] On the other hand, Watson's father is also described as telling his son to get an education and to get out of Painted Post, both good pieces of advice.[101] Watson seemed to have a reasonably affectionate relationship with his immediate family. His mother was also Scots-Irish. His four sisters, "strong-willed, competent women"[102] named Effie, Jennie, Emma, and Louella, were schoolteachers.

Watson himself gave some thought to teaching school, but one day as a substitute changed his mind about that. His ill-educated father wanted him to go to law school, but he wanted to go into business. At his father's urging, Watson studied at the Miller School of Commerce, a small, local institution, before launching his career.[103]

At some point—it is not clear when, but apparently in his late teens—Watson took the measure of his father. "I was absolutely sure that I was a smarter man than my father," he said years later. "I was positive of that. I felt I could prove it, if I were called upon to prove it."[104] By his early twenties, Watson was for all intents and purposes the head of his household. When he went to Buffalo in the mid-1890s, his family followed. When he became the NCR agent in Rochester in 1899, Jennie Watson assisted him. Effie married an NCR salesman and moved in with him. All his life Watson wanted to be surrounded by others.[105]

When the big 1903 promotion to Dayton came through, Watson hurried back to Rochester to visit his family and especially to see his ailing father. His father, with graciousness and generosity, expressed pleasure and pride in his son's accomplishments. That night, he died.[106] John Patterson was the real father figure in Watson's life. It was only with the severing of that relationship that Watson was completely independent of the preceding generation. Nevertheless, Watson's early mastery of his father may have sown in him the fear that his own son would do the same to him.

Unemployed at the age of forty and with family responsibilities to a wife, a son, and a mother, one would think that Watson would have jumped at the first good job offer he received. However, he did not. Offers came in from big, famous companies like Frigidaire, Montgomery Ward, Remington Arms, Electric Boat, and Dodge.[107] It is a commentary on the growing importance of managerial ability as a discrete asset that Watson received offers from firms in industries with which he had no experience. Perhaps the very number of these offers made it easier to turn each one down. Nevertheless, as his eldest son later observed, "I've always been impressed with how picky he was about what he'd do next." His father "explained this by saying he was sure he'd find a job because he had a reputation for being able to sell almost anything."[108] At a time when others would have been downcast and felt defeated to the point of paralysis, Thomas J. Watson was a self-confident man. He had won one of the toughest battles of life.

This sales ability had not come to Watson without a struggle.

He was a good example of Patterson's dictum that salesmen are made and not born. He had experienced his share of failures in early attempts at selling in the countryside around Painted Post and then with the Cash in Buffalo. Even at Dayton, tall, impressive, and physically prepossessing as he was, Watson was known to stammer at large public presentations.[109]

Watson had outgrown his father when he was twenty. When he was three months shy of forty, he parted company with his surrogate father, Patterson. Patterson, too, had been forty years old when he bought the Cash. Watson's break with Patterson had not been entirely unprovoked. Watson felt that he was destined for great things, and he knew that great things would never be accomplished playing second fiddle to anyone. Perhaps it was because of this burgeoning faith in his own talent that Watson felt he negotiated from strength even in situations in which cold, hard facts suggested that this posture was not justified. Perhaps that is why his life's pace, although fantastically frenetic and filled with constant travel well into his old age, retained a certain stately aspect.

Watson was a man who knew how to learn and knew when it was time to lead. He knew how to wait. His first day with the firm which was to be his next, and final, employer, Computing-Tabulating-Recording (CTR), was May 1, 1914. But he did not become chief executive officer until December of 1924, at the age of fifty, despite the fact that he was unquestionably the business leader of a company becoming ever more prosperous. It was wise to wait, however, so he did.

Watson had a volcanic temper, and as he aged and grew more successful there were fewer people to force him to contain himself. His anger attacks would sometimes be followed by remorse just as acute. This man, who plastered THINK signs everywhere in the world that his company marched, was often out of control emotionally. What he never did, however, was to panic. Even two brushes with bankruptcy (in 1932 and 1937) did not shake his faith in his business destiny.[110]

Watson knew what he wanted. He wanted to be the boss in fact, even if not at first in name. And he wanted money. Specifically, he wanted his compensation tied to CTR's performance. Watson got what he wanted. His pay package included a salary of $25,000, an option on 1,220 shares of stock, and a profit escalator to be negotiated in the future.[111] Twenty-five thousand dollars was a very substantial salary in 1914. The salary was even more impressive when one considers that Watson's conviction for antitrust violations was still on appeal and that CTR was not a strong company at the time.

Watson was recruited for CTR by its creator, an arms merchant, international high liver, and corporate manipulator named Charles R. Flint. Flint got involved in merging companies in the same industry in 1880 and continued to do so gleefully (which is the way he did everything) until he retired in 1931. At a time when "trusts" were universally reviled, Flint enjoyed being dubbed their father by Chicago newspapers after he delivered a speech in their defense.

In his memoirs, Flint claimed to have "acted as organizer or industrial expert in the formation of twenty-four consolidations. . . ."[112] He offered as a defense of horizontal combinations that they captured economies of scale and that they increased efficiency in numberless ways—from manufacturing to marketing to inventory management to consulting fees. These things would be true only if the firms being combined were in the same line of business. Flint was not an apostle of what in later years would come to be called unrelated diversification.

Flint did, however, assert that "consolidating the manufacturers of similar but not identical products" could achieve economies. His first effort in this area was CTR in 1911. In 1923, he wrote that although CTR "is not the largest of the consolidations in which I have acted as organizer, it has been and is the most successful."[113]

CTR's president in 1911 was George W. Fairchild, a self-made man who had been involved in the time recording business for almost twenty years. He became chairman of the board when Watson was hired and remained titular chief executive. He was an early investor and apparently an active manager in his early years. His attention, however, must have been more than a little diverted by the fact that he was elected to the House of Representatives in 1906 (as a Republican) and served from 1907 to 1919.[114]

CTR did not do well in its early years, and Flint soon felt it was time for new talent. The company itself had become an odd, wayward assortment of dozens of establishments more related in Charles Flint's mind than anywhere else.

Flint had engineered horizontal mergers in the computing scale industry and the time recording industry at the turn of the century. He came to believe there was a connection between the measurement of time and of weight; and so in 1911 he decided to merge the time recording and computing scale manufacturers into a single business. Precisely how the merger of companies in these two industries would produce the economies of which he boasted he never made clear.[115]

The Tabulating Machine Company was thrown into the mix in 1911 at the last moment. This "haphazard organization"[116] marketed a device invented by Dr. Herman Hollerith for recording census data. Hollerith had gotten involved in tabulating back in 1880. At that time, it was realized that population increases were rendering the census so outdated that it was losing much of its value. The tenth census, begun in 1880, took a decade to compile. If ever necessity were the mother of invention this was the time. Hollerith developed his electrical tabulating system by 1889, making the tenth census the final one to be manually assembled. In 1896, the Tabulating Machine Company was established with Hollerith the manager and principal stockholder.[117]

The obstacles Watson faced at CTR in May of 1914 ran the gamut from daunting to seemingly insuperable. The company itself was a mess. Flint's fine philosophizing to the contrary notwithstanding, the company was so utterly bereft of organization that it took twenty years to sort it all out. CTR was the parent company; but it had as a companion another holding company. Various subsidiary companies had bought interests in other firms with no strategic coordination.

Assets of some of the firms of which Watson had become general manager

> were little more than legal fictions, but each of the ten companies Watson found himself dealing with had its own corporate structure with a board of directors, separate accounting system and sales offices, and often its own intracompany feuds and patent litigation. Factories, some little more than sheds, were scattered throughout the country. . . . Even the main offices were widely separated. . . .[118]

Financially, things could also have been a good deal better. CTR's bonded indebtedness was, at its inception, twenty-five times its assets. Its "assets" were to a large degree accounting conventions. Fortunately, however, the accounting system itself was so misleading that "Watson was spared having to face all the bad news at once."[119] For

all Flint's airy sermonizing about the real economic advantages of consolidation, CTR was a typical example of an industrial mirage summoned up for the sake of promoters' profits. If the company had
failed, it would have been very easy to point to reasons why.

Watson's biggest problem has not yet been mentioned. It was
Watson himself. Flint hired him when he was still snared amid the
toils of the law, prompting one director to ask: "What are you trying to do? Ruin this business? Who is going to run this business
while he serves his term in jail?"[120]

Watson's first meeting with the board was what today would be
called a "stress interview." He was asked why he had left NCR. He
responded, "Because Mr. Patterson asked for my resignation."[121]
His first speech at a company meeting was not, at its outset, any
pleasanter. It "was received coldly, with no applause. . . ."[122] In both
instances, however, Watson quickly succeeded in winning the
doubters over. His innate self-confidence served him well at this critical moment. Having sold himself to himself, he was able—despite
his occasional stammer—to sell himself to others.

On March 13, 1915, the federal circuit court of appeals reversed
the conviction of Watson and his confederates at NCR for antitrust
violations. A new trial was ordered but never held, because the Cash
signed a consent decree agreeing not to engage in the practices
which had so upset the government in the first place. Watson
refused to sign the decree. He maintained always that he was innocent of any wrongdoing and that signing the decree would have at
least implied the contrary. Since he was no longer at the Cash, his
consent to a different policy there was moot. The government therefore simply dropped the case.[123]

The next business day, Monday, March 15, the CTR board
elevated Watson's title. He had been cleared, and he was at the
company to stay. But he never escaped the shadow of this episode
completely. He never told Tom Jr. about it. His son found out from
an IBM executive by chance sometime shortly after World War II.
He was shocked to the marrow. The discovery cost him sleep.[124]

FROM CTR TO IBM: MOLDING THE FIRM

There is no substitute in business for fundamental insight. It is wor-
thy of note how many great companies have had at their core a busi-

ness motto which was both descriptive and inspiring. In two of the cases already discussed in this book, we see this phenomenon clearly. At Kodak, "You press the button and we do the rest." At Ford: "A car for the common man." Other firms from the 1880s onward were able to enunciate the same kind of core value. At Coca-Cola, for example, "The pause that refreshes." At General Motors: "A car for every purse and purpose." At American Telephone and Telegraph: "One Policy—One System, Universal Service."

These slogans not only stuck in the minds of consumers. They also helped train the sales force and organize its thinking. They seemed to endow the sales force with a belief that they were doing more than pushing products onto reluctant customers. They were serving humankind. The rhetoric of service to society suffused corporate America, especially in the 1920s.[125]

Watson did not develop a single phrase like the ones mentioned above. (He employed dozens of them.) But he did use a single word which became the company's signature, the banner behind which it marched. That word was "think." Concentration on this word became a powerful force uniting the company.

Like so much else at IBM, THINK had its origins at NCR. Watson "was trying to command full attention to some sales message." Probably standing onstage, he wrote THINK on one of the omnipresent NCR easels. Patterson happened by and liked the effect so much he had THINK signs made up and posted around the office.[126] THINK migrated with Watson to CTR, where it became enshrined. It was engraved on the top stair of the "Steps of Learning" at IBM's staged playlets in its school building. (The other four stairs were labeled, in descending order: OBSERVE, DISCUSS, LISTEN, and READ.)[127]

THINK is a puzzling battle cry. What did the word mean in the context of IBM's business practices? Business is about action, not cogitation. THINK did not mean "think independently." When Watson said THINK, he did not mean "think for yourself." He meant "think like me." Watson was no "organization man" in a "gray flannel suit." He positioned himself as the leader with the answers. What IBM employees were supposed to think about were the views and attitudes of President Thomas J. As a journalist put it in the *Saturday Evening Post*: "Thomas J. Watson well might typify the day of one-man rule in business. Within his organization, his executives say that

President Watson *is* the International Business Machines Corporation. . . . In the IBM parlance, the company's president is not the president but the leader."[128] Watson placed a lot of faith in three assistants to update him on the state of the business by the early 1940s because, according to a reporter, "their entire careers have been spent under his tutelage, and they think as he does."[129]

Purely by chance, the product that was to enable Watson to achieve business greatness was a thinking machine. The word "think" is not meant to suggest a machine that "played" with ideas. Rather, it was one which assembled objective data and performed calculations with those data.

Of the three components of CTR, it was the "T"—the Tabulating Machine Company—which, it will be recalled, was thrown into the combination almost as an afterthought at the last minute. The "C" which stood for "computing" in the company's name, was not the forerunner of the computer. Rather, it manufactured and marketed scales for a variety of uses. The "recording," for which the "R" stood, was the time clock business.

It was that "T," for tabulating, where the real potential lay. Here was a machine which could benefit mightily from further development. It was a machine that might cut some of the most unproductive costs any business faced: the costs of counting and keeping track of things. Hollerith had already proven its worth through his work on the census. With modification and refinement, what else might such a marvelous machine do?

The supreme insight of Watson's whole career was the potential of tabulating machines. Like Carnegie, Eastman, and Ford, and like the other CEOs profiled in this book, Watson had a gift for not being blinded by the past or by the present. He did not march backward into the future. Rather, he imagined what might be and labored mightily to put his company on the crest of the wave. In 1920, tabulating machines were still the smallest of CTR's three businesses. Most profitable was time equipment, with scales second.[130]

But that was the past and the present. For the future, Watson saw that machines which could cut human labor in the office had a limitless potential.[131] The most important decision any company makes is what markets it elects to serve with what products. Watson's breakthrough insight was that the products to push were the tabulating machines, and the markets to serve were not only companies but also governments. Without this strategic insight, Watson probably would have been a success anyway, but he would not have become the monumental figure in business that he did.

In 1933, International Business Machines (which is what Watson renamed CTR in 1924) sold "more than 700 aids to modern business." These included meat slicers and coffee grinders. Tabulating equipment, last in sales in 1920, had moved into first place. It was there to stay.[132]

By 1940, tabulating, organized into the Electric Accounting Machine Division, generated three-quarters of IBM's sales and "the overwhelming bulk of profits." The coffee grinders and meat slicers had been sold off, and what remained of the old International Scales Division had been folded into the Time Recording Division, which included time clocks, fire alarms, and a limited line of commercial scales.[133] Tabulating was the future in 1940, and the future looked bright.

The electric accounting machine was the principal product of the division which bore its name. IBM held an 85 percent unit share of market of this product line. Remington Rand had the rest. There was no third player, nor did one seem likely to enter the list. According to *Fortune*, "Because volume is now necessary to profitable operation, and because the most effective features are covered by patents, and manufacturing processes take years to perfect, and the builder's reputation is worth a lot, it is unlikely that a newcomer will usurp the field. . . ."[134]

Another barrier to the entry of new competition was the fact that all the products of the Electric Accounting Machine Division, with the single exception of the punch cards that ran through them, were leased, not purchased. The practice of leasing was instituted by happenstance before the turn of the century. The government wanted Hollerith's tabulators for the census, but for nothing else. It cost a lot less to rent than to buy, so that was what the government did.

What happened by accident turned into an important marketing tool. A lower price for a government rental was also a lower price for rental to a private company. That lower price was a form of penetration pricing which increased the size of the market and led to economies of scale and the learning curve, just as it did with the Model T Ford.

All marketers know that understanding the customer is a critical part of their job. This is true whether they sell a product with a service contract or they lease the product. Yet the desire to understand the customer might increase if the marketer's company still owned the product that the customer was using. You are going to work a little harder to help the customer maintain the machine properly.

Flowing directly from leasing was IBM's insistence that only punch cards which it manufactured and marketed be used in its machines. The cards were fabulously profitable. In the late 1930s, the company was selling 4 billion of them a year. In 1938, the gross dollar sales of cards was equal to one-fifth the rental income from electric accounting machines.[135] In the 1930s, the card business was said to account for a third of IBM's profits.[136]

The federal government was not only one of IBM's biggest customers, it was also the nation's principal antitrust enforcement institution. Tying the sale of IBM cards to the sale (as opposed to the lease) of an IBM machine would have constituted a violation of the Clayton Antitrust Act. If, on the other hand, IBM owned the machines being used by others, it could plausibly argue that it had a right to see that they were well maintained. Poorly made punch cards might damage IBM property. IBM in fact made this argument and charged higher rentals for any customer using other cards. The government brought suit, and in 1936 the Supreme Court decided that IBM's right to protect the machinery it owned did not give it the right to demand that renters use its cards. The Court did, however, grant the company the right to establish the specifications for the cards used in its machines.

The net result of all this maneuvering seems not to have been very detrimental to the company.[137] Although the federal government was a major customer of IBM not only for the census but, after 1935, for the management of the social security system, and although it did make some of its own cards, IBM's dominance in this market was never seriously threatened. The manufacture of these cards was very difficult. If exacting specifications were not met, incorrect calculations might result or machines might jam altogether.[138] These hurdles helped keep competition from entering this burgeoning market.

The relationship with the customers which leasing facilitated helped smooth IBM's earnings. The company was not, as was sometimes said, "depression-proof." Earnings grew from a million dollars in 1921 to $7.4 million in 1930. Thereafter, they flattened out, dropped to a low of $5.7 million in 1933, and then fought their way back to a healthy $9.4 million in 1940. Considering the state of other businesses during this dreadful decade, this was a performance of which the firm could well be proud.

By the beginning of the war, new product ideas, resulting in part from heavy research expenditures, began to bubble up and hold out the promise of profit for the future. A remarkable variety of new applications were being developed for government, indeed for any institution—public or private, profit or nonprofit—for which sorting and tabulating mattered. The need to count, to file, to calculate, was everywhere, not just in large organizations but in small ones, not just in the United States but all over the world.

IBM's machinery cut costs so dramatically that if one competitor in an industry invested in it others could not afford to be without it. The work it eliminated was boring, repetitive, and mind-numbing, yet important. The cost of an accounting or an actuarial mistake is potentially very high indeed. Organizations get little credit for accuracy in those areas. It is expected. But they catch a lot of grief for mistakes. Of IBM's products, *Fortune* observed in 1940 that their "historic function, like that of the most memorable inventions, is to allow men to invest less manpower in drudgery, to save labor."[139] Or, as an IBM slogan of later years put it: "Machines should work. People should think."

When Alfred P. Sloan Jr. was starting out in business at the turn of the century, John Wesley Hyatt, the founder of the ball-bearing firm Sloan's father bought for him, said that he "should find a market for antifriction bearings anywhere there was a turning wheel."[140] At the dawn of the automobile age, that meant everywhere. The same kind of limitless expanse of possibility spread out before Watson in 1940. What was needed was to develop the market, to engross it, to defend it.

IBM's expenditures on products designed to open up new markets; its glistening manufacturing facilities, especially the gleaming complex located on the seven-hundred-acre industrial estate it owned in what Watson called the "Valley of Opportunity" in Endicott, New York, not far from Painted Post; its vigor in pursuing global opportunities; its sheer luck in being in the right business at the right time in 1941 as the government expanded its own administrative responsibilities (IBM's second-largest branch sales office was in Washington, D.C.) and as the government also forced, through regulation, increased recordkeeping on business—all these assets paled in comparison to the company's sales force as a factor for growth and competitive superiority.

Watson has sometimes been portrayed as a stranger to technology. It is true that he never invented anything, and by 1941 would not have been able to "plug up a board" of one of the electric accounting machines which his company made.[141] Compare this to George Eastman taking pictures in 1878 or Henry Ford building the quadricycle in 1896.

Nevertheless, it should be acknowledged that in the prime of his life Watson had a clear understanding of how the machinery which he sold worked. He may not have had much of an understanding of computers in, say, 1952. Few people did. But in 1912, he was well informed on the workings of the cash register and other contemporary mechanical equipment. He had to be, if only to understand how best to sabotage the machines of competitors.

It really is striking how, even late in life when he had completed his rise from poverty and obscurity to great wealth and fame, Watson was keeping his eye on the future. Like Carnegie, Watson invested and built when times were bad and prices were low. In July of 1932, at the nadir of the Great Depression, Watson broke ground for a new research and engineering laboratory in Endicott, saying, "We have realized from experience that the future of our business largely depends on the efforts, brain, and ability of our engineering department" (which included research).[142] The company's leading engineers reported directly to Watson, "who thought of them as *his* inventors. If a disagreement between an inventor and Commercial Research was escalated to Watson, he was likely to side with the inventor."[143] This is a further indication that the eulogist at his funeral missed the mark by speaking of Watson's devotion to the past.

Capitalists, as we mentioned in the introduction, are "people who make bets on the future."[144] If "an orientation toward the future" is the test, Watson, quite unlike Henry Ford, remained a capitalist until the end of his life. In stark contrast to Ford, Watson knew that change was in the nature of things. "This war," he said of World War II in 1943, when he was nearing seventy, "is changing everything."[145] He knew that a key to mastering change was reliance on education (which reached "no saturation point")[146] and alliances with institutions of higher education (Harvard and especially Columbia) and the government. Despite having little formal education himself, he became the most important person on the board of trustees of Columbia and played a key role in making Dwight D. Eisenhower president of the university after World War II.[147]

Even when it came to electronics during and after the war, Watson seemed to be willing in his mid-seventies to make fundamental change. The evidence here is mixed. Tom Watson Jr. said in his autobiography that electronics was "the only major issue" on which he and his father "didn't fight." But the son's own narrative did not make the change sound as if it were easily accomplished.[148]

Once again, the influence of Patterson and NCR can be felt in Watson's attitude toward new products and the future. Patterson established the Future Demands Committee at NCR around the turn of the century. Watson became a member, and it is there that he met Charles F. Kettering, the inventor of the electric self-starter for the automobile. An electrical engineer, Kettering founded the Dayton Engineering Laboratories (Delco) in 1909 and, after its purchase by General Motors, served as GM's director of research for more than a quarter of a century. From such men Watson learned "respect for the specialized knowledge of engineers."[149]

It was Watson's very love of selling which made at least some product knowledge essential. The sales force pulled new products out of the laboratories because they wanted more to sell. Because of the success of his sales force motivation and management, Watson put more pressure on his inventors and engineers than he may have intended.

How to sell was what Watson knew best. He knew how to sell his company's products to its customers, his salesmen to their accounts, his company to its salesmen and to its other employees, and his company to a remarkable variety of constituencies around the nation and the world.

One example was the world of art. "It is our opinion," he wrote in 1939, "that mutual benefit would result if the interest of business in art and of artists in business should be increased. . . ."[150] Wealthy people patronizing art was nothing new. J. P. Morgan, reminiscent of the Medicis, assembled a magnificent collection of paintings, drawings, and books. Henry Clay Frick also purchased artworks of surpassing beauty, housed today in the Frick Museum on Fifth Avenue in New York City.[151] But there was a difference between the attitude of these and other collectors from Watson.

Watson saw the art world as another avenue for bringing global recognition to IBM. His connection with art was not limited to painting. The IBM Symphony composed by Vittorio Gianinni premiered on January 18, 1938, on the occasion of the dedication of IBM's twenty-story World Headquarters Building in New York City. It was also performed by the Philadelphia Orchestra on IBM Day at the New York World's Fair on May 4, 1939, which marked Watson's twenty-fifth year with the company. *Fortune* described it as "gratifyingly short, and not hard to listen to."[152] The melody of the most often sung of IBM's songs, "Ever Onward," was woven in to the symphony's second movement.[153] Art was but another way of expressing Watson's view of his enterprise. "The IBM is a world institution," he repeated endlessly, "and is going on forever."[154] He said this in words; but he wanted it said in music as well, tone-deaf though he was.

For many years, McGraw-Hill's business publications ran an advertisement the purpose of which was to encourage institutional advertising in their trade magazines. The advertisement features a gimlet-eyed, highly skeptical purchasing agent staring out at the reader and asking, or rather demanding:

I don't know who you are.

I don't know your company.

I don't know your company's product.

I don't know what your company stands for.

I don't know your company's customers.

I don't know your company's record.

I don't know your company's reputation.

Now—what was it you wanted to sell me?[155]

The moral of this advertisement was that sales began before a sales call, which is why business-publication advertising was a good idea. Watson succeeded in answering all the purchasing agent's questions for his salesmen without having to pay for the advertising it suggested.

Indeed, IBM was a very noisy company.[156] From 1931 through 1940 there was an average of twenty entries per year for Thomas J. Watson in the *New York Times Index*. In 1940, the company did a little over $46 million in business, netted $9.4 million in profits, and had $83 million in assets. It was a big company in the American business world and the biggest firm in its industry. It was, however, Lilliputian when placed in the land of the giants. Sales of General Motors in 1940 were $1.8 billion, profits $196 million, and assets $1.5 billion. The assets of American Telephone and Telegraph were about sixty-six times IBM's. Its profits were about twenty-four times greater.

At the New York World's Fair in 1939 and in 1940, IBM positioned itself, in terms of the space and expanse of its exhibit, in the same class with General Motors and General Electric (which had sales in 1940 of just under $412 million and profits of over $55 million). Peter Drucker, who at the time was a New York correspondent for some British newspapers, wanted to file a story on Watson and IBM because of the size of its pavilion. Drucker "thought a story on so small a frog behaving like a big shot might be amusing. 'Forget it,' my editor wrote back. 'We are not interested in a story on an unsuccessful company which as far as anyone can tell is never going to amount to much.'"[157]

Unfazed, Watson felt that he had the formula for the future. The secret of that formula was his method of selecting, training, and motivating his sales force. When Watson had started selling back in Painted Post in the early 1890s, the job was as unsystematic and unscientific as it had been from time immemorial. The salesman taught himself the tricks of the trade. And there were plenty of tricks to learn. He sold himself as much as he did a product.

Watson saw Patterson transform this sometimes sleazy method of operation into a systematic, quantifiable business assignment. Self-esteem—that is what Patterson wanted his salesmen to feel. They could only feel it if they earned it. And they could only earn it if he helped. Watson was Patterson with the craziness removed. With most of the craziness removed, that is.

The IBM schoolhouse in the Valley of Opportunity graduated 10,000 people from its inception in 1927 to World War II. Among the graduates were machinists and technicians, but the salesmen were the elite.

The creation of an IBM salesman began literally before the train pulled into the station. Future salesmen were recruited on college campuses, the selection criteria consisting, reportedly, predominantly of "good looks and manners." (Some things are more difficult to change than others, and it was perhaps concluded that even a course at Endicott could not make an ugly man handsome.) Like George Eastman, Watson never attended a college (other than a vocational school); but also like Eastman, he came to see colleges and universities as abodes of the elect which could be of great benefit to his firm.

Describing the curriculum at Endicott in 1941, a journalist noted that it included visits to the plant,

> where engineers explain the electric accounting machine, a complicated maze of some seventy-five miles of wire and 55,000 separate parts, surmounted by a sort of typewriter which prints the results of the machine's calculations. . . . The instructors show the boys how to plug up a sort of telephone switchboard connecting the wires in many different combinations.[158]

And "the boys" were tested on their ability to plug up a board, even though they would rarely be called upon to do so, such work being consigned to maintenance men under normal circumstances.

As for the actual selling process, there were three basic steps: the approach, the demonstration, and the closing. By the time the salesman made the approach, his first call, he was expected to know more about the prospect's accounting than the prospect himself. This knowledge was acquired "by talking to friendly minor employees of the prospect, examining his available records, and sometimes by discussing him with business rivals who already are using I.B.M. installations."[159] Here we see one example of the advantages of market share. Far more firms used IBM than anything else, so far more such opportunities for information gathering were available.

After investigating the decision-making process in the firm to see how and by whom decisions to spend money on the type of equipment IBM marketed were made, the salesman sent his card to the appropriate party, along with a letter from a satisfied customer in a similar business. Usually, the salesman got the interview he requested because IBM had the reputation for sending people "to serve," not "to sell." Once inside the organization, the salesman was expected to learn every aspect of the prospect's accounting system and be able to present persuasively any deviations from best practice to the boss.

The next step was to speak with the chief accountant or head bookkeeper. This required exquisite tact, and "many hours at Endicott are spent in rehearsing 'delicate situations.'"[160] The delicacy resulted from the fact that the top accountant often feared that the size of his staff would be diminished if machines replaced human labor. This fear was justified. That was the point of installing them.

Watson had encountered a dilemma similar to this back at NCR in the 1890s. The people closest to the cash registers—bartenders or soda jerks who actually handled cash—hated the machines. They might not be able to prevent their bosses from purchasing them, but they were adept at sabotage once they were in place.

Even greater than the chief accountant's fear that his staff might shrink in size was the terror, also quite reasonable, that IBM's machines placed even him in danger of being downsized. Yet the salesman was trained to explain that mastery of the new machinery could increase the chief accountant's importance in his company. Encomiums to IBM from former bookkeepers who had risen in the ranks, some all the way to CEO, were standard weapons in the selling arsenal. Once again, market share helped here. The more companies that used IBM, the more such examples there were.

This was not all. The salesman was authorized to offer the top accountant a course for customer administrators at Endicott, where he would be treated as an "honored guest," "meeting coming executives from other companies, bowling and playing golf at the country club, and generally accumulating facts and social background which will make the boss sit up and take notice when he gets home."[161]

Once the chief accountant was on board, the salesman undertook "the survey." It was this aspect of the selling process which, according to one journalist, "takes the I.B.M. salesman out of the knocker-on-doors class; they are efficiency engineers."[162] The survey took up to a half a year to complete. Its goal was to show how IBM's equipment could provide more accurate information at greater speed and lower cost than was otherwise possible.

The simple fact was that this was true. All the puffery which so often has surrounded selling, all the exaggeration which stopped ever so short of the outright lie, was not necessary. It is not clear whether IBM's product was superior to Remington Rand's. Its market share would suggest it was. But it was without question superior to the person-intensive manual methods of information gathering and retrieval that preceded it.

Management information, the IBM salesman understood, extended well beyond accounting. Its importance reached into all the corners of the business. Take the sales force, for example, or inventory management: "The great argument . . . is that the head of a sales organization . . . may know at any moment the state of his inventory—or may check up on his individual salesmen. Using hand methods, he might not know his business was on the downgrade till months after the inventory was overstocked or the sales force became lax."[163]

Rosser Reeves, a famous advertising agent of the 1950s and 1960s, used to describe the toughest problem he faced as follows. A prospective client walks into your office and puts two identical half dollars on your desk. The prospect says: "Mine is the one on the left. You prove it's better."[164] This is precisely the problem the IBM salesman did *not* have. He was pushing no "me-too" product. IBM had genuine advantages over the manual methods it was replacing.

With the survey completed, the IBM salesman went back to management. "Already the battle [was] more than half won" because the salesman had thoroughly examined the prospect's information systems.[165] The salesman accompanied management to the local IBM branch office to demonstrate his wares. The demonstration thus took place on home turf.

If one can picture the scene, one can envision how by this time the salesman had the prospective customer in his grip. He knew (or should have known) as much about the customer's business as the customer himself. He probably knew a lot more about the latest systems in the customer's industry and in other industries as well. We are not speaking now of a drummer or a Willy Loman figure. We are speaking of an expert selling an expert system to a man who had the option of buying it or of being left behind by the rest of the business world.

Here is where all the training up at Endicott was brought to bear. The customer might buy, or, rather, lease, one or two machines of the type IBM was selling during the course of his career. The salesman, by contrast, leased them every day. He was trained in what by World War II was the finest school of its kind. At that school, all these salesmen pooled their experiences. They prepared themselves for every contingency.

Closing, that moment of truth so famous in sales lore, was not, apparently, a moment of which most IBM salesmen stood in dread. An often-asked question was: "Why do we have to sign a one-year lease?" This was the only time the prospect asked that question, but the salesman heard it every day. He was prepared. "We'll send our customer service men around to inspect them [i.e., IBM's products] regularly; we're selling service, not machines."[166]

The IBM salesman did not merely knock on doors. He was part of a powerful system. A system which drove sales from $26.2 million in 1936 to $46.3 million in 1940 . . . from $62.9 million in 1941 to $138.2 million at World War II's end . . . from a dip to $115.6 million in the reconversion year of 1946 to $214.9 million in 1950 . . . from $266.8 million in 1951 to $563.5 million in 1955.

Thomas J. Watson Sr. stepped down as chairman of the board of directors and chief executive officer of the International Business Machines Corporation on May 8, 1956. He turned the reins of the company over to his son and namesake, Tom Jr. He was eighty-two years of age. A few weeks later, his life came to an end.

On May 1, 1914, when Watson assumed his position at Computing-Tabulating-Recording, it was a small, disorganized collection of establishments employing fewer than four hundred people. There was no reason to believe that it would grow into a successful enterprise and plenty of room to doubt whether it would survive.

What if you had purchased 100 shares of CTR in 1914? The price would have been $2,750. If you had exercised the rights attached to those shares through 1925, you would in that year have owned 153 shares at a total cash cost to you of $6,364. At the time of Watson's death, you would have held 3,990 shares of IBM with a market value of $2,164,000, and you would have enjoyed $209,000 in dividends.[167] Your investment (calculating from 1925) would have increased at a compound annual rate of growth of 21 percent for a period of more than three decades.

IBM's sales in 1956 were $734.3 million and its profits $68.8 million. It ranked forty-eighth on *Fortune*'s list of the nation's largest firms. It price/earnings ratio was over forty-one. The first line of Watson's front-page obituary in the *New York Times* described him as the man "who built the fabulous International Business Machines Corporation." The adjective was well-chosen.[168]

Watson was not a technologist. IBM was sometimes not a product leader. But he was a great businessman. His first earned income as a youth was $6 a week. No one ever gave him anything. He had a talent, a drive, an optimism in situations where men with more common sense would have been downcast, which won the day.

The puzzle is this: Did Watson need the relentless adulation which he demanded of all who worked for IBM in order to succeed? Or did he succeed in spite of the lockstep conformity, which was an iron law at the company. IBM had so many songs that the company published books of them. Here is the first verse of what has been called its anthem, "Ever Onward":

> There's a thrill in store for all,
> For we're about to toast
> The corporation in every land.
> We're here to cheer each pioneer
> And also proudly boast
> Of that "man of men," our friend and guiding hand.
> The name of T. J. Watson means a courage none can stem:
> And we feel honored to be here to toast the "IBM."[169]

Company songs were far more common in the early 1900s in American companies than they are today. The cultural artifact just quoted must be seen in context. At Coca-Cola, a century ago, for example, it was commonplace to sing "Onward Christian Soldiers" at the end of sales meetings.[170] The unstated implication was that you were doing God's work when you sallied forth to sell the magic elixir.

Even in recent times there has been plenty of cheering, not only in foreign companies but in American firms such as the Saturn Division of General Motors. There has been a lot of singing and cheering at Wal-Mart, the most successful retail phenomenon of the second half of the twentieth century. Sam Walton was known to exact promises with the concluding oath: "So help me Sam." A corporation as an extension and amplification of the ego of a single individual is a common sight. And the rah-rah culture of many firms helps to ward off the cynicism and perhaps the even-more-menacing boredom of which business, like any other pursuit, has its share. Moreover, singing and sophomoric enthusiasm have hardly been unique to the business world. Many an academician who sniffs at such things in corporations grows misty-eyed when his college's alma mater is played or when his school scores an upset in the big game.

With all that said, with all the allowances one can think reasonably to make, I have never seen anything quite like the degree of slavish devotion directed not merely to IBM as an institution but to Watson personally in any other large organization in the free world. The constant, unending chorus of praise, some of it personally orchestrated by Watson himself, was without parallel. The endless dinners with endless speeches conferring meaningless awards as the chorus sang on cue verses such as:

> With Mr. Watson leading,
>   To greater heights we'll rise . . .[171]

The endless tributes, honorary degrees, certificates, encomiums, etc. . . . The tongue-lashings administered to those who did not sit at attention in rapturous admiration as they listened to yet more boilerplate. . . . Examples of comparable behavior do not spring to mind.

At IBM celebrations, which were lavish, common, and endless, Watson would often be presented with various tokens such as plaques. He "would sometimes choke up at these presentations, his eyes shimmering with tears—even though he had previously inspected the inscription and approved the expenditure for engraving it."[172] What was he weeping about? Did he, like Carnegie, have the power of "selective amnesia" which permitted him to believe that the words he was hearing represented the sincere feelings of his employees? Were they tears of joy about how far he had traveled from his youth in East Campbell, New York? Were they tears of relief that no one would ever again be able to do to him on a podium what Patterson had once done to him? Were they tears of laughter at the absurdity of the situation? What explains his entry in

Who's Who, at one and three-quarters columns said to be the longest in the volume?[173] People listed in *Who's Who* write their own entries.[174] Why was it important to Watson that the world know he became in 1946 "Grand Officer, grand Ducal Order of the Crown of Oak, Luxembourg" or that in 1949 he received the "Elroy Alfaro Internat. Found. Cross, Republic of Panama." Was it conceit? Was it insecurity? No one will ever know.

Surely scores if not hundreds of creative men were repulsed by all this phony ecstasy. Surely IBM must have sacrificed the services of many whose simple common sense revolted at the servility which was part of the life of everyone in the company who crossed Watson's path. His son and heir, Tom Jr., believed so. "The longer I worked at IBM," he wrote in his memoirs, "the more I became convinced that my father's style silenced too many people."[175]

As the 1940s turned into the 1950s, Watson became progressively more difficult to argue with. The reason is that IBM's spectacular growth was making headlines, and to Watson personally must go much of the credit. Perhaps the company would have been even more successful had Watson been just a bit more of a democrat at heart. But perhaps not. Tom Jr. observed twice in his autobiography that business is a "dictatorship." The government has checks and balances, but the dictatorial license in a business, he wrote, "is what makes it really move."[176] And Tom Sr. was the dictator. Like Henry Ford, he disdained organization charts.[177] In essence, the whole company reported to him, and he was no respecter of a chain of command when he wished to speak with anyone at IBM about anything or to promote people over the heads of others.

Watson's pictures were everywhere. So were the magazines he published. So were his aphorisms. (As one of his sons observed, "In 1915 we started the singing . . . and we've been in the black ever since so we're afraid to quit.")[178] The company came to bear an uncomfortable resemblance to *1984.* Unlike Ford in his later years, it should be emphasized that Watson was a benevolent dictator. He had a human and humane side which served as a counterpoint to his aloofness and uncontrollable temper. But it was he who determined when he would play which role. He exercised the power of unpredictability.[179]

Watson was a hard taskmaster. As was the case with Patterson, the closer one approached, the more dangerous he became. Biographers Thomas G. and Marva R. Belden have written that difficult though this experience often was, "the men who stuck it out, survived his jealousy if they lived too well, his contempt if they lived too poorly, his desire for good fellowship, his suspicion of cliques, his need for ability, and his mistrust of too much of it—if they stuck it out, they had one of the most rewarding careers in American business. . . . [A]lmost everyone who came in contact with Watson surpassed his expectations of himself."[180] The question is: Why was the price so high to be one's best? Does the reason lie in Watson? Was this simply the way of big business in the mid-twentieth-century United States?

Today, empowerment of subordinates is advanced as proper managerial technique. No modern business school would teach the human relations policies of IBM as they were practiced during the apex of Watson's power as a model for modern business building. Yet they unquestionably worked. Have times changed? In what specifics?

Tom Jr. put his finger on an even more important attribute of IBM. It was indeed a dictatorship without checks and balances. Yet the whole point of founding the United States was to live in the very kind of freedom that no employee at IBM enjoyed. IBM was the rule in this regard, not the exception. The American citizen was born politically free, it would seem, but got his living in corporate hierarchies where, if not in chains, he was certainly not free either. From 1914 to 1956 there was a grand total of one free man at IBM.

When Alexis de Tocqueville visited the United States in 1831, he was astonished by the equality of condition he encountered compared to the class structure which was the fundamental fact of the Old World. Perhaps he would have been less astonished had he visited a hundred years later. Very, very few people anywhere lived the life of privilege and command enjoyed by Thomas J. Watson Sr. at the flood tide of his life. And few lived the life of his successor.

FATHER AND SON

Thomas J. Watson Jr., born the year his father took the job at CTR, became the CEO of IBM the day his father stepped down. He was forty-two years of age and had been groomed for this position for a decade.[181] In 1957, young Tom's first full year at the helm, IBM's sales topped $1 billion. It had taken forty-six years to reach that mark. But a mere six years later sales topped $2 billion. The following year, 1964, sales topped $3 billion.

Young Tom resigned as CEO in 1971, having piloted the company to the apex of the world of computerized data processing through the introduction of the 360 series and its successors. The year he stepped down, sales topped $8 billion and profits were greater than sales had been in 1957.

In his novel *Ragtime*, E. L. Doctorow described J. P. Morgan as "that classic American hero, a man born to extreme wealth who by dint of hard work and ruthlessness multiplies the family fortune till it is out of sight. . . ."[182] Watson succeeded his father in as spectacular a fashion as did Morgan. But both were exceptions. Far more common in big business is to see the son of a great man fail. The Sarnoff story at RCA is the rule; the Watson story at IBM, the exception.

The vehicle for young Tom's triumph, the IBM System/360, was a remarkable gamble. IBM invested $5 billion in this product, which was presented to the market in 1964. IBM's total *revenues* in 1960 were less than a third the cost of this product launch. Its success in terms of market leadership and profit dollars has led one scholar to call it "the most successful big-ticket product introduction . . . since the Model T Ford."[183]

Young Tom resigned from the executive committee in 1979. Sales that year were $22.9 billion and profits topped $3 billion. IBM seemed beyond competition in its industry worldwide. It set a standard for liberal treatment of its hundreds of thousands of employees and for constructive corporate conduct that made its logo an icon for those believing in the harmony of interests between the private, profit-seeking enterprise and the public good.

The price of this success was high. It is difficult for those of us who live a more-or-less normal existence to imagine what life is like for people with riches and power. People who own multiple, palatial dwellings. People with a cadre of servants. People who can telephone anyone anywhere and have the call returned. People with so much money that the thought of it does not cross their minds. People who own their own airplanes. People who don't have to waste time. People who don't have to smile when they don't want to. People who know other people like themselves. These are the people who seem to "have everything."

Of course, they do not. What they have is everything we want when our own house needs repair, when all we can get on the other end of the telephone is a computerized voice response, or when we are being jostled as we wait in line to see if we will get a seat on a dirty, oversold, overcrowded airplane.

These special people, the true royalty of the modern world, have problems of their own. Where do they fit in a democratic age? How can they know themselves when no one around them shows a true face? How do you keep all that money and power from interfering with true, human communion? Stories about poor little rich girls or boys are common and tend to evoke little sympathy. On the other hand, alcoholism and suicide are not strangers to the rich.

For Tom Watson Jr., locating himself within his family of origin, with regard to his wife, and with regard to International Business Machines was not easy. Watson's childhood and youth were extravagant, not very happy, and not very stable. He was born at a turning point in his father's life. He and IBM (at the time, CTR) entered T. J. Sr.'s life the same year. His father was so single-mindedly committed to business success that it would have taken a miracle for him to serve as the ideal family man. That miracle did not happen. His relationship with his wife exemplifies the strain.

The usually astute and critical author William Rodgers wrote this of T. J. Sr.'s marriage. "Tom Watson and Jeannette Kittredge together represented more strength and perseverance than was possible for them singly. . . . As the wife of a man like Watson, she was unsurpassable."[184]

That was the way the marriage looked to the outside world. From the inside, the truth was different. In his memoirs, Tom Jr. wrote:

> My mother wasn't necessarily cut out to be married to a socially ambitious businessman. In spite of her [upper-class] upbringing and her boarding-school education, she was strong on prairie virtues that were unusual in Short Hills [the swanky New Jersey suburb to which the Watsons had moved from Dayton]. . . .
>
> The closer I got to my mother, the more upset I was at the way I thought Dad treated her. This was when IBM was at a critical stage, demanding a lot of Dad's attention. In his office he could press the button on his desk, a fellow would come in, Dad would say "Send a letter," and boom, it would hap-

pen. When he wasn't thinking he expected Mother to obey him in the same way. She found that hard to put up with, so in the years when Dad was most intense about his work there was enormous tension in our household. I remember incessant arguments between them. The door to their bedroom would be closed but my brother and sisters and I would hear angry, muffled voices rising and falling. Father would be rude to her and then half an hour later he'd give us a lecture about how we ought to be good to our mother. I never had the guts to say, "Then why aren't you."[185]

Tom Jr. remembers "about ten years of strife" between his parents which suddenly ended "around the time I was fourteen."[186] The timing is a bit odd. Why would the fighting have begun four years into the marriage?

Tom was shocked by the sudden rapprochement between his parents. He thought his mother had "stopped standing up for herself." In fact, she later told him, she had come to find the marriage so impossible that she asked for a divorce. T. J. Sr. was so thunderstruck that, convinced of his love, she decided to accept her role in his life and in the life of the company. She never mentioned divorce again.[187] Needless to say, this is hardly the idyll presented to the rest of the world.

Thomas J. Watson Sr. and Jeannette Kittredge Watson had four children: Tom Jr., Jane, Helen, and Arthur (known as "Dick"). Family relations were Darwinian. Tom Jr., the oldest, was a troubled child who lived the life of a playboy until World War II enabled him to grow into adulthood. After the war, there seems to have been no doubt that Tom Jr. would eventually succeed his father as CEO of IBM, even though this was far from a family firm. The Watsons owned a tiny percentage of the equity, but the company had experienced as much success as anyone could have wished. Moreover, at the time shareholders had nothing like the power in the large, publicly held firm that they began to assume toward the end of the century. The question was: How long would it be before Tom Jr. took the helm? He rejoined IBM in 1946. (He had worked briefly for the company before the war.) He was thirty-two years old. Watson Sr. was seventy-two. Had it not been for Tom Jr. the logical successor was Charles A. Kirk, forty-one, the executive vice president known as Tom Sr.'s number two. The men worked closely together. Watson

Sr. gave Kirk the responsibility of training his son. If there was any recognition of the exceptionally difficult position Kirk was thus put into, there is no record of it.

Kirk and his pupil got along reasonably well at first, but that could not and did not last. Kirk began to realize that Tom Jr.'s playboy days were over and that he had the skills to run the company. Tom Jr. did not want to work for Kirk, did not want to wait decades for Kirk to retire, and envied Kirk's close relationship to his father. The inevitable tension mounted. Kirk and Tom Jr. traveled to Europe in mid-1947. The trip was a disaster. Tensions and tempers were raw and inflamed, approaching physical violence. These tensions ended when Kirk died of a heart attack during the trip.[188] Kirk was not the first or last man to give his life for the company.

On January 15, 1952, Tom Jr. became president of IBM. His father continued on as chairman of the board, and the gut-clutching pattern of vituperation, remorse, and reconciliation between the two persisted. Finally, feeling his age, Watson Sr. resigned from IBM and turned the company over to his son. Watson Sr. was eighty-two. He had spent one year more than half his life transforming IBM from a motley collection of unconsolidated cats and dogs with no strategic direction into a firm better positioned to compete for the future than any other in its industry.

The cause of Tom Sr.'s death that year was malnutrition resulting from intestinal blockage. The blockage could have been relieved by surgery, and there is a reasonable likelihood that his life could have been prolonged. But Watson had never had surgery, and he did not want it. In a way, his death was similar to George Eastman's. Eastman took his own life when his health was failing. Watson elected passively to let his life be taken.[189]

Tom Watson Jr. ran IBM from 1956 until his heart attack in 1971. His self-expressed "desire to have total command" was at last fulfilled.[190] *Fortune* called Watson Jr. the "greatest capitalist who ever lived," but also observed: "A tough boss, Watson helped set the high-stress tone of IBM in the 1950s and 1960s. Though he was paternal with ordinary employees, he often treated his lieutenants roughly. He trained executives by reshuffling them and pushing them into jobs that were over their heads. For those who erred he devised the so-called 'penalty box'—a temporary but humbling transfer off the company's fast track."[191]

The best example of an executive so treated was Watson's brother, Dick. Watson said he loved his brother, which was doubtless true. But to be loved by Watson was to be an endangered species. In 1948 and 1949 when Watson Sr. was reorganizing IBM, he wanted to put Dick Watson in charge of a subsidiary, IBM World Trade. His instinct told him that Dick needed a protected niche. But Tom Jr. argued that World Trade was being given too much responsibility. In Tom Jr.'s words, after an acrimonious meeting: "Dad rose up and thundered, 'What are you trying to do, prevent your brother from having an opportunity?' Those words killed me. They set me up against my brother, who was right there. Dad would say that kind of thing without thinking, because he always aimed to win."[192]

Later events suggested that there might have been some truth in the father's accusation. In 1962, Tom Jr. brought Dick Watson back to the United States from IBM World Trade, where he had been very successful. In his autobiography, Tom Jr. wrote that this was "the worst business and family mistake I ever made. I should never have forced my brother into a horse race with others for the top job. . . ."[193]

The result was that leadership for the crucial System/360 program was divided between Dick Watson and the ferocious T. Vincent Learson. The friction between the two "got completely out of hand." Dick's gifts, like his brother's and his father's, were in the area of selling and motivation. But Tom Jr. put him in charge of manufacturing and engineering for the System/360, something which neither knew anything about. Tom Jr. felt forced to replace his brother with Learson; and a rift was created which never healed.[194]

Dick Watson became ambassador to France in 1970. In 1974, he suffered a household accident in his home in New Canaan, Connecticut. Tom Jr. and his wife rushed to his bedside, but Dick spent a week without regaining consciousness before dying. Watson's grief at his brother's death was real and touching. His guilt feelings did not present themselves as unwarranted.[195]

EVER ONWARD

Thomas J. Watson Jr.'s remarkable autobiography has given us a valuable window into life at the corporate pinnacle. The business accomplishments of two generations of Watsons are as impressive as any father/son combination one can name. What one asks is: Were these achievements in spite of the personal turmoil that surrounded them? Was this personal tension the price of these achievements? How different would the Watson story have been if the family were German or Japanese or English rather than American? Are emotional explosions to be expected when people from the same family work closely together in business? Is the discord worth it?

There are no answers to these questions. Perhaps there are, as Benjamin Franklin put it, no gains without pains. Perhaps the conflicts of the Watsons are not so different from those of the rest of us, but seem so because they are played out on such a grand canvas. Perhaps that temper which seemed to flow from Patterson to Watson Sr. to Watson Jr. was so overwhelming because it was allowed to grow unchecked. These people had no outside forces containing them. They were compelled to control themselves, and they did not do a very good job.

Americans are raised to believe in equality. More than once, people whose talent or luck has raised them to a position of eminence have not known how to act.

A FINAL NOTE

As this manuscript was being prepared for publication, a new book appeared in which the author, Edwin Black, accuses IBM of going to great lengths to do business with Nazi Germany from its beginning in 1933 until its collapse at the end of the war. Black, the son of Holocaust survivors, seeks to document the use of IBM equipment in the location, transportation, torture, and murder of millions of people. He alleges that IBM did business as usual with Hitler's heinous regime.[196] A word needs to be said about Black's thesis, especially since I discussed in some detail the anti-Semitism of Henry Ford.

First, it is true (and has long been known) that IBM did a lot of business with Nazi Germany. It is also true that Watson accepted a medal from the Nazis in 1937, the Merit Cross of the German Eagle, at a time when informed people had plenty of evidence of who and what Hitler was. Watson returned the medal in 1940. It is not an excuse for IBM—but an important comment on capitalism—that many other non-German companies did business with Nazi Germany as well. Businesspeople have often been willing to do business with the Devil as long as the check clears.

It hardly needs saying that one wishes this were not so, but it is.

In his attitude toward Jews, Watson was, however, altogether different from Ford. Ford was a genuine anti-Semite. He simply hated Jews. His bigotry embarrassed many who wanted to be his friend, and it cost his company money.

As Black himself writes, "IBM's business was never about Nazism. It was never about anti-Semitism. It was always about the money."[197]

Watson, a sponsor of the National Conference of Christians and Jews, was not an anti-Semite, and Black never says that he was. He was a business executive selling important products to murderers. The willingness to do so, not only on Watson's part but by many others as well, raises profound questions, not so much about Watson as about business.

THOMAS J. WATSON SR.

February 17, 1874	Watson is born.
c. 1895	Watson is hired as a salesman for National Cash Register's Buffalo office.
1899	Watson becomes the NCR agent in Rochester.
1908	Watson is promoted to sales manager.
February 22, 1912	Watson, Patterson, and other executives are indicted for violating the Sherman Antitrust Act.
February 13, 1913	Watson and others are sentenced.
April 17, 1913	Watson marries Jeannette Kittredge.
1913	Watson is fired from NCR.
May 1914	Watson joins Computing-Tabulating-Recording.
1915	Watson becomes president.
March 13, 1915	Conviction is reversed by federal circuit court of appeals.
February 14, 1924	CTR is renamed International Business Machines Corp.
1949	Watson resigns as president and becomes chairman.
May 8, 1956	Watson steps down as CEO.
June 19, 1956	Watson dies.

5 CHARLES REVSON AND REVLON

Consumer Packaged Goods and the Television Revolution

[T]he reason women buy cosmetics is because they buy hope.[1]

IT TAKES ALL KINDS

David Packard, co-founder with William Hewlett of Hewlett-Packard and one of the most admired business leaders of the twentieth century, recalls in his autobiography walking around one of HP's machine shops with the shop manager. The two of them stopped to observe a machinist intently at work making a polished plastic mold die. Absentmindedly, Packard reached down and touched the die and left a mark on it. "Get your finger off my die!" the machinist said. The manager accompanying Packard quickly asked: "Do you know who this is?" Replied the machinist: "I don't care!" Packard's comment on this encounter was that the machinist "was right and I told him so. He had an important job and was proud of his work."[2]

Compare the above encounter with the following.

In the late 1960s, Revlon had a policy that everyone signed in when they came to work. Charles Revson himself signed in, though his example could not have served as much of an inspiration, since by the late 1960s he did not show up at the office before 11 A.M. One morning, he walked in and began looking over the sign-in sheet to see who had arrived when. The receptionist politely told him that he was not supposed to look at the sheet. "Yes, I can," said Revson. "No sir," she replied. "I have strict orders that no one is to remove the list; you'll have to put it back." The receptionist was new on the job. She was polite, but firm. At length, Revson said: "Do you know who I am?" "No, sir, I don't," she replied. "Well, when you pick up your final paycheck this afternoon, ask 'em to tell ya."[3]

These stories typify Packard and Revson. They were different in almost all respects. Packard was physically prepossessing at six feet five inches in height. Revson was about five feet eight.[4] Packard was an athlete and an outdoorsman. Revson was neither. Hewlett-Packard has always been a firm which prided itself on motivation through inspiration, personal responsibility, and trust. Revlon during Revson's day was characterized by fear and unpredictability. Both William Hewlett and David Packard were men of the West. They were hunters who also raised livestock on their extensive ranch lands. Revson was an easterner and a dedicated indoorsman. His story and Revlon's were preeminently wrapped up in New York City, which has always been the nation's fashion capital. What engineers were to Hewlett and Packard, advertising agents were to Revson. Packard was a "man's man" who owned a company that sold to men. Revson was a sexually confused man who owned a company that sold to women.

That said, HP and Revlon did have one thing in common. One important, vital thing. They were able to change with the times. When Bill Hewlett and David Packard set up shop in Silicon Valley in 1939, there were no computers. Over the years, computers came to be the heart of their business. When Revlon opened for business in 1932, there was no television. By the 1950s, however, television, which, like fashion, was headquartered in New York City, was rapidly diffusing throughout the United States. Both companies became masters of new technologies which were developed by others but to which they had to adapt.

We will return to Silicon Valley at the end of this book through a discussion of Robert Noyce of Intel, a discussion which will include references to the HP story as well. In this chapter, we will examine a New York company in a New York industry[5] which, through its innovative products and its mastery of television, made its principal owner very rich, though not very happy.

THE EARLY YEARS

"Thanks from Revlon" is the title of a full-page advertisement placed in *Toilet Requisites and Druggists' Sundries* magazine in January 1939. The advertisement features separate photographs against a cheerful red background of four young men. They are

Charles Revson, "President, and said to be the Revlon 'Spark-Plug'"; Charles Lachman, "Vice President, and creator of *the* manicure preparations extraordinary"; Joseph Revson, "General Manager and 'Watch Dog' of the treasury"; and Martin Revson, "Sales Manager, and self-appointed guardian of Revlon's good name." Part of the text of the ad reads as follows:

> It has been a long journey from our modest beginning in a small, one room office to our present position of leadership in manicure preparations sold through department stores. When the three of us, Charles Revson, Charles Lachman, and Joseph Revson started Revlon seven years ago (Martin Revson joined us [in 1935]) we had very little money. And . . . none of us has a long gray beard even today. But we did have a fixed determination to offer you the best manicure preparations ever offered in this country, or anywhere else. From this policy we have never wavered for one instant. And that, we believe, is why Revlon is now the fastest moving merchandise of its kind in fine department stores everywhere.

This straightforward statement has an appealing air about it. It is low-keyed, friendly, and even somewhat jocular until it speaks of the company's unwavering commitment to high quality. The advertisement concludes by graciously thanking all the people, "toilet goods buyers, the girls behind the counters, and all our friends in the toilet goods industry," for helping to make Revlon's success possible.[6] The proprietors of the Revlon Nail Enamel Corporation[7] did indeed have much to be thankful for in 1939. They had managed to place their fledgling company on reasonably firm ground despite the trials of the Great Depression and the special difficulties caused by the peculiarities of the cosmetics industry.

The Revlon Nail Enamel Company was founded on March 1, 1932. The brothers Charles and Joseph Revson supplied the paid-in capital of $300. Their partner, Charles Lachman, was a chemist whose wife's family owned the small Dresden Chemical Company in New Rochelle, New York. Dresden produced nail polish for other firms to market. Lachman wanted his own brand, which is why he decided to throw in with the Revsons. His contribution was not to be capital, but rather nail enamel from Dresden to Revlon on credit. This credit apparently never amounted "to more than a few thousand dollars."[8]

Lachman was described in the advertisement quoted above as "creator of *the* manicure preparations extraordinary" (surely *extraordinaire* was the word these unsophisticated folks had in mind); and, in addition to financing Revlon's inventory, he was supposed to supply his technical know-how, "such as it was."[9] For his contribution, he received 50 percent of the company. Charles and Joseph Revson split the remaining half.

Charles Revson was twenty-five years old when Revlon was founded. Joseph Revson was sixteen months Charles's senior. Lachman was thirty-five.[10] These men chose what was probably the worst single year (with the possible exception of 1933) in the twentieth century in which to found a business in the United States. Nineteen thirty-two was the trough of the Great Depression. Real gross national product had fallen a calamitous 26.8 percent since 1929 and would decline further the following year. Investment, a key barometer of the confidence with which businesspeople face the future, sank from $16.2 billion in 1929 to a sickening $0.8 billion (measured in 1929 dollars) in 1932 and would fall yet further the following year.[11] From an index level of 100 in July 1926, the stock prices on the New York Stock Exchange peaked at 216 in September of 1929. In March 1932, when Revlon was founded, this index stood at 54. By June, it dropped to 34.[12] The worst blow was the employment situation. Three percent of the workforce was unemployed in 1929. A staggering one-quarter could not find work the year Revlon was founded, the worst performance in the history of the American economy.[13]

The magnitude of this disaster cannot be overstated. The unemployed worker—"the worm that walked like a man," in the phrase of one journalist[14]—was the symbol of the depression. "To be unemployed in an industrial society is the equivalent of banishment and ex-communication," one historian has written.

A job established a man's identity—not only what other men thought of him but how he viewed himself; the loss of his job shattered his self-esteem and severed one of his most important ties to other men. Engulfed by feelings of inferior-

ity, the jobless man sought out anonymity. He withdrew
from the avocations he had had before he lost his job, even
tried to escape the company of friends and neighbors whose
opinions he respected.[15]

Thus, the depression had a psychological as well as an economic
impact. Optimism turned to doubt; hope to fear. By 1932, the leadership in Washington had proven itself defeated by the crisis. Not
only had jobs disappeared, relief and welfare for the unemployed
were evaporating as well. The Great Depression was "profound and
terrifying."[16] As year passed into gloomy year people began to face
the startling prospect that they might never work again.

One of the remarkable aspects of Franklin D. Roosevelt's first
inaugural address, delivered on March 4, 1933, was his understanding of the psychological dimension of the Depression with his
famous declaration: "So, first of all, let me assert my firm belief that
the only thing we have to fear is fear itself—nameless, unreasoning,
unjustified terror which paralyzes needed efforts to convert retreat
into advance." (What Roosevelt did not mention was that fear in
and of itself was worth being afraid of.) Roosevelt also understood
the worst aspect of the Depression: "Our greatest primary task," he
told a very nervous nation, "is to put people to work."[17]

Charles Revson took many risks in his business life. Every new season, every new advertisement, every new product, every new color was
a risk. But the biggest risk he took in the time between his birth on
October 11, 1906, and his death on August 24, 1975, was when he
walked out on a paying job and decided to found his own business. He
had a high school education, next to no capital, no real plan, and no
connections outside of a family skirting the edge of penury.

On top of this, Revson had chosen two partners who were very
limited people. His brother Joseph, described by journalist and Revson
biographer Andrew Tobias as being "in his own way . . . even stranger
than Charles,"[18] had a good memory and was a competent bookkeeper. But it would take a lot more than that to build a nail polish
company into a cosmetics giant in the depths of the Depression.

As for Charles Lachman, he seems to have suffered from a massive lack of talent. Martin Revson said Lachman "didn't know his
ass from a hole in the ground about chemistry." After the first year
in business, Martin Revson said Lachman "was asked to do noth-

ing." He "was put on the shelf. Absolutely nothing."[19]

Lachman's most important contribution to the company was the first letter of his last name. That "l" is the "l" in "Revlon." For this he was given 50 percent of the company. His stake was scaled back to 30 percent in 1938.[20] Never did a man amass a multimillion dollar fortune with less effort. "I've got a rake, and I rake it in" is what he would come to say he did at the firm.[21] That "l" bothered Charles Revson quite a lot in later years. He came to want the company to have his name on it, like Elizabeth Arden, Max Factor, and Helena Rubenstein.

If Revlon were to succeed against the heavy odds it faced it would be all up to the "Spark-Plug," as the 1939 advertisement described Charles.

Charles Revson was born in Boston, Massachusetts, and grew up in Manchester, New Hampshire. His parents were both Russian-born Jews and both arrived in the United States in the late nineteenth century. Samuel Morris Revson emigrated in his early twenties to avoid service in the Russian army. In Manchester, he hand-rolled the "724" cigar for the R. G. Sullivan Company. His wife, Jeanette Weiss Revson, was brought to the United States as an infant by her parents. While the family lived in Manchester she worked nights sporadically at a dry goods store. Revson's father apparently was an impractical dreamer, while his mother was more dynamic and realistic.[22]

There is precious little else known about Revson's family in the early years. The three brothers (Joseph, Charles, and Martin) seemed to get along with one another well enough and did well academically at Manchester Central High School, from which Charles graduated at the age of sixteen in 1923. The family appears to have been reclusive. They were isolated to some degree by their religion. Only one other Jewish family lived nearby. They did not become part of a Jewish community. Martin Revson has said that being a Jew in that place at that time was not particularly easy. Although firmly Jewish in ethnic identity, there was no formal religion in the family. None of the three boys was bar mitzvahed.[23]

There was more than the typical amount of tension between the parents. "I don't think there was a great marriage between my mother and father," Martin recalled in later life.[24] After graduating from high school, Charles went to work in the garment district in New York City. His employer was the Pickwick Dress Company, owned by a cousin, where he began as a salesman and worked his way up to a piece goods (i.e., fabric) buyer by 1930. "He supposedly became proficient," according to Andrew Tobias, "in differentiating between shades of black, which demands a sensitive eye."[25] This is noteworthy because Revson came to acquire a reputation as a "color genius," an elusive phrase if ever there was one. If indeed he possessed this particular trait, it was perhaps during his seven years in the "rag trade" that he acquired it.

It is rather odd that Revson, who made an important part of his living from sensitivity to color, left no record of any interest in it during his youth. As a wealthy man in his later years, when he could afford the third-largest privately owned yacht in the world (after Onassis and Niarchos) and had forty-four in help,[26] he was not known as a collector of serious art. If he was a "color genius," that characteristic was a matter of impulse and instinct.

In 1930, he was, it is said, fired from Pickwick for overbuying a fabric which he liked. The fabric sold out; but by the time it did he had decamped to Chicago with a bride, one Ida Tompkins, "show girl" daughter of a Pennsylvania farmer. He got a job peddling sales promotion materials. Business was bad; and, at the time, food was scarce. Martin Revson has said Charles was "literally starving to death" in Chicago.[27] Within months, he was back in New York. He had the same job, but no better luck. His marriage ended; and he moved in with his family, which had left Manchester first for Brooklyn and then for 173rd Street and Amsterdam Avenue in Manhattan. Revson's next job was with Elka cosmetics in Newark.[28]

INTO THE COSMETICS INDUSTRY

In either 1930 or 1931, Charles Revson, having failed at selling sales material, got a job with the Elka Company in Newark, New Jersey. Elka was a tiny—"pitiful," Martin Revson remembered it as being—firm in the nail polish business. Charles was to be the distributor in "Greater New York."[29]

Why this company? Why this industry? Why this product line? How did he get the job? On what basis was he paid—salary plus commission? Commission only? We do not know.[30] Revson would have been a reasonable candidate for a job selling cosmetics. He had spent seven years in the ladies' garment business. Like cosmetics, ladies' garments were highly fashion sensitive and dominated by small firms.[31] He had experience selling, even though not all that experience was successful. He was not concerned with what his acquaintances considered the "sissyish" nature of the product; and he was skilled at selling to women—"bringing out sexual instincts in some and motherly instincts in others."[32]

Charles had enough faith in himself to persuade his brother Joseph to leave his job at the General Motors assembly plant up the Hudson in Tarrytown, New York, and join him distributing Elka's products from their New York headquarters. These "headquarters" were a small corner of another cousin's lamp factory at 38 West Twenty-first Street in Manhattan. This was a remarkable move for Joseph. Jobs were getting harder to find by the day in 1931. It did not take a genius to predict whether Elka or General Motors had a better chance to survive the depression. The two young men were taking quite a risk, Joseph more than Charles because Joseph had more to lose.

We now come to a key point in Revson's career. This man who became world famous as one of the great marketers in business encountered a product with which he felt he could change the industry. We will never know for certain how or where he came across this product. Tobias writes that Elka had developed it.[33] When I tried to find the answer to this question in 1970 and 1971 through interviews and reading the trade press, I was led to believe that the product was developed either by the much-maligned (but by 1970, very wealthy) Charles Lachman or perhaps by his wife, whose family owned the chemical company for which Lachman worked.[34]

By 1932, Charles Revson had been working for a living for nine years. What gave him the courage to strike out on his own after a decade working for others? The immediate cause for his leaving Elka was that he wanted the rights to serve as the company's national distributor, rather than being restricted to the New York metropolitan area. Elka turned him down. That kind of business judgment is all that is needed to explain why no one is writing chapters about that company today. Indeed, Revson may have felt he was taking a bigger risk staying with Elka than starting his own firm.

Perhaps Revson did encounter the product and the vision of how to market it at Elka, and that inspiration prompted him to set up his own business. This sequence assumes that Elka's product was not patented and that Revson knew how to manufacture it. It further assumes that Revson went into business by marketing Elka's product with his brand on it. If, on the other hand, Lachman and his wife or a chemist working for their firm developed the product itself,[35] they may have done so by following Revson's suggestions concerning the properties that a nail polish had to have to be marketable.

Let us move on from what we can only guess at to what we know. Charles Revson changed the cosmetics industry. As Tobias writes, Revson "entered a fledgling, highly unprofessional industry of one-man shows (one-woman shows, really) and, more than anyone else, was responsible for building it into a $5 billion industry [by the mid-1970s]."[36] To be sure, in economic terms, cosmetics have always been compared to giant industries which can make or break economies. However, for (literally) obvious reasons, the social impact of the cosmetics business has been far greater than that of other industries its size.[37] The marketing expenditures of these companies have been high as a percentage of sales.[38] Cosmetics have mattered in many ways. Revson is therefore a more important figure in American history than he would have been had he built a firm similar in sales to Revlon which marketed not cosmetics but steel flanges.

We know that as of March 1, 1932, Revson was in business with a product which, in a "me, too" competitive environment, delivered something special.

> It was opaque. All the other nail polishes on the market were transparent. [There was] potential in the difference. The others were made with dyes and were limited to three shades of red—light, medium, and dark. Revson felt that "polish"— "cream enamel," it came to be called—made with pigment so that it would really cover the nails, and made in a wide variety of shades, could capture the market.[39]

Revson was not out to market a better version of nail polish already being sold. He wanted fundamentally to change the meaning of the product to the woman who wore it. That is putting it mildly. Many people in the early 1930s associated red nail polish with prostitutes.[40] "At that time, many women did not wear liquid nail polish. If they did . . . it was generally colorless. The transparent polish then in use did not allow for subtle shades. The only reds were almost black red, which were not considered in good taste."[41] Most American women in 1930 would no sooner have bought stylish nail polish than stylish lightbulbs. Revlon revolutionized this part of the cosmetics business with its creamy, opaque enamels. Revson possessed the entrepreneurial imagination.[42]

THE REVLON NAIL ENAMEL COMPANY, 1932–1939

Let us recall the aforementioned famous phrase of Franklin D. Roosevelt in his first inaugural address in 1933: "The only thing we have to fear is fear itself." During the preceding year, an increasing number of Americans were living in shacks in what came to be known as Hoovervilles. In big cities, once self-confident people were chasing garbage collectors hoping to grab a scrap of food. Farmers were doing worse, if that was possible. They were losing their land to banks foreclosing on their mortgages. Their only harvest was the "grapes of wrath." People by the hundreds of thousands were on the road, either by jalopy or by hopping freight trains, going . . . nowhere.

Charles Revson was on the move, too; but he was going somewhere. He was running from beauty parlor to beauty parlor talking to owners and manicurists and responding to complaints. Revson did not suffer from the "nameless, unreasoning, unjustified terror" of which Roosevelt spoke. He was not afraid of fear. His fears were all too concrete. One fear dealt with the wondrous new nail enamel itself of which he was now the proud proprietor. Sometimes, it did not quite perform up to expectations. Revlon's "control of color was imperfect. When it was first applied it looked fine, but in a short time, it turned yellow."[43]

This kind of failure did not occur in every instance, but it happened often enough to keep Revson scurrying from salon to salon. He would sit down at a table and "[pull] out little bottles of liquid. He mixed little globules of color together and watched them closely as they cohered."[44] "Bring me all your complaints," Revson told a salon owner.[45]

If Revson were going to sell not "Dark Red Nail Polish" but rather "Tropic Sky Nail Enamel" and price the product as aggressively as he did, quality had to be unquestionable. He did not turn such an important matter over to a chemist; he handled it himself. Lachman's Dresden Chemical Company could not meet Revson's standards, and he switched suppliers in 1937.[46]

It is difficult to say whether product quality or money was a bigger problem—a greater and very real fear—in the early years. Revlon was a shoestring operation in 1932 and 1933, but even shoestrings cost money. Revson borrowed space from relatives and also labor from them. His mother worked briefly for the fledgling firm. She died in 1933 of a streptococcal infection.[47]

Revson could not borrow money from family members. They did not have any to lend. Banks were not much help. There was no collateral for a loan, and they were not in a risk-taking frame of mind in 1932. The venture capital industry we know today did not exist at the time. In a word, no one was investing in anything. To keep going, Revson turned to loan sharks. "The first year or so," he later said, "we gave the Shylocks plenty of business—we used to pay 2 percent a month to stay alive."[48]

In its first ten months in business, Revlon posted sales of $4,055.09.[49] Annualized, if we assume sales to have been steady throughout the year, this figure becomes $4,866.11. Is this good or bad? The performance was not good enough for Martin Revson to leave his $35-a-week job as a clerk with a Wall Street firm. Revlon was a gamble, and the family wanted one of its members to be making money.[50]

On the other hand, despite everything, Revlon had survived what would be its most difficult year until 1984, well after Charles's death. Many start-up firms did not stay in business for ten months, especially during the Depression.

Revlon sold through salons exclusively until 1935. This means that it probably sold most of its merchandise through beauty supply wholesalers rather than to individual beauty parlor owners. Revson must have learned while working for Elka who the wholesalers were that he needed to see. Perhaps the wholesalers knew him and were already familiar with the product when Revlon was founded.

Four thousand dollars' worth of nail polish probably means that Revson, representing a new firm with a product that was either new or, at best, not really proven, must have made sales to at least three dozen people, perhaps twice that many. In the spring of 1934, Revson sold $400 worth of product directly to the beauty salon in Marshall Field in Chicago. That was the largest single order received up to that time.[51] Orders in 1932 must have been far smaller.

Revson must have made a lot of person-to-person sales calls. What was his hit rate? How many calls did he make per sale? Five? Ten? More? We do not know, but common sense suggests that he must have suffered a lot of rejection trying to sell a new, expensive nail polish in the Depression.

How many bad debts did Revson have to swallow? Tobias writes that "Revlon collected cash on delivery."[52] This cannot have been true for all his business. Indeed, Tobias also recounts an incident in 1933 in which Revson waited "a long time" to speak to Bernard Latz, whose firm, Seligman and Latz, either owned or supplied thirty or forty beauty salons, concerning $48 worth of Revlon Nail Enamel which Seligman and Latz had bought on credit.[53]

There must have been unpaid bills. Large firms have been known not to pay small firms promptly. They have been known not to pay them in full. Or at all. Especially if the product did not perform. Once again we must emphasize that this was the Depression. Revson must have made sales to firms run by honest, well-meaning people who went bankrupt.

If we speculate that Revson made forty sales to wholesalers and perhaps a few large individual salons (such as the Waldorf Astoria, the Plaza, and other big hotels in Manhattan), that meant that there might have been about a hundred outlets where manicurists were applying Revlon Nail Enamel to customers willing to try something new. That means a hundred different shops where something might be going wrong—where a customer might be complaining about yellowing color or where the manicurists did not know the proper way to apply the product. That meant Charles Revson must have been a very busy man.

"The mechanics of the manicurist," an employee of Seligman and Latz in the 1930s told Tobias in the 1970s, "were certainly different then from today. . . . The idea was to have the moon and the tips of the nail white, and the center, red." The woman who explained this also mentioned that "I think they got twenty-five dollars a week then plus a small percentage over a certain level."[54]

This is not a lot of money. Some of these manicurists probably had to support families with their earnings. They therefore must have welcomed gladly any "push money" (which will be discussed later in this chapter) from a supplier. Revlon had no funds to spare for this purpose in 1932. It did two decades later. Fortunately, Revlon's competition had limited funds as well at this time. Indeed, I can think of only one brand of nail polish other than Revlon (that brand is Cutex)[55] which was on the market in 1932 and is still on the market today. Barriers to the entry of new firms in this business were small. So were barriers to exit. Others came and went. Revlon came and stayed. In this context, performance in 1932 was impressive.

The next year sales jumped to $11,246.98. Expenses incurred to achieve these sales were:

Merchandise purchased	$4,792.26
(nail enamel, bottles, caps, brushes, etc.)	
Wages	813.80
Rent	330.00
Miscellaneous	161.29
Trucking and parcel post	345.67
Shipping supplies	71.71
Advertising (in trade journals)	978.32
Telephone	136.88
Traveling and miscellaneous	772.13
TOTAL	$8,402.06

That left $2,844.92 for the three partners to enjoy as profit. Lachman received half, and the two Revson brothers split the other half.[56]

This was not bad, and things got even better fast. In 1935, Martin Revson left his job as a clerk and joined the firm. He could provide some of the sales support for which neither his oldest brother Joseph nor Lachman was suited. Revlon had sales of $68,000 that year, a remarkable rate of increase.[57] In 1938, Charles took home $39,000 in total compensation, close to a tenfold increase over *sales* in 1932. The following year, sales doubled as Revlon introduced its first major new product line, lipstick.[58]

The company did what it did with a flair unique to the industry. It introduced the idea of coordinating the color of lipstick and nail polish with its "Matching Lips and Fingertips" campaign.[59] In the context of this industry, this was breakthrough thinking. It publicized this idea with heavy expenditures for color advertisements placed in high-fashion women's magazines. This may not seem like an earth-shattering idea when considered in the great scheme of the whole economy, but it showed a special creativity and cleverness. The rewards were princely. Sales in 1940 were $2.8 million, a notable increase in less than a decade.

When Revlon got started, it had to solve a host of problems. The company needed a product that performed; it needed money to pay its suppliers; it needed a method of informing the trade and the consumer about the product's putative benefits; and it needed a channel by which to move this product from the laboratory to the factory to the warehouse to the consumer. What requires emphasis is that all these problems had to be solved at once. And they had to be solved in the face of a doubting, sometimes derisive, world. Why do business with Revlon, a name no one had heard of selling a product which was composed primarily of one man's imagination in an industry with a well-earned reputation for being full of fly-by-night operations?

Revson trusted himself. If he could get a foot in the door, he felt he could get the product in the door as well. But which door? Nail polish was retailed through a variety of outlets during the 1930s, including drugstores, department stores, and five-and-ten-cent stores (such as Woolworth), as well as beauty salons.

Revson selected beauty salons, a decision which, in the words of a business journalist, "really launched the company."[60] The manicurist, a Revlon executive reflected later, was "the expert, the professional who decided for the woman what she was going to have." Her recommendation acted as "built-in advertising." Women used Revlon in a beauty salon and then asked for it at a retail outlet. Enough such inquiries would make it a lot easier for Revson to approach a department store buyer and ask for retail space.[61]

Although there is no record of Revson discussing it at the time, we can infer his strategy from his actions. The essence of his approach was to make nail polish part of the world of fashion. He wanted the American woman to think of nail polish as being as important a part of her wardrobe as blouses or shoes or handbags.

If Revson could succeed in making nail polish a fashion item, a whole new range of options would open to him which his competitors could not even consider. First was price. Consumers do not think the same way about price when they are buying fashion goods as opposed to commodities. Consumers will only pay so much for a bottle that contains a mixture of chemicals. But how much will they pay for glamour, for mystery, for sexuality? More.

By transforming nail polish from chemicals to fantasy, Revlon changed the nature of the appeal to buy from the rational to the emotional. Revson detached the selling price from the cost of goods sold. The key to making this change was his imagination and the imagination of a corps of outstanding copywriters and merchandisers whom he hired over the years.

Revlon did not sell merely a product, it sold a story. Beatrice Castle, who worked in advertising for the firm in the 1950s and 1960s, had this to say about a campaign in which she was involved for a color called Persian Melon: "We envisioned a whole scene at the Shah's pool of madam lying down there, and you know that the Shah's just about to come in with a great new emerald necklace for his baby. Now don't you think that Mrs. Middle America is dreaming in her bathtub of such a thing? Of course she is."[62]

From the beginning, Revlon priced aggressively. Dreams are not made in the Woolworths of this world, and there was no thought of selling through those outlets. It was manicurists first. Next were the high-fashion department stores. The first account through which Revlon sold bottled nail enamel at retail (as opposed to selling to manicurists working in department stores) was Saks Fifth Avenue.

The company blew its whole 1935 advertising budget of $335.56 on an advertisement in *The New Yorker* for "Summer Shades in Nail Polish." The summer shades in question were Sun Rose and Chestnut, described as "new exciting exclusive" and "[o]riginated by a New York socialite." The latter claim was as fanciful as the "Shah" with his "emerald necklace." "Ask your manicurist" was the concluding sentence.[63]

This advertisement illustrates the Revlon strategy quite well. The product was special. It was upper-class. But in addition to this appeal to emotions, the reader was invited to satisfy her skepticism as well. She should ask her manicurist, the expert, who had been presold by Charles. Note also that Revlon was introducing two summer shades, not one. The very idea that you needed a summer shade was new.

In a fashion item, price often signifies value. Thus, a high price justifies itself. This advertisement would have made no sense if it announced the product's availability at Woolworth for a dime. Interestingly, it does not mention price at all. "Willing to gamble, or confident that his way was right, Revson set a price of 50 cents for a bottle of nail enamel when his competitors' prices were 10 cents. He introduced Revlon lipstick at one dollar when other lipsticks sold at 49 cents. Advertisers warned Revson that he would never succeed at that price. But he succeeded in raising the price level of all cosmetics."[64]

Revson was an admirer of General Motors. In a way, this is absurd. Two people could hardly have been more different than he and Alfred P. Sloan Jr., nor two companies run more differently than Revlon and General Motors. In a couple of particulars, however, Revson did emulate Sloan. The practices that Sloan adopted which caught Revson's eye were planned obsolescence and a product line offering, rather than a single product, which was aimed, as the saying went, at "every purse and purpose."

The less expensive products came later in Revlon's history. The best example was the remarkable success of "Charlie," a moderately priced fragrance which became the best-selling brand in its category in the world.[65] But in the early years, Revlon entered the market at the top. A lot of the sales price fell straight to the bottom line. Revlon's cost of goods sold was typically about 10 percent of what the consumer spent at the sales counter.[66]

Revlon not only advertised extensively by the late 1930s, it also merchandised through packaging, displays, and tie-ins with the fashion themes of the department stores which carried its products. Revson understood early "how thoroughly he could promote through the women's fashion magazines. He set promotion tie-ups between a magazine, a manufacturer [of women's wear], and key department stores in major American cities. He used every sort of point-of-purchase display in these stores, and dramatic window displays, to show Revlon products 'as seen in the magazines.'"[67]

Planned obsolescence, new products, high prices, "news"— these were all critical components of Revson's approach to the market.[68] A commodity is used until it is used up. Before Revson, a woman might own one bottle of nail polish until it was empty. After Revson, she might own two—for example, both Sun Rose and Chestnut—and throw away whatever spring shades she might previously have been applying long before they were used up. How far can one go down this road? In 1952, Revlon was telling the business press that "it has nearly 5,000 nuances of . . . various reds to choose" in order to capture "the feminine mood for fall."[69] There probably are not many women who own 5,000 shades of nail polish. On the other hand, it is probable that most women who use nail polish today own more than one color. Revson created a market.[70]

In order to service that market, distribution was critical. After joining the company, Martin Revson built a sales force very quickly. By the end of the decade, Revlon was apparently available nationally. In addition to beauty salons, in which it "had a near-monopoly" by 1941,[71] Revlon had opened up drugstore accounts as well as department stores.

The drugstores to which Revlon was willing to sell were characteristically in the better neighborhoods. Revlon played hardball with retailers. It wanted them to sell its products exclusively, or at the very least to favor them in terms of shelf space and display. The company was devoutly committed to fair trade.[72] No customer would believe that Revlon was "like Cadillac," as Charles put it,[73] if its products were shoved into dusty corners with garish "Reduced to 39¢" signs above them.

Some of what went on when a Revlon salesperson visited a retail outlet was not very nice. According to Tobias:

> If a Chen-Yu nail enamel color chart somehow walked out of a store in a salesman's briefcase . . . well, it could always be replaced by a Revlon color chart. If the bottle caps on some Chen-Yu nail enamel were loosened a bit and the enamel hardened . . . well, the store, or the consumer, would know not to buy an inferior brand again. If, in an attempt to secure counter space, a salesman should spread his arms out, accidentally sweeping the competitive product off either end of the counter onto the floor . . . well, the salesmen were authorized to buy up the damaged merchandise at the retailer's cost and replace it with Revlon product.[74]

As Revlon became the hottest name in the industry toward the end of the 1930s and the beginning of the 1940s, the problem of controlling the channels of distribution became more urgent. In the beauty salon trade, Revlon insisted that wholesale suppliers carrying its lines distribute no competing products. The Federal Trade Commission held these agreements to be in violation of the Robinson-Patman Act in 1954, after a five-year battle, and they were terminated. According to a business journalist in 1956, the nullification of these agreements "has not shaken the company's hold on the salons; it estimates today that more than 90 percent of them still use Revlon enamel exclusively, and argues from this fact that the restrictive agreements were never of real importance."[75] Revlon's argument raises the question of why the company violated the antitrust laws if it could have beaten the competition without doing so.

In the drugstores, controlling the product was even more difficult for Revlon. Remember that Revson was selling drama and dreams. Product sloppily displayed, sold in sloppily managed stores, or, worst of all, displayed with prices slashed in order to entice customers into a store, perhaps to be persuaded by the owner to buy something else—such practices struck at the heart of the spell Revson was trying to cast. The solution from Revlon's point of view was carefully monitored selective distribution.

Through the retailer's eyes, on the other hand, Revlon's creation of a high-fashion, high-margin brand presented an opportunity. A retailer with the franchise to carry Revlon products could itself enter the wholesaling business. It could "double wholesale" or "bootleg" Revlon products by overbuying, marking up the excess, and selling to stores with which Revlon refused to deal. The franchised store would turn an immediate profit by selling Revlon at a higher price than it paid. The store which had been unable to purchase Revlon would now have the products, and with them, a chance to satisfy its customers and improve its own image.

Everyone benefited . . . except, of course Revlon, which was fighting not to improve the image of stores on the wrong side of the tracks but rather to benefit from well-heeled establishments. The outcome of bootlegging would be more intensive distribution than Revlon wanted and eventually price competition. The end result would be the cheapening of the brand. The gossamer foundations of Revlon's castle in the air could disappear in a heartbeat.

What to do? There are no court cases, sworn testimony, or convictions to prove it; but there is reason to believe that Revlon coped with this dilemma the old-fashioned way—through muscle. Stories were still circulating in the 1970s about the bad things that happened to retailers who bootlegged on their franchise in the early years of the company. There was talk of "goon squads" who did more than merely purloin color charts or sabotage competitive products, but who physically beat up offending retailers. At the least, threats of such beatings would have been quite in character for the company.[76]

At the end of the 1930s, there was still plenty of skepticism in the investment community about the cosmetics industry. Because of the unavoidably high advertising-to-sales ratio, according to one article, the industry was among the "most economically unsound in the world."

> All told, the cosmetic industry is essentially speculative. While still growing, it is beset by intense competition, a constantly lower scale of prices and high taxation. To top it off, it is subject to the whims of American women and even the highest paid executives in the business have often "missed the boat" in gauging the reception that would be afforded a new product.[77]

Revson wanted to make Revlon less "speculative" by bringing fashion to the fore and maintaining fashion leadership. Unfortunately, fashion intensity has the defects of its virtues. Margins may be high, but fashion is volatile and unpredictable by definition. The successful firm must become a "fashion maker" rather than a "fashion taker." General Motors brought fashion to the automobile industry in the 1920s, but exercised such control over the industry that it reaped the rewards without suffering the setbacks which befell other automobile firms during the Depression. This was another reason for Revson to admire GM. He also wanted to dictate fashion, rather than be dictated to by it.

THE WAR YEARS AND AFTERMATH, 1939–1950

World War II affected every business in the United States, and Revlon was no exception. The macroeconomic situation was transformed almost overnight. Real gross national product rose 93 percent from 1939 to 1944. With skyrocketing output and the dramatic growth of the armed forces, unemployment disappeared.[78] Three million women entered the workforce during this period. Women had worked for money wages in factories since the days of the Lowell, Massachusetts, textile mills in the 1820s, but never had so many women begun to earn good wages in such a brief span of time. If you were in the cosmetics business, this was an important development.

Staffing was affected at all businesses due to wartime demands, and Revlon was no exception. Joseph Revson joined the army; but doubtless a bigger loss was Martin, who enlisted in the army in April of 1943, three months after being elected president of the National Beauty and Barber Association.[79]

Charles remained a civilian. He became a military contractor. Revlon produced first-aid kits, and Revson formed the Vorset Corporation in 1942 for the manufacture of hand grenades for the U.S. Army and dye markers for the U.S. Navy. Both services were well satisfied with the firm, which won an "E" award in July of 1944[80] for its excellent record. Not much is known about Vorset, which is a pity because its successful operation suggests that Revson was a capable manager. The army was not in the market for high-fashion hand grenades, nor did the navy want a choice of five thousand shades of red for its dye markers. This was defense contracting in wartime. The products marketed had to work. Lives were at stake. Vorset received official recognition for getting the job done.

As far as the cosmetics business was concerned, the war posed problems well before Pearl Harbor. As early as December 1939, the industry was complaining of shortages of various oils and packaging materials.[81] After the United States entered the war, things at first looked even worse. Early in 1942, the War Production Board slapped restrictions on the industry.[82] But these were revoked only a few months following their imposition "after some high pressure selling by industry representatives."[83] The argument was that cosmetics were important for the morale of women on the home front.[84]

Cosmetics thus continued to be sold in the United States, as they did in Britain and Germany during the war. In fact, in the United States cosmetics sales increased briskly, from $400 million in 1940 to $659 million in 1945, according to one source.[85] The United

States was alone among the principal warring powers in seeing aggregate consumer spending grow. In real terms, it increased 22 percent from 1938 to 1944, while declining 20 percent in Britain over the same years.[86]

Referring to women working in defense plants or married to newly employed factory workers, Revson noted rather bluntly that "now and for the first time in their lives these suddenly rich women have the money to indulge themselves in beauty products they've heard so much about: the cosmetics their bosses' wives use, the good grooming preparations their rich friends buy."[87]

The fashion industries, speaking generally, were not nearly as vibrant during the war as they were afterward. The War Production Board wanted to conserve fabric and sought to reassure "the women and girls of America that there will be no extremes in dress styles during this war . . . and that their present wardrobes will not be made obsolete by radical fashion changes."[88]

Thus, there were limits to the breadth of the coordination with which any fashion-intensive product could be merchandised. But fashion did not go away in the United States during World War II. Hollywood did not stop making movies, and mindfulness of new films could tip off a shrewd marketer on how to capture the advantages of the free publicity the film generated.

In 1942, for example, MGM released *Mrs. Miniver.* This movie, "MGM's wartime salute to gallant England," was a big hit, winning five Academy Awards.[89] According to Helen Golby, Revlon's advertising and promotion director, who was described in the trade as "a brilliant, highly nervous girl who habitually threatened to resign but continued to project her ideas of color in cosmetics through department stores as they had never been pushed before":[90]

> [W]ithout solicitation from the movie companies, Revlon plucked the rose out of the memorable movie success, "Mrs. Miniver," and created one of the great colors of the year in "Mrs. Miniver Rose" . . . a name that soon saw print fabrics develop, leathers dyed, artificial and real roses develop, and a whole new type of woman emerge in the fashion world based on the unforgettable Mrs. Miniver, and exploited by leading stores all over America.[91]

Six short months after it had begun this $500,000 campaign, Revlon deemphasized the unforgettable Mrs. Miniver and featured a new shade with a new name.[92] Perhaps in this case at least, planned obsolescence was for the best. *Mrs. Miniver* was and remains a terrible movie. Pauline Kael, the nation's leading movie critic, described it as "one of the most scandalously smug of all Academy Award winners" and Greer Garson as "the excruciatingly proper paragon-heroine."[93]

There is plenty of puffery in Golby's account. And no wartime campaign such as "Mrs. Miniver," "Pink Lightning," or "Fatal Apple" was able to marshal such a synchronized, total fashion program as took place after the war. But these promotions do make clear that the War Production Board did not quite get its wish that the world of fashion and planned obsolescence should stop spinning during the war.

In 1946, any inhibitions caused by wartime were obviously in the past; and Revlon attacked the market vigorously. The spring promotion was "Bachelor's Carnation," for "the first Spring that the boys were home from overseas, out of uniform, sporting red carnations in their civvies. . . ." This was good news for florists, who tied in the Revlon campaign with their window displays. In October, it was "Ultra Violet," and once again there was free publicity to accompany it, with the popular young singer Dinah Shore cutting a record of a song entitled "Who'll Buy My Ultra Violets?"[94]

For each of its two promotions a year, Revlon developed a calendar for the launch and even greater skill at publicity and joint marketing arrangements. Often, Revlon would continue to market previous shades as it launched new ones. Thus it increased its variety and clogged the distribution channels. The company was trying to bring a systematic approach to a highly unpredictable business. There remained, however, an irreducible element of guesswork no matter how large the advertising budget and how widespread the publicity. Even Golby acknowledged in 1947 that "in the shade and the name is the great gamble."[95] A decade later, when Revlon was a household word, a *Fortune* journalist could still comment that "any major promotion can turn into a company-wide crisis."[96]

The guessing was Charles's department, and he had to guess right. Revlon was still a fashion taker rather than a fashion maker.

TRIUMPH AND TRAVAIL: THE 1950s

Revlon became a publicly traded company on December 7, 1955; and from that date, for the first time in its history, there are audited financial statements available. The data in public offering documents go back to 1949. Selected statistics are presented in Table 5.1.

TABLE 5.1   Selected Financial Data for Revlon, 1949–1960

	Net sales	Advertising, promotional, selling, and administrative expenses	Net income
Year ended Dec. 31:			
1949	$ 16,929,484	$ 6,511,537	$ 1,132,055
1950	19,147,286	7,188,014	1,417,435
1951	22,392,062	8,896,728	987,273
1952	25,490,613	10,167,805	1,188,365
1953	28,306,898	12,837,548	983,330
1954	33,604,037	15,335,919	1,297,826
1955	51,646,612	22,598,733	3,655,950
1956	85,767,651	34,411,395	8,375,502
1957	93,656,256	N/A	8,999,337
1958	108,762,302	N/A	9,688,307
1959	123,115,147	N/A	10,836,797
1960	134,443,070	N/A	11,321,095

Sources: Years 1949 through 1956 are taken from Reynolds & Co., "Prospectus: 241,020 Shares, Revlon, Inc., Common Stock," April 1, 1957. Years 1957 through 1960 are taken from Revlon, Inc., *Annual Report 1961*, December 31, 1961, pp. 13–14. The years from 1949 through 1956 and from 1957 through 1960 are drawn from different sources and are not strictly comparable. The Revlon *Annual Reports* provide sales of $50,769,530 and $84,302,366 in 1955 and 1956 respectively. These differences with Table 5.1 are slight. The *Annual Reports* and the "Prospectus" provide identical numbers for net income.

Looking at the numbers presented in Table 5.1, it would seem unfair to ask for better performance. But these numbers were delivered at a price. Revlon's dirty little secrets were neither little nor secret by 1960. During these years, Revlon launched the "Fire and Ice" promotion and sponsored *The $64,000 Question* television program. Both deserve our attention.

Fire and Ice

Revlon demanded that its advertising agencies comprehend the company's image; the agencies had to produce Revlon's semi-yearly promotions with their theme, the "Revlon Look." This look centered around an "exotic and expensive" woman, described by an advertising man as one who "only goes out at night and looks at first like a high class tramp, but you know, somehow, that she's really a nice girl."[97] According to a Revlon executive, Revson believed that in every woman there was a little evil, an urge for the wild and dangerous. It was to this putative impulse that he aimed his advertisements.[98]

The most memorable of Revlon's promotions during these years, and one which has made a permanent impression on the cosmetics business, was the Fire and Ice campaign of the fall of 1952. Planning for this campaign began early, right after the new year, with a meeting of what Revlon called its Creative Planning Board. Plans for the spring promotion had just been completed; and even though "Paint the Town Pink," as the spring promotion had been christened, would not be put before the public for another month, the time had come to start thinking about the fall.

The Creative Planning Board convinced itself that the final quarter of 1952 would witness a rebellion against current styles. American women, the board believed, were weary of the girdle and the tiny waist which confined them. The new look in fashion "would be the natural, free-flowing look of the mermaid." Now Revlon had to choose a shade for its lipstick and nail polish which would express this new mood. From the thousands of possibilities which the company claimed were at its disposal, Charles Revson chose "a lush and passionate red, the richest red the company had ever made."[99]

This, at least, was the way Revlon described its new shade to *Business Week* magazine. However, one woman who was closely associated with the Fire and Ice promotion recalled the shade quite differently. Beatrice Castle, Revlon's fashion director, whose job it was, along with Kay Daly of the advertising agency, to dream up a name for the campaign, was not nearly so impressed with the new shade: "We were faced with a nothing color. There was nothing about the color itself which would make a divine name spring to your mind. . . . Here was a red red . . . a medium red red, nothing new about it, nothing exciting about it."

According to Castle, she and Daly would meet at Rubens Delicatessen each morning at 8:30 to discuss possible names. Charles had suggested the name Four Star Red, having in mind the four stars on a general's shoulder. "Well, of all the things you would never do," commented Castle, "it would be that!" Castle and Daly discussed a number of other names such as True Red and Red Is It. In a "last gasp effort," Castle suggested the "corny" title of Fire and Ice: ". . . the two sides of every female which were suggested to me by the new Italian movie stars . . . on the one hand . . . , all woman and involved in a million affairs; and on the other hand, toughest babies who ever lived when it came to money and contracts."

Daly liked the idea and suggested they include a questionnaire in the advertisement. If the reader answered in the affirmative to a number of questions, Fire and Ice was for her. With the help of Martin Revson, the advertisement was further refined. Eventually, fifteen questions were selected, questions which "were answered by every woman in the civilized world. It was like having a cheap analysis."[100]

In addition to the copy, there were two aspects of this magazine advertisement which were of critical importance. First, Revlon had to find a model who would symbolize the Fire and Ice look; second, it had to select suitable clothing and hairstyling for her. Kay Daly chose Dorian Leigh as the model and had a forelock of her black hair streaked to suggest ice. Leigh wore a skin-tight, all-rhinestone, silver halter neck dress especially designed for the advertisement. Over the dress she wore a red cloak, to suggest fire, which matched the color of her lipstick and nail polish.

That is one version of events. Tobias interviewed Kay Daly and writes that her narrative "of the genesis of 'Fire and Ice' differs [from Bea Castle's] only on the essentials."[101] Daly was the vice president and creative director of Norman, Craig, and Kummel, one of the advertising agencies Revlon used in the 1950s. In 1961, she became vice president of creative services at Revlon; for over a decade she was the sole woman among Revlon's corporate officers. She died shortly after Revson.[102] At any rate, Daly said Fire and Ice was her idea and that Castle did not like it and contributed very little to it. The truth will never be known. What is certain is that the campaign was not Charles's idea.[103]

In November of 1952 the Fire and Ice double-page color advertisement at last broke in *Vogue, Ladies' Home Journal, Life, The New Yorker, Glamour,* and other magazines. The left-hand page featured the photograph of Ms. Leigh wearing the costume described above. Across her body, about waist high, was written:

> For you who love to flirt with fire . . .
> who dare to skate upon thin ice . . .

> ## Revlon's "Fire and Ice"

> For lips and matching fingertips. A lush and passionate scarlet . . . like flaming diamonds dancing on the moon!

The right-hand page copy asked:

> ARE YOU MADE FOR "FIRE AND ICE"?

> Try this quiz and see.

> What is the American girl made of? Sugar and spice and everything nice? Not since the days of the Gibson Girl! There's a new American beauty. . . . She's tease and temptress, siren and gamin, dynamic and demure. Men find her slightly, delightfully baffling. Sometimes a little maddening. Yet they admit she's easily the most exciting woman in all the world! She's the 1952 American beauty with a foolproof formula for melting a male! She's the "Fire and Ice" girl. (Are you?)

> Have you ever danced with your shoes off?

Did you ever wish on a new moon?

Do you blush when you find yourself flirting?

When a recipe calls for <u>one</u> dash of bitters, do you think it's better with <u>two</u>?

Do you secretly hope the next man you meet will be a psychiatrist?

Do you sometimes feel that other women resent you?

Have you ever wanted to wear an ankle bracelet?

Do sables excite you, even on other women?

Do you face crowded parties with panic—then wind up having a wonderful time?

Does gypsy music make you sad?

Do you think any man <u>really</u> understands you?

Would you streak your hair with platinum without telling your husband?

If tourist flights were running would you take a trip to Mars?

Do you close your eyes when you're kissed?

Can you honestly answer "yes" to at least eight of these questions? Then you're made for "Fire and Ice"![104]

This advertisement was striking, dramatic, and original. (It was also more than a little odd.) But advertising is only a part of what is involved in selling cosmetics. Fire and Ice indelible cream lipstick, regular lipstick, frosted nail enamel, and improved formula nail enamel were marketed through thousands of franchised drugstores and hundreds of high-fashion department stores across America. Revlon made every effort to see that retailers gave Fire and Ice as much window display space and as much personal selling attention as possible.

In drugstores and in smaller department stores where Revlon did not employ a demonstrator, the company could now afford to pay saleswomen an allowance called push money. In the early 1950s, this practice came into its own. According to Martin Revson, "The purpose of a girl getting paid p.m. money, or pm's as we put it, is to interest her sufficiently in a product so she will want to talk about it to a customer instead of just handing it over."[105] Thus, the saleswoman, whom the ordinary customer believed to be working for the store, was working for Revlon as well and would make an extra effort to move Revlon merchandise. Cosmetics customers often asked saleswomen, "What's new?"[106] Influenced by push money, the saleswoman would very likely reply, "Fire and Ice." Revlon was by no means the only cosmetics company to pay p.m.'s, but the company was said to have used this tool more extensively and expertly than the competition.[107] During the Fire and Ice campaign, the company was paying more money to more saleswomen than any competitor. In the fall of 1952, commented *Business Week*, "Push money was being paid to salesgirls everywhere. . . ."[108]

In the summer of 1952, Revlon sent representatives to department stores around the country to suggest Fire and Ice as a theme to sell products throughout the store, especially in the women's apparel departments. Between three hundred and five hundred department stores responded enthusiastically to the idea. In the windows of Pogue's in Cincinnati, for example, "sequins, spangles, embroidery, beads, gleaming satin in both flaming and frosty colors and rhinestone jewelry . . . combined to give their own rendition of the 'Fire and Ice' theme." Inside the store:

> Tie-in displays of ready-to-wear with spot setups of the new lipstick and enamel reached through the store's Third Floor of Fashions, the Rose Room, Junior Shop, Moderate Priced Dresses, Lingerie, Sportswear, and Millinery. Spot displays featuring Revlon were also shown in the accessories departments—Hosiery, Handbags, Jewelry, Gloves, Shoes, Belts, and Sweaters. Twenty-six elevator and escalator landing signs and elevator interior signs were used.[109]

In addition to its own advertising and cooperative advertisements with the store, Revlon received free publicity for Fire and Ice from Cincinnati's news media. A *Cincinnati Enquirer* columnist wrote a humorous description of the promotion at Pogue's, and local radio and television commentators and a local hotel-circulated weekly magazine gave it plentiful attention.

The perspective of half a century makes it, if anything, more difficult to decode what was really going on with a promotion like Fire and Ice. What did it mean to have a "Creative Planning Board" in January of 1952 guess what "the mood of the American woman" would be the following fall? What did it mean for Revlon to "select a shade" which "expressed that mood"? Would it really have mattered if a different shade had been chosen? Recall that when Beatrice Castle first saw the color selected from the supposed five thousand possibilities, she was underwhelmed—"a red red . . . a medium red red, nothing new about it, nothing exciting about it."[110]

One wants to conclude that the color meant nothing—that with its experience, connections, market power, push money, and advertising, Revlon could have matched lips and fingertips in bright green. A fashion maker rather than a fashion taker at last. One's common sense rebels at the notion that a group of businesspeople cloistered in a Manhattan office building in January 1952 could guess what "fashion's color" would be in November.

A lot happened between January and November of 1952. President Truman seized the steel mills in April to avoid a strike, but the owners regained control not long thereafter when the seizure was ruled unconstitutional. In July, the Republicans nominated Dwight D. Eisenhower for the presidency. Eisenhower had defeated Robert A. Taft, a U.S. senator from Ohio and a native of the "Queen City of the West" (i.e., Cincinnati). Was the mood of anybody shopping at Pogue's affected by this unpredictable turn of events? On November 4, Eisenhower was elected president, the first Republican to win the White House since Herbert Hoover in 1928. Did that affect anybody's mood?

Internationally, the United States was mired in the stalemate of the Korean War. On the battlefield, red meant not fashion but blood. Politically, red meant Communist; and 1952 was the height of the paranoia generated by Senator Joseph R. McCarthy. In no published account and in no interview concerning the planning and execution of Fire and Ice have I encountered any mention of these developments.

Then there is the advertisement itself. The model, Dorian Leigh, looks (to me, anyway) like a creature from outer space, perhaps the offspring of an extraterrestrial and a vampire. She brings to mind the lyrics of "Hard-Hearted Hannah—The Vamp of Savannah. She'd pour water on a drowning man."[111]

Kathy Peiss, a historian of cosmetics, has written: "Strikingly, Fire and Ice portrayed a moment of pure glamour, featuring . . . a model 'totally floating in space . . . in a complete world of her own.' There was no heterosexual encounter here, no romantic scene, just a self-absorbed—or self-sufficient woman." Peiss emphasizes the persona of "'Tough' but 'all woman'" suggested by the advertisement. There was a remarkably inward, asocial quality to this presentation, a weirdly perverse suggestion of what was to become feminism in the 1970s.[112] Is this really what "Mrs. Middle America" was "dreaming about in her bathtub"?

Facing this melodramatic photograph, what do we encounter but a test. A quiz. Yet another form to fill out. It is hard to imagine anything more prosaic. The net effect is disorienting. On the other hand, it should be acknowledged that it is always difficult to evaluate fairly yesterday's fashions.[113] In the summer of 1999, beauty salon operators were saying that the hot nail polish was OPI. When asked why, they said: "They've got the colors."[114]

There is something to it when it comes to choosing the right color in fashion merchandising. Whatever that something might be, more than one successful executive has suggested that it is beyond analysis. Kay Daly asked: "Can you afford . . . to put all those horn-rimmed, crew-cut, method-trained young men from the Harvard School of Business into positions of authority in a business which is more madness than method? . . . Wherever we find this type *showing* up we find our business *slowing* up."[115]

For all the hype about Fire and Ice, the numbers Revlon reported do not indicate dramatically improved performance. To be sure, sales increased in 1952 (recall that the Fire and Ice promotion broke in November of that year) and in 1953. However, the increases were not extraordinary compared to previous performance, as Table 5.2 illustrates.

The modest but respectable birthplace of Andrew Carnegie in Dunfermline, Scotland. The family would take a giant step down from this, to Slabtown, before beginning its upward climb. (*Photo courtesy of Corbis/Bettmann Archive ©*)

The kind of place you wouldn't be ashamed to bring a friend. Skibo Castle, Carnegie's summer home in the Scottish Highlands. Fully modernized, it functions today as a club and a retreat for the wealthy. Rock star, actress, and oddity Madonna was married at Skibo on December 22, 2000. One doubts she and Carnegie would have gotten along well. (*Photo courtesy of Carnegie Library of Pittsburgh*)

Photography before George Eastman. (*Photo courtesy of George Eastman House*)

Photography after George Eastman. (*Photo courtesy of George Eastman House*)

Nineteen thirty-one, a year before his death, Eastman (second from left) is the guest of honor at the annual banquet of the Society of the Genesee. The toastmaster and host for the evening: Thomas J. Watson Sr. (third from left), also a native of upstate New York. (*Photo courtesy of George Eastman House*)

Assembling a Model T.
Highland Park, Michigan.
Birthplace of the moving
assembly line. This is the
engine drop at the Highland
Park plant in the autumn of
1913. (*Photo courtesy of
Corbis/Bettmann Archive* ©)

Henry Ford with his
son Edsel driving the
15 millionth Model T
off the assembly line.
Ford's posture says it
all. He knows the
Model T is doomed.
(*From the Collections
of Henry Ford
Museum &
Greenfield Village*)

A blot that will never be
erased . . . never fade. Henry
Ford accepting the Grand
Cross of the German Eagle,
the highest "honor" the
Third Reich bestowed on
foreigners. Ford certainly
earned the award because of
his anti-Semitism. July 31,
1938. Detroit, Michigan.
(*Photo courtesy of
Corbis/Bettmann Archive* ©)

The most famous photograph of Watson, with his message emblazoned above him. (*Photo courtesy of Hulton Getty/Archive Photos*)

Watson doing what he did best—motivating the sales force. Here he is personally congratulating each member of the 100% Club—those salespeople who met or beat their quota for the previous year. (*Photo courtesy of IBM*)

Watson with a man he did not need to motivate—Dwight D. Eisenhower. Watson played a key role in securing for Eisenhower the presidency of Columbia University, a position he held between the armed forces and the presidency of the United States. (*Photo courtesy of Corbis/Bettmann Archive ©*)

Passing the baton. May of 1956, Tom Watson Sr. turns the reins of IBM over to his son, Tom Jr. The next month, Watson Sr. died. (*Photo courtesy of Corbis/Bettmann Archive ©*)

Projecting the "Revlon look" was glamorous Suzy Parker, Dorian Leigh's sister. Here are Parker and Revson together. (*Photo courtesy of Leonard McCombe/Timepix*)

Charles Revson with lipstick on his left hand. Suzy Parker with nail polish on her left hand. Next to her is Martin Revson. At the rear is advertising director George Abrams. To his right, Beatrice Castle of Fire and Ice. (*Photo courtesy of Leonard McCombe/Timepix*)

A Ben Franklin store not unlike the one in Newport, Arkansas, where Samuel Moore Walton got his start in the retail trade in 1945. His ambition: to become the best variety-store merchant in the state. (*Photo courtesy of Corbis/Joseph Sohm* ©)

One of the nation's richest men making a spectacle of himself because he lost a bet. Sam Walton doing the hula on Wall Street on March 15, 1984, because his company's achievements deserved unorthodox recognition. (*Photo courtesy of John McGrail/Timepix*)

The "Traitorous Eight" at Fairchild Semiconductor (surprisingly formally dressed). They have a lot to smile about. They are rich, getting richer, and doing work they love. Noyce is front and center. Third from the right: Gordon Moore. (*Photo courtesy of Intel*)

A magic moment. November 1, 1956. William Shockley, having just learned he has won the Nobel Prize in physics, hosts a champagne breakfast for some of the staff of Shockley Semiconductor at Dinah's Shack on El Camino Real in Palo Alto. Shockley is seated at the head of the table. His golden boy, Robert Noyce, is standing behind and to the left of Shockley (as you view the photo). In his right hand is a glass raised for a toast. (*Photo courtesy of Intel*)

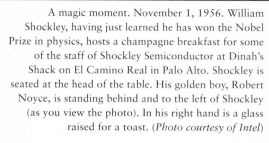

Bob Noyce at Fairchild with artifacts from his profession. (*Photo courtesy of Ted Streshinsky/Timepix*)

TABLE 5.2 Increases in Sales and Earnings for Revlon, 1950–1960

	Change in sales	Change in earnings
1950	$ 2,217,802	$ 285,380
1951	3,244,776	(430,162)
1952	3,098,551	201,092
1953	2,816,285	(205,035)
1954	5,297,139	314,496
1955	18,042,575	2,358,124
1956	34,121,039	4,719,552
1957	7,888,605	623,835
1958	15,106,046	688,970
1959	14,352,845	1,148,490
1960	11,327,923	484,298

Source: Calculated from Table 5.1.

As Table 5.1 shows, Revlon's advertising, promotional, selling, and administrative expenses increased almost 15 percent from 1951 to 1952 and over 25 percent from 1952 to 1953. The push money and other expenses took a bite out of the income statement.

Revlon's sales increased steadily from 1949 through 1954. The compound annual growth rate in sales during those years was a vigorous 14.7 percent, with the result that in five years sales almost doubled. But the year-to-year changes for 1952 and 1953, the Fire and Ice years, were not out of line with the trend. Indeed, the dollar sales increase in 1953 was lower than in 1952; and in 1952 it was lower than in 1951. So despite all the noise, the results in terms of sales and profits must have been disappointing.

To see the effect of a real blockbuster advertising and promotion effort, one need merely look at the sales increases in 1955 and 1956. They were 54 percent and 66 percent respectively, while earnings jumped 182 percent and 129 percent. This was internal growth, not the result of acquisitions. Revlon's compound annual growth rate from 1954 through 1959 was 29.7 percent in sales and 52.9 percent in earnings.[116] The sales growth came on a higher base than the years from 1949 through 1954. As for earnings, they had been going nowhere. In 1954, they were below what they had been in 1950. But by 1956, Revlon had become one of the nation's largest companies.[117]

There can be no more dramatic demonstration of what television advertising could do for a consumer products company in the 1950s than the numbers just cited. On June 7, 1955, *The $64,000 Question* made its debut on the CBS Television Network. Revlon was the sponsor, and Revlon's sponsorship put it on the map of corporate America.

Charles Revson grew up in a marketing-driven industry, the ultimate expression of which was the full-color glossy layout in the high-fashion woman's magazine. It was the color and the model that piqued interest, established image, and sold product. Dorian Leigh as "Hard-Hearted Hannah" in an androgynous "moment of pure glamour," "totally floating in space," was the quintessence of the kind of advertising Revson had been immersed in for more than two decades. With Fire and Ice, he had mastered cosmetics advertising and the promotional programs that bolstered it. The Fire and Ice campaign was a symphony. Revson was the composer. Revlon as a company was the conductor. They were the best.

Then, all of a sudden, a new technology came on the scene which was to change all the rules not only in cosmetics but in the environment of all consumer product marketing from the most inexpensive of products to automobiles.

This new technology was television. Just after Revson won the old game played under the old rules, the rules changed because of developments external to the firm and to the industry. This was more than a "disruption"; it was an earthquake. The one constant law of business—adapt or die—was being enforced with a vengeance at this crucial moment.

For all the impact that Fire and Ice undoubtedly had in the trade, for the contribution it made toward establishing Revlon as an industry leader, and for all the money it made for the company, it is hard to make the case looking at the numbers in Table 5.1 that it changed the world. Looking at the numbers following the embrace of television, it is easy to make that case. Fire and Ice was "normal science"; *The $64,000 Question* was a new "paradigm."[118] Writing in 1967, John Kenneth Galbraith asserted, "The industrial system is profoundly dependent on commercial television and could not exist in its present form without it.[119] The Revlon story supports his view.

How did Revson negotiate such a fundamental change in an industry as unstable as cosmetics? He was winning at the old game. How would he, at the age of fifty, adapt rather than die when a pillar of his business—advertising—was fundamentally transformed?

The $64,000 Question

Charles Revson was, as we have seen, touted from the beginning as Revlon's "color genius." The company was said to have at its disposal thousands of shades of red, along with the capability to construct stories with appropriate labels based on each one. Color that could shock, color that could soothe, color that could speak was the essence of what was being sold. The perfect medium for this man and his message was the high-fashion woman's magazine, with its sumptuous, lush, glossy, multicolored pages all designed to be suggestive. Without color, the Fire and Ice advertisement would have been a nonevent.

Television was a very different medium from these magazines. First and most important, television was transmitted in black and white, not in color, during the 1950s. Second, the content of broadcasts, including commercials, was regulated by the Federal Communications Commission (FCC). Third, and at least as important as potential regulatory action, no one knew how people would react to a device such as the television, which brought not only sound (as, of course, the radio had been doing for decades) but live images directly into the living room of the person who owned it.

Radio was commercialized after World War I and television after World War II. From the point of view of the business world in general, the two media shared a number of features. They both brought the spoken word right into the home. Anyone who owned a receiver could hear the spoken word free of charge. The whole nation could listen to the same thing at the same time.

Printed communications could be read and re-read. They could be easily stored for future reference. Because print could be delivered in color, it could appeal dramatically to the eye (as radio could not) and could represent reality in a way that television could not until the mid-1960s.

Nevertheless, first radio and then television were immediately world-transforming. They were intimate. They were democratic in that they required no education on the part of the listener. They were accessible to the illiterate. They were accessible to children. They were truly mass media. Radio and television were real time, and they were exciting.

There were, it should also be said, important historical differences between radio and television. Radio came first; and many of the issues which would have agitated the world of television in the 1940s and 1950s were settled in the radio arena in the 1920s and 1930s. The basic pattern of public regulation of private use of public airwaves, for example, was established with the creation of the Federal Communications Commission by the Communications Act of 1934.[120]

The central profit model for broadcasting was also established during the radio regime; and as with federal regulation, this was no small matter. Radio was not invented by or for the business world. Guglielmo Marconi invented wireless telegraphy on his family's estate in Italy in 1895 for reasons which were personal and unique. It did not take long for governments and armies and navies around the world to grasp what wireless meant to them.[121]

Businesspeople were slow to follow. Everyone knew that radio was unprecedented; everyone knew that it was big; everyone knew that it was here to stay. The world had changed and would not change back. Things would never be the same. In these ways, radio was like the Internet a century later.

What no one knew was how best to use radio to make money, another similarity to the Internet. Would communication be point to point, as in a telephone call or telegraph message, or point to mass? If it were point to mass, would the mass be families in private homes or groups gathered in public places? What, precisely, would be communicated by this new communications system? Where was the value in the value chain? Was radio going to be about content or conduit? How much money was to be made by obtaining a license to operate a station? Should stations be linked in a network? How much money was to be made from the manufacture of radio receivers? How should receivers be priced? Looking back at the post–World War I era, General Electric researcher William C. White confessed to being "amazed at our blindness . . . we had everything except the idea."[122] Someday, perhaps in the not distant future, an engineer or operations researcher trying to commercialize interactive home shopping for grocery retailing will be speaking words similar to these.

One answer to the conundrum of commercialization which seemed to be ruled out early in radio's development was the broadcasting of paid advertisements. Herbert Hoover stated at the Washington Radio Conference in 1922 that "it is inconceivable that we should allow so great a possibility for service to be drowned in advertising chatter."[123] This declaration is noteworthy for a number of reasons. Our image of Hoover is clouded by his failed presidency during the Great Depression, but in 1922 he was probably the most prestigious public figure in the nation. A self-made millionaire, his humanitarian work during World War I, especially in providing food relief for Belgium, was extraordinarily efficient and universally admired. He participated in the Versailles Peace Conference, after which John Maynard Keynes wrote that he "was the only man who emerged from the ordeal of Paris with an enhanced reputation."[124]

Moreover, Hoover was secretary of commerce in 1922, a post he held from 1921 until he ran for the presidency in 1928. Unclear and untested though it was, what federal regulatory power which existed over radio was established by the Radio Act of 1912 and resided in Hoover's office.[125] This man's words had weight.[126] Erik Barnouw's authoritative histories of broadcasting are studded with expressions of incredulity about the possibility of paid advertising as the key to radio's financial and social future. It would be "positively offensive to great numbers of people," according to one publication.[127]

Radio stations and licenses were valueless unless radios were in the hands of the mass buying public. They were purchased with speed that very few people—RCA's David Sarnoff was among the exceptions—predicted. Annual expenditures on radios grew by more than an order of magnitude—from $60 million to $840 million—between 1922 and 1929.[128] Sixty thousand American households had a radio in 1922. Seven years later, 10.25 million households had one.[129]

With radios in everyone's homes, ideas about how to sell products to all those listeners were percolating through the business world. The solution came when advertising pioneer Albert D. Lasker placed "reason why," "unique selling proposition," hard-sell advertising for Pepsodent toothpaste on the air to sponsor the radio serial *Amos 'n' Andy.* By 1929, when Lasker purchased this property for Pepsodent, it was being beamed over the air not by a single station but by the newly formed (as of 1926) radio network of the National Broadcasting Company (NBC), a wholly owned subsidiary of the Radio Corporation of America. Within weeks, sales tripled. These results answered a lot of questions about the future of radio.[130]

Television's growth was stunted by World War II; but when the war ended, things changed. Television became the center of national attention with fantastic speed. Eight thousand American households owned television sets in 1946. In 1956, about 35 million did.[131] There was never any doubt that television would be commercial, as it was not in many other countries.[132]

It takes a leap of imagination for the modern television viewer to appreciate the impact of a TV commercial in the mid-1950s. In those days, there were no remote-control devices. Therefore, if you watched television, you watched commercials unless you got out of your chair. You could not push a button to turn the set off or to mute the sound. Nor could you channel surf. Even if you did turn the channels, there was not much else on the air other than what you were watching. Only the nation's largest metropolitan areas had more than three channels. Many cities had one or two.

The commercials you saw were not like those broadcast today. They were usually live, not prerecorded. They lasted not ten seconds but as long as two minutes or even more. The advertiser sometimes had its name on the show. On *Coke Time,* for example, the show's star, Eddie Fisher, sang a song that included Coca-Cola slogans. The whole program was not much more than an advertisement.

These commercials had enormous authority. They seemed so real. It was unthinkable that someone would send a message into your own living room that was untrue. The nation had recently emerged from World War II—the good war, the just war. It was fighting another equally good and just war in the 1950s, although this one was "cold" rather than "hot." This was an innocent, pre-Vietnam, pre-Watergate, pre-Clinton era. The president was a heroic war leader. "Play hard, have fun doing it, and despise wickedness," was what Eisenhower told the American people.[133] They believed him, and they believed in him.

They also believed television, about which they were sadly naive. Television was manipulated in ways they could not begin to guess. As had been the case with radio, it was customary for the sponsor not only to pay the bills but to exercise a veto over program content. Cigarettes, for example, were to be "smoked gracefully, never puffed nervously" on *Man Against Crime,* a drama series sponsored by R. J. Reynolds's Camel cigarettes. Writers were informed not to "have the heavy or any disreputable person smoking a cigarette. Do not associate the smoking of cigarettes with undesirable scenes or situations plot-wise." Arson was not one of the crimes man was against on *Man Against Crime,* because it might remind viewers of fires caused by cigarettes. It went further. There was to be no coughing on this program.[134]

Reynolds was equally strict with news. On its *Camel News Caravan* with John Cameron Swayze, no newsworthy figure could be filmed smoking a cigar with the exception of Winston Churchill. No shots of "No Smoking" signs were permitted.[135]

Television could enhance a corporation's reputation as well as sell consumer goods. For United States Steel and Alcoa, television spelled public relations benefits. For Coca-Cola and Procter & Gamble, it meant sales. The true magic of television was dramatized by what it could do for previously unknown products. Hazel Bishop sold $50,000 worth of lipstick in 1950. In 1952, thanks to television advertising, its sales hit $4.5 million.[136]

Results like this caught the attention of the cosmetics industry. No one was more vigorous in the pursuit of the right program for his product than Charles Revson. In 1955, he found it. Thus our story returns to June 7 of that year, when *The $64,000 Question* made its debut on the CBS television network.

There was nothing new about the idea behind this program.[137] Since the mid-1930s, radio had been exploiting the American passion for facts with contests and games. For years, small amounts of cash or manufacturer-donated merchandise had been given away through various formats. What was new about *Question* was the size of the purse. The giveaway had taken a "quantum jump"; losers received a Cadillac as a consolation prize.[138]

Question's format was simple. The producers selected a contestant who chose a subject about which he or she answered increasingly difficult questions which were assigned monetary values ranging from \$64 to \$64,000. Contestants could quit without attempting the succeeding plateau, but if they chose to continue and missed, they forfeited their winnings and were left with only their Cadillac.

By a few deft touches, the producers heightened the aura of authenticity and tension. The questions used were deposited in a vault of the Manufacturers Trust Company and brought to the studio by a bank officer flanked by two armed guards. As the stakes increased, the contestant entered a glass-enclosed "isolation booth" onstage to the accompaniment of "ominous music which hinted at imminent disaster"[139] in order to prevent coaching from the audience. Since the contestant returned week after week rather than answering all the questions on one broadcast, the audience was given time to contemplate whether he or she would keep his or her winnings or go on to the next plateau, and also a chance to worry about how difficult the next question might be.

The \$64,000 Question offered the largest amount of cash ever awarded by a radio or television show up to that time.[140] A contestant, who had been selected from thousands of applicants for the amount of factual material he or she knew in a certain subject area, was asked questions by the show's master of ceremonies. Although the public was aware that contestants were intensively screened, the nature of this screening process was not made clear. The show's producers led the public to believe that the questions used were prepared by a professor at Northwestern University and that their secrecy was closely guarded.

The program became an immediate hit. In September, an estimated 55 million people, over twice as many as had seen Richard Nixon's famed Checkers speech, viewing 84.8 percent of the television sets in operation at the time, saw Richard S. McCutchen, a twenty-eight-year-old marine captain whose category of expertise was gourmet foods, become the first grand prize winner.[141]

Most early contestants were seemingly average folks who harbored hidden knowledge of a subject far removed from their workaday lives. Thus McCutchen was asked about haute cuisine rather than amphibious assault. This separation was no accident.[142] Its purpose was not only to increase the novelty of the show by providing something odd to the point of being freakish, but also to integrate the viewer more intimately into the video melodrama. Everyone who had ever accumulated a store of disconnected, useless information could fantasize about transforming it into a pot of gold.

In a few months, *Question* had created a large new "consumption community," historian Daniel Boorstin's label for the nonideological, democratic, vague, and rapidly shifting groupings which characterized twentieth-century American society. Suddenly, a large fraction of the country had a common bond about which total strangers could converse. Paradoxically, in order to belong to this community, the individual had to isolate him or herself physically from others. Families stayed at home to watch the show, rather than celebrating it in the company of a large crowd.[143] Movie theaters reported a precipitous decline in business, and stores and streets were empty when it came on the air.

Everyone whose life was touched by the show seemed to prosper. In addition to their prize money, some contestants received alluring offers to do public relations work for large companies or to star in movies. *Question*'s creator, an independent program packager named Louis Cowan, became president of CBS-TV, an indication of how pleased the network executives were to broadcast so successful a property. Even the banker who brought the sealed questions from the vault found himself promoted to a vice presidency. But the greatest beneficiary was the sponsor.

In March 1955, the show was purchased by Revlon, and soon after *Question*'s debut in June, the company began reaping the rewards of well-constructed advertising on a popular television program. At the end of 1955, Revlon went public.[144]

Question's greatest liability was its own success; it spawned imitators around the world. In the United States, a spate of programs featuring endless variations of gift giving for answering questions further retarded "TV's already enfeebled yearning to leaven commercialism with culture."[145] Most of these have mercifully been consigned to oblivion, but one rivaled *The $64,000 Question* in its impact on the nation.

That program, *21*, was developed by another firm of independent program producers, Barry and Enright. The format was different, especially in having two contestants compete against each other with no limit on their winnings; but the basic idea was the same. Questions were given point values, and the points were worth money. Once again, the "wiles of a riverboat gambler" were combined with the memory of sundry bits of information which was passed off as intellectual acumen, with the result a spectacularly profitable show.

Barry and Enright leased *21* to Pharmaceuticals, Incorporated,[146] and it first appeared on NBC on October 12, 1956. Pharmaceuticals, whose most well known product was Geritol, soon had good reason to be pleased with its quiz show. *21* did not quite attain the ratings of *Question,* but it competed successfully against *I Love Lucy,* one of the most popular programs in television history, and attracted much notice. Although Pharmaceuticals' advertising director was reluctant to give it complete credit for the increased sales of Geritol, it could hardly have hurt. Sales in 1957 bettered the previous year's mark by one-third.[147]

Unlike *Question, 21* did not shun the highly educated; and one of its contestants became a symbol to the nation of the profitability of intellectual achievement. Charles Van Doren provided evidence that an intellectual could be handsome, that he could get rich, and that he could be a superstar. Like a football player, the intellectual athlete could win fame and wealth.

Van Doren's family could lay genuine claim to membership in an American aristocracy of letters. Descended from seventeenth-century Dutch immigrants, Van Doren's uncle Carl was a literary critic whose biography of Benjamin Franklin won a Pulitzer Prize in 1939.[148] His father, Mark, won the 1940 Pulitzer Prize for poetry,[149] and he was equally famous for his accomplishments in the classroom as a professor of English at Columbia. The wives of the Van Doren brothers were also literary, rounding out a remarkably cultivated quartet. Van Doren's family divided its time between a country estate in Connecticut and a Greenwich Village town house, where guests over the years included Sinclair Lewis, Mortimer Adler, Joseph Wood Krutch, and Morris Ernst. The family was a symbol of intellectual vitality.[150]

The most remembered of the quiz shows from the 1950s is *The $64,000 Question.* The most remembered of the contestants is Charles Van Doren (who, like so many others, was eventually exposed).[151] At this writing, some people still think that Van Doren appeared on *Question,* though he never did.

The greatest coup in Revlon's history was its sponsorship of *The $64,000 Question* and *The $64,000 Challenge* television programs. The company sponsored *Question* from June 1955 to November

1958 and *Challenge* (a spin-off from *Question*) from October 1955 to September 1958; and sales and earnings skyrocketed.[152] During the height of its popularity *Question* was watched by more Americans than any other program in television history up to that time.

Precisely how much Revlon's sales increases were due to *Question* is difficult to determine. During the years it sponsored the program, Revlon continued its promotions, hired the most talented people in the cosmetics industry, and introduced many new products. Yet there can be little doubt that *Question* and its companion *Challenge,* but especially the former, must be given most of the credit for the company's remarkable growth during these years.[153]

In March 1955, *Question* had been offered to and rejected by other prospective sponsors before Revson purchased it. When the show premiered, he was angry with his advertising agency for recommending what he was sure would prove an expensive failure.[154] The *New York Times* agreed with him: "Hal March is the quizmaster on the show. On the stage there was also a bank official who drew questions from a safety deposit box. He was flanked by two armed guards. They didn't get Cadillacs [as did the show's contestants] and they looked pretty grim about the whole outlandish business."[155]

Revson may have been pessimistic about *Question* after its premiere, but he did approve the purchase of the program nevertheless. *Question* became popular beyond anyone's predictions. Even the president of Hazel Bishop admitted that it "unexpectedly captured the imagination of the American public."[156] The program succeeded, according to one view, because it was real, dramatic, unpredictable, and appealed to the intelligence of the viewers; it "reached people intimately, directly, and warmly."[157]

George F. Abrams, Revlon's vice president for advertising, used only superlatives in describing what *Question* did for the company:

> It is doing a most fantastic sales job. It certainly is the most amazing sales success in the history of the cosmetics industry. There isn't a single Revlon item that hasn't benefited. . . . It has been of tremendous merchandising value at the retail level. The show has been a door-opener for our salesmen. Retail accounts that originally were tough are now easy. And picking up new retail outlets is no problem. Our big problem today is handling complaints about back orders. Several

department stores have used special window displays with $64,000 in cash as the center of attention. [One] store built a whole day's promotion around the program[158]

The company claimed that some Revlon products posted sales increases of up to 500 percent after being advertised on *Question*.[159] One Revlon lipstick shade, Love That Pink, sold out across the country as a result of the show. *Question*, believed *Barron's*, was also at least partially responsible for the increased sales of some of Revlon's competitors because it "was making women more conscious than ever of their appearance and drawing them to cosmetics counters like a magnet, to the benefit of all the producing firms."[160]

Question was indeed a display of the awesome ability of television advertising to sell merchandise. Each week the nation watched an actress named Barbara Britton sell Revlon products. "If women believe in her [Britton], it's only because she's real," *Printers' Ink* magazine reported. "She neither sells nor acts before those who see her. She chats." Revlon's *Question* advertising placed the company "in the vanguard of commercial development which combined a personality spokesman with glamour in persuasive product demonstrations." In the opinion of *Printers' Ink*, Britton, despite her beauty, was accepted rather than resented by the women who watched her low-pressure selling approach. Her seemingly natural reality before the camera was not, however, achieved without considerable exertion on the part of Revlon and its agencies. They managed every aspect of her appearance and demeanor with great care.[161]

One of the puzzling aspects of the *Question* story is the stark contrast between the Revlon of *Question* and the Revlon of Fire and Ice. Same company. Same product. Totally different image. Fire and Ice model Dorian Leigh certainly did not "sell by being herself." (There was never anyone quite like the person portrayed in that advertisement.) Nor did she "chat." There was nothing of the "vamp," on the other hand, about Barbara Britton. She was positioned as the sweet, unthreatening next-door neighbor. There was nothing androgynous about her. Revlon had migrated from the vamp to Betty Crocker.

To watch *Question* today is to see a program which seems achingly boring. The advertisements are plain vanilla. No wonder that when Revson first saw the program he was sure it was a loser. According to a partner in the advertising agency who sold him the show, Revson thought it "was a long way from cosmetics and wasn't conducive to the emotional aura and surroundings in which he'd like to see his products."[162]

Revson could not have been more right. The *Question* program and advertisements were a far cry from what he had spent his life creating. But the sales spoke for themselves, and he was quickly won over.

When Revlon bought *Question,* it was apparently an honest program.[163] After approximately six weeks, a new firm began to produce the show; and this firm controlled questions and contestants in a way unbeknownst to the public. The executives of this firm, Entertainment Productions, Incorporated (EPI), sought not only to secure interesting and colorful contestants; they sought to keep these contestants on the program as long as possible and to eliminate those in whom the public did not take an interest. To achieve this objective, Merton Koplin, an executive with EPI who produced *Question* for two years and *Challenge* for nine months, would visit each prospective contestant and have an extensive discussion of his or her field of knowledge. From this discussion, Koplin would gain an idea of what the contestants knew and thus could often keep them on the show or get them off by asking the appropriate question. Sometimes a contestant knew either more or less than Koplin suspected; as a result, his system of control was, he estimated, only 80 percent effective.[164] "It was not a matter of coming in and saying here are the questions, here are the answers," Koplin stated. "The questions at enormous effort were created out of the matrix of the contestant's existence." Koplin's methods were supposedly so subtle that some contestants themselves were, it is said, unaware of what was happening.[165]

Each week the producers met with George Abrams and Martin Revson of Revlon and representatives of Revlon's advertising agency to discuss *Question.* The precise nature of these meetings was a topic of sharp disagreement among the witnesses who testified before the House subcommittee which investigated the quiz shows.

According to George Abrams, who was vice president for advertising for Revlon at the time of the premiere of *Question,*

The primary purpose of these meetings was to discuss methods of keeping the ratings high, or raising them. Charts were maintained which showed the contestants then on the program and the "audience draw" while they were appearing. At these meetings we would discuss with the producers and the advertising agency whether individual contestants were interesting personalities, or dull and unexciting, and what publicity appeal they had as indicated by the current newspaper clippings. If a contestant was interesting, it was generally the consensus of opinion that he remain on the show. If he was dull, we would suggest to the producer that it would be desirable that the contestant not continue in the future.[166]

We understood that the technique for controlling the destiny of a contestant was to ask questions ranging from tough to easy, based on the producer's knowledge of the expertness of the contestant in certain areas within his chosen category as determined in their screening operation. If a contestant or match did not come out as we had suggested, the sponsor and agency representatives would be upset and express displeasure—often in a very heated fashion. . . .

The producers carried out the sponsor's wishes most of the time.[167]

Steve Carlin (Merton Koplin's boss at EPI) spoke of these weekly meetings without much nostalgia in his subcommittee testimony.

Q: Would you say that it would have been hard if not impossible, to say "No" to a suggestion made by Revlon, the sponsor?

Carlin: There is a tradition in television . . . of trying to please the client. If you have a client whom you see once in thirteen weeks,[168] pleasing him becomes a relatively simple matter. But if you have a client whom you see each week, a very persuasive client, pleasing him becomes far more difficult. You have to please him every week, not every thirteen weeks. We were willing to please the client.[169]

Revlon pressured Carlin in a way that the co-sponsor of *Challenge*, cigarette maker P. Lorillard and Son, did not. In 1959, Carlin admitted that "we were foolishly nervous" about the possibility of Revlon's termination of its sponsorship because *Question*'s popularity would have made it easily marketable to other sponsors. He also said, however, that "whether you have a hit show or not, as you begin approaching that cancellation date, a set of jitters sets in." Moreover, Revlon purchased *The $64,000 Challenge* (along with Lorillard) soon after *Question*, so "[w]e were now dealing with a client that had two of our shows. . . . We had some feeling that the sponsor identification with the *Question* show was so great that this was a negative in trying to sell it."[170]

Shirley Bernstein (the sister of Leonard Bernstein), who served as the producer of *Challenge* from January of 1958 and who reported to Carlin, wrote questions for the show, as did Merton Koplin. She testified that she believed Revlon was dictating who should win and lose on her program at the weekly meetings. "There were many meetings with the sponsor," she declared, "where Mr. Carlin would come back white with anger."[171]

Bernstein said she was not completely effective at delivering the results Revlon wanted because, unlike the case with *21*, neither *Question* nor *Challenge* was perfectly stage-managed. EPI worked assiduously to learn what the contestants knew and supplied the master of ceremonies with questions designed to keep popular contestants coming back and to get rid of unpopular contestants.[172]

The subcommittee was loaded for bear when Martin Revson took the stand on November 4, 1959; but Martin did not give an inch. Yes, he attended the weekly meetings. Yes, he did indeed make suggestions which "ranged from the broadest possible policy matters to the narrowest details." But as to the rigging of the shows— about this he knew nothing. "[I]t never entered my mind that the producer could control the losing or winning."[173]

George Abrams and the EPI people had testified that questions were prepared in house by EPI with the purpose of pleasing the sponsor, as represented by Martin Revson, when the ratings of *Question* and *Challenge* were analyzed with regard to the popularity of the contestants. Martin was closely questioned on this point by one congressman in particular:

Q: George Abrams was a very close friend of yours in addition to being a close associate, was he not?

Martin: He still is a friend of mine. . . .
Q: Why would he lie under oath?
Martin: I don't know.
Q: Are you saying he lied under oath?
Martin: I didn't say he was lying. I said I don't agree with the
           statement. . . .
Q: Did you not know that every winner over $32,000 had
           been coached or controlled?
Martin: Absolutely not. Absolutely not; I never knew it.
Q: Somebody is not telling the truth here.[174]

As far as the statements by the representatives of EPI were concerned, Martin expressed shock:

Q: Didn't you understand that possibly the producer would
           control the show to the extent of either asking a hard
           question or an easy question . . . ?
Martin: Absolutely not. It was our understanding that these ques-
           tions were made up by Dr. Bergen Evans [of Northwest-
           ern University].[175]

On this matter, Martin asserted he had been taken in by EPI. Commenting on the testimony of Merton Koplin, Martin said he was
"amazed and surprised . . . , because at the meetings he hardly ever
opened his mouth. He was like a mouse at the meetings."[176] As far
as Shirley Bernstein was concerned, "if I met her it was so slight that
I do not recall it."[177]

Citing Revlon's contract with EPI, Martin Revson made clear
his view of who held the whip hand with regard to *The $64,000
Question* and *The $64,000 Challenge:*

> To whom did the shows belong? I can tell you simply: They
> were not Revlon's. Rather, the shows had been conceived
> and produced by Entertainment Productions, Inc., EPI, and
> EPI owned and operated them. We only leased the contrac-
> tual right to telecast them as they were prepared by EPI. . . .
>
> In short, EPI was boss. They had the last word on every-
> thing about the shows. If we didn't like it, there was nothing
> we could do about it.

> EPI's people made it clear that they did not need Revlon. They told us constantly that we were lucky to have the show, that other sponsors were lined up at their door.[178]

George Abrams was questioned by the subcommittee after the submission for the record of his written affidavit and after Martin Revson's testimony. He was asked to reconcile the differences between what he and Martin said. He could not. Anyone attending those meetings, he asserted, could not have helped knowing that the contestants were being manipulated. "Frankly," he said, "I was amazed at the testimony because I consider Martin a very honest person. I have worked with him now for about 4 years. I frankly don't understand his answer unless he was preoccupied [during the meetings with his many other responsibilities]."[179]

On the other hand, an advertising agent named James Webb, president of an agency which had some of Revlon's business, supported Martin before the subcommittee.

Webb: I was extremely surprised at hearing Mr. George Abrams' affidavit read into the record of this meeting. It seems as though we attended different meetings.

Q: Your recollection of the meetings is the same as that of Martin Revson?

Webb: Yes, sir.[180]

This was not what the subcommittee wanted to hear. Webb's credibility was challenged because he still handled Revlon business and had met with Revlon's lawyers prior to his testimony.[181] Abrams, in sharp contrast, was congratulated for what was characterized as "a very honest and very frank and very reasonable" summation of the relationship between the sponsor and the producer.[182]

The subcommittee held open hearings (and they were very well publicized) on the sixth through the tenth and on the twelfth of October, and the second through the sixth of November. Not until Wednesday, November 4, immediately after Martin Revson completed his testimony, did Charles Revson, accompanied by his counsel, Washington heavy-hitter Clark Clifford, appear before the subcommittee.

Revson's testimony, which accounts for a mere 33 pages of a 1,156-page record, was very similar to his brother's (and James

Webb's). For example: "Entertainment Productions, Inc., was the boss. . . ."[183] Revson told the subcommittee that he was shocked that the quiz shows that his firm sponsored were fixed. He had no knowledge of the rigging until the knowledge became general.

From a business point of view, knowingly sponsoring fixed shows made no sense: "We have too much at stake [in terms of public acceptance of Revlon products] to do anything . . . which would reflect unfavorably upon us as a company."[184] From a personal point of view, Revson said he was just like everybody else:

> I never missed a show if I could possibly help it. I would walk out of a play just to watch the show on Tuesday nights. I would walk out of banquets when I should have been listening to the speeches, to make sure that I'd see whether the Italian shoemaker would win $32,000 by answering a question on Italian opera. . . .
>
> If I had known that these shows were fixed, crooked, rigged, do you think that I would have watched or bothered this way?[185]

Charles Revson attended the meetings only rarely and then only for a few minutes. Claiming to be "absolutely flabbergasted" when he discovered that *Question* and *Challenge* were fixed, he said that he had been fooled with the rest of the American public into believing the shows to be legitimate.[186] He asserted that the producers of the programs were trying to place the blame for their wrongdoing on Revlon. He pointed out first of all that Revlon did not have the power to rig the shows: "We did not own either of these programs. We leased them from Entertainment Productions, Inc. . . . which owned the show and . . . had complete control of everything on it except the commercials. In other words, Entertainment Productions, Inc. was the boss; we paid the bills, and we had the right to make suggestions. We had no other right. . . ." Secondly, Revlon had assiduously cultivated a good reputation, and "it wouldn't make sense to risk the goodwill built in 24 years by putting and keeping on a phony quiz show—no matter how good the ratings were."[187] When "another program on another network, 'Twenty-one,' had come under attack," Revson suggested that quiz show producers should form an association and appoint a "czar" to guarantee honesty, "the same as in baseball." Revson said he made this suggestion repeatedly, but it never gained acceptance.[188]

When the complete record is examined, we are left with many contradictions concerning who exercised power at whose behest and what form the exercise of that power took. True, EPI owned *Question* and *Challenge;* but EPI was a small outfit peddling ideas to advertising agencies, which in turn peddled them to sponsors. Yes, EPI controlled the shows; but to what degree could this little company, which was similar to lots of other little companies selling programming ideas in the early days of commercial television, afford to antagonize a major advertiser? There would be other programs in years to come.

True, Revlon monitored the ratings of these shows and the popularity of the contestants with a microscopic scrutiny which was out of the ordinary. Revlon's co-sponsor, Lorillard, did not conduct weekly meetings with the producers about *Challenge,* the show in which it had a half interest. On the other hand, is it not simply good business to watch how one's money is being spent? At the outset, *The $64,000 Question* cost Revlon "about $75,000 to $80,000 a week," according to Martin's testimony. This included "the commercials and everything else." Fifteen thousand dollars a week was set aside for awards.[189] This was a lot of money. Herein lay a large part of the appeal of television quiz and game programs. They attracted attention because of the sums awarded winning contestants. Even losers, as we have noted, received a Cadillac, an automobile which few Americans could aspire to own in 1955.[190] But this was actually not that expensive when compared to financing a prime-time drama or a Hollywood-produced horse opera (i.e., a western).

As far as the networks were concerned, they claimed to have been duped along with the public, as did the Federal Communications Commission. Both the networks and Congress did respond to the scandal. Congress passed a law governing the conduct of quiz shows.[191] The network response was twofold.

First, the networks assumed greater control over the content of what they broadcast than ever before in the history of either television or radio. From their point of view, no matter who bore the principal responsibility for the scandal—the independent production companies or the sponsors—this fantastic money machine called commercial broadcasting was being jeopardized. Television was too valuable to be left in the hands of the content creators (i.e., the producers) or of the people who paid for it (i.e., the advertisers).

The second action the networks took was to provide free airtime to the two major political parties to stage a series of four debates during the 1960 presidential race. These debates—between candidates Richard M. Nixon and John F. Kennedy—are the direct ancestors of the "debates" to which the public is subjected every presidential year. Historian Daniel Boorstin has remarked that the debates bore about as much relation to the task of governance as did the mindless spouting of quiz show trivia to genuine intellectual endeavor. Indeed, to Boorstin the debates bore a comical similarity to the quiz shows themselves. Answer some questions well and win as a prize a four-year job with an annual salary of $100,000.[192] No matter. This gesture could be interpreted as a bow in the direction of the often-cited but just as often ignored clause in the Communications Act of 1934, which declared that broadcasting should operate in accord with the "public's interest, convenience, and necessity."[193] What better way to curry favor with potentially powerful politicians than to provide them with free access to the airwaves?

Looking at the quiz show phenomenon more broadly than "Who did what to whom?" and with the perspective of almost a half century, what can we make of it? The answer, I believe, is that witnesses whose testimony seemed so contradictory in the moment were actually saying much the same thing. Everyone knew these programs were managed. Not everyone knew the extent of this management. Indeed, the extent varied on different programs. It is also plausible that Martin Revson made suggestions which the producers interpreted as orders. One is reminded of Henry II's famous remark to four of his retainers: "Will no one rid me of this parish priest?" The four rode off and murdered Thomas à Becket in Canterbury Cathedral. Henry had not given them a direct order, but his wish was their command. Like EPI, they, too, were in the business of pleasing the customer.

Yet another question which historical perspective brings to the fore: Why were public figures so upset about the quiz show scandals? And many leading politicians and columnists were upset indeed. President Eisenhower compared the fraud to the "Black Sox" throwing the World Series in 1919.[194]

The truth is that no one knew what impact the scandals would have on the general public. Television, after all, came right into people's living rooms. The federal government had the right to regulate it because broadcast frequencies traveled through the air, and the air in the United States belongs to every American. If some very small group of Americans are going to be granted a monopoly on certain frequencies for the purpose of making money for themselves, they are going to have to conduct their business in a regulated environment and, in theory at least, in furtherance of the public interest. It is hard to argue that phony quiz shows meet that standard.

Interestingly enough, the public at large (as opposed to public figures) took the revelations of quiz show fraud very much in stride, as far as these things can be determined.[195] Thus, although many people were upset, it is also true that many people were not. The blithe attitude of so many in the general public was in itself a cause for concern among the elite. People may have been amazed at their own gullibility; but there had been victimless crimes before in the United States, and a lot of people seemed resigned to the idea that there would be victimless crimes again.[196]

Because of the nature of radio waves, broadcasting has some of the aspects of a natural monopoly. Monopolists are regulated in the United States. The broadcasters knew that with the quiz shows they had stepped over the line. They scurried back quickly. Television has always been about access. The networks wanted to control that access, and they succeeded.

From the point of view of Revlon's welfare, the decision to buy *The $64,000 Question* was a stroke of genius. Thanks to *Question*, Revlon firmly established its supremacy over all other cosmetics companies doing business through retail outlets (as opposed to selling house to house, as Avon Products did). In December 1955, Revlon stock was offered on the New York Stock Exchange at $12 per share. The stock quickly rose to $30 and became "a triumph . . . so great it was almost embarrassing."[197] The quiz show scandal caused the stock to drop five and one-half points in one day, but it quickly recovered. Neither sales nor the precious company image was tarnished in the long run. Immediately after the hearings, *Time* magazine ran a story describing Charles as the "undisputed genius of the flamboyant world of cosmetics."[198]

"I venture to say that I don't know where we would have been without that show," Martin Revson once said about *The $64,000*

Question.[199] He was right in that before *Question*, Revlon was one among many in its competitive set. Afterward, it stood alone at the head of the class.

How should Charles Revson's role in *The $64,000 Question* be assessed? He did not create the program. When it was aired, he did not like it. This was not what the cosmetics industry meant to him. Far preferable were the blurred sexual boundaries suggested in so many Revlon magazine advertisements to the *Brady Bunch* image projected by Barbara Britton in the unimaginative television commercials, so colorless in every sense. But Revson was in business above all to make money, and a great deal was to be made from the sponsorship of these television shows. Revson's business judgment did not lead him to these programs; but, once there, it led him to commit himself and his firm to them.

What about the fixing of these shows? Was Charles Revson the culprit? Yes and no. It is not difficult to understand why he avoided meetings with the producers about fixing the shows. They were boring. It is also easy to see why anyone working for him would understand that he wanted results at any cost. Revlon was spending a lot of money on these television shows. For the commercials to move merchandise, a lot of people had to see them. For those people to tune in, the contestants had to excite their interest. The details of how the ratings were to be maintained Revson left for others.

It was that simple. Revson had been in business for himself for over two decades by the time *The $64,000 Question* was first aired. Everyone understood who he was and what he demanded. It was as natural to fix a quiz show for Charles Revson as it would have been unnatural to do something similar for David Packard.

Advertising by itself, however, does not a company make. Even advertising on a program into which, at its peak, 82 percent of American television sets were tuned. Even advertising in as advertising-intensive an industry as cosmetics. We know this because Hazel Bishop beat Revlon to the punch in television. With an advertising man as president, Hazel Bishop put half of each sales dollar into advertising, most of it on television. The program *This Is Your Life* put the company on the map.[200] But not long thereafter, the company sank like a stone. It takes management, not just advertising, to sustain a successful business.

PUTTING PEOPLE LAST

It is around the issue of management that Revlon's history is so puzzling. From 1932, the year the company was founded, until 1975, the year Charles Revson died, Revlon was a malevolent dictatorship. Every precept taught in America's business schools, every practice employed by its most admired companies, was violated by Revson. The wonder is that the firm not only survived, but prospered in spite of a working environment that was, to be blunt, appalling.

What were the financial consequences of Charles's management practices? Charles died on a Sunday. The previous Friday, August 22, 1975, Revlon had a market capitalization of $988,455,000.[201] This was a very large sum for a company in this industry to be worth at this time.

To say Revson's reputation on Madison Avenue was not a favorable one is an understatement. Advertising agencies wanted the Revlon account because it was large and kept growing, but they did not relish the idea of dealing with Charles Revson. Described as "insanely particular" concerning advertising, Revson and Revlon made the most stringent demands upon their agencies' talent and time.[202]

When Revlon withdrew its $8,000,000 account from Batten, Barton, Durstine, and Osborn in the late summer of 1957, a stalwart executive reported: "My hand is not shaking. I am alert and cheerful. I face life with optimism. This agency will go on."[203] While Revlon was between agencies, *Time* magazine reported:

> Even as they panted after Revlon, the most dynamic cosmetic maker in the United States, veteran admen gulped their gibsons nervously at the thought of also taking on . . . Charles Revson . . . the most feared, cheered, and jeered advertising client since the late George Washington Hill of American Tobacco fearlessly sent Lucky Strike Green to war. . . . The biggest problem with BBD&O was that client Revson demanded top-quality advertising and simply worked too hard for the admen to keep up. The weary admen began agreeing with Revson's bad ideas as well as his good ones in order to crawl home to the wife and kiddies. His brand of rugged individualism overpowered those accustomed to the grey-flanneled politeness of modern, managerial-type clients.[204]

Revson began to earn his reputation as a "genius [but] . . . also a bombastic, terribly hardworking, frantic guy who just chews people up"[205] in the late 1940s. Revlon itself was in a state of constant turmoil during these years. At one point, executive turnover reached 130 percent annually, with one important executive position being filled by six different people in one year.[206] Revson was as tough on his advertising agencies as he was on his own executives and on himself. Between 1944 and 1948, Revlon had eighteen different account executives at McCann-Erickson.[207]

Revson was always eyeing competitors with a view to doing what they themselves were trying to do, except more skillfully and in order to spirit away from them their most valued talent. According to a former employee: "Charles . . . is one of the greatest copy artists in America or in the world, because he will copy a thing . . . but he will make it better—better quality, better packaging, better pricing, and better advertising. . . . So if his competition comes out with something good, he'll make it better."[208] His interest in the promotional plans of other companies resulted in suits against Revlon by Coty in 1955 and by Juliette Marglen, a division of Fabergé, in 1958, for corporate espionage, and also generated rumors that Revlon tapped the phones of Hazel Bishop.[209]

Revson employed highly capable people, according to some observers the most capable in the cosmetics business. He found many of these executives by determining who was responsible for the growth of his competitors and hiring them away with promises of high salaries and stock options. He was reputed to pay the highest salaries in the industry. However, he found it extremely difficult to get along with many of the talented people he hired.

Revson tried to exercise an inordinate amount of control over his own people. Since his executives were high-strung themselves, they often found Revson intolerable.

Examples of Revlon's, and particularly Charles's, attempts to control employees can be found in the company's relationships to its salespeople all the way up to its top executives. In the late forties and early fifties, Revlon used what it called the "Psycho-Revlon Method" for improving sales performance. At the annual sales meetings, Martin Revson and the sales district supervisor talked to individual salespeople to determine how they could increase productivity.

Further than that [explained Martin], we show scenes—action scenes and motion pictures of live actors, depicting the mental blocks that arise in a salesman's mind and we try to remove those blocks. We feel that if a man has the proper amount of intelligence and drive, and he wants to get out and work and does work, and if he is not a success, there must be mental blocks. In other words, he is not imposing his will sufficiently upon his customer, and we have to probe into what the reasons are—whether he has trouble at home or whether he doesn't feel that he should be that strong.[210]

These are high-pressure tactics, but they can justifiably be considered one way to get the best out of employees. In November of 1955, however, a New York State legislative committee on wiretapping discovered that Revlon was monitoring its own phones. Most of the phones monitored were in the order department, and a company spokesman explained that the wiretapping was designed to give better service to the public. The telephone company at this time provided a monitoring service for airline reservation desks, so this practice was not unknown. Revlon, however, also tapped the phone of one of its own executives whose loyalty was in question. This tap was not installed by the telephone company, and the conversations were monitored by Revlon's controller, "a curious assignment for any controller."[211]

Charles hounded all his executives, including his brothers; and his conduct seemed to deteriorate as Revlon became more successful. Joseph ceased active participation in the company in 1955, not long before the company went public. (He thus deprived himself of millions of dollars.) Martin left on bad terms in 1958. By the time of the quiz show hearings in 1959, Charles and Martin were not on speaking terms, a situation which caused some embarrassment and confusion.[212] Two years later, Martin sued Charles for swindling him out of $600,000. Martin's suit alleged that

Charles Revson engaged in a practice of mistreating executives of Revlon, Inc., and abusing them personally to such extent that men of proven capacity who held high positions in nationally known corporations before and after their employment by Revlon, Inc. suffered humiliation and impaired efficiency and left Revlon, Inc. to escape mistreatment. The rate of turnover of Revlon executives became a subject of ribald humor.[213]

Martin stated that he chose to leave Revlon in 1958 because he believed that Charles's personnel policies were endangering the future of the company. This striking condemnation from Charles's own brother, a man who had worked for the company since 1935, is not without corroboration.

There is little debate over the manner in which Charles treated many of his employees. Numerous executives complained of the personal abuse that they and their staffs suffered at his hands. Even those who liked him said that he maintained an atmosphere of "controlled fear" and intense internal competition. He believed that this approach benefited that which he loved above all else—his company.

Martin should have been right, but he was not. Charles's personnel policies did not lead to the demise of Revlon. Whether it would have grown even faster without these policies is difficult to determine.

I conducted research on Revlon in 1970 and 1971. During those years, Charles Revson was a name to conjure with in Midtown Manhattan. The stories of his cruelty were legion. Below I recount one description of how he ran his company. The narrator, a respected executive at the time, was a top man at Revlon but left the company:

> I remember one particular incident in which out of his [Revson's] own mouth he articulated his [management] policy. We used to have an advertising meeting with him once a week. . . . My advertising department was divided into brand groups, and I would bring up the head of each of the brand groups who had advertising to present. . . . Of course I had screened all this material ahead of time and had worked on it with the individual brand managers.
>
> And I recall I needed a bright brand manager . . . and I found a girl in San Francisco who was working for an advertising agency out there as one of the head copy writers. After

a great deal of persuasion, I got her to move to New York and take the job. Revson had never met her. She was a very nice girl and a very talented girl. I let her get about a month under her belt in the organization before I took her to one of the advertising meetings with Revson.

She was presenting a campaign at this particular meeting, first time she ever presented one. . . . For some reason he [Revson] decided to take out after her, and he used every four-letter word imaginable to describe what she was presenting. She sat there in total shock. She had never been talked to, I think, in her life this way. She was a very genteel, soft-spoken . . . highly talented young lady. But completely a lady; and for a man to use that kind of language to describe her efforts completely threw her.

As soon as he took out after her, I could see her tense up; and then she finally got to tears. She didn't know how to handle this kind of a situation. So I stepped in and I said, "Now wait a minute, Charles. I approved this campaign and Miss ——— is presenting it because I have approved it, and I have worked with her on it. And anything you've got to say about this—say it to me, not to her." By this time she's sitting down at the end of the table dabbing her eyes. She's completely at a loss. . . .

Charles reached over and he put his hand on mine, patted it and he said, "Look, kiddie, I built this business by being a bastard. I run it by being a bastard. I'll always be a bastard, and don't you ever try to change me."

Now there is the man's total management philosophy. He has the idea that the harder you beat on people and the more miserable you make them, the more they're going to perform for you.[214]

This story would sound familiar to anyone who knew Revson. This is how he acted. Yet his company succeeded while others failed. After he died, his handpicked successor, Michel Bergerac, took the helm. Bergerac was a true professional manager who headed ITT/Europe prior to Revson's recruiting him in 1974. One wonders why Revson hired an outsider, a man whose background and manner of dealing with others was so different from his own, to run his company.[215]

At any rate, Revlon prospered under Bergerac until the early 1980s. It then fell into a swift decline.[216] It was the subject of a hostile takeover by Ron Perelman in 1984 and 1985. Today, Perelman cannot figure out what to do with it.[217]

A company that was a leader has become an also-ran. In what form it will survive is very much in doubt.

Charles Revson could not get along with other men. He never got along with himself. And some who knew him well believe that he really hated women.[218]

The contrast between Revson and Mary Kay Ash, the founder of Mary Kay Cosmetics, could hardly be more complete. They were in the same industry: beautifying women. But Mary Kay Ash conceived of her cosmetics company at least in part as a way to liberate women from being held back in what she saw as very much a man's world. She envisioned her company not solely as a profit-making organization, but also as a movement, a cause, a way of life. Cynicism and depression were absent from her world. You could will yourself to happiness.

The function of cosmetics in Ash's view was as a tool to help people feel good about how they presented themselves to the world. The leap she made was the belief that the "outer" you could and did become the "inner" you: "You see—the funny thing about putting on a happy face is that if you do it again and again, pretty soon that happy face is there to stay. *It becomes the real you.*" She was, in other words, selling not hope but fulfillment for her sales directors, her consultants, and their customers. Her pink-packaged products carried with them her own unquenchable optimism. "Every entrepreneur I've ever met," she said, "has been an incurable optimist." She must never have met Revson, who was quite the reverse.[219]

When one reads all the stories, only a few of which have been recounted here, one comes to feel that Revson had a seriously unbalanced personality. The mystery is not only that he held this company together but that he built it while at the same time isolating himself from everyone around him. It sounds harsh to say so, but he seems to have worked at making himself repulsive and succeeded. And he died one of the wealthiest and most successful business tycoons of his time.[220]

CHARLES REVSON

October 11, 1906	Revson is born. The name on the birth certificate is Hyman Charles Revson.
1923	Revson graduates from high school; starts as a salesman at the Pickwick Dress Company.
1930	Revson is married, but only for several months.
c. 1931	Revson is hired as a distributor for the Elka Company.
March 1, 1932	Revlon Nail Enamel Company is founded.
November 1952	Fire and Ice campaign is launched.
June 7, 1955	*The $64,000 Question* debuts on CBS.
December 7, 1955	Revlon becomes a publicly traded company.
August 24, 1975	Revson dies.

PART THREE

Our
Own
Times

SAM WALTON

ROBERT NOYCE

INTRODUCTION

The rise of the American economy, the organization of its business enterprises, and the innovativeness of its citizenry had attracted notice as long as a century and a half ago. At the Crystal Palace Exhibition in 1851, Londoners saw on display American methods of manufacturing which were sufficiently new to provoke comment. Parliamentary reports were written to examine the not-yet-labeled "American System of Manufactures."[1] At every industrial exhibition after 1851, there was plain and plentiful evidence that the United States was leading the way to a new and more efficient method of producing things. By 1880, soulful characters in Russian novels were conceding that Americans were "wonderful at machinery."[2]

The Orient was as impressed by American technology as the Occident. Not long after the Crystal Palace Exhibition in London, the government of Japan entertained a very unwelcome guest in Tokyo harbor. It was Commodore Matthew C. Perry with an American fleet whose purpose was to open Japan's ports for commerce.[3] The Japanese and the Americans exchanged gifts to symbolize a newly formed ersatz friendship. The Japanese gave the Americans seashells, flower holders, and coral. The Americans gave the Japanese rifles, telegraph equipment, and a model railroad train. If the Japanese were to avoid being victimized by the imperialistic West, they quickly realized, they were going to have to make some big changes and make them quickly. When the Meiji Restoration took place in 1868 and Japan set out upon its policy of "rich country, strong army," Japanese students were sent abroad to learn modern ways; and the United States was one of the nations in which they studied. At century's turn a Briton, Fred A. McKenzie, published *The American Invaders: Their Plans, Tactics and Progress.* It was 1901, the year Queen Victoria died and the climax of the British Empire. McKenzie observed:

> The most serious aspect of the American industrial invasion lies in the fact that these incomers have acquired control of almost every new industry created during the past fifteen years. . . . What are the chief new features in London life?

They are, I take it, the telephone, the portable camera, the phonograph, the electric street car, the automobile, the type-writer, passenger lifts in houses, and the multiplication of machine tools. In every one of these, save the petroleum automobile, the American maker is supreme; in several he is the monopolist.[4]

Had this passage been written a decade later, McKenzie would not have excepted the "petroleum automobile."[5]

By the 1960s, the belief that the American economy was going to overrun the world was becoming general. What Henry Luce had celebrated as the American Century looked like the American Challenge through French eyes. "The problem," according to French journalist Jean-Jacques Servan-Schreiber in 1967, "is a subtle one for many reasons. It is not that we are being inundated by an excess of U.S. dollars which the Americans can not use and which flow to the common market only because of temporary circumstances. On the contrary, it is something quite new and considerably more serious—the extension to Europe of an art of *organization* that is still a mystery to us."[6] Henry Luce's dream had indeed seemed to come true, brought to fruition by the power of American business.

Then, all of a sudden, America's position at the pinnacle of power became wobbly. By 1975, the year Charles Revson died, the United States no longer appeared to be the self-confident nation it was only a few years previously. In 1961, John F. Kennedy had pledged that America would land a man on the moon and return him safely to earth within a decade.[7] This was a breathtaking declaration, made publicly before the whole world so there could be no backing away from it. The moon is a long way away. It has been up there for quite a while, and when Kennedy spoke those words no human being had ever spent any time on it. Kennedy knew as little about rocketry as Roosevelt had known about aircraft manufacture when he made his public pledge that the nation would turn out fifty thousand planes a year. Both men felt the details could be safely left to others. The point was that each was president, this was America, and the job would get done.

For a variety of reasons, the "swinging sixties" turned into the "sobering seventies," by the end of which President Jimmy Carter complained that the nation had sunken into a "malaise."[8] This loss of self-confidence was startling. Politically, the dreadful combination of the Vietnam War and the Watergate scandal transformed the way Americans viewed themselves and helped produce a yawning gap between the older and younger generations. The nation's elected leaders had taken bribes (in the case of Vice President Spiro T. Agnew), they had persisted in a war which they themselves knew could not be brought to a successful conclusion (Robert S. McNamara stands out here, but he had plenty of company), and they had countenanced activities which had struck at the heart of constitutional freedoms which Americans had taken for granted since the Revolution. In 1974, Richard M. Nixon became the first president forced from office. All this chaos and disaster made the self-assurance of an earlier day difficult indeed to recapture in one's thoughts.

From a business point of view, the situation in the 1970s seemed steadily to deteriorate. The whole economy was rocked by the oil shocks of 1973 and 1979. Servan-Schreiber to the contrary notwithstanding, it began to seem that the secret of business organization was possessed by the Japanese, not by the Americans.

During the 1950s, Americans had gotten used to imported Japanese textiles and a few other products, usually of low-technology content and often of low quality. "Made in Japan" became a synonym for shoddiness, and it was no surprise when the first Japanese automobiles marketed in the United States were so poor they had to be withdrawn from the market. *Time* magazine chose Harlow Curtice, CEO of General Motors, as its Man of the Year in 1955,[9] a year in which almost no foreign automobiles were sold in the United States.

By the 1970s, the picture had changed completely. Efficient and appealing Japanese automobiles returned to the United States, and with a vengeance. Not only the automobiles themselves but the whole value chain (tires, for example) experienced import penetration which a decade earlier would have been unimaginable. The United States began to run a huge trade deficit with Japan in automobiles alone. By 1980 Japan, rather than the United States, had become the world's leading automobile-producing nation. The United States had led the industry since 1908. Chrysler lost $1.7 billion in 1980 and would have gone bankrupt without federal loan guarantees. Ford lost $1.5 billion and seemed next in line.

In other industries as well, the United States was not only losing out in global competition; its own home market was also falling prey to foreign products. The United States led the world in steel manufacture for decades but lost that lead to the Japanese. The home entertainment industry—phonographs, radios, televisions—was invented and developed in the United States. Today, no televisions are manufactured by companies headquartered in this country.

So, by the late 1970s, it was Japan which appeared to have cracked the code of global economic conquest. This seemed true not only in old industries like textiles or industries of the present like automobiles, but also industries which would determine national wealth in the future. A perfect example is semiconductors. "Japan, Inc." drove Intel out of memory chips, an industry Intel created.

During the 1970s and 1980s, the foreign challenge to American economic power came almost exclusively in manufacturing, more so than in research and far more so than in distribution. The greatest retailer in American history and perhaps in world history, Sam Walton, is the subject of the first chapter of this section.

From early in life, Walton showed extraordinary energy, personal magnetism, and an overwhelming desire to win. He had an innate confidence that he could win at anything on which he decided to concentrate. All through school, his athletic endeavors and student activities brought him success. One of the distinguishing characteristics of this remarkable man was that he did not succumb to the complacency or to the swelled head which so often accompanies achievement. He always felt there were new worlds to conquer and that the key to this conquest was knowledge.

Sam Walton believed you could learn from anybody, and he spent his life in the quest for more knowledge about retailing. He had a genuine affection and respect for people regardless of social class, and he also had an ardent desire to be liked. Retailing is the classic "people" business—Wal-Mart became the largest private employer in the nation—and these traits served him well.

Like all industries, retailing has been affected by the revolution in data processing through computerization which has taken place in the past half century. Walton embraced the new technology, but always with a healthy dose of skepticism. He knew how to put technology in its place. It was a means to an end and not an end in itself. The end was serving the customer.

Walton served the customer so well that Wal-Mart blew right through the stagflation "malaise" of the 1970s which was so hard on so many other retailers. He showed what inspired, astute, dynamic leadership can do even when the times in general are challenging.

"Buy globally, sell locally" has been a retail strategy for years. To achieve leadership, this saying has been honed to "Buy intergalactically, sell by zip code plus four digits." Buying globally keeps prices down. Selling locally caters specifically to the individual desires of the consumer. Consumer knowledge is so crucial to retail sales that retailers have had a great deal of trouble operating stores profitably in foreign countries. Wal-Mart was thus relatively unaffected by the Japanese incursions into the American market. In fact, Wal-Mart in the 1990s moved abroad more vigorously than any other retailer in history.

With the semiconductor industry, the story is quite different. Even more than automobiles, this was an industry born and bred in the United States. Semiconductors and the microprocessors they made possible are essential for technological growth in the twenty-first century. The semiconductor was invented simultaneously but independently by Jack Kilby at Texas Instruments and by the subject of our final biographical essay, Robert Norton Noyce.

Like Sam Walton, Noyce was born in the middle of the country, in Denmark, Iowa. Walton was a son of the middle border with a strong southern identification. He was born in Kingfisher, Oklahoma. Wal-Mart was headquartered in Arkansas, one of the eleven states which seceded from the Union to form the Confederate States of America in 1860 and 1861. Noyce was a midwesterner who even after studying and living in the East for a number of years and then moving out to California, never fully left the Midwest behind.

Noyce was a polymath. He sang madrigals, flew his own airplane, founded companies, and co-invented the integrated circuit. Although many could lay plausible claim to such a designation, it is not unfair to assert that Noyce was more responsible for the creation of the cluster of high-technology companies south of San Francisco in what has come to be known as Silicon Valley than any other individual. His creativity, charisma, and technical knowledge combined to produce a potent brew from which many of the brightest people in the United States and the world over wanted to drink.

Noyce asked not what he could do for a company (to paraphrase John F. Kennedy's inaugural address) but rather what a company could do for him. This is not to suggest that Noyce was a selfish man. Quite the contrary. It is merely to say that he envisioned the corporation as working for profit, of course, but working for larger goals as well. For Noyce, a corporation was a tool for the fulfillment of his personal goal, which was pushing back the technological frontier.

The firm Noyce co-founded, Intel, has played a key role in the technological revolution of recent years. But it almost did not. In the early and mid-1980s, it was forced out of its leadership position in an important market by the onslaught of Japanese competition.

Not only Intel but the whole semiconductor industry knew that creative ways had to be found to compete globally or the United States would fall behind other economies, perhaps permanently. Yet the institutional barriers to industry cooperation were daunting both in law and in custom. The very element that Jean-Jacques Servan-Schreiber had specified as America's greatest strength, the art of organization, was looking like its greatest weakness when compared to the resources Japan was able to deploy in order to overrun an industry.

America's high technology community needed a universally respected leader to step forward and help firms work together for the good of the industry and the nation. In a remarkably selfless act, Noyce agreed to play this role. It was he who became the first head of the industry consortium, Sematech, a job he did not want but was ideally suited to perform. It was toward the end of his tenure at Sematech, in the summer of 1990, that he died suddenly of a heart attack.

6 **SAM WALTON** All-American

SAM WALTON AND BEN FRANKLIN

Benjamin Franklin was seventy-nine years of age when he at last, after repeated requests, obtained the permission of Congress to relinquish his post as minister to France and sail home to the United States. Franklin was the most well known American in the world. His life had been marked by such peaks of achievement in numerous, unrelated endeavors that it is impossible to confine his genius to one or two categories. Jack-of-all-trades and master of all. He rose from unlettered, penniless vagabondage to become a great scientist, a best-selling author, a wealthy entrepreneur, the first citizen of his adopted city of Philadelphia and state of Pennsylvania, a great inventor, a great diplomat, a great revolutionary, and one of the six great founding fathers of a great nation (the other five being James Madison, Alexander Hamilton, Thomas Jefferson, George Washington, and John Adams). When Jefferson arrived in France to present his credentials as the next American minister, he was commonly greeted by the question: "It is you, Sir, who replaced Dr. Franklin?" To which Jefferson usually replied: "No one can replace him, Sir: I am only his successor."[1]

Franklin's character and career cast a very long shadow. His homilies, his wit, and his wisdom, often honored as much in the breach as in the observance but honored nonetheless, became woven into the fabric of nineteenth-century America. Entrepreneurs and educators pointed to his inspiration as a key factor in their elevating themselves to success.[2] Down to this very day, Franklin's image and achievements—especially his rise from obscurity and his homespun democracy—are with us still.

How did this great man—one wears out the word "great" in discussing Franklin—while away the days on shipboard between Le Havre and Philadelphia as he returned from France for the final time? He wrote three essays, two of which were eminently practical: "On the Causes and Cure of Smoky Chimneys" and "Description of a New Stove for Burning of Pitcoal, and Consuming all the Smoke."[3]

Celebrations greeted Franklin upon his return to Philadelphia. After they subsided, he continued his work in government; and he also enlarged his house, turning it into a more "commodious" dwelling. On September 17, 1787, he delivered the closing address to the Constitutional Convention, suggesting that each member "doubt a little of his own infallibility."[4]

However, what is of interest is not the continuity of Franklin's public life but rather the continuity of his private demeanor. Jefferson once speculated that seven years of diplomatic service abroad was enough to ruin an American. Franklin spent more than three times that long without losing his interest in smoky chimneys and stoves and without losing the common touch in general. "Acclaimed and decorated as no other American had ever been, he returned to Philadelphia and was immediately at home again, easily recognizable by his neighbors as the man they had always known: Ben Franklin, printer."[5]

Franklin died in 1790. Samuel Moore Walton died in 1992. If Walton were alive today, he would be astonished and probably appalled to see his name and Benjamin Franklin's in the same sentence. Nevertheless, the two shared some traits. Both possessed the common touch to an uncommon degree. Both were acutely aware of the importance of understanding the psychology of the people with whom they dealt. Both were shrewd. Both knew how to get what they wanted. Neither was primarily motivated by money. Both were born leaders. Both were revolutionaries.

I like to think that it was more than mere coincidence that the first store Sam Walton ever operated was named "Ben Franklin." Located in Newport, Arkansas, it was part of a chain of five-and-ten-cent stores owned by the Butler Brothers of Chicago.

BEGINNINGS

On Friday, March 29, 1918, Samuel Moore Walton was born in a farmhouse near Kingfisher, Oklahoma. Sam's father, Thomas Gibson Walton, was twenty-six years old at the time, and his mother, the former Nannia Lee Lawrence, was nineteen. She was a farmer's daughter and dropped out of college when she was wed. The couple set up house on a small farm which Thomas had acquired.

Thomas Walton never knew his parents. His mother, Clara, and his father, Samuel W. Walton (after whom Sam Walton was named), both died within a few months of one another just over a year after his birth. Thomas was brought up by relatives. His childhood could not have been easy. The Waltons were a family of the upper South and border states. The founding father, William P. Walton, had moved from Virginia to a farm just outside of LaMine in central Missouri. His son Sam became LaMine's postmaster as well as the proprietor of a small general store. Thus, it was Sam Walton's grandfather and namesake who was the family's first merchant.[6]

On his mother's side, Tom Walton was part of the Moore family, providing Sam Walton's middle name. Like the Waltons, the Moores had a history that straddled the border between North and South. Joseph T. Moore was born in Giles County, Tennessee, from which he migrated to Marshfield, Missouri. A Union sympathizer and a Republican, Moore served in the Eighth Missouri Cavalry and saw action at Pea Ridge, about ten miles north of Bentonville in northwestern Arkansas, and elsewhere. In the 1880s, he served two terms in the Missouri legislature.[7]

When Thomas Walton finished high school he joined the farm loan business owned by a relative, J. W. Walton. J. W. had taken part in the Oklahoma land rush of April 22, 1889, and staked out land seven miles from where government surveyors had planned to establish the town of Kingfisher. According to reporter and author Bob Ortega, J. W. decided that there were "less backbreaking" ways than farming to make a living. As he watched other homesteaders go bankrupt and lose their land, he "decided to get in on the lending end of things and became a farm loan agent." Ortega speculates that he served as the representative for an insurance company or state bank.[8]

This was a key move. It meant that J. W. was not going to become an "Okie," drifting further west, farming again, and failing again. It meant that he had a chance to prosper; and because he did, he had the chance to preside over the gathering together of his family, rather than watching it drift apart in search of a competence. In the most famous advice a father ever gave to his son, Polonius told Laertes in *Hamlet:* "Neither a borrower nor a lender be." What J. W. figured out was that if circumstances forced you to make a choice between the two, lending was better.

J. W.'s choice put him on the right side of history. America was born in the country. At the time of the Revolution, there were only two cities, Philadelphia and New York, with a population of more than twenty-five thousand. But the nation moved to the city, slowly but inexorably. The movement took a long time to reach consummation. A far higher percentage of America's population lived the rural life into the twentieth century compared to other countries which industrialized early. Not until the 1920 census did a majority of the population reside in urban territory, defined as cities and towns with a population of twenty-five hundred or greater.[9] In the first federal census of 1790, 97 percent of the respondents classified themselves as farmers. In the 1990 census, 3 percent did.[10]

America's heart was on the farm. "Those who labour in the earth are the chosen people of God, if ever he had a chosen people . . . ," Jefferson wrote in *Notes on the State of Virginia.*[11] Unfortunately, America's heart was also broken on the farm. It had taken considerable shrewdness to flourish as a farmer, especially prior to the massive federal welfare and subsidy programs of the second half of the twentieth century. A man had to own a lot of land, grow the right crops, raise the right livestock, and manage his finances with care.

We will meet such a man presently. His name was Leland Stanford Robson of Claremore, Oklahoma. Robson was as much a businessman and government official as he was a farmer and rancher. He was a very big man in a very little town. Years later, Wal-Mart would rise to dominance by building very big stores in very small towns. Robson's daughter, Helen Alice Robson, became Sam Walton's wife on February 14, 1943. It was Valentine's Day.

Tom Walton began his working life in the employ of his uncle, J. W. Walton.[12] But Tom did not like the business, so, as as we have seen, he married and took up farming near Kingfisher, Oklahoma, in 1917. Sam was born the following year; and on December 20, 1921, Nan Walton gave birth to the couple's other child, James L., known as "Bud."

The 1920s were hard times for farmers, and Tom Walton was no exception to the trend. He gave up after a few years and went to work for his half brother Jesse Walton, whose Walton Mortgage Company apparently represented Metropolitan Life in Springfield, Missouri. Jesse dispatched Tom to Marshall, Missouri, in the center of the state.[13] Soon thereafter, Tom decided to go into the farm mortgage business himself. He failed, but fortunately Jesse took him back into his agency. Tom moved the family to Shelbina, Missouri, as Jesse wished. Springfield is the first town of which the mature Sam Walton had a recollection. He started school there and moved with the family to Marshall and Shelbina before ending up in Columbia. Columbia is the home of the main campus of Missouri's state university, from which Walton graduated with a B.A. in economics in 1940.[14]

At the end of his life, Walton collaborated with *Fortune* editor John Huey on his autobiography. He had often been approached to write a book and had often rebuffed the offers. His family finally prevailed upon him to work on one with a writer from the *Wall Street Journal* named Eric Morgenthaler. He did not enjoy the experience; and upon being diagnosed with terminal cancer, he decided that he had to "simplify my life" by "get[ting] rid of things I don't want to do." The Morgenthaler project fell into that category; and Walton terminated it, paying Morgenthaler to turn over his work product to the family and buying out the contract.

Once again, however, prodded by family and friends and knowing that an unauthorized account of his life was in progress, Walton agreed to cooperate on a book. Because of his failing health, it is doubtful that he gave it as much attention as he otherwise might have. It is an interesting, though too brief, book.[15] Here is what Walton had to say about his father: "My dad . . . was an awfully hard worker who got up early, put in long hours, and was honest. Completely, totally honest, remembered by most people for his integrity. He was also a bit of a character, who loved to trade, loved to make a deal for just about anything. . . ."

Walton said his father had "that unusual instinct" of knowing the limits to which he could push in a negotiation. Some of his father's offers were so low that they embarrassed Walton, who asserted that he himself was not the world's greatest negotiator (an observation with which many people who negotiated with him would probably disagree). Walton said his brother and partner, Bud, inherited his dad's ability to haggle.

Walton believed that

> Dad never had the kind of ambition or confidence to build
> much of a business on his own, and he didn't believe in tak-
> ing on debt. . . . Dad became the guy who had to service . . .
> old farm loans, most of which were in default. In twenty-
> nine and thirty and thirty-one, he had to repossess hundreds
> of farms from wonderful people whose families had owned
> the land forever. I traveled with him some, and it was tragic,
> and really hard on Dad too—but he tried to do it in a way
> that left those farmers with as much of their self-respect as
> he could. All of this must have made an impression on me as
> a kid, although I don't ever remember saying anything to
> myself like, "I'll never be poor."[16]

This passage is notable for how little of note there is in it. It reads as
if Huey kept nagging Walton to say something, anything, about his
father. Bud Walton is quoted as saying that his brother had "a lot of
our mother's characteristics."[17] However, Walton's comments about
his mother are as flat as those about his father.[18]

Neither mother nor father as individuals seemed to have been
much of a factor in Walton's life, with two exceptions. The first was
the single point upon which his parents agreed: "One thing my
mother and dad shared completely was their approach to money:
they just didn't spend it."[19] The second exception was that Tom and
Nan Walton were a mismatch. They did not get along. They were,
reported Walton,

> always at odds, and they really only stayed together because
> of Bud and me. After we were grown, they even split up and
> went their separate ways for a while. . . . Growing up as the
> oldest child, I felt like I took a lot of the brunt of this domes-
> tic discord. I'm not exactly sure how this situation affected
> my personality—unless it was partly a motivation to stay so
> busy all the time—but I swore early on that if I ever had a
> family, I would never expose it to that kind of squabbling.[20]

Tom and Nan Walton were married for thirty-three years. The
marriage ended in the fall of 1950 with Nan's death from cancer at

the age of fifty-two. Tom Walton died on August 15, 1984. He was ninety-two and had lived well into the era of Wal-Mart's greatness. Two years before his death, he made a few remarks at the grand opening of the Wal-Mart in Kingfisher.[21]

Walton seems to have learned more from his family about how not to behave than the opposite. Don't squabble like your parents. Think big, unlike your father. It was not until the spring of 1942, when he met his future father-in-law, Leland Stanford Robson, that Walton acquired a model from his parents' generation.

Listening to L. S. Robson, Walton said,

> was an education in itself. He influenced me a great deal. He was a great salesman, one of the most persuasive individuals I had ever met. And I am sure his success as a trader and a businessman, his knowledge of finance and the law, and his philosophy had a big effect on me. My competitive nature was such that I saw his success and admired it. I didn't envy it. I admired it. I said to myself: maybe I will be as successful as he is someday.[22]

Robson was fifty-eight and Walton was twenty-four when Walton met him in the process of courting his daughter and Walton's future wife, Helen. Robson was born and raised in Georgia and found his way to Oklahoma by 1909 as, according to Ortega, an "itinerant peddler of pots, pans, bibles, and picture frames."[23] It has been said that the most difficult item to sell is a Bible because everyone who wants one already owns one. At any rate, Robson returned to Georgia, where he put himself through law school, and then went back to Oklahoma with plans to practice in Tulsa. He decamped from there to the town of Claremore, twenty miles to the northwest.

It was in Claremore that Robson became a success. His

> law practice . . . flourished, and as prominent citizens often do in small towns, he soon had his fingers in a passel of pies. He served as city attorney for twelve years. During the Great Depression, he snapped up 18,500 acres of land on the cheap and began ranching. In 1936 he became the founder of the Rogers County Bank in Claremore, which he ran as a director, president, and chairman over the following three

decades. During World War II, he angled successfully for a seat on the Oklahoma Highway Commission. He wound up with interests in coal-mining, farming, and other industries, as well.[24]

But we are skipping an important part of our story. By the time Sam Walton met L. S. Robson, in 1942, he had already learned how to learn. He had also learned how to lead. From early in life, he was intensely ambitious. In an unintentionally amusing juxtaposition, Walton says on one page of the Walton/Huey book that as early as fifth grade he learned that teamwork was what life was all about: "One person seeking glory doesn't accomplish much. . . ." On the preceding page he informs us that in 1931, when he was thirteen, he became the youngest Eagle Scout in the history of the state of Missouri, thus winning a bet with some of his friends; and on the following page, he remarks of his basketball playing that "I liked running the team, I guess."[25]

By the time he got to Hickman High School in Columbia, Missouri, Walton had already had about four years of experience in team sports. He was five feet nine inches tall; but despite his size, he was "drafted" by the basketball team. How did the team do? An undefeated season capped by a state championship.

This was matched by performance on the gridiron. Walton started playing peewee football in fifth grade. At Hickman High, he played linebacker on defense and was a quarterback on the other side of the ball. How did the team do? Also an undefeated season capped by a state championship. Walton never played in a losing football game. "It never occurred to me that I might lose," he explained. "To me, it was almost as if I had a right to win." Walton, by his own description, was not a gifted athlete. As he put it, "I guess I was just totally competitive . . . , and my main talent was probably the same as my best talent as a retailer—I was a good motivator."[26]

Walton also says he was not a great student, "but I worked really hard and made the honor roll." In addition to his sports and schoolwork, Walton was the president of the student body and participated in numerous clubs. He was also voted "Most Versatile Boy."[27] It is a pity that the actual tally is not known. He must have finished way ahead of whoever came in second.

The transition to college was seamless. The first thing most freshmen learn at a big university is that high school stars are a dime a dozen. This is especially true if the freshman is, like Walton, a "townie" whose family was in straitened circumstances financially. Despite all this, Walton eagerly plunged into life at the University of Missouri and was accepted with open arms. "I had decided," he explains, that

> I wanted to be president of the university student body. I learned early on that one of the secrets to campus leadership was the simplest thing of all: speak to people coming down the sidewalk before they speak to you. I did that in college. . . . I would always look ahead and speak to the person coming towards me. If I knew them, I would call them by name, but even if I didn't I would still speak to them. Before long, I probably knew more students than anybody in the university, and they recognized me and considered me their friend. I ran for every office that came along. I was elected president of the senior men's honor society . . . , and officer in my fraternity, and president of the senior class. I was captain and president of Scabbard and Blade, the elite military organization of ROTC.[28]

In his spare time, Walton ran a large Bible class on Sundays (he was a Methodist). He also earned money through paper routes (some of which he subcontracted) to finance tuition, fraternity dues, and his social life. He paid for his own clothes. By 1939 and 1940, he reports that he was making $4,000 to $5,000 a year,[29] which was probably a good deal more than his professors and indeed was a very high sum at the time. Inflation adjusted, $5,000 equals about $61,500 in 2000. Author Vance Trimble interviewed a schoolmate of Walton's named Everett Orr in Shelbina, Walton's home prior to moving to Columbia. Orr remembered Walton as making friends easily "even though he was shy; people sort of flickered towards him. . . . How such a shy guy could become a leader, I just can't understand."[30] There is no other evidence that Walton was shy as a youth, so the most likely possibility is that Orr's perception is simply incorrect. On the other hand, it is intriguing to think that Walton may have adopted behavioral methods, such as speaking to people before they spoke to him, in order to overcome whatever shyness he may have felt.

Walton graduated from the University of Missouri on May 31, 1940. He had job offers from Sears and from J. C. Penney. He chose the latter and began as a management trainee at the Des Moines, Iowa, store at $75 a month.[31] From the beginning, he loved retailing. He was a born salesman, a natural with customers. He spent some time checking out the nearby store even at this early stage of his career. The climax of the experience was meeting Mr. James Cash Penney himself.[32]

Walton was working at the Penney's in Des Moines when the United States entered World War II. As a graduate of ROTC, he was already a second lieutenant in an artillery unit of the U.S. Army Reserve. One gathers it was possible to hold such a position without having undergone a physical. When Walton finally did, early in 1942, the doctors "gave him a surprise and a shock." He was diagnosed with a "partial bundle branch block," a heart defect which impacts the conduction system of the heart and could lead to an irregular heartbeat. He could still join the army, but he was cleared for "limited duty" only and did not leave the United States during the war.[33] Brother Bud, by contrast, shipped out as a torpedo bomber pilot aboard the *Manila Bay* and saw action during the invasion of Okinawa.[34]

Walton left Penney's after eighteen months in anticipation of joining the service. He proceeded, according to the Walton/Huey account, to "[wander] south, toward Tulsa, with some vague idea of seeing what the oil business was like." Instead, he got a job at a munitions plant in Pryor, not far from Tulsa. Apparently, there was no lodging to be found in Pryor; so, as Walton put it, he took the only room he could find, which was "nearby, over in Claremore."[35]

It was on an April night in 1942 that Sam Walton went bowling in Claremore. There was a pretty girl bowling in the next lane. Sam smiled at her and said, "Haven't I met you somewhere before?" I guess there actually was a time when boys with roving eyes used that line to break the ice with pretty girls. This particular pretty girl was Miss Helen Alice Robson.

Why did Walton leave Penney's before being called up for service? The answer could be that he had become romantically involved with a cashier at the Des Moines Penney's named Beth

Hamquist. This presented Walton with two dilemmas. One, Miss Hamquist was under the impression that she and Walton were engaged. Two, there was a company policy at J. C. Penney that "associates"—as employees were called at the company—were not to date one another.

So convinced was Miss Hamquist that Sam Walton was her fiancé that she followed him to Claremore. There she stayed for between two days and two weeks. The woman who provided lodging for her is reported by one author as saying: "Sam broke his engagement. Oh, the girl was terribly upset. It was kind of a big row. The girl left on the next train."[36]

This account has been cobbled together from fleeting facts, and it leaves many issues unresolved. Why would Sam Walton, who loved retail so much that he was happy to take a two-thirds cut in income to work full-time for Penney's, leave not only Penney's but also retailing? Why would he look for jobs with two big oil refineries (Carter and Humble)? Both oil companies turned him down because, it is said, they knew he would soon be in the army. The job he finally landed at the Du Pont gunpowder works in Pryor was as a field investigator who checked up on job applicants, which could hardly have been much fun for a man of Walton's temperament.

Why did Walton "wander," to use his word, all the way from Des Moines to Tulsa, a distance of 396 miles? Was the oil industry all that appealing? His parents had separated. His father was living in Fulton, Missouri, 22 miles east of Columbia and 93 miles west of St. Louis, where his mother was living (as of 1943). There is no report of his visiting either of them, even though a glance at a map shows that it is difficult to get from Des Moines to Tulsa while avoiding Missouri.

In 1942, in his twenty-fourth year, Sam Walton was effectively homeless. His return to Oklahoma cannot be interpreted as any sort of search for roots. True, he was born in Kingfisher; but that lies 115 miles west of Tulsa. It is closer to Oklahoma City (by 14 miles), insofar as it is close to any place.

There are also questions about Walton's relationship with Beth Hamquist. Was she justified in considering herself his betrothed? Were the two lovers? How did she discover that he was living in Claremore, Oklahoma? Why is she not even mentioned in the book on which he worked with John Huey?

I have dwelt at some length on these questions because this seems to me to be the only time in Walton's life that he was out of focus and drifting. Here is a man whose father, though not a failure, was not a success and not a role model. Worse, his family was not a success. As soon as his brother left home, Walton's parents separated and did not spend much time with one another thereafter. He came of age in a series of small towns. How many people reading this book could locate on a map or have ever previously heard of Kingfisher or Claremore or Pryor, Oklahoma, or of Marshall or Shelbina (is the "i" long or short?), Missouri? The discord in his family was probably known about in each town in which he lived.

As if this were not enough, Walton grew up during the Great Depression; and the region in which he grew up was particularly hard hit. As he recalled many years later, good people whose families had worked the land for as long as anyone could remember were being dispossessed. Of course this was not his father's fault, but his father was an agent of the dispossessors. As reporter Ortega put it, Tom Walton was "a repo man. It wasn't cheery work; but it was all too steady."[37]

Despite everything, Sam Walton was a ball of fire through high school and college. He had multiple job offers, selected one of the nation's most prestigious retail companies in which to train, and even met the great man, J. C. Penney himself, personally. I remember a college football coach describing his quarterback and team leader as neither a great runner nor a great passer, but a born winner. That was the image that Sam Walton managed to develop of himself despite some imposing obstacles. He was a positive thinker. "Thinking like that often seems to turn into a sort of self-fulfilling prophecy," he asserted, sounding not unlike Mary Kay Ash.[38]

In 1941 and 1942, Walton was walloped by three blows in quick succession. After years of domestic warfare, it became undeniable that his parents were married in name only. Family was very important to Walton. He remained close to his brother his whole life, he cherished the family he built with his wife,[39] and he often used the family metaphor when building Wal-Mart. Second, his relationship with Beth Hamquist, whatever its nature, obviously did not turn out well. Its ending, in a noisy "row," could not have failed to bring to Walton's mind how his own parents had failed to get along.

Finally, and this might have been most important of all, there was the "surprise" of the army physical.[40] For all his unparalleled talent as a motivator, Walton does not seem to have been an introspective or psychologically minded man. As he said, "I've always had a strong bias toward action. . . ."[41] He was not contemplative, and he did not appear really to know himself very well. The unexamined life was perfectly well worth living for him.

Whether you choose to know it and think about it or not, however, the news that you have something wrong with your body is not good. And the heart is heavy with symbolic meaning and psychological significance. Moreover, unlike his weight, which he overcame in football, or his height, which he overcame in basketball, this physical fact was going to have an impact which no amount of positive thinking could change. The army said that Sam Walton, who had been the president of Scabbard and Blade in ROTC in college, could never see action, never build and lead a team, never be a hero in the biggest war in history. "I wish I could recount a valiant military career—like my brother Bud . . . ," he later remarked, "but my service stint was really fairly ordinary time spent as a lieutenant and then as a captain doing things like supervising security at aircraft plants and POW plants. . . ."[42]

RETAILING

The years in the service were not a total waste. Walton had learned two big things: "I not only knew I wanted to go into retailing, I also knew I wanted to go into business for myself."[43] His ambition had not lain idle during the war. He read voraciously about retailing. At war's end, he and Helen, whose first child, Samuel Robson Walton (known as Rob), was born in 1944, agreed that they should not return to Claremore. They both admired Helen's father, but neither wanted Sam to start out in L. S.'s shadow. They also agreed, at Helen's wish, that they should live in a small town. "I'll go with you any place you want so long as you don't ask me to live in a big city," she told him as he resumed civilian life. "Ten thousand people is enough for me."[44]

Sam and Helen Walton settled in Newport, Arkansas, in the fall of 1945. This little town, with a population of between 4,301 in 1940 and 6,254 in 1950, is about seventy-eight miles northwest of Memphis and about eighty-nine miles northeast of Little Rock.[45] It is located on the White River and is the county seat of Jackson County. "Railroad shipping, cotton, pecans, a shoe factory, a metal mill, and some other industries formed the basis of its economy."[46]

Newport had not been Walton's first choice as a place to call home. He had a friend from college days, his roommate at the Beta Theta Pi fraternity house, Tom Bates. At war's end, Bates was working in the shoe department of Butler Brothers in St. Louis. Butler Brothers was a wholesaler which franchised a department store chain (Federated) and a chain of variety stores (Ben Franklin). Bates suggested that he and Walton each invest $20,000 to buy a Federated department store on Del Mar Avenue in St. Louis—"a great idea," thought Walton. His share would come partly from the $5,000 he and his wife had saved, "and I knew we could borrow the rest from her father."[47] Walton had not inherited his father's aversion to debt.

Helen, however, "spoke up and laid down the law" about small towns and big cities. That ruled St. Louis out. She was opposed to partnerships as well, having seen a few "go sour." These were the reasons Walton advanced for going back to Butler Brothers to see what else was available. For an up-front fee of $25,000, Butler Brothers would make Samuel M. Walton its franchisee in Newport, which is how he, his wife, and his young son wound up there.[48]

Walton was twenty-seven years old when he opened his five-thousand-square-foot variety store "in the heart of town, looking out on the railroad tracks" on September 1, 1945. He was full of vigor and optimism, just raring to go. "I've always believed in goals, so I set myself one: I wanted my little Newport store to be the best, most profitable variety store in Arkansas within five years."[49]

This seemingly simple story is noteworthy for a host of reasons. The first is access to capital. Twenty-five thousand dollars was a considerable sum to be able to invest in 1945. Inflation-adjusted, it is the equivalent of almost $240,000 in 2000.

If we assume that Walton's $5,000 share of this fee was half his and half Helen's (a not unreasonable assumption—he earned money in college, after college, and in the army; and her father was a man of means), then one-tenth of the funds required for Walton to open up shop was his own equity. All of which is to say that when Walton later wrote of Helen's "[laying] down the law," it might have been a little more than the standard figure of speech. It is questionable whether he would have been able to raise the necessary funds through a bank or through other sources were it not for his wife and father-in-law. His own parents certainly did not have the capital to finance him.

The second important aspect of this story is the amount of capital required. This $25,000 was a cover charge. Butler Brothers had strict rules for their franchisees. They "wanted us to do things literally by the book—their book. They really didn't allow their franchisees much discretion."[50] Eighty percent of a franchisee's merchandise had to be purchased through Butler Brothers, which marked up their goods fairly high. It was, in other words, virtually prohibited by economics for a Butler Brothers franchisee to become a discounter.

By far the most remarkable part of the story comes down to two words: Newport, Arkansas. Arkansas was simply not a state to which people, especially ambitious people, were attracted in 1945. As one of the state's historians has remarked, "Unless one owned land or a business, those who left Arkansas to help fight World War II or for a well-paying defense job had little economic reason to return to the state [at the end of the war]."[51]

Arkansas was a small, poor state in the process of growing smaller in the poorest section of the country. The population in 1940 was 1,949,387; by 1950, it had dropped to 1,909,511. This was a decline of 2 percent in a nation that grew during that same decade from 131,669,275 to 150,697,361 or almost 15 percent. Arkansas ranked twenty-fourth among the forty-eight states (Alaska and Hawaii were not admitted to the Union until 1959) in population in 1940 and thirtieth in 1950. It is true that the population of Newport increased during the 1940s; but we do not know when (during the war? after the war? steadily?) or why. There is no evidence that Walton selected Newport because he saw a potential for growth in the town. As late as 1990, Newport's population was only 7,459.

In 1929, per capita income in Arkansas was less than half the national average, $306 compared to $705. In 1940, the numbers were $254 for Arkansas and $592 for the nation as a whole. Per capita income in Arkansas increased dramatically in the decade of World War II as opposed to the Depression decade, from $254 to $825. The state still badly lagged the nation, however. Per capita income in the United States reached four figures in 1950 at $1,496. Keep in mind that this took place in the context of a growing national population, while Arkansas's population declined.[52]

Arkansas "was not a typically southern state."[53] Its farms were smaller; its people, poorer. The proportion of African Americans declined from 24.7 percent of the population in 1940 to 22.3 percent in 1950,[54] far lower than such southern "Black Belt" states as South Carolina, Georgia, Alabama, and Mississippi.[55] Arkansas, along with those four states and six others,[56] seceded to form the Confederate States of America in 1861. The Civil War is merely a dim memory at this writing[57]; but it was a vivid reality, especially in the states that lost, in 1945.

History had "happened" to the eleven states of the Old Confederacy.[58] They had lost the defining armed conflict of the United States. Their political culture wallowed in their defeat. The racism which came hand in glove with the Confederacy's "noble" failure besmirched American society. Needless to say, racism was a national phenomenon, not restricted to the South. De jure segregation and denial of the franchise did, however, predominate there.

Here is how one historian described politics in Arkansas during the depression:

> A politician did not rise because he took a stand on issues, but because in an election he had the right people behind him (local leaders who could turn out votes and rich supporters who could supply him with campaign funds) and because he knew what to say in a campaign—recall the past, the "wah" of the 1860's and the grasping Yankees who ever since it had oppressed the South, and perhaps allude to the ever-present "nigger" menace.[59]

Such demagogy would, of course, do the average citizen of the nation's second-poorest state no good.[60] But that was the politics of this segregated, one-party state,[61] and it would be many years before things changed. Orval E. Faubus "served" as governor for six terms, from 1955 to 1967. It was Faubus whose gross mismanagement of the era of school integration forced President Eisenhower to mobilize elements of the 101st Airborne (a unit which had fought at Normandy) and deploy them in Little Rock.[62]

In a state in a city in a store which were primitive by contemporary standards in most other places in America, Sam Walton launched his career in retailing. The store's previous owner was a "guy from St. Louis" for whom "things weren't working out at all. . . ."[63] Under the previous owner the preceding year, the store had done $72,000 in business. Across the street there was another variety store, part of the long-forgotten Sterling chain, which did $150,000, slightly over twice Walton's store's volume. Clearly on that September day in 1945 in which Walton's Ben Franklin opened up, its new owner had a very long way to go to become the most successful five-and-dime operator in Newport, never mind the whole of the great state of Arkansas. The previous owner of Walton's store "was losing money," Walton later recalled, and "I was the sucker Butler Brothers sent to save him."[64]

Sam Walton's first store was a second-rate store in a second-rate town in what no one would have classified as a first-rate state. Millions, literally, of small stores failed during the course of the twentieth century in America. There were about 1.7 million retail establishments in the United States in 1945.[65] Why wouldn't this one be among the many that didn't make it?

Surely, any analyst of the situation in 1945 would have found in Walton a good candidate for failure. As he himself put it, "For all of my confidence I hadn't had a day's experience in running a variety store. . . ."[66] He could have added that he had not had a day's experience in running a business of any kind. He paid a price for this inexperience and excessive enthusiasm before his store even opened. He had selected the wrong store and paid too much for it. "Only after we closed the deal, of course, did I learn that the store was a real dog."[67] The rent for this "dog" was 5 percent of sales. This sounded fine to Walton; but after signing the lease, he discovered that this "was the highest rent anybody'd ever heard of in the variety store business. No one paid 5 percent of sales for rent."[68] Here was another economic factor which was going to make it difficult to use low prices as a competitive weapon. And there were more problems with the lease, serious problems, which it would take Walton another half decade to discover.

Walton seemed to have a lot of strikes against him. But he was a spectacular success in his first store. Why? Much of what was to make him the great merchant he became was evident from the very beginning. First he learned all the rules. Then he broke all the rules which did not make sense to him—which meant almost all of them. Everything he did seems so obvious. It seems that way because it was. Sam Walton did not become a billionaire because he was a genius (although he was without question smart, shrewd, and astute). The real explanation for his success was that he had the courage of his convictions.

Butler Brothers had a training program for variety store franchisees, so Walton was off to Arkadelphia, Arkansas, for two weeks of education prior to opening his store. He found it useful. "You can learn from everybody," he said,[69] and one of the key characteristics of his career was that he kept learning until the day he died. He learned from Butler Brothers, from retail publications, and from his competitor, John Dunham, with his Sterling Store. According to Helen Walton, "Of course, what really drove Sam was that competition across the street—John Dunham over at the Sterling Store. Sam was always over there checking on John. Always. Looking at his prices, looking at his displays, looking at what was going on. . . . I'm sure it aggravated him quite a bit early on."[70]

It did not take long for Walton to begin to chafe under the tight controls of Butler Brothers. He began scouting around for less expensive suppliers, and he found them. If there was inspiration in his business strategy, it lay in the next step. Having found less expensive suppliers than Butler Brothers, he did not sell his products at prevailing prices. Instead, he discounted his merchandise, passing the savings he achieved on to the consumer, and made his profit on volume rather than on margin. "Simple enough," as Walton himself admitted. But it took him a decade to appreciate fully the power of the idea. Once he had seized on it, never wavering from it became the centerpiece of Wal-Mart's greatness.

That was still a long time in the future. Butler Brothers was not thrilled by Walton's freelancing ways, but the numbers he was putting up seemed to mollify them. Sales increased more than 45 percent to $105,000 in his first full year of ownership. The following year, sales were up another third to $140,000. The year after that he surpassed his rival Dunham as sales increased 25 percent to $175,000. After thirty months in business, Walton was able to repay his father-in-law's loan in full. In his fifth year at the Ben Franklin on Front Street in Newport, Arkansas, Sam Walton—the sucker Butler Brothers had been looking for—sold $250,000 worth of merchandise and made a profit of between $30,000 and

$40,000.[71] His loser of a store in the middle of nowhere had posted a compound annual growth rate in sales of over 28 percent. He was the leading variety store operator in Arkansas, and probably in the adjacent states as well.

And then, in a heartbeat, he lost everything.

The problem was the lease Walton had signed back in 1945 for his Front Street store. It contained no renewal clause. Options to renew were standard features of leases such as the one Walton had originally entered into.[72] L. S. Robson was reportedly shocked by Walton's mistake.

Not only had Walton built a successful business in Newport, he had invested a lot of himself in the town. He was an active member of the Rotary Club, a member of the board of deacons of the Presbyterian church ("even though I was a Methodist, it worked out real well"), and president of the Chamber of Commerce.[73]

Equally important, Helen loved the town. Three of her four children—John Thomas (1946), James Carr (1948), and Alice (1949)—were born during those five years. "We had built a life there," she recalled in 1992. "I still have good friends from those days."[74] Now they were going to have to leave because there was no other space available to relocate the store.

"It was the low point of my life," Walton recalled.

> I felt sick to my stomach. I couldn't believe it was happening to me. It was really like a nightmare. I had built the best variety store in the whole region and worked hard in the community—done everything right—and now I was being kicked out of town. It didn't seem fair. I blamed myself for getting suckered into such an awful lease, and I was furious at the landlord. Helen, just settling in with a brand-new family of four, was heartsick at the prospect of leaving Newport. But that's what we were going to do.[75]

There is a great deal to be learned from Walton's assessment of the situation. First of all, this really hurt. Second, he blamed himself. Third, he had been a sucker—there is that word again. Fourth, even though he took responsibility, he found something fundamentally unfair in what had befallen him. He had "done everything right," yet his reward was exile.

Many another great entrepreneur suffered similar setbacks. Many made mistakes for which they had only themselves to blame. Many encountered situations in which their failure to achieve their goals was experienced as fundamentally unfair. Great entrepreneurs are, speaking generally, people of enormous, innate optimism. (Charles Revson was quite exceptional in this regard.) They believe that honest, intelligent effort will be greeted by appropriate reward. What they do not believe is that life is unfair. When they do everything right, and the result turns out wrong, the cause is a temporary cosmic misunderstanding which will be corrected in due course. Sometimes corrected with a vengeance.

Thus, when George Eastman was passed over for promotion at the Rochester Savings Bank in 1881, he did not merely accept the setback fatalistically. He rebelled. He rebelled because, as he said using language not dissimilar from Walton's, "It wasn't fair. It wasn't right; it was against every principle of justice."[76]

Also like other great entrepreneurs, Walton traveled light. He did not ruminate. "I've never been one to dwell on reverses, and I didn't do so then. . . . I know I read my leases a lot more carefully after that, and maybe I became a little more wary of just how tough the world can be. . . . But I didn't dwell on my disappointment."[77]

It is worth asking why Mr. P. K. Holmes, Walton's landlord, did not renew his lease. There were some obvious reasons for him to keep rather than evict Walton. His flair was creating a lot of what Newport had precious little of, excitement. Walton was repeating his high school and college experiences, becoming the most popular man around. And there was what cannot have been the completely insignificant question of money. Before Walton, the local Ben Franklin did $72,000 in sales. Five years into Walton's tenure, it did a quarter of a million. At a rental fee of 5 percent of sales, that meant the difference between $3,600 and $12,500 or $8,900 for Mr. Holmes. That $8,900 in 1945 is, inflation adjusted, over $85,000 in 2000. Mr. Holmes received this bounty for doing nothing whatever himself. It was pure luck for him that Helen Walton wanted to live in a small town, that Butler Brothers needed to unload the local Ben Franklin, and that the "sucker" on whom it was unloaded turned out to be the greatest merchant ever.

Think about the future. Let's say that Walton's store eased from its 28 percent compound annual growth rate in sales down to 18 percent. In five years, the sales of that store would be about $572,000. Five percent of that is over $28,000. Not a bad income for sitting around and watching the grass grow. One can imagine worse tenants.

The fact that Walton had acquired the lease to a store in Newport that Kroger was vacating and then set up a small department store himself, which he called the Eagle Store, might not have been completely irrelevant in Holmes's thinking. Walton did not intend to go into the department store business in a serious way. He bought the lease to prevent his "friendly" rival John Dunham from acquiring the property and expanding his Sterling Store. Newport already had a couple of department stores. One of these was owned by P. K. Holmes. Walton's transaction did not go unnoticed.

However, Walton believed, probably correctly, that Holmes refused to renew his lease at any price because he saw how well the Ben Franklin was doing. He purchased the store's inventory and fixtures at what Walton himself concedes was "a fair price," $50,000.[78] So Walton did not leave Newport empty-handed. With the store intact, Holmes gave it to his son. Thus, Walton suffered from nepotism in a sense just as Eastman had. Holmes must have figured there was no particular reason to be content with 5 percent of something when he could have 100 percent of that same thing all in the family.

Eastman returned to the Rochester Savings Bank as a director after he had made his fortune. Walton never came back to Newport as a resident, but he did as a merchant. This is what he had to say:

> Wal-Mart No. 18 . . . opened in 1969, and it marked our return to Newport . . . nineteen years after we had basically been run out of town. By then, I was long over what had happened to us down there, and I didn't have revenge in mind. . . . As it happened, we did extraordinarily well with our Newport Wal-Mart, and it wasn't too long before the old Ben Franklin store I had run on Front Street had to close its doors. You can't say we ran that guy—the landlord's son—out of business. His customers were the ones who shut him down. They voted with their feet.[79]

Perhaps Walton did not have revenge uppermost in mind. But odds are it was there somewhere. He found room to mention Wal-

Mart No. 18 in his autobiography, which was written on his deathbed.

BENTONVILLE

Despite the bitter disappointment, anger, and self-reproach which accompanied the loss of the Newport lease, great things had been done. Walton had competed in a come-from-behind situation and had won. He had learned the importance of rule breaking.

In merchandise procurement, for example, he had done an end run around the Butler Brothers system, venturing as far afield as New York City to buy goods for less. He had created excitement in his store by passing those savings along to his customers. Newport was not the poorest place in Arkansas, but it and the surrounding trading area were among the poorest in the nation. Low prices—bargains—attracted attention.

Walton had also learned a lot about how to merchandise a store. Once again, the emphasis was on excitement, on the unexpected, on what had not been done before. The story is told best in his own words:

> We tried a lot of promotional things that worked really well. First, we put a popcorn machine out on the sidewalk, and we sold that stuff like crazy. So I thought and thought about it and finally decided what we needed was a soft ice cream machine out there too. I screwed my courage up and went down to the bank and borrowed what at the time seemed like the astronomical sum of $1,800 to buy that thing.[80] That was the first money I ever borrowed from a bank. Then we rolled the ice cream machine out there on the sidewalk next to the popcorn machine, and I mean we attracted some attention with these two. It was really new and different—another experiment—and we really turned a profit on it.[81]

Walton said that "most everything I've done I've copied from someone else."[82] He did indeed copy from others much of what he did. He gives ample credit to other merchants for various of the measures he took to build Wal-Mart into the leader it became.

Nevertheless, Walton was a bit modest about copying. Plenty of what he did in his career was quite new. We see this novelty from the start. The popcorn and ice-cream machines are good illustrations. No one had done that before in his neck of the woods. In 1983, when Wal-Mart put up a satellite to facilitate communications, no other retailer had done that before, either.

Thus, Walton had some solid accomplishments under his belt by the time he decamped to Bentonville, Arkansas, with his wife and four young children. The trip and everything associated with it were not much fun. Helen Walton liked Newport. To her, it was "a thriving cotton town not a backwater." "I hated to leave," she said bluntly.[83]

It was difficult to tell yourself a happy story about Bentonville.[84] It is in the Ozarks, in the far northwestern corner of Arkansas, 174 miles away from Newport, squeezed in between Missouri and Oklahoma. Bentonville's population was 2,359 in 1940 and 2,912 in 1950, when the Walton family moved there.[85]

Bentonville was not the first choice. Walton had tried to buy a store in Siloam Springs, right on the Oklahoma border, but had failed to come to terms with the store's owner. When he and his father-in-law first drove into Bentonville and looked around, what greeted them was a bit on the dreary side. The best thing Helen Walton could think to say about it was that it had a railroad track.

"I remember," she said, "I couldn't believe this was where we were going to live."[86] It almost wasn't. Walton had a hard time leasing a store there, and it was his father-in-law who made the deal with "two old widows from Kansas City who owned it [and who] wouldn't budge."[87] Robson negotiated a ninety-nine year lease for Walton. There would be no repeat of the Newport fiasco.

The Bentonville store was a step down not only from the point Walton had reached in 1950 in Newport, but also from where he had begun in 1945. The store did $32,000 in sales the year before he bought it. Despite the fact that Bentonville was half the size of Newport, it had three variety stores. "It didn't matter that much," Walton later wrote, "because I had big plans."[88]

These big plans hatched in a little town came to fruition quickly. Walton immediately expanded, leasing the barbershop next door and knocking down the wall between them. He now had fifty feet looking out at the town square, where there was a statue the like of which could be seen in only a few other states—a Confederate soldier. The expanded store was four thousand square feet, almost all of which was selling space.[89] This expansion was undertaken without any evaluation of market demand. It was based on intuition.

Walton's 5 & 10, as the new store was known despite the fact that it was still part of the Ben Franklin chain, opened for business with a "remodeling sale" in July 1950. The cost of the store and the remodeling was $55,000, or $5,000 more than Walton would receive in payment for the fixtures in the Newport store.[90] So he was betting the proverbial farm.

Walton did not vacate the Newport store until the end of 1950. He and his family moved to Bentonville in January of the following year. Thus, he commuted between the two towns for about six months. Although the distance is 174 miles as the crow flies, it was more than 250 miles over the winding two-lane roads of the Ozarks. Walton and his family always had the reputation for being heavy-footed, but this drive took even him eight to ten hours one way.[91] He was a man in a hurry, and losing a day this way must have aggravated him considerably. Thoughts of his own airplane entered his mind early in his career, thoughts which struck fear into the hearts of his friends who knew his driving habits.[92]

In the midst of all this activity—running two stores, uprooting his family to the great disappointment of his wife and probably also of those of his children who were old enough to have made friends in Newport—came word from St. Louis that Nan Walton, Sam's mother, needed surgery for cancer. "Sam and Bud rushed there," according to one of Walton's biographers.[93] We do not know if her husband was present. Nan Walton died soon after her operation.[94]

Interestingly, there is no mention of his mother's death taking place at this time in Walton's autobiography. It is, however, easy to see how he might have been especially moved by it at this moment. He was thirty-two years old, only twenty years younger than she. He had already learned that there was an issue with his heart. Walton was in a hurry. One wonders whether his mother's death at this particular point might have pushed him to hurry even faster.

As of January 1, 1951, Walton was back down to running a single store. From a standing start in Bentonville, he proved once again that he could make something out of nothing. Soon that store, the sales of which were about the same as the profits from the Newport store, had tripled its volume. Walton was immediately in the hunt for more stores and more ideas about how to turn them into big successes. He sought, and he found. There were over a million and a half stores in the United States. Breakthrough thinking could be anywhere.

Developments in Pipestone and Worthington, Minnesota, provide an example. Always a voracious reader of anything dealing with the trade, Walton got wind of the fact that self-service was being implemented in the Ben Franklins in those two towns. Walton always kicked the tires—he had to see, feel, touch—so he hopped on a bus to inspect these stores for himself. Worthington, Minnesota, is 506 miles from Bentonville, and Pipestone is 32 miles farther as the crow flies. As the bus drives, it was a longer trip, but it was well worth making.[95]

What Walton saw were stores which replaced a cash register at each counter with one central checkout register. This was noteworthy for a number of reasons. It meant fewer cash registers, which lowered costs. It meant fewer clerks tending those cash registers. Payroll has always constituted a significant portion of retail expenses, and anything that reduced it was news. The fewer the employees handling cash, the less chance for mistakes or pilferage. These savings could be passed along to the customers, with lower prices increasing volume.

Fewer transactions meant less time paying for items and more time shopping for them. It meant that your attention was less often called to the cost of what you were buying. It turned out that the average shopper in a variety store spent more per trip when the format was self-service. Walton recognized this quickly and implemented the concept.[96]

Walton opened his second variety store in Fayetteville, Arkansas, twenty miles south of Bentonville, on October 30, 1952. Like Bentonville and also like Newport, Fayetteville was the small county seat of a small county. It was also the home of the University of Arkansas. Self-service was such a success at Fayetteville that Walton remodeled the Bentonville store and introduced it there as well. The following year, Walton acquired yet another variety store, this one in the Kansas City suburb of Ruskin Heights, two hundred miles north of Bentonville.

At all his stores, Walton's magic touch evinced itself immediately. Sales and profits grew beyond what anyone had a right to expect. Amidst this success, the idea of the shopping center caught his eye. His instincts were unerring. Shopping centers were indeed the future of retail commerce in the United States in the 1950s. But Walton did not have the funds to become a shopping center entrepreneur; and after two years and $25,000 of effort, he went back to what he knew best. His variety store empire grew at a torrid pace. He bought himself an airplane in 1957 so he could be everywhere at once. Without private planes, it probably would not have been possible to manage a company that became as large as Wal-Mart from a location as remote as Bentonville.

By the early 1960s, Walton had achieved an altogether remarkable record: "That whole period—which scarcely gets any attention from people studying us—was really very successful. In fifteen years time, we had become the largest independent variety store operator in the United States."[97] In his early forties, Sam Walton was already a rich man, and he had learned a lot of lessons which were to stand him in good stead in the future.

Retailing is the quintessential people-intensive business. People choose to buy a product at a particular store for a host of reasons, not all of which they themselves are fully aware. Merchandise assortment and price are key variables, but other factors play important roles as well. The feeling you get in the store, the welcome you receive, the look of the place, the helpfulness of the staff, and the reputation of the proprietor all matter.

In order not only to manage the merchandise but also the less tangible aspects of retailing, Walton knew he had to hire the best store managers he could. This was not easy. First, he had to be able to spot the talent. Since outstanding store managers were invariably already managing stores, he had to lure them away from their present employment to work for him. Walton was unexcelled at both tasks. His appreciation of retail talent was innate. He had a lifelong habit of visiting all kinds of retailers wherever he traveled. He quickly developed an eye for a store that "is looking real fine out there."[98] As he put it, from early in his career Walton would do what he would always "do for the rest of my run in the retail business without any shame or embarrassment whatsoever: nose around other people's stores searching for good talent."[99]

Walton kept that talent loyal to the company by giving them a piece of the action in both monetary and psychic terms. Monetarily, store managers and later the "associates" who staffed the stores benefited from a generous profit-sharing program. The psychic reward derived from the fact that Walton gave his store managers considerable latitude in how they ran their stores. He was not going to make the same mistake that Butler Brothers and so many other chains made of thinking that they and they alone knew the one best way to run a store. After all, what point would there be in finding the people with the best ideas if one then prevented them from implementing those ideas?

Walton entered a mature, declining business in a backwater part of the country and showed how imagination could create success. By 1960, he was doing $1.4 million in sales through fifteen stores. He was the nation's largest independent variety store operator— wealthy and successful—with every reason to believe the future promised more of the same.

"BUY IT LOW, STACK IT HIGH, SELL IT CHEAP"

Around the fringes of respectable, main street retailing, there had been for years by 1960 the phenomenon of discounting. Discounting simply means selling products below what most other competitors sell them for. Great fortunes had been made in this way, including the Rosenwalds' at Sears and the Hartfords' at the A&P. It was a proven formula for success. Price may be only one factor in the determination of where a consumer shops; but it is very important for a number of reasons.

First and most obviously, if you cannot afford a product you cannot buy it, no matter how much you might want it or how pleasant you might find the store's ambience. Second, there are many people who have a visceral dislike of paying $1.39 for a tube of toothpaste that is being sold for $1.19 a couple of blocks away, even though twenty cents does not mean much to them.

Opportunities to discount abounded in the United States in the twentieth century. Among the factors facilitating it were that many goods traveled a long and tortuous path from the manufacturer's plant to the consumer's home. Wholesalers, jobbers, truckers, sales representatives—depending upon the product, all of these middlemen have been involved in distributing merchandise. All have taken a "cut," thus raising the price. The retailer who could combine business savvy with volume purchases could circumvent some of these middlemen. If he chose to pass his savings along to the consumer with the view to make up in volume what he sacrificed in margin, he was a discounter.

Two other factors created opportunities for discounters during the past hundred years. One was the rise of manufacturer-branded, nationally advertised products. Crest is, after all, Crest. It is the same toothpaste in Portland, Maine, as it is in Portland, Oregon. Why pay more? A tough question to answer. Second, the manufacturer's advertising dollar could now exercise an unprecedented impact first through radio and then through television. We have examined television advertising in our chapter on Revson.

In addition to all this, distribution in general and retailing specifically have long served the purpose of an "employment sponge" in the United States and in other nations as well. By that, I mean that any mom and pop who could scrape up a little capital and were willing to work long hours and cultivate the goodwill of their neighbors could open up the proverbial "mom and pop" store. Such stores were redolent with economic inefficiencies and thus constantly in danger of well-managed, low-price competition. Every mom and pop did, however, have a vote; and for years there was a battle over so-called fair trade, a policy whereby manufacturers could determine the price at which their goods could be sold. This policy benefited inefficient retailers because it protected them from low-price retail competition.

Many manufacturers also felt that fair trade was of benefit to them. They spent a lot of money to establish a reputation for their brand in the mind of the consumer. If discounters featured their brand at a very low price, the effect might be to tarnish the brand's image. Retailers who were trying to sell the product at the manufacturer's suggested retail price would be angered that the same product was being sold for less at another retail outlet. These are the reasons that Revlon was always on the lookout for retailers who bootlegged on their franchise.

The result of using a manufacturer's brand as a "price football"—that is to say, kicking it around—might thus be to erode the value of the brand over the long term. Mainstream retailers might no longer be able to afford to sell a standard brand on which they were being underpriced. And the discounters might use the bait and switch, enticing the consumer to their stores with the promise of low prices on well-known brands but then stocking out of those brands and leaving consumers to purchase the retailer's own private-label merchandise.[100]

In a word, discounting meant disorder in distribution. To many, profits would be assured if order were maintained. To others, to the Sam Waltons of the world, disorder meant opportunity. (As a mature company, Wal-Mart broke the mold by creating a well-ordered discounting environment.)

Different nations have handled the challenge of discounting in different ways. For the most part, there has been a bias in favor of viewing the citizen as an employee or a proprietor and against viewing that same individual as a consumer. This has meant zoning laws and other restrictions which have protected small, inefficient distributors and forestalled the development of the large, bulk-distributing discounter. Japan is an oft-cited example.[101]

In the United States, by contrast, the consumer has been king. No one in the nation was better positioned to compete in such a context than Sam Walton, whose endlessly repeated mantra was "serve the customer." Note how he described his return to Newport, Arkansas, in 1969 with Wal-Mart No. 18. He didn't put that Ben Franklin out of business. The customers shut the old store down: "They voted with their feet." Walton was a fervent believer in consumer democracy. Consumers have choices in a free country. They "vote" for us by patronizing our stores.

Because of the importance of the consumer in the United States, there was always plenty of pressure pushing back against fair trade or resale price maintenance, known simply as price fixing to its opponents. The fair trade laws had draconian implications, but they were difficult to enforce. State by state, these laws were repealed during the 1950s and 1960s; and in 1975, Congress enacted legislation ending the practice.[102]

Despite his success in the variety store business, Walton was always on the lookout for new and better ways to do things. He knew that the world would not stop turning just because he was successful. Walton was always willing to discard old ways of operating even when they had proven successful and to embrace the new.

Notwithstanding his accomplishments in variety stores, he took stock in the early 1960s and wasn't thrilled by the result: "The business itself seemed a little limited. The volume was so little per store that it really didn't amount to that much. I mean, after 15 years—in 1960—we were only doing $1.4 million in fifteen stores. By now, you know me. I began looking around hard for whatever new idea would break us over into something with a little better payoff for all our efforts."[103]

Walton was restless. He was looking for answers to the problem of how to grow. He sensed that other retailers were asking the same question. If he failed to grow, his competitors might do so at his expense.

He stumbled upon one clue to the future in the first Walton Family Center, opened in St. Robert, Missouri, in 1962. Located near the Fort Leonard Wood army base, St. Robert had a population of only fifteen hundred. Nevertheless, Walton opened a very large store there, thirteen thousand square feet. Business boomed; and before the end of the year, Walton enlarged the store to twenty thousand square feet. Annualized sales in its first year in business were $2 million, or more than his entire chain of fifteen variety stores in 1960. Soon thereafter, Walton opened another large variety store in a small town, this one a thirteen-thousand-square-foot store in Berryville, Arkansas, population two thousand.

In 1962, Walton proved to himself that very small towns could support very big stores. This, then, was to be his path to growth. His immediate problem was that other stores, especially discounters, were attempting to grow aggressively at this time as well. Everywhere he looked there were tigers devouring the old world of retail. In the Northeast, there were E. J. Korvette, Ann and Hope, Two Guys from Harrison, among others. In the West there was Sol Price, whose Fed-Mart Walton much admired. In his own backyard, there was Herb Gibson—"a barber from over in Berryville"—who had gone into discounting in Texas and had invaded northwest Arkansas in 1959. Having a national rather than a local view of retail trends, Walton knew the threat Gibson posed. He was not an isolated phenomenon but part of a broad trend. It was Gibson whose stores were focused around the concept "Buy it low, stack it high, sell it cheap." "I knew the discount idea was the future," Walton later wrote.[104]

In 1962, a number of others thought as Walton did. Woolworth, a variety chain founded in 1879 in Lancaster, Pennsylvania, by Frank W. Woolworth, established a discount arm, Woolco. The midwestern department store giant Dayton-Hudson founded Target. Most menacing of all, another midwestern retailer, S. S. Kresge, founded Kmart. This move was made after years of study by a man Walton described as "one of the leading retailers of all time," Harry B. Cunningham.[105] All this took place in 1962. That same year, on July 2, Sam Walton opened his first Wal-Mart, in Rogers, Arkansas.

Imagine the following question being asked were a poll taken in 1962: "Of the following four firms, which will emerge as the power retailer of the twentieth century: Woolco, Target, Kmart, or Wal-Mart?" How many people would have answered Wal-Mart? Probably not too many. "Sometimes," said Walton, "even I have trouble believing it."[106]

Walton was certainly right about discounting. It was the future. Moreover, it was a future in which by virtue of his background, abilities, and temperament, Walton was particularly suited to compete. In order to understand why, a few observations about the discount industry are in order.

First, let's look at what discounting is not. Discounting is not glamorous. Your merchandise is not glamorous. Neither are your stores. Nor are your employees. Nor your customers. Think of Rodeo Drive, the Rue du Faubourg St. Honoré, Savile Row. Everything represented by these famous avenues is what discounting is not.

Your merchandise consists of staples. From small-ticket items such as health and beauty aids all the way up to household appliances and automobile accessories, you sell what people need to make it through the day. Your selection in these product categories is unimaginative. You have to stock the most well known brands for two reasons. First, the sole appeal of your store is price; and well-known brands are widely enough available so that prices can be easily compared. Second, in pursuit of the low cost structure which is absolutely essential to your operations, you cannot hire too much sales help; and the salespeople you do employ will receive the minimum wage, if that. A large percentage of your employees must be part-timers, so you don't have to pay benefits. With no training and, speaking generally, no motivation, such salespeople are unable to explain why one brand of a product might be better than another. From toilet tissue to oil filters, your products have to sell themselves.

Everything about your stores must be as cheap as possible. Rent, fixtures, lighting, rest rooms—everything. Your customers are shopping to procure goods at the lowest possible price. They are not out for entertainment or excitement.

Your customers are going to be bargain hunters. Most will look for the cheapest goods by necessity. A few by inclination. But none of them will be loyal. These are people transacting business, not building relationships. Many of them have more time than money, and as soon as they locate an item at a lower price than yours they are out the door.

This competitive environment could be extraordinarily profitable. Returns on equity for top discounters have been the envy of the retail world.[107] The problem is that discounting is unforgiving. When you lose your focus on what must be your sole goal, provisioning your customer at a lower price than everybody else, you have a big problem. Time after time, discounters have lost that focus and lost their business as a result. A look at a list of leading discounters in 1965 shows a lot of names, such as E. J. Korvette, Interstate, Gibson Products, Zayre, GEM International, Vornado, S. Klein, Food Fair, which had disappeared by the turn of the century.[108] Why?

In order to deliver goods profitably at the lowest prices, you have to have the lowest costs in the business. The history of retailing illustrates that maintaining a low-cost position over an extended period of time is extraordinarily difficult. The efficiency of suppliers changes over time. Consumers move to new locations. New roads are built, changing your trading area and perhaps exposing you to new competition. New technology is developed which may lower costs eventually by, for example, facilitating inventory management. But how do you know what to invest in? How do you know whether your investment will pay off? What if you make investments in a technology which does not perform as promised? What if, on the other hand, you decline to invest but your competitors do and the technology does perform?

Added to all this is the ego of the discount entrepreneur. Many discounters start their business in no-frills, no-fixtures warehouses (literally warehouses or abandoned mills) because they can not afford anything else. Once they begin to enjoy some success, the feeling creeps up on them that their stores ought to look a bit better. Better signage, some carpeting, and nicer executive offices make it more enjoyable to bring family and friends by to admire the store.

This sounds simple, but it is a powerful engine which time and again drives up costs and therefore prices. Here is what Walton said: "In 1962, the discount industry was full of high-living, big-spending promoters driving around in Cadillacs—guys like Herb Gibson— who had the world by the tail. But it had very few of what you'd call good operators. . . ."[109]

For many entrepreneurs—especially those who had to pull themselves up from nothing and succeed against heavy odds—living high, spending big, and driving around in a Cadillac was the whole point of going into business. To the end of his days, Walton regarded this kind of extravagant, conspicuous consumption as antithetical to what he was trying to build:

> The fact is, a lot of folks in our company have made an awful lot of money. . . . And it just drives me crazy when they flaunt it. . . . I don't think big mansions and flashy cars are what the Wal-Mart culture is supposed to be about. It's great to have the money to fall back on, and I'm glad some of those folks have been able to take off and go fishing at a fairly early age. But if you get too caught up in that good life, it's probably time to move on, simply because you lose touch with what your mind is supposed to be concentrating on: serving the customer.[110]

There is a great deal about Walton and his success wrapped up in this observation. The problem with discounters, the reason that the early success so many enjoyed turned to failure later on, is that they lost their focus on the customer. When they did, they lost their discipline. Discipline is the key to success in discount merchandising. New ways have to be found every day to cut costs. When cost savings are achieved, the savings have to be passed along to the customer. This formula must become a religion. Walton believed it should characterize the private lives of his executives as well as how they handled their jobs at the company. Many Americans would bridle at the idea that their boss's on-the-job preferences should follow them home when the day's work is done. If you felt that way when you worked for Walton, well then, as he bluntly put it, "it's probably time [for you] to move on." Wal-Mart, in other words, was not for everyone. If you wanted to march with the righteous few to lead the customer out of the high-priced house of bondage to the low-priced promised land, Wal-Mart was the company for you. If you were less fervent, there were plenty of other nice companies which were happy to spend on their executives rather than save for their customers where you were welcome to find employment.

WAL-MART

The first Wal-Mart opened its doors in Rogers, Arkansas, on July 2, 1962. Sam Walton had entered the discount retailing business. He would eventually change the way America shops. But in the period leading up to the grand opening and on the day itself, almost everyone who did not know Walton personally was distinctly underwhelmed. Walton had tried to interest Butler Brothers in backing him. No sale. He had gone to Herb Gibson in the hopes of becoming a Gibson franchisee. Gibson "peremptorily rebuffed" Walton, seeing him "as a bush-league variety-store merchant who possessed neither the finances nor the experience necessary to succeed in the Gibson chain."[111]

Walton was, however, incapable of discouragement; and he had no fear of debt. He had discovered that small towns could support big stores if properly merchandised. And he had that special ability to see the future, vouchsafed to so few. The future was discounting, but only if carried out with the strictest discipline. As the signs in Wal-Mart stores put it, "Always the low price . . . *Always.*" What Walton understood was that the consistent achievement of low prices meant constant change because the world was changing.

The variety store business is a good case in point. Walton could see that selling so many different product lines in small stores put a permanent limit on their ability continually to lower costs. Any discount merchant selling a wide range of products had fixed expenses and operational problems. These included the store itself, the fixtures in it, the hiring and training of employees, the management of the supply chain through which goods were procured, to name a few. To keep costs down, fixed costs must be amortized over as high a volume as possible, turning over as quickly as possible. A variety store format, featuring, as it did, small stores in small towns doing business in a small trading area, could never compete against larger stores. When combined with Walton's understanding that a big store that sold low-priced goods could do a lot of business in a small town (because people would drive from many miles away to shop there), this meant that variety stores were doomed.

After opening his first Wal-Mart in 1962, Walton began to exit the variety store business. This redeployment of his assets and his attention took place slowly. As late as 1970, he still operated fourteen variety stores which accounted for 26 percent of the company's income.[112] Not until 1978 was Walton's last variety store, a family center in Waynesville, Missouri, closed.[113]

The significance of this migration from variety stores to the new Wal-Mart format cannot be overemphasized. Walton had already achieved the seemingly impossible. First in Newport, then in Bentonville, then in town after town he had turned nothing stores in unlikely places into winners. Why not continue? Walton was forty-four years old in 1962 and supporting a family of six. Why change?

Most people in Walton's situation would not change. We know this because most variety store operators at the time did not change. They approached each day, month, and year with the expectation that it would be pretty much like the preceding one. They were doing what most people do—marching backward into the future. P. K. Holmes and his son with their Ben Franklin in Newport were like that. Indeed, so was Ben Franklin and its parent, Butler Brothers. No one hears of these firms anymore.

Variety store operator W. T. Grant went bankrupt in 1976. F. W. Woolworth was once one of the nation's great retailers. Its home office in New York City, the Woolworth Building, was the tallest building in the world from 1913 to 1930. Woolworth announced in 1997 that it was closing its five-and-dime stores.

Sam Walton could tell the difference between the seemingly impossible and the genuinely impossible. These others could not. For them, a retail store or chain was an annuity. For him, the end, the goal that organized his business, was serving the customer. He understood that serving the customer best was a moving target.

To hit the target, Walton opened Wal-Mart: "Mart" for "market" and "Wal" because it is the first syllable of Walton's last name.

The store's name was suggested by Bob Bogle, the first manager of the Bentonville five-and-ten-cent store, who pointed out that the shorter the name, the fewer the letters to be bought.[114] Frugality began on the first day of operation. On one side of the sign was a smaller one saying "Satisfaction Guaranteed" and on the other a sign announcing "We Sell for Less."[115] The policy was obvious from the outset.

Wal-Mart No. 1 was sixteen thousand square feet in size and sold everything from boys' apparel to books to automobile supplies. The store had twenty-five clerks who made between $0.50 and $0.60 an hour, less than the minimum wage.[116] Store manager Don Whitaker trumpeted to the world prices on nationally branded merchandise between one-quarter and one-half below other retailers. Newspaper advertisements claimed that Wal-Mart sold only "first-quality merchandise. There's [sic] no seconds or factory rejects in the store—our policy forbids it." How, then, was Wal-Mart able to grasp the holy grail of retailing, selling the best for less? "We have been able," explained Whitaker, "to cut out the middleman. Most of our goods were purchased directly from the manufacturer, allowing us to pass on our savings to the consumer."[117]

Fair trade was pretty much a dead letter in most product categories by 1962. If it had not been, Wal-Mart would not have been possible. Even so, sourcing goods was a serious problem for the company and would remain so for more than a decade. It is doubtful that everything for sale at Wal-Mart No. 1 at its grand opening was actually purchased direct from the manufacturer. Here are Walton's words: "It was a little frustrating there for a while, being out on our own. In addition to no basic merchandise assortment, we had no real replenishment system. . . . We had no established distributors. No credit. . . . I don't mind saying that we were the victims of a good bit of arrogance from a lot of vendors in those days. They didn't need us, and they acted that way."[118]

Getting goods to sell was probably Wal-Mart's biggest problem, but there were a myriad of others. Despite them all, the store's success was immediate. For reasons which are unclear, perhaps because Walton was stretched so thin financially, Wal-Mart No. 2 was not opened for twenty-five months. As Walton put it, "Once we opened Rogers, we sat there and held our breath for two years."[119]

The grand opening of Wal-Mart No. 2 has been made famous

by the description of an observer named David D. Glass, who worked for Crank Drugs (yet another company that no one knows of today) in Springfield, Missouri. The location of Wal-Mart No. 2 was Harrison, Arkansas, with a population of six thousand. The time was August of 1964. This store was unprepossessing on a good day: concrete floor, eight-foot ceiling, wooden plank fixtures, no rest rooms in a building located in the midst of what was once a cattle yard. Walton himself described it as "highly promotional, truly ugly."[120] And the day Glass visited was not a good day. As he put it,

> It was the worst retail store I had ever seen. Sam had brought a couple of trucks of watermelons and stacked them on the sidewalk. He had a donkey ride out in the parking lot. It was about 115 degrees, and the watermelons began to pop and the donkey[s] began to do what donkeys do, and it was all mixed together and ran all over the parking lot. And when you went inside the store, the mess just continued, having been tracked in all over the floor. He was a nice fellow, but I wrote him off. It was just terrible.[121]

True, Wal-Mart No. 2 was a rude affair. However, it was selling the same merchandise as the lovely Sterling store in the center of Harrison, but for 20 percent less.[122] The store was a tremendous success.

Walton now began to open more Wal-Marts very quickly. Two in 1964, another in 1965, two more in both 1966 and 1967, five more in both 1968 and 1969, and two more by the date of the initial public offering in 1970.[123] That made twenty Wal-Marts in addition to the remaining variety stores. From Morrilton, Arkansas, to Sikeston, Missouri . . . From Neosho, Missouri, to Claremore, Oklahoma . . . From Tahlequah, Oklahoma, to Van Buren, Arkansas, Wal-Marts were springing up in town after town that no one else had ever heard of. As Walton knew, there was a lot of business in these towns. The fact that they were unknown places hidden up in or near the Ozarks was much more of an opportunity than it was a problem. They could support one big discounter; but Walton knew this part of the world better than any other retailer, and he well understood that none of these towns could support two stores of Wal-Mart's size.

Once he was there, no comparable discounter could move in. This comes as close as possible to the definition of a phrase so often used in the Internet age—"first-mover advantage." If I am there, you cannot be. In an ever-expanding circumference from Bentonville, Wal-Mart was gaining monopoly power over a market the potential of which only Walton really understood.

Obtaining and distributing goods to these stores scattered in the remote reaches of a big country was often a trial and a challenge. It took a long time for these problems to be solved.

Here is how the issue presented itself to Claude Harris. Harris was Wal-Mart's first buyer. He was one of Walton's many discoveries. "We found Claude over in Memphis running a Woolworth store," Walton explained. "He was from Muskogee, Oklahoma, and about one-quarter Indian, and he had started with Woolworth out of high school."[124] According to Harris:

> We used to get in some terrific fights. You can't let them get by with anything because they are going to take care of themselves, and your job is to take care of the customer. I'd threaten Procter & Gamble with not carrying their merchandise, and they'd say, "Oh, you can't get by without carrying our merchandise." And I'd say, "You watch me put it on a side counter, and I'll put Colgate on the endcap at a penny less, and you just watch me." They got offended and went to Sam, and he said, "Whatever Claude says, that's what it's going to be."[125]

Between 1969 and 1979 Wal-Mart constructed a number of distribution centers to handle the increasing volume of goods it was purchasing and to ship the appropriate merchandise to each store. The first one was located a mile south of Bentonville. It was sixty thousand square feet and cost just over half a million dollars to build. Early in 1975, another center over twice this size opened in Bentonville. In 1978, the 390,000-square foot Searcy, Arkansas, distribution center was opened. Another 390,000-square-foot center was opened in Bentonville in 1979; and yet another was under construction during that year in Palestine, Texas.[126]

The ability to buy, the network of stores, and the network of large distribution centers through which to supply those stores all became part of Wal-Mart's first-mover advantage. Arkansas, southern Missouri, eastern Oklahoma, and southeastern Texas constituted part of the national market that was largely ignored by the giant national discounters like Kmart and the more upscale general merchandise chains like Sears. Walton was far more dedicated and focused—he had a much better idea of what he was doing—than regional discounters like Gibsons or the variety stores like Woolworth.

Walton was forced to build these large distribution centers and eventually to put together his own trucking fleet because he was not centered in, nor did he serve, major metropolitan areas. Trucking companies did not have regular routes to Tahlequah, Oklahoma, or Neosho, Missouri. Nor did big discounters like Kmart have large distribution centers which could serve such towns economically. Walton was systematically creating a hub-and-spoke distribution network (with the main hub originally located in Bentonville) which allowed his trucks to carry far fuller loads not only out to the stores, but back to the distribution centers from the stores in order to redistribute merchandise. Wal-Mart's trucks always had fuller loads on back-haul than any competitor.[127]

Walton was possessed of a searing insight which—again—can be expressed in one phrase: "serving the customer." His logistics system was an integral part of that strategy. "Serving the customer" is, like so much of what Walton did, deceptively simple. Indeed, there are few companies that conceive of themselves as not serving the customer. The difference is that at Wal-Mart, to an important degree because of Walton's own personal leadership and inspiration, those three words were given a meaning they had at few other companies.

The stories about buying and logistics illustrate how "serving the customer" was woven into the fabric of the company. Buying from arrogant companies is difficult. It's hard to make a good bargain, and it's bruising to the ego. But if you are like Claude Harris and you conceive of yourself as being on a mission to save your customers a penny—and, moreover, if you know that your boss will always back you up in this noble quest—it's a little easier.

Hauling freight is not a particularly romantic aspect of retailing. But a penny saved there is the same as a penny saved anywhere else. The customer neither knows nor cares how the products she or he purchases arrive at the store shelf. But as a retailer, you better care a lot. If your trucking costs are lower than the competitors', that is an advantage that leads directly to lower prices, greater volume, and a better reputation among consumers. Walton was always aggressive not only in keeping distribution costs down. He was equally keen to find inexpensive ways to keep morale up. He spent plenty of time at the distribution centers and with his truckers. He often attended drivers' safety meetings. In 1970, Wal-Mart instituted a profit-sharing plan; and Walton promised truckers financial rewards over the long term that seemed incredible to them. Eventually, he delivered far more than he promised.[128]

One of the intriguing aspects of retailing is that a great deal of what goes into a retail firm is visible for all to see. Anybody can walk into any store anytime. Merchandise mix, prices, visual display, and everything else are in plain view. The location of the store is obvious, and so is the location of a warehouse. If you are going to build 390,000-square-foot warehouses in places like Searcy, Arkansas, or Palestine, Texas, anybody with an interest can find out.

Secret products and processes, sometimes protected by patents, played a critical role in the development of the business economy in the twentieth century. The Eastman Kodak and IBM stories are good cases in point. So also is the story of the man we will meet in the next chapter, Robert Noyce. High-technology companies have been and remain highly security conscious.

Walton did what he could to avoid calling attention to himself and the growth of his company. A heritage of jokes grew up that can be characterized as: Walton, who? Wal-Mart, what? Bentonville, where? Walton liked that very much. He wanted to fly under everybody's radar. "The best thing we ever did," he once said, "was to hide back there in the hills and eventually build a company that makes folks want to find us."[129] But a success of the magnitude Walton was making could not be kept secret forever.

When Walton went to the public markets to sell stock, theretofore private information was published in accord with securities laws. This information was fairly interesting. It showed, for example, that in 1966 Wal-Mart operated sixteen stores which generated $6,246,000 in sales and $246,000 in profits; while in 1970, the company operated twice as many stores, enjoyed sales increases of almost a factor of five, and profit growth just under a factor of six. Walton had begun his career creating stores out of nothing. Now he was creating an empire out of nothing.

This kind of success not only continued, it accelerated at a torrid pace. Wal-Mart was still tiny in 1970 compared to Sears, J. C. Penney, many regional discounters, and what was viewed as the king of the discount world, Harry Cunningham's creation, Kmart. In 1980, Wal-Mart was not the biggest in the business, but it was certainly not small. It consisted of 276 stores generating $1,248,176,000 in sales and $41,151,000 in profits.

The growth continued through the 1980s. In 1990, Wal-Mart operated 1,525 stores (counting 123 Sam's Clubs); sales were $25,810,656,000; and profits topped one billion dollars for the first time in the company's history, at $1,075,900,000. The following year, Wal-Mart surpassed Sears as the nation's largest retailer. Sears had held that position since it surpassed the A&P in 1965. Both these firms, Sears and the A&P, started out as discount merchants. Both lost their way.[130] It was Sam Walton's gift that he was able, to paraphrase Lenin, to keep the revolution forever young.

Sam Walton died on April 5, 1992, three weeks after President George Bush and Mrs. Bush traveled to Bentonville to award him the Presidential Medal of Freedom, an event which Walton called the "highlight of our entire career."[131] The year of Walton's death, Wal-Mart ran 1,928 stores (including 208 Sam's Clubs). Sales of $43,886,902,000 were more than $11 billion higher than the previous year. Profits reached $1,608,476,000. Walton had been named the nation's richest man by *Forbes* magazine as early as 1985; and by 1992 his family, which held a great deal of Wal-Mart wealth, was among the richest in the world.

Seventy-four years previously, Samuel Moore Walton had been born in Kingfisher, Oklahoma, to a family indistinguishable from millions of others in the United States. He had decided to make a career in retailing, a business not amenable to a "magic bullet" of a product which one could own and prevent others from using. It is the most transparent of all industries. No place to run; no place to hide. The goal of every retailer in the world is the same and simple to state: getting the right product to the right place at the right time for the right price.

At his death, Walton had arguably established himself as the most successful retailer in American history. More than that, he was arguably the nation's most successful executive. How had this happened?

THE PHENOMENON OF SAM WALTON

There is, of course, no satisfactory answer to the previous question. We can, however, achieve some understanding of his success by taking a look specifically at some of the roles he played.

Walton was a born leader. His leadership took many forms. He led by example. He loved his work because he loved to learn, to improve, and to compete. He loved those "crazy" moments, those altogether unorthodox sales promotions which all the strategizing in the world would not have led one to undertake, but which simply sprang from the creativity of some Wal-Mart store manager. Wal-Mart was well known for its outlandish promotions in its early years: the mountains of Tide it would sell or the deep discounts on antifreeze it would take.

These promotions served a number of purposes. They became news, thus generating a lot of free publicity and drawing in new customers from many miles around. They gave Wal-Mart's executives and associates (i.e., hourly employees) the feeling that each new day might be quite unlike the last. They infused the whole company with a sense of possibility. What is more, they were fun.

No one at Wal-Mart worked harder or longer hours than did Sam Walton. Probably no one has ever visited more retail outlets—not only his own, but competitors' and also stores in classes of trade in which he did not compete. The more he worked, the more fun he had.

Others entered into that spirit. Wal-Mart's rah-rah culture was real. Its Saturday morning meetings in which success was celebrated were rare indeed in the 1970s in their unbridled enthusiasm. They harked back to the motivational meetings that Thomas J. Watson Sr. held in the early years of IBM,[132] and back further than that to the camp meetings of the religious revivalists. This was "charismatic capitalism."[133]

Spontaneous association was a characteristic of Americans that de Tocqueville noted when he visited the United States in the 1830s, and there was plenty of such activity at Wal-Mart in the early years. Take, for example, the Shrinkettes. The mortal enemy of all retailers, shrinkage refers to the disappearance of merchandise by theft or misplacement. In order to fight shrinkage, a group of women at the Wal-Mart in New Iberia, Louisiana, got together as a cheerleading squad with cheers such as "WHAT DO YOU DO ABOUT SHRINKAGE? CRUSH IT! CRUSH IT!" Walton, with obvious pleasure, said the Shrinkettes "stole the show" at an annual meeting with such cheers as:

CALIFORNIA ORANGES, TEXAS CACTUS,
WE THINK K-MART COULD USE SOME PRACTICE![134]

Why did people organize themselves into groups like the Shrinkettes? The profit-sharing plan that Walton instituted in 1971 to cover all the associates was one reason. A large portion of the profit-sharing funds was invested in Wal-Mart stock. As the stock soared through the 1970s and 1980s, people from humble backgrounds who never dreamed that they would be able to accumulate capital found themselves with holdings of hundreds of thousands and in some cases over a million dollars. If ever there was an example of ordinary people doing extraordinary things, or, from another point of view, if ever there was an example of the discovery that many ordinary people out there in the United States who had not gone through the society's standard credentialing system (e.g., who never went to college) were in fact not ordinary at all, surely it was the commitment of the managers and associates of Wal-Mart in the 1970s and 1980s.

The creativity and enthusiasm of the Wal-Mart workforce cannot be bought with money alone. Some things are not for sale. Walton may have admired some of T. J. Watson's motivational methods, but there was much that Watson did that Walton would not have dreamed of. There was a great deal of ersatz celebration at Watson's IBM, of forced enthusiasm, of compulsory fun. There was extreme centralization of power in a man who could be tyrannical as well as kind. Charles Revson may have been able to buy people who had already proved their talent, but he was unable to keep most of them. It is difficult to build a company governed primarily by fear and expect it to last long in a free country.

Walton seems to have harbored genuine respect and admiration for strivers and achievers. He believed his own greatest strength was as a motivator, and he took a lot of pride in helping people achieve their fullest potential. When they did, they felt good about themselves. Money can not buy this kind of psychological reward.

Walton led by example. When the silly season rolled around, he was a player-coach. He did not merely watch and cheer from the sidelines. In 1984, he made a bet with David D. Glass, the same David Glass who had written Walton off as a well-meaning incompetent back in 1964 but who was now second man in Wal-Mart, that Wal-Mart would not turn in a pretax profit of greater than 8 percent. It did, Walton lost, and Glass insisted that he pay up. The stakes were to dance the hula wearing a grass skirt on Wall Street, an event that drew a lot of media attention and doubtless gales of laughter among Wal-Mart's associates. "Most folks probably thought we just had a wacky chairman who was pulling a pretty primitive publicity stunt," Walton wrote. "What they didn't realize is that this sort of stuff goes on all the time at Wal-Mart. . . . We always have tried to make life as interesting and as unpredictable as we can, and to make Wal-Mart a fun proposition."[135]

Walton confessed that the hula episode was a little too much for him. He was sixty-six years old, doing "a pretty fair hula," accompanied by a group of hula dancers and musicians. "It was one of the few times one of our company stunts really embarrassed me."[136] Walton endured this embarrassment at a time when he was fabulously wealthy and successful. He did something he did not want to do because he was being held to a bet by people he could have fired in an instant. When this incident took place, Walton was very well known in the investment community and among retailers; but he and his firm were not yet a major presence in the East. He must have looked quite ridiculous to the average New Yorker seeing this little display on the news.

Why did he do it? When one thinks of the great American business tycoons from John Jacob Astor through Jack Welch, it is hard to imagine any of them making such a bet or living up to it once lost. They were all too self-important, too dignified, too hidden, or simply too used to having things their own way. It is hard to imagine people around these leaders holding them to their word on such a matter. "But at Wal-Mart, when you make a bet like I did . . . you always pay up," Walton said. And, besides, the hula "was nothing compared to wrestling a bear," which is what a warehouse manager had to do when he lost a bet about productivity.[137]

To some degree this was Wal-Mart's answer to the staid, button-down business world of the Northeast and Midwest. It was the

Arkansas version of what in Silicon Valley was to become the culture of sex, drugs, and rock-'n'-roll. Breaking rules in the 1970s was not a bad way to think because the people making the rules in public and private life were not working or living up to expectations. The people who played by the rules brought us Vietnam and Watergate. The principal characteristic of the leader in both public life and private enterprise seemed to be dullness. Sears is a good example of a company for which it had become unalloyed drudgery to work.[138] The old ways were not delivering results. The Shrinkettes, hula dancing, and bear wrestling were a refreshing approach.

More than that, with his Wall Street hula dance Walton showed by doing something it was clear he did not want to do that he put the company and those who worked for it above his own particular desires. Wal-Mart the institution was thus bigger than Walton the man.

Whenever a great, charismatic leader arises to create a new institution, the inevitable question is: What next? Often, usually, the answer is: Nothing good. Sometimes the answer is: Nothing at all. More than once, as with the aged Henry Ford or Tom Watson Sr. the organization can come to feel that it can neither do without the leader nor with him. Indeed, some great men seem to want to destroy what they have created before they die. Henry Ford, the example of so much that was corrosive in American business life, exemplified this tendency.

Walton wanted Wal-Mart to live on. He felt a kinship with his associates to a degree probably unique in retail, and he was an ardent believer in Wal-Mart's mission to serve the customer.

It was Wal-Mart's happy fate to be consistently underestimated. Walton was such a unique businessperson, and Wal-Mart's success was so extraordinary, that it was easy to believe that the latter could not exist without the former. Helen Walton had wanted her husband to limit his business activities fairly early in his career. Accounts of their lives suggest that she was never happier than when they were together as a family in Newport, where her husband busied himself not only with his store but also with his family and with the community.

As it became apparent that he had a special gift as a retailer, Walton felt compelled to exploit that gift in order to lead a satisfying life. Taking the company public, which was an essential step in funding its distribution infrastructure, was upsetting to Helen because it meant opening up their private world to the outside. When are we big enough? When are we successful enough? How much does the family have to sacrifice for the sake of the company?

His wife's opinion always carried a lot of weight with Walton, and in 1974 he decided to take the action she wished. He had spent almost three decades in business, and perhaps the time had come to follow other avenues. Together, Walton and his wife were worth about $130 million at the time,[139] which was probably sufficient to support a family in Bentonville in style.

Walton selected Ron Mayer, a hard-charging, technologically fashion-forward executive to be chairman of the board and chief executive officer. He appointed Ferold Arend (the kind of name one runs across either at Wal-Mart or Princeton—no place in between) as president and chief operating officer. The year 1974 was a tough one for the retail trade in general. There was a recession. OPEC hiked oil prices in the wake of the Arab-Israeli Yom Kippur War. Nevertheless, the Mayer-Arend team grew sales and profits at a rapid pace.

The problem was that the Mayer-Arend team was not a team at all. Each formed the core of a clique. One executive reported that "we thought we were going to hell in a handbasket. I'm not exaggerating. I mean we really did."[140] Walton told Mayer in June 1976 that he was returning as chairman of the board and CEO. He asked Mayer to remain with Wal-Mart as a senior executive, but Mayer resigned.

It is not unknown for founders to return to their businesses when they perceive their businesses to have gone astray. In the wake of poor performance at the company he co-founded, David Packard assumed greater responsibilities at HP in 1990 after a lengthy absence. Henry Ford attempted to run the Ford Motor Company following the death of his son, Edsel, in 1943. So Walton's grasping the operational reins of the company, given the power he had through ownership and given his own character, was neither unprecedented nor surprising. Nevertheless, it did carry consequences.

When Ron Mayer left, a number of other key people left with him. Yet another group of managers left soon thereafter. Walton estimated that Wal-Mart lost a third of its senior managers in the wake of his retaking the helm.[141] It had seemed that the "old man" had left active management. To many high executives in the firm, that may have been good news. They may have felt that Walton was fine for his time; but that his time—with its penny-ante promotions at rural five-and-dimes, donkey rides, and exploding watermelons—was over. Walton's rejection of high living must have been a bore to some people. What the company needed now was a new breed of young Turks who would bring modern merchandising methods and computerization to a growing firm and who did not mind the big spending that accompanied success.

When the old man decided that he still had it in him to run the company, a lot of people felt that they did not want to wait any longer for their turn at bat. They left; and it looked to the world like Wal-Mart, which had seemed too good to be true, would not prove to be a distance runner. As it turned out, the company had a lot of bench strength, enough to fill the lineup with first-string performers. The man and his company had been underestimated again, as Wal-Mart's onward march continued almost without a hiccup.

The fate of Mayer and his confederates was interesting. With the help of financial backers, some closely attached to Wal-Mart, Mayer took over an Indianapolis-based discount retailer called Ayr-Way. Here was his chance, unencumbered by the archaic ways of the past, to be the next Sam Walton. Mayer lasted fewer than four years. The company went nowhere, and he was forced out. He continued to live in Indianapolis, running some inconsequential local retail shops.[142]

Mayer's defection and ensuing failure were yet another tribute to Walton and a case study of the fate of management without leadership. Mayer was as much of an insider as anybody at Wal-Mart. He knew the strategy, the implementation, the people. He knew about the hard and soft sides of what had made Wal-Mart great. He knew Walton's shortcomings, and he knew state-of-the-art managerial techniques. But of that special magic Walton had, Mayer apparently possessed very little. His goal was to do to Walton and Wal-Mart what they were doing to Kmart. But it turned out that the Walton formula without Walton did not work, while Walton without his top executives could do just fine. Wal-Mart could not easily be transplanted.

An economist once defined the chief executive officer as the person who made decisions that could not be delegated.[143] In Walton's case, the CEO was the one man who could infuse the winning spirit into the company.

Though a personal tribute to Walton, Wal-Mart's survival of the mass exodus and the failure of the defectors had to worry both Walton and his company's investors. No one lives forever, and someday Wal-Mart would have to run without Walton. Charles Revson failed to hand his company off successfully. Few entrepreneurs do better. There was no particular reason to believe that the executives who remained at Wal-Mart were more able retailers than those who left.

At any rate, Walton came back and Wal-Mart roared ahead. Through the first half of the twentieth century, mid-market retailing was dominated by Sears and Ward. In the 1970s and 1980s, Sears lurched from one initiative to the next. What resulted was one mistake after another. By the late 1980s, rumors were circulating that Sears might be an inviting target for a hostile takeover. As for Ward, it had ceased to exist as an independent entity by 1980.

In the 1970s, Kmart appeared to be the retailer to watch; but it, too, lost its way in the following decade. Wal-Mart, by contrast, seemed to be able to do no wrong. In sales, profits, and market value, the 1980s were great years for the firm. So Walton's reemergence as the chief operating officer as well as chief executive officer in 1976 was a complete success. He also occupied a position seen on few corporate organization charts. He was the chief spiritual officer of the firm, and the question of who would follow him never went away.

It has been said of Napoleon that he did not set out to conquer the world, he only wanted to defeat the country next to his. Sam Walton did not plan to conquer the world, either. "Well, now, Sam," Ferold Arend once asked him, "how big do you really want this company to be? What is your plan?" "Ferold," Walton answered, "we're going to take it as it comes, and if we can grow with our own money, we'll maybe add a store or two."[144] In 1992, the year of Walton's death, Wal-Mart ran over nineteen hundred stores with over 430,000 employees. Sales topped $55 billion, making it the world's largest retailer, and profits approached $2 billion.

Walton began the process of passing the baton to new management in the mid-1980s. On February 1, 1988, he turned over the position of CEO to David Glass. He remained as chairman of the board and continued to visit stores and instill the company's values in an organization that was growing very fast. This time, unlike the aborted retirement of the mid-1970s, Walton meant it. He was going to let Glass run the company.

Walton nevertheless remained highly visible within the firm and more visible to outsiders than he liked. Indeed, he became something of a national icon. In a world of phonies, Sam Walton seemed to be the real thing.

After Walton's death, Wal-Mart did encounter some bumps in the road. The stock price flattened out, and morale suffered. Probably more important, no one could succeed Sam Walton as a motivator. Perhaps that is why the selection of Glass was a good one. His values were similar, but his personality was so different that there could be no question of his even attempting to imitate the spiritual role Walton played.

Walton seemed to be a man completely at home with himself. Glass was not similarly endowed with a personality that could project itself with such seeming effortlessness onto the public platform. When he appeared on television, the result was a sharp public relations setback. All the pent-up anger of small-town retailers put out of business by the Wal-Mart juggernaut and of small suppliers who felt brutalized by their giant customer could find an outlet with Glass as CEO that would not have been available against Walton. Big firms also saw opportunity in Walton's departure. One example: After Walton died, Target attacked Wal-Mart for publishing what it asserted were misleading price comparisons and asserted that "this never would have happened if Sam Walton were alive."[145]

"You can't replace a Sam Walton," observed Glass shortly after his death, "but he has prepared the company to run well whether he's there or not."[146] This was not the case in the 1970s, when Walton's attempt to retire led to turmoil within the executive ranks. By the late 1980s, with the company running so very well, Walton succeeded in one of the most difficult tasks any entrepreneur faces: handing his company, his creation, off to a successor. Why?

Walton failed in his attempt to withdraw from the business in the mid-1970s. He wasn't ready, the company wasn't ready, and Ron Mayer overestimated himself. By the late 1980s, things had changed.

Walton was diagnosed with hairy cell leukemia in 1981.[147] His mother, recall, had died of cancer at an early age. He was less than a decade older than she at his own diagnosis. His treatment was successful, and the disease went into remission. But as anyone will tell you who has had firsthand experience, cancer punctuates your life. Things are never quite the same afterward. Although he maintained his grueling schedule and never seemed to have sought sympathy, this is news that changes one's outlook on the future.

In David Glass, moreover, Walton had found a man who, despite his differences in personality, understood what had made Wal-Mart great and had a sense of how to make it greater. He appreciated the role that technology could play in transforming the retail world. He also appreciated that technology unaccompanied by hands-on experience could never sustain a retailer's performance. Both Sears and Kmart proved that.

Walton was an outstanding manager because his managerial philosophies and methods dovetailed so well with his leadership and his vision. As a manager, Walton epitomized the low-overhead operator.

Store visits by top executives were constant and often unannounced. The problem of "national versus local," a permanent challenge in the retailing world, was solved not through the establishment of regional offices but through the company's private air force. In the early 1990s, regional vice presidents, buyers, and dozens of corporate officers were on board one of the company's fifteen aircraft every Monday morning, taking off from Bentonville to visit stores. They were supposed to come back "with at least one idea which would pay for the trip."[148]

The trip itself was Spartan. Executives slept two to a room and drove about in the cheapest cars they could rent.[149] This was true for executives personally worth tens of millions of dollars, men who could have traveled in style on their own account while hardly making a dent in their assets. But that would have violated the company culture and brought frowns from Sam.

Walton, according to two Harvard Business School professors,

> described his management style as "management by walking and flying around." Others at Wal-Mart described it as "management by wearing you down" and "management by looking over your shoulder." On managing people, Walton said, "You've got to give folks responsibility, you've got to trust them, and then you've got to check up on them." Wal-Mart's partnership with its associates meant sharing the

numbers—Walton ran the business as an open book and maintained an open-door policy. Wal-Mart aimed to excel by empowering associates, maintaining technological superiority, and building loyalty among associates, customers, and suppliers.[150]

Walton was a tough manager. He held his people to the highest standards both in terms of quantitative results and in the manner in which they conducted themselves. Of all major corporations in twentieth-century America, the distinction between management and leadership was probably less sharp at Wal-Mart while Walton lived than at any other.

The original strategy was brilliant. Walton sensed a market imperfection. Rural and small-town America was being underserved by retailers. He systematically exploited that imperfection, growing even stronger in the process. He never let his success go to his head, and he did not tolerate its spoiling anyone else. The way he managed his business kept everyone sharp every day.

The travel policy is a good example. Travel meant sacrifices in personal comfort and also in spending so much time away from hearth and home. However, traveling from Bentonville rather than maintaining regional offices saved the company 2 percent of sales annually.[151] Some of those savings flowed right to the bottom line, doing wonders for the price of the stock. Some went to the consumer in the form of lower prices, stimulating sales. There were dozens of such virtuous circles in Wal-Mart. A competitor could see and understand them. But it was extraordinarily difficult to emulate them.

Indeed, no one ever did. Sam Walton, the disciplined discounter, defined the rules and endlessly explained them to his adoring associates and executives. He made retailing his game. No one could beat him at it.

SAM WALTON

March 29, 1918	Walton is born.
May 31, 1940	Walton graduates from the University of Missouri.
1940	Walton begins working for J. C. Penney; stays for eighteen months.
February 14, 1943	Walton marries Helen Alice Robson.
September 1, 1945	Walton opens his first variety store in Newport, Arkansas.
1950	Walton starts over in Bentonville, Arkansas, with a new store, Walton's 5&10.
July 2, 1962	Walton opens Wal-Mart, his first discount store, in Rogers, Arkansas.
October 31, 1969	Wal-Mart is incorporated.
1974	Walton selects Ron Mayer to replace him as CEO; Walton returns to the office two years later.
1988	Walton turns over the position of CEO to David Glass.
April 5, 1992	Walton dies.

7 ROBERT NOYCE AND SILICON VALLEY

Toward a New Business World

THE REPUBLIC OF TECHNOLOGY

From the Stone Age two and a half million years ago to the present day, technology has been an avenue through which man has sought to tame nature and to extend his power over other men as well. From the first, the uses of technology for peace and war have been closely intertwined. The sharpened edge of a stone could be used to skin an animal. Or it could be used to kill a man who had just skinned an animal.

What in retrospect seems a slight technological edge has at times meant the difference between suzerainty and slavery throughout history. A better sail could change the balance of power on the seas. The stirrup transformed the horse into a weapon of war with consequences for whole societies.[1]

In Britain and in the United States during the twentieth century, technological progress was hastened by World War II and, especially in the United States, by the Cold War (and the space race, which was part of it) that followed. In the United States, Defense Department contracts were instrumental in transforming the valley south of San Francisco and north of San Jose in northern California from the center of the nation's prune-growing industry[2] to the technological hotbed of the world by the end of the century.

The history of business in the United States since the Civil War has been driven by technological change to a greater extent than in any other part of the world and in any other period in world history. Throughout this book, we have seen that the key to success in American business has lain in either the creation of or the adaptation to new technologies. Steel was once a scarce metal. But Andrew Carnegie, by investing capital in previously unheard of amounts and by understanding the key success factors in the business, created what might be called a "revolution in maximum." He built the world's biggest steel mills, located them strategically, scrapped and rebuilt with an abandon that shocked competition and transformed the industry.

In what has come to be known as Silicon Valley, a revolution of equal import gripped the nation and the world in the latter part of the twentieth century. This was a "revolution in miniature."[3] There are no giant mills in the valley. There is nothing like the Edgar Thomson works or Kodak Park or the River Rouge. There are few if any plush office buildings. Many of the companies fairly revel in the absence of conspicuous display. When I interviewed Gordon Moore—one of the nation's leading technological minds, multibillionaire, co-founder of Intel—for this book, I found him working not in an office but in a tiny cubicle. He has never owned a custom-made shirt.[4]

Intel, perhaps more than any other firm, represented what the Valley was in the late 1960s. It was a start-up in 1968. Just as the United States had from the beginning meant a "new world," a rebirth, another chance, a new beginning for foreigners, the California dream was a new beginning, a new frontier for Americans. The Valley was the perfect place for Intel, and Intel was the perfect firm for the Valley. Its name was said to be short for "integrated electronics." That was the business it was in. Some believed, however, that it was short for "intelligence," a quality its two founders—Gordon Moore and Robert Noyce—did not see enough of in the management of their previous employers. (There was some thought to calling the firm "Moore-Noyce," but that sounded a bit too much like "more noise" and was discarded.)

Moore and Noyce and the firm they founded did not break laws. Neither did they necessarily abide by them. Rather, they made them. Or they discovered them. In 1965, Gordon Moore wrote an article for the thirty-fifth anniversary of *Electronics* magazine predicting that the number of transistors, capacitors, diodes, and resistors that could be "crammed" onto an integrated circuit (or "chip") would double at a predictable rate. This was just a guess, a hunch based on the recent past. In the previous six years, the number of transistors on a chip had increased from one to sixty-four. This had taken place with no increase in price, resulting in vast productivity gains. Moore, a remarkably modest, straightforward man, did not fully believe the implications of his own prediction. It meant that by 1975, sixty-five thousand transistors could be crammed onto an

integrated circuit. Astonishingly, to Moore and to others, the prediction came true. Thus was born "Moore's Law." In 1975, memory
chips were being produced with 65,536 transistors. "I still have a
tough time believing that we can make these things," said Moore in
1975. That was only the beginning.[5]

The integrated circuit on a silicon chip has matured in ways few
could have imagined and has become an essential element of the
information revolution that gripped the world as the twentieth
century drew to a close. Without the breakthroughs in physics and
electronics necessary to create the integrated circuit, the eventual
development of a whole range of silicon chips, including the microprocessor, the brains of the computer, would not have been possible.
In large part, because of the line of inventions which followed the
integrated circuit, millions of people have computers in their homes
and offices. From that infrastructure, the Internet has developed.
Data are now being transmitted globally in a volume and with a
speed unprecedented in history.

The twentieth century drew to a close in an atmosphere of acute
uncertainty because no one could predict with any degree of confidence where this new world would lead. In fact, what we can learn
from history is that we cannot even guess at what is over the horizon. What we do know is that the world lives on transportation and
communication; and anything which makes them faster, more pro-
ductive, more efficient, and more immediate exercises an impact on
every business and on every individual in society.

Technological change takes place with its own rational, irre-
versible randomness. The rational element is perfectly captured by
Moore's Law. Moore saw no reason to believe that the trend, which
became known as his "Law," would not continue—even though, if
it did, the number of transistors would increase by three orders of
magnitude in the decade following his observation.

The irreversibility of technological change is evident all around
us. There will never be a world without steel, photography, television, or the computer, just as there will never be a world without the
railroad, no matter what that industry's financial problems may be.
Technological and industrial revolutions stand in stark contrast in
this regard to political revolutions. Germany today is more like the
Germany of the Weimar Republic in the 1920s than it is like the
years of the Nazis or of the Second Reich (1871–1918). But with

technology, the genie is never shoved back into the bottle. The knowledge and the ability to split the atom are here to stay.[6]

The randomness of technological change derives in part from the interaction of disparate technologies which converge as they mature. When the steam engine was invented, no one had the railroad in mind. When the railroad was invented, no one had refrigeration in mind. But when refrigerated railroad cars were perfected, beef could be economically slaughtered in Chicago and consumed in eastern cities a thousand miles away.

Or consider the stirrup. The stirrup transformed the horse from a means of transportation to a mobile instrument of warfare because it permitted the horseman to brace himself and thus to wield a sword or lance effectively without losing his balance. Horses became a vital military asset; but keeping them was expensive because, among other reasons, land was required to provide fodder to feed them. An elaborate hierarchy of landholding and loyalty grew up as a result. This "military-agricultural complex" came to be called feudalism. The stirrup was the "revolution in miniature" of feudalism. It was an analogue of the silicon integrated circuit—one small artifact which transformed the world.

The inventor of the integrated circuit with a silicon substrate[7] (referred to hereinafter as the silicon integrated circuit) was Robert N. Noyce.

The silicon integrated circuit gave its name to a geographic region. Silicon Valley, once known as the Santa Clara Valley, is more than merely a spot on the map. It has become shorthand for a new industry—some as-yet-undefined amalgam of computers, component manufacturers, and internet portals. The first California gold rush of 1848–1849 took place after gold was discovered near Sutter's Mill, about 150 miles from Intel's headquarters in Santa Clara. One need merely drive the freeways of Silicon Valley today to see the insignia of the second gold rush: Intel, Apple, SUN, Yahoo!, Hewlett-Packard, Oracle, and on and on. In the midst of these, there are as many start-ups as money can fund—most of which will fail, a handful of which will be the giants of the future. Silicon Valley in the 1980s and 1990s was a high-tech hothouse.

Early in the twentieth century, Silicon Valley was an area of intense natural beauty. Its fertile soil and year-round temperate climate made it ideal for fruit growers, and there were orchards of apricots, dates, and plums.

By the 1940s, the Valley had become home to defense contractors specializing in high-technology electronics. In 1938, David Packard and his wife, Lucile, moved into their new home at 367 Addison Avenue in Palo Alto. Behind the house, William Hewlett rented a cottage, and the two Stanford classmates began working together in a small garage on the lot which in 1989 was designated as the "birthplace of Silicon Valley" by the California Landmarks Commission.

Hewlett-Packard (the order of the names was determined by the toss of a coin) became an anchor tenant of Silicon Valley. HP has grown into a leading player in the world of high technology, employing by 1996 (the year Packard died; Hewlett died in 2001) 112,000 people with sales of $38.4 billion, profits of $2.6 billion, and a market capitalization on March 26, 1996, the day of Packard's death, of $47.4 billion.

The company Hewlett and Packard built is probably better seen as a precursor than as the exemplar of what was to come in the Valley. It presaged the future in that its founders were committed to more than solely financial success. From the start, HP was dedicated, in Packard's words, "toward making important technological contributions to the advancement of science, industry, and human welfare. It was a lofty, ambitious goal. But right from the beginning, Bill and I knew we didn't want to be a 'me-to' company merely copying products already on the market."[8]

Hewlett was born and bred in San Francisco. Packard was from Pueblo, Colorado. Both were men of the West, and there is a wide-open sense of possibility about them and their start-up. Both were children of the Great Depression (Hewlett was born in 1912; Packard in 1913); and as it did on so many Americans, the Depression imprinted itself on them and their company.

This imprint was probably deeper on Packard than on Hewlett. Hewlett came from an upper-middle-class family. Packard's circumstances were more modest. But both men had seen "its devastating effects on people, including many families and friends who were close to us." Not altogether unlike the experience of Sam Walton and his father, Packard's father, a lawyer, had been named the bankruptcy referee for the state of Colorado. "When I returned to Pueblo during the summers of the 1930s, I often helped my father in looking up the records of those companies that had gone bankrupt."[9]

Like Walton, Packard never thought that bankruptcy might intrude upon his career. The possibility of failure seemed never to have crossed his mind. Nor, like Walton, did he resolve as a result of the Depression that he himself would never be poor. But the experience did matter to Packard, as it did to Walton. Hewlett-Packard was to be conservatively financed in its early years (no long-term debt) because the Depression had shown Packard how debt could lead to bankruptcy and thence to foreclosure.

Hewlett-Packard came to stand for much of what is good in late-twentieth-century American business. Founded by westerners, HP was a creature of the West. It was more democratic in atmosphere than, for example, General Electric, an old-line eastern firm where Packard had worked after graduating from Stanford. The work the company took on had to have meaning—to use technology to break new ground. Employees were expected to take pride in anything and everything they did. The managers themselves, starting with Hewlett and Packard, understood the work of the firm on a technical level. They could thus evaluate the quality of their employees simply by walking around and watching them. Indeed, Hewlett-Packard is the home of the term "management by walking around,"[10] a practice which would be of precious little use if the manager walking around did not have the technical ability to evaluate what he was looking at.

There was, moreover, an "HP way" of doing things. The essence of the HP way was integrity and commitment. HP, from the beginning, aspired to be more than just another business. The goal was profit, as it must be in all businesses, but it was also the development of a sense of mission. This is not to say that the company or its founders were somber. But they were serious.

It is not surprising to learn that David Packard served as deputy secretary of defense in the Nixon administration during the Vietnam War. Hewlett-Packard, like so many other companies in the Valley, had lived off Defense Department contracts for years by the time Packard was tapped for the job in 1969. It is not surprising that the Packards were friends of Herbert Hoover.

Think of these observations; and now think of Steve Jobs and Steve Wozniak and Apple Computer, founded just up the road from

Palo Alto in Cupertino four decades after Hewlett and Packard formed their partnership. It is difficult to imagine Jobs or "Woz from Oz" holding public office. Hewlett and Packard had a certain resemblance to Sam Walton (born in 1918) in that all three were liberal minded in the way they ran their companies but quite conservative politically and in matters of home and family. Hewlett and Packard were philanthropic by nature. They did not need a public relations adviser to tell them it was good for their reputations.

Hewlett and Packard were technologists, but no one would label them "nerds." Packard grew up in a tough town, played football at Stanford, and was a physically rugged man. He, Hewlett, and their friends were outdoorsmen. Camping, rock climbing, hunting, and fishing were their pastimes. (Sam Walton, too, was an avid, passionate hunter.) Hewlett, Packard, and Walton were not only children of the Great Depression but also of World War II, the good and just war. Hewlett and Walton were veterans.

What a difference half a century makes. Steve Jobs was born a decade after World War II ended, the year before William Shockley moved from Bell Labs back out west to his hometown of Palo Alto to found Shockley Semiconductor. Jobs was nine when Mario Savio launched the "free speech" movement at the University of California at Berkeley, when the '60s became "the '60s."[11] He was 12 when *The Graduate*, a movie of the '60s, of California, of Berkeley, and of the idiocy of adults, premiered.

The world of Steve Jobs was wholly different from that of Hewlett and Packard. It was a world of fast cars, conspicuous display, and the "big score" in every sense of that phrase. One facet that these worlds had in common was networking. Even in the 1980s, with its exploding population from all over the world, there was an aspect of the small town about Silicon Valley. As opposed to New York City, the most anonymous of places, people in Silicon Valley knew each other. Doors were open. Ideas and people were shared, borrowed, stolen. In this center of capitalism there has run a theme of cooperation as part of the landscape.

AnnaLee Saxenian, a scholar of the Valley and a refugee from the East, has asserted that the "Valley's engineers developed stronger commitments to one another and to the cause of advancing technology than to individual companies or industries."[12] This sounds a bit too good to be true. Plenty of people in the Valley wanted plenty of money and wanted it fast. They lived in a world of "drug and alcohol abuse, workaholism, debt, alienation, divorce and the ultimate frustration of a life based on achievement and not on human relationships."[13] With the stodginess of old-line eastern companies came a stolidity and stability which one jettisons at one's peril.

That said, there has been and remains something special about Silicon Valley. There are other centers of creativity in business in the United States—around Boston, around Austin, and in the Seattle area. Not only in America but the world over, municipalities, counties, and nations are seeking to crack the code and reproduce or surpass the wealth creation and technological progress which Silicon Valley has come to represent.

It is, I think, no accident that Silicon Valley has been a phenomenon of the United States. In a nation which for so much of its history suffered from a labor shortage, technology has played a key role in taming a continent. Europeans came to America looking for gold. What gold they eventually found was as nothing compared to the mineral and agricultural resources which the virgin land would yield if it could be linked to mills and to markets. The railroad and the telegraph made that possible. They were object lessons in the power of technology to transform the economy and change the world.

Inventors hold a special place in America's pantheon.[14] An invention is without human prejudice. If it works and makes life better, that is all that matters. Whether the inventor is male or female, black or white, foreign or native-born is of no account. What matters is the invention and the intelligence behind it. To honor inventiveness is to celebrate merit.

It is this celebration of merit which has been and is the beating heart of Silicon Valley. Capital may have no heart, as a former president of Mexico once said, but it also has no hatred or prejudice. A true capitalist cannot afford bigotry. Steve Jobs and Steve Wozniak deserved a hearing from financial backers no matter how bizarre their self-presentation by the usual metrics of button-down businessmen.

Robert Noyce and Gordon Moore founded Intel in 1968. The third employee, hired by Moore, was Andrew S. Grove, who matured into one of the greatest CEOs in American business history. Moore had hired Grove to work at Fairchild Semiconductor in 1963. Grove was born in Hungary in 1936, a terrible year for a Jew to be born in that country. He somehow escaped the Holocaust and fled to the West after the Soviet invasion of Hungary in 1956. He worked his way through City College of New York and then, disliking the eastern winters, took his Ph.D. in chemical engineering at Berkeley in three years.

Why did Moore hire Grove? Moore was not only bred in Silicon Valley, he was born very near it, one of the few people his age who made it in high tech of whom that could be said.[15] He was quiet, cautious, and brilliant. Grove was not only not a Californian; he was not a westerner, he was not American-born, and he was not a Christian. In 1963, he looked like a young fellow who had spent a little too much time in what came to be called the "People's Republic of Berkeley." He must have spoken English with a marked accent. He described himself as "a hotheaded 30-year-old running around like a drunken rat."[16] In short, two people from more different backgrounds than Moore and Grove could hardly be imagined. Given all this, I once asked Moore how he was able to look past all the obvious differences and make the job offer. He leaned back in his chair and with a beatific look on his face said, "It didn't matter." Grove was brilliant. That alone was what counted. Grove worked for Moore in apparently perfect harmony and mutual respect for years, and the two have built a great corporation in three decades from a standing start.

Moore's hiring Grove was Silicon Valley at its best. The man who helped make this and countless other such episodes possible was Robert Noyce.

EARLY YEARS

Robert N. Noyce stood at the center of Silicon Valley during its early growth and maturation as a haven for high technology. Less conservative than Hewlett or Packard, more civilized than Jobs, less self-effacing than Moore, less egomaniacal than Larry Ellison of software giant Oracle, less of a manager than Grove, less of a mismanager than Shockley, Bob Noyce was a man you could trust.

Noyce was phenomenally talented at a remarkable variety of activities. He possessed a thorough understanding of the most advanced work in electronics in the 1950s. He himself was, for a time, in the vanguard of inventing the future. U.S. Patent No.

2,981,877 is Noyce's patent for the integrated circuit. Jack Kilby at Texas Instruments and Noyce went through a tedious dispute about who was first. They and the rest of the world decided that they should be thought of as co-inventors.[17] It was Noyce's idea to embed the integrated circuit in silicon rather than germanium, which was the material of choice for the early transistor radios of the 1950s. Both germanium and silicon were semiconductors. Germanium was easier to work with, but failed at high temperatures. Silicon was more brittle but held up at high temperatures.[18] Silicon won the day, which is why the area between San Francisco and San Jose is not called Germanium Valley.

Noyce was born on December 12, 1927, in either Burlington or Denmark, Iowa (the sources differ), the third of four boys. He was a small-town boy of the plains and prairies, just like millions of other Americans. He did not stay in Denmark long, only six weeks, but the thought of his starting out in a town of that name is a pleasant one. The Dane Niels Bohr, one of the greatest physicists in the history of science and an outstanding humanitarian, was awarded the Nobel Prize in physics in 1922, five years prior to Noyce's birth.

Noyce's father was a Congregationalist minister (as were both his grandfathers). The family left Denmark so that his father could tend a new flock, this one in Atlantic (an odd name for a town in Iowa) at the other end of the state. The family lived there for eight years. "My earliest memory of that period was that it was Depression time. The church wouldn't pay Dad, so they paid him in produce."[19]

In the 1930s, Sam Walton and Bob Noyce lived in adjacent states, not all that far from one another as distance is thought of west of the Mississippi. Walton was a decade older, and the Depression made a deeper impression on him. It could not have been easy for Noyce's father to support a family of six with no cash income, but rural Iowa in the 1930s was a place where people knew how to make do. Poverty never seems to have been a problem for the Noyce family. After Atlantic, Iowa, it was on to Decorah in 1935. Noyce had thus lived in three of the four corners (all but the northwest) of a large state. Two years after Decorah came the call to Webster City. When Noyce was twelve, it was on to Rennow. The following year, the family moved to Grinnell. In the first thirteen years of his life, Noyce lived in six towns.

Grinnell was the home of the Iowa Conference of Congregational Churches, and Bob's father became the associate superintendent in one of the least hierarchical of religious denominations. Grinnell was to be the family home for about seven years, "afford[ing] Bob and his brothers a measure of stability in their lives. Now they could weave themselves into the fabric of their community, become Boy Scouts and develop their reputations in organized sports, attend dances, meet girls and lead their lives free from the ever present fear of having to pack up and leave everything they thought mattered."[20] From what one can gather, Noyce's parents were loving and devoted to one another and to their four sons. They had their family and their faith; but through much of Noyce's youth, he was an itinerant. He did not seem to mind, though one wonders whether this constant migration might have contributed to a streak of shyness that impressed those closest to him in his later years.

Grinnell is fifty miles east of Des Moines, squarely in the center of the vastness of America's great plains. Surrounded by cornfields and rural to its core, the town was subjected each year to the biting, seemingly endless, dark, brutal winters of that part of the country. Not only was this little town in the middle of nowhere the headquarters, if that is not too grandiose a term, for the state's Congregationalist churches; it was also, however improbably, the home of one of the nation's great colleges.

Grinnell College, named for Congregationalist minister Josiah Grinnell, was founded in 1846. It is one of those elite institutions, like Reed College in Oregon (from which Steve Jobs was a dropout), which is not widely known to the average American but which has developed an enviable reputation for excellence among cognoscenti. Noyce came to love Grinnell. He would credit the town, "stiff, Republican, and religious" though it may have been, and the gem of a college therein with much of his eventual success. One journalist has written that Grinnell was "Noyce's first—and perhaps only—real home." He later shared his fortune generously with the school, as well as donating to it his time, connections, and enthusiasm.[21]

In his youth, Noyce developed the habits of doing, of earning, and of tinkering. He does not seem to have seen himself as a man of destiny early on. He just liked doing things, and had the time and space to be playful with mechanical contrivances. He also developed a certain fearlessness. He was resourceful and mechanically talented, but he did not see his tinkering as anything remarkable. "It was just sort of the way life was. Dad always managed to have some sort of workshop in the basement. And it was the usual rural environment of harvesting in the summer and canning in the winter." Nothing special.[22]

It was toward the end of high school that Noyce "began to feel that maybe I had [a] little bit more than average ability. . . ." His special gift lay in a field that would transform the century, physics, and in mathematics as well. He was taking courses at Grinnell College while still in high school because he needed the challenge. Noyce was extraordinarily active his whole life; and while excelling at his high school studies he was also doing farm work, delivering newspapers, mowing lawns, and baby-sitting for the townsfolk. One of his customers was the chairman of the physics department at the college, Professor Grant O. Gale.

For the Noyce family it was time to move again, this time finally breaking Iowa's borders into Illinois. But Bob stayed behind. He had decided to study physics with professor Gale at Grinnell. It was the autumn of 1945, and with his high school record Noyce could have attended any university in the nation. But he loved physics, got along very well with Gale, and was happy in Grinnell. Why leave?

Silicon Valley has for decades been taken to exemplify the advantages of intense clusters of related economic activity. Grinnell, in sharp contrast, illustrates the advantages of widely dispersed outposts of excellence dotting the landscape. In the midst of the Corn Belt, many miles from any other college (not to mention any major research university), Grant Gale was one of the most well informed physicists in the country. Judging from his impact on Noyce, who years later donated a quarter of the funds for an observatory for the college in Gale's name, he must also have been an outstanding teacher.

One of Gale's college classmates at the University of Wisconsin was a man named John Bardeen. Bardeen was also a physicist. On December 23, 1947, Bardeen, working with Walter H. Brattain under the supervision of William B. Shockley (and not always working harmoniously), invented the transistor.[23]

The transistor is a device with three terminals that regulates or amplifies current or voltage and can act as a switch. Ernest Braun and Stuart MacDonald, in their *Revolution in Miniature,* are undoubtedly correct in their observation that it is "unrealistic to see the transistor as the product of three men, or of one laboratory, or of physics, or even of the forties. Rather its invention required the contributions of hundreds of scientists working in many different places, in many different fields over many years."[24]

Quite true. The transistor was, in its broadest context, the culmination of the history of the "invention and development of wireless telegraphy and all that it led to in radio and television, the success of [vacuum tube] electronics, which widened the scope of electronics far beyond the original wireless telegraphy applications, and finally, pure research in solid state physics which had, from time to time, almost by accident, brought about various solid state devices."[25] Some of these developments can be traced back to the seventeenth century.

On the other hand, it is also true that on December 22, 1947, there was no such thing as a transistor and on December 24 there was. There were a lot of problems associated with integrating the transistor into the world of electronics, and there was some early skepticism about the utility of the device. But its value quickly became apparent for a number of applications, such as hearing aids; and its inventors were honored in the world of physics by being awarded the Nobel Prize in 1956. John Bardeen, the friend of Noyce's professor Grant Gale, won the Nobel Prize again in 1972 for his work on superconductivity. Clearly, Bardeen was a good man to have as a friend if you were a physicist who wanted to be on the cutting edge of your profession.

Though the transistor was the result of streams of research that had been carried on for centuries, its invention and its diffusion marked a step-function increase in the power of electronics. The most important thing about the transistor is that it is not a vacuum tube. Vacuum tubes are very large relative to transistors. They are bulky, unwieldy, delicate. They demand far more power than a transistor because of the necessity for heating the filament or metal tube which serves as the cathode. They are slow to turn on because it takes time to heat the cathode. They emit heat, which means they cannot be placed close together, and if a great many of them are used, as many as were required by early computers, the rooms in which they are stored have to be cooled. They also emit light, which attracts insects. The word "de-bug" was originally used to describe the removal of moths from the vacuum tubes of computers which were, of necessity, so large that they occupied huge rooms.

The transistor episode of the revolution in miniature was a breakthrough moment. It was not merely a smaller, more efficient vacuum tube. The "radically different way in which the transistor worked . . . was to make feasible a radical new sort of electronics. . . ." Here was "not simply a new sort of amplifier but the harbinger of an entirely new sort of electronics with the capacity not just to influence an industry or scientific discipline, but to change a culture."[26]

Some people glimpsed what the transistor might mean. Or at least they understood that its implications were unfathomable but undoubtedly titanic. One of these was Grant Gale. Because of his friendship with Bardeen, Gale was one of the first physicists to study transistors and examine them with his students. He had two transistors in 1948. One of the students with whom he studied them was Noyce.

Noyce loved Grinnell, where he excelled in his double major of physics and mathematics and in everything else as well. Handsome and athletic with an appealing baritone voice, he acted in a local radio soap opera, won a varsity letter in swimming and was a state champion diver, played the oboe, and sang in choral groups. He graduated at the top of his class and won the Brown Derby Award for getting the best grades while doing the least work.[27]

The old saying that a minister's son is a son of a gun rings true in Noyce's case. He once stole a twenty-five-pound pig for a dormitory party with a Hawaiian luau theme. The party was a big success, but the authorities were not amused. Noyce was suspended from Grinnell for a term. The punishment might have been more severe had it not been for Gale's vigorous advocacy of his cause.

Noyce spent his enforced absence from college in New York City. He had been in New York and its environs during summer vacations, so the city was not a shock to him. His oldest brother, Donald, was studying at Columbia, so he was not completely isolated. While in New York, he learned enough statistics to become an actuary and get a job with Equitable; and he learned enough about the insurance business to discover that, for him at least, "it was a terribly boring place to be."[28]

Noyce certainly was not swept away by New York, overawed or intimidated by it. What he wanted was to finish up at Grinnell, and he wanted especially to get back in touch with the transistor. Noyce was one of those who quickly understood the potential of the device: "It was simply astonishing. Just the whole concept that you could get amplification without a vacuum. It hit me like the atom bomb. It was one of those ideas that just jolts you out of the rut, gets you thinking in a different way."[29]

The next step after Grinnell was graduate school. He chose MIT, where, it turned out, "there were no professors around who knew anything about transistors."[30] Grinnell was more advanced than the nation's premier technical institution because of the personal connections and vibrant curiosity of Gale. Noyce proceeded to get a Ph.D. in physics anyway, with a thesis entitled "A Photoelectric Investigation of Surface States on Insulators." Though not directly concerned with the transistor, the thesis did cite work by Shockley, Bardeen, and Brattain and helped Noyce familiarize himself further with semiconductors as well as with the technical vocabulary which was essential for what was to be his life's work. "The major problems in the field at that time were electron emission from cathode-ray and vacuum tubes. But still they had many of the same physical properties [as transistors]; you had to learn the language, the quantum theory of matter and so on."[31]

"Noyce's life," one author has written, "is basically a narrative of one outstanding success after another. . . ."[32] In Noyce's professional undertakings, there is a lot of truth to this observation. He not only cleared every academic hurdle, but left a lot of light between himself and the bar. He did not just graduate from high school, he was valedictorian. He did not just graduate from college, he was Phi Beta Kappa. He did not attend just any graduate institution, he received a Ph.D in a hard science from the nation's premier technical institute, which he sailed through without breaking stride. He worked as a teaching assistant, an assistant in the research laboratory for electronics, won a fellowship, and was elected to Sigma Xi.[33] Once in business, we will see the same pattern, from mountaintop to mountaintop.

Noyce lived life in the fast lane, and any description which suggests a linear progression from one activity to another would slight the remarkable variety of activities in which this omnicompetent man engaged. While at MIT, for example, he attended the few professional conferences there dealing with transistors. The number of such conferences would increase quickly as the importance of semi-conductors became widely appreciated. He maintained his lifelong interest in music and theater. Typically, that interest was pursued as a participant not as a spectator.

Noyce did not merely attend plays, he acted in them. At one of these, a musical put on at Tufts, the costume changer was a young woman named Elizabeth Bottomley. They met and married not long thereafter, in 1953. Betty and Bob Noyce were to have four children. Twenty-one years after this wedding, in another part of the country and in such a different era that it seemed another world, they were divorced. To outward appearances, the marriage had been a happy one; but its failure, keenly felt, was a sharp exception to the generalization that Noyce's life skipped from one outstanding success to another. We will speak more of his personal life presently.

Noyce maintained a relationship with MIT through the years, but the school did not seem to have been anything special to him. His reaction seemed to be similar to how he handled New York City. It was interesting, even noteworthy, but not awesome. They knew more about transistors in the Corn Belt. His thesis supervisor, Professor Wayne B. Nottingham, is mentioned in no writing by Noyce or about him that I have seen.

With degree in hand, it was time to find a job. Apparently, the academic life never crossed Noyce's mind, nor did he show any interest in working for the government or for any nonprofit research institution. He was going into business. With his record, he had the pick of the crop: GE, RCA, Bell. He chose instead to work for "lowly Philco" because, as he said, "the way I put it to myself at the time was that they really needed me. At other places they knew what was going on. They knew what they were doing." Equally important, according to journalist Michael S. Malone, Noyce preferred being a big fish in a relatively little pond. He did not want to get lost at a behemoth like Bell Labs. Philco paid the lowest salary among his choices; but there he would "be able to wear many hats, including those of both scientist and businessman, and be able to hop around to different projects."[34]

"Hopping around" is something Noyce did a lot of. He has, indeed, been criticized for a certain lack of depth. The confrontations which are an inescapable part of running a business always left him acutely uncomfortable. When firings were called for at firms in which he held positions of responsibility, they were usually carried out by others, often when he was out of town.[35] "I don't run large organizations well," he once said. "I don't have the discipline to do that, have the follow through."[36]

The hopping around became even more apparent as Noyce grew older. The world, for him, was an invitation. Everywhere he hopped, he found success; and he made it look easy. His successes extended beyond work to play. He took up skiing as an adult and he became so good at it that friends suggested he enter organized competition. He was a skilled pilot and scuba diver, in addition to being a seeming natural on stage, either acting or singing.

All that having been said, Noyce must have been a man of outstanding native ability who also possessed the self-control to mobilize that ability all by himself, late at night, when no one else was around. Slow though it may have been to grasp the importance of the transistor, MIT was an institution with standards; and a Ph.D. in physics earned there was not nothing. Noyce's thesis was, of course, sole authored.

Noyce has been presented to the world as a "tinkerer." He tinkered with box kites and engines as a youth. He would solve problems in the workshop of the family home in Grinnell and bring the results to his encouraging father. "In a small town," he said, "when something breaks down, you don't wait around for a new part, because it is not coming. You make it yourself."[37] When one reads Noyce's description of his invention of the integrated circuit, one encounters the same sense of the practical tinkerer.

It is true that Noyce's inclination was more to the practical than the theoretical, and it is better to think of him as an engineer than as a scientist. From what I can gather, however, this was a matter of inclination rather than of intellectual limitation. Growing up the way he did, in an environment in which problems could not be solved by ordering a new part "because it is not coming," practical problem solving was the order of the day.

No one can argue with the choices he made. Look at the results. It does seem to me worth remarking, however, that had he turned his talent toward theory rather than practice, the results in this different realm might have been equally remarkable. In 1970, Noyce said, "Don't be encumbered by history. Go off and do something wonderful."[38] The academic disciplines (not least the history profession) are as much in need of this message as the practical world.

Noyce's job at Philco, according to one source, provided him with "a chance to practice serious science." He presented various papers on semiconductors at professional conferences. His work was state of the art. In 1955, he presented a paper on "base widening punch-through" to the American Physical Society. In the audience was William Bradford Shockley.

NOYCE AND SHOCKLEY SEMICONDUCTOR

If Noyce was at the cutting edge of semiconductors, Shockley was the tip of the blade. "He was absolutely the most important person in semiconductor electronics," Noyce later said. In January 1956, Shockley phoned Noyce with the news that he was going to leave Bell Labs and set up his own firm in Palo Alto, California (where he had been brought up), and bring advanced transistors to the market. He wanted to know if Noyce would be interested in interviewing for a position. After serving his apprenticeship in the minors at Philco, "getting that job," Noyce said, "meant you would definitely be playing in the big leagues."[39]

Noyce had a wife and two children (Bill was two years old and Penny six months) to support and apparently no money in the bank to speak of. Nevertheless, it did not take much persuading. He left a secure position at an established firm and an employment future as predictable as such things can be and hurried out to what was still known as the Santa Clara Valley to interview with a firm that did not yet exist. The year was 1956, the same year that journalist William H. Whyte published his influential book *The Organization Man*,[40] the thesis of which was that American business executives did not do this sort of thing.

Noyce arrived in Palo Alto,[41] bought a house that morning, and went to see Shockley that afternoon. This sequence is often cited as being highly revelatory. Specifically, he bought the house *before* he had his job interview. This house was located in a region of the country he had never even visited, although his oldest brother, Donald, who had studied at Columbia, was teaching at Berkeley at the time "and, you know, his letters were stories of sunshine and lovely weather. . . ."[42]

Noyce, of course, got the job; and Shockley kept on hiring. The people he hired were remarkable, among them three physicists, Jean Hoerni, Jay Last, and Noyce; a metallurgist, Sheldon Roberts; a mechanical engineer, Julius Blank; an electrical engineer, Victor Grinich; an industrial engineer, Eugene Kleiner; and Gordon Moore, a physical chemist.[43] "It was the greatest collection of electronics genius ever assembled—and all of them were under thirty, at the height of their powers."[44] What expectations would be too great for such a team with the world's top expert in the field as its leader? What breakthrough was too ambitious? What future would be denied Noyce, the handsome, self-assured, delightful, incisive talent who seemed naturally to gravitate to the position of Shockley's favorite?[45]

Noyce once said that Silicon Valley "holds the keys to the kingdom." What kingdom? "It has often been said that just as the Industrial Revolution enabled man to apply and control greater physical power than his own muscle could provide, so electronics has extended his intellectual power."[46] The folks in the Valley were thinking big.

Shockley Semiconductor, funded by Arnold Beckman and his Beckman Instruments Company, opened for business in 1956. On the morning of November 1, Shockley received a phone call that he, along with Brattain and Bardeen, had been awarded the Nobel Prize for their invention of the transistor. Shockley came to work that day, closed up shop, and took everyone in the firm out for a champagne breakfast at Dinah's Shack on El Camino Real in Palo Alto.

There is a remarkable photograph of that event with a handsome Shockley sitting at the head of the table looking like a benign paterfamilias being toasted by his employees/acolytes. The photograph brings to mind the St. Crispin's Day speech that Shakespeare had Henry V deliver to his army on the day of Agincourt: "We few, we happy few, we band of brothers. . . ."[47] It was a magic moment and a photograph which Noyce kept long afterward. It captured an ambience representative of a new way of doing business. No one was wearing a suit. Only two men wore ties. This was the West, not the East. Working in a converted apricot barn (Shockley Semiconductor's headquarters) and decamping to a local greasy spoon to celebrate a Nobel Prize—this was the new way. High on achievement; low on formality and display.

Unfortunately, Shockley Semiconductor was already running amok by the time this photograph was taken. Some of the young men in that picture were probably only too happy to begin the day drunk. Shockley turned out to be a very strange man. Although he was said to be a skilled manager while at Bell Labs, whatever talent he may have had on that dimension evaporated by the time he returned to Palo Alto.

As a theoretical physicist and an engineer (he held over ninety patents) Shockley's abilities were unquestioned. Where phenomena were knowable, where the world had rules, Shockley was profoundly impressive. Noyce said he "had this wonderful ability to make the right simplifying assumption, to get the math out of the way until you had a basic visual image of what was happening. . . ."[48] Hans Queisser, a German solid-state physicist who worked with Shockley, noted his "extremely quick grasp of scientific problems. . . . His strategy was to get to the heart of the matter very quicky."[49]

Shockley proved, as had been proven many times, that brainpower alone does not a business make. He humiliated his employees in dozens of ways, large and small. When one of them came to him with an idea, he would, in his presence, phone his friends back at Bell Labs to see if the idea was worth pursuing, rather than showing him the respect his intellect merited. He administered psychological tests to everyone because he wanted to weed out the 10 percent of the population that he had convinced himself was psychotic. (Rumor had it that Noyce's test indicated that he was a very talented physicist but a poor manager.)[50] This was the beginning of Shockley's interest in psychology, an interest which proved wasteful and offensive and made him a pariah. Shockley had no head for business at all. His product ideas were unworkable and his marketing hopeless.

Oddly enough, one of Shockley's obsessions became thinking. In the 1960s, he taught a freshman seminar at Stanford on "Mental Tools for Scientific Thinking" in which was assigned Shockley's essay "THINKING about THINKING improves THINKING."[51] The oddity lies in the similarity to T. J. Watson Sr.'s obsession with the word "think" and his pasting it all over IBM as if its repetition would achieve some purpose. It is perhaps not surprising that scientists and engineers in this industry should become obsessed by thinking. They built machines that mimicked human thinking, and a whole field of study called artificial intelligence has grown up around this idea.[52]

Disillusion with Shockley came quickly. By 1957, seven of the top scientists and engineers at the firm were looking for somewhere else to work. These seven could have found work individually, but they wanted to continue together as a team. This was not unprecedented in American business history. The "Whiz Kids," the young hotshots who had done statistical work for the U.S. Army Air Corps during World War II, sought employment as an ensemble in private industry at war's end. They wound up at Ford.[53] But the automobile industry was a known quantity at the time and almost half a century old. The semiconductor business was new.

One of the seven who were discontented got in touch with the Wall Street investment bank of Hayden Stone in their search for a corporate home. At Hayden Stone, they caught the attention of Arthur Rock. An easterner born and bred, Rock was from George Eastman's hometown of Rochester, attended Syracuse University, and graduated from the Harvard Business School in 1951. He peddled the talents of the group to almost two dozen companies without much success.

Meanwhile, the seven defectors from Shockley had become eight. Noyce was well aware of the discontent and shared it, but it seems to have been a little more difficult for him to make the break. Shockley was brilliant but plainly unhinged. However, there seems to have been a childlike innocence about his cruelty. In a world of selfishness, greed, and mindless ambition, Shockley had a streak of non-nerdish charm. "He was an enthusiast, a raconteur, and a showman" with a winning sense of humor.[54] There was, in other words, an appealing side to Shockley's personality; and Noyce, his handsome "golden boy," probably saw more of that than the others did. Noyce never lost his respect for Shockley's genius as a scientist and an engineer. No one could deny, though, that he was an utter failure as an entrepreneur. Arthur Rock said he was simply impossible to deal with in a business setting. Shockley Semiconductor never turned out a viable product.

Some men are born great, some achieve greatness, and some have greatness thrust upon them, the old saying goes. There is an element of all three in most great people, but Noyce seems to have had greatness thrust upon him to an exceptional degree. Shockley, for example, picked him out of a pretty impressive crowd. Moreover, the seven who decided to leave, as well as their investment banker, felt that Noyce brought something special to the new venture which everyone needed. There seems to have been a spontaneous consensus that starting a new business needed a spark that only Noyce could provide. They approached him, and he agreed to leave with them. Arthur Rock, after having more than twenty doors closed in his face, finally found a backer for the eight. It was a "bachelor bon vivant" named Sherman Fairchild who lived with his Aunt May in a fashion-forward town house on East Sixty-fifth Street in Manhattan. "The place looked like something from out of the Crystal Palace of Ming in *Flash Gordon*."[55] This was a far cry from the homes of executives at RCA or GE.

Fairchild was an aviator and his company, headquartered in Syosset, on Long Island, specialized in aerial photography. He was very rich. He and his Aunt May owned the company. What is more, Sherman owned the largest block of stock in a company we have seen before, IBM. He owned more than either Watson Sr. or Jr. The reason was that he was the only child of George Winthrop Fairchild, a journalist and congressman from upstate New York who for reasons unknown was tapped by Charles Ranlett Flint to be the chief executive officer of Computing-Tabulating-Recording, which, it may be remembered, became IBM after Flint replaced Fairchild with Thomas J. Watson Sr. Obviously, the Fairchilds had opted to keep the stock originally granted in the family. The happy result was vast wealth.[56]

With Fairchild's funding, a new company was founded in Silicon Valley in October of 1957—the Fairchild Semiconductor Corporation. Noyce, who by now had become the first among equals from a managerial and organizational point of view, became the director of research and development. Each of the eight technologists was asked to invest $500 as "earnest money" with the understanding that the company retained the option to purchase their stock at its discretion. Fairchild's offices were at 844 Charleston Street in Palo Alto.[57]

The day the Fairchild announcement was made, Shockley issued a statement that the departure of the eight "has no real effect on the Shockley lab."[58] In one sense, that was true. The Shockley lab had been barren of accomplishment up to that time because of its mercurial boss. Nothing was lost due to the defection because nothing had been achieved. The departure did, however, seal the company's fate. Nothing would ever be done. The company was sold in 1960, sold again in 1965, and closed down in 1968, twelve years after the happy band of brothers toasted Shockley and his Nobel Prize at Dinah's Shack.

What we call Silicon Valley today really began in the converted apricot barn that was Shockley Semiconductor. The commercialization of a scientific/engineering breakthrough. Dreaming big dreams. The mind-bending problem of manipulating physical objects so small and through which particles moved so quickly that no metaphor could make what you were doing comprehensible in terms of daily reality. (Noyce, speaking with the voice of an engineer, said that in the world in which he lived people had to become "reconciled" to unimaginable speed. They did not have to understand it. Think of a nanosecond, 1/1,000,000,000, or one billionth, of a second. Then think of a femtosecond, 1/1,000,000,000,000,000, or one quadrillionth, of a second.)[59] The overweening ambition. The clash between intellect and character. Shifting loyalties. The desire not only for fame and money but to make a difference, to change the world. The willingness to walk out and start something new without being paralyzed by the fear of failure.

His press release to the contrary notwithstanding, Shockley was utterly thunderstruck at the departure of the young men. He labeled them the "traitorous eight," a nickname that stuck. Silicon Valley would come to be a great testing ground for the idea of loyalty in the years to come. As for Shockley, "feeling forsaken and deceived, depression crippled him for months."[60] Shockley was through in the Valley, finished as a businessman and even as a scientist. He spent the rest of his life propounding ugly, pseudoscientific theories about race and making himself anathema among intelligent people.

The legacy of Shockley Semiconductor, in contrast to its founder, proved lasting. A corporate genealogy in 1981 showed seventy-five firms tracing their origins back to that converted apricot barn. Of these, Fairchild Semiconductor was the first to become famous.

FAIRCHILD AND THE INTEGRATED CIRCUIT

From its founding through most of the 1960s, Fairchild was a leader in silicon technology. Looking back three decades after he and Noyce left Fairchild to found Intel, Gordon Moore wrote that

Fairchild "introduced the first silicon mesa transistor to be made commercially, the first planar transistor, and the first commercial integrated circuit, as well as performed much of the research that has led to stable interfaces necessary for today's metal-oxide-semi-conductor (MOS) transistors."[61]

"We divided the work," Moore explained,

> to fit the backgrounds of the group. Roberts took responsibility for growing and slicing silicon crystals and for setting up a metallurgical analysis laboratory. Noyce and Last took on the lithography technology development, including mask making, wafer coating, exposure, development, and etching. Grinich set up electrical test equipment, consulted with the rest of the group on our electronic questions, and taught us how to measure various transistor parameters. Kleiner and Blank took charge of the facilities and set up a machine shop to make the equipment and fixtures we could not purchase. I took on the diffusion, metallization, and assembly technology development. Hoerni, our theoretician, sat at his desk and thought.[62]

Hoerni, a Swiss immigrant with two Ph.D.s, one from the University of Geneva and one from Cambridge, must have gotten a kick out of that last sentence in Moore's enumeration of responsibilities. Some of Hoerni's thoughts turned out to be pretty important. One of these was the development of the "planar process" for diffusing the circuitry of a transistor onto the flat surface of silicon, rather than constructing transistors using a sedimentary or "mesa" model, which had been the standard up to that time.[63] Fairchild had already shipped one hundred mesa transistors to IBM's Government Systems Division in Owego, New York, in January 1958. The mesa process itself was new.[64] Things were moving fast.

Flatter. Smaller. More compact. More efficient. That was the direction of the transistor and semiconductor in 1960, and it has remained the direction for four decades. Unlike the Shockley Lab, Fairchild, on minimal funding from its sponsor back east, was shipping product; and the first customer was a prestigious one.

The style of work at Fairchild could also be described as flat, small, compact, and efficient. Although the expertise of each individual scientist or engineer naturally led them to gravitate to certain tasks, they were nevertheless not reluctant to ask for help. Moore, for example, described an instance in which he was "out of ideas"; so he decided to try one of Noyce's suggestions, even though it did not seem very promising. As with so many of Noyce's ideas which seemed to come out of nowhere, this worked.

The emphasis was on getting things done rather than on necessarily understanding why or how things worked. In discussing some of his experiments with aluminum, for example, Moore observed: "While it was several years before we understood the physics involved, that was not important at the time. What was important was that we had a reproducible process to make contacts to our transistors."[65]

As far as management was concerned, there does not seem to have been a great deal of it. None of the "traitorous eight" had any experience running a business. They apparently did not think very much about money. Insofar as they did, they had simply assumed they would work for a salary all their lives. With Fairchild, they suddenly realized, in Noyce's words, that "they could get some equity in a start-up company. That was a great revelation—and a great motivation too."[66] Stock, not salary, would become the mother's milk of Silicon Valley.

Fairchild Camera had invested $1.5 million in Fairchild Semiconductor, and the feeling grew that all these young geniuses, the "Fairchildren" as they came to be known, could do with some adult supervision. In 1958, Fairchild Semiconductor was reported to have hit a half a million dollars in sales. It employed one hundred people. It was beginning to look like a real business.

Real businesses need real business managers, and in March of 1958 Ed Baldwin, from the semiconductor division of Hughes Aircraft, was hired to play that role. But he himself left the following year, not because he was fired but because he heard the siren song of entrepreneurship. He and some friends decamped to found Rheem Semiconductor.[67] Here was another way in which Fairchild provided a harbinger of the way of the Valley. Loyalty to a company was a concept out of the alien East. In Silicon Valley, the idea was to get your own thing and to get it now. Companies would come and go, but the people hung around. That was the Silicon Valley way.

In 1958 or 1959 (the date is uncertain), John Carter, president and chief executive officer of Fairchild Camera and Instrument Corporation, paid a visit to Fairchild Semiconductor. In his article on Bob Noyce, Tom Wolfe used this visit as another example of the differences between eastern and western methods of running a company; and Wolfe's description is amusing enough to deserve quotation at length. Carter arrived at Mountain View (Fairchild Semiconductor's home in the Valley)

> in the back of a black Cadillac limousine with a driver in the front wearing the complete chauffeur's uniform—the black suit, the white shirt, the black necktie, and the black visored cap. That in itself was enough to turn heads at Fairchild Semiconductor. Nobody had ever seen a limousine and a chauffeur out there before. But that wasn't what fixed the day in everybody's memory. It was the fact that the driver stayed out there for almost eight hours, *doing nothing*. He stayed out there in his uniform, with his visored hat on, in the front seat of the limousine, all day, doing nothing but waiting for a man who was somewhere inside. John Carter was having a terrific chief executive officer's time for himself. He took a tour of the plant, he held conferences, he looked at figures, he nodded with satisfaction, he beamed his urbane Fifty-seventh Street Biggie CEO charm. And the driver sat out there all day engaged in the task of supporting a visored cap with his head. People started leaving their workbenches and going to the front windows. It seemed that bizarre. Here was a serf who *did nothing all day* but wait outside a door in order to be at the service of the haunches of his master instantly, whenever those haunches and the paunch and the jowls might decide to reappear. It wasn't merely that this little peek at the New York–style corporate high life was unusual out here in the brown hills of the Santa Clara Valley. It was that it seemed *terribly wrong*.[68]

Wolfe's little East meets West drama is not altogether fair. Plenty of Silicon Valley executives came to relish high living; while some in the East—such as Ken Olsen, the man who founded the Digital Equipment Corporation, guided it to greatness, and then presided over its collapse—lived modest lives. Speaking generally, however, the emphasis on work as opposed to perks, especially in the late 1950s and early 1960s and especially in this industry, seemed greater in the West than in the East. It is hard to believe that the expansive intellectual ferment of Xerox PARC could have occurred if the facility had been located in New Haven, as was first considered.[69]

In the midst of this minor social revolution, great things were being accomplished at Fairchild Semiconductor. Most important among these was Noyce's invention of the integrated circuit. Jean Hoerni had transformed what had been a three-dimensional object, the transistor, virtually into two dimensions. Height had been, if not quite completely eliminated, greatly reduced as a limiting factor in the efficiency of the transistor. By late 1958, Fairchild was turning out planar, not mesa, transistors. The question was: What next to achieve the goals of flatter, smaller, more compact, more efficient? One barrier was the necessity of connecting the negative-positive-negative elements of a transistor with wires in order to make the flow of electrical current possible and then wiring the transistors themselves to one another. "Here we were in a factory," Noyce said, "that was making all these transistors in a perfect array on a single [silicon] wafer, and then we cut them apart into tiny pieces and had to hire thousands of women with tweezers to pick them up and try to wire them together."

Now we hear Noyce the problem solver. In order to be a problem solver, you have to spot the problem that must be solved. "It just seemed so stupid," he said of Fairchild's production system. "It's expensive, it's unreliable, it clearly limits the complexity of the circuits you can build. It was an acute problem. The answer, of course, was don't cut them apart in the first place—but nobody realized that then."[70]

Step by step, by small increments, Noyce moved toward solving this "stupid problem." His method was trial and error, experimental, inductive—more in the style of the solo inventors of the late nineteenth century than of the scientists working in research and development at major corporations. Now that Hoerni had transformed the transistor into something close to a two-dimensional device, why not run wires across the top of it? Any wire, however, even one the width of a fraction of a human hair, would take up more space than no wire at all. Perhaps a metal which would serve the purpose of a wire could be printed on the oxide coating the transistor. Thus, no need for a wire as wires had previously been known, but merely a printed line.

One thought led to another. If you could connect different regions of a transistor (i.e., positive and negative) with a printed line of metal, why not connect transistors that way? And why not connect resistors, capacitors, and various other electrical devices as well? Why not put a complete integrated circuit on a silicon chip, thus solving the "stupid" problem of hundreds of people implanting large wires where space was at a desperate premium? Why not, indeed?[71]

The idea for the integrated circuit was much in the air in the late 1950s. Noyce's invention was virtually simultaneous with Jack Kilby's invention of a very similar device at Texas Instruments. Kilby was a man with a certain offbeat charm who lived in a world of his own. He was not the kind of man to attract a cult following. Noyce was and did. The integrated circuit added enormously to his already growing luster. This was the device that put Fairchild Semiconductor on the map. By the mid-1960s, the company hit $130 million in sales, employed twelve thousand people, and had facilities around the world.[72] Fairchild put Silicon Valley's semiconductor industry on the map.

The two men who had invented the integrated circuit had never met. They worked at different companies two thousand miles apart (Texas Instruments is headquartered in Dallas). Neither man was working for one of the lavishly funded major research and development facilities of the nation's largest companies. Kilby was a maverick in a maverick company who did some of the critical work on his invention when everyone else was on vacation. Fairchild was a start-up. Texas Instruments was an upstart, much larger than Fairchild but not nearly the size of GE or Westinghouse in 1959.

The tendency of industrial research and development in large, established companies, was in general biased "toward improvements of existing systems rather than toward the inauguration of new ones."[73] To be sure, this is not always the case. Nylon was invented at Du Pont, and the transistor at Bell Labs.

Speaking generally, however, the environment of privately funded research moved from hunches or genius to inventions based on science financed by highly trained experts working for major corporations. The nylon and transistor developments came to be more the exception than the rule. A fundamental technological breakthrough is not necessarily good news for a company that has invested a fortune to build a system designed around yesterday's technology. Great profits were to be realized from the transistor by a host of companies; but for many of those companies heavily invested in systems built around the vacuum tube, great costs would be incurred first. The integrated circuit was a fundamental development. It is not surprising that its invention came from Kilby and Noyce, rather than from the "patent machines" of the corporate laboratories of the nation's biggest firms. Fairchild had a great deal to gain and very little to lose by moving from a mesa transistor connected by wires to a wireless planar integrated circuit etched on silicon.[74] The same could not be said for larger companies, which had much to gain but much to lose as well.

Noyce liked to speak of himself not as an engineer, a scientist, or a businessman but as a "technologist," which he described as "the kind of person who is comfortable with risk." "No businessman," he said, "would have developed the telephone. It's got to be a maverick—some guy who's been working with the deaf and gets the crazy idea that you could actually send the human voice over a wire. . . . A businessman would have been out taking a market survey, and since it was a nonexistent product he would have proven conclusively that the market for a telephone was zero."[75]

This kind of thinking illustrates why the invention and commercialization of radically new technology sometimes (not always) calls for the creation of a whole new company with new entrepreneurs, new investors, and a new vision. That is what Fairchild was about in the late 1950s.

"The successful solution" to a problem, Noyce explained, "comes about because somebody was able to fire up his imagination and try something new. . . . If you want to achieve something worthwhile, you have to jump to the new idea."[76] To be able to "jump to the new idea," you first must be able to choose the problems you want to solve. It was a lot more probable that you would have that opportunity at Fairchild than at Bell Labs.

It is true, as just noted, that nylon was invented at Du Pont and the transistor at Bell Labs, both huge research installations at two of the nation's largest companies. But as the twentieth century progressed, these sites were not designed to produce this kind of step-function advance. Some industrial R&D operations became more concerned with obtaining patents than with the true commercial potential of what was being patented.

It is worth looking at what happened to the men who invented the transistor and nylon. Shockley did not remain at Bell Labs. He left to form his own company. The inventor of nylon, Wallace H. Carothers, was an extraordinary talent who was more of a maverick than Kilby. He was tragically disturbed emotionally, and he warned the Du Pont executive who recruited him from the Harvard Chemistry Department that he suffered "neurotic spells of diminished capacity." Carothers committed suicide on April 29, 1937, convinced that he was a failure as a scientist. He was forty-one years old and being spoken of as a potential Nobel Prize winner at the time.[77]

The great difference between Noyce and his cohort at Fairchild on the one hand, and Edison and his generation on the other, is that the top people at Fairchild were, in fact, more than just instinctive tinkerers "hunting and trying" one thing after another. They were that, but they were also formally trained in the finest educational institutions. They had both the independent inventor's self-starting, driving curiosity as well as a knowledge of and respect for high theory, even though they had no interest in pursuing it. They combined the best of both worlds. The result was the planar process, the integrated circuit, and a good deal more besides.

The "new alchemists"[78] were transforming not lead into gold, but rather the most common elements on the planet into a device far more valuable than any metal.[79] In Gordon Moore's words:

> We were really looking for materials that were inherently inexpensive, and generally available. Oxygen is the most prevalent, but it's a gas, so we couldn't use that directly. But we learned that when you combine oxygen with the earth's second most common element, silicon, at about the ratio that they occur in nature, you end up with silicon dioxide for an insulator, and for the conductor, we added aluminum, which is the third most common element.[80]

Noyce liked to say that the integrated circuit was the product of his annoyance at an obnoxious situation. "The integrated circuit came out of my own laziness. We took those transistors that were all nicely arranged on a piece of silicon, cut them up into little pieces, and then shipped them to the customers. So I thought, why not cut out that middle ground and just put them together while they were still on the silicon. So that is what we did."[81]

Neither the idea not the execution were quite as simple as Noyce suggested. The result, however, was one of the basic building blocks of the world as it has developed since the invention. The executives at Fairchild Camera and Instrument back in Syosset, New York, were sufficiently impressed with what was going on out in Palo Alto that on September 24, 1959, they exercised their option to purchase all the stock of Fairchild Semiconductor. In other words, Fairchild Semiconductor ceased to exist as an independent firm and became a wholly owned division of Fairchild Camera. This transaction was carried out by an exchange of stock. Holders of Fairchild Semiconductor stock surrendered their stock in that entity and in return received a total of 19,901 shares of stock in Fairchild Camera.[82]

What all those words in the paragraph above mean is that each of the "traitorous eight," who for $500 in "earnest money" had formed Fairchild Semiconductor in 1957, were, less than twenty-four months later, worth $250,000 in marketable securities. A quarter of a million dollars in 1959 is, inflation adjusted, more than $1.5 million in 2000. These eight young men, who did not come from inherited wealth, who had thought of themselves as paycheck-to-paycheck kind of guys, and who did not seem to think as much about the money they were earning as the work they were doing, had just backed into a small fortune in almost no time. The streets in the former Santa Clara Valley were indeed paved with silicon.

With their newfound wealth, three of the original "traitorous eight" who had left Shockley for Fairchild (Hoerni, Roberts, and Kleiner) now left Fairchild to found their own firms. As quickly as people left, however, others signed on, most notably, Charles Sporck. Most of those going and coming were remarkably talented and would amass fortunes greater than they had imagined possible just a few years earlier. Assessing the history of computer and communications technology during the twentieth century, a historian observed:

At the start of the 1960s, communications technologies were more tightly controlled than at any other time during the twentieth century. Three networks dominated television, with programming that differed only superficially from one another. AT&T, which had monopolized telephone service for over half a century, was rapidly replacing the postal service as the primary conveyor of personal communications in the United States. . . . The dynamic industry spawned by the powerful new tool of data-processing, the computer, was dominated by a single firm: IBM controlled 85 percent of the market. . . . Communications seemed inextricably linked to these organizations and the large systems they operated.[83]

At the very moment when computers and communications seemed encased in the concrete of five huge firms—AT&T, IBM, RCA, CBS, and ABC—forces of fission and fusion were at work in Silicon Valley which would lead to fundamental changes in these industries between 1960 and 2000. An observer looking at these industries in 1960 would have seen a structure seemingly as immovable as a huge mountain. What the observer might not have realized was that the mountain was in fact a volcano, and that underneath it molten lava was increasing the pressure until the lid finally blew off. AT&T would be the first to fall, in 1982. RCA would be the next, gobbled up by General Electric. RCA's television network, NBC, would, along with its competitors CBS and ABC, find themselves in a fluid, unpredictable world. IBM, which had seemed the most invincible company in the country as late as the 1980s, almost collapsed in the early 1990s.[84]

This process of corporate fission and fusion which came to symbolize the Silicon Valley way had its start at Shockley and Fairchild. The products that were to eventuate from the offspring of these companies, especially the microprocessor, which was the descendant of the transistor,[85] were the furnace heating the lava which was to blow the mountain of the computer and communications industries to bits. In 1960, at the heart of the fiery furnace heating the lava was Fairchild Semiconductor. And at the heart of Fairchild was Bob Noyce.

Noyce was a man who craved stimulation and hated boredom. He loved to see smart people be smart and derived great satisfaction from developing talent. Above all, he comes down to us as a man who wanted to be free. Everything about him bespeaks this desire for freedom. The clearest physical manifestation was his love of flying, his purchase of his own airplane, and his skill as a pilot. Arthur Rock said you could not tell Bob Noyce that something could not be done because he would take that as a challenge and prove you wrong by doing it himself. Think once again of the remark stenciled on the T-shirt: "Don't be encumbered by history. Go off and do something wonderful." Noyce communicated a message of vibrant, electric liberation to some of the most able people in the nation—people who had a horror, as did he, of being stifled by the hierarchy and rituals of traditional eastern corporate America.

Noyce really did seem to have a magic touch. Later in his life, in the 1980s when there was a parade of people to his office wanting to see him—wanting a piece of him—some would leave those meetings and not wash their hand after shaking his. People would talk about kissing his ring. Without doing anything particularly exceptional in a fifteen-minute meeting, he seemed able to induce a euphoric sense of possibility. The intensity of this magic quality is like nothing I have ever encountered in studying other business leaders.

Noyce's desire for freedom in part conflicted with the need for order to accomplish his goals. Piloting your own plane may suggest a desire for freedom. It usually takes a lot of self-control, however, to earn the money necessary to buy your own plane. And once you are at the controls, concentration and rules are vital. Undisciplined pilots do not live long. Noyce described Intel to the *Harvard Business Review* as a highly disciplined organization, and he was proud of it:

> The people we want to attract are . . . high achievers. High achievers love to be measured . . . because otherwise they can't prove to themselves that they're achieving.
>
> Yes, the fact that you are measuring them says that you do care. Then they're willing to work. . . . We've had people come in who have never had an honest review of their work.[86]

When Fairchild was in its prime, this sense of discipline was yet to be achieved. Rather, it was a world of enormous effort, high risk, and high reward. In the words of a journalist: "It was a high-pressure, long-hours place, where employees were expected to exhibit almost superhuman endurance and energy. Then, when the day was over, everybody retired to a nearby restaurant-bar, the Wagon Wheel, and boozed and talked business until all hours of the night."[87]

Fairchild was a roller coaster. Bigger competitors—HP, Motorola, Texas Instruments, Raytheon, RCA—were on its tail. Its record from 1957 through 1968 was enviable, despite the inevitable bumps in the high-tech road. By 1967, Fairchild Semiconductor accounted for "well over half" the sales of parent Fairchild Camera. The parent's sales that year were almost $210 million, so the semiconductor division was well into nine figures in sales in a decade.[88] Some years were more profitable than others; but overall, the performance in terms of sales, market position, and technical progress was remarkable. Tom Wolfe wrote that the semiconductor division had between 1957 and 1968 "generated tremendous profits for the parent company back east;"[89] but no statistics on profitability (as distinct from sales) have survived. People of great talent left the division, but enormously talented people also signed on.

Noyce was at the center of this strange amalgam of strict discipline and informality, of intense concentration and after-hours alcohol. Wolfe described him as "the administrator or chief coordinator or whatever he should be called."[90] In Noyce's world, there was no chain of command, no hierarchy, no expensively decorated offices. Noyce hired smart people, told them to do whatever was necessary to get the job done, and then let them sink or swim.

> The young engineers who came to work for Fairchild could scarcely believe how much responsibility was suddenly thrust upon them. Some twenty-four-year-old just out of graduate school would find himself in charge of a major project with no one looking over his shoulder. A problem would come up, and he couldn't stand it, and he would go to Noyce and hyperventilate and ask him what to do. And Noyce would lower his head, turn on his 100-ampere eyes, listen, and say: "Look, here are your guidelines. You've got to consider A, you've got to consider B, and you've got to consider C." Then he would turn on the Gary Cooper smile: "But if you think I'm going to make your decision for you, you're mistaken. Hey . . . it's *your* ass."[91]

If this was the kind of freedom you had craved all your young life, Fairchild was the place for you. If you experienced it as "repressive tolerance," it was not.

As the years passed, Noyce was awarded promotion after promotion: from vice president and general manager of Fairchild Semiconductor in 1959 to a vice presidency of parent Fairchild Camera in 1962, to group vice president of Fairchild Camera in 1965, to a seat on the board of directors in 1967. What would have seemed like a golden staircase to the average organization man became progressively less appealing to Noyce. He did not take any pleasure in the upper reaches of business management. Fairchild Camera was involved in a lot of different products and services in which Noyce had no interest. The purpose of top management was to see to it that the company made money. Noyce liked money as much as the next man, and he knew how to spend it. But he was preeminently a product person and, as he said, a technologist. He wanted to make money his way, doing what he enjoyed. Eastern business practices struck him as bloated, archaic, and lazy. People observed protocol, in his view, based not on merit but on some other metrics in which he had no interest.

The most valuable asset in Silicon Valley in the 1960s was neither a patent nor a production facility. It was Bob Noyce. By taking him further away from what he loved, Fairchild was alienating him and also threatening the viability of the Semiconductor Division, where discontent seemed to increase in direct proportion to Noyce's distance from it. Top talent, like Charlie Sporck, began to leave.

Arthur Rock, who knew and liked Noyce (the two got quite a kick out of one another), said that Noyce had "strokes of genius."[92] He did, and they meant the world to him. But these ecstatic moments would occur in the lab at a workbench, in a meeting room with fellow technologists, or perhaps on a ski slope or while piloting his plane. Where they would not occur was in a boardroom. The promotions Fairchild was giving him he did not particularly want, and he was being deprived of the chance for those peak moments of insight for which he had already built a reputation.

Noyce was a playful man, and he was a man who needed variety in his work and in his life. That is why he skied, piloted a plane, took up scuba diving, acted, sang madrigals, and so on. What he could not abide was being stuck in a room full of men in suits and ties, stuck in a suit and tie himself, trapped in discussions of accounting profits. He could not stand to be bored.

INTEL

Time for something new. The year was 1968, a tumultuous year around the world. In Europe, there were riots in Paris. France, a newspaper reported, was bored. In August, the Prague Spring was terminated by Soviet tanks as the attempt of liberals in Czechoslovakia to create "socialism with a human face" was crushed by the assertion of the Brezhnev Doctrine: once a Communist country, always a Communist country. China was in the midst of the Cultural Revolution, a sociopolitical upheaval with an incalculable cost in lives.

Adjacent to China's southern border lay Vietnam, and 1968 was a turning point in that catastrophic war. The North Vietnamese and the Vietcong launched the Tet Offensive on January 30. Although its military cost was staggering, the offensive's psychological victory over the United States was impressive. In April, violent riots broke out at Columbia University in opposition to the war and in response to other issues. More riots took place on college campuses in May. On the evening of the California Democratic Party presidential primary, June 5, the winner, Robert F. Kennedy, was shot at his campaign headquarters hotel in Los Angeles. The following day he died. More riots accompanied the Democratic National Convention in late August, probably the most raucous political gathering in the United States since the Democratic National Convention in Charleston, South Carolina, in the spring of 1860, on the eve of the Civil War.

The country seemed to be coming apart. The mood of unease, confusion, and anger, permeated many institutions—companies and families as well as universities and political parties. Perhaps this general ambience contributed to Noyce's own sense that Fairchild was not pursuing the beckoning technological frontier as it should. He was unimpressed by his own promotions. He was not put on earth to climb a corporate ladder. He quit.

"I remember," he said,

> standing out in my front yard talking to Gordon and telling
> him that I was resigning. He was probably the closest person

left in the organization to me; I mean, he'd been part of the original founding team of Fairchild and I felt I had to tell him about it.

And we got discussing, you know, "What are you going to do?" that sort of thing, sort of speculating on what would be the next big thing in this field. And that sort of planted the seeds in our minds that it might make sense to do something together.[93]

Intel was incorporated on July 16, 1968. On August 2, the *Palo Alto Times* ran a front-page article about the new venture. Unsolicited, Noyce and Moore "began to receive resumés, calls, and letters of application from talented engineers all over the country who knew of Noyce's work on the integrated circuit or of Moore's achievements at Fairchild. Finding good employees willing to join a start-up—usually one of the hardest tasks facing most entrepreneurs—was clearly not going to be a problem. . . ."[94]

Raising money, a far tougher challenge for a new business in 1968 than it would be in the 1990s, proved to be no problem either. Arthur Rock had relocated from New York and Hayden Stone to San Francisco and his own venture capital firm. Noyce's name attracted money like a magnet. "Bob just called me on the phone," Rock later recalled. "We'd been friends for a long time. . . . Documents? There was practically nothing. Noyce's reputation was good enough. We put out a page-and-a-half little circular, but I'd raised the money even before people saw it."[95]

This was the way Noyce liked it. "It may shock a lot of people to find this out, but we never wrote a business plan, never wrote a prospectus. We just said, 'We're going into business; would you like to support it?'"[96] People who knew what they were doing did not need reams of a legal document to communicate with one another. The investors included Noyce, Moore, Rock, Noyce's beloved alma mater Grinnell, and a few others. No one regretted it.

Along with Moore, Andy Grove came over from Fairchild to become Intel's director of operations. Tim Jackson, a journalist who is a harsh critic of Grove, observed that given that Noyce and Moore could have chosen anybody as Intel's Director of Operations, the selection of Grove "was so bizarre that it mystified most of the people who were watching their new business take shape.

They offered the director ops job to a guy who had no manufacturing experience at all—who was more a physicist than an engineer, more a teacher than a business executive, more a foreigner than an American"[97]

If the unnamed "people who were watching" the new venture were surprised at Grove's selection, so was Grove. "When I came to Intel," he said,

> I was scared to death. I left a very secure job where I knew what I was doing and started running R&D for a brand-new venture in untried territory. It was terrifying. I literally had nightmares. I was supposed to be director of engineering, but there were so few of us that they made me director of operations. My first assignment was to get a post office box so we could get literature describing the equipment we couldn't afford to buy.[98]

Intel's first three employees were profoundly different people. Noyce was a man capable of intense concentration early in his life, but he was more interested in indulging his wide range of interests as he grew older. Rock, who once described Noyce as "the most complicated man I ever met,"[99] said "he couldn't stick to anything." Moore, in Rock's view, "was the opposite. He didn't invent things, but he certainly saw the way to get somewhere. He more than anyone else set his eyes on a goal and got everybody to go there."[100]

Of Moore, Grove said that he "knew what he was doing, and he guided me." Many things have been said about Andy Grove, but no one has ever called him soft and sentimental. Nevertheless, he said of Moore that "he was kind of Uncle Gordon."[101] It is hard to imagine Grove describing any other professional relationship in such an intimate and openly vulnerable fashion. Moore and Grove are both brilliant men who share a respect for technology. Their personalities, however, are strikingly different. They look different and their boiling points are different. What worried them was different. It is a long way from Pescadero (Moore's birthplace) to Budapest. Moore was confident that Intel would succeed; and confident that if it did not, he would land on his feet. Grove had landed on his feet after the Nazis and after the Soviets. Was it wise to tempt fate again? He was appalled at the challenges the new company faced.

Like anyone who had spent time in the Valley, Grove had seen companies with very smart people at the helm fail. Indeed, in 1968, the very year Intel was founded, Shockley Semiconductor was finally liquidated. The Nobel Prize–winning inventor of the transistor had failed. Here was a shot across the bow for any budding entrepreneur.

As for Noyce, he founded Intel because of the excitement of it. He had already succeeded with one start-up, Fairchild. And he had been with that company long enough to see how difficult it was to keep the revolution forever young. A new company was needed, one whose goal was "to push the edge of product design and be the first to market with the newest devices."[102] He wanted a company where he could see the results of his efforts and not have to put up with the "frustration" and the "massive inertia" of a large organization.[103] Noyce knew that meant, in his words, "working on the edge of disaster."[104] But what more exciting place could there be in which to work?

Arthur Rock, who acted as the financial midwife of Intel, served on the board of directors from the date of its founding, and knew all the dramatis personae as well as they permitted themselves to be known, put it this way: "In order to succeed, Intel needed Noyce, Moore, and Grove. And it needed them in that order."[105] Noyce: the visionary, born to inspire. Moore: the virtuoso of technology, the man without a needy ego, the calm at the center of the storm, an island of reason in a sea of passion—just your average fellow who happens to be a technical genius and who happens to have amassed a fortune of a couple of billion dollars (he made more money from Intel than anyone else). Grove: the technologist turned management scientist, the man who became fascinated with how organizations run and how they interact, the man who did not need to be liked, who understood that bad things can happen to good companies, the man whose life was almost forfeit as a child (he had scarlet fever) and as a youth (during World War II) and as an adolescent (during the 1956 Hungarian uprising) and who was determined to live as many lives as he could.

With his flair, his genius, his charm, his track record, and his Rolodex, Noyce was undoubtedly the best person in the industry to start a new company in 1968—to put the people together with the funding, to establish the vision, and to hold things together during the mistakes which are inevitable in the early years. In fact, Intel's first two products, introduced in 1969, were technically advanced but commercially unsuccessful.[106] Rumors began to circulate that three strikes and you're out.

In 1971, however, Intel introduced the 1103, a dynamic random access memory chip which by the following year was the best-selling semiconductor product in the world.[107] The company was on the way, though it would have its share of crises in the years ahead.

In 1971, Intel went public, issuing 307,472 shares to raise $6.8 million. In its description of Intel's business, the initial public offering document explained that "Intel has placed primary emphasis on the development and sale of LSI [large-scale integrated] circuits designed to perform the memory function in digital equipment." Semiconductor memories were in the process of replacing magnetic core memory in mainframe computers. They were more efficient. The market was promising.

As of August 31, 1971, Intel had 382 full-time employees, 88 of whom were involved in product and process development engineering, 242 in manufacturing, 34 in marketing, and 18 in administration. Nine Ph.D.s were on the payroll. Since its inception three years earlier, the company had accumulated losses of $4.1 million. It was still in a start-up investment mode; and it had raised sufficient funds so that the accumulated deficit it carried on its balance sheet was $1.8 million. Total shareholder equity was $7.2 million, and total assets were $8.6 million.

There is, of course, no guarantee that a company will ever get out of "investment" mode and see the red ink on the income statement turn to black. But the presence of Robert Noyce inspired a lot of confidence in Intel's future. He served as the president, treasurer, and CEO. He owned 419,000 shares of the company, or 18.6 percent of the shares outstanding on August 31, 1971. The price of a share as of the date of the prospectus was $23.50. So Noyce had almost $10 million of his own money in this company. He probably had other investments, but it is reasonable to assume that this represented the bulk of his wealth. Intel had been kind to Noyce. Three years previously, in August 1968, he had invested half a million dollars in it.

Gordon Moore, the executive vice president, had also invested half a million dollars in Intel in 1968. He owned twenty-five hundred more shares than Noyce when the company went public in 1971, so the company had been good to him, as well. Arthur Rock, the chairman of Intel's board, was also a major investor. Other investors included at least four of the "traitorous eight" who had left Shockley Semiconductor with Noyce and Moore back in 1957.[108]

Noyce's intense involvement with Intel's daily operations lasted from its founding through about 1975, when he moved up from president and CEO to chairman of the board, and Gordon Moore assumed his office. During these seven years, Intel laid the foundations for becoming one of the most profitable and, from the point of view of technological progress, one of the most important companies in the world. Noyce's talent and distinctive mix of informality and rigor left a lasting imprint on the firm. So did his close collaboration with Gordon Moore, who is Intel's Chairman Emeritus and largest stockholder.

What was it like to be at Intel in its early years? That depends on what job you had and on your own personality. For Gordon Moore, it was hard work but fun. For Andy Grove, it was extremely hard work and nerve-racking. For the average new employee, it was the chance of a lifetime. Noyce was liberal with stock options. Profit sharing, he felt, provided an incentive to make things better by small increments. Stock options got people thinking about home runs.[109] This is what the top people at Fairchild either did not understand or did not want.

Both of Noyce's parents lived into their nineties, and he said he planned on living that long as well. Yet when one reads about him, one has the feeling that he sensed the brevity of life. Noyce wanted to score; he did not have time for singles, walks, and errors. He was an intensely competitive man, and when he came to bat, it was to hit a home run.

I mean this literally as well as metaphorically. His daughter Penny remembers a father/daughter softball game at which he did hit a home run. He felt great rounding the bases. It was only after he had passed home plate that it was explained to him that the idea was to make the children look good, not the parents.[110]

At Intel, the youngsters were well taken care of. It was not just stock options. It was the absence of the trappings of office which at other companies seemed specially designed to boost the egos of people who already had excessively high opinions of themselves and to diminish newcomers who needed some encouragement. Thus, no limousines, executive dining rooms, fancy offices, or reserved parking places. "If you come late," Noyce said, "you just have to park in the back forty."[111]

Noyce liked meetings, and any meeting in which he took part was an exciting event. He would

> set the agenda. But after that, everybody was an equal. If you were a young engineer and you had an idea you wanted to get across, you were supposed to speak up and challenge Noyce or anybody else who didn't get it right away. This was a little bit of heaven. You were face to face with the inventor, or the co-inventor, of the very road to El Dorado, and he was only forty-one years old, and *he* was listening to *you*.[112]

Pretty heady stuff.

By 1973, Intel posted sales of $66 million and employed a workforce of over twenty-five hundred. Noyce's stock was worth about $18.5 million that year,[113] equivalent to almost $70 million in 2000 dollars. The 1103 had made him a rich man and the recently invented microprocessor bade fare to make him richer still. Intel had success written all over it.

In Noyce's personal life, things were not, unfortunately, progressing as smoothly. His relationship with his wife was deteriorating. Almost alone among the people who knew him, she seemed to find it possible not to like the man Arthur Rock called "impossible not to like."[114] It has been reported that she wanted "a life independent of the company and Bob's achievements," that she wanted an identity and accomplishments she could call her own.[115] After a "monumental row" at the couple's summer home in Maine, they decided to divorce. She got the house in Maine, he kept the house in Los Altos, and they split the Intel stock fifty-fifty.

In 1974, after twenty-one years of marriage and four children (Bill, Penny, Polly, and Margaret), this man whose life looked to outsiders like "one outstanding success after another"[116] had failed at home. Divorces were common in Silicon Valley in the 1960s and 1970s; and there were plenty of jokes, none very funny, about them. Noyce did not use the metaphor of family often in his business life the way Sam Walton, for example, did. Intel was never a family firm as Wal-Mart was in its early years.

Nevertheless, the collapse of his marriage must have caused Noyce a great deal of pain. He was unused to failure; yet here was a problem, than which nothing was more important, that he did not know how to fix. To the outside world, Noyce seemed picture perfect. As one Intel manager remarked, "Bob could stand up in front of a roomful of securities analysts and tell them we were facing a number of major problems in our business, and the stock would go up five points."[117] But this man who was greeted every day by an admiring if not downright idolatrous world could not find peace at home.

Betty Noyce returned to her native New England at last. "We were under the distinct impression that we would try it for a year and if I didn't like it, we wouldn't stay," she later said of the family's move to California in the mid-1950s. "We stayed 19 years."[118] She found the breakup of her marriage "hugely debilitating," according to her lawyer and friend Owen Wells.[119]

In time, Betty Noyce became deeply attached to Maine. As her Intel stock appreciated, she also became very wealthy. She gave away a fortune to causes in Maine and was beloved by many whom she helped. Betty Noyce died of a heart attack at her home, a fifty-acre estate in Bremen, Maine, where she lived year-round, on September 17, 1996. She was sixty-five years old.

The following week, a memorial service was held for her in Portland. Maine, it turned out, had embraced her as she had embraced the state. More than a thousand people, including the state's top political figures as well as former president George Bush were in attendance. Her daughter Penny said, "Maine healed her. She loved the rocks and the shore. She told me she woke up every morning happy to be here."[120] Among her bequests was $200 million to the Libra Foundation, which she had established in 1989, to make grants only to Maine-based organizations.[121]

Betty Noyce had not remarried. She had been found dead in her home by a caretaker. Her ex-husband remarried in 1975. His second wife, Ann S. Bowers, was born in Pittsburgh and migrated to Silicon Valley by way of San Francisco, where she had worked in human resources at Macy's of California. By 1970, as Intel was beginning its spurt of rapid growth, she was the head of human resources.

Bowers's first encounter with Noyce was not auspicious. The expanding company was moving from its original location, a former Union Carbide plant in Mountain View, south to Santa Clara. Real estate prices were still reasonable there, and the twenty-six-acre site selected for the Santa Clara I chip fabrication facility was covered by fruit trees, which had to be uprooted. ("They paved paradise," in the words of popular singer Joni Mitchell about California, "and put in a parking lot.")

The new property had its share of problems. Streets were poorly lit and laid out. Their names were not terribly cheering for a new company either. Intel was to be located on Coffin Road. Ann Bowers was asked to have the name changed. Semiconductor Street or Memory Boulevard (Intel was making memory chips) sounded appealing. Bowers applied to the Santa Clara government for a change, and it obliged by simply using the name of the street on the other side of the expressway which bisected the property. That name happened to be Bowers. When Bob Noyce discovered that the request for a change in the name of the street on which his company was located had resulted in his working on Bowers Avenue, he marched over to Ann Bowers and told her he was not very happy. She replied that this was the first she had heard of the name change, and the selection was merely coincidental. He was mollified, yet "there seemed no reason to spoil a good story—so most of the company's employees believed, for years afterwards, that Ann Bowers had so much influence in Santa Clara that she managed to have the company's permanent address named after her."[122]

Noyce had told both Moore and Grove that he was getting a divorce, and he had assumed that word had filtered down to Bowers. Apparently, however, Moore and Grove did not mention this development to anyone else in the company. Their discretion, especially given the fact that the divorce would have not only personal but business implications because of the disposition of Noyce's stock, is an indication of the respect in which they held him. Both Moore (whose wife is also named Betty) and Grove have been married for life. They knew that for Noyce divorce meant pain. This was not a matter for hallway chitchat (in which neither of them indulged anyway).[123]

Bowers had met Noyce in 1970; and like so many others, she was smitten. But he was, to outward appearances, a happily married man and therefore off limits. She had determined to keep her distance. Now, all of a sudden, he was available.[124] The two were married soon after Noyce's divorce.

Ann Bowers married Noyce at quite a different point in his life than did his first wife. The first Mrs. Noyce, Elizabeth Bottomley Noyce, was born in Auburn, Massachusetts, of a working-class family. Her father held two jobs during the Depression to make ends meet. She may have been the first member of her family, or at least a member of the first generation of her family, to attend college. When she was in her early twenties majoring in English at Tufts, she hoped to write novels and short stories. She met Noyce in his "liberal arts" guise, working on a play together. He was a graduate student at MIT, not a rarity in Boston. He had no money, making his way through graduate school with the help of grants.

When Ann Bowers met Noyce, he was already a wealthy and famous man and a proven leader. She herself was a career woman— shrewd, hardworking, independent, and with gumption enough to talk back to Andy Grove when the occasion called for it.[125] Bowers and Noyce were established professionals in the business world when they married. The union proved a lasting one. She elected to leave Intel; the wife of the boss serving as the head of human resources was not a really great idea. The year they married, 1975, was the year that Noyce began, in a sense, to leave Intel as well. He became chairman of the board that year, and Gordon Moore was elected president and CEO. In 1979, Moore was elected chairman of the board as Noyce became vice chairman. There were always two people running Intel. At first it was Noyce and Moore. By 1979, it was Moore and Grove, who that year became president and chief operating officer and was to mature into one of the great CEOs of the century.

Noyce continued to play the role of Intel's face to the outside world, a responsibility he discharged with incomparable panache. His interests and activities were becoming so broad, however, that Intel was becoming more his base of operations than a company in whose daily activities he was intimately involved.

INDUSTRIAL STATESMAN

As early as 1983, journalist Michael Malone interviewed Noyce and later wrote that "he has come as close to immortality as any engineer."[126] Had Noyce lived to the year 2000, he would have come even closer. In October of that year, seventy-six-year-old Jack Kilby was awarded the Nobel Prize in physics for his role in the invention of the integrated circuit. If Noyce had lived to 2000, he would have been seventy-two years old; and he would have shared the award with Kilby. Both had agreed long ago to take joint credit for the invention. It is not, moreover, meant as any reflection on Kilby's genius to suggest that Noyce's version of the integrated circuit was more capable of being produced in commercial quantities and thus to exert a broader impact on society. The Nobel Prize is not awarded posthumously, which is a pity.

By the early 1980s, Noyce was becoming a spokesman for the industry and a citizen not only of the nation but of the world. Michael Malone asked him late in 1983 to describe how he spent his time. The reply:

> Let's see, to take a snapshot of a week or so. Last week I was in Washington at this conference on high technology, a government conference on trade and the SIA [Semiconductor Industry Association], was releasing a report on Japanese targeting. The week before that I was skiing—at least I skied on Thursday and Friday at Aspen. This week I was here [at Intel] Monday, Tuesday, and Wednesday. I have a board meeting tomorrow and Saturday at Grinnell College. Then I'm heading to Japan Sunday morning for a series of conferences and meetings with customers on Tuesday and Wednesday. Then I'm leaving Tokyo Wednesday afternoon and coming back here to a University of California regents meeting on Thursday and Friday. . . .[127]

No question about it, he was busy. Through this welter of activities, a subject which began to take progressively more of his time and attention as the '70s turned into the '80s was the issue of "Japanese targeting."

Japanese companies, with plenty of help from their government, began making inroads into the U.S. semiconductor market in the mid-1970s. This was an era during which the United States was losing not only global market share but sales in its home market to foreign companies in industries in which it had thought itself preeminent as if by divine right since before World War II. These included consumer electronics and the set of industries based upon the mass-marketed automobile. The idea that high-tech Silicon Valley industries, a sector which seemed to hold the future of national economies in the balance, would also fall to the Japanese was hard to accept. The loss of leadership in semiconductor electronics to Japan had educational, economic, and psychological implications. The potential loss of this industry also posed a serious problem for America's military defense as well as for such high-profile, national-prestige-enhancing enterprises as the space program.

When it came to industry targeting, the truth is that the United States was second to none, although its methods were different from other nations. The federal government constituted the first major semiconductor market and indeed the sole market for integrated circuits until as late as 1964. Defense and space were the two keys. As Noyce observed, "The missile program and the space race were heating up. What that meant was there was a market for advanced devices at uneconomic prices . . . so there was a lot of motivation to produce this thing."[128]

"Advanced devices at uneconomic prices"—demand like that does not come along every day. The need was for zero defects and the condition was price insensitivity. John F. Kennedy's 1961 declaration that the United States should land a man on the Moon and return him to Earth before the decade was over was the statement of a price-insensitive customer. The goal was inconceivable without the work of Noyce and Kilby and their companies. "Only the existence of a miniature computer, two feet long, one foot wide, and six inches thick—exactly three thousand times smaller than the old ENIAC and far faster and more reliable—made the flight of *Apollo 8* possible."[129] A computer that size would have been impossible without the integrated circuit. It is no wonder Jack Kilby won the Nobel Prize.

As for the Defense Department, it was the same story. The Minuteman II intercontinental ballistic missile was the breakthrough. In 1962, the decision was made to use the chip for this weapon. The floodgates opened at both the navy and the air force. "About 500,000 integrated circuits were sold in 1963; sales quadrupled the next year, quadrupled again the year after that, and quadrupled again the year after that."[130] "From a marketing standpoint, Apollo and Minuteman were ideal customers," said Kilby. "When they decided that they could use these Solid Circuits, that had quite an impact on a lot of people who bought electronic equipment. Both of

those projects were recognized as outstanding engineering operations, and if the integrated circuit was good enough for them, well,
that meant it was good enough for a lot of other people."[131]

This background should be kept in mind when evaluating American manufacturers' complaints about Japanese inroads into the
memory business in the late 1970s. With cheap capital, free R&D,
and a protected home market, Japanese firms overwhelmed American semiconductor manufacturers in the late 1970s and 1980s.[132]

The American semiconductor firms faced an even bigger prob-
lem than the often complained of "uneven playing field" created by
Japan's industrial policy. The simple sad fact was that by 1980,
Japanese firms were turning out a higher-quality product than their
American competitors.

The fact that America had fallen behind in quality was dramatized on the "black day" of the American semiconductor industry:
March 28, 1980. That was the day Richard W. Anderson, a division
manager at Hewlett-Packard, revealed the results of performance
tests for three hundred thousand memory chips, half of which came
from HP's three Japanese suppliers and half from American firms.
The results: All of the Japanese firms outperformed the best American firm. Concluded Anderson: "So that's a remarkable, and I would
think to American suppliers, perhaps a frightening set of statistics."
He was right. His presentation became known as "The Anderson
Bombshell."[133] Even Intel, which had based so much of its success on
its memory chip business, was forced to exit in 1984 and 1985.[134]

As the best-known and most well connected person in the industry, Noyce found himself drawn into issues of trade and product
quality which Japanese penetration of the American market forced
upon the domestic industry. He was worried because of the pride he
took in the industry he helped create and because he believed the
promise of the industry to bring a better life to people was without
limit. Noyce was also a patriot, and the thought that the United
States might not take a leadership position in the future which
glowed just beyond the horizon was very distressing. "Tariffs and the
other obvious issues aren't really the problem," he noted. "It is more
like the mechanisms of the Industrial Revolution." As he saw it:

The character of *this* industry, this industrial revolution—
innovation intensive, rapidly growing, intensely competi-

tive—really played into America's hands. Because America is an enterprise where the pioneer is still admissible. We won the game. Other societies not organized to promote innovation and entrepreneurial activity got left behind. But as the business becomes more mature, in the sense that it's becoming more capital intensive, the elements of success are changing, too. And several of the elements are playing into the hands of the Japanese winning the next round.[135]

There seemed to Noyce and to other executives in other industries a historical inevitability about Japanese success. As we saw earlier in this book, the United States overtook Britain (which had a long head start) in the steel industry not because of "tariffs and the other obvious issues," to use Noyce's words, but because it had a business system which was more appropriate to the technology of the product and because "the pioneer [was] still admissible."

In the 1980s, it appeared that the keys to long-term success in high technology included cheap capital, obsession with the highest possible quality in manufacturing, cooperative research and development, long-term commitments to the workforce during the valleys of a cyclical industry, strategic government support, and society-wide dogged determination. On all these dimensions, Japan was besting the United States. It was not just that one company was doing better than its counterpart in the United States. It was that the Japanese had constructed a planned, rational, integrated system to attack an industry.

Noyce was a competitive man, and this prospect was disturbing. Some kind of coordinated industry effort which had not only government permission but financial backing was called for. However, industry associations had, generally speaking, been ineffectual in the United States. As long ago as the 1870s, John D. Rockefeller called them "ropes of sand."[136]

The problems with coordinated industry efforts included legal restrictions, political alliances, and the different interests of the various members of the industry coalition. Legally, there are certain agreements that antitrust regulations prevent. Indeed, the sharing of information about aspects of businesses in the same industry can be illegal. Politically, different executives in different parts of the country may have different allegiances and traditions. Economically, companies in the same industry are almost bound to have different interests depending upon the nature of their business. Are they vertically integrated, for example? Do they have operations abroad? Are they full-line or niche producers? Are they in the commodity or specialty end of the industry? Are they big or small?

Except in the most general sense, there is no "business community" in the United States. There are shifting congeries of interests. This is not to say that business does not influence government or that business executives do not act in concert. A glance at the daily newspaper shows the impact of private special interests on public policy. It is merely to say that when one gets beyond the most obvious issues, industry associations break up. It is the most skilled operators within industries, usually a small subset of the whole, that manage to get what they want.

On top of all this, even if everyone in an industry agrees that cooperation is necessary and public policy should be shaped a certain way not only for the industry's welfare but for the national interest, the question then becomes: Who will be willing to work for the industry association? Will the businesses that belong be willing to send their most talented technologists? Will talented technologists be willing to leave a lucrative job with a promising future and a big paycheck in order to work for an industry association offering no career path and precious little excitement? To ask such questions is to answer them.

The Semiconductor Industry Association (SIA) had been founded back in 1977 as a forum for mutual concerns of five firms in the industry which otherwise were very competitive and spent a lot of time suing one another. In June 1986, as Japanese inroads continued, the SIA asked Charlie Sporck, a semiconductor manufacturing expert who had worked for Noyce back at Fairchild and had gone on to run National Semiconductor, to investigate the need for industry cooperation.

Over the course of the next two years, Sematech (derived from *S*emiconductor *Ma*nufacturing *Tech*nology) took shape. As Sematech's historians have observed, the consortium was founded because "Japan was close to dominating the industry, and it would require pooled resources to respond to that threat."[137] It was, however, a very long way from understanding that cooperation was necessary to actually bringing it into being. Funding. Staffing. Location. These and many more issues provided plenty of opportunity for disagreement in the industry.

Because of his interests and his standing, Bob Noyce became deeply involved in Sematech at an early stage. Along with Jerry

Sanders, CEO of Advanced Micro Devices, Noyce co-chaired the executive search committee. Here was Sematech's biggest problem. Who would staff it? Who would lead it?

Everyone wanted Noyce himself to take the job. Everyone, that is, except Noyce. In the 1980s, he had finally found the freedom for which he had been looking all his life. He had the time and the money to indulge his interests. He had in Ann Bowers a companion who could share those interests and who knew how to be the wife of a great man. He felt sufficiently secure with her to reveal his own vulnerabilities. There was a shy side to his personality which few who encountered his public face would have guessed but which he could safely reveal to her. Everything he had, he earned himself. Sematech promised to be a difficult endeavor and a cauldron of contention. In 1987, Noyce, still youthful and athletic, celebrated his sixtieth birthday. Why take on an assignment of this nature, which, not incidentally, would require his leaving his Los Altos Hills home and moving to Austin, Texas, Sematech's headquarters, at this stage of his life?

"We went to Aspen specifically for the purpose of making the decision," recalled Ann Bowers.

> We postponed it until Sunday afternoon. Finally, we went up [on the mountain] and sat up there in this howling wind, and decided. We came down off the mountain, and Bob called Charlie Sporck. It was in July, 1988. A week later we were in Washington making the announcement, and Bob was physically on the job the first of August. It was like a two-week time span from yes to *here*.[138]

This is a perfect example of Noyce's having greatness thrust upon him. This was not a job he wanted, but it was a job he knew had to be done if the industry to which he had devoted his life really was as important as he believed and if he was a patriot. His willingness to become CEO of Sematech got the project off the ground. Staffing was Sematech's biggest challenge; and in the words of an executive, Noyce "basically made it okay for people in the industry to come to Sematech. If Bob Noyce was willing to come . . . and it was that important to the industry, then maybe I should leave my job for two years and go serve a national cause which is also a cause for my company."[139]

Noyce's move to Austin gave Sematech instant credibility in

Washington (which meant financial support) and in the industry worldwide. He had two principal goals: to sell Sematech to Washington and to assure the commitment of the companies which belonged to it.[140] By April of 1990, two years later, he felt these goals had been achieved, so he informed the Sematech board that he intended to step down as CEO at the end of that year.

On June 1, 1990, Sematech held "Bob Noyce Day" to mark his contributions to it. Everyone got a T-shirt with Noyce's likeness and the phrase "Teen Idol" stenciled on it. Tapes and photographs of the event suggest a very good time was had by all, not least Noyce.

On the morning of June 3, Noyce went for a swim in his pool. Feeling fatigued afterward, he lay down on a couch in his home. He never arose. His death from a heart attack was sudden and shocking. He had undergone a complete physical the previous week indicating he was in fine health. He was, however, a smoker; and it is possible that tobacco contributed to his death.

Noyce, the child and grandchild of preachers, had taken the job at Sematech out of a sense of duty to the larger community. But why did all the interested parties want so much for him to take the job?

Was it because of his reputation as a technologist? Was it because of his success as an entrepreneur? Was it because of his charisma? Was it because of his sense of fun and playfulness at work? Was it because they saw in him what Andy Grove—an extraordinarily clear-eyed man about everything and everyone, including Noyce—observed, that "Bob was always six or ten steps ahead of the rest of us?"[141] Was it because of all these things?

Perhaps.

But it seems to me that the real reason everyone wanted to be on Robert Noyce's team was that everybody trusted him. He earned that trust. He was a pioneer in a new industry with no rules. Yet day in and day out, from one deal to the next, from one project to the next, and from one enterprise to the next, Noyce instinctively knew how to act.

An executive at the investment bank which took Intel public once described Noyce as "a national treasure."[142] He was not without flaws and faults. But when one considers his life, one feels one is encountering America at its best.

ROBERT NOYCE

December 12, 1927	Noyce is born.
1949	Noyce graduates from Grinnell College.
1953	Noyce marries Elizabeth Bottomley; Noyce becomes a research engineer at Philco.
1954	Noyce receives a Ph.D. in physics from MIT.
1956	Shockley Semiconductor begins business with Noyce as employee.
1957	Fairchild Semiconductor is founded by Noyce and others; Noyce is director of research.
1958–1959	Integrated circuit is invented by Kilby and Noyce independently.
1959	Noyce becomes vice president and general manager; Fairchild Semiconductor becomes a division of Fairchild Camera.
1962	Noyce becomes vice president of Fairchild Camera.
1965	Noyce becomes group vice president.
1967	Noyce joins the board of directors.
1968	Intel is founded by Noyce and Moore with Noyce as president.
1971	Intel introduces the 1103 dynamic random access memory chip; Intel goes public.
1974	Noyce divorces his wife Elizabeth.
1975	Noyce marries Ann S. Bowers; Noyce becomes chairman of the board of Intel and is replaced by Moore as president and CEO.
1979	Noyce becomes vice chairman of Intel.
1988	Noyce becomes first CEO of Sematech.
June 3, 1990	Noyce dies.

CONCLUSION PROGRESS AND PROFITS

CHANGE AND CONTINUITY

The past, it has been said, is another country. We would find it easier to make a list of what has *not* changed between the era of Carnegie to the time of Noyce than what has. Railroads and steel were the new industries in Carnegie's day. It was an era of "things" that you could touch and feel. No one was talking about virtual this or that. Carnegie's era marked the coming of truly big business to American industry. Everything he built was of a scale not theretofore encountered. The capital he invested, the number of workers he employed, the mills he erected, the ore ships that brought raw materials to them, the customers to whom he sold—all were big. The Brooklyn Bridge and other huge structures were built with Carnegie steel, as were innumerable railroads.

In Carnegie's world, things moved from big to bigger. When he sold his company to J. P. Morgan for the creation of United States Steel, he came into possession of what was believed to be the largest fortune in private hands in the world, $300 million worth of gilt-edged securities. United States Steel itself was like nothing that had ever been seen. Capitalized at $1.4 billion in 1901—an amount equal to two-thirds of all the money then in circulation in the United States[1]—it was the first corporation to number its assets in ten figures. Soon after its formation, U.S. Steel employed a quarter of a million men, more than served in the army and the navy combined.

To place this scale in sharp relief, we can compare Carnegie to John Jacob Astor. Astor died in 1848, the same year Carnegie emigrated to the United States. Like Carnegie, Astor was an unlettered immigrant when he landed on these shores. He started life peddling musical instruments. When he died, he left an estate valued at about $20 million, making him the nation's richest man. At the height of his business life, when he was running the American Fur Company and investing in Manhattan real estate, he had only a handful of employees, the most important of whom was his son, William B.

Astor. His "headquarters" consisted of a few clerks working in a room the size of a hotel suite. During the War of 1812, when the British blockade of American ports made foreign commerce impossible, he stopped trading and turned to speculating in securities. In February of 1814, he said he intended to "withdraw from almost every kind of business & I mean to remain so."[2]

Carnegie numbered his employees in five figures, six once the merger creating U.S. Steel was consummated on his retirement in 1901. His fortune of $300 million dwarfed Astor's, even allowing for change in the value of a dollar over the intervening half century. With so many employees and such vast physical facilities, Carnegie needed managers at many levels, from foremen who directed gangs of workers, to mill and furnace managers, to money managers (both accountants and financiers), to salesmen and marketing specialists to manage them, all the way up to partners, of which Carnegie had as many as two dozen with some equity in the firm.

The second half of the nineteenth century, as the railroads matured and the giant enterprises they helped make possible (such as Carnegie Steel and Rockefeller's Standard Oil) burst upon the scene, saw the birth of the business manager in the United States. In Astor's era, ownership and management were one and the same. Such an arrangement was possible because businesses were small, transactions few, and the pace of life in general slow.

All this changed decisively with the railroad, the telegraph, and the steam ship. Suddenly, business could be conducted on a new scale. New products could be developed and the costs and prices of current products reduced. To make this new scale possible, vast sums of capital had to be invested in special-purpose assets.

The result was that to succeed in business you needed high volume and high market share, rather than high margins. That is why Carnegie kept saying, "Cut the prices; scoop the market; run the mills full. . . ." and "Run our works full; we *must* run them at any price."

Carnegie did not have the luxury of simply calling a halt to his business the way Astor did to his trading during the War of 1812. The bulk of Carnegie's costs were fixed; he spent a fortune on his works every day whether he sold any steel or not. That is why he was so vulnerable to strikes. "Strike" is a word John Jacob Astor never used in his half a century in business.

All this seems obvious in retrospect. But the transformation of business and the reallocation of capital from variable to fixed costs represent among other things an intellectual revolution—a change in the conception of how to compete—of the first magnitude.

As the world changed, the individuals changing it became wealthy beyond imagining. They also became famous. Carnegie was known around the world by the 1880s. Rockefeller was as well. So profound was their impact that the names of these two men are still well known in the twenty-first century.

Compare private enterprise in the late nineteenth century to politics and public affairs. Are the presidents who served in the 1880s well known today? Five men occupied the White House during the 1880s. Can anyone reading these pages name them?[3] Can anybody name one of them? Business was big; government small. By the 1990s, business remained a major force in our lives; but even political advocates of small government understand that the private sector will never overshadow the public sector to the extent it did in the late nineteenth century.

Interestingly enough, the very measures of what makes a business big—or at least the ranking of those measures—have changed. By the 1990s, the first question addressed in assessing the importance of a business was not the number of people it employed, nor even its current profits. The first question was its market capitalization—the price of its stock multiplied by the number of its shares. During the last quarter of the twentieth century in the United States, Microsoft was for a number of years the highest flier among American companies; and Bill Gates, its CEO, one of the nation's most famous men. For some years, Gates was the nation's richest man.

Yet by many of the measures of Carnegie's era, Microsoft would be considered a small and unimportant company. Compared to the giant steel companies and railroads, its sales and assets were small, its employees few. (Of course, its profits as a percentage of sales and its return on those assets were very high.) Indeed, Microsoft's products were not considered to be in the touch, feel, and kick category. It was a service firm. It sold information. Its high market capitalization was an index of the move from the economy of goods of Carnegie's day to today's emphasis on services in the economy as a whole.

Particularly important in modern times has been the rapid communication of large volumes of information. The information revolution is among the reasons for Microsoft's high market capitalization. The integrated circuit and Robert Noyce were at the center of this revolution. The new world of information technology has been aptly characterized as a "revolution in miniature," a nice contrast to the world of Carnegie, which was all about things getting bigger. From the vacuum tube to the transistor to the integrated circuit to the microprocessor, computer-related technology has generated ever-greater power in ever-smaller packages. From the mainframe to the minicomputer to the personal computer, vast volumes of information have been placed at the fingertips of millions of people around the world. The people who make these machines speak in terms of fractions of microns, small percentages of the width of a human hair. One result of this revolution in miniature is that any man or woman can open a global business today with next to no capital simply by putting a web page on the internet. (How long that business will last is another question.)

One could write volumes about the changes in business from Carnegie to Noyce. One point, however, stands out when we discuss the titans who mastered change. The seven people portrayed in this book, along with a few select others, either created new technology or welcomed it. All of them exploited it more skillfully than the competition.

During the crisis of the Union, Abraham Lincoln said, "As our case is new, so we must think anew, and act anew."[4] Although Lincoln was fighting to preserve the Union, his statement is that of a true revolutionary. Most businesspeople, most people in any walk of life, tend to think that today is going to be pretty much like yesterday. Most people march backward into the future. In our seven biographies, by contrast, we have seen time and again the adaptation to or the actual creation of a whole new future. It is this ability to be oriented toward a future beyond imagining to others—to think anew and act anew—which defines these men as genuine visionaries.

Often, the visions of these visionaries were as much the product of personal revelation as of reason. Sometimes, as with Henry Ford, the revelation was there from the beginning. The automobile, to reach its potential, had to be mass-produced and mass-marketed. Sometimes, as with George Eastman, the revelation only came after having spent some time in the industry. It took Eastman a number of years to understand that he would have to create a mass market for the camera but that once he did, it could prove a bonanza. Sometimes, the revelation came from a sense of sheer annoyance, as when Bob Noyce invented the integrated circuit because of his sense of the wastefulness of manually connecting wires.

In each case, the point is there was something special, a bright beam of light which illuminated a previously unseen landscape. What these men realized was that the changes they could make or that others were making were their friend, not their enemy.

THE VANTAGE POINT

President Harry S. Truman had a sign on his desk which said, "The buck stops here." Theodore Roosevelt called the presidency a "bully pulpit." These phrases tell us a lot about the conception that each of these men had of his job. For Roosevelt, it was a place from which to preach. For Truman, it was a place at which you had to take responsibility.

Each of the seven business leaders we have discussed had their own particular conception of what their job was. But each had one thing in common. Only they had their vantage point.[5] Only they knew what it meant to have virtually absolute power within their businesses.

In fact, they had a lot more power in their companies than all but a few presidents have had in the nation. These businessmen either had control through ownership or through a docile board of directors. They lived lavish lives and had to account to no one. All seven of these men could, by virtue of their money, position, and acumen, exercise a great deal of discretionary power.

What this means is that most of us can never know what the world looks like to people like them. They are surrounded by courtiers. It is impossible for it to be otherwise. We, on the other hand, must govern ourselves with care. There is no lawyer or public relations executive willing to put his or her career on the line to clean up the messes we make.

The most powerful men in our business world have posed something of a conundrum to our society. America has celebrated equality since the Declaration of Independence. Americans are born free, but everywhere get their living in hierarchies. These select few about whom we have read look at a nation worshiping equality from their vantage point at the peak of a hierarchy, richly endowed with privileges of which the rest of us can only dream. This is important. It means we cannot see the world through the eyes of these people. It is important for us to understand that we cannot understand them.

By the same token, these men at the pinnacle cannot see the world through our eyes. This is true even of those who started life in poverty and powerlessness. Perhaps it is even truer of them. Andrew Carnegie was poor when he was thirteen in 1848, and all his life he thought poverty to be a static condition with which he was intimately familiar. But when he wrote about "The Advantages of Poverty" in 1891, the world had changed and so had he. Carnegie probably knew a lot more about wealth in 1848 than he did about poverty in 1891.

For a vivid illustration of what mischief the vantage point can wreak on a business executive of unsurpassed shrewdness, think of Thomas J. Watson Sr. Here is a man who would engineer company celebrations at which he was the individual being celebrated. He would read citations praising him before they were delivered. And then when they were publicly presented, he was known to weep. If this were simply the story of a rich playboy who wanted to hear nice things said about himself or if it were the actions of an emotionally unbalanced man who somehow had acquired great wealth, it would be understandable. The conundrum lies in the combination of this dreamworld with an intense comprehension of the realities of business.

Watson constructed himself from nothing: no education, no effective parenting, no connections. Then at the age of forty, just emerging from the possibility of a term in prison, he embarked on his life's true calling, the building of International Business Machines into the giant of information processing. If you had invested in IBM when Watson joined what was then Computing-Tabulating-Recording, a post he took in the face of an extremely skeptical board of directors, and held on to that investment until he finally stepped down in 1956 at the age of eighty-two, you would have been very happy. The Fairchild family, as we saw in the chapter on Bob Noyce, certainly was.

We have special knowledge of the derangement of power in Watson's case because of the in-part unintentionally revealing autobiography of his son and successor, Thomas J. Watson Jr. A moment's thought would have prevented the disastrous grand tour of Europe in 1947 during which, at Watson's direction, Charles Kirk chaperoned T. J. Jr. The tensions between these two rivals became predictably unbearable. The trip ended when Kirk died of a heart attack.

This disavowed, dictatorial cruelty did not stop at the threshold of hearth and home. Recall the following. "Father would be rude to her [mother], and then half an hour later he'd give us a lecture about how we ought to be good to our mother," Watson Jr. recalled bitterly. "I never had the guts," he reproached himself, "to say, 'Then why aren't you?'"

Watson Jr. should not have thus reproached himself. (There was much else about which he did have reason to feel guilt, especially his treatment of his brother.) No one told Watson Sr. the truth to his face, certainly not in a way that he could take it in. You could shout at him, as his son sometimes did; but he would merely shout back. He would not change his personality. It was his personality, after all, which had brought him remarkable and undeniable success in the world of affairs. That success put food on the table of a lot of employees, and they were sincerely grateful for it. Lest we be too harsh in our judgment, this fact is worth keeping in mind.

Unchecked power may be a great tool to see that the work of the world gets done. As the old saying goes, you can't make an omelette without breaking eggs.

The men in this book broke a lot of eggs. But, especially late in life, from their vantage point, all they saw was the omelette. Despite essays with titles like "The Advantages of Poverty," they had quite lost the ability and perhaps the desire to take the point of view of the egg.

The derangement of power. It is very common among the powerful and very destructive. When Henry Ford arrived in Norway aboard his "peace ship" *Oscar II* and started talking about tractors, a Norwegian observed that one must have to be a very great man to say such foolish things. Norwegians have, in fact, a word for this syndrome. It is *stormannsgalskap*, which can be translated as "great men's madness."[6]

GOODNESS AND GREATNESS

Can a businessman be both good and great? Greatness is not that difficult to define and to recognize. It consists of succeeding beyond expectation, beyond imagination, in the field to which one has elected to devote oneself. What are the chances that a poor man with no backing could found a nail polish company in the depths of the Great Depression and grow it into an industry leader located in sumptuous offices on top of Fifth Avenue and become a defining force in the beauty industry? The answer is obvious. The chances are slim. But Charles Revson did it. In the world in which he lived, which he in part created, it is fair to call him a great man.

Was he a good man? Goodness is more difficult to define than greatness. But we can safely say that goodness includes honesty, generosity, a sense of fairness, and respect for others. It means appreciating that other people have a right to seek happiness in their own way. It means understanding that there are certain requests and demands which are out of bounds because although they may seem vital to you, they are destructive to the person of whom they are being made. It means remembering those who have helped you achieve your goals even when you no longer need them. It means giving back to society some of what you have been able to achieve because of how society is organized. Perhaps goodness comes down to nothing more than doing unto others what you would have them do unto you.

All our seven executives qualify as great. But when we apply the tests of goodness just described, the results are more problematic.

Of course, no one is flawless. Even Bob Noyce, who is referred to by one author as "St. Bob,"[7] avoided some of the more unpleasant aspects of being CEO. He did not like interpersonal conflict. When the time came to fire someone who was underperforming, he was often nowhere to be found. This is understandable. No decent person wants to be the bearer of bad news. On the other hand, there has never been a successful business which did not have to let some people go; and if Noyce did not take care of this part of the job, it only meant that somebody else had to play the heavy and do so.

To be a success in business, one is simply forced to do things which are hard on others. This is true within the organization not only with underperformers but also with talented people who want greater rewards in terms of rank and remuneration than may be good for the firm. It can be true of the workforce. Look at the relationship between Carnegie Steel and the Amalgamated Association of Iron and Steel Workers which led up to the Homestead lockout.

It is true of competitors. Win/win situations are often spoken of in business; and it is true that if one looks carefully enough, one can find such situations in unexpected places. On the other hand, business is at the end of the day (or the quarter or the year) about money. If I get a contract or make a sale, you will not. Competitors are often on a seesaw: "I'm up, you're down." Business is about competition. There is nothing inherently bad about competition. It brings out the best in many of us. The questions in business become: "What are the rules?" "What are you willing to do to win?"

Every great businessperson has been in some way a rule breaker. He or she has done new things or has done old things in a new way. Rules are often little more than the unconscious assumptions of unimaginative people. When rules go beyond conventional thinking and are codified as laws, those laws are invariably written for the benefit of people who have done well in the past and are doing well in the present. They are not written to enable breakthrough thinkers to turn the world upside down.

The financier Michael Milken was a great man, little short of a financial genius. More than anyone else—some would say single-handedly—he brought into being a new market for securities that had previously been worth very little because slow-thinking rating agencies adhering to accepted analytical rules had disregarded them as below investment grade. By creating a market for these high-yield securities (known as junk bonds) Milken, an outsider who did his own analysis rather than relying on conventional wisdom, made funding available to a host of businesses in the 1980s which would otherwise have been denied it.

The problem with Milken was that the more money he made for his clients, his associates, and himself, the less willing or able he became to distinguish between rules and customs which existed because of a lack of imagination and laws which were vital to the efficient functioning of the capital markets. He became hypercompetitive. He engaged in illegal activity and wound up in jail. He has always maintained that he did no wrong but rather was brought down by those not as skilled as he. From what one can gather, he still does not understand the gravity of his violations.[8]

Warren Buffett, perhaps the most successful investment manager in the twentieth century, has said that to succeed in business you need three strengths: brains, energy, and character. He then added that without the third of these, the first two will kill you. Part of character is knowledge of self, knowing who you are, what your impact is on others, and how others view you. Buffett has proposed an interesting standard. How many tycoons could pass it?

THE AMERICAN BUSINESS TRADITION

In the Republican Era of ancient Rome, there existed a fairly clear track—"career path" as we would say today or *cursus honorum* as the Romans put it—for advancement in the Senate. Generally speaking, one served as quaestor for a set period of time, then advanced to tribune, then to aedile, then to praetor, then to consul, and at last to the top, censor. By the hard and fast standards of ancient Rome or by those of a modern army, there is no "American Business Tradition." In a looser sense, however, such a tradition can be said to exist. For example, there are career tracks within corporate hierarchies; but these have often been derailed during the past quarter century as big business has gone through a major period of restructuring. This book has dealt not with CEOs of typical corporations, but with towering figures who have very few peers in American society. For membership in this inner circle, there are fewer, not more, ticket-punching requirements; but those requirements are very strict, indeed.

If a young man or woman was sufficiently intelligent and well connected in the United States during recent years, there did exist a track for a certain kind of job. One might start at a private day school or one of a handful of famous prep schools. The next step would be an elite private university, an Ivy League school, Stanford, or MIT. One would major in a branch of engineering, a hard science, or economics. The next step would be to hire on at a consulting firm or an investment bank for three to four years. Some of that time should be spent outside the United States. Along the way, one should become fluent in at least one foreign language. Next, at age twenty-five or twenty-six, it was time to apply to business school. Harvard was your best bet. Stanford was certainly acceptable. After graduation, it was time to return to an investment bank or consulting firm and start working your way up from associate to partner.[9] Salaries were high; hours long.

What I have just outlined was a well-known track for the American elite at the end of the twentieth century. Indeed, the president of the United States, before he entered politics, followed just such a track. Born into a fabulously well connected family (his grandfather was a wealthy Republican senator from Connecticut who was a golfing buddy of President Eisenhower; his father was a successful businessman who became vice president and then president), George W. Bush graduated from Andover and Yale. After a couple of years in the Air National Guard (far from Vietnam), he attended the Harvard Business School. After some problems in business, he was kicked up the ladder of success—finally, like his father, to abandon business for politics.

A key element of the American Business Tradition is that it has not been necessary to complete any prescribed *cursus honorum* in order to reach the apex of the business world. The man who came the closest to so doing among the seven in this book was Robert Noyce, who attended Grinnell College and earned a Ph.D. from MIT. MIT did open doors for him when he was looking for his first job, but it exercised a minimal impact on his career. I have not seen any reference to networking with other MIT alumni in writings by or about him.

Grinnell was more important to Noyce than MIT; and, though an elite institution, its name does not shout at the average American the way Harvard or Stanford does. What was most important about Grinnell was Noyce's mentor Grant Gale, and Gale's early familiarity with the transistor. Indeed, one can cite even Noyce's background as evidence that you do not need credentials prescribed by society to make it to the top in American business. His family had no connections. And Gale knew about the transistor not because he knew someone at MIT or Caltech, but because he knew someone at the University of Wisconsin, John Bardeen. The University of Wisconsin is a great institution; but it is a state-funded, land-grant school with none of the social cachet of, say, Princeton.

The tycoons in this book were far more important to the nation's credentialing institutions than those institutions were to the tycoons. Andrew Carnegie, with next to no formal education, founded Carnegie-Mellon University, one of America's most prestigious universities. George Eastman did not graduate from high school, but donated a fortune to MIT. Neither did Thomas J. Watson Sr. graduate from high school; but he was a major donor to Columbia, served on its board of trustees for almost a quarter century, and played a key role in making Dwight D. Eisenhower president of the University,[10] from which position he moved on to become president of the United States. Columbia needed Watson far more than he ever needed it.

This tradition is alive and well right now. Bill Gates did come from an established, influential upper-class family in Seattle. He attended Lakeside, a private day school; and Lakeside was important to him because it facilitated access to computers years ahead of public schools. He and Paul Allen, co-founder of Microsoft, donated a building to Lakeside in the late 1980s.[11] Gates attended Harvard. His development is beginning to look like it followed the modern *cursus honorum*. However, he dropped out. He never completed a college education. He did not need one to found and build the business that conquered the mighty IBM and played a pivotal role in changing the computer industry forever. I have never seen any reference to Gates making use of a Harvard network. In 2000, the Bill and Melinda Gates Foundation donated $25 million to the Harvard School of Public Health. Harvard needs Gates more than ever Gates needed Harvard.

There are a number of similar stories. Michael Dell, founder of the computer company bearing his name and one of the nation's richest men, dropped out of the University of Texas after his freshman year. Steve Jobs, the moving force behind Apple Computer and a central figure in Silicon Valley, dropped out of Reed College, a school in Oregon not dissimilar in quality and reputation from Grinnell.

These people are exceptional, but the point is that they exist. There are clearly marked career paths in large corporations and professional service firms. But brains, energy, and character—or at the very least brains and energy—have always trumped pedigree in the race for greatness in the American business world. It is an important component of the American Business Tradition that you do not have to punch a ticket to get to the top. It is also true, however, that in many cases punching the right ticket can give you a head start in the race. That is why it is so difficult to get into the Harvard Business School today. The successful completion of the *cursus honorum* can serve you well in the race for high position in the American business world. It cannot, however, help you become a titan, nor do titans have to run a *cursus honorum*. The people in this book were born, not made. At the least, they were made in such a way that their peers wanted to thrust greatness upon them. This magic, which Noyce, for example, had, cannot be learned.

This chapter and the whole book have been making the case that openness is a key component of the American Business Tradition. But how are we to think of the groups not represented in any of our biographies? No women or African Americans. No Latinos. If we look at the *Fortune* 500 today and in the past we find the same story. The questions thus arise: "Who's in and who's out?" and "Openness for whom?"

To respond to these questions, let us broaden our discussion to include not only world-famous figures such as Carnegie or Ford, but top business leadership more generally. When we look at the most important executives of the most important American companies over the years, there can be no question that the demographic profile of the occupants of these privileged positions has not reflected the population as a whole. My own study of the CEOs in the two hundred largest industrials in the country in 1917 showed many anomalies. The CEOs were disproportionately born in the Northeast and Midwest, with the South very underrepresented. They came from urban, economically advantaged backgrounds. They were all male Caucasians. Eighty-six percent were Republicans. Almost two-thirds of them were either Episcopalians (34 percent) or Presbyterians (28 percent). Roman Catholics accounted for only 7 percent. Interestingly enough, Jews were actually overrepresented at 5 percent.[12]

Anyone with a cursory familiarity with American history would know that it was simply beyond the realm of consideration to have a woman or an African American running a corporation such as, say, the Pennsylvania Railroad in 1917. Less well known would have been the extent of prejudice with regard to political affiliation and religion. The CEO of the Pennsylvania Railroad from 1913 to 1925 was Samuel Rea. Some of the Pennsylvania's directors staunchly opposed Rea's promotion because they "recoiled at the prospect of turning over railroad affairs to any person who had not pledged allegiance to Republican politics and who was not even an Episcopalian (Rea was a Presbyterian)."[13]

It is hard to believe that the board of directors of a modern company of importance comparable to the Pennsylvania in the first quarter of the twentieth century would have either felt or voiced the kind of sentiment which Rea's candidacy provoked. Even if someone felt it, he would have voiced it at his peril. Passing over a candidate for promotion on the grounds of race, gender, or religion is illegal, and has been since legislation which has its roots in the 1960s. At this writing, a woman, Carly Fiorina, is the CEO of Hewlett-Packard. Two of the most admired CEOs of the 1990s, Andy Grove and Jack Welch, departed from the pattern of the first quarter of the twentieth century. Welch is the son of a conductor on the Boston and Maine Railroad. He is a Roman Catholic whose undergraduate education was at the University of Massachusetts and who earned his Ph.D. at the University of Illinois, both publicly funded, land-grant universities. Grove, who made a vital contribution to Intel's growth as its CEO, is a foreigner (not even born in western Europe, but in Hungary) and a Jew. He was educated at the City College of New York and the University of California at Berkeley, both supported by public funds. Few, if any, shareholders complained about Welch or Grove because they did not have "white-shoe" backgrounds.

That having been said, it is also true that there are in the year 2001 only a few firms among the five hundred largest in the nation with CEOs who are women, blacks, or Latinos. If openness is at the heart of the American Business Tradition, what explains the obvious disparity between the makeup of the population as a whole and the makeup of the population of CEOs? One answer, no less true because it is obvious, lies in the fact that openness is now and always has been at war with prejudice in the American business world. Law or no law, there are people in power who are reluctant to see members of groups out of power advance. Another explanation is the problem of the "pipeline." Here it is useful to reintroduce our distinction between the CEO of the large corporation and the towering tycoon of the type with which this book concerns itself. It is in the large corporation, as in any bureaucracy, where there still exists to some extent a *cursus honorum*, a prescribed way to the top. Pedigree still matters.

In the case of the businessperson of national repute who brings something very rare and special to the industry in which he or she competes—the kind of person profiled in this book—the prescribed career path can be dispensed with. It is in this realm that one sees openness most dramatically. Dozens of examples could be cited, but no illustration would be better than Oprah Winfrey.[14]

Without punching any traditional tickets, Winfrey has become one of the wealthiest and most powerful people in the United States and one of the best-known Americans in the world. She is a black woman. She does not come from an "old" family. She did not go to Exeter, Princeton, and the Harvard Law School. Few indeed are the people in business who do not admire her acumen, success, and power.

Even in established companies, the *cursus honorum* has been over the past quarter of a century giving way to talent. During the middle of the twentieth century, even including the Great Depression, most large companies were controlled more by managers than by owners. Ownership was dispersed among thousands of shareholders who had little knowledge of how the firm in which they had invested actually operated and less influence on the strategies the firm pursued.

For a variety of reasons, owners began to assert their claims on the corporation more effectively in the final quarter of the twentieth century. Shareholders were growing restive with the relatively disappointing performance of their holdings. And shareholders even in the largest of companies were far less dispersed and uninformed by 1990 than they had been a quarter of a century earlier. Pension funds had accumulated large holdings and were able to speak with one voice. They demanded an acceptable return on their investment, and they did not care about the demographic background of the CEO who delivered these returns or how many years and how many jobs and how much of his life he had devoted to the company. These new pressures of ownership, facilitated by the new financial instruments created by Michael Milken and others, have transformed the American corporation in recent years.

George Eastman took little note of the price of Kodak's shares. But even a titan like Sam Walton was very concerned about Wal-Mart's performance on Wall Street. In the entrepreneurial culture which has spread from the Silicon Valley of Bob Noyce all over the nation, it is performance, not pedigree, that counts. CEOs who perform are rewarded with great wealth. Those who do not—even if they run such traditional stalwarts of corporate America as General Motors, Procter & Gamble, or IBM—are out.

Are the riches of American capitalism equally available to all?

No. Are they more equally available now than they were in the United States a half century ago? Yes. Are they more equally available than in other societies? The United States measures up well. There is more openness now than there once was and than there is in global comparison.

In the 1940s, the economist Joseph A. Schumpeter described capitalism as an economic system characterized by a "perennial gale" of "creative destruction."[15] In the 1990s, the *Economist,* sounding very much like Schumpeter, wrote in its "Survey of American Business":

> Underpinning all of this [recent productivity growth] is something distinctive in American society and politics. No other rich country gives companies quite such a free hand to lay off workers [including, it might have added, executives at all levels] and shift resources from declining industries into growing ones. No other country refreshes itself in quite the same way by continuous waves of immigration. . . . For as long as Americans are willing to put up with the mass lay-offs and accompanying social dislocation, these are incomparable wealth-creating advantages.[16]

Is the *Economist*'s description of the American economy true? Yes. Is it good? Does the economy so described produce a good society? These latter are questions concerning which reasonable people can differ.

The story of American business from 1970 to 2000 can be captured in three words: decline and rebirth. It is hard to see how the rebirth could have taken place absent the ability of the American corporation to sail with the "perennial gale" at its back rather than against the wind. But the price of the rebirth has been high. The truth is that Americans are not "willing to put up with the mass lay-offs and accompanying social dislocation." America is an armed camp with violence and crime, often gun related, that would be wholly unacceptable in any other wealthy nation. The willingness to which the *Economist* referred is illusory, caused by the fact that anger and rebellion are usually expressed in random acts of everyday lawlessness rather than in an organized political fashion.

At the heart of the American Business Tradition is a contradiction. Business is about money. Money is perhaps the most unequal element in a nation born in the service of equality. Some people have more than others.

The contradiction lies in the fact that money is in itself morally neutral and without prejudice. It does not care what race you are, what religion you practice, or how far back you can trace your lineage. Everyone is precisely the same in the opinion—if it could express one—of a dollar bill.

"A ploughman on his legs," Benjamin Franklin wrote in *The Way to Wealth,* in 1754, "is higher than a gentleman on his knees."[17]

NOTES

Introduction: The Big Picture

1. Daniel J. Boorstin, *The Americans: The National Experience* (New York: Vintage, 1965), epigram.
2. Gabriele D'Annunzio, *"In Morte Di Giuseppe Verdi"* (Milan: Fratelli Treves, 1901), p. 23. D'Annunzio's verse was *Pianse ed amò per tutti.* The literal translation is "He wept and loved for all." Francis Toye, *Giuseppe Verdi: His Life and Works* (New York: Knopf, 1946), p. 195. See also "verdiana." http://www.r-ds.com/verdiana.htm at this writing.
3. Quoted in Henri Troyat, *Tolstoy* (New York: Harmony, 1967), p. 311.
4. Samuel Eliot Morison and Henry Steele Commager, *The Growth of the American Republic* (New York: Oxford University Press, 1942), vol. 2, p. 134.
5. Stanley Elkins and Eric McKitrick, *The Hofstadter Aegis: A Memorial* (New York: Knopf, 1974), p. 305.
6. Quoted in Edward C. Kirkland, *Industry Comes of Age* (Chicago: Quadrangle, 1961), p. 323.
7. I am conducting such a study, the working title of which is "The American CEO in 1917: Demography and Career Path." My co-authors are Courtney Purrington, Ph.D., and Kim Bettcher, Ph.D.
8. This is the same study referred to in note 7.
9. Frank W. Taussig and Carl S. Joslyn, *American Business Leaders: A Study in Social Origins and Social Stratification* (New York: Macmillan, 1932), p. 245.
10. This well-known phrase was coined by Nathan Glazer and Daniel Patrick Moynihan in *Beyond the Melting Pot: The Negroes, Puerto Ricans, Jews, Italians, and Irish of New York City* (Cambridge, Mass.: MIT Press and Harvard University Press, 1963).
11. For an excellent introduction to Sarnoff, see Thomas K. McCraw, *American Business, 1920–2000: How It Worked* (Wheeling, Ill.: Harlan Davidson, 2000), pp. 115–146, and the accompanying Bibliographical Essay on pp. 236–239.
12. The best place to begin for the history of African American business is Juliet E. K. Walker, *The History of Black Business in America: Capitalism, Race, Entrepreneurship* (New York: Macmillan, 1998). A noteworthy study of a single African American company is Walter B. Weare, *Black Business in the New South: A Social History of the North Carolina Mutual Life Insurance Company* (Urbana: University of Illinois Press, 1973). For women in business, see Mary A. Yeager, ed., *Women in Business,* 3 vols., (Cheltenham, U.K.: Edward Elgar, 1999), and Angel Kwolek-Folland, *Incorporating Women: A History of Women and Business in the United States* (New York: Twayne, 1998). See the helpful bibliographical references in McCraw, *American Business,* pp. 228–229, 235–236.

13. Thomas K. McCraw, ed., *Creating Modern Capitalism: How Entrepreneurs, Companies, and Countries Triumphed in Three Industrial Revolutions* (Cambridge, Mass.: Harvard University Press, 1997), p. 4.

14. Alfred D. Chandler Jr. and Richard S. Tedlow, *The Coming of Managerial Capitalism: A Casebook on the History of American Economic Institutions* (Homewood, Ill.: Irwin, 1985), p. 582.

15. "The Tire Industry: Spinning Out of Control?" *Sales Management*, April 1, 1970, p. 21; Donald N. Sull, Richard S. Tedlow, and Richard S. Rosebloom, "Managerial Commitments and Technological Change in the US Tire Industry," *Industrial and Corporate Change*, vol. 6, no. 2 (1997), pp. 461–501.

16. Glenn Rifkin and George Harrar, *The Ultimate Entrepreneur: The Story of Ken Olsen and Digital Equipment Corporation* (Rocklin, Calif.: Prima Publishing, 1990).

17. "Computers: DEC's Olsen Stuns Industry by Resigning," *Wall Street Journal*, July 17, 1992.

18. "Compaq, Digital Make It Official; Decision to Sell Maynard-Based Company Finalized at Emotional Shareholder Meeting," *Boston Globe*, June 12, 1998.

19. According to a report which appeared in the *Wall Street Journal* in March 2001, General Electric's stock was down 30 percent since August of 2000 "thanks to the steady decline in the market and some doubts about G.E.'s pending $33 billion acquisition of Honeywell International, Inc., its largest ever." Matt Murray, "Shares of GE Climb as Chairman Predicts Earnings Growth of at Least 10 Percent in 2001," *Wall Street Journal*, March 14, 2001, p. B7. For a succinct summary of Welch's views on transforming a company he acquires, see Jeffrey E. Garten, *The Mind of the CEO* (New York: Basic, 2001), pp. 2–3.

20. See Howard H. Stevenson, Michael J. Roberts, and H. Irving Grousbeck, *New Business Ventures and the Entrepreneur* (Homewood, Ill.: Irwin, 1989), pp. 1–19.

21. This article is quoted in Stephen E. Ambrose, *Nothing Like It in the World: The Men Who Built the Transcontinental Railroad, 1863–1869.* (New York: Simon & Schuster, 2000), p. 177.

22. John Locke, "Fundamental Constitutions of Carolina: March 1, 1669." This document is on the web at http://www.yale.edu/lawweb/avalon/states/nc05.htm. For a brief but useful discussion, see Alan Brinkley, *The Unfinished Nation: A Concise History of the American People* (New York: Knopf, 1997), pp. 48–50.

23. According to Article I, Section 9 of the U.S. Constitution, "No Title of Nobility shall be granted by the United States. . . ."

24. David L. Lewis, *The Public Image of Henry Ford: An American Folk Hero and His Company* (Detroit: Wayne State University Press, 1976), pp. 476–477.

PART ONE: THE RISE TO GLOBAL ECONOMIC POWER

Introduction

1. Andrew Carnegie, *Triumphant Democracy, or Fifty Years' March of the Republic* (New York: Scribner's, 1886), p. 1.

2. A. J. P. Taylor, *The Struggle for Mastery in Europe, 1848–1918* (New York: Oxford University Press, 1954), p. xxx.
3. James J. Flink, *The Automobile Age* (Cambridge, Mass.: MIT Press, 1988), p. 136.

Chapter 1: Andrew Carnegie

1. Mark Twain to Andrew Carnegie. The letter was dated February 6, but no year was provided. It was probably sent in the late 1890s. Joseph Frazier Wall, *Andrew Carnegie* (New York: Oxford University Press, 1970), pp. 825, 1101, n. 62.
2. Ibid., pp. 323, 615, 419. Wall recalls this anecdote on page 615 and states that the response to Carnegie's letter came "[w]ithin two days" of its being sent, which seems hardly possible prior to the era of Federal Express. In a footnote, Wall writes: "This is a well known Carnegie story, told to me by several persons who were friends of the Carnegie family." Ibid., p. 1087, n. 77. Neither Carnegie's letter nor the response to it have survived. It is possible that there is a little more legend than fact to this story. The story has survived, however, because it reveals (in a humorous way) Carnegie's skill as a manipulator, especially with regard to money.
3. Joseph Frazier Wall, ed., *The Andrew Carnegie Reader* (Pittsburgh: University of Pittsburgh Press, 1992), p. 115. In his autobiography, Carnegie wrote, "No pangs remain of any wound received in my business career save that of Homestead." Andrew Carnegie, *Autobiography of Andrew Carnegie*, John C. Van Dyke, ed. (Boston: Houghton Mifflin, 1920), p. 232.
4. "An Employer's View of the Labor Question" reprinted in Wall, *Carnegie Reader*, p. 96.
5. "Results of the Labor Struggle" reprinted in ibid., p. 112.
6. Wall, *Carnegie*, p. 525.
7. Paul Krause, *The Battle for Homestead, 1880–1892: Politics, Culture, and Steel* (Pittsburgh: University of Pittsburgh Press, 1992), pp. 124–125.
8. This story is recounted in both Wall, *Carnegie*, pp. 475, 486–488, and Burton J. Hendrick, *The Life of Andrew Carnegie* (London: Heinemann, 1933), pp. 261–262.
9. Wall, *Carnegie*, pp. 474–475.
10. Harold C. Livesay, *American Made: Men Who Shaped the American Economy* (New York: Harper and Row, 1979), p. 107.
11. Krause, *Homestead*, pp. 240–251.
12. Wall, *Carnegie*, p. 553. Wall's source for this quotation is J. Bernard Hogg, "The Homestead Strike of 1892" (unpublished doctoral dissertation, University of Chicago, 1943), p. 242. Unfortunately, Hogg does not footnote this quotation, so it is difficult to document the extent to which the partner quoted was expressing the outlook of the firm as a whole.
13. Mark Van Doren, ed., *The Portable Walt Whitman* (New York: Viking, 1945), p. 134. This passage is from "Song of Myself."

14. Betty Boyd Caroli, *The Roosevelt Women* (New York: Basic Books, 1998), p. 234.
15. A. J. P. Taylor, *The War Lords* (New York: Penguin, 1983), p. 98.
16. Wall, *Carnegie*, pp. 819–822.
17. Ron Chernow, *Titan: The Life of John D. Rockefeller, Sr.* (New York: Random House, 1998), p. 48.
18. Wall, *Carnegie*, p. 33.
19. Ibid., pp. 36–37. Wall uses the comparison to an organist, and it is quite appropriate.
20. See, for example, Wall's description of Will Carnegie attending a church service in which the subject of the sermon, the Sunday after the birth of his first child, was infant damnation. Ibid., p. 34.
21. Wall, *Carnegie*, p. 695. See also Robert L. Beisner, *Twelve Against Empire: The Anti-Imperialists, 1898–1900* (New York: McGraw-Hill, 1968), pp. 165–185.
22. Wall, *Carnegie*, p. 65.
23. Ibid., p. 71.
24. The city of Pittsburgh annexed Allegheny in 1907. See Stefan Lorant, ed., *Pittsburgh: The Story of an American City* (Garden City, N.Y.: Doubleday, 1964), p. 474.
25. Wall, *Carnegie*, p. 88; Carnegie, *Autobiography*, pp. 35–36.
26. Harold C. Livesay, *Andrew Carnegie and the Rise of Big Business*, 2nd ed. (New York: Longman, 2000), p. 17.
27. Wall, *Carnegie*, pp. 97–99.
28. Daniel J. Boorstin, *The Americans: The Democratic Experience* (New York: Vintage, 1973), pp. 1–87.
29. Carnegie, *Autobiography*, pp. 62–63.
30. Livesay, *Carnegie*, p. 21. See, for example, Carnegie's speech to students at Pittsburgh's Curry Commercial College on June 23, 1888. In his discussion of "conditions essential to success," he said: "Do not be afraid that I am going to moralize or inflict a homily upon you. I speak upon the subject only from the view of a man of the world, desirous of aiding you to become successful businessmen." Andrew Carnegie, "The Road to Business Success: A Talk to Young Men" in Wall, *Carnegie Reader*, p. 43.
31. Wall, *Carnegie*, p. 105.
32. Abraham Zaleznik in conversation with me, February 1999. See Abraham Zaleznik and Manfred F. R. Kets de Vries, *Power and the Corporate Mind: How to Use Rather Than Misuse Leadership* (Chicago: Bonus Books, 1985). For an eye-opening treatment of Carnegie's psychology, see Zaleznik's "Charisma and Guilt in Leadership—Andrew Carnegie," in idem, *Learning Leadership: Cases and Commentaries on Abuses of Power in Organizations* (Chicago: Bonus Books, 1993), pp. 193–239. See also Margaret Ann Farrah, "Andrew Carnegie: A Psychohistorical Sketch" (unpublished doctoral dissertation, Carnegie-Mellon University, 1982).
33. Wall, *Carnegie*, p. 2.
34. Carnegie, *Autobiography*, p. 10.
35. Wall, *Carnegie*, pp. 400–420.
36. Ibid., pp. 404, 1073 n. 10. "Memoir" of Burton J. Hendrick, Columbia

University Oral History Collection, p. 47. On Louise Carnegie, see Burton J. Hendrick and Daniel Henderson, *Louise Whitfield Carnegie: The Life of Mrs. Andrew Carnegie* (New York: Hastings House, 1950).

37. Carnegie, *Autobiography,* p. 63.
38. See the thought-provoking comments about Charles M. Schwab, one of Carnegie's "geniuses," a word he used almost as often as "heroes," in whom he later lost faith, in Glenn Porter, "A Picture from Life's Other Side: Pocket Robber Baron," *Reviews in American History,* vol. 4, no. 3 (September 1976), pp. 415–420.
39. Carnegie described his hero fund as "my pet." "I don't believe there is a nobler fund in the world," he asserted. Early recognition was won, for example, by "one man (fisherman) [who] rescued seven men when the Life Boat crew declared it impossible." Wall, *Carnegie,* pp. 894–897. See also John A. Garraty's review of the Wall biography in the *Journal of American History,* vol. 58, no. 2 (September 1971), pp. 475–476.
40. Wall, *Carnegie,* pp. 117–119.
41. Livesay, *Carnegie,* p. 28.
42. Wall, *Carnegie,* pp. 397, 687.
43. Carnegie, *Autobiography,* p. 25.
44. Wall, *Carnegie,* p. 399. Italics added.
45. Ibid., p. 33.
46. Tom was married in the "late Summer of 1867." Ibid., p. 221.
47. Tom was born in Dunfermline on October 2, 1843, and died in Homewood, Pennsylvania, on October 19, 1886.
48. Carnegie, *Autobiography,* p. 56.
49. Quoted in Zaleznik, *Leadership,* p. 195.
50. George H. Burgess and Miles C. Kennedy, *Centennial History of the Pennsylvania Railroad Company* (Philadelphia, Pennsylvania Railroad, 1949), pp. 341–342.
51. James A. Ward, *J. Edgar Thomson: Master of the Pennsylvania* (Westport, Conn.: Greenwood Press, 1980), p. 95.
52. Andrew Carnegie, "How I Served My Apprenticeship," *Youth's Companion,* April 25, 1896, reprinted in Wall, *Carnegie Reader,* p. 35.
53. Carnegie, *Autobiography,* p. 63.
54. Ibid., pp. 66–67.
55. Ibid., p. 67.
56. Ibid., p. 70.
57. Ibid., p. 71; Wall, *Carnegie,* p. 124.
58. This incident is recounted in Carnegie, *Autobiography,* pp. 70–72.
59. Ibid., p. 79.
60. Ibid.
61. Ibid., pp. 79–80; Wall, *Carnegie,* pp. 132–135, 145, 189, 223.
62. Carnegie, *Autobiography,* pp. 90–91.
63. The story is recounted in Wall, *Carnegie,* pp. 143–144, and Carnegie, *Autobiography,* pp. 91–92.
64. The quoted word is typical Carnegie. See his *Autobiography,* p. 92.
65. Wall, *Carnegie,* p. 138; Hendrick, *Carnegie,* pp. 81–82.
66. Livesay, *Carnegie,* p. 80.
67. Wall, *Carnegie,* pp. 223–224.

68. Ibid., p. 224 and pp. 217–226. The italics in the quotation from Carnegie are added.
69. James P. Baughman, "J. P. Morgan," in Alfred D. Chandler, Jr., Thomas K. McCraw, and Richard S. Tedlow, *Management, Past and Present: A Casebook on the History of American Business* (Cincinnati: South-Western, 1996), pp. 2-52–2-69.
70. Carnegie, *Autobiography,* pp. 172–173.
71. Maury Klein, *Union Pacific: Birth of a Railroad, 1862–1893* (Garden City, N.Y.: Doubleday, 1987), pp. 19–22.
72. Dodge is discussed at length in Ambrose, *Nothing Like It in the World: The Men Who Built the Transcontinental Railroad, 1863–1869* (New York: Simon and Schuster, 2000).
73. Ward, *Thomson,* p. 206. Ward describes William Thaw as "Scott's financial ally," Henry Houston as the Pennsylvania's general freight agent, and John McManus as "a prominent iron master." Ward provides no description of the position of Matthew Baird. See Ward, *Thomson,* pp. 154, 161–162, 206. The only individual other than Scott that Carnegie mentions as having attended the meeting was J. N. McCullough, "vice-president of the Pennsylvania Railroad at Pittsburgh." Carnegie, *Autobiography,* p. 173. Ward does not mention McCullough's attendance. McCullough was a vice president of the Pennsylvania Company, which was a wholly owned subsidiary of the Pennsylvania Railroad, from 1873 to 1891. Thaw was a vice president of the Pennsylvania Company from 1871 to 1889. Burgess and Kennedy, *Pennsylvania Railroad,* pp. 795–796.
74. Wall, *Carnegie,* p. 297.
75. Burgess and Kennedy, *Pennsylvania Railroad,* p. 348.
76. The extent to which Carnegie was endangering the financial well-being of his new partners by investing in Scott's Texas and Pacific is difficult to determine. Carnegie thought Scott's railroad was a bad idea. There is no question about that. But if the railroad had gone bankrupt, would Carnegie also have gone bankrupt? Would the railroad's creditors have been able to reach beyond whatever amount Carnegie had actually invested to his other assets as well if their losses had exceeded the amount of his investment? Would creditors have been able to reach beyond all Carnegie's assets to those of his partners in his steel venture, such as Phipps, Kloman, and his brother Tom, whom he mentions specifically in his autobiography? This is an important question. How legitimate was his appeal to his "duty" to his new partners? Was this a reason or an excuse?

    We can only guess at the answers to these questions. The Texas and Pacific was organized as a corporation with limited liability. Carnegie therefore risked only the money he invested. Creditors would not have had access to his other assets. Carnegie had, before the meeting took place, as the paragraph in the text following this note explains, already invested a quarter of a million dollars of his own money in the Texas and Pacific at Scott's request. If the railroad went bankrupt, that was all the money he could have lost.

    If, however, Carnegie were to have invested in Scott's railroad not as an individual but as a member of the Carnegie Steel partnership he was forming, those organizations and the partners in them would have been in jeopardy. Carnegie's partnerships were unincorporated. Liability was unlimited. The law apparently assumed that one partner could speak for all, so all the partners would have been "jointly and severally" liable not only for the full amount of Carnegie's investment but for the full amount of the losses of the creditors. In other words, it appears possible that Carnegie could have bankrupted his partners by making an investment without their consent.

Though theoretically possible, the above chain of events is unlikely. If Carnegie were to have invested in the railroad, it seems that he could have done so without endangering his new partners directly. However, they were depending upon his capital and his acumen. None of them could have created Carnegie Steel without him. If Carnegie had allowed a failed investment to ruin him, he would have indirectly ruined his new partners by depriving them of his resources both financial and as a leader.

The complexities of this subject are only hinted at in this note. But the complexities are important because they throw into sharp relief a question which is part of the Carnegie-Scott story. That is: Did Carnegie turn Scott down in his hour of need because he had no choice? Or did he make his decision because, despite Scott's numberless favors, the effort of managing a large investment of which he disapproved required more time, money, and energy than he felt he owed his former mentor? The only way we could be certain of the answer would have been if Carnegie had played the role of Scott's savior and made the requested investment, the railroad had gone bankrupt nevertheless, and Carnegie had been sued. Carnegie never had any intentions of risking such an outcome.

The literature on partnerships, corporations, and the evolution of limited liability is very large. Among the most useful sources are James Willard Hurst, *The Legitimacy of the Business Corporation in the Law of the United States, 1780–1970* (Charlottesville: University Press of Virginia, 1970); Herbert Hovenkamp, *Enterprise and American Law, 1836–1937* (Cambridge: Harvard University Press, 1991); Morton J. Horwitz, *The Transformation of American Law, 1870–1960: The Crisis of Legal Orthodoxy* (New York: Oxford University Press, 1992); Ronald E. Seavoy, *The Origins of the American Business Corporation, 1784–1855: Broadening the Concept of Public Service during Industrialization* (Westport, Conn.: Greenwood Press, 1982); Donald J. Weidner, "The Existence of State and Tax Partnerships: A Primer," *Florida State University Law Review,* vol. 11, no. 1 (spring 1983).

The Byzantine history of the "notorious" Texas and Pacific Railway can be traced with the help of Albert V. House Jr., "Post–Civil War Precedents for Recent Railroad Organization," *Mississippi Valley Historical Review,* vol. 25, no. 4 (March 1939), pp. 505–522. House labels the Texas and Pacific "notorious" on p. 509. See also Texas and Pacific Railway, *From Ox-Teams to Eagles: A History of the Texas and Pacific Railway* (Dallas: Texas and Pacific Railway, 1946[?]), pp. 6–21; John F. Stover, *The Railroads of the South, 1865–1900: A Study in Finance and Control* (Chapel Hill: University of North Carolina Press, 1955), pp. 99–121. It is noteworthy that none of these sources (nor any of the other sources I have examined) mention Carnegie or the 1873 meeting. This could be taken as evidence that Carnegie overemphasized his importance.

77. Quoted in Wall, *Carnegie,* p. 303.
78. Livesay, *Carnegie,* p. 107.
79. Carnegie, *Autobiography,* p. 174.
80. Wall, *Carnegie,* pp. 306, 302–306 passim.
81. Historian James Ward has written that "for the rest of his life Carnegie regretted that he abandoned his friends in their hour of need, admitting later that he was a cause for Scott's 'premature death.' He could have added, for Thomson's also." Ward, *Thomson,* p. 207.
82. Ibid., pp. 207–208.
83. Henrietta M. Larson, *Jay Cooke, Private Banker* (Cambridge, Mass.: Harvard University Press, 1936), pp. 412–433; Stuart Bruchey, "Cook, Jay" in John A. Garraty with Jerome L. Sternstein, eds., *Encyclopedia of American Biography* (New York: Harper and Row, 1974), pp. 217–218.
84. Ward, *Thomson,* p. 208.
85. The following month Scott died, "never to see," according to Gould's most recent biographer, "Gould complete in short order the line he [Scott] had fumbled for years to create." Maury Klein, *The Life and Legend of Jay Gould* (Baltimore: Johns Hopkins University Press, 1986), p. 265. See also Robert E. Riegel, *The Story of the Western Railroads* (New York: MacMillan, 1926), pp. 120, 179–184, 195.
86. Burgess and Kennedy, *Pennsylvania Railroad,* p. 348. According to Scott's obituary in the *New York Times,* Scott's debts at one point amounted to about $17 million. The *Times* also reported that Scott "eventually redeemed it all, dollar for dollar." "A Railroad Prince Dead," *New York Times,* May 22, 1881, p. 1.
87. The standard source on labor turmoil at this time is Robert V. Bruce, *1877: Year of Violence* (Indianapolis: Bobbs-Merrill, 1959). A very interesting, recent interpretation of the meaning of the 1877 strikes in Pittsburgh is provided in Krause, *Homestead,* especially pp. 124–156.
88. Burgess and Kennedy, *Pennsylvania Railroad,* p. 382. According to James A. Ward, in 1878 Scott "suffered the first of three strokes that would eventually kill him." James A. Ward, "Thomas A. Scott," in *Railroads in the Nineteenth Century,* Robert L. Frey, ed. (New York: Facts on File, 1988), p. 362.
89. Burgess and Kennedy, *Pennsylvania Railroad,* p. 383. In Scott's lengthy *New York Times* obituary, there was no mention of the meeting about which Carnegie wrote. In fact, there was no mention of Carnegie at all. "Prince," *Times.*
90. Wall, *Carnegie,* p. 238.
91. Carnegie, *Autobiography,* p. 174. Italics added.
92. Wall Carnegie, p. 306. Italics added.
93. Carnegie wrote that "Wagner was revealed to me in 'Lohengrin'." Carnegie, *Autobiography,* pp. 49–50. If Carnegie was familiar with *Lohengrin,* he doubtless became familiar with the *Ring,* of which Siegfried is the protagonist.
94. Hendrick, *Carnegie,* p. 170.
95. Wall, *Carnegie,* p. 303.
96. Hendrick, *Carnegie,* p. 171.
97. Ibid., pp. 173.
98. Ibid., pp. 171.

99. Wall, *Carnegie,* pp. 188–189.
100. Ibid., p. 189.
101. Ibid., pp. 228–229.
102. Wall provides an excellent recounting of this trip in ibid., pp. 229–239.
103. Ibid., pp. 233–234.
104. The story of iron and steel is critical to the rise of modern civilization and has been told many times. The most accessible academic study for the United States remains Peter Temin, *Iron and Steel in Nineteenth-Century America: An Economic Inquiry* (Cambridge, Mass.: MIT Press, 1964). This can be usefully supplemented by Paul F. Paskoff, ed., *Encyclopedia of American Business History and Biography: Iron and Steel in the Nineteenth Century* (New York: Facts on File, 1989). For context, see Peter Mathias, *The First Industrial Nation: The Economic History of Britain, 1700–1914* (London: Routledge, 1993), and David S. Landes, *The Unbound Prometheus: Technological Change and Industrial Development in Western Europe from 1750 to the Present* (London: Cambridge University Press, 1969). For the general reader, a good source is Robert Raymond, *Out of the Fiery Furnace: The Impact of Metals on the History of Mankind* (University Park: Pennsylvania State University Press, 1986).
105. Sir Henry Bessemer, *An Autobiography* (Offices of "Engineering," 35 and 36, Bedford Street, Strand, W. C., 1905), p. 138.
106. A brief and useful description is William H. Becker, "Bessemer Process," in Paskoff, ed., *Encyclopedia,* pp. 32–33.
107. This paper is reprinted in its entirety in Bessemer, *Autobiography,* pp. 156–161.
108. Matthew Josephson, *Edison: A Biography* (New York: McGraw-Hill, 1959), p. 355.
109. Kenneth Warren, *Triumphant Capitalism: Henry Clay Frick and the Industrial Transformation of America* (Pittsburgh: University of Pittsburgh Press, 1996), pp. 1–55. See especially pp. 9–10. Temin, *Iron and Steel,* pp. 195–196.
110. By my mother.
111. Warren, *Capitalism,* pp. 383–384.
112. Livesay, *Carnegie,* p. 130.
113. Sir Isaiah Berlin, "The Hedgehog and the Fox," in idem, *Russian Thinkers* (New York: Viking, 1978). This is an essay on Tolstoy's view of history. The fox, in Berlin's essay, knows many things. The hedgehog knows one big thing.
114. I am adopting this phrase from Wall, who writes of the "material structure of civilization" in a slightly different context from that used here. See his *Carnegie,* p. 504.
115. Ibid., pp. 318–319.
116. Ibid., p. 324. According to a publication in 1879, the Pennsylvania specified "that the length of rails at 60 deg. Fahr. shall be kept within 1/4 in. of the standard lengths, which are 30 ft., 27½ ft., and 25 ft." James Dredge, *The Pennsylvania Railroad: Its Organization, Construction, and Management* (New York: John Wiley and Sons, 1879), p. 35.
117. Wall, *Carnegie,* pp. 320.
118. Warren, *Capitalism,* p. 386.

119. Livesay, *Carnegie*, p. 125.
120. Carnegie, *Autobiography*, p. 182.
121. Livesay, *Carnegie*, p. 124–126.
122. Ibid., p. 129.
123. Ibid., pp. 129–130.
124. Ibid., p. 113.
125. Wall, *Carnegie*, p. 584.
126. Livesay, *American Made*, p. 119.
127. Wall, *Carnegie*, pp. 259, 490.
128. F. Scott Fitzgerald, "The Rich Boy" in idem, *All the Sad Young Men* (New York: Scribner's, 1926), p. 1.
129. Ernest Hemingway, "The Snows of Kilimanjaro," in *The Fifth Column and the First Forty-Nine Stories* (New York: Scribner's, 1939), p. 170.
130. John Emerich Edward Dalberg-Acton, First Baron Acton, *Essays in the Study and Writing of History*, vol. 11, J. Rufus Fears, ed. (Indianapolis: Liberty Classics, 1985), p. 383.
131. I am indebted for this insight to Judge Sandra Lynch of the First Circuit Court of Appeals in Boston.
132. Mel Gussow, *Don't Say 'Yes' Until I Finish Talking: A Biography of Darryl F. Zanuck* (Garden City, N.Y.: Doubleday, 1971).
133. Quoted in Edith Hamilton, *The Greek Way* (New York: Norton, 1983), p. 31.
134. This amendment abolished slavery in the United States.
135. On this point, see generally Richard Sennett, *The Corrosion of Character: The Personal Consequences of Work· in the New Capitalism* (New York: Norton, 1998).
136. For Carnegie and Junius Morgan's son, John Pierpont, see Vincent P. Carosso, *The Morgans: Private International Bankers, 1854–1913* (Cambridge, Mass.: Harvard University Press, 1987), pp. 466–471.
137. The standard biography of Frick is Warren, *Capitalism*. See also the remarkable narrative of the attempt to assassinate Frick in Wall, *Carnegie*, pp. 562–563.
138. See Zaleznik, *Leadership*, pp. 193–239.
139. Wall, *Carnegie*, p. 365.
140. Carnegie, *Autobiography*, p. 339.
141. Wall, *Carnegie*, p. 391.
142. Richard Hofstadter, *The American Political Traditiion: And the Men Who Made It* (New York: Knopf, 1948); p. xxxix.
143. Richard Hofstadter, *Anti-Intellectualism in American Life* (New York: Knopf, 1963), pp. 24–29. Italics in original. See also the discussion of "Business and Intellect" on pp. 233–252.
144. Wall, *Carnegie*, p. 223.
145. Livesay, *Carnegie*, p. 206.
146. Wall, *Carnegie*, p. 789.
147. Ibid., p. 879.
148. See, for example, ibid., pp. 941–942.
149. Ibid., pp. 688–689.
150. Ibid., p. 948. For Skibo, see also Hendrick, *Carnegie*, pp. 673–689.
151. Wall, *Carnegie*, pp. 856–857; Hendrick, *Carnegie*, pp. 599–617.

152. *Nineteenth Century,* no. 169 (March 1891), pp. 367–385.
153. Remarks Hendrick: "It might be imagined that a man who was unable to sleep nights for the ticking of his watch and who habitually stuffed cotton in his ears to protect them against trivial noises, would find himself discomfited in the Edgar Thomson Steel Works." Hendrick, *Carnegie,* p. 208.
154. Wall, *Carnegie,* p. 924.
155. Ibid., p. 926. Italics in original.
156. Hendrick, *Carnegie,* pp. 645–646.
157. Gordon A. Craig, *The Politics of the Prussian Army, 1640–1945* (New York: Oxford University Press, 1964), pp. 238–242; Erich Eyck, *Bismarck and the German Empire* (New York: Norton, 1958), pp. 299–300.
158. Carnegie, *Autobiography,* p. 371.
159. The autobiography incorrectly dates this event as 1912 rather than 1913.
160. This phrase is Harold Livesay's. See his *Carnegie,* p. 2.
161. When Carnegie told Henry Clay Frick on January 10, 1900, that he intended to force Frick out of Carnegie Steel through exercise of the Iron Clad Agreement, Frick shouted at him: "For years I have been convinced that there is not an honest bone in your body. Now I know that you are a god damned thief. . . ." Frick clenched his fists and moved toward Carnegie, who quickly left the office. Warren, *Capitalism,* p. 257.

Chapter 2: George Eastman

1. Harold Gleason, "Please Play My Funeral March," University of Rochester *Library Bulletin,* vol. 26, no. 3 (Spring 1971), pp. 122–123. The literature on suicide among business executives is not as extensive as one would expect. Some suggestive articles include: Harry Levinson, "On Executive Suicide," *Harvard Business Review* (July–August 1975), pp. 118–122; idem, "At Their Own Hands," *Executive,* vol. 5, no. 2 (March 1979), pp. 30–33; Bruce Horovitz, "Suicide: An Executive Suite Hazard?" *Industry Week,* March 9, 1981, pp. 41–44; and Herbert Hendin, "Fall from Power: Suicide of an Executive," *Suicide and Life Threatening Behavior,* vol. 24, no. 3, pp. 293 ff. With the collaboration of Courtney Purrington, Ph.D., and Kim Bettcher, Ph.D., I have examined the demographics and career paths of the chief executive officers of the 200 largest industrial firms in the United States in 1917. Of those, we have identified five who took their own lives. They are Knowlton Lyman Ames of Booth Fisheries Company, August Anheuser Busch Sr. of the brewery by that name, Albert Russell Erskine of Studebaker, William M. Wood of the American Woolen Company, and Eastman. It is possible that this represents an undercounting. The suicide of an important individual in an organization is a catastrophic event for many, with both emotional and legal ramifications. Richard S. Tedlow, Courtney Purrington, and Kim Bettcher, "The American CEO in 1917: Demography and Career Path," manuscript in author's possession.
2. Eastman had once asked his personal physician, Dr. Audley Stewart, about strychnine. He also once asked Stewart: "Audley, you're always

listening to my heart. Just where is it?" Stewart responded by percussing the borders of the heart (as physicians percuss the lungs for fluid). Not satisfied, Eastman then requested that Stewart "outline it for me." Elizabeth Brayer, *George Eastman: A Biography* (Baltimore: Johns Hopkins University Press, 1996), pp. 516–517.

Elizabeth Brayer is the first scholar to be given full access to the papers of George Eastman. This chapter relies heavily on her work in order to understand the basic facts of Eastman's life. Brayer has also provided extensive footnotes and bibliographic references, and her book serves as an excellent guide to the primary sources on George Eastman's life. Other sources of biographical information include: Carl W. Ackerman, *George Eastman* (Boston: Houghton Mifflin, 1930), the only full-length authorized biography of Eastman and extensively edited by Eastman himself; Bernard Weisberger, "You Press the Button, We Do the Rest," *American Heritage,* vol. 23, no. 6 (October 1972); Brian Coe, *The Birth of Photography: The Story of the Formative Years, 1800–1900* (London: Ash and Grant, 1976); Brian Coe, *George Eastman and the Early Photographers* (London: Priory Press, 1973); Reese V. Jenkins, *Images and Enterprise: Technology and the American Photographic Industry, 1839 to 1925* (Baltimore: Johns Hopkins University Press, 1975); Blake McKelvey, *Rochester on the Genesee: The Growth of a City* (Syracuse: Syracuse University Press, 1973); Blake McKelvey, *Rochester: The Water-Power City, 1812–1854* (Cambridge, Mass.: Harvard University Press, 1945); Blake McKelvey, *Rochester: The Flower City, 1855–1890* (Cambridge, Mass.: Harvard University Press, 1949); Blake McKelvey, *Rochester: The Quest for Quality, 1890–1925* (Cambridge, Mass.: Harvard University Press, 1956); Blake McKelvey, "George Eastman," in *Dictionary of American Biography,* vol. 21, supp. 1 (New York: Scribner's, 1944), pp. 274–276; Albro Martin, "George Eastman," in John A. Garraty, with Jerome L. Sternstein, eds., *Encyclopedia of American Biography* (New York: Harper and Row, 1974); Genesee Book Club, *Rochester and Monroe County* (Rochester: Scrantons', 1937); twelve articles in the University of Rochester *Library Bulletin,* vol. 26, no. 3 (Spring 1971); George E. Norton, "My Friend George Eastman," University of Rochester *Library Bulletin,* vol. 23, no. 1 (Fall 1967), pp. 3–13; O. N. Solbert, "George Eastman, Amateur," *Image,* vol. 2, no. 8 (November 1953).

3. Brayer, *Eastman,* p. 10.
4. Ibid., pp. 15–16.
5. Ibid., pp. 15–19.
6. Ibid., pp. 15–16.
7. Ibid., p. 17.
8. Ibid., p. 19.
9. Ibid.
10. Ibid., p. 20.
11. Ibid., p. 19; see also p. 541 n. 29.
12. Ibid, p. 20.
13. Allan Nevins makes this observation about John D. Rockefeller. It is true of both Rockefeller and Eastman. See Nevins, *Study in Power: John D. Rockefeller, Industrialist and Philanthropist,* vol. 1 (New York: Scribner's, 1953), p. 18.

14. "Oliver Optic" was the pseudonym for William T. Adams. To place this literature in context, see John G. Cawelti, *Apostles of the Self-Made Man: Changing Concepts of Success in America* (Chicago: University of Chicago Press, 1965), pp. 101–123, 265–266.

15. Brayer, *Eastman*, p. 21. The "Oliver Optic" adventure published that year was *Make or Break: or, The Rich Man's Daughter* (Boston: Lee and Shepard, 1869).

16. Richard S. Tedlow, "Nineteenth-Century Retailing and the Rise of the Department Store," in Alfred D. Chandler Jr., Thomas K. McCraw, and Richard S. Tedlow, *Management, Past and Present: A Casebook on the History of American Business* (Cincinnati: South-Western, 1996), pp. 3-8.

17. Brayer, *Eastman*, pp. 24–25.

18. Ibid., p. 25.

19. Ibid.

20. Carl Van Doren, *Benjamin Franklin* (New York: Garden City Publishing, 1941), p. 782.

21. Alfred D. Chandler, Jr., "The Standard Oil Company—Combination, Consolidation, and Integration" in Chandler, McCraw, and Tedlow, *Management*, pp. 3-47.

22. Harold C. Livesay, *Andrew Carnegie and the Rise of Big Business* (Boston: Little, Brown, 2000), p. 209.

23. Sir Henry Bessemer, *An Autobiography* (London: Offices of "Engineering," 35 and 36 Bedford Street, Strand, W.C.), p. 138.

24. David Riesman and Eric Larrabee, "Autos in America," in Riesman, ed., *Abundance for What? And Other Essays* (Garden City, N.Y.: Doubleday, 1964), p. 293.

25. Alfred D. Chandler, Jr., *Giant Enterprise: Ford, General Motors, and the Automotive Industry* (New York: Arno, 1980), p. 26.

26. Nevins, *Power*, vol. 1, pp. 10–17; Richard S. Tedlow, *The Rise of the American Business Corporation* (Chur, Switz.: Harwood Academic Publishers, 1991), pp. 30–31.

27. Brayer, *Eastman*, photograph 6, following p. 118.

28. Donald R. Howard, *Chaucer: His Life, His Work, His World* (New York: Fawcett, 1987), p. 172.

29. Brayer, *Eastman*, p. 24.

30. Four decades later, Eastman cruised the shoreline of Santo Domingo at Samana Bay, which had been his destination in 1877. Francis S. Macomber, "A Different Sort of World," University of Rochester *Library Bulletin*, vol. 26, no. 3 (Spring 1971), p. 94.

31. This picture is reproduced in Richard Calvocoressi, *Magritte* (New York: Phaidon, 1979), plate 30.

32. Weisberger, "You Press the Button," pp. 84–85.

33. Eastman's name does not appear in the index of Alan Trachtenberg's authoritative *Reading American Photographs: Images as History, Mathew Brady to Walker Evans* (New York: Hill and Wang, 1989). Suggestions for the interested reader include Nancy Martha West, *Kodak and the Lens of Nostalgia* (Charlottesville: University Press of Virginia, 2000) and Douglas Collins, *The Story of Kodak* (New York: Abrams, 1990).

34. The phrase is that of my colleague, Professor Susan Fournier.

35. Justin Kaplan, *Mr. Clemens and Mark Twain* (New York: Simon and Schuster, 1966), p. 379.

36. Weisberger, "You Press the Button," p. 90.

37. Bessemer, *Autobiography*, p. 1.

38. Collodion is "a solution of guncotton [nitrocellulose] in ether, or alcohol and ether. The guncotton was formed by dissolving cottonwool in a mixture of nitric and sulphuric acids." Coe, *Birth of Photography*, p. 137.

39. Ibid., p. 138. A negative is "the image formed after exposure and development. The tones of the subject are reversed, the light parts being dark in the negative, the dark light."

40. Ibid., p. 137. Fixing is "the process of removing the unused light-sensitive salts from exposed and developed photographic materials, in order to make the image permanent."

41. Helmut Gernsheim, *A Concise History of Photography* (New York: Grosset and Dunlap, 1965), pp. 34–35.

42. Brayer has written that Eastman read of Bennett's work in the first issue of the *British Journal of Photography*, which he received in February 1878. Brayer, *Eastman*, p. 27. Brayer was so informed by the retired head of the Patent Museum at the Eastman Kodak Company. At my request, Ms. Kathy Connor, curator at the George Eastman House, reviewed this publication for February and found no article by Charles Bennett. News of Bennett's work was, however, reported by and discussed in the *Journal's* issues for March 15, March 22, March 29, and April 5, 1878. Ms. Connor has kindly supplied me with copies of these articles. See especially Charles Bennett, "A Sensitive Gelatine Emulsion Process," *British Journal of Photography* (March 29, 1878), pp. 146–147.

43. Brayer, *Eastman*, p. 27.

44. James J. Flink, *The Automobile Age* (Cambridge, Mass.: MIT Press, 1988), pp. 51–55; William Greenleaf, *Monopoly on Wheels: Henry Ford and the Selden Automobile Patent* (Detroit: Wayne State University Press, 1961).

45. Brayer, *Eastman*, pp. 26–27. Further purchases of "sundries and lenses" increased his initial expenditures for camera and associated equipment to $94.36. Ackerman, *Eastman*, p. 15.

46. Weisberger, "You Press the Button," p. 84.

47. For a picture of the Brownie, see Jenkins, *Images*, p. 238.

48. George Bernard Shaw, *The Doctor's Dilemma, Getting Married, and the Shewing-Up of Blanco Posnet* (New York: Brentano's, 1911). See "Preface on Doctors," p. lxxix.

49. Brayer, *Eastman*, p. 28.

50. "Memorandum" from William A. Sahlman to the faculty of the Harvard Business School, September 27, 1996. See also Howard H. Stevenson, Michael J. Roberts, and H. Irving Grousebeck, *New Business Ventures and the Entrepreneur* (Homewood, Ill.: Irwin, 1989), pp. 4–20.

51. Weisberger, "You Press the Button," p. 85.

52. Brayer, *Eastman*, p. 28.

53. Ibid., pp. 30–31.

54. Ibid., p. 33.

55. Ibid., p. 32.

56. For the story of Marshall Field, see Robert W. Twyman, *History of Marshall Field & Co., 1852–1906* (Philadelphia: University of Pennsylvania

Press, 1954); and Nancy F. Koehn, *Brand New: How Entrepreneurs Earned Consumers' Trust from Wedgwood to Dell* (Boston: Harvard Business School Press, 2001), pp. 91–130.

57. Nevins, *Power*, vol. 1, p. 39.
58. Ibid., pp. 58–59.
59. Brayer, *Eastman*, pp. 39–40 and p. 545 n. 1. See also Martin, "George Eastman," pp. 317–319.
60. Quoted in Livesay, *Carnegie*, p. 103. Mark Twain liked this line so much he used it in *Pudd'nhead Wilson*. See Mark Twain, *Pudd'nhead Wilson and Those Extraordinary Twins* (New York: Collier, 1893), p. 130.
61. "Elder John Strong's Descendants Holding Reunion," *Rochester Times-Union*, August 16, 1986; McKelvey, *Rochester on the Genesee*, pp. 15, 17, 21, 23, 34, 40, 53, 68, 94; Paul E. Johnson, *A Shopkeeper's Millennium: Society and Revivals in Rochester, New York, 1815–1837* (New York: Hill and Wang, 1978), pp. 29, 31, 63, 65, 125–129.
62. Brayer, *Eastman*, p. 36; "Strong, Woodbury & Co.," *The Industries of Rochester*, p. 166; "Henry A. Strong," *History of Rochester and Monroe County*, p. 543.
63. Brayer, *Eastman*, p. 37.
64. Ibid., p. 64.
65. Ibid., pp. 36–37.
66. What we do not know is whether Carnegie could in fact have saved Scott from failure. We do know he was not willing to take the chance necessary to find out.
67. Brayer, *Eastman*, p. 140.
68. Ibid., pp. 140–142, 215.
69. Ibid., pp. 106, 175, 350.
70. Ibid., pp. 106, 350; Eastman to Pinkerton Detective Agency, September 19, 1887, George Eastman Papers, Eastman House, Rochester, N.Y.; Jenkins, *Images*, p. 198.
71. Marion Gleason, "The George Eastman I Knew," University of Rochester *Library Bulletin*, vol. 26, no. 3 (Spring 1971), p. 97.
72. George Eastman Papers, Eastman House, Rochester, N.Y.
73. The Tedlow-Purrington-Bettcher 1917 CEO database referred to in note 1 reveals that 195 out of the 200 CEOs of the 200 most important industrial firms in the United States in 1917 were married at some point in their lives. We are uncertain about two of the CEOs in the database. That leaves three who we are certain never married. Eastman is one of these three.
74. Brayer, *Eastman*, p. 259.
75. Ibid., p. 178.
76. Ibid., p. 138.
77. These thoughts are expressed in the vocabulary of Michael E. Porter, *Competitive Advantage: Creating and Sustaining Superior Performance* (New York: Free Press, 1985).
78. Jenkins, *Images*, pp. 104–106.
79. For the story of this development at Du Pont, see Alfred D. Chandler, Jr., and Stephen Salsbury, *Pierre S. duPont and the Making of the Modern Corporation* (New York: Harper and Row, 1971), pp. 112–114.
80. Ackerman, *Eastman*, p. 74.

81. See, for example, James C. Collins and Jerry I. Porras, *Built to Last: Successful Habits of Visionary Companies* (New York: HarperBusiness, 1994), pp. 91–114.

82. Jenkins, *Images*, p. 112.

83. Thomas S. Kuhn, *The Structure of Scientific Revolutions*, 2nd ed. (Chicago: University of Chicago Press, 1970), pp. 149–150.

84. Quoted in Jenkins, *Images*, p. 112. Eastman made this observation during his testimony in the Goodwin suit. *Goodwin Film & Camera Company v. Eastman Kodak Company*, Transcript of Record, vol. 1, p. 353.

85. Jenkins, *Images*, pp. 112–116.

86. "An invasion of armies can be resisted, but not an idea whose time has come." Victor Hugo, *Histoire d'un Crime* (Paris: J. Hetzel, 1883), p. 240.

87. Jenkins, *Images*, p. 116.

88. Ibid.

89. Ibid., p. 120.

90. Ibid., p. 131.

91. Ibid., p. 178.

92. Mark Twain, *A Connecticut Yankee in King Arthur's Court* (New York: Signet, 1963), p. 58.

93. Jenkins, *Images*, p. 184.

94. Brayer, *Eastman*, p. 341.

95. Ibid., p. 222.

96. See p. 101.

97. See the interesting approach to the meaning of the Kodak revolution in West, *Kodak*.

98. I am indebted to my colleagues Professors Susan Fournier and John Deighton for this insight.

99. For the distinction between richness and reach, see Philip Evans and Thomas S. Wurster, *Blown to Bits: How the New Economics of Information Transforms Strategy* (Boston: Harvard Business School Press, 2000).

100. http://www.kodak.com. See references to Brownie camera.

101. http://members.aol.com/Chuck02178/brownie.htm at this writing.

102. Jenkins, *Images*, p. 308.

103. Horatio Alger, *Fame and Fortune: The Progress of Richard Hunter* (Boston: Loring, 1868), p. 278. The hero of this book, Mr. Richard Hunter, in addition to this salary, also received income from $2,000 savings and $5,000 from a lot he sold uptown.

104. Quoted in A. J. P. Taylor, *The Origins of the Second World War*, 2nd ed. (New York: Fawcett, 1961), p. 223.

105. Rebecca W. Voorheis and Laura Bures under the supervision of Nancy F. Koehn, "H. J. Heinz: The Rise of a Global Food Giant," HBS Case Services #9–796–115; revised April 9, 1996.

106. The reader should be warned that not all sources paint Eastman as such a liberal-minded employer and citizen. According to Merle Curti and Roderick Nash in *Philanthropy in the Shaping of American Higher Education* (New Brunswick, NJ: Rutgers University Press, 1965), p. 153: In 1900 when Rush Rhees became president of the University of Rochester, Eastman "displayed no particular interest in education. He

was one of the self-made men who deprecated formal education as impractical and useless, and he especially disdained the higher education of women, his ideal being the old-fashioned type represented by his beloved mother."

Elizabeth Brayer, who is probably more familiar with Eastman's papers than anyone else today, has this to say about his attitude toward Jews. After three days of negotiating with Leonard Jacobi for the purchase of his Nepera Chemical Company, Eastman found Jacobi so difficult that his

> casual and latent anti-Semitism surfaced. "Mr. Jacobi, who is of Semite origin, with all the characteristics of his race, evidently thinks the combine must purchase his business at his own price but I think we can attain our object . . . by the expenditure of much less." (Eastman's prejudice, which seems largely the product of ignorance and provincialism, was not as mean-spirited as that of Thomas Edison, nor as virulent as that of Henry Ford, but if a Jew proved just as hard a bargainer as himself, then out it would pop. In later years, when he would deal more with people of varied cultural backgrounds, his attitude improved.) Brayer, *Eastman*, pp. 200–201.

When Mortimer Adler, a Jewish apparel manufacturer in Rochester, approached Eastman for aid to Eastern European Jewish refugees during World War I, Eastman, Adler recalled, "was at once vitally interested and asked me to submit him data on just what we were raising money for, and how it was to be disbursed. Promptly on receipt of that data, he mailed me a check for $5,000, and set an example which a considerable number of non-Jews in the Community followed." Mortimer Adler to F. W. Lovejoy, May 16, 1940, University of Rochester Library Archives. For perspective, $5,000 in 1916 is the equivalent of almost $80,000 in 2000. By 1929, Eastman had apparently established cordial relations with Julius Rosenwald, the Jewish philanthropist who possessed a fortune from Sears, Roebuck. Brayer, *Eastman*, pp. 409, 426.

107. Jenkins, *Images*, p. 182.
108. Alfred D. Chandler, Jr., *Scale and Scope: The Dynamics of Industrial Capitalism* (Cambridge, Mass.: Harvard University Press, 1990).
109. Brayer, *Eastman*, p. 178.
110. Quoted in John A. Garraty, "The United States Steel Corporation versus Labor," *Labor History*, vol. 1, no. 1 (Winter 1960), p. 1.
111. Victor Hugo, *Les Misérables* (New York: Barnes and Noble, 1986), p. 140.
112. Brayer, *Eastman*, p. 498.
113. Jenkins, *Images*, p. 329.
114. Marion B. Folsom, "A Great Man," University of Rochester *Library Bulletin*, vol. 26, no. 3 (Spring 1971), p. 65.
115. Howard Hanson, "Music Was a Spiritual Necessity," University of Rochester *Library Bulletin*, vol. 26, no. 3 (Spring 1971), p. 87.
116. Quoted in John Morton Blum, *The Republican Roosevelt* (New York: Atheneum, 1954), p. 161.

Chapter 3: Henry Ford

1. David L. Lewis, *The Public Image of Henry Ford: An American Folk Hero and His Company* (Detroit: Wayne State University Press, 1976), pp. 43, 494–495 n. 14. This statement was probably made during the period between 1903, the founding of the present day's Ford Motor Company, and 1906, the year of the introduction of the Model N, precursor to the Model T.
2. This view, which is predominant among students of the subject, is disputed in Donald Finlay Davis, *Conspicuous Production: Automobiles and Elites in Detroit, 1899–1933* (Philadelphia: Temple University Press, 1988), pp. 206–208 passim. See also Richard S. Tedlow, *New and Improved: The Story of Mass Marketing in America* (Boston: Harvard Business School Press, 1996), pp. 112–130.
3. Harold C. Livesay, *American Made: Men Who Shaped the American Economy* (New York: Harper and Row, 1979), p. 180.
4. Thomas K. McCraw, "Henry Ford and Alfred Sloan," in Alfred D. Chandler Jr., Thomas K. McCraw, and Richard S. Tedlow, *Management, Past and Present: A Casebook on the History of American Business* (Cincinnati: South-Western, 1996), pp. 6–12.
5. The lawyer representing the Dodge brothers was the "adroit and dynamic" Elliott G. Stevenson. Allan Nevins and Frank Ernest Hill, *Ford: Expansion and Challenge, 1915–1933* (New York: Scribner's, 1957), p. 95.
6. I am indebted to McKinsey consultant and former FCC chairman Reed E. Hundt for this insight.
7. *Dodge v. Ford Motor Co.*, 204 Mich. 459; 170 N.W. 668; 1919 Mich. LEXIS 720; 3 A.L.R. 413, February 7, 1919, decided. Italics added.
8. Nevins and Hill, *Ford: Expansion*, pp. 86–113.
9. André F. Perold, "Ford Motor Company's Value Enhancement Plan," Harvard Business School Case Services no. N9–201–079.
10. For Ford's reputation in rural America especially, see Reynold M. Wik, *Henry Ford and Grass-roots America* (Ann Arbor: University of Michigan Press, 1972).
11. McCraw, "Ford," in Chandler, McCraw, and Tedlow, *Management*, p. 6-12.
12. Richard Hofstadter, *The American Political Tradition: And the Men Who Made It* (New York: Vintage, 1973), p. 119.
13. Allan Nevins with the collaboration of Frank Ernest Hill, *Ford: The Times, the Man, the Company* (New York: Scribner's, 1954), p. 585.
14. Anne Jardim, *The First Henry Ford: A Study in Personality and Business Leadership* (Cambridge, Mass.: MIT Press, 1970), p. 63. For Ford's overwhelming market share in rural states, see Wik, *Grass-roots*, p. 42.
15. Wik, *Grass-roots*, p. 9.
16. Ibid., pp. 1–13; Davis, *Conspicuous*, pp. 126–127.
17. Gerald R. Ford, *A Time to Heal: The Autobiography of Gerald R. Ford* (Norwalk, Conn.: Easton, 1979), p. 112.
18. Jonathan R. T. Hughes, *The Vital Few: The Entrepreneur and American Economic Progress* (New York: Oxford University Press, 1986), p. 294.
19. Ibid., p. 321.

20. Davis, *Conspicuous*, p. 5.

21. Ibid., p. 1.

22. The books are *My Life and Work* (with Samuel Crowther) (Garden City, N.Y.: Doubleday, 1922); *Today and Tomorrow (Being a Continuation of "My Life and Work")* (with Samuel Crowther) (Garden City, N.Y.: Garden City Publishing, 1926); *Ford Ideals: Being a Selection from "Mr. Ford's Page" in the Dearborn Independent* (Dearborn, Mich.: Dearborn Publishing, 1926); *My Philosophy of Industry* (New York: Coward-McCann, 1929); *Moving Forward* (with Samuel Crowther) (Garden City, N.Y.: Doubleday, 1930); and *Things I've Been Thinking About* (New York: Fleming H. Revell, 1936). The magazine Ford owned was the *Dearborn Independent*.

23. John B. Rae, *Henry Ford* (Englewood Cliffs, N.J.: Prentice-Hall, 1969), p. 2.

24. Lewis, *Image*, pp. 93–112.

25. The three basic volumes in this project are Nevins with Hill, *Ford: The Times*; Nevins and Hill, *Ford: Expansion*; Nevins and Hill, *Ford: Decline and Rebirth, 1933–1962* (New York: Scribner's, 1963). Other volumes that grew out of the Nevins and Hill research effort include Mira Wilkins and Frank Ernest Hill, *American Business Abroad: Ford on Six Continents* (Detroit: Wayne State University Press, 1964); William Greenleaf, *Monopoly on Wheels: Henry Ford and the Selden Automobile Patent* (Detroit: Wayne State University Press, 1961); and idem., *From These Beginnings: The Early Philanthropies of Henry and Edsel Ford, 1911–1936* (Detroit: Wayne State University Press, 1964). The Nevins and Hill project also generated a remarkable oral history archive. As with any interviews, however, the historian must use these reminiscences with care. See, for example, David A. Hounshell's discussion in *From the American System to Mass Production, 1800–1932: The Development of Manufacturing Technology in the United States* (Baltimore: Johns Hopkins University Press, 1984), pp. 244–246.

26. Nevins with Hill, *Ford: The Times*, pp. 576–577.

27. Jardim, *Ford*, p. 243. Italics added.

28. The observation about Franklin appears in Carl Van Doren, *Benjamin Franklin* (New York: Garden City Publishing, 1941), p. 782.

29. This is the same George B. Selden from Rochester whom we encountered briefly in the previous chapter.

30. George S. May, *R. E. Olds: Auto Industry Pioneer* (Grand Rapids, Mich.: William B. Eerdmans, 1977), p. 55.

31. Ibid., pp. 108–111.

32. Ibid., p. 127.

33. Ibid., p. 141 provides a review of low-priced cars from 1899 to 1903.

34. A "runabout" has been defined as a "two-seater, which in most instances amounted to a horseless carriage with an engine mounted underneath." Davis, *Conspicuous*, p. 43.

35. Come away with me Lucille,
    In my merry Oldsmobile,
Over the road of life we'll fly
    Autobubbling you and I,
To the church we'll swiftly steal,

And our wedding bells will peal,
You can go as far as you like with me,
In our merry Oldsmobile.

This has been called "the best known song ever written about the auto-mobile." David L. Lewis, "Sex and the Automobile: From Rumble Seats to Rockin' Vans," in David L. Lewis and Laurence Goldstein, eds., *The Automobile and American Culture* (Ann Arbor: University of Michigan Press, 1983), p. 125.

36. Glenn A. Niemeyer, "Ransom Eli Olds," in *Dictionary of American Biography,* supp. 4 (New York: Scribner's, 1974), p. 638.
37. Davis, *Conspicuous,* p. 55. See also May, *Olds,* pp. 187–188.
38. Davis, *Conspicuous,* p. 53.
39. Vanessa O'Connell and Joe White, "After Decades of Brand Bodywork, GM Parks Oldsmobile—for Good," *Wall Street Journal,* December 13, 2000, p. B1.
40. Davis, *Conspicuous,* p. 55.
41. Sophocles, *Antigone,* in E. F. Watling, trans., *Sophocles: The Theban Plays* (Baltimore: Penguin, 1960), p. 135.
42. This example is derived from the discussion by Marc Bloch in *The Historian's Craft* (New York: Vintage, 1953), pp. 113–116.
43. This is the figure Nevins and Hill use. See *Ford: The Times,* pp. 193–194. Statistics on the early manufacture of automobiles vary with the source from which they are taken.
44. Davis, *Conspicuous,* following p. 83.
45. Quoted in Jardim, *Ford,* p. 35. See also Lewis, p. 230. Lewis and Jardim both report this quotation as fact. This quotation is provided in Harry Bennett with Paul Marcus, *Ford: We Never Called Him Henry* (New York: TOR, 1987), p. 83.
46. Davis, *Conspicuous,* p. 124.
47. Jardim, *Ford,* p. 133; Nevins and Hill, *Ford: Expansion,* p. 23.
48. Nevins and Hill, *Ford: Expansion,* p. 23.
49. Ibid., p. 24.
50. Jardim, *Ford,* p. 133.
51. Lewis, *Image,* p. 90.
52. Louis P. Lochner, *Henry Ford—America's Don Quixote* (New York: International, 1925), pp. 214–220; Nevins and Hill, *Ford: Expansion,* pp. 55 and 26–85 passim.
53. Nevins and Hill, *Ford: Expansion,* pp. 82–85.
54. Quoted in Jardim, *Ford,* p. 133.
55. David Hackett Fischer, *Historians' Fallacies: Toward a Logic of Historical Thought* (New York: Harper and Row, 1970), p. 14.
56. Nevins and Hill, *Ford: Expansion,* pp. 1–85.
57. Ibid., pp. 32–34.
58. Harry Barnard, *Independent Man: The Life of Senator James Couzens* (New York: Scribner's, 1958), pp. 3–6, 99–100.
59. Nevins and Hill, *Ford: Expansion,* pp. 53–54.
60. Barnard, *Independent Man,* p. 100.
61. Ibid.
62. Nevins and Hill, *Ford: Expansion,* p. 29.

63. Davis, *Conspicuous*, p. 177.
64. Nevins and Hill, *Ford: Expansion*, p. 120.
65. Davis, *Conspicuous*, p. 183.
66. Nevins and Hill, *Ford: Decline*, pp. 166–167.
67. See, e.g., the review of the Jardim book by Robert J. Brugger in the *Business History Review*, vol. 48, no. 4 (Winter 1974), pp. 565–567. It is important for the historian to extract insight from psychiatry and psychology without forcing his or her subject into the sometimes procrustean models of those disciplines. For a thought-provoking discussion, see Fred Weinstein and Gerald M. Platt, "The Coming Crisis in Psychohistory," *Journal of Modern History*, vol. 47 (June 1975), pp. 202–228.
68. Erik H. Erikson, *Young Man Luther: A Study in Psychoanalysis and History* (New York: Norton, 1958), pp. 170–222.
69. Jardim, *Ford*, p. 133. Italics added. The preceding discussion of Ford's pacifism draws heavily on Jardim's observations.
70. Lewis, *Image*, p. 139. David L. Lewis provides the best summary of Ford's anti-Semitism. See especially pp. 135–159.
71. Ibid., pp. 138–139.
72. Ibid., p. 139.
73. Ibid., p. 143.
74. Ibid., quoted on p. 143.
75. Von Schirach was sentenced to twenty years in prison.
76. Lewis, *Image*, pp. 143, 135–159 passim., and the accompanying footnotes on pp. 509–513.
77. See, for example, Lewis, *Image*, pp. 135–159; Albert Lee, *Henry Ford and the Jews* (New York: Stein and Day, 1980).
78. For the Nevins and Hill treatment of Ford's anti-Semitism, see *Ford: Expansion*, pp. 311–323.
79. For an excellent example, see the letter from Ernest Kanzler to Ford in 1926, which was soon followed by Kanzler's firing. Jardim, *Ford*, pp. 217–220.
80. John Côté Dahlinger with Frances Spatz Leighton, *The Secret Life of Henry Ford* (Indianapolis: Bobbs-Merrill, 1978), pp. 1–32. John C. Dahlinger has written not only about the affair his mother, Evangeline Côté Dahlinger, had with Ford; he has bluntly asserted: "I am Henry Ford's son." This may be true, although, as he has also written, "I was not there to witness my conception." Evangeline Dahlinger was married to Raymond C. Dahlinger, a Ford employee.
81. Lewis, *Image*, pp. 365–377, 407–408.
82. Samuel S. Marquis, *Henry Ford: An Interpretation* (Boston: Little, Brown, 1923), p. 160.
83. Peter Collier and David Horowitz, *The Fords: An American Epic* (New York: Summit, 1987), p. 437.
84. Nevins with Hill, *Ford: The Times*, p. 40.
85. Ibid., p. 31.
86. For Detroit statistics, see *Report of the Social Statistics of Cities* (Washington, D.C.: Government Printing Office, 1887), p. 598. For Michigan statistics, see *The Ninth Census of the United States—A Compendium* (Washington, D.C.: Government Printing Office, 1872), pp. 8–9.

87. This discussion draws on Nevins with Hill, *Ford: The Times,* pp. 1–53. The idea of referencing de Tocqueville came from Robert Lacey, *Ford: The Men and the Machine* (Boston: Little, Brown, 1986), pp. 3–4. See Alexis de Tocqueville, *Democracy in America* (New York: Vintage, 1945) and George W. Pierson, *Tocqueville and Beaumont in America* (New York: Oxford University Press, 1938), pp. 239, 282–293.

88. Nevins with Hill, *Ford: The Times,* p. 42.

89. Ibid.

90. Ibid., pp. 49–50.

91. Justin Kaplan, *Mr. Clemens and Mark Twain* (New York: Pocket Books, 1966), pp. 395–396.

92. Nevins with Hill, *Ford: The Times,* pp. 52 and 51–53 passim.

93. Ibid., p. 51.

94. Ibid., p. 54.

95. Ibid., pp. 72–73.

96. Ibid., p. 58.

97. Elizabeth Brayer, *George Eastman: A Biography* (Baltimore: Johns Hopkins University Press, 1996), p. 409.

98. Nevins with Hill, *Ford: The Times,* pp. 653–655. See Margaret Ford Ruddiman, "Reminiscences," in the Henry Ford Museum Archives, Dearborn; and idem, "Memories of My Brother Henry Ford," *Michigan History,* vol. 37, no. 3 (September, 1953), pp. 225–275.

99. At least they do for Jardim and for me. James T. Patterson, one reviewer of Jardim's book, found Jardim's reliance on Ruddiman ("who argued retrospectively [in the 1950s!]—as well a dutiful daughter might—that Ford got along with his father") less than satisfying. James T. Patterson, "The Uses of Techno-Psychohistory," *Journal of Interdisciplinary History,* vol. 2, no. 4 (Spring 1972), p. 475.

100. Quoted in Jardim, *Ford,* pp. 167–168.

101. Ibid., pp. 170–171. Once again, this account closely follows Jardim's, by which I am very impressed.

102. Tedlow, *New,* p. 161.

103. Knudsen made this observation when he left. Nevins and Hill, *Ford: Expansion,* p. 168.

104. Jardim, *Ford,* p. 189.

105. Ibid., p. 216.

106. Collier and Horowitz, *Fords,* pp. 195–196.

107. Nevins with Hill, *Ford: The Times,* pp. 64–65 and 74–91.

108. Ibid., p. 107.

109. Ibid., p. 152.

110. Lacey, *Ford,* p. 39.

111. Bruce Lansky, *10,000 Baby Names* (New York: Meadow Brook, 1985), p. 94.

112. The best book on the Edsel is G Gayle Warnock (apparently there is no period after the first initial in Mr. Warnock's name), *The Edsel Affair* (Paradise Valley, Ariz.: Pro West, 1980).

113. Nevins with Hill, *Ford: The Times,* pp. 154–157.

114. Hughes, *Few,* p. 286.

115. Nevins with Hill, *Ford: The Times,* p. 160.

116. Quoted in Jardim, *Ford,* p. 184.
117. Nevins with Hill, *Ford: The Times,* pp. 166–167.
118. Davis, *Conspicuous,* p. 62.
119. Nevins with Hill, *Ford: The Times,* p. 176.
120. Ibid., p. 177.
121. Ibid., pp. 175–193; Davis, *Conspicuous,* p. 62.
122. Nevins with Hill, *Ford: The Times,* pp. 175–177, 184, 190–191, 202–207, 213, 237–239.
123. Tedlow, *New,* pp. 115–118.
124. Donald T. Critchlow, *Studebaker: The Life and Death of an American Corporation* (Bloomington: Indiana University Press, 1996), pp. 44–45.
125. See Robert Paul Thomas, "Business Failures in the Automobile Industry, 1895–1910," *Papers Presented at the Annual Business History Conference* (Kent, Ohio: Kent State University Press, 1965), pp. 11–30.
126. Barnard, *Independent,* pp. 41–42; Nevins and Hill, *Ford: Expansion,* p. 110.
127. The company built the three-story brick plant on Piquette Avenue in 1905. Charles E. Sorensen with Samuel T. Williamson, *My Forty Years With Ford* (New York: Norton, 1956), pp. 72–73.
128. Hounshell, *Mass Production,* p. 226.
129. Nevins with Hill, *Ford: The Times,* p. 648.
130. Nevins and Hill, *Ford: Expansion,* pp. 200–216, 279–299. Workforce statistics appear on p. 687.
131. Lewis, *Image,* p. 43. Lewis notes that Ford's partner James Couzens was making similar statements in 1906. Ibid., pp. 494–495, n. 14. The television text of Ford's statement is ". . . so low that no man or woman making a good salary . . ."
132. Nevins with Hill, *Ford: The Times,* p. 271.
133. For the financing of the Ford Motor Company in 1903, see Davis, *Conspicuous,* pp. 118–120.
134. Nevins with Hill, *Ford: The Times,* pp. 275–276.
135. These issues are discussed in Tedlow, *New,* pp. 112–181 passim.
136. Sorenson, *Ford,* p. 76.
137. Nevins with Hill, *Ford: The Times,* p. 275.
138. Ibid., pp. 323–353, 387–414.
139. Nevins and Hill, *Ford: Expansion,* pp. 430–432, 409–436 passim.
140. Hounshell, *Mass Production,* p. 223.
141. Sorenson, *Ford,* pp. 54, 45–55.
142. Nevins with Hill, *Ford: The Times,* pp. 576–577.
143. John Kenneth Galbraith, "Was Ford a Fraud?" in *The Liberal Hour* (Boston: Houghton Mifflin, 1960), pp. 117–137. See also Robert Paul Thomas, "The Automobile Industry and Its Tycoon," *Explorations in Entrepreneurial History,* vol. 6, no. 2 (1969), pp. 139–157, and Keith Sward, *The Legend of Henry Ford* (New York: Atheneum, 1968).
144. Nevins with Hill, *Ford: The Times,* p. 243. For Couzens's biography, see Barnard, *Independent.* Norval Hawkins, the able Ford sales manager, said of Couzens in 1927, "Mr. Couzens was a very remarkable man, as remarkable in many ways as Mr. Ford. Mr. Couzens was responsible for at least half of the success of the Ford Motor Company. . . ." Ibid., p. 7.

145. A statement to this effect is quoted in a review of *Ford: The Times,* by Harold U. Faulkner in the *American Historical Review,* vol. 59, no. 4 (July 1954), pp. 956–957. I have not been able to locate the quotation to which Faulkner refers in the Nevins book itself.

146. John A. Byrne, *The Whiz Kids: The Founding Fathers of American Business—and the Legacy They Left Us* (New York: Doubleday, 1993), pp. 343–344.

147. Nevins with Hill, *Ford: The Times,* p. 452. From 1908 to 1912 and again from 1925 to 1927 the Model T was made available in a small selection of colors. See ibid., pp. 394–395, and Nevins and Hill, *Ford: Expansion,* p. 400.

148. The precise statistic is 435,676 according to Jerry Heasley, *The Production Figure Book for U.S. Cars* (Osceola, Wis.: Motorbooks International, 1977), p. 41.

149. I have learned, much to my surprise, that many people under the age of thirty-five do not know that "Tin Lizzie" was the jocularly affectionate nickname for the Model T Ford. It is short for "Tin Limousine." William and Mary Morris, *Dictionary of Word and Phrase Origins* (New York: Harper and Row, 1967), vol. 2, p. 97.

150. Collier and Horowitz, *Fords,* p. 291.

151. William J. Abernathy, *The Productivity Dilemma: Roadblock to Innovation in the Automobile Industry* (Baltimore: Johns Hopkins University Press, 1978), p. 18.

152. Nevins and Hill, *Ford: Expansion,* p. 388.

153. Nevins with Hill, *Ford: The Times,* p. 388.

154. Lewis, *Image,* p. 95.

155. For mass production in the automobile industry, see Nevins with Hill, *Ford: The Times,* pp. 447–480; Hounshell, *Mass Production,* pp. 216–330; and James P. Womack, Daniel T. Jones, and Daniel Roos, *The Machine That Changed the World: The Story of Lean Production* (New York: HarperPerennial, 1990), pp. 21–47.

156. Quoted in Tedlow, *New,* p. 123.

157. Abernathy, *Dilemma,* p. 219. Writing in 1978, Abernathy explained: "[B]oth the Oldsmobile and Ford's Model T were initially well-defined and unique entities. Today, however, little is communicated about a car by saying it is an Oldsmobile. To say that it was produced in a General Motors assembly plant for midsized Buicks, Oldsmobiles, and Pontiacs (a 'BOP' plant) is much more informative." Ibid., p. 48.

158. The prices can be found in Nevins with Hill, *Ford: The Times,* pp. 646–647. Pictures of the various body types can be found in Michael Allen, *Ford Model T: Super Profile* (Sparkford U.K.: Haynes Publishing Group, 1987), pp. 17–56. For a useful description of body style designations with accompanying drawings, see Pat Chappell, *Standard Catalog of Chevrolet, 1912–1990* (Iola, Wis.: Krause, 1990), pp. 7–9.

159. Nevins with Hill, *Ford: The Times,* p. 647.

160. Lewis, *Image,* p. 122.

161. Womack, Jones, and Roos, *Machine,* p. 38. This advice appears on p. 6 of the sixth edition of the *Instruction Book for Model T Cars,* a reprinted copy (March 1954) of which is available in Baker Library of the Harvard Business School.

162. The phrase is Daniel Bell's in "The Company He Keeps," *New York Review of Books,* March 19, 1964, p. 13.

163. Jonathan Hughes, *American Economic History* (Glenview, Ill.: Scott, Foresman, 1987), p. 233.

164. Womack, Jones, and Roos, *Machine,* p. 38.

165. Allen, *Ford Model T,* pp. 11–12.

166. Ibid., p. 8.

167. Hounshell, *Mass Production,* pp. 273–276. See also Abernathy, *Dilemma,* pp. 13–19, 183–222 and Hounshell's comment on Abernathy in *Mass Production,* p. 378, n. 9.

168. Hounshell, *Mass Production,* p. 276.

169. Alfred P. Sloan Jr., *My Years with General Motors* (Garden City, N.Y.: Doubleday, 1972), p. 186.

170. Hounshell, *Mass Production,* p. 275. Italics added.

171. In the words of Kim B. Clark and Takahiro Fujimoto, "A product begins as a concept, part of a strategy for attracting and satisfying customers." *Product Development Performance: Strategy, Organization, and Management in the World Auto Industry* (Boston: Harvard Business School Press, 1991), p. 129.

172. Hounshell, *Mass Production,* p. 275.

173. Ibid.

174. Nevins with Hill, *Ford: The Times,* pp. 387–414.

175. Tedlow, *New,* p. 125.

176. Hounshell, *Mass Production,* p. 233.

177. Ibid., p. 233; Nevins with Hill, *Ford: The Times,* p. 464.

178. Tedlow, *New,* p. 137.

179. Womack, Jones, and Roos, *Machine,* pp. 26–27.

180. Hounshell, *Mass Production,* pp. 222–223, 239.

181. Sorensen, *Ford,* p. 128.

182. Ibid., p. 131.

183. Hounshell, *Mass Production,* pp. 246–247.

184. Ibid., pp. 247–248.

185. Alfred D. Chandler, Jr., *Giant Enterprise: Ford, General Motors, and the Automotive Industry* (New York: Harcourt, Brace and World, 1964), p. 26.

186. Hounshell, *Mass Production,* p. 228.

187. Nevins with Hill, *Ford: The Times,* p. 447.

188. Lewis, *Image,* pp. 69–77. It should be noted that the International Workers of the World, a radical labor organization, had been encouraging labor unrest in Detroit during 1913. Daniel M. G. Raff, "Looking Back at the Five-Dollar Day," *Harvard Business Review* (January–February, 1989), pp. 180–182.

189. Lewis, *Image,* p. 70.

190. Daniel M. G. Raff and Lawrence H. Summers, "Did Henry Ford Pay Efficiency Wages?" *Journal of Labor Economics,* vol. 5, no. 4, pt. 2 (1987), p. 563.

191. Ibid., pp. 583–584.

192. Lewis, *Image,* p. 75.

193. Ibid., pp. 76 and 69–77.

194. For Coca-Cola and its formula, see Tedlow, *New,* pp. 22–111, 344–375; Roger Enrico and Jesse Kornbluth, *The Other Guy Blinked: And Other*

Dispatches from the Cola Wars (New York: Bantam, 1986); Thomas Oliver, *The Real Coke, the Real Story* (New York: Random House, 1986). See also "Ten Years Later, Coca-Cola Laughs at 'New Coke'" *New York Times,* April 11, 1995.

195. Nevins and Hill, *Ford: Expansion,* pp. 171–199.
196. Sloan, *General Motors,* p. 23.
197. Nevins and Hill, *Ford: Expansion,* p. 197.
198. Heasley, *U.S. Cars,* p. 58.
199. Chandler *Enterprise,* p. 33.
200. Tedlow, *New,* p. 313.
201. Ibid., p. 139.
202. Ibid., p. 137.
203. Hughes, *Few,* p. 329.
204. Nevins and Hill, *Ford: Expansion,* p. 415.
205. Ibid., p. 437
206. William J. Abernathy and Kenneth Wayne, "Limits of the Learning Curve," *Harvard Business Review* (September–October 1974), pp. 111–112.
207. Nevins and Hill, *Ford: Expansion,* p. 451.
208. This phrase is from David Riesman and Eric Larrabee, "Autos in America," in David Riesman, ed., *Abundance for What? And Other Essays* (Garden City, N.Y.: Doubleday, 1964), p. 293.
209. For the shutdown at the Rouge, see Hounshell, *Mass Production,* pp. 281–282.
210. Abernathy and Wayne estimate the cost at $200 million. "Learning Curve," p. 115. Nevins and Hill estimate $250 million. *Ford: Expansion,* p. 458. Abernathy and Wayne state that Ford "laid off 60,000 workers in Detroit alone." "Learning Curve," p. 115. Nevins and Hill acknowledge that Ford dealers "suffered, some becoming bankrupt . . ." waiting for the Model A. Nevertheless, they assert that dealer turnover was lower in 1927 than it had been in either of the preceding two years. *Ford: Expansion,* p. 457.
211. Nevins and Hill, *Ford: Expansion,* p. 454.
212. Unit share of the domestic automobile market in 1925 was: Ford—40.02 percent, General Motors—19.97 percent, and Chrysler—3.6 percent. In 1927 share figures were: Ford—9.32 percent, General Motors—43.49 percent, and Chrysler—6.22 percent. Chandler, *Enterprise,* p. 3.
213. This account is based upon Nevins and Hill, *Ford: Expansion,* pp. 437–478, and Hounshell, *Mass Production,* pp. 275–301.
214. Hounshell, *Mass Production,* p. 281. See also Tedlow, *New,* p. 163, and Jardim, *Ford,* p. 240.
215. Hounshell, *Mass Production,* p. 292.
216. Ibid., p. 297.
217. Heasley, *U.S. Cars,* p. 34.
218. Nevins and Hill, *Ford: Decline,* p. 59.
219. Chandler, *Enterprise,* p. 3. This was in a rising market. Nineteen thirty-seven was a false dawn of the return of prosperity. Domestic passenger car sales of almost 4 million were higher than they had been since 1929 and higher than they would be again until 1949. Ibid., p. 4.
220. Ibid., pp. 3–7.

221. Nevins and Hill, *Ford: Decline,* p. 64.
222. Ibid., p. 67.
223. Ibid., p. 75. According to Nevins and Hill, Zephyr sales in 1937 were 25,186. According to another source, they were 29,997. Heasley, *U.S. Cars,* p. 67. A "model year" traditionally begins in the autumn of the previous year. Thus, the 1939 model year began in the autumn of 1938.
224. Nevins and Hill, *Ford: Decline,* pp. 119, 129.
225. Ibid., p. 119. Italics in original.
226. Ibid., pp. 120–132; Chandler, *Enterprise,* p. 4.
227. Quoted in Sidney Fine, *Sit-Down* (Ann Arbor: University of Michigan Press, 1969), p. 133. The classic discussion of divisionalization at General Motors during this period and of the relationship between diversification and divisionalization in general is Alfred D. Chandler, Jr., *Strategy and Structure: Chapters in the History of the American Industrial Enterprise* (Cambridge: MIT Press, 1962), pp. 52–162 and passim.
228. Sloan, *General Motors,* pp. 63–77.
229. Ibid.
230. Nevins and Hill, *Ford: Decline,* pp. 119–120.
231. Ibid., p. 132.
232. Ibid., pp. 109–132.
233. Bennett's career is well chronicled in Nevins and Hill, *Ford: Expansion* and *Ford: Decline.* Bennett's view of his career, for what it may be worth, is presented in Bennett, *Henry.*
234. Nevins and Hill, *Ford: Decline,* pp. 242, 272.
235. Ibid., p. 243.
236. Ibid., pp. 246–248.
237. Collier and Horowitz, *Fords,* p. 197.
238. Henry Ford II was born on September 4, 1917.
239. Nevins and Hill, *Ford: Decline,* p. 257.
240. Ibid., p. 268.
241. Collier and Horowitz, *Fords,* p. 218.
242. Nevins and Hill, *Ford: Decline,* p. 255. Italics in original.
243. Collier and Horowitz, *Fords,* p. 222.
244. Ibid.
245. Ibid., p. 191.
246. Ibid., pp. 94–95.
247. Lewis, *Image,* p. 407.
248. Ibid.
249. Collier and Horowitz, *Fords,* pp. 435–436.
250. Lewis, *Image,* p. 473.
251. Collier and Horowitz, *Fords,* p. 226.
252. Lewis, *Image,* p. 473.
253. Ibid., p. 476.
254. Davis, *Conspicuous,* p. ix.
255. James A. Ward, *The Fall of the Packard Motor Car Company* (Stanford, Calif.: Stanford University Press, 1995), p. 9.
256. Ibid., p. 37.
257. Ibid., p. 10.
258. Lewis, *Image,* p. 476.
259. Galbraith, *Liberal,* p. 129.

260. See Sigmund Diamond, *The Reputation of the American Businessman* (Cambridge, Mass.: Harvard University Press, 1955), pp. 142–175. According to the obituary in the *New York Times*, "To a peculiar degree [Ford] was the embodiment of America in the industrial revolution. . . ." Ibid., p. 143.
261. Ibid., pp. 164–165.
262. Brugger, review of Jardim's *Ford*, p. 566.

PART TWO: THE HEART OF THE AMERICAN CENTURY
Introduction

1. Henry R. Luce, "The American Century," *Life*, February 17, 1941, pp. 61–65. For reactions to Luce's essay, see James L. Baughman, *Henry R. Luce and the Rise of the American News Media* (Boston: Twayne, 1987), pp. 130–133.
2. Thomas K. McCraw, *American Business: 1920–2000: How It Worked* (Wheeling, Ill.: Harlan Davidson, 2000), pp. 73–102.
3. Richard S. Tedlow, *The Rise of the American Business Corporation* (Chur, Switzerland: Harwood Academic Publishers, 1991), pp. 1–2.
4. See David M. Potter, *People of Plenty: Economic Abundance and the American Character* (Chicago: University of Chicago Press, 1954).
5. Lawrence G. Foster, *Robert Wood Johnson: The Gentleman Rebel* (State College, Penn.: Lillian Press, 1999). See pages 466–467 for Johnson's comments on Revlon advertising.
6. Mark S. Foster, *Henry J. Kaiser: Builder in the Modern American West* (Austin: University of Texas Press, 1989); idem., "Giant of the West: Henry J. Kaiser and Regional Industrialization, 1930–1950," *Business History Review*, vol. 59, no. 1 (Spring 1985), pp. 1–23.
7. See Thomas Parke Hughes, *American Genesis: A Century of Invention and Technological Enthusiasm* (New York: Viking, 1989).

Chapter 4: Thomas J. Watson Sr.

1. "Thomas J. Watson Sr. Is Dead; IBM Board Chairman Was 82," *New York Times*, June 20, 1956, pp. 1, 31.
2. "Watson Funeral Attended by 1,200," *New York Times*, June 22, 1956.
3. "Multifarious Sherman Fairchild," *Fortune* (May 1960), p. 171.
4. "Watson Funeral," *New York Times;* "President Pays Tribute," *New York Times*, June 20, 1956.
5. Louise Whitfield Carnegie was born on March 7, 1857, and died on June 24, 1946. See "Oakland: Louise Whitfield Carnegie," http://www.clpgh.org/exhibit/neighborhoods/oakland/oak_n 101.html.
6. According to journalist Paul Carroll, IBM was in the early 1990s "easily the biggest employer" in the Hudson River valley, "with ten times as many jobs in some counties as the next-largest employer." In the early 1980s, unemployment in the region was 3 percent. It jumped to 7 percent following the massive layoffs of the early 1990s. Paul Carroll, *Big Blues: The Unmaking of IBM* (New York: Crown, 1993), p. 364.

7. "Watson Funeral," *New York Times.*

8. Emerson W. Pugh, *Building IBM: Shaping an Industry and Its Technology* (Cambridge, Mass.: MIT Press, 1995), pp. 109, 112, and 109–116 passim.

9. Thomas J. Watson, *Men—Minutes—Money: A Collection of Excerpts from Talks and Messages Delivered and Written at Various Times* (New York: International Business Machines, 1934), p. 82. Italics in original.

10. Brayer, *Eastman,* pp. 513–514, 581, n. 6.

11. Thomas J. Watson, "George Eastman, Pioneer," in Watson, *Men,* pp. 477, 474–478.

12. Thomas Graham Belden and Marva Robins Belden, *The Lengthening Shadow: The Life of Thomas J. Watson* (Boston: Little, Brown, 1962), pp. 19–20.

13. William Rodgers, *Think: A Biography of the Watsons and IBM* (New York: Stein and Day, 1969), p. 30.

14. Belden and Belden, *Shadow,* pp. 23–24.

15. Ibid., pp. 26–27.

16. Rodgers, *Think,* p. 41; *Trow's General Directory of the Boroughs of Manhattan and Bronx* (New York: Trow, 1904), p. 145.

17. Rodgers, *Think,* p. 44.

18. Rodgers uses the term "competition department." *Think,* p. 43. On its own stationery, this department used the more blunt "Opposition Department." See for example, "Circular Letter," February 4, 1892, reproduced in Richard L. Crandall and Sam Robins, *The Incorruptible Cashier: The Formation of an Industry, 1876–1890,* vol. 1 (New York: Vestal Press, 1988), p. 35. According to the expert on this company, Walter A. Friedman, an "opposition department" was established in November 1891 and the name was later changed to "competition." "Building an Efficient Pyramid: John H. Patterson and the Sales and Competition Strategy of the National Cash Register Company, 1884–1922" (unpublished manuscript, author's possession). See also Friedman's "John H. Patterson and the Sales Strategy of the National Cash Register Company, 1884 to 1922," *Business History Review,* vol. 72, no. 4 (Winter 1998), pp. 552–584. I have benefited from numerous conversations with Walter Friedman about selling various kinds of products including cash registers and adding machines during the late nineteenth century.

19. According to Judge Howard C. Hollister of the United States District Court for the Western Division of the Southern District of Ohio:

> Of course, acts of violence by agents of the National Cash Register Company upon agents of its competitors are not immediately involved in the question under discussion, because upon objection by the defendants to the introduction by the Government of testimony tending to show instances of fisticuffs between the agents of the National and the agents of competitors, the testimony was excluded from the consideration of the jury, for the reason, among others, that it might be difficult to determine who was immediately to blame for such occurrences, and it would be wandering from the issues to try incidental issues raised by charges of assault or assault and battery.

United States v. Patterson et al. (District Court, S.D. Ohio, W.D., February 3, 1913), 205 *Federal Reporter,* 301.

20. Crandall and Robins, *Cashier,* p. 35.

21. "Knocker Catalogue" (Dayton, Ohio: National Cash Register Co.) This document is available in Baker Library at the Harvard Business School.

22. Belden and Belden, *Shadow,* p. 68.

23. Rodgers, *Think,* p. 54; *United States v. Patterson et al.,* 201 Fed. Rep., 697.

24. Rodgers, *Think,* pp. 59–60. The sentences are published in Roger Shale, comp., *Decrees and Judgments in Federal Anti-Trust Cases, July 2, 1890–January 1, 1918* (Washington, D.C.: Government Printing Office, 1918), pp. 795–798; $5,000 in 1913 is the equivalent of almost $87,000 in 2000.

25. For a more moderate treatment of these issues, see Friedman, "Pyramid."

26. Thomas J. Watson Jr. and Peter Petre, *Father, Son & Co.: My Life at IBM and Beyond* (New York: Bantam, 1990), p. 12. For the history of interpersonal selling, see Walter A. Friedman, "The Peddler's Progress: Salesmanship, Science, and Magic, 1880–1940" (unpublished doctoral dissertation, Columbia University, 1996). Friedman's bibliography is especially useful. For a late-nineteenth-century exposé of selling scams, see Bates Harrington, *How 'tis Done: A Thorough Ventilation of the Numerous Schemes Conducted by Wandering Canvassers Together with the Various Advertising Dodges for the Swindling of the Public* (Chicago: Fidelity Publishing Company, 1879).

27. Samuel Crowther, *John H. Patterson: Pioneer in Industrial Welfare* (Garden City, N.Y.: Garden City Publishing, 1926), p. 29. This quotation bears a similarity to Carnegie's attitude about useful knowledge. On a cruise in the Pacific in 1878, Carnegie, out of idle curiosity, decided to attend a sermon delivered by a missionary on his way to the Orient. His comment: "The sermon is over. Pshaw! He spent the morning attempting to prove to us that the wine Christ made at the marriage feast was not fermented, as if it mattered, or as if this could ever be known!" Wall, *Carnegie,* p. 367.

28. Crowther, *Patterson,* p. 29.

29. Stanley C. Allyn, *My Half Century with NCR* (New York: McGraw-Hill, 1967). Apparently, Patterson had convinced himself that Wisconsin's students were, in Allyn's words, "[c]ountry boys who knew how to work and wanted to work. . . ." Ibid., pp. 9–10.

30. Crowther, *Patterson,* pp. 34–35.

31. Ibid., pp. 34–51.

32. Ibid., pp. 43–48.

33. Ibid., pp. 71–72.

34. Ibid., pp. 79–80.

35. Ibid., p. 59.

36. Friedman, "Pyramid."

37. Crowther, *Patterson,* p. 81.

38. Ibid., pp. 81–82.

39. Richard H. Grant Jr. and Teri E. Denlinger, *Freewheeling: Eighty Years of Observations by the Patriarch of Reynolds and Reynolds* (Dayton, Ohio: Landfall Press, 1994), p. 45.

40. Crowther, *Patterson*, p. 104.
41. Allyn, *Half Century*, p. 68.
42. Ibid.
43. There is a very large literature on Taylor. The place to begin is with Daniel Nelson, *Frederick W. Taylor and the Rise of Scientific Management* (Madison: University of Wisconsin Press, 1980).
44. Ibid., p. 7.
45. Ibid., p. 8.
46. Ibid., p. 20.
47. For small-scale merchants and credit in the history of retailing (in this case in Canada), see David Monod, *Store Wars: Shopkeepers and the Culture of Mass Marketing, 1890–1939* (Toronto: University of Toronto Press, 1996).
48. Crowther, *Patterson*, p. 94.
49. Ibid., p. 92.
50. Ibid., pp. 87–88.
51. Ibid., p. 119.
52. Ibid., pp. 163–164.
53. Ibid., p. 230.
54. Ibid., p. 118.
55. Ibid., pp. 211–212.
56. Rodgers, *Think*, pp. 46–49.
57. Crowther, *Patterson*, p. 261.
58. For a description of the quota system at NCR, see Roy W. Johnson and Russell W. Lynch, *The Sales Strategy of John H. Patterson* (Chicago: Dartnell, 1932), pp. 252–262.
59. Crowther, *Patterson*, p. 88.
60. Ibid., pp. 160–161.
61. Alfred D. Chandler, Jr., *The Visible Hand: The Managerial Revolution in American Business* (Cambridge, Mass.: Harvard University Press, 1977), pp. 285–314.
62. Johnson and Lynch, *Strategy*, pp. 253–254. Italics added.
63. Ibid., pp. 254–255.
64. Isaac F. Marcosson, *Wherever Men Trade: The Romance of the Cash Register* (New York: Dodd, Mead, 1948), p. 32.
65. Ibid., p. 39.
66. Crowther, *Patterson*, p. 105.
67. Ibid., p. 111.
68. Grant and Denlinger, *Freewheeling*, p. 45.
69. Crowther, *Patterson*, pp. 128–129.
70. Ibid., pp. 116–117. Italics added.
71. Alfred P. Sloan Jr., *My Years with General Motors* (Garden City, N.Y.: Doubleday, 1972), p. 326.
72. Crowther, *Patterson*, pp. 166–167.
73. Ibid., p. 124.
74. Johnson and Lynch, *Strategy*, p. 231.
75. Crowther, *Patterson*, p. 238.
76. Rodgers, *Think*, p. 48.
77. Johnson and Lynch, *Strategy*, facing p. 243.
78. Crowther, *Patterson*, p. 136.

79. Rodgers, *Think*, pp. 50–51.
80. Ibid., pp. 50–54.
81. Ibid., p. 56.
82. Crowther, *Patterson*, pp. 302–303.
83. Rodgers, *Think*, p. 64.
84. Ibid., pp. 64–65.
85. For a good discussion, see Friedman, "Pyramid."
86. Johnson and Lynch, *Strategy*, facing p. 288. In 1913, $50,000 was the equivalent of almost $870,000 in 2000.
87. Rodgers, *Think*, p. 66.
89. Belden and Belden, *Shadow*, p. 10.
90. Rodgers, *Think*, p. 66.
91. Leo Tolstoy, *The Death of Ivan Ilyich* (Toronto: Bantam, 1981), p. 37.
92. Watson to Grant, November 29, 1913, photocopied in Grant and Denlinger, *Freewheeling*, p. 25.
93. Watson, *Father*, p. 14.
94. Ibid. For Deeds, see Isaac F. Marcosson, *Colonel Deeds: Industrial Builder* (New York: Dodd, Mead, 1947).
95. Watson, *Father*, p. 14. It is noteworthy that the son remembered Watson as continuing to refer to Patterson as "Mr."
96. Rodgers, *Think*, p. 102.
97. Ibid., p. 194.
98. Emerson W. Pugh, *Building IBM: Shaping an Industry and Its Technology* (Cambridge, Mass.: MIT Press, 1995), pp. 250–251.
99. Belden and Belden, *Shadow*, p. 4.
100. Ibid., p. 31.
101. Ibid., pp. 5, 11.
102. Ibid., p. 24.
103. Ibid., p. 5.
104. Ibid.
105. Ibid., pp. 24–25.
106. Ibid., p. 31.
107. Ibid., p. 89; Watson, *Father*, p. 15.
108. Watson, *Father*, pp. 14–15. According to the Tedlow/Purrington/Bettcher database on CEOs in 1917 (described in note 1 of Chapter 2, on George Eastman), 105 had substantial experience in production, 60 in finance, and 55 in sales. These numbers cannot be translated into percentages due to double counting. Many of our CEOs had substantial experience in more than one functional area. Slightly over two-fifths of our sample had no experience in a family business. One-fifth attained their position because of their managerial success in another company.

    When placed in context, Watson's high standards in selecting new employment and the quality of the offers he received are not surprising. He had built a career as a proven salesman and a proven manager at a widely respected and well-known company. His teacher and mentor was regarded as an eccentric genius.
109. Rodgers, *Think*, p. 64.
110. Belden and Belden, *Shadow*, p. 181.
111. Ibid., p. 94. In 1914, $25,000 was equivalent to just over $430,000 in 2000.

112. Charles R. Flint, *Memories of an Active Life: Men, and Ships, and Sealing Wax* (New York: Putnam, 1923), p. 309.

113. Ibid., pp. 312–314.

114. "George Winthrop Fairchild," *Biographical Directory of the United States Congress, 1774–1989,* Bicentennial ed. (Washington, D.C.: U.S. Government Printing Office, 1989), p. 980.

115. Belden and Belden, *Shadow,* p. 92; Saul Engelbourg, *International Business Machines: A Business History* (New York: Arno, 1976), pp. 1–58.

116. Belden and Belden, *Shadow,* p. 92.

117. Engelbourg, *International Business Machines,* pp. 20–27. For Hollerith's biography, see Geoffrey D. Austrian, *Herman Hollerith: Forgotten Giant of Information Processing* (New York: Columbia University Press, 1982). Hollerith is discussed in James W. Cortada, *Before the Computer: IBM, NCR, Burroughs, and Remington Rand and the Industry They Created* (Princeton: Princeton University Press, 1993), pp. 44–63. The best brief treatment is Pugh's *Building IBM,* pp. 1–28.

118. Belden and Belden, *Shadow,* pp. 102–103.

119. Ibid., pp. 103–104.

120. Ibid., p. 93.

121. Pugh, *Building IBM,* p. 29.

122. Belden and Belden, *Shadow,* pp. 94–95.

123. Rodgers, *Think,* pp. 76–77.

124. Watson, *Father,* pp. 148–149.

125. For what "service" meant in the business context, see James W. Prothro, *The Dollar Decade* (Baton Rouge: Louisiana State University Press, 1954). For a brilliant discussion of how businesses present themselves to the public, see Roland Marchand, *Creating the Corporate Soul: The Rise of Public Relations and Corporate Imagery in American Big Business* (Berkeley: University of California Press, 1998).

126. Rodgers, *Think,* p. 52.

127. Watson, *Father,* photograph following p. 114; "International Business Machines," *Fortune* (January 1940), p. 130.

128. Gerald Breckenridge, "Salesman No. 1," *Saturday Evening Post,* May 24, 1941, pp. 10, 11. See Abraham Zaleznik, "Managers and Leaders: Are They Different?" *Harvard Business Review,* vol. 55 (1977), pp. 67–78.

129. Gerald Breckenridge, "Market-Maker: IBM's Watson Proves He's Still Salesman No. 1," *Saturday Evening Post,* May 31, 1941, p. 117.

130. Watson, *Father,* photograph and caption following p. 114.

131. Belden and Belden, *Shadow,* p. 111.

132. Watson, *Father,* photograph and caption following p. 114.

133. The Computing Scales Company was least interesting to Watson and did not do well. He sold it off in 1935 and—to his chagrin—it began making money under its new ownership. The time equipment business did make money, but it became a progressively marginalized distraction. IBM sold it off in 1958. Pugh, *Building IBM,* p. 28.

134. "International Business Machines," *Fortune,* pp. 124, 126.

135. Ibid., p. 126.

136. Belden and Belden, *Shadow,* p. 301.

137. Ibid.; Engelbourg, *IBM,* pp. 272–276.

138. This subject is a lot more interesting than it sounds. There is a useful collection of IBM educational pamphlets in the Baker Library at Harvard Business School. See, for example, *Machine Methods of Accounting: A Manual of the Basic Principles of Operation and Use of International Electric Bookkeeping and Accounting Machines* (New York: IBM, 1936), pp. 3-1–4-15.

139. "International Business Machines," *Fortune*, p. 126.

140. Alfred P. Sloan Jr., *Adventures of a White-Collar Man* (New York: Doubleday, Doran, 1941), pp. 24–25.

141. Breckenridge, "Salesman," p. 38.

142. Pugh, *Building IBM*, p. 55.

143. Ibid., p. 63.

144. Thomas K. McCraw, "Introduction" in idem., ed., *Creating Modern Capitalism: How Entrepreneurs, Companies, and Countries Triumphed in Three Industrial Revolutions* (Cambridge, Mass.: Harvard University Press, 1997), p. 4.

145. Pugh, *Building IBM*, p. 118.

146. Ibid., p. 58.

147. Rodgers, *Think*, pp. 203–210; Stephen E. Ambrose, *Eisenhower: Soldier and President* (New York: Simon and Schuster, 1990), pp. 234–235.

148. Watson, *Father*, pp. 199–220; Pugh, *Building IBM*, pp. 149–150, 357 n. 12; Robert Sobel, *I.B.M.: Colossus in Transition* (New York: Quadrangle, 1981), pp. 120–123.

149. Pugh, *Building IBM*, pp. 109–110. For the Kettering story, see Stuart W. Leslie, *Boss Kettering* (New York: Columbia University Press, 1983). See pp. 41–42 for the founding of Delco.

150. Breckenridge, "Market-Maker," p. 117.

151. Martha F. S. Sanger, *Henry Clay Frick: An Intimate Portrait* (New York: Abbeville Press, 1998).

152. "International Business Machines," *Fortune*, pp. 43, 124.

153. Rodgers, *Think*, p. 193.

154. "International Business Machines," *Fortune*, p. 132.

155. Thomas F. Garbett, *Corporate Advertising: The What, the Why, and the How* (New York: McGraw-Hill, 1981), p. 100.

156. "International Business Machines," *Fortune*, p. 128.

157. Peter F. Drucker, "Thomas Watson's Principles of Modern Management," in *Fifty Who Made the Difference* (New York: Villard Books, 1984), pp. 135–136.

158. Breckenridge, "Salesman," p. 38.

159. Ibid., p. 38.

160. Ibid.

161. Ibid.

162. Ibid.

163. Ibid., p. 41.

164. Martin Mayer, *Madison Avenue, U.S.A.* (New York: Harper & Brothers, 1958), p. 53.

165. Breckenridge, "Salesman," p. 41.

166. Ibid.

167. In 1965, $2,164,000 was the equivalent of $13,700,000 in 2000. In 1956, $209,000 was the equivalent of $1,323,000 in 2000.

168. "Watson Sr. Is Dead," *New York Times*. Most of the above data come from the lengthy obituary in the *Times*.
169. Rodgers, *Think*, pp. 114–115.
170. Richard S. Tedlow, *New and Improved: The Story of Mass Marketing in America* (Boston: Harvard Business School Press, 1996), pp. 30–41.
171. Rodgers, *Think*, p. 115. This analysis relies heavily on William Rodgers's *Think*. For the reader seeking a more favorable treatment of Watson and IBM, see William W. Simmons with Richard B. Elsberry, *Inside IBM: The Watson Years* (Bryn Mawr, Penn.: Dorrance, 1988) and Kevin Maney, "Technology: IBM Founder Wasn't the Bad Guy Book Portrays," *USA Today*, February 14, 2001, p. 10B.
172. Rodgers, *Think*, p. 119.
173. "Watson, Thomas John," in *Who Was Who in America: A Companion Biographical Reference Work to Who's Who in America*, vol. 3 (Chicago: A. N. Marquis, 1960), p. 895; Reese V. Jenkins, "Watson, Thomas John," in John A. Garraty, ed., *Dictionary of American Biography*, supp. 6 (New York: Scribner's, 1980), p. 675.
174. Cedric A. Larson, *Who: Sixty Years of American Eminence* (New York: McDowell, Obolensky, 1958), pp. 120–129, 316–327.
175. Watson, *Father*, p. 162.
176. Ibid., pp. 148–149, 328.
177. Ibid., p. 110.
178. Belden and Belden, *Shadow*, p. 136.
179. For an intriguingly different way of looking at the world, see Howard H. Stevenson, *Do Lunch or Be Lunch: The Power of Predictability in Creating Your Future* (Boston: Harvard Business School Press, 1998).
180. Belden and Belden, *Shadow*, pp. 147–148.
181. Watson, *Father*, p. ix.
182. E. L. Doctorow, *Ragtime* (New York: Bantam, 1975), pp. 158–159.
183. Rowena Olegario, "IBM and the Two Thomas J. Watsons," in McCraw, *Capitalism*, p. 368 (this is the source for the quotation); Carliss Y. Baldwin and Kim B. Clark, *Design Rules: The Power of Modularity*, vol. 1 (Cambridge, Mass.: MIT Press, 2000), pp. 169–194; Emerson W. Pugh, *Memories That Shaped an Industry: Decisions Leading to IBM System/360* (Cambridge, Mass.: MIT Press, 1984). See also Steven W. Usselman, "IBM and Its Imitators: Organizational Capabilities and the Emergence of the International Computer Industry," *Business and Economic History*, vol. 22, no. 2 (Winter 1993), pp. 1–35.
184. Rodgers, *Think*, p. 61.
185. Watson, *Father*, pp. 18–22.
186. Ibid., p. 22.
187. Ibid.
188. Ibid., pp. 137–155.
189. Ibid., pp. 289–297.
190. Ibid., p. 285.
191. "The Greatest Capitalist in History," *Fortune*, August 31, 1987, pp. 24, 24–35.
192. Watson, *Father*, p. 189.
193. Ibid., p. 369.
194. Ibid., pp. 369–384.

195. Ibid., p. 432.
196. Edwin Black, *IBM and the Holocaust: The Strategic Alliance between Nazi Germany and America's Most Powerful Corporation* (New York: Crown, 2001).
197. Ibid., p. 377.

Chapter 5: Charles Revson

1. This quotation is from an interview in 1950 with Martin Revson, Charles's younger brother. Martin was, at the time, Revlon's vice president for sales. This statement is usually attributed to Charles rather than Martin and is usually rendered: "In the factory, we make cosmetics, in the store, we sell hope." See, for example, Andrew Tobias, *Fire and Ice: The Story of Charles Revson—the Man Who Built the Revlon Empire* (New York: William Morrow, 1976), p. 107 and Theodore Levitt, *The Marketing Imagination* (New York: Free Press, 1983), p. 128. This has come to be viewed as one of the classic formulations of the relationship between an actual, physical product and the benefit the consumer perceives the product to be delivering. The formulation has also gained a certain currency as an explanation for why women do, in fact, buy cosmetics. Thus, historian Kathy Peiss entitled her history of cosmetics *Hope in a Jar: The Making of America's Beauty Culture* (New York: Henry Holt, 1998). She refers to this as "Charles Revson's famous phrase" (p. 200). Martin Revson has told me that this statement was first made by him. He cites a *Business Week* article: "Revlon's Formula: Smart Words, Quality, and Freud," *Business Week* (August 12, 1950), pp. 70–76. Soon after this article appeared, as Revson pointed out to me, author S. J. Perelman wrote a part humorous, part serious reaction to the *Business Week* article in *The New Yorker:* S. J. Perelman, "Salesman, Spare that Psyche," *The New Yorker,* November 11, 1950, pp. 40–43. Telephone interview with Martin Revson, January 2, 2000. Peiss's *Hope* contains illuminating discussions of why different segments of America's female population purchased cosmetics and how the nature of demand changed over time.
2. David Packard, *The HP Way: How Bill Hewlett and I Built Our Company* (New York: HarperBusiness, 1995).
3. Tobias, *Fire,* p. 99.
4. Ibid., p. 28.
5. Not only fashion in general but the cosmetics industry specifically was headquartered in New York City through the twentieth century. Helena Rubinstein, Estée Lauder, Elizabeth Arden, and many other independent cosmetics firms (i.e., cosmetics firms which were not divisions of large consumer product or health care companies such as Procter & Gamble and Johnson & Johnson) were founded in New York City. Even Avon Products, the largest and one of the oldest cosmetics companies in the United States, was founded in New York City and is headquartered there at this writing, despite the fact that from its incorporation in 1886 to 1939 Avon's name was the California Perfume Company. See "Avon Products Inc.," in Kimberly N. Hunt and Annamarie L. Sheldon, *Notable Corporate Chronologies,* 2nd ed. (Detroit: Gale Press, 1999),

pp. 157–158, and "Avon," in Tina Grant, ed., *International Directory of Company Histories,* vol. 19. (Detroit: St. James Press, 1998), pp. 26–29. There are, of course, exceptions. Max Factor was founded in Los Angeles and Mary Kay in Dallas.

6. *Toilet Requisites and Druggists' Sundries,* January 1939, p. 25. This was a well-known trade journal. It changed its name to *Beauty Fashion* in 1941, a sign of changing times.

7. When the advertisement just quoted was published, the firm was known as the Revlon Nail Enamel Corporation. Later in 1939, the name was changed to Revlon Products Corporation. *Toilet Requisites and Druggists' Sundries* (May 1939), p. 62.

8. Tobias, *Fire,* p. 50.

9. Ibid.

10. Joseph Revson was born on June 6, 1905. Charles Revson was born on October 11, 1906. According to his birth certificate, his name was Hyman Charles Revson. Martin Revson was born on June 15, 1910. Charles Lachman was born on May 10, 1897. Ancestry.com.

11. The statistics above are from Peter Temin, *Did Monetary Forces Cause the Great Depression?* (New York: Norton, 1976), p. 4.

12. Charles P. Kindleberger, *The World in Depression, 1929–1939* (Berkeley: University of California Press, 1986), pp.110–111.

13. Thomas K. McCraw, *American Business, 1920–2000: How It Worked* (Wheeling, Ill: Harlan Davidson, 2000), p. 38.

14. Heywood Broun, quoted in Irving Bernstein, *Turbulent Years: A History of the American Worker, 1933–1941* (Boston: Houghton, Mifflin, 1971), p. 131.

15. William E. Leuchtenburg, *Franklin D. Roosevelt and the New Deal, 1932–1940* (New York: Harper and Row, 1963), p. 119.

16. Stephen K. Bailey, *Congress Makes a Law: The Story Behind the Employment Act of 1946* (New York: Columbia University Press, 1950), p. 6.

17. Roosevelt's first inaugural address is reproduced in its entirety in the standard edition of Roosevelt's public papers: Samuel I. Rosenman, ed., *The Public Papers and Addresses of Franklin D. Roosevelt* (New York: 1938–1950—vols. 1–5, Random House; vols. 6–9, Macmillan; vols. 10–13, Harper and Brothers).

18. Tobias, *Fire,* p. 26.

19. Ibid., p. 51.

20. Ibid., p. 52.

21. Ibid., p. 50. Martin Revson interview.

22. Ibid., pp. 26–29.

23. Martin Revson interview.

24. Tobias, *Fire,* pp. 28–29.

25. Ibid., p. 29.

26. Ibid., p. 44.

27. Martin Revson interview.

28. Most of this information on Charles's early years and on the Revson family is based upon Andrew Tobias's account in *Fire and Ice,* a book about which a word should be said. Some of Tobias's information is corroborated by secondary sources, such as trade magazines and Revlon's own publicity. Much of what he has written is original. His book is

based on interviews. He lists over a hundred interviewees, but also observes that "not all [the people to whom he spoke] would want their names to appear [on his pages]." The typed transcripts of these interviews "run to around a million words" (pp. 7–8).

In his acknowledgments, Tobias thanks "[t]he late Charles Revson himself" for cooperating with an "unauthorized" book which "he knew would be at best not a totally flattering portrait" and also for making Tobias his guest "for three magnificently pampered days on his yacht." Tobias does not state that Revson himself was interviewed, nor does he seem to quote Revson directly except insofar as Revson's words are provided by other sources. It is therefore not clear whether Revson's cooperation meant that he himself answered specific questions from Tobias (perhaps with the proviso that the answers not be used verbatim), or whether it meant merely that Revson facilitated access to people who would not have spoken with Tobias otherwise. Indeed, it is not even clear whether Revson was on his yacht when Tobias was his guest.

Tobias is a graduate of the Harvard Business School (Class of 1972), and he was writing for *New York* magazine at the time he produced this book. Despite occasional lapses, *Fire and Ice* is astute and valuable. Tobias's observations, for example, about the gender confusion resulting from men selling a woman's product to women and Revson's own hypersexuality teach us a lot about the man, his company, the industry, and the times. And Tobias's instincts are shrewd. He spotted, for example, the similarity in temperament between Revson and Martin Revson's older son, Peter, the famous automobile racer who was killed in a crash in 1974 (pp. 277–278).

Tobias displays a playful and becoming modesty in the face of what he would like to know but cannot be known. One chapter is entitled "Separating Myth from Legend" (pp. 18–30). He appreciates the problems of arriving at the truth through interviews about a powerful man who was a mystery to those who knew him and to himself as well.

All that having been said, one finishes the book thirsting for answers, for meaning, and for context. Why did any talented person work for Revson? What held this company together? How did it grow despite the manifest pathology at the top? Where do man, company, and industry fit in the context of the American business world? As for Revson himself, was he merely a bundle of symptoms with a knack for guessing right about two things—color and fashion—that drove his industry? Is there any coherence hidden beneath the incoherence of his public utterances and his, at times, disgusting conduct? See Marilyn Bender's critique of *Fire and Ice* in "Books: Was That All There Was to Revson?" *New York Times,* August 22, 1976, sec. 3, p. 12. See also Richard R. Lingeman, "Making It the Revson Way," *New York Times,* August 25, 1976, p. 33 and Tobias's response to Bender in a letter to the editor of the *New York Times,* August 22, 1976, sec. 3, p. 12, col. 7.

29. Tobias, *Fire,* p. 49.
30. Ibid., pp. 48–49; "Revson, Charles Haskell," *Who Was Who in America* (Chicago: Marquis Who's Who, 1976), p. 342; Richard S. Tedlow, "An American Autocrat: Charles Revson and the Rise of Revlon" (unpublished master of arts thesis, Columbia University, 1971), p. 17.

31. There is no cosmetics or ladies' apparel firm on Alfred D. Chandler, Jr.'s list of the two hundred largest American industrial enterprises ranked by assets in 1930. Alfred D. Chandler, Jr., *Scale and Scope: The Dynamics of Industrial Capitalism* (Cambridge, Mass.: Harvard University Press, 1990), pp. 644–650.

32. Tobias, *Fire*, pp. 49 and 61.

33. Ibid.

34. Tedlow, "American Autocrat," p. 25. Lachman died on August 11, 1978, leaving an estate valued at $30 million. *Washington Post*, August 13, 1978, p. B6. He was eighty-one. "Widow to Get Half of Estate Worth Millions," *Toronto Globe and Mail*, August 10, 1979, p. 11.

35. Tobias, *Fire*, p. 51.

36. Ibid., p. 20. Kathy Peiss cites the rise of a mass market for cosmetics between the wars as perhaps the principal reason for the ascendancy of men over women in the industry. Men had better access to capital and were more conversant with the demands of business management in general, especially with regard to advertising and distribution strategies. See Peiss, *Hope*, pp. 106 esp. and 97–133 passim.

37. For an authoritative historical treatment, see Peiss, *Hope*, passim.

38. Determining Revlon's advertising to sales ratio and comparing it to other firms and other industries is not easy. According to a prospectus issued in 1957, Revlon's "consolidated expenditures on advertising and promotion" in 1954 were $6,145,374. (I choose 1954 because it was the year prior to the spike in sales caused by sponsorship of *The $64,000 Question*.) See Table 5.1 below. Revlon's sales in 1954 were $33,604,037, yielding an 18.3 percent ratio of advertising "and promotion" to sales. According to the same Prospectus, "advertising, promotional, selling and administrative expenses" in 1954 were $15,335,919, or 45.6 percent of sales. Overall marketing expenses were far higher than expenses for paid advertising alone. "Prospectus: 241,020 Shares, Revlon, Inc., Common Stock," April 1, 1957. In 1974, the last full year of Charles Revson's life, Revlon, according to *Advertising Age*, spent $40,250,000 on "advertising and promotion." Its sales that year were $638.6 million (*Advertising Age* incorrectly reported Revlon's sales as $605.9 million), yielding an advertising to sales ratio of 6.3 percent. According to *Advertising Age*, Revlon was the nation's fifty-sixth largest national advertiser that year. It ranked seventy-fifth in advertising and promotion to sales ratios. Merle Kingman, "Top 100 Advertisers Spend Record $6 Billion," *Advertising Age*, August 18, 1975, pp. 29–30. In *Brand New: How Entrepreneurs Earned Consumers' Trust from Wedgwood to Dell* (Boston: Harvard Business School Press, 2001), Nancy F. Koehn writes that in the late 1940s and early 1950s, "[m]ost of these companies [i.e., Avon Products, Max Factor, Coty, Elizabeth Arden, Helena Rubinstein, and Revlon] devoted between 20 and 25 percent of net sales to advertising" (p. 174). Her source is Association of National Advertisers, *Advertising Expenditure Trends* (New York: Association of National Advertisers, 1953), appendix. It is difficult for me to arrive at that statistic from any source dealing specifically with Revlon. The Association of National Advertisers collaborated with the National Association of Cost Accountants to study the distribution costs of 312 manufacturers of "twenty-nine distinct

kinds of products" back in 1931. The study grouped drugs with "toilet articles" and arrived at marketing costs of 38.8 percent of net sales, highest of the 29 types of products. The ratio of sales to "advertising and promotion" was 18.4 percent, more than 10 percentage points higher than the next product group. Paul W. Stewart and J. Frederic Dewhurst, *Does Distribution Cost Too Much? A Review of the Costs Involved in Current Marketing Methods and a Program for Improvement* (New York: Twentieth Century Fund, 1939), pp. 200–202, 394. In recent years, advertising to sales ratios in the cosmetics industry have varied widely by product, by competitive situation, and by method of distribution. Thus Mary Kay Cosmetics and Avon, both of which are direct sellers and one of which (Avon) has long been the largest firm in the cosmetics industry in terms of sales volume, were reported to have spent less than 1 percent of sales and 1.2 percent of sales respectively on advertising in 1981. These are tiny ratios for mass marketed, small-ticket consumer goods. L'Oreál's Plenitude, by contrast, was costing the company $0.46 out of every dollar in 1995 for advertising and an additional 14.4 percent in promotion. See John A. Quelch, "Mary Kay Cosmetics, Inc: Marketing Communications," Harvard Business School (HBS) Case Services #9–583–065, Rev. 8/85, with the accompanying Teaching Note, HBS Case Services #5–583–065, Rev. 8/85. See also Robert J. Dolan, "L'Oreál of Paris: Bringing 'Class to Mass' with Plenitude," HBS Case Services #9–599–017, Rev. July 10, 1998, with the accompanying Teaching Note, HBS Case Services #5–599–017, Rev. July 10, 1998.

39. Tobias, *Fire,* p. 49.
40. "Revlon's Revson Dies; Was Demanding Ad Critic," *Advertising Age,* September 1, 1975, p. 35.
41. "The Revson Story: He Knows What Women Want," *Printers' Ink,* November 15, 1957, p. 53. Peiss, *Hope,* p. 190.
42. Tedlow, "American Autocrat," pp. 28–31. For a cogent, useful, and brief treatment of entrepreneurship, see Howard H. Stevenson, Michael J. Roberts, and H. Irving Grousbeck, *New Business Ventures and the Entrepreneur* (Homewood, Ill.: Irwin, 1985), pp. 1–19. For what will become the standard book-length treatment, see Amar V. Bhide, *The Origin and Evolution of New Business* (New York: Oxford University Press, 2000).
43. "Revson Story," p. 53.
44. Ibid., p. 53.
45. Ibid. As noted, Martin Revson joined the firm in 1935. Speaking to him six and a half decades later, it is impressive and touching to learn how difficult it was to make these rounds. The words he used were "demanding," "unnerving," "humiliating." Martin Revson interview. See also the exceptionally shrewd discussion of men in a "woman's" business in Peiss, *Hope,* pp. 114–122. She refers to a "taint of effeminacy and homosexuality that marked men who beautified women" (p. 114).
46. Tobias, *Fire,* p. 51.
47. Ibid., p. 29.
48. Daniel Seligman, "Revlon's Jackpot," *Fortune,* April 1956, p. 236.
49. Seligman, "Jackpot," p. 236. Tobias says this figure accounts for sales in

the first nine months; but since the firm was founded at the beginning of March 1932 rather than at the end, Seligman is probably right.

50. Ibid., p. 236.
51. Tobias, *Fire*, pp. 63–66.
52. Ibid., pp. 50.
53. Ibid., pp. 44–46.
54. Ibid., pp. 45–46.
55. According to one source, Cutex "introduced the first tinted liquid nail polish, made from natural resins coloured with dyes," in 1917. Susannah Conway, "The History of . . . Nail Varnish," *Independent* (London), November 8, 1998, p. 9. For Cutex in recent times, see "Chesebrough Purchase by Unilever Done," *Chicago Sun-Times*, February 12, 1987; "Cutex Helps Bring Sales Turnaround in Nail Care Market," *Chain Drug Review*, June 21, 1993, p. 130; "Carson Sells Cutex to Shansby for $30 Million," *Los Angeles Times*, December 11, 1998, p. C-2. Peiss, *Hope*, p. 163.
56. Tobias, *Fire*, p. 43–44.
57. "It's the Ad that Sells Cosmetics," *Business Week* (December 13, 1952), p. 69; Tobias, *Fire*, p. 47.
58. Sources differ concerning whether Revlon introduced lipstick in 1939 or 1940. Tobias, *Fire*, p. 47, says 1940. The *Dictionary of American Biography* says 1939. From what I have been able to gather, 1939 is more likely. See Barbara Gerber, "Revson, Charles Haskell," *Dictionary of American Biography*, supp. 9 (New York : Scribner's, 1994), pp. 648–649. A prospectus prepared by Lehman Brothers and Reynolds and Company for the sale of 130,000 shares of Revlon in 1960 contains the following statement concerning the company's history:

> When the Company changed its name in 1939 from the Revlon Nail Enamel Corporation to Revlon Products Corporation . . . , the change was symptomatic of the growth and diversification of the business. In that year the company began the manufacture of lipstick. Under the slogan "Matching lips and fingertips," the company marketed identical new shades for lipsticks and nail enamels under [the same] names. . . .

See "Prospectus. 130,000 Shares. Revlon, Inc., Common Stock," December 14, 1960, p. 6. This prospectus is available from the Baker Library at the Harvard Business School.
59. Gerber, "Revson," p. 648.
60. Seligman, "Jackpot," p. 236.
61. Tedlow, "American Autocrat," pp. 27–28.
62. Ibid., p. 64.
63. Tobias, *Fire*, pp. 108–109. Tobias reproduces this advertisement in his book. Although he says it appeared in the summer, I have not been able to find it in any summer issue of *The New Yorker* in 1935.
64. "Revson Story," p. 54.
65. Roy Rowan, "Revlon's Smell of Success," *Fortune*, December 31, 1979, p. 31.
66. See Tobias, *Fire*, pp. 111–114.
67. "Revson Story," p. 54. Such co-marketing arrangements were not new

when Revson employed them. See, e.g., Peiss, *Hope,* p. 129. It would appear, however, that Revson was particularly effective in their use.

68. Helen Golby, "Rise of Revlon," *Advertising & Selling,* March, 1947, p. 105.

69. "Ad That Sells," p. 66.

70. According to one report in 1939, nail polish was sold to 80 percent of American women that year. La Rue Applegate, "Drug and Cosmetic Industry Still Expanding, Despite Decline in Earning Power," *Annalist,* August 17, 1939, p. 205.

71. Seligman, "Jackpot," p. 236. By 1956, according to a prospectus, the Retail Sales Division accounted for 85.52 percent of Revlon's net domestic sales. The Salon Sales Division brought in 13.79 percent. However, the prospectus explained that the "Salon Sales Division has an importance to the Company beyond the direct sales volume derived from its activities, since it brings Revlon products to the attention of the many women who patronize beauty salons." "Prospectus," April 1, 1957, p. 6.

72. For the best recent discussion of the history of fair trade, see Thomas K. McCraw, "Competition and 'Fair Trade': History and Theory," *Research in Economic History,* vol. 16 (Greenwich, Conn.: JAI Press, 1996), pp. 185–239.

73. Lawrence M. Hughes, "The Many Shades of Revlon's Revson," *Sales Management,* March 3, 1961, p. 96.

74. Tobias, *Fire,* p. 68.

75. Seligman, "Jackpot," p. 236.

76. See Tobias's description of Mark D. Soroko, who was a gun-toting "street fighter." "No one knew exactly how Mickey [as Soroko was known] did what he did—there were plenty of rumors—but he got things done." Tobias, *Fire,* pp. 68–69. See also Tedlow, "American Autocrat," pp. 45–47.

77. Applegate, "Cosmetics Industry," p. 205. For the growth in advertising expenditures in the 1910s and 1920s, see Peiss, *Hope,* pp. 105–106. Common sense suggests that advertising to sales ratios must have been high in the cosmetics industry. However, in the case of Revlon, it is difficult to argue that expenditures solely for national advertising, as opposed to expenditures for the total marketing effort, were so outrageously high as to make the company "economically unsound" by nature. See note 38, above.

78. McCraw, *American Business,* pp. 88–89.

79. Tobias, *Fire,* p. 80; Tedlow, "American Autocrat," p. 43.

80. Tobias, *Fire,* p. 80; Tedlow, "American Autocrat," pp. 43–44.

81. "War versus Glamour: From Cosmetics to Hair Pins, the Beauty Trade Feels Pinch of Blockage and Requirements of Essential Defense Industries," *Business Week,* May 17, 1941, p. 56.

82. "Cosmetics Output Spirals," *Business Week,* August 24, 1946, p. 68.

83. Ibid.

84. For morale and cosmetics during World War II, see Peiss, *Hope,* pp. 238–245.

85. Gilbert Vail, *A History of Cosmetics in America* (New York: Toilet Goods Association, 1947), p. 138. According to another source, retail sales of makeup, fragrances, and toiletries rose from $450 million in

1940 to $711 million in 1945. Koehn, *Brand New,* p. 165. For a note-worthy comparative treatment of women during World War II, see Leila J. Rupp, *Mobilizing Women for War: German and American Propa-ganda, 1939–1945* (Princeton, N.J.: Princeton University Press, 1978).

86. McCraw, *American Business,* pp. 92–93.

87. "To the Future," *Beauty Fashion,* January 1943, pp. 26, 50. There is now a considerable literature on American women at work during World War II. See Koehn, *Brand New,* and the sources she cites, including: Claudia Goldin, "The Role of World War II in the Rise of Women's Employment," *American Economic Review,* vol. 81, no. 4 (September 1991), pp. 741–756; Karen Anderson, *Wartime Women: Sex Roles, Fam-ily Relations and the Status of Women during World War II* (Westport, Conn.: Greenwood, 1981); Sherna Berger Gluck, *Rosie the Riveter Revisited: Women, the War, and Social Change* (Boston: Twayne, 1987). For a comprehensive history of women in the workforce, see Alice Kessler-Harris, *Out to Work: A History of Wage-Earning Women in the United States* (New York: Oxford University Press, 1982). For World War II, see pp. 273–299 and the accompanying notes on pp. 379–383. "Rosie the Riveter" was the name of a song during the war years. See pp. 275–276.

88. Quoted in McCraw, *American Business,* p. 91.

89. Pauline Kael, *5001 Nights at the Movies* (New York: Holt, Rinehart and Winston, 1984), p. 381. The awards were best picture; best director, William Wyler; best actress, Greer Garson; best supporting actress, Teresa Wright; and cinematography.

90. "Revson Story," p. 54.

91. Golby, "Revlon," p. 106. In the spring of 1944, the company announced its "Tournament of Roses," marketing "Mrs. Miniver Rose, Hothouse Rose, Rosy Future, and Bright Forecast." *Beauty Fashion,* May 1944, facing p. 32. The use of motion pictures to publicize cosmetics dates to the 1920s. Peiss, *Hope,* pp. 126–127.

92. Tedlow, "American Autocrat," p. 39.

93. Kael, *Movies,* p. 381.

94. Golby, "Revlon," pp. 106–107.

95. Ibid., p. 106.

96. Seligman, "Jackpot," p. 137.

97. Ibid., p. 138.

98. Interview with a former Revlon executive, 1971. Tedlow, "American Autocrat," p. 54.

99. "Ad That Sells," pp. 63–69, passim.

100. Interview with Beatrice Castle, 1971. Tedlow, "American Autocrat," pp. 56–57. Questionnaires had been used as gimmicks in marketing cos-metics as early as 1929. Peiss, *Hope,* p. 144.

101. Tobias, *Fire,* p. 122.

102. Kay Frances Daly died on October 16, 1975. She was fifty-six years old. "Daly, Kay Frances" *Who Was Who,* vol. VI (Chicago: Marquis Who's Who, 1976), p. 101. A quarter of a century later, Martin Revson still spoke with great respect of Daly's talent. Telephone interview with Mar-tin Revson, January 2, 2000.

103. For Kay Daly, see Kay Daly, "How Do You Advertise Cosmetics to

Women? Combine Razz-Matazz with Truth, Kay Daly Advises," *Advertising Age,* May 22, 1961, pp. 101–102; "How Revlon's Kay Daly Works Magic at Retail," *Printers' Ink,* September 24, 1965, pp. 23–24, 29.

104. *Vogue,* November 1, 1952, pp. 28–29.

105. "Revlon's Formula," pp. 72–73.

106. See Tedlow, "American Autocrat," p. 60. The demonstrator, in Peiss's words, "mingled the intimate and the commercial." Peiss, *Hope,* pp. 131–133. An even more radical integration "of the domestic and economic spheres reminiscent of pre-industrial America" can be seen in the operation of direct selling organizations such as Mary Kay.

107. Tedlow, "American Autocrat," pp. 60–61.

108. "Ad That Sells," p. 69.

109. "'Fire and Ice' at Pogue's," *Beauty Fashion,* December 1952, p. 36.

110. See p. 271.

111. "Hard hearted Hannah, the vamp of Savannah, the meanest gal in town. . . . Leather is tough but Hannah's heart is tougher; / she's a gal who loves to see men suffer. To tease 'em and thrill 'em, to torture and kill 'em, is her delight they say." This song was composed and the lyrics written in 1924 by Jack Yellin, Milton Ager, Bob Bigelow, and Charles Bates. Leo Schofield, "Savannah Vamp," *Sydney Morning Herald,* July 16, 1992, p. 25; Alan Stewart, "Between the Sexes: Women Men Love to Hate," *Toronto Globe and Mail,* September 27, 1980, p. F2.

112. Peiss, *Hope,* pp. 249–252.

113. In one of his books, Stanley Marcus (of Nieman-Marcus) reports "Laver's Law," which he attributes to English writer and fashion expert James Laver:

Laver's Law

The same costume will be:

Indecent	10 years before its time
Shameless	5 years before its time
Outré (daring)	1 year before its time
Smart	————
Dowdy	1 year after its time
Hideous	10 years after its time
Ridiculous	20 years after its time
Amusing	30 years after its time
Quaint	50 years after its time
Charming	70 years after its time
Romantic	100 years after its time
Beautiful	150 years after its time

Stanley Marcus, *Minding the Store* (Boston: Signet, 1974), pp. 226–227. For James Laver, see the brief but useful essay by Doris Langley Moore in Lord Blake and C. S. Nichols, eds., *The Dictionary of National Biography, 1971–1980,* (Oxford: Oxford University Press, 1986), pp. 483–484.

114. Interview with a beauty salon operator, summer 1999.

115. Daly, "Razz-Matazz," p. 102. Italics in original.

116. Revlon did not make any acquisitions in 1955 or 1956. In 1957, it purchased Knomark Manufacturing Company, makers of Esquire Shoe Pol-

ish, and made a substantial investment in the Schering Corporation, a manufacturer of pharmaceuticals. The following year it acquired 20 percent of Schick, which produced electric shavers. In 1959, Revlon increased its interest in Schick to 26.7 percent, purchased Bressard Distributors (hair color preparations), AsthmaNefrin Company (asthma relief products), Pinex Company (cough medicine), and became the distributor in the United States and Canada of Paris-based Parfums Revillon. Despite these acquisitions, the bulk of Revlon's sales growth came from its own traditional operations.

117. Revlon's 1955 sales entitled it to rank 486 on *Fortune* magazine's list of the 500 largest companies in the United States that year. As table 5.1 shows, Revlon posted sales of $51,646,612. This should have placed it just after Mullins Manufacturing with sales of $51,668,000 which was ranked 485 and before Commercial Solvents with sales of $51,608,000 on the list *Fortune* published for that year. "The Fortune Directory," *Fortune,* July 1956, pp. 1–10. But *Fortune* skipped Revlon altogether for unknown reasons. Revlon did make the 500 for 1956. Thus, in 1957, *Fortune* ranked Revlon number 384 in sales for 1956 and noted without comment that the company was not present on the 1955 list. "The Fortune Directory," *Fortune,* July 1957, pp. 1–19. In 1958, *Fortune* ranked Revlon 378 in sales for 1957 and stated that it was the sixth-most-profitable public firm that year, with a return on invested capital of 31.6 percent. "The Fortune Directory," *Fortune,* July 1958, pp. 139 and 131–150.

118. These terms were introduced by Thomas Kuhn in *The Structure of Scientific Revolutions* (Chicago: University of Chicago Press, 1970).

119. John Kenneth Galbraith, *The New Industrial State* (Boston: Houghton Mifflin, 1967), p. 208.

120. Public Law no. 416, June 19, 1934, 73rd Cong.

121. See Debora Spar, *Ruling the Waves: Cycles of Invention, Chaos, and Wealth* (New York: Harcourt Brace, 2001).

122. This quotation is from Erik Barnouw, *A Tower in Babel: A History of Broadcasting in the United States, vol. 1: To 1933* (New York: Oxford University Press, 1966), pp. 73–74. Barnouw's works are the definitive histories of broadcasting. His other books which have been consulted and used extensively in this chapter include: *The Golden Web: A History of Broadcasting in the United States, vol. 2: 1933 to 1953* (New York: Oxford University Press, 1968); *The Image Empire: A History of Broadcasting in the United States, vol. 3: From 1953* (New York: Oxford University Press, 1970); *Tube of Plenty: The Evolution of American Television* (New York: Oxford University Press, 1975); and *The Sponsor: Notes on a Modern Potentate* (New York: Oxford University Press, 1978). For a clear and interesting discussion of the early history of wireless transmissions and the development of the transistor, see Ernest Braun and Stuart MacDonald, *Revolution in Miniature: The History and Impact of Semiconductor Electronics* (Cambridge, U.K.: Cambridge University Press, 1982), esp. pp. 1–60.

123. Barnouw, *Tower,* p. 96.

124. Keynes is quoted in Richard Hofstadter, *The American Political Tradition: And the Men Who Made It* (New York: Random House, 1989), p. 369.

125. Public Law no. 264, August 13, 1912, 62nd Cong.
126. Barnouw's assessment of Hoover is that the secretary was, in the final analysis, unclear in his attitude and actions with regard to the development of broadcasting.

> He seemed to many a bulwark against commercialization, sometimes making quotable, sardonic statements on the subject. At the third Washington [radio] conference in October 1924, he said: "If a speech by the President is to be used as the meat in a sandwich of two patent medicine advertisements, there will be no radio left." Yet he had given toll broadcasting its most important boost in providing it with a clear channel. And when the 1925 Washington conference went on record as deprecating "the use of radio broadcasting for direct sales effort," it also adopted, at the urging of Secretary Hoover himself, another resolution: "The problem of radio publicity should be solved by the industry itself, and not by Government compulsion and legislation." Barnouw, *Tower,* pp. 177–178.

127. Barnouw, *Tower,* pp. 107–108.
128. Ibid., pp. 125, 210, 229.
129. *Historical Statistics of the United States from Colonial Times to 1970,* Series R 93–105, p. 796. There were 25,687,000 households in the United States in 1922 and 29,582,000 in 1929. *Historical Statistics,* Series A 350–352, p. 43.
130. Barnouw, *Tower,* pp. 221–231, 272–274; Barnouw, *Web,* pp. 9–18; John Gunther, *Taken at the Flood: The Story of Albert D. Lasker* (New York: Harper, 1960); Richard S. Tedlow, "Albert D. Lasker," *Dictionary of American Biography,* supp. 5 (New York: Scribner's, 1977), pp. 410–412.
131. *Historical Statistics,* Series R93–105, p. 796. The 8,000 number is a bit strange. According to the same source from which it was taken, the authoritative *Historical Statistics of the United States,* compiled by the U.S. Bureau of the Census, only 6,000 television sets were produced in 1946. Since none were produced commercially during World War II, only a handful were produced prior to the war (and it would be surprising indeed if any of those were still in working order by 1946), only a skilled amateur could build one him- or herself, and none were imported, one wonders where the remaining 2,000 households acquired their sets. There were 38,370,000 households in the United States in 1946 and 48,902,000 households in the United States in 1956. U.S. Bureau of the Census, Current Population Survey, "Household and Family Characteristics: Table 1.4—Households by Type: 1947 to 1997," p. 13, provides households for 1956. The 1946 number comes from *Historical Statistics of the United States.*
132. For an interesting illustration of the differences in marketing strategy adopted by the same company in a nation in which television was commercialized as opposed to a nation in which commercial advertisements were not permitted on television, see Robert D. Buzzell and Jean-Louis LeCocq, "Polaroid France (SA)," in Steven H. Star, Nancy J. Davis, Christopher H. Lovelock, and Benson P. Shapiro, *Problems in Marketing,* 5th ed. (New York: McGraw-Hill, 1977), pp. 191–213.

133. Quoted in William E. Leuchtenburg, *A Troubled Feast: American Society since 1945* (Boston: Little, Brown, 1983), p. 84.

134. Barnouw, *Empire*, p. 23.

135. Ibid., p. 43.

136. Ibid., pp. 5–6.

137. This discussion of *The $64,000 Question* is based upon the following sources: Tedlow, "American Autocrat," pp. 65–79; Richard S. Tedlow, "Intellect on Television: The Quiz Show Scandals of the 1950s," *American Quarterly*, vol. 28, no. 4 (Fall 1976), pp. 483–495; U.S. House of Representatives, 86th Cong., 1st Sess., Special Subcommittee on Legislative Oversight of the Interstate and Foreign Commerce Committee, *Investigation of Television Quiz Shows, Hearings* (Washington, D.C.: Government Printing Office, 1960) [cited hereafter as *Hearings*]; Barnouw, *Empire*, pp. 122–129; Kent Anderson, *Television Fraud: The History and Implications of the Quiz Show Scandals* (Westport, Conn.: Greenwood Press, 1978); William F. Boddy, *Fifties Television: The Industry and Its Critics* (Urbana: University of Illinois Press, 1990), pp. 214–255; and Tobias, *Fire*, pp. 145–160.

138. Barnouw, *Web*, p. 102; idem, *Empire*, p. 57.

139. Jack Gould, "Rise and Fall of the Quiz Empire," *New York Times Magazine*, September 23, 1958, p. 64.

140. *New York Times*, March 16, 1955, p. 48.

141. "Semper Chow," *Time*, September 26, 1955, pp. 17–18.

142. *Hearings*, pp. 779, 784.

143. Daniel J. Boorstin, *The Americans: The Democratic Experience* (New York: Vintage, 1974), pp. 89–164.

144. Seligman, "Jackpot," pp. 240, 244; Tedlow, "American Autocrat," pp. 68–79; *Hearings*, pp. 809–810.

145. "Quiz Crazy," *Time*, February 27, 1956, pp. 74–75; "Fort Knox or Bust," *Time*, August 22, 1955, p. 47.

146. Pharmaceuticals, Inc. changed its name to the J. B. Williams Company. This privately held company was sold to Nabisco in the early 1970s. Nabisco sold it to Beecham in the late 1970s. After a merger, Beecham became SmithKline Beecham. In 2000 SmithKline Beecham merged with Glaxo to become GlaxoSmithKline. At this writing, GlaxoSmithKline is still marketing Geritol.

147. *Hearings*, pp. 156, 164–168, 176.

148. Carl Van Doren, *Benjamin Franklin* (New York: Viking, 1938).

149. Mark Van Doren, *Collected Poems, 1922–1938* (New York: Henry Holt, 1939).

150. "The Wizard of Quiz," *Time*, February 11, 1957, pp. 44–46.

151. For Charles Van Doren, see *Hearings*, pp. 623–646 (in which Van Doren was treated with exaggerated sympathy bordering on deference by many, but not all, of his interrogators); Anderson, *Fraud*, pp. 53–75, 139–143, 147–149, and 168–169; Tedlow, "Intellect," passim.

152. In 1953, Revlon's closest competitor in the retail cosmetics business was Helena Rubinstein, which had sales of $20,473,124, compared to $28,306,898 for Revlon. In 1958, Revlon's closest competitor was Max Factor, whose sales were approximately $45,000,000 as compared to $108,762,302 for Revlon. *Hearings*, p. 811.

153. Ibid., pp. 809–811, 889; Seligman, "Jackpot," p. 136.
154. Seligman, "Jackpot," p. 240. Interview with a former Revlon executive, 1971. Tedlow, "American Autocrat," p. 68.
155. *New York Times,* June 8, 1954, p. 59.
156. "Revlon Lipsticks Paint a Gaudy Report, but Hazel Bishop Finds Consolation," *Business Week,* January 28, 1956, p. 62.
157. *New York Times,* August 21, 1955, sec. 4, p. 30.
158. "Printers' Ink Shoots Some $64,000 Questions," *Printers' Ink,* November 18, 1955, p. 24.
159. J. Richard Elliott Jr., "Beauty Contest," *Barron's,* August 29, 1955, p. 3.
160. David A. Loehwing, "Search for Beauty," *Barron's,* August 20, 1956, p. 3.
161. "She Sells By Being Herself," *Printers' Ink,* November 8, 1957, pp. 54, 58.
162. Tobias, *Fire,* p. 146.
163. *Hearings,* p. 748. There were questions raised at the hearings (seemingly inadvertently) by Charles Revson about the extent of the "controls" or "rigging" which characterized *Question* from its inception. See *Hearings,* pp. 877–885. See also, however, Anderson's exoneration of Cowan in *Fraud,* pp. 161–162.
164. *Hearings,* pp. 742–744.
165. Ibid., pp. 747–748.
166. Ibid., p. 979. By the time of his testimony before the House subcommittee, Abrams had moved on to the presidency of the cosmetics and toiletries division of Warner-Lambert Pharmaceuticals.
167. Ibid., pp. 849–850.
168. Thirteen weeks was the usual length of a contract between a sponsor and a production company in television in the 1950s. Sometimes, at renewal, that period might be doubled. Thus, Revlon bought *Question* from the producer for thirteen weeks twice and then increased the run of the contract to twenty-six weeks. Ibid., p. 794.
169. Ibid., pp. 794–795.
170. Ibid., p. 796.
171. Ibid., p. 925.
172. Ibid., pp. 922–926.
173. Ibid., pp. 806–807.
174. Ibid., pp. 846–847.
175. Ibid., p. 816. One point all were able to agree upon during the contentious questioning of Martin Revson was that Northwestern was "one of the great universities in this country. . . . A very honorable institution." Ibid., pp. 841–842.
176. Ibid., pp. 814–815.
177. Ibid., p. 829.
178. Ibid., pp. 805–806.
179. Ibid., pp. 979–988.
180. Ibid., p. 861.
181. Ibid., pp. 861–870.
182. Ibid., p. 988.
183. Ibid., p. 879.
184. Ibid., p. 878.

185. Ibid. Apparently, Charles's initial negative reaction to the shows, alluded to above, was rather quickly and dramatically transformed.
186. Ibid., pp. 878, 879.
187. Ibid., p. 879.
188. Ibid., pp. 880–881.
189. Ibid., p. 825.
190. In 1955, Cadillacs accounted for 141,038 out of a total of 7,169,908 automobiles sold in the United States. Lawrence J. White, *The Automobile Industry Since 1945* (Cambridge, Mass.: Harvard University Press, 1971), pp. 292–293.
191. See "Communications Act Amendments," House of Representatives Report no. 1800, 86th Cong., 2nd sess., September 13, 1960.
192. Daniel J. Boorstin, *The Image: A Guide to Pseudoevents in America* (New York: Harper and Row, 1964), pp. 41–44; Tedlow, "Intellect," pp. 493–494.
193. Public Law No. 416, June 19, 1934, 73rd Cong.
194. Tedlow, "Intellect," pp. 489–490.
195. Anderson, *Fraud*, pp. 175–183; Tedlow, "Intellect," p. 495.
196. See Eric Goldman, *The Crucial Decade—And After* (New York: Vintage, 1960), pp. 324–326; Tedlow, "Intellect," pp. 491–493.
197. Seligman, "Jackpot," p. 244.
198. "The Unflabbergasted Genius: Charles Haskell Revson," *Time*, November 16, 1959, p. 106.
199. Tobias, *Fire*, p. 145.
200. Murray Spitzer, "To Feed the Dynamic Cosmetic Market," *Printers' Ink*, July 19, 1957, p. 34.
201. Data from Baker Library business information analyst Jeffrey C. Cronin, August 27, 1999.
202. "Agency Shakeup Follows Martin Revson's Exit as Revlon Executive Vice President," *Advertising Age*, June 9, 1958, p. 70.
203. "$16,000,000 Challenge," *Time*, September 30, 1957, p. 88.
204. Ibid.
205. Ibid.
206. Hughes, "Shades," p. 41.
207. "$16,000,000," p. 88.
208. Interview, former Revlon executive, 1971. Tedlow, "American Autocrat," p. 82.
209. Walter Goodman, "The Lipstick War: All's Fair—Even Wiretaps," *Nation*, January 21, 1956, pp. 47–49.
210. "Revlon's Formula," pp. 74, 76.
211. Seligman, "Jackpot," p. 243.
212. *Hearings*, pp. 894–896. The two were said to have achieved a reconciliation after Joseph Revson's death in 1971.
213. "A Family Affair," *Time*, March 28, 1960, pp. 97–98
214. Former Revlon executive, interview. Tedlow, "American Autocrat," pp. 95–96.
215. "Revlon Appoints New President," *New York Times*, July 18, 1974, p. 55.
216. Marylin Bender, "Bergerac Chosen as Revlon Chief," *New York Times*,

May 2, 1975, p. 47. Bergerac's compensation package was sufficiently lavish to provoke a question at the shareholders meeting at which it was announced.

217. "Revlon Takes Down 'For Sale' Sign as Shares Sink 34 percent; Perelman Now Plans to Sell Parts of Business, Rejuvenate Company Himself," *Wall Street Journal,* October 4, 1999, p. B6.

218. See, for example, Tobias, *Fire,* pp. 192–193.

219. Mary Kay Ash, *Mary Kay* (New York: Harper and Row, 1987), pp. 8, 23, 29, 56, 109–110, 120, 157, 174. The quotations are on pp. 56 and 120. Italics added. See also Nicole Woolsey Biggart, *Charismatic Capitalism: Direct Selling Organizations in America* (Chicago: University of Chicago Press, 1989), pp. 112–113 and passim.

220. Revson owned 10.33 percent of Revlon's stock in 1975, the year he died. Bender, "Bergerac," p. 47.

PART THREE: OUR OWN TIMES

Introduction

1. David A. Hounshell, *From the American System to Mass Production, 1800–1932: The Development of Manufacturing Technology in the United States* (Baltimore: The Johns Hopkins University Press, 1984), pp. 15–25; Nathan Rosenberg, ed., *The American System of Manufactures: The Report of the Committee on the Machinery of the United States, 1855, and the Special Reports of George Wallis and Joseph Whitworth, 1854* (Edinburgh: Edinburgh University Press, 1969), pp. 87–389.

2. Fyodor Dostoyevsky, *The Brothers Karamazov* (New York: Random House, 1950), p. 926. The phrase is Dmitri Karamazov's.

3. Peter Booth Wiley, *Yankees in the Land of the Gods: Commodore Perry and the Opening of Japan* (New York: Viking, 1990).

4. Fred A. McKenzie, *The American Invaders: Their Plans, Tactics, and Progress* (New York: Street & Smith, 1901), p. 31.

5. Mira Wilkins, *The Emergence of Multinational Enterprise* (Cambridge, Mass.: Harvard University Press, 1970), pp. 215–217.

6. Jean-Jacques Servan-Schreiber, *The American Challenge* (New York: Atheneum, 1969), p. 10. Italics in original.

7. President John F. Kennedy, "Special Message to the Congress on Urgent National Needs," May 25, 1961.

8. James L. Sundquist, "The Crisis of Competence in Our National Government," *Political Science Quarterly,* vol. 95, no. 2 (summer 1980), pp. 183–208; Seymour Martin Lipset and William Schneider, "The Decline of Confidence in American Institutions," *Political Science Quarterly,* vol. 98, no. 3 (autumn 1983), pp. 379–402.

9. "Man of the Year: First Among Equals," *Time* (January 2, 1956), p. 54.

Chapter 6: Sam Walton

1. Thomas Jefferson to William Smith, in Thomas Jefferson, *Writings* (New York: Library of America, 1984), p. 975.

2. Leonard W. Labaree et al., eds., *The Autobiography of Benjamin Franklin* (New Haven, Conn.: Yale University Press, 1964), pp. 10–11.
3. The third essay was "Maritime Observations." Carl L. Becker, "Benjamin Franklin," *Dictionary of American Biography*, vol. 6 (New York: Scribner's, 1931), p. 595.
4. William G. Carr, *The Oldest Delegate: Franklin in the Constitutional Convention* (Newark: University of Delaware Press, 1990), pp. 119, 159–161.
5. This sentence and the description of Franklin's house in the previous paragraph as "commodious" are from Becker, "Franklin," pp. 595, 597.
6. Bob Ortega, *In Sam We Trust* (New York: Random House, 1998), pp. 16–18.
7. Vance H. Trimble, *Sam Walton: The Inside Story of America's Richest Man* (New York: Dutton, 1990), pp. 19–20.
8. Ortega, *Sam*, p. 17; Trimble, *Walton*, pp. 10–16.
9. U.S. Census, *Historical Statistics of the United States*, p. 11. For the census's definition of "urban" and "rural," see ibid., pp. 2–3. The observation about America's being born in the country and moving to the city was Richard Hofstadter's.
10. Ibid.
11. Thomas Jefferson, *Notes on the State of Virginia* (New York: Penguin, 1999), p. 170.
12. Ortega, *Sam*, p. 18. See also Trimble, *Walton*, pp. 14–15. The relationship between Jesse Walton and J. W. Walton is altogether unclear. What we do know is that Sam Walton's father worked for a relative in the home and farm mortgage business during the Great Depression.
13. Ortega, *Sam*, p. 18.
14. Sam Walton with John Huey, *Sam Walton: Made in America, My Story* (New York: Bantam, 1993), p. 4; Sandra S. Vance and Roy V. Scott, *Wal-Mart: A History of Sam Walton's Retail Phenomenon* (New York: Twayne, 1994), p. 2.
15. The book has already been cited. At the end of it, Huey appends a brief "Co-author's Note" in which he mentions none of the information just provided. Walton with Huey, *Walton*, pp. 333–334. In "A Postscript," Walton's oldest son, Rob, makes some reference to the earlier book project. Ibid., pp. 329–332. The source for this information is Ortega, *Sam*, pp. 13, 220.
16. Walton with Huey, *Walton*, pp. 4–5.
17. Ibid., p. 14.
18. Ibid., pp. 4–6, 14–15.
19. Ibid., p. 6.
20. Ibid., p. 87.
21. Trimble, *Walton*, pp. 212–213.
22. Walton with Huey, *Walton*, p. 7
23. Ortega, *Sam*, p. 9. The date of Robson's birth was January 21, 1884. Why parents of a child born that year in Georgia would name him after Leland Stanford is a puzzle. Stanford (1824–1893) was a merchant, politician, and railroad tycoon in California. He was a Republican, which could hardly have made him generally popular in the Georgia of the 1880s.

24. Ibid., p. 10. See also Frank C. Robson, "Robson," in *The History of Rogers County, Oklahoma* (Claremore, Okla.: Claremore College Foundation, 1979), entry 492. This document was made available through the courtesy of Ms. Linda Smith, Reference Librarian, Will Rogers Library, Claremore, Oklahoma.
25. Walton with Huey, *Walton*, pp. 15–17.
26. Ibid., pp. 17–18.
27. Ibid., p. 17.
28. Ibid., p. 19.
29. Ibid., p. 20.
30. Trimble, *Walton*, p. 22.
31. This figure is puzzling. Walton provides it in the Walton/Huey book on page 22. There is no mention of sales commissions. Ortega states Walton's salary was $75 per week, rather than per month, plus commissions of an unspecified amount (Ortega, *Sam*, p. 22). The monthly figure sounds far more likely. Trimble puts the figure at $85 per month plus commissions, which, quoting Trimble, "brought his income up to about $115 per month, Sam remembers" (Trimble, *Walton*, p. 35). Oddly, no one mentions that even at $115 a month, Walton was making $3,600 a year less than he was making working part-time while in college running a newspaper distributorship. (His income from his newspaper distributorship is, if accurate, extraordinarily high.) Even though one would expect a trainee to be paid meager wages, this is a very large pay cut in 1940 dollars. Some part of this story must be merely lore.
32. Walton with Huey, *Walton*, pp. 22–24. Trimble, *Walton*, pp. 32–36, gives a more complete treatment. However, the fact that Trimble did not investigate the salary issue and his reference to James Cash Penney as "John" does not inspire confidence in his account.
33. Trimble, *Walton*, pp. 36 and 41.
34. Ibid., p. 44.
35. The towns are seventeen miles apart.
36. Trimble, *Walton*, p. 43.
37. Ortega, *Sam*, p. 18.
38. Walton with Huey, *Walton*, p. 18.
39. Ortega notes some of the difficulties which Walton's family encountered. See especially the problems of Walton's daughter, Alice. Ortega, *Sam*, pp. 198–201.
40. Walton with Huey, *Walton*, p. 24.
41. Ibid., p. 16.
42. Ibid., pp. 25–26.
43. Ibid., p. 26.
44. Ibid., p. 27.
45. U.S. Bureau of the Census, *Number of Inhabitants, Arkansas*, rev., January 22, 1998. The mileage is from Bali Online.
46. Vance and Scott, *Wal-Mart*, p. 5.
47. Walton with Huey, *Walton*, pp. 26–27.
48. Ibid., pp. 27–28.
49. Ibid., pp. 28–29.
50. Ibid., p. 30.

51. Michael B. Dougan, *Arkansas Odyssey: The Saga of Arkansas from Prehistoric Times to Present* (Little Rock: Rose Publishing, 1994), p. 573.

52. Statistics from Dougan, *Arkansas,* p. 592, and also from Harvard Business School business information analyst Jeffrey C. Cronin.

53. T. Harry Williams, *Huey Long* (New York: Knopf, 1969), p. 623.

54. Dougan, *Arkansas,* p. 592.

55. In Mississippi, for example, the African American population in 1940 was 49.2 percent of the total. U.S. Census, *Population,* Series A195–209, pp. 24–37.

56. The six others are Texas, Louisiana, Tennessee, Florida, North Carolina, and Virginia. South Carolina seceded late in 1860; the others in 1861.

57. Fewer than one-third of American seventeen-year-olds surveyed in the mid-1980s were able to identify correctly the *half century* in which the Civil War took place. Diane Ravitch and Chester E. Finn Jr., *What Do Our Seventeen-Year-Olds Know? A Report on the First National Assessment of History and Literature* (New York: Harper and Row, 1987), pp. 49–51.

58. C. Vann Woodward, *Origins of the New South, 1877–1913* (Baton Rouge: Louisiana State University Press, 1971). See the epigraph by Arnold Toynbee at the beginning of the book.

59. Williams, *Long,* pp. 614–615.

60. At least from 1929 through 1948, and perhaps for longer, Mississippi was the nation's poorest state in terms of per capita income; and Arkansas was next on the list. U.S. Bureau of the Census, *Statistical Abstract of the United States: 1950,* 71st ed.

61. Arkansas did not vote for a Republican at the presidential level from the end of Reconstruction in 1876 until the second election of Richard Nixon in 1972.

62. Dougan, *Arkansas,* pp. 493–507.

63. Walton with Huey, *Walton,* p. 28.

64. Ibid., p. 28.

65. According to the U.S. Bureau of the Census, there were 1,770,335 "retail establishments" in the nation in 1939 and between 1,688,479 and 1,769,540 in 1948. *U.S. Census,* Series T79–196 p. 843.

66. Walton with Huey, *Walton,* pp. 28–29.

67. Ibid., p. 28.

68. Ibid.

69. Ibid., p. 29.

70. Ibid., pp. 29–30.

71. Ibid., p. 38.

72. Ortega, *Sam,* p. 29.

73. Walton with Huey, *Walton,* p. 37.

74. Ibid., p. 40.

75. Ibid., pp. 38–39.

76. See chapter 2, p. 89.

77. Walton with Huey, *Walton,* p. 39.

78. Ibid., p. 38; Ortega, *Sam,* p. 29.

79. Walton with Huey, *Walton,* pp. 225–226.

80. It is not clear when this ice-cream machine was purchased. If we assume it was 1949, its cost of $1,800 would be slightly over $13,000 in 2000 dollars.

81. Walton with Huey, *Walton*, pp. 34–35.
82. Ibid., p. 47.
83. Ibid., p. 40. See also Trimble, *Walton*, p. 45.
84. But Trimble makes an effort. See his *Walton*, pp. 65–70.
85. Statistics from U.S. Census as supplied by Harvard Business School information analyst Jeffrey C. Cronin.
86. Walton with Huey, *Walton*, p. 41.
87. Ibid.
88. Ibid., pp. 41–42.
89. Of this we can not be certain. Walton kept a sixty-four-square-foot office at the back of his store. We do not know how much space was devoted to storing merchandise. Vance and Scott, *Wal-Mart*, p. 10.
90. Fifty-five thousand dollars in 1950 is worth about $393,000 in 2000 dollars.
91. Trimble, *Walton*, p. 71.
92. Ibid., p. 64.
93. Ibid.
94. Nan Walton's funeral took place on October 2, 1950, at the Presbyterian church in Columbia, Missouri. Why a Presbyterian church was chosen, given that the family was Methodist, is unknown.
95. My assistant, Christopher J. Albanese, has consulted Mapquest to determine the road mileage from Bentonville to Worthington and Pipestone. The distances are 584.5 miles and 629.5 miles, respectively. This, however, is for the year 2000. It is reasonable to assume that a half-century earlier the trip was longer and, with the dearth of four-lane highways, demanded a good deal more time than in recent years.
96. Vance and Scott, *Wal-Mart*, pp. 11–12. See also Terry P. Wilson, *The Cart that Changed the World: The Career of Sylvan N. Goldman* (Norman, Okla.: University of Oklahoma Press, 1978), p. 84.
97. Walton with Huey, *Walton*, p. 53.
98. Harold Seneker, "A Day in the Life of Sam Walton," *Forbes*, December 1, 1977, p. 45.
99. Walton with Huey, *Walton*, p. 45.
100. Thomas K. McCraw, "Competition and 'Fair Trade': History and Theory," *Research in Economic History*, vol. 16 (1996), pp. 185–239. Also useful is Thomas R. Overstreet Jr., *Resale Price Maintenance: Economic Theories and Empirical Evidence*, Bureau of Economics Staff Report to the Federal Trade Commission (November 1983).
101. See, for example, Thomas K. McCraw and Patricia A. O'Brien, "Production and Distribution: Competition Policy and Industry Structure," in Thomas K. McCraw, ed., *America versus Japan* (Boston: Harvard Business School Press, 1986), pp. 77–116; and Jeffrey R. Bernstein, "7-Eleven in America and Japan," in Thomas K. McCraw, ed., *Creating Modern Capitalism: How Entrepreneurs, Companies, and Countries Triumphed in Three Industrial Revolutions* (Cambridge, Mass.: Harvard University Press, 1997), pp. 492–530.
102. The Miller-Tydings and McGuire Acts (which permitted resale price maintenance) were repealed by the Consumer Goods Pricing Act of 1975 (Public Law 94–145, Sect. 1, 89 Stat. 801).

103. Walton with Huey, *Walton*, p. 53.
104. Ibid., pp. 53–55.
105. Ibid., p. viii; Vance and Scott, *Wal-Mart*, pp. 30–32.
106. Walton with Huey, *Walton*, p. 63.
107. The returns on equity of the seven top discounters in 1993, for example, ranged from 13.8 percent for Kmart to 31.2 percent for Wal-Mart. They were thus all above the average return of 13 percent for all corporations in the United States. Stephen P. Bradley and Pankaj Ghemawat, "Wal-Mart Stores, Inc.," Harvard Business School Case #9–794–024, rev. August 6, 1996, p. 17 and Stephen P. Bradley, "Wal-Mart Stores, Inc.: Teaching Note," Harvard Business School Case #5–395–225, June 12, 1995, p. 1.
108. Vance and Scott, *Wal-Mart*, p. 36.
109. Walton with Huey, *Walton*, pp. 62–63.
110. Ibid., pp. 218–219.
111. Vance and Scott, *Wal-Mart*, p. 43.
112. Ibid., pp. 52–53.
113. Ibid., p. 63.
114. Ibid., p. 44.
115. Walton with Huey, *Walton*, pp. 56–57.
116. It is not clear whether these wages were in violation of the law. In 1962, some workers—those covered by the Fair Labor Standards Act—received a federally mandated $1.15 per hour. Only with the 1961 amendments to this act, however, were "employees in large retail . . . enterprises" covered by the minimum wage, and its level was $1.00 per hour. Whether the first Wal-Mart would have qualified as a "large retail enterprise" and whether its employees worked enough hours to be covered by the statute is not known. U.S. Department of Labor, "History of Federal Minimum Wage Rates . . . ," http://www.dol.gov/dol/esa/public/minwage/chart.htm.
117. Vance and Scott, *Wal-Mart*, pp. 43–45.
118. Walton with Huey, *Walton*, p. 66.
119. Ibid., p. 58.
120. Ibid., p. 59; Vance and Scott, *Wal-Mart*, p. 46.
121. Walton with Huey, *Walton*, p. 58.
122. Ibid., p. 59.
123. Prospectus, Wal-Mart Stores, Inc., October 1, 1970, p. 8.
124. Walton with Huey, *Walton*, p. 70.
125. Ibid., p. 236.
126. Vance and Scott, *Wal-Mart*, pp. 51, 71.
127. By 1993, Wal-Mart owned and operated a fleet of two thousand trucks which ran 60 percent full on backhauls. Wal-Mart's inbound logistics expenses that year were estimated at 3.7 percent of sales, far less than the 4.8 percent for its competitors. Bradley and Ghemawat, "Wal-Mart," pp. 6–7.
128. Walton with Huey, *Walton*, pp. 169–170.
129. Vance and Scott, *Wal-Mart*, p. 51.
130. Richard S. Tedlow, *New and Improved: The Story of Mass Marketing in America* (Boston: Harvard Business School Press, 1996); Donald R. Katz, *The Big Store: Inside the Crisis and Revolution at Sears* (New York: Viking, 1987).

131. Walton with Huey, *Walton,* pp. 330–331.
132. Ibid., p. 201. Walton knew of Watson's motivational meetings.
133. This phrase is the title of an interesting book by Nicole Woolsey Biggart, who uses it in a slightly different sense. See her *Charismatic Capitalism: Direct Selling Organizations in America* (Chicago: University of Chicago Press, 1989). For a useful review of the concept of charisma in business, see Alan Bryman, *Charisma and Leadership in Organizations* (London: Sage, 1992).
134. Walton with Huey, *Walton,* p. 206.
135. Ibid., p. 203.
136. Ibid.
137. Ibid.
138. Katz, *Store,* passim.
139. The couple's assets are provided by Ortega, *Sam,* p. 79.
140. Ibid., p. 81.
141. Vance and Scott, *Wal-Mart,* pp. 76–77.
142. Ortega, *Sam,* p. 83.
143. Robert A. Gordon, *Business Leadership in the Large Corporation* (Washington, D.C.: Brookings, 1945), pp. 75, 67–98 passim.
144. Walton with Huey, *Walton,* p. 274.
145. Bradley and Ghemawat, "Wal-Mart," p. 14.
146. Ibid., p. 14.
147. Ortega, *Sam,* p. 144.
148. Bradley and Ghemawat, "Wal-Mart," p. 10.
149. Ibid.
150. Ibid., p. 4.
151. Ibid., p. 10.

Chapter 7: Robert Noyce

1. The classic account is Lynn White Jr., *Medieval Technology and Social Change* (Oxford: Clarendon Press, 1962). And see generally William H. McNeill, *The Pursuit of Power* (Chicago: University of Chicago Press, 1982).
2. Gray Allen, *Sunsweet at Seventy-five: The Sunsweet Story Continues* (Yuba City, Calif.: Sunsweet Growers, 1992), pp. 23–24.
3. The phrase is that of Ernest Braun and Stuart MacDonald, *Revolution in Miniature: The History and Impact of Semiconductor Electronics in an Updated and Revised Second Edition* (Cambridge, U.K.: Cambridge University Press, 1982).
4. "Profile: Gordon E. Moore: No Goodbyes for World's Mr. Chips," *Observer,* August 8, 1999, p. 5.
5. The literature on "Moore's Law" is large, and the phenomenon itself is more complex than can be explained here. A good place to begin is with T. R. Reid, *The Chip: How Two Americans Invented the Microchip and Launched a Revolution* (New York: Simon and Schuster, 1984), pp. 123–124.
6. Many of the above observations are drawn from Daniel J. Boorstin, *The Republic of Technology: Reflections on Our Future Community* (New

York: Harper and Row, 1978), pp. 1–35. Gordon Moore has said that "the basic technology used in the industry is fundamental and will be around essentially forever . . . [T]he technology used for making microstructures will continue to be used for a variety of things—electronic and beyond." "Profile: Gordon E. Moore."

7. As will be discussed below, Jack Kilby at Texas Instruments invented an integrated circuit with a germanium substrate independently of, but simultaneously with, Noyce.

8. David Packard, *The HP Way: How Bill Hewlett and I Built Our Company* (New York: HarperBusiness, 1995), p. 93.

9. Ibid., p. 84.

10. Ibid., p. 155, states that this phrase "was coined . . . by one of our managers, though the technique itself goes back to my days at General Electric."

11. Todd Gitlin, *The Sixties: Years of Hope, Years of Rage* (Toronto: Bantam, 1987). "A demographer might have noticed that 1964 was the year the first cohort of the baby boom was reaching college in force" (pp. 163–164).

12. AnnaLee Saxenian, *Regional Advantage: Culture and Competition in Silicon Valley and Route 128* (Cambridge, Mass.: Harvard University Press, 1999), p. 36. The academic literature on Silicon Valley is growing fast. See especially Leslie R. Berlin, "Robert Noyce and the Rise and Fall of Fairchild Semiconductor, 1957–1968," *Business History Review,* vol. 75, no. 1 (spring 2001), pp. 63–101; and Christopher Lécuyer, "Making Silicon Valley: Engineering Culture, Innovation, and Industrial Growth, 1930–1970" (unpublished doctoral dissertation, Stanford University, 1999). Berlin and Lécuyer have well-informed and quite divergent views about the valley. This work and the sources they cite are invaluable.

13. Michael S. Malone, *The Big Score: The Billion-Dollar Story of Silicon Valley* (Garden City, N.Y.: Doubleday, 1985), p. 393.

14. See Thomas Parke Hughes, *American Genesis: A History of the American Genius for Invention* (New York: Penguin, 1989).

15. Moore was born on January 3, 1929, in San Francisco. He was brought up in Pescadero, where his father was the deputy sheriff.

16. Brian O'Reilly, "From Intel to the Amazon: Gordon Moore's Incredible Journey," *Fortune,* April 26, 1999.

17. Reid, *Chip,* pp. 79–95.

18. Ibid., p. 63.

19. Malone, *Score,* p. 74.

20. Ibid., pp. 75 and 73–84.

21. Ibid., p. 75.

22. Ibid., p. 74.

23. Braun and MacDonald, *Revolution,* p. 46.

24. Ibid., p. 49.

25. Ibid., p. 11.

26. Ibid., p. 60.

27. Malone, *Score,* p. 76.

28. Ibid., p. 77.

29. Reid, *Chip,* p. 72.

30. Malone, *Score,* p. 78.

31. Ibid.
32. Reid, *Chip,* p. 71.
33. Robert Norton Noyce, "A Photoelectric Investigation of Surface States on Insulators" (unpublished doctoral dissertation, Massachusetts Institute of Technology, 1953), p. 79.
34. Malone, *Score,* pp. 78–79. The description of Philco as "lowly" and the final quotation are Malone's. The other quoted remark is Malone quoting Noyce.
35. Ibid., pp. 81–82.
36. Quoted in Berlin, "Noyce," p. 100.
37. Tom Wolfe, "The Tinkerings of Robert Noyce," *Esquire,* December 1983, p. 372.
38. These sentences are stenciled on T-shirts that are presently sold in Intel's museum shop at corporate headquarters in Santa Clara, California, in the heart of Silicon Valley. The headquarters is named the Robert Noyce Building.
39. Reid, *Chip,* p. 73.
40. New York: Simon and Schuster, 1956.
41. It is typical of stories about Noyce, perhaps indicative of the legendary status he achieved later in life, that details such as the encounter with Shockley and the trip from Philadelphia to Palo Alto are often recounted differently by different authors. One author says Shockley heard Noyce deliver his paper in 1956, and Noyce took the "red eye" out to California (Malone, *Score,* p. 79). Another says Noyce delivered the paper in 1955, that it "caught [Shockley's] eye," and that he took the train out west (Reid, *Chip,* pp. 72–73). Both these authors appear to have gotten this disparate information from interviews with Noyce himself.
42. Malone, *Score,* p. 79.
43. Gordon E. Moore, "The Role of Fairchild in Silicon Technology in the Early Days of 'Silicon Valley,'" *Proceedings of the IEEE,* vol. 86, no. 1 (January 1998), p. 53.
44. Malone, *Score,* p. 69.
45. John N. Ingham and Lynne B. Feldman, *Contemporary American Business Leaders: A Biographical Dictionary* (New York: Greenwood Press, 1990), p. 448.
46. Quoted in Dirk Hanson, *The New Alchemists: Silicon Valley and the Microelectronics Revolution* (Boston: Little, Brown, 1982), p. xv.
47. William Shakespeare, *The Life of King Henry the Fifth,* act 4, scene 3, line 60.
48. Reid, *Chip,* p. 70. See also Eugene S. Ferguson, *Engineering and the Mind's Eye* (Cambridge, Mass.: MIT Press, 1992).
49. Hans Queisser, *The Conquest of the Microchip* (Cambridge, Mass.: Harvard University Press, 1988), p. 91.
50. Malone, *Score,* p. 69; Queisser, *Microchip,* p. 87.
51. Reid, *Chip,* pp. 45–46; William B. Shockley, "THINKING about THINKING improves THINKING," *IEEE Student Journal* (September 1968), pp. 11–16.
52. Andrew Hodges, *Alan Turing, the Enigma* (New York: Simon and Schuster, 1983).
53. John A. Byrne, *The Whiz Kids: The Founding Fathers of American Business—and the Legacy They Left Us* (New York: Currency, 1993).

54. Wolfe, "Tinkerings," p. 354.
55. Ibid., p. 356. See also "Multifarious Sherman Fairchild," *Fortune,* May 1960, and Berlin, "Noyce," passim.
56. "Fairchild, George Winthrop," *National Cyclopedia of American Biography* (New York: J. T. White, 1922), vol. 14, pp. 247–248.
57. "8 Leave Shockley to Form Coast Semiconductor Firm," *Electronic News,* October 20, 1957.
58. Ibid.
59. Reid, *Chip,* p. 152.
60. Queisser, *Microchip,* p. 87.
61. Moore, "Early Days," p. 53
62. Ibid., pp. 55–56.
63. Michael S. Malone, *The Microprocessor: A Biography* (New York: Springer-Verlag 1995), pp. 56–58. Mesa devices are still in use for some purposes.
64. Moore, "Early Days," p. 57; Malone, *Microprocessor,* p. 56.
65. Moore, "Early Days," p. 56.
66. Hanson, *New Alchemists,* pp. 91–92.
67. Malone, *Score,* p. 90. For Baldwin, see George Rotsky, "The Transistor: A Biography," *Electronic Engineering Times* (October 30, 1997). See also Fairchild Camera and Instrument Corporation, *Annual Report 1957,* p. 16.
68. Wolfe, "Tinkerings," p. 359.
69. Michael Hiltzik, *Dealers of Lightning: Xerox PARC and the Dawn of the Computer Age* (New York: HarperBusiness, 1999), pp. 31, 36–37.
70. This quotation and the one in the previous paragraph are from Reid, *Chip,* p. 76.
71. This account is summarized from ibid., pp. 76–78.
72. Malone, *Score,* p. 100.
73. Hughes, *Genesis,* p. 172.
74. It is a noteworthy indicator of how quickly even a new company can become committed to a product, thus making mobility to something new difficult. According to Jean Hoerni, who invented the NPN (i.e., negative-positive-negative) planar transistor at Fairchild, Noyce's decision to move the company from the mesa to the planar product was not an easy one. "That was quite a decision to take," he said. "There was resistance throughout the company, in the production and engineering departments. Yields would be much lower on the planar structure, and we already had orders for the mesa parts. But he supported it wholeheartedly, and after that everybody else followed." Rob Ristleheuber, "Noyce Remembered: Unusual Ideas, Unusual Approaches," *Electronic News,* June 11, 1990, p. 4.
75. Reid, *Chip,* p. 70.
76. Ibid., p. 71.
77. Hughes, *Genesis,* pp. 175–180; John K. Smith and David A. Hounshell, "Wallace H. Carothers and Fundamental Research at Du Pont," *Science,* vol. 279 (August 2, 1985), pp. 436–442.
78. The phrase is Dirk Hanson's, coined in his book by that name.
79. This observation was made by George Gilder.
80. Anthony B. Perkins, "The Accidental Entrepreneur," *Red Herring,* September 1, 1995.

81. Louise Kehoe, "Robert N. Noyce: 1990 Award for Achievement," *Electronics* (December 1, 1990), p. 49.
82. Fairchild Camera and Instrument Corporation, *Annual Report, 1959,* p. 6.
83. Steven W. Usselman, "Computer and Communications Technology," in Stanley I. Kutler, editor in chief, *Encyclopedia of the United States in the Twentieth Century,* vol. 2 (New York: Scribner's, 1996), p. 819.
84. An interesting journalistic account of the travails of IBM is Paul Carroll, *Big Blues: The Unmaking of IBM* (New York: Crown, 1993).
85. The microprocessor was invented at Intel by engineer Marcian "Ted" Hoff. The first microprocessor was marketed in 1971 and contained 2,300 transistors in a $200 chip "smaller than a baby's thumbnail." Gordon E. Moore, "The Microprocessor: Engine of the Technology Revolution," *Communications of the ACM,* vol. 40, no. 2 (February 1997).
86. Lynn Solerno, "Creativity by the Numbers: An Interview with Robert N. Noyce," *Harvard Business Review,* May–June 1980, p. 124.
87. Malone, *Score,* pp. 97, 87–113 passim.
88. Fairchild Semiconductor and Camera, *Annual Report for 1967,* pp. 4, 6.
89. Wolfe, "Tinkerings," p. 364.
90. Ibid., p. 360.
91. Ibid. Italics in original.
92. Brian O'Reilly, "From Intel to the Amazon: Gordon Moore's Incredible Journey," *Fortune,* April 26, 1999, pp. 166 ff.
93. Malone, *Score,* pp. 138–139.
94. Tim Jackson, *Inside Intel: Andy Grove and the Rise of the World's Most Powerful Chip Company* (New York: Penguin, 1998), p. 23.
95. Ibid., p. 22.
96. Solerno, "Creativity," p. 130.
97. Jackson, *Intel,* p. 31.
98. Peter Botticelli, David Collis, and Gary Pisano, "Intel Corporation: 1968–1997," Harvard Business School Publishing Case #9-797-137, rev. October 21, 1998, p. 2.
99. Interview with Arthur Rock, January, 2000.
100. O'Reilly, "From Intel to Amazon," *Fortune,* pp. 166 ff.
101. Ibid.
102. Botticelli, Collis, and Pisano, "Intel," p. 2.
103. Solerno, "Creativity," p. 130.
104. Ibid., p. 129.
105. Rock interview.
106. Bollicelli, Collis, and Pisano, "Intel," p. 2.
107. Ibid.
108. The financial information above is from C. E. Unterberg, Towbin Co., "Prospectus: 350,000 Shares Intel Corporation Capital Stock," October 13, 1971.
109. Wolfe, "Tinkerings," p. 367.
110. Interview with Pendred Noyce, M.D., January 2000.
111. Wolfe, "Tinkerings," p. 360.
112. Ibid., p. 368.
113. Ibid., pp. 367, 371.
114. Rock interview.

115. Jackson, *Intel,* p. 165.
116. Reid, *Chip,* p. 71.
117. Jackson, *Intel,* p. 188.
118. Ellen Debenport, "She Put $50 Million to Work so Maine Could Produce Jobs," *St. Petersburg Times,* October 5, 1996, p. 1A.
119. Steven G. Vegh, "Noyce's 'Economic Philanthropy' Makes Itself Widely Felt," *Portland Press Herald,* September 14, 1997, p. 1A.
120. John Richardson, "State Bids Goodbye to 'Best Friend,'" *Portland Press Herald,* September 24, 1996, p. 1A.
121. "'Economic Philanthropy,'" p. 1A.
122. Jackson, *Intel,* p. 61. At this writing, the address of the Robert Noyce Building, Intel's headquarters, is 2200 Mission College Boulevard in Santa Clara.
123. Ibid., p. 164.
124. This account is from Ibid., pp. 163–164. See also Robert McG. Thomas Jr., "Elizabeth B. Noyce," *New York Times,* September 20, 1996, sec. B, p. 7.
125. Jackson, *Intel,* pp. 67–68.
126. Malone, *Score,* p. 84.
127. Ibid., p. 83.
128. Reid, *Chip,* p. 121.
129. Wolfe, "Tinkerings," p. 362.
130. Reid, *Chip,* p. 121.
131. Ibid., pp. 121–122.
132. See David B. Yoffie with Alvin G. Wint, "The Global Semiconductor Industry, 1987," Harvard Business School Publishing #9–388–052, rev. March 22, 1993, and John J. Coleman under the supervision of David B. Yoffie, "The Semiconductor Industry Association and the Trade Dispute with Japan (A)," Harvard Business School Publishing #9–387–205, rev. March 11, 1991; "(B)" Harvard Business School Publishing #9–387–195, rev. February 16, 1988; and "(C)" Harvard Business School Publishing #9–388–049, rev. January 9, 1992.
133. Reid, *Chip,* pp. 176–177.
134. An excellent treatment of this decision is Robert A. Burgelman, "Fading Memories: A Process Theory of Strategic Business Exit in Dynamic Environments," *Administrative Science Quarterly,* vol. 39, no. 1 (March 1994), pp. 24 ff.
135. Hanson, *New Alchemists,* pp. 191–192.
136. Alfred D. Chandler Jr., "The Standard Oil Company—Competition, Consolidation, and Integration," in Alfred D. Chandler Jr., Thomas K. McCraw, and Richard S. Tedlow, *Management, Past and Present: A Casebook on the History of American Business* (Cincinnati: South-Western, 1996), pp. 3–50.
137. Larry D. Browning and Judy C. Shetler, *Sematech: Saving the U.S. Semiconductor Industry* (College Station: Texas A&M University Press, 2000), p. 202.
138. Ibid., p. 81.
139. Ibid.
140. Ibid., pp. 138–139.
141. Ibid., p. 138.
142. Wolfe, "Tinkerings," p. 373.

Conclusion: Progress and Profits

1. Bertie C. Forbes, *Men Who Are Making America* (New York: B.C. Forbes Publishing, 1917), pp. 144–145.
2. Patricia Denault and Thomas K. McCraw, "John Jacob Astor, 1763–1848," in Alfred D. Chandler, Jr., Thomas K. McCraw, and Richard S. Tedlow, *Management, Past and Present: A Casebook on the History of American Business* (Cincinnati: South-Western, 1996), p. 1-42.
3. Rutherford B. Hayes, James A. Garfield, Chester A. Arthur, Grover Cleveland, and Benjamin Harrison.
4. Abraham Lincoln, "Annual Message to Congress," December 1, 1862.
5. This phrase is the well-chosen title of the book President Lyndon Johnson wrote after leaving office: *The Vantage Point: Perspectives of the Presidency* (New York: Holt, Rinehart and Winston, 1971).
6. *Stor* means "great." A *stormann* is a "chieftain," a "great man," or a "notable." *Galskap* means "insanity" or "madness." *Stormannsgalskap* is sometimes translated as "megalomania." I am grateful to Judge Sandra Lynch of the First Circuit Court of Appeals in Boston for this reference.
7. Michael S. Malone, *The Big Score: The Billion-Dollar Story of Silicon Valley* (Garden City, N.Y.: Doubleday, 1985), pp. 73–84.
8. Nancy Koehn and Rowena Olegario, "Michael Milken," in Chandler et al., *Management*, pp. 6-31–6-83.
9. For changes in this career path with the surge of entrepreneurship at the close of the twentieth century, see William A. Sahlman, "The New Economy Is Stronger Than You Think," *Harvard Business Review* (November–December 1999), pp. 99–106.
10. Reese V. Jenkins, "Watson, Thomas John," in John A. Garraty, ed., *Dictionary of American Biography, Supplement Six, 1956–1960* (New York: Scribner's, 1980), p. 675.
11. Stephen Manes and Paul Andrews, *Gates: How Microsoft's Mogul Reinvented an Industry—and Made Himself the Richest Man in America* (New York: Simon and Schuster, 1994), p. 46.
12. Richard S. Tedlow, Courtney Purrington, and Kim Bettcher, "The American CEO in 1917: Demography and Career Path" (manuscript in author's possession).
13. Michael Bezilla, "Samuel Rea," in Keith L. Bryant Jr., ed., *Railroads in the Age of Regulation, 1900–1980* (New York: Facts on File, 1988), p. 361.
14. See, for example, Janet Lowe, *Oprah Winfrey Speaks: Insight from the World's Most Influential Voice* (New York: John Wiley, 1998).
15. Joseph A. Schumpeter, *Capitalism, Socialism, and Democracy* (New York: Harper and Row, 1950), pp. 90 and 61–163, passim.
16. Quoted in Thomas K. McCraw, ed., *Creating Modern Capitalism: How Entrepreneurs, Companies, and Countries Triumphed in Three Industrial Revolutions* (Cambridge, Mass.: Harvard University Press, 1997), p. 348.
17. Quoted in Chandler et al., *Management*, p. 1-12.

BIBLIOGRAPHICAL ESSAY

The endnotes to this book are designed to provide a clear guide to the sources used so that the reader wishing to explore specific subjects discussed can do so. The goal of this brief essay is to focus on certain books which I relied upon extensively.

Carnegie. For Andrew Carnegie, the place to begin is Harold Livesay, *Andrew Carnegie and the Rise of Big Business* (Boston: Little, Brown, 2000). Brief (213 pages and not a lot of print per page) and vibrant, it captures much of the drama of Carnegie's life. Joseph Frazier Wall's *Andrew Carnegie* (Pittsburgh: University of Pittsburgh Press, 1989) represents an investment for the reader, weighing in at over a thousand pages with a lot of print per page. But it is a great book: authoritative, comprehensive, and obviously a labor of love for the author. It repays the investment the reader makes, manyfold.

Useful, also, is Wall's *The Andrew Carnegie Reader* (Pittsburgh: University of Pittsburgh Press, 1992), a judicious selection of Carnegie's writing accompanied by interesting observations by Wall. And then there is Carnegie's *Autobiography,* edited by John C. Van Dyke (Boston: Houghton Mifflin, 1920). This is a long, rambling book but with some fascinating passages.

Eastman. Essential is Elizabeth Brayer's *George Eastman: A Biography* (Baltimore: The Johns Hopkins University Press, 1996). Brayer's authoritative account of this hidden man is based upon careful examination of an abundance of source material. For the technological world in which Eastman lived, the best source is Reese V. Jenkins, *Images and Enterprise: Technology and the American Photographic Industry, 1839 to 1925* (Baltimore: The Johns Hopkins University Press, 1975). Jenkins's mastery of this highly complex subject is evident on every page.

Ford. It is a pity there is no analogue for Ford to Livesay's book on Carnegie. The best place to start for the general reader is Peter Collier and David Horowitz, *The Fords: An American Epic* (New York: Summit, 1987). For a special angle of vision on Ford's problematic personality, I recommend Anne Jardim, *The First Henry Ford* (Cambridge, Mass.: MIT Press, 1970) and the lengthy but always interesting *The Public Image of Henry Ford: An American Folk Hero and His Company* (Detroit: Wayne State University Press, 1976) by David L. Lewis. An outstanding study of American technology climaxing in Fordism is David A. Hounshell, *From the American System to Mass Production, 1800–1932: The Development of Manufacturing Technology in the United States* (Baltimore: The Johns Hopkins University Press, 1984). A classic (but mighty long) study is Allan Nevins with Frank Ernest Hill, *Ford: The Times, the Man, the Company* (New York: Scribner's, 1954) and two succeeding books by Nevins and Hill, *Ford: Expansion and Challenge, 1915–1933* (New York: Scribner's, 1957) and *Ford: Decline and Rebirth, 1933–1962* (New York: Scribner's, 1963).

Watson. The place to begin is with the lengthy, much praised autobiography of Thomas J. Watson Jr., written with Peter Petre, *Father, Son & Co.: My Life at IBM and Beyond* (New York: Bantam, 1990). But be warned.

502 Bibliographical Essay

Like all important autobiographies, especially of businesspeople, this is a seductive book. It should be supplemented with the now forgotten but very useful volumes by William Rodgers, *THINK: A Biography of the Watsons and IBM* (New York: Stein and Day, 1969) and Thomas Graham Belden and Marva Robins Belden, *The Lengthening Shadow: The Life of Thomas J. Watson* (Boston: Little, Brown, 1962).

Revson. The book to read on Revson is Andrew P. Tobias, *Fire and Ice: The Story of Charles Revson—the Man Who Built the Revlon Empire* (New York: Morrow, 1976). Shrewd, astute, and an easy read. Highly entertaining. For the cosmetics industry, accessible and authoritative is Kathy Peiss, *Hope in a Jar: The Making of America's Beauty Culture* (New York: Henry Holt, 1998). For television at the time of the quiz shows, the outstanding volumes remain those by Erik Barnouw, especially *The Golden Web: A History of Broadcasting in the United States, Volume II—1933 to 1953* (New York: Oxford University Press, 1968) and *The Image Empire: A History of Broadcasting in the United States—from 1953* (New York: Oxford University Press, 1970).

Walton. Begin with the underrated Sam Walton with John Huey, *Sam Walton: Made in America, My Story* (New York: Bantam, 1993). The previous caveat about autobiographies applies. This should be supplemented at least with journalist Bob Ortega's *In Sam We Trust* (New York: Random House, 1998) as well as with a company history, Sandra A. Vance and Roy V. Scott, *Wal-Mart: A History of Sam Walton's Retail Phenomenon* (New York: Twayne, 1994).

Noyce. There is no first-class book about Noyce, which, given his importance, is incredible. A very good article on Noyce has been published in an academic journal called the *Business History Review* by Leslie R. Berlin, "Robert Noyce and the Rise and Fall of Fairchild Semiconductor, 1957–1968" (vol. 75, no. 1). An article which became quite famous—Tom Wolfe, "The Tinkerings of Robert Noyce," *Esquire*, December 1983—is much admired by some who knew Noyce but dismissed by others as shallow and too clever by half. Noyce's story has to be pieced together.

A Last Word. The inspiration for this book is Richard Hofstadter, *The American Political Tradition: And the Men Who Made It.* I read this work in 1964, and its impression on me is permanent. First published in 1948, it has gone through multiple editions, deservedly so. It is a book of incandescent brilliance.

INDEX

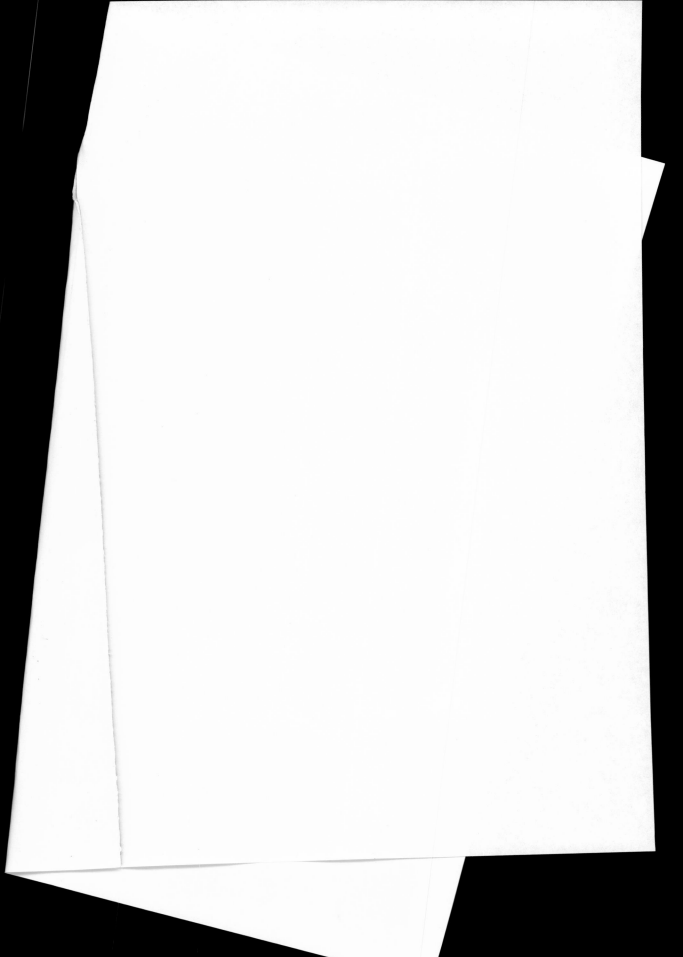